T5-DHJ-223

ALMANAC*of*
ARCHITECTURE
AND DESIGN
2000

MARCH 2000

SUN	MON	TUES	WED	THURS	FRI	SAT
			1 Thomas Hastings	2	3	4
5	6 Michaelangelo	7	8	9 Edward Durell Stone	10	11
12 Andre´ LeNotre	13	14	15	16 Aldo Van Eyck	17	18
19	20	21 Eric Mendelsohn	22	23	24 William Morris	25
26	27 Ludwig Mies van der Rohe	28	29 Edwin Lutyens	30	31	

Notes for Events & Anniversaries

APRIL EVENTS AND DEADLINES

Technology Watch and Innovation in the Construction Industry
Brussels, Belgium
April 5 - 6
www.cobomedia.be/technologywatch/

International Home Furnishings Market
High Point, NC
April 6 - 14
www.furnituremarket.com

National Home Show
Toronto, Ontario, Canada
April 7 - 16
www.southex.com

Canadian Facility Management Conference & Design Expo
Toronto, Ontario, Canada
April 13 - 14
(416) 236-5856

Australian Urban/Planning History Conference
Adelaide, Australia
April 13 - 15
christine.garnaut@unisa.edu.au.

International Window Coverings Expo
Baltimore, MD
April 14 - 16
www.heimtextil.de

ISFE (International Society of Facilities Executives) Annual Conference
Cambridge, MA
April 16 - 18
www.isfe.org

Business Week/Architectural Record Awards
Submissions due April 18
(888) 242-4240 or (202) 682-3205

Austro Glas: International Trade Fair for Glass, Glass Processing and Architecture
Salzburg, Austria
April 27 - 29
www.reedexpo.com

Conference on Design Management in the Digital Environment
Pasadena, CA
April 30 - May 2
www.dmi.org/conferences/index.shtml

APRIL 2000

SUN	MON	TUES	WED	THURS	FRI	SAT
						1
2 Pierre Charles L'Enfant	3	4	5	6 William Strickland	7	8 Richard Neutra
9	10	11	12	13 Thomas Jefferson	14 Mary Jane Colter	15 Leonardo DaVinci
16	17	18	19 Passover	20	21 Humphry Repton	22 James Stirling
23 Easter	24	25	26 I.M. Pei	27	28	29
30						

Notes for Events & Anniversaries

MAY EVENTS AND DEADLINES

SIBEX: Southeast Asia Int'l Building Expo
Singapore
May 3 - 6
www.reedexpo.com

**AIA (American Institute of Architects)
Expo 2000**
Philadelphia, PA
May 4 - 6
www.e-architect.com

FEDfacilities
Washington, D.C.
May 9 - 10
www.reedexpo.com

LightFair 2000
New York City, NY
May 9 - 11
www.lightfair.com

Victorian Society in America Annual Mtg.
Philadelphia, PA
May 10 - 13
www.libertynet.org/vicsoc/

**EDRA 30 (Environmental Design
Research Assoc.) Annual Conference**
San Francisco, CA
May 10 - 14
www.edra.org

**RAIC (Royal Architecture Institute of
Canada): Ottawa 2000 Festival of Arch.**
Ottawa, Ontario, Canada
May 11 - 13
www.raic.org

**International Conference on Building
Education and Research (CIB)**
Atlanta, GA USA
May 16 - 18
http://murmur.arch.gatech.edu/~bear2000/

**SEGD (Society for Environmental
Graphic Design) 2000 Annual Conf.**
Portland, OR
May 17 - 20
www.segd.org

EnvironDesign4
Denver, CO
May 18 - 20
www.isdesignet.com

**Third National Conference on Women
and Historic Preservation**
Washington, D.C.
May 19 - 21
womenpres@hotmail.com

**ICFF (International Contemporary
Furniture Fair) 2000**
New York City, NY
May 20 - 23
www.glmshows.com

Surtex
New York City, NY
May 21 - 23
www.glmshows.com/glmshows/surtex

**ILCDES 2000: International
Symposium on Integrated Life-Cycle
Design of Materials and Structures**
Helsinki, Finland
May 22 - 24
www.ril.fi/ilcdes.htm

Heimtextil Americas
Miami, FL
May 24- 26
www.heimtextil.de

**CSC (Construction Specifications
Canada) CONFERENCE 2000**
Montreal, Quebec
May 25 - 27

**SOIS: Southwestern Ontario Industrial
Show**
Kitchener, Canada
May 30 - June 1
www.reedexpo.com

**AIA (American Institute of Architects)
Architecture Firm Award**
Submissions due in May
for additional info: www.e-architect.com

MAY 2000

SUN	MON	TUES	WED	THURS	FRI	SAT
	1 Benjamin Latrobe	2	3 Aldo Rossi	4	5	6
7	8 Hans Knoll	9	10	11	12	13
14	15	16	17	18 Walter Gropius	19	20
21	22 Robert A.M. Stern	23	24	25	26	27
28 Charles F.A. Voysey	29 *Memorial Day*	30	31			

Notes for Events & Anniversaries

JUNE EVENTS AND DEADLINES

AEC Systems Show
Chicago, Illinois
June 5 - 8
www.aecsystems.com

**VAF (Vernacular Architecture Forum)
2000 Annual Meeting**
Duluth, MN
June 7 - 10
www.vernaculararchitecture.org

**ACSA (Association of Collegiate Schools
of Architecture) Int'l Conference**
Hong Kong
June 10 - 14
www.acsa-arch.org/

**International Corporate/Brand Identity
Conference**
Montreal, Quebec
June 11 - 13
www.dmi.org/conferences/index.shtml

World Workplace 2000 (IFMA)
Glasgow, Scotland
June 11 - 13
www.worldworkplace.org

**European Project Management
Conference (Project Management
Institute)**
Jerusalem, Israel
June 11 - 16
www.ortra.com/pmi/

Decorex USA
Chicago, Illinois
June 12 - 14
www.decorexusa.com

NeoCon World's Trade Fair 2000
Chicago, IL
June 12 - 14
800/677-6278 or 312/527-7600

International Design Conference
Aspen, CO
June 14 - 17
info@idca.org

**LHAT (League of Historic American
Theaters) Annual Conference**
San Francisco, CA
June 14 - 17
www.lhaf.org

Designing for the 21st Century II
Providence, RI
June 14 - 18
www.adaptenv.org/21century

**SAH (Society of Architectural
Historians) Annual Meeting**
Miami, FL
June 14 - 18
www.sah.org

**Solar 2000 (ASES: American Solar
Energy Society)**
Madison, WI
June 16 - 21
www.ases.org/

**BOMA (Building Owners & Managers
Association) Annual Convention/Office
Building Show**
San Diego, CA
June 18 - 20
registrar@boma.org

**Int'l Conf. on Implementation of
Construction Quality and Related
Systems: A Global Update (CIB)**
Lisbon, Portugal
June 19 - 21
www.civil.ist.utl.pt/~ldias/cibtg36/index_n.htm

EuroSun 2000
Copenhagen, Denmark
June 19 - 22

Continued on pg. 14

JUNE 2000

SUN	MON	TUES	WED	THURS	FRI	SAT
				1 Norman Foster	2	3
4	5	6	7 Charles Rennie Mackintosh	8 Frank Lloyd Wright	9	10 Antonio Gaudi
11	12 John Roebling	13	14 Kevin Roche	15	16	17 Charles O. Eames
18	19 Charles Gwathney	20	21 Paolo Soleri	22 Alison Smithson	23	24
25	26 Matthew Nowicki	27	28	29	30	

Notes for Events & Anniversaries

JUNE EVENTS AND DEADLINES (CON'T)

Buildings - New York
New York, NY
June 20 - 21
www.reedexpo.com

Interior Lifestyle
Tokyo, Japan
June 21 - 23
www.heimtextil.de

PMI (Project Management Institute) Research Conference 2000
Paris, France
June 21 - 24
www.pmi.org/research/conference.htm

VIDA Country 2000: Fourth Forum on Suburban Development
Buenos Aires, Argentina
June 21 - 25
www.uli.org

CSI (Construction Specifications Institute) CSI 2000
Atlanta, GA
June 22 - 25
www.csinet.org/confer/conhome.htm

International Conference on Construction Information Technology
Reykjavik, Iceland
June 28 - 30
http://cit2000.rabygg.is/

IBEX: The 16th International Building Exposition
Hong Kong
June, 2000
for additional info: www.reedexpo.com

JULY EVENTS AND DEADLINES

Good Design Competition
Submissions due July 1
www.chi-athenaeum.org/

Renewable Energy 2000
Brighton, U.K.
July 2 - 4
www.reedexpo.com

Urban 21: Global Conference on the Urban Future
Hanover, Germany
July 4 - 6
www.urban21.de/english/index.html

Roomvent 2000: 7th International Conference on Air Distribution in Rooms
Reading, U.K.
July 9 - 12
www.rdg.ac.uk/rv2000/

AIBD (American Institute of Building Design) Convention
San Diego, CA
July 12 - 16
www.aibd.org

APPA Educational Conference & Annual Meeting
Ft. Worth, TX
July 16 - 18
www.appa.org

AIAS (American Institute of Architecture Students) Grassroots
Washington, D.C.
July 27 - 30
www.aiasnatl.org/

IESNA (Illuminating Engineers Society of North America) Annual Conference
Washington, D.C.
July 31 - August 2
www.iesna.org

JULY 2000

SUN	MON	TUES	WED	THURS	FRI	SAT
						I Josep Lluís Sert
2	**3**	**4** *Independence Day*	**5**	**6**	**7**	**8** Philip Johnson
9 Michael Graves	**10**	**11**	**12** Buckminster Fuller	**13**	**14** Moshe Safdie	**15**
16	**17**	**18**	**19** John Hejduk	**20**	**21**	**22**
23 Richard Rogers	**24**	**25**	**26**	**27**	**28**	**29**
30	**31**					

Notes for Events & Anniversaries

AUGUST EVENTS AND DEADLINES

Healthy Buildings Conference 2000
Espoo, Finland
August 6 - 10
www.hb2000.org

SCA (Society for Commercial Archeology) 2000 Conference
Maniton Springs, CO
August 24 - 26
www.sca-roadside.org

Orlando Furniture & Decorative Accessory Market
Orlando, FL
August 25 - 27
www.kemexpo.com

IFLA (International Federation of Landscape Architects) Eastern Regional Conference
Hyogo Prefecture, Japan
August 30 - September 2
www.ifla.kee.hu/ifla/

AIA (American Institute of Architects) Institute Honor Awards for Architecture
Submissions due in August
for additional info: www.e-architect.com

AIA (American Institute of Architects) Institute Honor Awards for Interior Architecture
Submissions due in August
for additional info: www.e-architect.com

AUGUST 2000

SUN	MON	TUES	WED	THURS	FRI	SAT
		1 Martin Roche	2	3	4	5
6	7	8 Charles Bullfinch	9	10	11 Peter Eisenman	12 Robert Mills
13	14	15	16	17	18	19 Henry Ives Cobb
20 Eero & Eliel Saarinen	21	22	23	24 Charles Follen McKim	25	26
27	28	29	30	31		

Notes for Events & Anniversaries

SEPTEMBER EVENTS AND DEADLINES

CTM 2000: Construction Technology Malaysia Expo
Kuala Lumpur, Malaysia
September 12 - 15
www.reedexpo.com

Alice Davis Hitchcock Book Award (SAH)
Submissions due September 15
www.sah.org

Antoinette Forrester Downing Award (SAH)
Submissions due September 15
www.sah.org

Philip Johnson Award (SAH)
Submissions due September 15
www.sah.org

SAH (Society of Architectural Historians) Founder's Award
Submissions due September 15
www.sah.org

Spiro Kostof Book Award (SAH)
Submissions due September 15
www.sah.org

Millenium Solar Forum 2000 (ISES International Solar Energy Society)
Mexico City, Mexico
September 17 - 22
www.ises.org

Docomomo Conference, Sixth International
Brasilia, Brazil
September 20 - 22
www.ooo.nl/docomomo/sixth.htm

IDSA (Industrial Designers Society of America) Annual Conference
New Orleans, LA
September 20 - 23
www.idsa.org

Frank Lloyd Wright Building Conservancy Annual Conference
Minneapolis, MN
September 20 - 24
www.swcp.com/flw

IIDEX/NeoCon Canada
Toronto, Ontario, Canada
September 21 - 22
www.iidexneoconcanada.com/overview.htm

Decorex International
London, U.K.
September 24 - 27
www.decorex.com

ACEC Fall Conference
San Diego, CA
September 28 - 30
www.acec.org

***Interiors* Magazine Awards**
Submissions due in September
for additional info: (212) 536-5193

AIA (American Institute of Architects) Honor Awards for Reg. and Urban Design
Submission due in September
for additional info: www.e-architect.com

AIA (American Institute of Architects) Twenty-Five Year Awards
Submission due in September
for additional info: www.e-architect.com

SEPTEMBER 2000

SUN	MON	TUES	WED	THURS	FRI	SAT
					1 William Holabird	2
3 Louis Sullivan	4 Kenzo Tange	5	6 Sebastiano Serlio	7	8	9
10 John Soane	11	12	13	14	15	16 Fumihiko Maki
17	18 Peter Smithson	19	20 Stanley Tigerman	21	22	23
24	25 William LeBaron Jenny	26	27	28	29	30 *Rosh Hashanah*

Notes for Events & Anniversaries

OCTOBER EVENTS AND DEADLINES

CERSAIE 2000: International Exhibition of Ceramics for the Building Industry and Bathroom Furnishings
Bologna, Italy
October 3 - 8
www.cersaie.it

Philconstruct
Manila, Philippines
October 5 - 8
www.convex-ph.com/

International Assoc. for the Study of Traditional Environments Conference
Italy
October 12 - 15
www-archfp.ced.berkeley.edu/cedr//

ACADIA (Association for Computer Aided Design in Architecture) Conf.
Washington, D.C.
October 19 - 22
www.acadia.org

orgatec
Cologne, Germany
October 19 - 24
orgatec@koelnmesse.de

Sustainable Building 2000
Maastricht, The Netherlands
October 22 - 25
www.novem.nl/sb2000/

DMI (Design Management Institute) International Design Management Conf.
Cape Cod, MA
October 22 - 26
(617) 338-6380

DesigNation3:ICE
Miami, FL
October 26 - 30
(202) 659-3918

ASLA (American Society of Landscape Architects) Annual Meeting
St. Louis, MO
October 28 - 30
www.asla.org

Metalcon
Atlanta, GA
October 31 - 11/2
www.metalcon.com

Urban Land Institute Fall Meeting
Chicago, IL
October 31 - November 4
www.uli.org

AIA (American Institute of Architects) Edward G. Kemper Award
Submissions due in October
for additional info: www.e-architect.com

AIA (American Institute of Architects) Honor Awards for Prof. Achievement
Submissions due in October
for additional info: www.e-architect.com

AIA (American Institute of Architects) Honors for Collaborative Achievement
Submissions due in October
for additional info: www.e-architect.com

AIA (American Institute of Architects) Thomas Jefferson Awards for Public Arch.
Submissions due in October
for additional info: www.e-architect.com

AIA (American Institute of Architects) Whitney Young, Jr. Award
Submissions due in October
for additional info: www.e-architect.com

AIA (American Institute of Architects) Young Architects Award
Submissions due in October
for additional info: www.e-architect.com

AIA (American Institute of Architects)/ACSA TOPAZ Medallion
Submissions due in October
for additional info: www.e-architect.com

OCTOBER 2000

SUN	MON	TUES	WED	THURS	FRI	SAT
1 Robert Smirke	2	3 Tadao Ando	4	5	6 Le Corbusier	7
8	9 Yom Kippur	10	11	12 Cesar Pelli Columbus Day	13 Edwin Lundie	14
15	16	17	18	19	20 Christopher Wren	21
22	23 Paul Philippe Cret	24	25	26	27	28
29	30	31 Charles Moore				

Notes for Events & Anniversaries

NOVEMBER EVENTS AND DEADLINES

Design.y.c.
New York, NY
November 1 - 3
www.designyc.com/

Interplan
New York City, NY
November 1 - 3
www.interplanshow.com/

Design2000: International Design Meeting
Paris, France
November 7 - 10
www.reedexpo.com

International Hotel/Motel & Restaurant Show
New York City, NY
November 11 - 14
(914) 421-3200

Build Boston
Boston, MA
November 14 - 16
(800) 544-1898

Chicago Design Show
Chicago, Illinois
November 2 - 5
www.chicagodesign.com

Symposium on Healthcare Design 2000
Anaheim, CA
November 29 - December 2
(508) 647-8637

International Forum on Design Management Research & Education (DMI)
Europe
November, 2000
for additional information:
www.dmi.org/conferences/index.shtml

NOVEMBER 2000

SUN	MON	TUES	WED	THURS	FRI	SAT
			1	2	3	4
5	6	7	8	9 Stanford White	10	11 James Renwick *Veteran's Day*
12	13	14	15	16	17	18
19	20	21	22	23 *Thanksgiving*	24 Walter Burley Griffin	25
26	27	28	29 Gottfried Semper	30 Andrea Palladio		

Notes for Events & Anniversaries

DECEMBER EVENTS AND DEADLINES

**AIAS (American Institute of
Architecture Students) Annual Forum**
Washington, D.C.
December 27, 2000 - January 1, 2001
www.aiasnatl.org/

**Rudy Bruner Award for Urban
Excellence**
Submissions due in December
For additional info:
www.brunerfoundation.org

DECEMBER 2000

SUN	MON	TUES	WED	THURS	FRI	SAT
					1	2
3	4	5 Ricardo Bofill	6	7	8	9
10 Adolf Loos	11	12	13	14	15 Oscar Niemeyer	16 Ralph Adams Cram
17	18	19	20 Calvert Vaux	21	22 *Hanukkah*	23
24	25 *Christmas*	26	27	28	29	30
31						

Notes for Events & Anniversaries

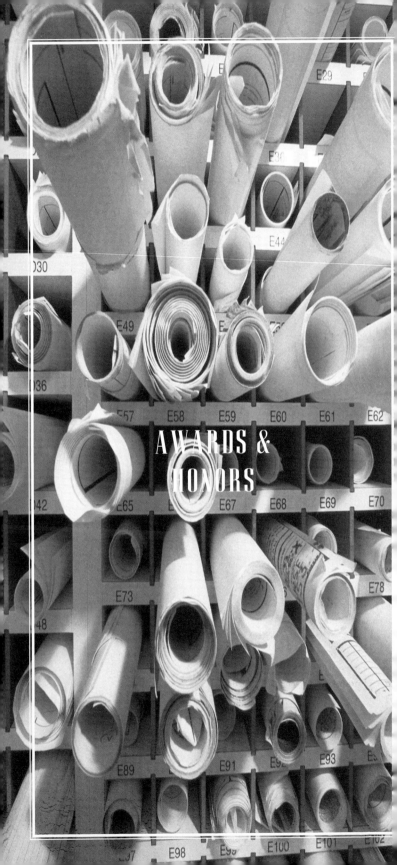

AWARDS & HONORS

AWARDS & HONORS

Abbott Lowell Cummings Award

The Abbott Lowell Cummings Award is presented annually by the Vernacular Architecture Forum (VAF), honoring outstanding books published about North American vernacular architecture and landscape. A review committee prioritizes submissions on new information, the role of fieldwork in research, critical approach and the model provided in writing and research methods. A founder of the VAF, Abbott Lowell Cummings was a prolific researcher and writer. He is best known for his magnum opus, *The Framed Houses of Massachusetts Bay, 1625-1725* (1979).

For additional information, visit the VAF's Web site at *www.vernaculararchitecture.org*.

1983
 "'In a Manner and Fashion Suitable to Their Degree': An Investigation of the Material Culture of Early Rural Pennsylvania,"* in Working Papers from the Regional Economic History Research Center, by Jack Michel

1984
 no award granted

1985
 Big House, Little House, Back House, Barn: The Connected Farm Buildings of New England by Thomas Hubka (University Press of New England)

1986
 Hollybush by Charles Martin (University of Tennessee Press)

1987
 Holy Things and Profane: Anglican Parish Churches in Colonial Virginia by Dell Upton (Architectural History Foundation)

1988
 Architecture and Rural Life in Central Delaware, 1700-1900 by Bernard Herman (University of Tennessee Press)

1989
 Study Report for Slave Quarters Reconstruction at Carter's Grove. Colonial Williamsburg Foundation

 Study Report for the Bixby House Restoration by Old Sturbridge Village

1990
 Manhattan for Rent, 1785-1850 by Elizabeth Blackmar (Cornell University Press)

 Building the Octagon by Orlando Rideout (American Institute of Architects)

1991
 Architects and Builders in North Carolina by Catherine Bishir, Charlotte Brown, Carl Lounsbury, and Ernest Wood, III (University of North Carolina Press)

Abbott Lowell Cummings Award (Con't)

1992

Alone Together: A History of New York's Early Apartments by Elizabeth Cromley (Cornell University Press)

A Place to Belong, Community, Order and Everyday Space in Calvert, Newfoundland by Gerald Pocius (University of Georgia Press)

1993

Homeplace: The Social Use and Meaning of the Folk Dwelling in Southwestern North Carolina by Michael Ann Williams (University of Georgia Press)

The Park and the People: A History of Central Park by Roy Rosenzweig and Elizabeth Blackmar (Cornell University Press)

1994

The Stolen House by Bernard Herman (University Press of Virginia)

1995

Living Downtown: The History of Residential Hotels in the United States by Paul Groth (University of California Press)

1996

An Illustrated Glossary of Early Southern Architecture and Landscape by Carl Lounsbury (Oxford University Press)

1997

Unplanned Suburbs: Toronto's American Tragedy, 1900-1950 by Richard Harris (Johns Hopkins University Press)

1998

City Center to Regional Mall : Architecture, the Automobile, and Retailing in Los Angeles, 1920-1950 by Richard Longstreth (MIT Press)

1999

The Myth of Santa Fe: Creating a Modern Regional Tradition by Chris Wilson (University of New Mexico Press)

Architecture of the United States by Dell Upton (Oxford University Press)

Source: Vernacular Architecture Forum

Did you know...
The Parthenon, built from 447 – 438 BC as a temple to the goddess Athena, is constructed of precisely fitted, mortarless marble blocks.

Aga Khan Award for Architecture

Granted once every three years, the Aga Khan Trust for Culture's Aga Khan Award for Architecture recognizes outstanding contributions to the built environment in the Muslim world. The diversity of winning projects includes individual buildings, restoration and re-use schemes, large-scale community developments, and environmental projects. In addition to the physical, economic, and social needs of a region, this award seeks to emphasize the importance of cultural and spiritual aspects of a project. The Steering Committee, comprised of internationally distinguished architects and scholars, governs this complex three-year process of nominations and technical review in addition to the selection of the Master Jury, which selects the final winning entries. Eligible projects must have been completed within the past 25 years and in use for a minimum of two years. An award of US $500,000 is apportioned between each cycle's winners.

For more information about this award and photographs, drawings and descriptions of the 1998 award recipients, visit the Aga Khan Award for Architecture's Web site at *www.akaa1998.org.*

1980

Agricultural Training Centre
Nianing, Senegal
UNESCO/BREDA (Senegal)

Medical Centre
Mopti, Mali
André Ravereau (France)

Courtyard Houses
Agadir, Morocco
Jean-François Zevaco (Morocco)

Sidi Bou Saïd
Tunis, Tunisia
Technical Bureau of the Municipality, Planners (Tunisia)

Halawa House
Agamy, Egypt
Abdelwahed El-Wakil (England)

Rüstem Pasa Caravanserai
Edirne, Turkey
Ertan Çakirlar (Turkey)

Ertegün House
Bodrum, Turkey
Turgut Cansever

Turkish Historical Society
Ankara, Turkey
Turgut Cansever and Ertur Yener
(Turkey)

Aga Khan Award for Architecture (Con't)

Inter-Continental Hotel and
    Conference Centre
Mecca, Saudi Arabia
Rolf Gutbrod and Frei Otto
    (Germany)

National Museum, Doha, Qatar
Michael Rice and Co. (England) and
    Design and Construction Group
    (Greece)

Water Towers
Kuwait City, Kuwait
VBB, Sune Lindström and Joe
    Lindström, Björn and Björn
    Design, Stig Egnell (Sweden)

Ali Qapu, Chehel Sutun and Hasht
    Behesht
Isfahan, Iran
ISMEO – Istituto Italiano per il
    Medio ed Estremo Oriente (Italy)

Mughal Sheraton Hotel
Agra, India
ARCOP Design Group (Canada)

Kampung Improvement Program
Jakarta, Indonesia
KIP Technical Unit (Indonesia)

Pondok Pesantren Pabelan
Central Java, Indonesia
Amin Arraihana and Fanani
    (Indonesia)

1983

Hafsia Quarter
Tunis, Tunisia
Association de Sauvegarde de la
    Médina de Tunis (Tunisia)

Darb Qirmiz Quarter
Cairo, Egypt
Egyptian Antiquities Organization
    and German Archaeological
    Institute (Egypt)

Sherefudin's White Mosque
Visoko, Bosnia-Herzegovina
Zlatko Ugljen with D. Malkin,
    Engineer (Bosnia-Herzegovina)

Residence Andalous
Sousse, Tunisia
Serge Santelli (France) and Cabinet
    GERAU (Tunisia)

Hajj Terminal, King Abdul Aziz
    International Airport
Jeddah, Saudi Arabia
Skidmore, Owings and Merrill
    (USA)

Ramses Wissa Wassef Arts Centre
Giza, Egypt
Ramses Wissa Wassef (Egypt)

Tanjong Jara Beach Hotel and
    Rantau Abang Visitors' Centre
Kuala Trengganu, Malaysia
Wimberly, Wisenand, Allison, Tong
    and Goo (USA) with Arkitek
    Bersikutu (Malaysia)

Great Mosque of Niono
Niono, Mali
Lassina Minta (Mali)

Nail Çakirhan Residence
Akyaka Village, Turkey
Nail Çakirhan (Turkey)

Aga Khan Award for Architecture (Con't)

Azem Palace
Damascus, Syria
Michel Ecochard (France) and Shafiq
al-Imam (Syria)

Tomb of Shah Rukn-i-'Alam
Multan, Pakistan
Awqaf Department (Pakistan)

1986
Social Security Complex
Istanbul, Turkey
Sedad Hakki Eldem (Turkey)

Dar Lamane Housing Community
Casablanca, Morocco
Abderrahim Charai and Abdelaziz
Lazrak (Morocco)

Mostar Old Town
Bosnia-Herzegovina
Stari-Grad Mostar (Bosnia-
Herzegovina)

Al-Aqsa Mosque
al-Haram al-Sharif, Jerusalem
Isam Awwad (Jerusalem) and
ICCROM (Italy)

Yaama Mosque, Yaama
Tahoua, Niger
Falké Barmou (Niger)

Bhong Mosque, Bhong
Rahim-Yar Khan, Pakistan
Rais Ghazi Mohammad, Patron
(Pakistan)

1986 Honorable Mentions
Shushtar New Town
Shushtar, Iran
DAZ Architects (Iran)

Kampung Kebalen Improvement
Surabaya, Indonesia
Surabaya Kampung Improvement
Program, with the Surabaya
Institute of Technology, and the
Kampung Kegalen Community
(Indonesia)

Ismaïliyya Development Projects
Ismaïliyya, Egypt
Culpin Planning (England)

Saïd Naum Mosque
Jakarta, Indonesia
Atelier Enam Architects and
Planners (Indonesia)

Historic Sites Development
Istanbul, Turkey
Touring and Automobile Association
of Turkey (Turkey)

1989
Great Omari Mosque
Sidon, Lebanon
Saleh Lamei-Mostafa (Egypt)

Rehabilitation of Asilah
Morocco
Al-Mouhit Cultural Association,
Patron (Morocco)

Grameen Bank Housing Program
Bangladesh
Grameen Bank (Bangladesh)

Citra Niaga Urban Development
Samarinda, Indonesia
Antonio Ismael Risianto, PT Triaco,
and PT Griyantara Architects
(Indonesia)

Aga Khan Award for Architecture (Con't)

Gürel Family Summer Residence
Çanakkale, Turkey
Sedat Gürel (Turkey)

Hayy Assafarat: Landscaping and Al-
Kindi Plaza
Riyadh, Saudi Arabia
Bödeker, Boyer, Wagenfeld and
Partners, Landscape Architects
(Germany)
Beeah Group Consultants, Architects
(Saudi Arabia)

Sidi el-Aloui Primary School
Tunis, Tunisia
Association de la Sauvegarde de la
Médina de Tunis (Tunisia)

Corniche Mosque
Jeddah, Saudi Arabia
Architect: Abdelwahed El-Wakil
(England)

Ministry of Foreign Affairs
Riyadh, Saudi Arabia
Henning Larsen (Denmark)

National Assembly Building, Sher-e-
Bangla Nagar
Dhaka, Bangladesh
Louis I. Kahn with David Wisdom
and Associates (USA)

Institut du Monde Arabe
Paris, France
Jean Nouvel, Pierre Soria and Gilbert
Lezénés, with the Architecture
Studio (France)

1992

Kairouan Conservation Program
Kairouan, Tunisia
Association de Sauvegarde de la
Médina de Kairouan (Tunisia)

Palace Parks Program
Istanbul, Turkey
Regional Offices of the National
Palaces Trust (Turkey)

Cultural Park for Children
Cairo, Egypt
Abdelhalim Ibrahim Abdelhalim
(Egypt)

East Wahdat Upgrading Program
Amman, Jordan
Urban Development Department,
Planners (Jordan)
Halcrow Fox Associates and Jouzy
and Partners, Feasibility Studies
(Jordan)

Kampung Kali Cho-de
Yogyakarta, Indonesia
Yousef B. Mangunwijaya (Indonesia)

Stone Building System
Dar'a Province, Syria
Raif Muhanna, Ziad Muhanna, and
Rafi Muhanna (Civil Engineer),
(Syria)

Demir Holiday Village
Bodrum, Turkey
Turgut Cansever, Emine Ögün,
Mehmet Ögün, and Feyza
Cansever (Turkey)

Panafrican Institute for Development
Ouagadougou, Burkina Faso
ADAUA Burkina Faso (Burkina
Faso)

Entrepreneurship Development
Institute of India
Ahmedabad, India
Bimal Hasmukh Patel (India)

Aga Khan Award for Architecture (Con't)

1995

Restoration of Bukhara Old City
Uzbekistan
Restoration Institute of Uzbekistan,
Tashkent, and the Restoration
Office of the Municipality of
Bukhara, Uzbekistan

Conservation of Old Sana'a
Yemen
General Organization for the
Protection of the Historic Cities of
Yemen (Yemen)

Reconstruction of Hafsia Quarter II
Tunis, Tunisia
Association de Sauvegarde de la
Médina (Tunisia)

Khuda-ki-Basti Incremental
Development Scheme
Hyderabad, Pakistan
Hyderabad Development Authority
andTasneem Ahmed Siddiqui
(Pakistan)

Aranya Low-Cost Housing
Indore, India
Vastu-Shilpa Foundation, Balkrishna
V. Doshi (India)

Great Mosque and Redevelopment of
the Old City Centre
Riyadh, Saudi Arabia
Rasem Badran (Jordan)

Menara Mesiniaga
Kuala Lumpur, Malaysia
T.R. Hamzah and Yeang Sdn. Bhd.
(Malaysia)

Kaedi Regional Hospital
Kaedi, Mauritania
Association pour le Développement
naturel d'une Architecture et d'un
Urbanisme Africains (Mauritania)

Mosque of the Grand National
Assembly
Ankara, Turkey
Behruz and Can Cinici (Turkey)

Alliance Franco-Sénégalaise
Kaolack, Senegal
Patrick Dujarric (Senegal)

Re-Forestation Program of the
Middle East Technical University
Ankara, Turkey
Middle East Technical University,
Landscaping and Planners

Landscaping Integration of the
Soekarno-Hatta Airport
Cengkareng, Indonesia
Aéroports de Paris, Paul Andreu
(France)

1998

Rehabilitation of Hebron Old Town
Hebron, Palestine
Engineering Office of the Hebron
Rehabilitation Committee
(Palestine)

Slum Networking of Indore City
Indore, India
Himanshu Parikh, Civil Engineer
(India)

Aga Khan Award for Architecture (Con't)

Lepers Hospital
Chopda Taluka, India
Per Christian Brynildsen and Jan
   Olav Jensen (Norway)

Salinger Residence
Bamgi, Selangor, Malaysia
Jimmy C.S. Lim (Malaysia)

Tuwaiq Palace
Riyadh, Saudi Arabia
OHO Joint Venture (Atelier Frei
   Otto, Buro Happold, Omrania)

Alhamra Arts Council
Lahore, Pakistan
Nayyar Ali Dada (Pakistan

Vidhan Bhavan
Bhopal, India
Charles Correa (India)

Chairman's Awards
On two occasions the Chairman's Award has been granted. It was established to honor the achievements of individuals who have made considerable lifetime achievements to Muslim architecture but whose work was not within the scope of the Master Jury's mandate.

1980 Hassan Fathy (Egypt)
1986 Rifat Chadirji (Iraq)

Source: The Aga Khan Trust for Culture

Teach us all to have aspiring minds (to) comprehend the wondrous architecture of the world.

Christopher Marlow, c.1587

AIA Gold Medal

The Gold Medal is The American Institute of Architects' highest award. Eligibility is open to architects or non-architects, living or dead, whose contribution to the field of architecture has made a lasting impact. The AIA's Board of Directors grants no more than one Gold Medal each year, occasionally granting none.

For more information, contact the AIA's Honor and Awards Department at (202) 626-7586 or visit their Web site at *www.e-architect.com.*

1907	Sir Aston Webb, RA, Hon. FAIA	1961	Le Corbusier (Charles Edouard
1909	Charles Follen McKim, FAIA		Jeanneret-Gris, Hon. FAIA)
1911	George Browne Post, FAIA	1962	Eero Saarinen, FAIA*
1914	Jean Louis Pascal, Hon. FAIA	1963	Alvar Aalto, Hon. FAIA
1922	Victor Laloux, Hon. FAIA	1964	Pier Luigi Nervi, Hon. FAIA
1923	Henry Bacon, FAIA	1966	Kenzo Tange, Hon. FAIA
1925	Sir Edwin Landseer Lutyens, Hon. FAIA	1967	Wallace K. Harrison, FAIA
		1968	Marcel Breuer, FAIA
1925	Bertram Grosvenor Goodhue, FAIA	1969	William Wilson Wurster, FAIA
1927	Howard Van Doren Shaw, FAIA	1970	Richard Buckminster Fuller, FAIA
1929	Milton Bennett Medary, FAIA	1971	Louis I. Kahn, FAIA
1933	Ragnar Ostberg, Hon. FAIA	1972	Pietro Belluschi, FAIA
1938	Paul Philippe Cret, FAIA	1977	Richard Joseph Neutra, FAIA*
1944	Louis Henri Sullivan, FAIA	1978	Philip Cortelyou Johnson, FAIA
1947	Eliel Saarinen, FAIA	1979	Ieoh Ming Pei, FAIA
1948	Charles Donagh Maginnis, FAIA	1981	Joseph Luis Sert, FAIA
1949	Frank Lloyd Wright, FAIA	1982	Romaldo Giurgola, FAIA
1950	Sir Patrick Abercrombie, Hon. FAIA	1983	Nathaniel A. Owings, FAIA
1951	Bernard Ralph Maybeck, FAIA	1985	William Wayne Caudill, FAIA*
1952	Auguste Perret, Hon. FAIA	1986	Arthur Erickson, Hon. FAIA
1953	William Adams Delano, FAIA	1989	Joseph Esherick, FAIA
1955	William Marinus Dudok Hilversum, Hon. FAIA	1990	E. Fay Jones, FAIA
		1991	Charles W. Moore, FAIA
1956	Clarence S. Stein, FAIA	1992	Benjamin Thompson, FAIA
1957	Ralph Walker, FAIA (Centennial Medal of Honor)	1993	Thomas Jefferson*
		1993	Kevin Roche, FAIA
1957	Louis Skidmore, FAIA	1994	Sir Norman Foster, Hon. FAIA
1958	John Wellborn Root, FAIA	1995	Cesar Pelli, FAIA
1959	Walter Gropius, FAIA	1997	Richard Meier, FAIA
1960	Ludwig Mies van der Rohe, FAIA	1999	Frank Gehry, FAIA

* honored posthumously
Source: American Institute of Architects

AIA Honor Awards

The American Institute of Architects' (AIA) Honor Awards celebrate outstanding design in three areas: Architecture, Interior Architecture, and Regional & Urban Design. Juries of designers and executives present separate awards in each category.

Additional information and entry forms may be obtained by calling the AIA's Honors and Awards Department at (202) 626-7586 or by visiting their Web site at *www.e-architect.com*.

1999 AIA Honor Awards for Architecture Recipients:
The AIA Honor Awards for Architecture have been presented annually since 1949 to projects which have best met their own requirements. Projects are judged individually and not against each other in one of two categories: design resolution and design advancement.

Brooks County Safety Rest Area
Brooks County, Texas
Richter Associates Architects Inc.

Byzantine Fresco Chapel Museum
Houston, Texas
François de Menil Architects P.C.

Carlson-Reges Residence
Los Angeles, California
RoTo Architects, Inc.

Inventure Place, Home of National Inventors Hall of Fame
Akron, Ohio
Polshek and Partners Architects LLP and TC Architects, Inc

Kiasma: Museum of Contemporary Art
Helsinki, Finland
Steven Holl Architects, with associate architect Juhani Pallasmaa

K J McNitt Construction, Inc.
Oklahoma City, Oklahoma
Elliot + Associates Architects

Minneapolis Pathways: A Health Crisis Resource Center
Minneapolis, Minnesota
Anmahian Winton Associates, Inc., with associate architect Shea Architects, Inc.

Nomentana House
Stoneham, Maine
Scogin Elam & Bray Architects, Inc.

Old State Capitol Restoration, The Center for Governmental and Political History
Baton Rouge, Louisiana
E. Eean McNaughton Architects

Olympic College Shelton
Shelton, Washington
The Miller/Hull Partnership

Robert L. Preger Intelligent Workplace, Carnegie Mellon University,
Pittsburgh, Pennsylvania
Bohlin Cywinski Jackson, with associate architect The Center for Building Performance and Diagnostics

AIA Honor Awards (Con't)

The Thomas Jefferson Building of
the Library of Congress
Washington, D.C.
The Architect of the Capitol, with
associate architect Arthur Cotton
Moore/Associates

The World Bank
Washington, D.C.
Kohn Pedersen Fox Associates PC,
with associate architect KressCox
Associates PC

Jury:
Robert J. Frasca, Chair
James P. Alexander
Susan Child
Krista Dean, Assoc
Joseph J. Hittinger
Steven D. Ehrlich
Nestor I. Infanzon
Julie V. Snow
Joseph M. Valerio

1999 AIA Honor Awards for Interior Architecture Recipients:

AIA Honor Awards for Interior Architecture honor excellence in interior design projects of all types and sizes, worldwide. The award's intent is to highlight the diversity of interior architecture projects. All architects licensed in the U.S. are eligible to submit entries.

The Denver Central Library
Denver, Colorado
Michael Graves Architect, with asso-
ciate architect Klipp Colussy Jenks
DuBois Architects, PC

Fifth Avenue Residence
New York City, New York
Shelton, Mindel & Associates

FILA Corporate Headquarters
Sparks, Maryland
Shelton, Mindel & Associates.

The Gagosian Gallery
Beverly Hills, California
Richard Meier & Partners

Jil Sander Showroom
Hamburg, Germany
Gabellini Associates

Jil Sander and Ultimo Boutique
San Francisco, California
Gabellini Associates

Little Village Academy
Chicago, Illinois
Ross Barney + Jankowski, Inc

M.C. Ginsberg Objects of Art
West Des Moines, Iowa
Herbert Lewis Kruse Blunck
Architecture

National Postal Museum
Washington, D.C.
KCF/SHG Inc.

Studio/Residence
Omaha, Nebraska
Randy Brown Architects

Urban Interface Loft
New York City, New York
Dean/Wolf Architects

Jury:
Lauren L. Rottet, Chair
Michael Bierut
Stanford Hughes
Mark C. McInturff
David D. Salmela

AIA Honor Awards (Con't)

1999 AIA Honor Awards for Regional and Urban Design Recipients:
The AIA Honor Awards for Regional and Urban Design seek to recognize the expanding role of architects in planning our communities. Owners, agencies, organizations, architects and others involved in projects may submit them to the competition. A U.S. licensed architect must be involved in the project.

Diggs Town
Norfolk, Virginia
Urban Design Associates, with associate architect CMSS Architects

42nd Street Now!
New York City, New York
Robert A.M. Stern Architects, with associate firm M & Co

South Dade Watershed Project
Miami, Florida
Daniel Williams, FAIA, with associate architects Chris Jackson, Mark Brown, Erick Valle, and Manuel Fernandez-Norall

Tacoma Campus Master Plan & Phase I Buildings
Tacoma, Washington
Moore Ruble Yudell, with associate architect Loschky Marquardt & Nesholm

Theater District Streetscape Master Plan
Boston, Massachusetts
Sheila Kennedy, Kennedy & Violich Architecture

Jury:
Harrison Fraker, Chair
Susan Chin
Stanton Eckstut
John E. Kaliski
Roger Schluntz

Source: The American Institute of Architects

Did you know...
Sir Norman Foster's Hong Kong and Shanghai Banking Corporation Headquarters features a computer-controlled "sun-scoop:" a mirrored panel which follows the sun and reflects its rays into the top of the central building's atrium, flooding the building with light.

AIA Honors for Collaborative Achievement

The American Institute of Architects (AIA) presents their Honors for Collaborative Achievement annually to recognize achievements in influencing or advancing the architectural profession. Recipients may be individuals or groups. Nominees must be living and may have been active in any number of areas, including administration, art, collaborative achievement, construction, industrial design, information science, professions allied with architecture, public policy, research, education, recording and illustration, and writing and scholarship.

For more information, refer to the AIA's Web site at *www.e-architect.com* or contact the AIA's Honors and Awards Department at (202) 626-7586.

1976
Edmund N. Bacon, FAIA
Charles A. Blessing, FAIA
Wendell J. Campbell, AIA
Gordon Cullen
James Marston Fitch
The Institute for Architecture and Urban Studies
New York City Planning Commission and New York City Landmarks Preservation Committee
Saul Steinberg
Vincent J. Scully Jr., Hon. AIA
Robert Le Ricolais, Hon. FAIA

1977
Claes Oldenburg
Louise Nevelson
Historic American Buildings Survey
Arthur Drexler
G. Holmes Perkins, FAIA
The Baroness Jackson of Lodsworth DBE (Barbara Ward)
Walker Art Center
City of Boston

Pittsburgh History & Landmarks Foundation
Montreal Metro System

1978
Frederick Gutheim, Hon. AIA
Richard Haas
Dr. August Komendant
David A. Macaulay
National Trust for Historic Preservation
Stanislawa Nowicki
John C. Portman Jr., FAIA
Robert Royston, FASLA
Nicholas N. Solovioff
Robert Venturi, FAIA

1979
Douglas Haskell, FAIA
Barry Commoner
John D. Entenza, Hon. AIA
Bernard Rudofsky
Steen Eiler Rasmussen, Hon. FAIA
National Endowment for the Arts
Christo
Bedford-Stuyvesant Restoration
Charles E. Peters, FAIA
Arthur S. Siegel (posthumous)

AIA Honors for Collaborative Achievement (Con't)

1980

Cyril M. Harris
Sol LeWitt
Robert Campbell
Committee for the Preservation of
    Architectural Records
Progressive Architecture Awards
    Program
The Rouse Company for Faneuil Hall
    Marketplace
John Benson
M. Paul Friedberg
Jack E. Boucher
Mrs. Lyndon B. Johnson

1981

Kenneth Snelson
Paul Goldberger
Sir Nikolaus Pevsner
Herman Miller, Inc.
Edison Price
Colin Rowe
Reynolds Metals Company
Smithsonian Associates

1982

"Oppositions" (Institute for
    Architecture & Urban Studies)
Historic New Harmony, Inc.
The MIT Press
Jean Dubuffet
Sir John Summerson, Hon. FAIA
The Plan of St. Gall
The Washington Metropolitan Area
    Transit Authority
William H. Whyte

1983

The Honorable Christopher S. Bond,
    Governor of Missouri
Donald Canty
Fazlur Khan (posthumous)
Knoll International
Christian Norberg-Schulz
Paul Stevenson Oles, AIA

1984

Reyner Banham
Bolt, Beranek & Newman
Cooper-Hewitt Museum
Inner Harbor Development of the
    City of Baltimore
His Highness the Aga Khan
T.Y. Lin
Steve Rosenthal
San Antonio River Walk
Bruno Zevi, Hon. FAIA

1985

Ward Bennett
Kenneth Frampton
Esther McCoy
Norman McGrath
The Hon. John F. Seiberling
Weidlinger Associates
Nick Wheeler
Games of the XXIII Olympiad
Cranbrook Academy of Art
Central Park

1986

Cathedral Church of St. John the
    Divine
Antoinette Forrester Downing
David H. Geiger
Gladding, McBean & Company
William H. Jordy
Master Plan for the United States
    Capitol
Adolf Kurt Placzek
Cervin Robinson
Rudolf Wittkower (posthumous)

1987

James S. Ackerman
Jennifer Bartlett
Steven Brooke
The Chicago Architecture
    Foundation
Jules Fisher & Paul Marantz, Inc.
Charles Guggenheim
John B. Jackson

AIA Honors for Collaborative Achievement (Con't)

Mesa Verde National Park
Rizzoli International Publications, Inc.
Carter Wiseman

1988
Spiro Kostof
Loeb Fellowship in Advanced Environmental Studies, Harvard University
Robert Smithson (posthumous)
Society for the Preservation of New England Antiquities
Sussman/Prejza & Company, Inc.
Robert Wilson

1989
Battery Park City Authority
American Academy in Rome
Eduard Sekler
Leslie E. Robertson
Niels Diffrient
David S. Haviland
V'Soske

1990
The Association for the Preservation of Virginia Antiquities
Corning Incorporated
Jackie Ferrara
Timothy Hursley
Marvin Mass
Mary Miss
Peter G. Rolland
Joseph Santeramo
Taos Pueblo
Emmet L. Wemple

1991
James Fraser Carpenter
Danish Design Centre
Foundation for Architecture, Philadelphia
The J.M. Kaplan Fund
Maguire Thomas Partners

Native American Architecture (Robert Easton and Peter Nabokov)
Princeton Architectural Press
Seaside, Florida
Allan Temko
Lebbeus Woods

1992
Siah Armajani
Canadian Centre for Architecture
Stephen Coyle
Milton Glaser
The Mayors' Institute on City Design
The Municipal Art Society of New York
John Julius Norwich
Ove Arup & Partners Consulting Engineers PC
Peter Vanderwarker
Peter Walker

1993
ADPSR (Architects/Designers/Planners for Social Responsibility)
Michael Blackwood
The Conservation Trust of Puerto Rico
Benjamin Forgey
The Gamble House
Philadelphia Zoological Society
The Princeton University Board of Trustees, Officers and the Office of Physical Planning
Jane Thompson
Sally B. Woodbridge
World Monuments Fund

1994
Joseph H. Baum
Beth Dunlop
Mildred Friedman
Historic Savannah Foundation
Rhode Island Historical Preservation Commission

AIA Honors for Collaborative Achievement (Con't)

Salvadori Educational Center on the
Built Environment
Gordon H. Smith
The Stuart Collection
Sunset Magazine
Judith Turner

1995

The Art Institute of Chicago,
Department of Architecture
ASAP (The American Society of
Architectural Perspectivists)
Friends of Post Office Square
The University of Virginia, Curator
and Architect for the Academical
Village/The Rotunda
Albert Paley
UrbanArts, Inc.
Dr. Yoichi Ando

1996

Boston by Foot, Inc.
William S. Donnell
Haley & Aldrich, Inc.

Toshio Nakamura, Hon. FAIA
Joseph Passonneau, FAIA, ASCE
Preservation Society of Charleston
Earl Walls Associates
Paul Warchol Photography, Inc.

1997

Architecture Resource Center

1998

Lian Hurst Mann, PhD., AIA
SOM Foundation
William Morgan, FAIA

1999

Howard Brandston
Jeff Goldberg
Ann E. Gray
Ronald McKay
Miami-Dade Art in Public Places
Monacelli Press
New York Landmarks Conservancy

Source: American Institute of Architects

Did you know...
**Eero Saarinen &
Associates's Deere
Company Administration
Center (1958, Moline, IL)
was the first architectural
use of weathering steel.**

Alice Davis Hitchcock Book Award

The Alice Davis Hitchcock book award has been granted annually by the Society of Architectural Historians (SAH) since 1949. It is given to a publication by a North American scholar, published within the preceding two years, that demonstrates a high level of scholarly distinction in the field of the history of architecture.

For more information contact the SAH at (312) 573-1365 or visit their Web site at *www.sah.org/awards.html*.

1949
Colonial Architecture and Sculpture in Peru by Harold Wethey (Harvard University Press)

1950
Architecture of the Old Northwest Territory by Rexford Newcomb (University of Chicago Press)

1951
Architecture and Town Planning in Colonial Connecticut by Anthony Garvan (Yale University Press)

1952
The Architectural History of Newport by Antoinette Downing and Vincent Scully (Harvard University Press)

1953
Charles Rennie Macintosh and the Modern Movement by Thomas Howarth (Routledge and K. Paul)

1954
Early Victorian Architecture in Britain by Henry Russell Hitchcock (Da Capo Press, Inc.)

1955
Benjamin H. Latrobe by Talbot Hamlin (Oxford University Press)

1956
The Railroad Station: An Architectural History by Carroll L. V. Meeks (Yale University Press)

1957
The Early Architecture of Georgia by Frederick D. Nichols (University of N.C. Press)

1958
The Public Buildings of Williamsburg by Marcus Whiffen (Colonial Williamsburg)

1959
Carolingian and Romanesque Architecture, 800 to 1200 by Kenneth J. Conant (Yale University Press)

1960
The Villa d'Este at Tivoli by David Coffin (Princeton University Press)

1961
The Architecture of Michelangelo by James Ackerman (University of Chicago Press)

1962
The Art and Architecture of Ancient America by George Kubler (Yale University Press)

1963
La Cathédrale de Bourges et sa Place dans L'archtietture Gothique by Robert Branner (Tardy)

1964
Images of American Living, Four Centuries of Architecture and Furniture as Cultural Expression by Alan Gowans (Lippincott)

Alice Davis Hitchcock Book Award (Con't)

1965
The Open-Air Churches of Sixteenth Century Mexico by John McAndrew (Harvard University Press)

1966
Early Christian and Byzantine Architecture by Richard Krautheimer (Penguin Books)

1967
Eighteenth-Century Architecture in Piedmont: the open structures of Juvarra, Alfieri & Vittone by Richard Pommer (New York University Press)

1968
Architecture and Politics in Germany, 1918-1945 by Barbara Miller Lane (Harvard University Press)

1969
Samothrace, Volme III: The Hieron by Phyllis Williams Lehmann

1970
The Church of Notre Dame in Montreal by Franklin Toker (McGill-Queen's University Press)

1971
no award granted

1972
The Prairie School; Frank Lloyd Wright and his Midwest Contemporaries by Allen H. Brooks (University of Toronto Press)

The Early Churches of Constantinople: Architecture and Liturgy by Thomas F. Mathews (Pennsylvania State University Press)

1973
The Campanile of Florence Cathedral: "Giotto's Tower" by Marvin Trachtenberg (New York University Press)

1974
FLO, A Biography of Frederick Law Olmstead by Laura Wood Roper (Johns Hopkins University Press)

1975
Gothic vs. Classic, Architectural Projects in Seventeeth-Century Italy by Rudolf Wittkower (G. Braziller)

1976
no award granted

1977
The Esplanade Ridge (Vol. V in The New Orleans Architecture Series) by Mary Louise Christovich, Sally Kitredge Evans, Betsy Swanson, and Roulhac Toledano (Pelican Publishing Company)

1978
Sebastiano Serlio on Domestic Architecture by Myra Nan Rosenfeld (Architectural History Foundation)

1979
The Framed Houses of Massachusetts Bay, 1625-1725 by Abbott Lowell Cummings (Belknap Press)

Paris: A Century of Change, 1878-1978 by Norma Evenson (Yale University Press)

1980
Rome: Profile of a City, 312-1308 by Richard Krautheimer (Princton University Press)

1981
Gardens of Illusion: The Genius of Andre LeNotre by Franklin Hamilton Hazelhurst (Vanderbilt University Press)

1982
Indian Summer: Luytens, Baker and Imperial Delhi by Robert Grant Irving (Yale Univ. Press)

Alice Davis Hitchcock Book Award (Con't)

1983
  Architecture and the Crisis of Modern Science by Alberto Pérez-Goméz (MIT Press)

1984
  Campus: An American Planning Tradition by Paul Venable Turner (MIT Press)

1985
  The Law Courts: The Architecture of George Edmund Street by David Brownlee (MIT Press)

1986
  The Architecture of the Roman Empire: An Urban Appraisal by William L. MacDonald (Yale University Press)

1987
  Holy Things and Profane: Anglican Parish Churches in Colonial Virginia by Dell Upton (MIT Press)

1988
  Designing Paris: The Architecture of Duban, Labrouste, Duc and Vaudoyer by David Van Zanten (MIT Press)

1989
  Florentine New Towns: Urban Design in the Late Middle Ages by David Friedman (MIT Press)

1990
  Claude-Nicolas Ledoux: Architecture and Social Reform at the End of the Ancien Régime by Anthony Vidler (MIT Press)

1991
  The Paris of Henri IV: Architecture and Urbanism by Hilary Ballon (MIT Press)
  Seventeenth-Century Roman Palaces: Use and the Art of the Plan by Patricia Waddy (MIT Press)

1992
  Modernism in Italian Architecture, 1890-1940 by Richard Etlin (MIT Press)

1994*
  Baths and Bathing in Classical Antiquity by Fikret Yegul (MIT Press)

1995
  The Politics of the German Gothic Revival: August Reichensperger by Michael J. Lewis (MIT Press)

1996
  Hadrian's Villa and Its Legacy by William J. MacDonald and John Pinto (Yale University Press)

1997
  Gottfried Semper: Architect of the Nineteenth Century by Harry Francis Mallgrave (Yale University Press)

1998
  The Dancing Column: On Order in Architecture by Joseph Rykwert (MIT Press)

1999
  Dominion of the Eye: Urbanism, Art & Power in Early Modern Florence by Marvin Trachtenberg (Cambridge University Press)

* *At this time the SAH altered their award schedule to coincide with their annual meeting. Thus, no award for 1993 is listed.*

Source: Society of Architectural Historians

Did you know...
Cass Gilbert's Woolworth Building was completed in 1913 at a cost of $13.5 million, which the F.W. Woolworth Company paid in cash.

American Academy of Arts and Letters Academy Awards

The American Academy of Arts and Letters grants their annual Academy Award to an architect(s) as an honor of their work and an encouragement to their ongoing creativity. The prize consists of a $7500 cash award. Recipients must be citizens of the United States. Members of the Academy are not eligible.

For more information, contact the American Academy of Arts and Letters at (212) 368-5900.

1991	Rodolfo Machado and Jorge Silvetti	1995	Mack Scogin and Merrill Elam
1992	Thom Mayne and Michael Rotondi, Morphosis	1996	Maya Lin
1993	Franklin D. Israel	1997	Daniel Libeskind
1994	Craig Hodgetts and Hsin-Ming Fung	1998	Laurie Olin
		1999	Eric Owen Moss

Source: American Academy of Arts and Letters

Did you know...
Sir Norman Foster's Commerzbank in Frankfurt, Germany is the only European skyscraper to be included in the world's top 50 tallest buildings.

American Academy of Arts and Letters Gold Medal for Architecture

The American Academy of Arts and Letters grants a gold medal in the arts in rotation among painting, music, sculpture, poetry, architecture, and many other categories. The entire work of the architect is weighed when being considered for the award. Only citizens of the United States are eligible.

For more information contact the American Academy of Arts and Letters at (212) 368-5900.

1912	William Rutherford Mead	1968	R. Buckminster Fuller
1921	Cass Gilbert	1973	Louis I. Kahn
1930	Charles Adams Platt	1979	I. M. Pei
1940	William Adams Delano	1984	Gordon Bunshaft
1949	Frederick Law Olmsted	1990	Kevin Roche
1953	Frank Lloyd Wright	1996	Philip Johnson
1958	Henry R. Shepley		
1963	Ludwig Mies van der Rohe		

Source: American Academy of Arts and Letters

Opposite: Sterling Music Library addition, Yale Univ., New Haven, CT, Shepley Bulfinch Richardson Abbott
Photograph © Peter Aaron/Esto.

American Architecture Awards

The American Architecture Awards are presented annually by the Chicago Athenaeum: Museum of Architecture and Design. The program was organized in 1998 to honor new architecture, built or unbuilt, in the United States and abroad, and designed by U.S. architectural firms, including corporate, institutional, commercial, and residential projects.

For more information, contact the Chicago Athenaeum at (312) 251-0175 or visit their Web site at *www.chi-athenaeum.org*.

1999 Awarded Projects:

Ballet Memphis
Memphis, Tennessee
Williamson Founders Architects P.C

St. Thomas More Catholic Church
Owensboro, Kentucky
Williamson Founders Architects P.C.

John Luce Contractor's Office
Omaha, Nebraska
Randy Brown Architect

Amoco Research Center Lobby Addition
Naperville, Illinois
Teng & Associates

Fifth Avenue Residence
New York, New York
Shelton, Mindel & Associates

Lerner Hall Student Center
New York, New York
Bernard Tschumi/Gruzen Samton Associated

Private House on Deer Isle, Maine
Peter Forbes and Associates

14th Street Student Housing, New York University
New York, New York
Davis Brody Bond, LLP

The New York Public Library, Main Reading Room Restoration
New York City, New York
Davis Brody Bond, LLP

National Data Processing Center, Bureau of the Census
Bowie, Maryland
Metcalf /Davis Brody (a joint Venture of Davis Brody Bond, LLP and Tobey + Davis)

Washington Monument Restoration Scaffolding and Interior Renovation
Washington, D.C.
Michael Graves Associates

Tour Hines at La Défense
Paris, France
Pei Cobb Freed & Partners Architects LLP

Roth Center for Jewish Life at Dartmouth College
Hanover, New Hampshire

American Architecture Awards (Con't)

R. M. Kliment & Frances Halsband Architects/Randall T. Mudge & Associates

Adam Joseph Lewis Center for Environmental Studies
Oberlin, Ohio
William McDonough + Partners

Spencer Theater for the Performing Arts
Alto, New Mexico
Antoine Predock Architect

Philadelphia Regional Performing Arts Center
Philadelphia, Pennsylvania
Rafael Vinoly Architects PC

Aldrich Museum Addition
Ridgefield, Connecticut
Alexander Gorlin Architect

Visual Arts Center at the College of Santa Fe
Santa Fe, New Mexico
Legorreta Arquitectos

Form & Function Headquarters
Chicago, Illinois
Mark Demsky Architects, Ltd.

Samsung Plaza and Rodin Museum Project
Seoul, Korea
Kohn Pedersen Fox Associates PC/Samoo Architects & Engineers

Lake Superior College
St. Paul, Minnesota
The Leonard Parker Associates

Dearborn Plaza
Chicago, Illinois
DeStefano and Partners

Diversey Driving Range
Lincoln Park, Chicago, Illinois
DeStefano and Partners

730 North Michigan Avenue
Chicago, Illinois
Elkus/Manfredi Architects Ltd.

Mitsui Muromachi Building
Tokyo, Japan
Skidmore, Owings & Merrill

Nancy Lee and Perry R. Bass Performance Hall
Fort Worth, Texas
David M. Schwarz/Architectural Services, Inc. and HKS, Inc.

Jury:
Elizabeth Sverbeyeff Byron
Neil Kozokoff
Susan Grant Lewin
Donald M. Rorke
Jill Vanderfleet Scott

Source: The Chicago Athenaeum

Architecture Firm Award

The American Institute of Architects (AIA) awards its Architecture Firm Award annually to an architecture firm for "consistently producing distinguished architecture." The highest honor that the AIA can bestow on a firm, the Board of Directors confers the award. Eligible firms must claim collaboration within the practice as a hallmark of their methodology and must have been producing work as an entity for at least 10 years.

For more information, visit the AIA on the Internet at *www.e-architect*.org or contact the AIA Honors and Awards Department at (202) 626-7586.

1962	Skidmore, Owings & Merrill	1984	Kallmann, McKinnell & Wood, Architects
1964	The Architects Collaborative		
1965	Wurster, Bernardi & Emmons	1985	Venturi, Rauch and Scott Brown
1967	Hugh Stubbins & Associates	1986	Esherick Homsey Dodge & Davis
1968	I.M. Pei & Partners	1987	Benjamin Thompson & Associates
1969	Jones & Emmons		
1970	Ernest J. Kump Associates	1988	Hartman-Cox Architects
1971	Albert Kahn Associates, Inc.	1989	Cesar Pelli & Associates
1972	Caudill Rowlett Scott	1990	Kohn Pedersen Fox Associates
1973	Shepley Bulfinch Richardson Abbott	1991	Zimmer Gunsul Frasca Partnership
1974	Kevin Roche John Dinkeloo & Associates	1992	James Stewart Polshek and Partners
1975	Davis, Brody & Associates	1993	Cambridge Seven Associates Inc.
1976	Mitchell/Giurgola Architects	1994	Bohlin Cywinski Jackson
1977	Sert, Jackson and Associates	1995	Beyer Blinder Belle
1978	Harry Weese & Associates	1996	Skidmore, Owings & Merrill
1979	Geddes Brecher Qualls Cunningham	1997	R. M. Kliment & Frances Halsband Architects
1980	Edward Larrabee Barnes Associates	1998	Centerbrook Architects and Planners
1981	Hardy Holzman Pfeiffer Associates	1999	Perkins & Will
1982	Gwathmey Siegel & Associates, Architects		
1983	Holabird & Root, Architects, Engineers & Planners		

Source: American Institute of Architects

Opposite: Grand Central Station restoration, New York, NY, Beyer Blinder Belle, restoration architects
Photograph © Peter Aaron/Esto.

Arnold W. Brunner Memorial Prize

The American Academy of Arts and Letters annually recognizes an architect who has contributed to architecture as an art with the Arnold W. Brunner Memorial Prize. A prize of $5000 is granted to each recipient. Eligibility is open to architects of any nationality.

For more information, contact the American Academy of Arts and Letters at (212) 368-5900.

1955	Gordon Bunshaft	1985	William Pederson and Arthur May
	Minoru Yamasaki, Honorable Mention	1986	John Hejduk
1956	John Yeon	1987	James Ingo Freed
1957	John Carl Warnecke	1988	Arata Isozaki
1958	Paul Rudolph	1989	Richard Rogers
1959	Edward Larrabee Barnes	1990	Steven Holl
1960	Louis I. Kahn	1991	Tadao Ando
1961	I. M. Pei	1992	Sir Norman Foster
1962	Ulrich Franzen	1993	Jose Rafael Moneo
1963	Edward Charles Basset	1994	Renzo Piano
1964	Harry Weese	1995	Daniel Urban Kiley
1965	Kevin Roche	1996	Tod Williams and Billie Tsien
1966	Romaldo Giurgola	1997	Henri Ciriani
1968	John M. Johansen	1998	Alvaro Siza
1969	Noel Michael McKinnell	1999	Fumihiko Maki
1970	Charles Gwathmey and Richard Henderson		
1971	John Andrews		
1972	Richard Meier		
1973	Robert Venturi		
1974	Hugh Hardy with Norman Pfeiffer and Malcolm Holzman		
1975	Lewis Davis and Samuel Brody		
1976	James Stirling		
1977	Henry N. Cobb		
1978	Caesar Pelli		
1979	Charles W. Moore		
1980	Michael Graves		
1981	Gunnar Birkerts		
1982	Helmut Jahn		
1983	Frank O. Gehry		
1984	Peter K. Eisenman		

Source: American Academy of Arts and Letters

Did you know...
At 147 meters, Japan's Kasumigaseki Building (1968) was the first building in Japan to exceed 31 meters, Japan's building height restriction until Japanese Building Standard Law was revised in 1963.

ASLA Medal

Every year the American Society of Landscape Architects (ASLA) awards its highest honor, the ASLA Medal, to an individual who has made a significant contribution to the field of landscape architecture. The following individuals were chosen for their unique and lasting impact through their work in landscape design, planning, writing and/or public service. Eligibility is open to non-members of the ASLA of any nationality.

For more information, contact the ASLA at (202) 898-2444 or visit their Web site at *www.asla.org*.

1971	Hideo Sasaki	1991	Meade Palmer
1972	Conrad L. Wirth	1992	Robert S. "Doc" Reich
1973	John C. Simonds	1993	A. E. "Ed" Bye, Jr.
1974	Campbell E. Miller	1994	Edward D. Stone, Jr.
1975	Garrett Eckbo	1995	Dr. Ervin Zube
1976	Thomas Church	1996	John Lyle
1977	Hubert Owens	1997	Julius Fabos
1978	Lawrence Halprin	1998	Carol R. Johnson, FASLA
1979	Norman T. Newton	1999	Stuart C. Dawson, FASLA
1980	William G. Swain		
1981	Sir Geoffrey Jellicoe		
1982	Charles W. Eliot, II		
1983	Theodore O. Osmundson		
1984	Ian McHarg		
1985	Roberto Burle Marx		
1986	William J. Johnson		
1987	Phillip H. Lewis Jr.		
1988	Dame Sylvia Crowe		
1989	Robert N. Royston		
1990	Ray Freeman		

Source: American Society of Landscape Architects

Did you know...
Biltmore House in Asheville, North Carolina (Richard Morris Hunt, 1895) is America's largest privately owned home with 250 rooms and 4 acres of floor space, the equivalent of approximately 4 football fields.

ASLA Professional Awards

The American Society of Landscape Architects' (ASLA) annual Professional Awards Program is intended to encourage the profession of landscape architecture by rewarding works of distinction and to generate increased visibility for the winners and the profession in general. Entries are accepted for placement in one of four areas: design, analysis & planning, research, and communication. Eligibility is open to any landscape architect or, in the case of research and communication, any individual or group. Awards are granted on three levels: Presidents Award of Excellence, the highest distinction with only one granted in each category; Honor Awards, given to no more than five percent of the total number of entries in each category; and Merit Awards, determined by the discretion of the jury. Juries for each category are comprised of landscape professionals and appointed by the ASLA's Professional Awards Committee. The following list contains the recipients of the Presidents Award for Excellence and Honor Awards for 1999.

For additional information, visit the ASLA's Web site at *www.asla.org* or contact them at (202) 898-2444.

1999 Design Awards Recipients:

Presidents Award for Excellence:
Crosswinds Marsh
Wayne County, Michigan
JJR Incorporated

Honor Awards:
Dayton Residence and Garden
Minneapolis, Minnesota
Hargreaves Associates

Cascade Crest, Oregon Zoo
Portland, Oregon
The Portico Group

Charleston Waterfront
Charleston, South Carolina
Sasaki Associates, Inc.
Water Pollution Control Laboratory

Portland, Oregon
Murase Associates

Jury:
Laurel Olin, ASLA; Mark Johnson, FASLA; Mario Schjetnan, FASLA

1999 Analysis & Planning Award Recipients:

Presidents Award for Excellence:
The Rockaway River and its Treasured Resources: Visions and Strategies for their Recovery
Morris and Sussex Counties, New Jersey
Roy Mann Associates, Inc. (firm) and Natural Resources Conservation Service (agency)

ASLA Professional Awards (Con't)

Honor Awards:
Feasibility Study for the Canopy
    Project
Southwestern Oregon
The Portico Group

The Barbados National Park Plan
Barbados, West Indies
Urban Strategies, Inc.

Jury:
Carol Franklin, ASLA; Peter Jacobs,
FASLA; Grant Jones, FASLA

1999 Research Award Recipients:
Presidents Award for Excellence:
Award not granted

Honor Awards:
Approaches to Ecological Planning
Forster O. Ndubisi, Ph.D., ASLA

Jury:
Randall Arendt, MRTPI (invited);
Darrel Morrison, FASLA; Sally
Schauman, FASLA

1999 Communications Award Recipients:
Presidents Award for Excellence:
Stream Corridor Restoration:
    Principles, Process, and Practices
Ronald Tuttle, FASLA, NRCS
    (retired); Gary Wells, NRCS; Rob
    Corry, Environmental Alliance for
    Senior Involvement (EASI);
    Jennifer Shepherd, EASI; Kevin
    McCardle, EASI

Honor Awards:
The California Landscape Garden
Mark Francis, ASLA

Jury:
Randall Arendt, MRTPI (invited);
Darrel Morrison, FASLA; Sally
Schauman, FASLA

Source: American Society of Landscape Architects

**Every child is an artist.
The problem is how to
remain an artist once he
grows up.**

Pablo Picasso

Auguste Perret Prize

The International Union of Architects (UIA) grants the triennial Auguste Perret Prize to an internationally renowned architect or architects for their work in applied technology in architecture.

For more information, visit the UIA's Web site at *www.uia-architectes.org.*

1961
  F. Candela (Mexico)
  Honorary Mention:
    The Architects of the British
    Ministry for Education Office and
    the Architects of the Office for the
    Study of Industrial and
    Agricultural Buildings of Hungary
1963
  K. Mayekawa (Japan)
  J. Prouvé (France)
1965
  H. Sharoun (GFR)
  Honorary Mention:
    H. and K. Siren (Finland)
1967
  F. Otto and R. Gutbrod (GFR)
1969
  Karel Hubacek (Czechoslovakia)
1972
  E. Pinez Pinero (Spain)
1975
  A.C. Erickson and team (Canada)
  Honorary Mention:
    J. Cardoso (Brazil)
1978
  Kiyonori Kitutake (Japan)
  Piano & Rogers (Italy/United
    Kingdom)

1981
  G. Benisch (GFR)
  Honorary Mention:
    J. Rougerie (France)
1984
  Joao Baptista Vilanova Artigas (Brazil)
1987
  Santiago Calatrava (Spain)
  Honorary Mention:
    C. Testa (Argentina)
1990
  Adien Fainsilber (France)
1993
  KHR AS Arkitekten (Denmark)
1996
  Thomas Herzog (Germany)
1999
  Ken Yeang (Malaysia)

Source: International Union of Architects

Did you know...
The Library of Congress' Jefferson Building was the largest library structure in the world when it was built in 1897.

Awards for Architectural Research

The Awards for Architectural Research are presented annually by *Architecture* magazine and the Initiative for Architectural Research (IAR), which is comprised of the Association of Collegiate Schools of Architecture (ACSA), The American Institute of Architects (AIA), and the Architectural Research Centers Consortium. The awards are designed to recognize outstanding research in architecture and urban design. Entries may be made in one of four categories: energy and sustainable design; history; behavioral and social sciences; and technology, computing, and materials. However, the jury does not consider categories during judging.

For additional information, contact *Architecture* magazine on the Web at *www.architecturemag.org* or at (212) 536-6221.

1999 Recipients:

Daylighting With Integrated Envelope and Lighting System, Lawrence Berkeley National Laboratory

Emeryville Resourceful Building Project, Siegel & Strain Architects

An Alternative Light Source for Architectural Spaces, The University of California, San Diego and the Chinese University of Hong Kong

1999 Citations:

The Hillside Elevators of Valparaiso, Chile: Neighborhood Transportation as a Generator of Urban Form, René Davids

CoOL Studio: Expanding the Discursive Space of the Design Studio With Educational Technology, Georgia Institute of Technology

1999 Jury:

Janet R. White
Robert Berkebile
Richard A. Eribes, Ph.D.

Source: Architecture magazine

Business Week/Architectural Record Awards

The *Business Week/Architecture Record* Awards recognize creative design solutions with an emphasis on the achievement of business goals through architecture. Co-sponsored by The American Institute of Architects, the awards are judged by a jury of business leaders, public officials, and designers. Eligible projects must have been completed within the past three years and must be submitted jointly by the architect and the client. Projects may be located anywhere in the world.

For additional information, call (202) 682-3205 or visit the AIA on the Internet at *www.e-architect.org*.

1999 Award Winners:

ABB Power Generation Ltd.
Baden, Switzerland
Theo Hotz AG Architect + Planner

Alcoa Corporate Center
Pittsburgh, PA
Design Alliance

Astra France Headquarters
Rueil Malmaison, France
Jean Paul Viguier SA d'Architecture

Helmut Lang Boutique
New York, NY
Gluckman Mayner Architects

La Marina Preschool
Manhattan Beach, CA
Studio 9one2

MIT School of Architecture and
    Planning
Leers Wein Zapfel Architects
Cambridge, MA

New Jersey Housing and Mortgage
    Finance Agency
Trenton, NJ
Gatsch/Johnson Jones

Robert L. Preger Intelligent
    Workplace
Pittsburgh, PA
The Center for Building
    Performance and Diagnostics

Republic Windows and Doors
Chicago, IL
Booth Hansen Associates

Jury:

Duke Oakley
William Pedersen, FAIA
Rafael Pelli, AIA
P. Richard Rittelman, FAIA
Kosar Rittelman
Julie V. Snow, AIA
Richard N. Swett, AIA
David Tieger
David Thurm

Source: Architectural Record/Business Week

Carlsberg Architectural Prize

The Carlsberg Architectural Prize is awarded every four years to a living architect or group of architects who has produced works of enduring architectural and social value. As part of Carlsberg's long-standing patronage of the arts, Carlsberg A/S established this prize in 1991 to promote the benefits of quality architecture. Nominations are culled from the international architectural press, and the jury is comprised of architects, scholars, and members of the press. Winners of this international award receive a prize amount equal to $220,000 US.

For more information visit the Carlsberg Web site at *www.carlsberg.com/info/*.

1992 Tadao Ando, Japan
1995 Juha Leiviskä, Finland
1998 Peter Zumthor, Switzerland

Source: Carlsberg A/S

Did you know...
The Cathedral of Learning at the University of Pittsburgh (1926-37) is the tallest school building in the western world, standing 535 feet (42 stories), and contains 23 authentically designed and decorated Nationality Classrooms developed and funded by the ethnic communities of the Pittsburgh area.

Design for Transportation Awards

Co-presented by the Department of Transportation (DOT) and the National Endowment for the Arts (NEA), the Design for Transportation Awards are presented every five years for functional, innovative transportation system projects which solve problems by uniting form and function. Both agencies established criteria for judging, which is carried out by a multi-disciplinary jury of professionals. Entries must achieve one or more of the following DOT goals: tie America together through intermodal and multimodal connections; enhance the environment through compatibility with community life and the physical surroundings; demonstrate sensitivity to the concerns of the traveling public; and provide a secure and safe traveling environment. Innovation, aesthetic sensibility, technical and functional performance, and cost efficiency must all be demonstrated. Awards are presented at two levels, the highest being Honor Awards, followed by Merit Awards. The following projects won an Honor Award in 1995.

Photographs and jury comments for each winner can be found on the Internet at *http://ostpxweb.dot.gov*.

1995 Honor Awards:

Denver International Airport
Denver, Colorado

Double Arch Bridge of the Natchez
Trace Parkway
Franklin, Tennessee

HAER Historic Bridges Program
Washington, D.C.

Interstate 70 in Glenwood Canyon
Glenwood Canyon, Colorado

MTA Arts for Transit: Graphics and
Art Programs
New York, New York

Rehabilitation of 30th Street Station
Philadelphia, Pennsylvania

South Embarcadero Waterfront
Transportation Projects
San Francisco, California

Staples Street Bus Stops
Corpus Christi, Texas

Urban Design Guidelines Handbook
Hudson-Bergen Light Rail Transit
System, New Jersey

U.S. Department of Veterans Affairs
Pedestrian Bridge
Portland, Oregon

Visitor Reception and Transportation
Center
Charleston, South Carolina

Design for Transportation Awards (Con't)

1995 Jury:

Denise Scott Brown, Chair

Architecture, Interior Design, and historic Preservation:
Denise Scott Brown, Chair
Marilyn Jordon Taylor
David Dillon
Geoff Goldberd
Gregory Baldwin

Engineering:
Satoshi Oishi, Chair
Nancy Rutledge Connery

James Lammie
Donald Hunt
Edward Cohen

Landscape Architecture, Urban Design, Planning, Art and Graphic Design:
David Lee, Chair
Joan Goody
Elaine Shiramizu
Joseph Brown

Source: U.S. Department of Transportation and National Endowment for the Arts

Design is about humanity and simplicity – a little help for daily life.

Andrée Putman

Designer of Distinction Award

The Designer of Distinction Award is granted by the American Society of Interior Designers (ASID) to an ASID interior designer whose professional achievements have demonstrated design excellence. Eligibility is open to members in good standing who have practiced within the preceding ten years. Nominations are accepted by ASID's general membership body and judged by jury selected by the National President. This is a merit based award and, thus, is not always granted annually.

For more information, visit the ASID on the Internet at *www.asid.org* or contact them at (202) 546-3480.

1979	William Pahlman, FASID	1988	Louis Tregre, FASID
1980	Everett Brown, FASID	1994	Charles D. Gandy, FASID
1981	Barbara D'Arcy, ASID	1995	Andre Staffelbach, ASID
1982	Edward J. Wormley	1996	Joseph Minton, ASID
1983	Edward J. Perrault, FASID	1997	Phyllis Martin-Vegue, ASID
1984	Michael Taylor, ASID	1998	Janet Schirn, FASID
1985	Norman Dehaan, FASID	1999	Gary E. Wheeler, FASID
1986	Rita St. Clair, FASID		
1987	James Merricksmith, FASID		

Source: American Society of Interior Designers

Did you know...
Raymond Loewy got his first major career boost in 1935 when Sears, Roebuck & Company asked him to design their first refrigerator, the Coldspot Super Six, which went on to become an industry leader.

Distinguished Professor Award

The Association of Collegiate Schools of Architecture's (ACSA) Distinguished Professor Award is presented annually for "sustained creative achievement" in the field of architectural education, whether through teaching, design, scholarship, research, or service. Eligible candidates must be living faculty of an ACSA member school for a minimum of 10 years or be otherwise allied with architectural education at an ACSA member school. Students or faculty of an ACSA member school may make nominations. Each year, an Honors and Awards Committee recommends a maximum of five candidates to the ACSA Board. Winners are entitled to use the title 'ACSA Distinguished Professor' for life.

For additional information about the ACSA Distinguished Professor Award, contact the Association at (202) 785-2324, or visit their Web site at *www.acsa-arch.org*.

1984-85
Alfred Caldwell, Illinois Institute of Technology
Robert S. Harris, Univ. of Southern California
Fay Jones, Univ. of Arkansas
Charles Moore, Univ. of Texas at Austin
Ralph Rapson, Univ. of Minnesota

1985-86
James Marston Fitch, Columbia Univ.
Leslie J. Laskey, Washington Univ.
Harlan McClure, Clemson Univ.
Edward Romieniec, Texas A & M Univ.
Richard Williams, U. of Illinois, Champaign-Urbana

1986-87
Christopher Alexander, Univ. of California, Berkeley
Harwell Hamilton Harris, North Carolina State Univ.
Stanislawa Nowicki, Univ. of Pennsylvania
Douglas Shadbolt, Univ. of British Columbia
Jerzy Soltan, Harvard Univ.

1987-88
Harold Cooledge, Jr., Clemson Univ.
Bernd Foerster, Kansas State Univ.
Romaldo Giurgola, Columbia Univ.
Joseph Passonneau, Washington Univ.
John G. Willams, Univ. of Arkansas

1988-89
Peter R. Lee, Jr., Clemson Univ.
E. Keith McPheeters, Auburn Univ.
Stanley Salzman, Pratt Institute
Calvin C. Straub, Arizona State Univ.
Blanche Lemco van Ginkel, Univ. of Toronto

1989-90
Gunnar Birkerts, Univ. of Michigan
Olivio C. Ferrari, Virginia Polytechnic Institute

Distinguished Professor Award (Con't)

George C. Means, Jr., Clemson Univ.

Malcolm Quantrill, Texas A & M Univ.

1990-91

Denise Scott Brown, Univ. of Pennsylvania

Panos Koulermos, Univ. of Southern California

William McMinn, Cornell Univ.

Forrest Wilson, The Catholic Univ. of America

David Woodcock, Texas A & M Univ.

1991-92

M. David Egan, Clemson Univ.

Robert D. Dripps, Univ. of Virginia

Richard C. Peters, Univ. of California, Berkeley

David L. Niland, Univ. of Cincinnati

1992-93

Stanley W. Crawley, Univ. of Utah

Don P. Schlegel, Univ. of New Mexico

Thomas L. Schumacher, Univ. of Maryland

1993-94

George Anselevicius, Univ. of New Mexico

Hal Box, Univ. of Texas at Austin

Peter McCleary, Univ. of Pennsylvania

Douglas Rhyn, Univ. of Wisconsin-Milwaukee

Alan Stacell, Texas A & M Univ.

1994-95

Blake Alexander, Univ. of Texas at Austin

Robert Burns, North Carolina State Univ.

Robert Heck, Louisiana State Univ.

Ralph Knowles, Univ. of Southern California

1995-96

James Barker, Clemson Univ.

Mui Ho, Univ. of California, Berkley

Patricia O'Leary, Univ. of Colorado

Sharon Sutton, Univ. of Minnesota

Peter Waldman, Univ. of Virginia

1996-97

Colin H. Davidson, Universite de Montreal

Michael Fazio, Mississippi State Univ.

Ben J. Refuerzo, Univ. of Calif., Los Angeles

Max Underwood, Arizona State Univ.

J. Stroud Watson, Univ. of Tennessee

1997-98

Roger H. Clark, North Carolina State Univ.

Bob E. Heatly, Oklahoma State Univ.

John S. Reynolds, Univ. of Oregon

Marvin E. Rosenman, Ball State Univ.

Anne Taylor, Univ. of New Mexico

1998-99

Ralph Bennett, Univ. of Maryland

Diane Ghirardo, Univ. of Southern California

Robert Greenstreet, Univ. of Wisconsin-Milwaukee

Thomas Kass, Univ. of Utah

Norbert Schoenauer, McGill Univ.

Jan Wampler, Massachusetts Inst. of Tech.

Source: Association of Collegiate Schools of Architecture

Did you know...
The dome on Thomas Jefferson's Monticello was the first to ever crown an American house.

Dubai International Award for Best Practices in Improving the Living Environment

The United Nations Center for Human Settlements (HABITAT), in conjunction with the Municipality of Dubai, United Arab Emirates, presents the Dubai International Award for Best Practices in Improving the Living Environment. This biennial prize is awarded for initiatives which have made outstanding contributions to improving the quality of life in communities around the world. The first Best Practices award was presented in 1996 following an international conference on best practices held in Dubai. A Technical Advisory Committee assesses the submissions' compliance with the three criteria for a Best Practice: impact, partnership, and sustainability. Outstanding entries are forwarded for consideration to a Best Practices Jury; all entries are listed in a Best Practices database (*www.bestpractices.org*) which contains over 650 solutions to the common problems of an urbanizing world. The award is open to all organizations, including governments and public and private groups. Winners receive a $30,000 prize, trophy, and certificate.

For more information, contact HABITAT at (212) 963-4200, or on the Internet at *www.unhabitat.org/blp/submit.htm*.

1998 Winners:

Comprehensive Improvement of the Urban Environment of Zhuhai, China

Urban Sub-centres for Citizen Life in the Low-income Areas of Medellin, Colombia

Household Solid Waste Management: Zabbaleen Garbage Collectors, Cairo, Egypt

Urban Governance in Environment and Public Health: Surat's Experience, India

The Kipepeo Project, Arabuko-Sokoke Forest, Kenya

Housing Programme for the Peripheral Areas of Xalapa, Vera Cruz, Mexico

Participatory Planning Initiatives in Naga City, Philippines

Programmes for Improving the Urban Environment in Malaga, Spain

Community Infrastructure Upgrading Programme, Dar-es-Salaam, Tanzania

Interface's Journey to Sustainability, Kennesaw, Georgia, United States

Source: United Nations Center for Human Settlements

Edward C. Kemper Award

Edward C. Kemper served as Executive Director of The American Institute of Architects (AIA) for nearly 35 years, from 1914 to 1948. The Edward C. Kemper Award honors an architect member of the AIA who has similarly served as an outstanding member of the Institute.

For more information, visit the AIA on the Internet at *www.e-architect.org* or contact the AIA Honors and Awards Department at (202) 626-7586.

1950	William Perkins, FAIA	1978	Carl L. Bradley, FAIA
1951	Marshall Shaffer, FAIA	1979	Herbert E. Duncan Jr., FAIA
1952	William Stanley Parker, FAIA	1980	Herbert Epstein, FAIA
1953	Gerrit J. De Gelleke, FAIA	1981	Robert L. Durham, FAIA
1954	Henry H. Saylor, FAIA	1982	Leslie N. Boney Jr., FAIA
1955	Turpin C. Bannister, FAIA	1983	Jules Gregory, FAIA
1956	Theodore Irving Coe, FAIA	1984	Dean F. Hilfinger, FAIA
1957	David C. Baer, FAIA	1985	Charles Redmon, FAIA
1958	Edmund R. Purves, FAIA	1986	Harry Harmon, FAIA
1959	Bradley P. Kidder, FAIA	1987	Joseph Monticciolo, FAIA
1960	Philip D. Creer, FAIA	1988	David Lewis, FAIA
1961	Earl H. Reed, FAIA	1989	Jean P. Carlhian, FAIA
1962	Harry D. Payne, FAIA	1990	Henry W. Schirmer, FAIA
1963	Samuel E. Lunden, FAIA	1991	John F. Hartray Jr., FAIA
1964	Daniel Schwartzman, FAIA	1992	Betty Lou Custer, FAIA*
1965	Joseph Watterson, FAIA	1993	Theodore F. Mariani, FAIA
1966	William W. Eshbach, FAIA	1994	Harry C. Hallenbeck, FAIA
1967	Robert H. Levison, FAIA	1995	Paul R. Neel, FAIA
1968	E. James Gambaro, FAIA	1996	Sylvester Damianos, FAIA
1969	Philip J. Meathe, FAIA	1997	Harold L. Adams, FAIA, RIBA, JIA
1970	Ulysses Floyd Rible, FAIA	1998	Norman L. Koonce, FAIA
1971	Gerald McCue, FAIA	1999	James R. Franklin, FAIA
1972	David N. Yerkes, FAIA		
1973	Bernard B. Rothschild, FAIA		
1974	Jack D. Train, FAIA	** Honored posthumously*	
1975	F. Carter Williams, FAIA	*Source: American Institute of Architects*	
1976	Leo A. Daly, FAIA		
1977	Ronald A. Straka, FAIA		

Engineering Excellence Awards

The American Consulting Engineers Council's (ACEC) Engineering Excellence Awards are an annual competition that begins at the state level, with finalists moving to the national competition. Each year one project receives the "Grand Conceptor" Award, and up to 23 other projects receive either Grand or Honor Awards. Projects are judged by a panel of 20 – 25 engineers and infrastructure experts on the basis of uniqueness and originality; technical value to the engineering profession; social and economic considerations; complexity; and how successfully the project met the needs of the client. Projects must be entered in one of nine categories: studies, research and consulting engineering services, building support systems; structural systems; surveying and mapping; environmental; water and wastewater; water resources; transportation; and special projects. Any firm engaged in the private practice, consulting engineering, or surveying is eligible to participate. Entries must be submitted to an ACEC Member Organization.

For more information and winning project descriptions, visit *www.acec.org/programs/1999eeaawards.htm* on the Internet.

1999 Grand Conceptor Award Winner:
　　Doernbecher Children's Hospital
　　Portland, Oregon
　　KPFF Consulting Engineers

1999 Grand Award Winners:
　　Activation of New York City's Third
　　　Water Tunnel
　　White Plains, New York
　　Malcolm Pirnie, Inc.

　　Cryptosporidium Inactivation Study
　　Pasadena, California
　　Montgomery Watson

　　Newport News Waterworks
　　Newport News, Virginia
　　Camp Dresser & McKee Inc.

Somerset Hills Interceptor
　　Rehabilitation
Edison, New Jersey
Camp Dresser & McKee, Inc

Terminal One, JFK International
　　Airport
New York City, New York
Joseph R. Loring and Associates, Inc.

Westside Hills Light Rail
Portland, Oregon
Parsons Brinckerhoff Quade &
　　Douglas, Inc.

WPCF Odor Management Facility
Burlington, Massachusetts
Fay, Spofford & Thorndike, Inc.

Engineering Excellence Awards (Con't)

1999 Honor Award Winners:

Arched Precast Library Walls
Minneapolis, Minnesota
Middleton Engineering Associates &
    CNA Consulting Engineers

Benaroya Hall
Seattle, Washington
Skilling Ward Magnusson Barkshire,
    Inc.

Brooks Landfill Air Sparging
Wichita, Kansas
Camp Dresser & McKee, Inc.

Central Artery/Tunnel Project
Boston, Massachusetts
Howard/Stein-Hudson Associates,
    Inc.

Cold Spring & Arroyo Quemado
    Bridge Retrofits
Walnut Creek, California
Buckland & Taylor Ltd.

Eastern Toll Road
Santa Ana, California
CH2M Hill

Ft. Point Channel Groundwater
    Control System
Seattle, Washington
Shannon & Wilson, Inc.

Miho Museum Bridge
Shiga, Japan
Leslie E. Robertson Associates, RLLP

49Quickly Deployed Emergency
    Bridge Lift System
Seattle, Washington
Hamilton Engineering, Inc.

Rebuilding Southfield Sewer
Detroit, Michigan
NTH Consultants, Ltd.

Salt Lake Valley Water Source
    Protection
Salt Lake City, Utah
CH2M Hill

South Carolina State House
    Renovation
Columbia, South Carolina
Atlanta Testing and Engineering and
    Stevens & Wilkinson

Stanford Art Museum Retrofit And
    Addition
San Francisco, California
Degenkolb Engineers

St. Casimir's Church Renovation
Latham, New York
C. T. Male Associates, P.C.

Wastewater Treatment Plant No. 2
Kansas City, Missouri
Archer Engineers

Source: American Consulting Engineers Council

Did you know...
The deepest point in the ocean, the Marianas Trench in the Pacific Ocean with a depth of 35,837 feet, is 29 times the height of the Empire State Building.

GOOD DESIGN® Competition

Billing itself as "the oldest in the world," the GOOD DESIGN® Competition was founded in Chicago in 1950 by Charles and Ray Eames, Ecro Saarinen, and Edgar Kaufmann. The original program ran until 1957, and was resurrected in 1990 by the Chicago Athenaeum. The annual awards are presented for design excellence for products ranging from office furniture, housewares, automotive products, and hardware to electronics and other products. There is also a category for graphic design. Any product produced and/or designed during the previous year may be entered in the competition. Juries select winners based on the criteria set forth by the competition's founders in 1950, measuring innovation, form, materials, construction, concept, function, and utility.

For additional information, an entry form, or to see photographs of the winning designs, visit the Chicago Athenaeum's Web site at *www.chi-athenaeum.org.*

1998 GOOD DESIGN® Winners

Electronic Equipment

Audible Player, 1997
Thomas Overthun

Samsung TFT400 Flat-Panel Display
Christopher Loew

JBL Harmony Radio
JBL Consumer Products

IS40 Interactive Music Workstation
MCA + Partners

CRK76 Backlit Remote Control
Tom Renk

Wind MIDI Controller (WX5)
Yamaha Product Design Laboratory

Hewlett-Packard Office Jet 500
Series
Hauser Inc.

Z27X31D 27" Color Television
Cesaroni Design Associates, Inc.

WAN Maker
Studio Red

Appliances (Kitchen/Bath)

Wash Table
Philippe Starck, Issy les Moulineaux

Thomas Reverse Washbasin
Industrielle Produkt, Hans-Joachim
Krietsch GmbH

Dessauer Gerätwereke Built-In
Kitchen Stove
Industrielle Produkt, Hans-Joachim
Krietsch GmbH

Livello and Gelee Bath Accessory
Line
Big Design, Inc.

GOOD DESIGN® Competition (Con't)

Pharo Shower Column
Phoenix Product Design

Pollux I Wash Basin Unit
Erik Demmer & Christian Schäffler

Kaz 4200 CoolMist Humidifier
Smart Design Inc.

Maytag Neptune Washer and Dryer
Maytag Appliances

Furniture

Tangent Shelving System
Mark Müller, Nienkämper

Carré Table Series
ITO Design

Gitano Home Office
Maurizio Duranti

Modus Basic Swivel Chair
Wiege

The Maya Lin Collection: the earth is
(not) flat
Maya Lin

Rover Seating Series
David Ryan and Associates

Gorka Stacking Chair
Jorge Pensi

Bellini Chair
Mario Bellini

Textiles

Freehand, Frequency and Foundation
Panel Fabric
Knoll Textiles Design Team

Veil Drapery Fabric
Suzanne Tick

Chicago Decorating Fabric
Barbara Brenner – nya nordiska

Meinecke Collection Area Rugs
Kurt Meinecke

Cadenza Woven Upholstery Textile
Ruth Adler-Schnee

Lighting

Glowblow Floor Lamp
Valvomo Design

Spot On Desk Lamp
Jean Pierre Généraux Design

Housewares/Tabletop

883 Colander
Luigi Prandelli

Moon: Cipango Blue Porcelain
Tableware
Jasper Morrison

Professional Knife System
Lutz Gebhardt

Toaster
Michael Graves Architect

Ovenworks
Tupperware Design Team

Rondo Shopping Bag
Hansjerg Maier-Aichen

Materia/Cutlery
Sieger Design

Wastepaper Basket
György Gyimóthy

OXO Good Grips Salad Spinner
Human Factors Industrial Design

Harmony Bowl
Peter Aldridge, Steuben

Twin Collection Cheese Knives
Michael Schneider Product Design

Ice Cream Scoop
Ron C. LaGro

Rondure Flatware
Gerald Gulotta

GOOD DESIGN® Competition (Con't)

Pocket Corkscrew
Ed Kilduff, Pollen Design, New York, NY

Children's Products/Toys
Smile Childrens Cutlery
Flex Development B.V.

Medical Equipment
Johnson & Johnson Nextep Contour Walker
Ecco Design, Inc.

Midwest Dental Air Touch
John Brassil, IDEO

DenOptix Digital X-Ray System
Lunar Design

Continuum of Care Fetal Monitor
Anderson Design, Inc.

The Wand – Local Anesthesia Delivery System
Herbst LaZar Bell Inc.

Microlet Finger-Lancing Device for Diabetics
Metaphase Design Group, Inc.

Personal Care
Brookstone Travel Hair Dryer
Smart Design Inc.

Protector Razor
Roche Harkins Design

Office Equipment
Boston Portable Pencil Sharpeners
Ecco Design, Inc.

Hannibal Tape Dispenser
Julian Brown

Jaws Mini Paper Shredder
Staubitz Design Associates

Shredmaster Shark 200 Shredder
Herbst LaZar Bell Inc.

Hardware/Tools
LumiLock
Nicole Zeller – Zelco Industries, Inc.

Merlin Garage Door Opener
Peter Haythornthwaite Design

Toro Coathook
Carsten Schmidt

Wire Rope Winch
Tesign

Universal Cutter
Olavi Linden, Fiskars Inc.

ZAG Rolling Workshop
500 Group

CFM Full-Flow Wafer Washer
Bresslergroup, Inc/CFM Technologies

Clocks/Watches
ADN Wristwatch
Les Ateliers du Nord

Sports/Recreation Equipment
SI Binding
Eleven LLC

Y-Tech Mountaineering Boot
Design Continuum Italia SRL

Transportation
BMW System 4 Helmet
BMW Motorcycle Design Team

Porsche 911 Carrera
Harm Lagaay, Style Porsche

Street Furniture
Multiple News Rack
JC Decaux

Miscellaneous Products
Wave Work Assist Vehicle
David B. Smith and Crown Design Center

GOOD DESIGN® Competition (Con't)

The San Francisco Ceiling Fan
Mark Gajewski

Water Spring
Peter A. Büchele

Graphic and Packaging Design
Moorman Firm Brochure
Heine/Lenz/Zizka

Audi TT Coupé Brochure
JvM Werbeagentur GmbH

Audi AL2 Brochure
JvM Werbeagentur GmbH

Museum of Turopolje Corporate
Identity
Likovni Studio C.O.O.

Masunaga Poster Series
Makoto Saito

The George Gund Foundation 1997
Annual Report
Nesnadny + Schwartz

Chairs Brochure
Torbjörn Lenskog

Tom Brochure
Concrete Design Communications
Inc.

Design Exchange Logo
Concrete Design Communications
Inc.

Virtu Catalogue
Concrete Design Communications
Inc.

Humane Village Congress – ICSID
'97 Poster
Concrete Design Communications
Inc.

Leatherman Tools 1998 Product
Catalogue
Hornall Anderson Design Works

Heartport 1997 Annual Report
Cahan & Associates

Vivus 1997 Annual Report
Cahan & Associates

Marketable Aspects of Color
Brochure
Designframe Incorporated

Immigrant Theatre Festival Poster
Luba Lukova

Virgil- Theatre Poster
Luba Lukova

Pin Me Up Business Card
Eduard ehovin

Graphic Designers Scrapbook
Designed by: Eduard ehovin, Tanja
Rade, Darko Miladinovi, Bo_tjan
Botas Kenda, Lena Pislak Balant,
Boris Balant, Bojan and Dalida
Hadihaliovi, Slavimir Stojanovi

Issey Miyake Holiday Bags
Designed by: Karim Rashid

Source: Chicago Athenaeum

GSA Design Awards

The U.S. General Services Administration (GSA) presents biennial Design Awards as part of its Design Excellence Program, which seeks the best in design, construction, and restoration for all Federal building projects. The Design Awards were developed to encourage and recognize innovative design in Federal buildings and to honor noteworthy achievements in the preservation and renovation of historic structures.

For additional information about the GSA Design Awards or to view photographs and descriptions of the 1998 winners, visit GSA's Web site at *http://designawards.gsa.gov/.*

1998 Honor Award Recipients:

Architecture

Ronald Reagan Building and
   International Trade Center
Washington, D.C.
Pei Cobb Freed & Partners
   Architects, LLP and Ellerbe
   Becket

National Data Processing Center,
   Bureau of the Census, U.S.
   Department of Commerce
Bowie, Maryland
Tobey + Davis/ Davis, Brody, Bond

Mark O. Hatfield U.S. Courthouse
Portland, Oregon
Kohn Pedersen Fox Associates, P.C.
   and BOORA Architects

U.S. Port of Entry
Point Roberts, Washington
The Miller/Hull Partnership

Graphic Design

Booklet, "United States Court of
   Appeals Building for the Ninth
   Circuit,"
San Francisco, California
Rightside Imaging

Signage, Mark O. Hatfield U.S.
   Courthouse
Portland, Oregon
Mayer/Reed

1998 Citation Recipients:

Architecture

Robert C. Byrd U.S. Courthouse
Charleston, West Virginia
Skidmore Owings and Merrill LLP

On the Boards

U.S. Courthouse and Federal
   Building
Central Islip, New York
Richard Meier & Partners and The
   Spectorgroup

U.S. Post Office and Courthouse
Brooklyn, New York
R.M. Kliment & Frances Halsband
   Architects

William J. Nealon Federal Building
   and U.S. Courthouse
Scranton, Pennsylvania
Bohlin Cywinski Jackson, Architects

GSA Design Awards (Con't)

Historic Preservation/Conservation
Edward Gignoux U.S. Courthouse
Portland, Maine
Leers Weinzapfel Associates
Architects

Restoration of Alexander Calder's
Flamingo
Chicago, Illinois
McKay Lodge Fine Arts and
Conservation Laboratory, Inc.

Engineering
"Engineering and Environmental
Study" for U.S. Courthouse and
Federal Building
Phoenix, Arizona
Ove Arup & Partners

Landscape Architecture
Jacob Javitz Plaza
New York, New York
Martha Schwartz, Inc.

Urban Planning
Urban Design Guidelines for
Physical Perimeter and Entrance
Security: An Overlay to the Master
Plan for the Federal Triangle
Washington, D.C.
Sorg and Associates, P.C.

"Governors Island Land Use Study,"
New York Harbor
New York, New York
Beyer Blinder Belle Consortium

Art
Federal Triangle Flowers, Ronald
Reagan Building and
International Trade Center
Washington, D.C.
Stephen Robin

Boundary Markers, National
Building Museum
Washington, D.C.
Raymond Kaskey

Justice, Warren B. Rudman U.S.
Courthouse
Concord, New Hampshire
Diana K. Moore

Africa Rising
290 Broadway, New York, New York
Barbara Chase-Riboud

Architectural Glass, Robert C. Byrd
U.S. Courthouse
Charleston, West Virginia
David Wilson

Lens Ceiling, Federal Building and
U.S. Courthouse
Phoenix, Arizona
James Carpenter

Graphic Design
"Renewing the Commitment," 30th
Anniversary of the Architectural
Barriers Act
Tullier Marketing Communications

Jury:
Robert A.M. Stern (Chair)
Charles Durrett
Leslie Gallery-Dilworth
Arthur Gensler
Paul Hawkes
Pamela Hellmuth
Fred Kelley
Tom Moran
Garth Rockcastle
Allison Williams

Source: U.S. General Services Administration

Hugh Ferriss Memorial Prize

The Hugh Ferriss Memorial Prize is awarded annually by the American Society of Architectural Perspectivists (ASAP) to recognize excellence in architectural illustration. This international awards program is open to all current members of the Society. A traveling exhibition, Architecture in Perspective, co-sponsored by the Otis Elevator Company, highlights the winners and selected entries and raises awareness of the field.

To see the winning drawings, visit the ASAP's Web site at *www.asap.org/aip.html.*

1986
   Lee Dunnette, AIA and James Record

1987
   Richard Lovelace, *One Montvale Avenue*

1988
   Thomas Wells Schaller, AIA, *Proposed Arts and Cultural Center*

1989
   Daniel Willis, AIA, *Edgar Allen Poe Memorial (detail)*

1990
   Gilbert Gorski, AIA, *The Interior of the Basilica Ulpia*

1991
   Luis Blanc, *Affordable Housing Now!*

1992
   Douglas E. Jamieson, *BMC Real Properties Buildings*

1993
   David Sylvester, *Additions and Renovations to Tuckerton Marine Research Field Station*

1994
   Rael D. Slutsky, AIA, *3rd Government Center Competition*

1995
   Lee Dunnette, AIA, *The Pyramid at Le Grand Louvre*

1996
   Paul Stevenson Oles, FAIA, *Hines France Office Tower*

1997
   Advanced Media Design, *World War II Memorial*

1998
   Wei Li, *Baker Library Addition, Dartmouth College*

1999
   Serge Zaleski, *Five Star Deluxe Beach Hotel*

Source: American Society of Architectural Perspectivists

I.D. Annual Design Review

I.D. magazine's Annual Design Review began in 1954 and today is considered America's largest and most prestigious juried design recognition competition for industrial design. Entries are placed in one of seven separate categories (consumer products, graphics, packaging, environments, furniture, equipment, concepts and student work) and reviewed by juries of leading practitioners. Within each category, projects are awarded on three levels: Best of Category, Design Distinction, and Honorable Mention. Winning entries are published in a special July/August issue of *I.D.* magazine. The following products received the Best of Category award.

For listing of all winners, including photographs and project descriptions, visit *I.D.'s* Web site at *www.idonline.com*.

1999 Best of Category Winners:

Consumer Products:
Audi TT Coupe
Audi AG

Apple iMac and G3 Computers
Apple Design Group

Jurors:
Bill Potts, President, Martha Sutyak, Tucker Viemeister

Graphics:
Dead Man on Campus Film Titles
Imaginary Forces Design and Production Co.

The Blue Books
Todd Waterbury, Peter Wegner, Andrew Reed

Jurors:
Barbara Dewilde, Bill Cahan, Peter Girardi, Stephen Doyle

Packaging
Issey Miyake 2-in-1 Travel Kit
Karim Rashid, Inc.

Comme des Garcons Christmas Pillow
Comme des Garcons

Jurors:
Jennifer Sterling, Patrick Li, Robert Valentine

Environments
Samsung Plaza and Rodin Museum
Seoul, Korea
Kohn Pedersen Fox Associates

The Architecture of Repose, San Francisco Museum of Modern Art
Kuth/Ranieri Architects

Jurors:
Ali Tayar, David Meckel, Louise Harpman, Tod Williams

Furniture:
Landscape Office System
Crinion Associates

Jurors:
Alice Park Yiu, Niels Diffrient, Tom Deacon

I.D. Magazine Annual Design Review (Con't)

Equipment

Crown Equipment Forklifts
Ergonomic Systems, Inc. and Crown
Equipment Corporation

IBM Netfinity Servers
IBM

Jurors:
Bert Heinzelman, David Karshmer,
Eric Chan, Principal

Concepts:

Gooru Educational System
Herbst LaZar Bell, Inc.

Student Work:

T2K Digital Camera
TAKA Design Group, Pratt Institute

Trinca Interactive Table and Storage
Unit
Anoek Minneboo, University of
Washington

Jurors:
Barbara Glauber, Bill Modggridge,
Don Carr, Mickey Ackerman

Source: I.D. Magazine

Did you know...

The exterior of IBM's Selectric I, the first electric typewriter, was designed by Eliot Noyes in 1959, a U.S. architect and industrial designer who worked for Marcel Breuer, Walter Gropius, and Norman Bel Geddes before opening his own office.

Industrial Design Excellence Awards (IDEA)

The Industrial Design Excellence Awards (IDEA), co-sponsored by *Business Week* magazine and the Industrial Designers Society of America (IDSA), are presented annually to honor the design excellence of nearly any product made or distributed in the United States. Nearly any product designed or distributed in the U.S. may be entered in one of nine categories. Each year a jury of business executives and design professionals issues as many awards as they deem necessary, evaluating over 1,000 entries on the following criteria: design innovation, benefit to the user, benefit to the client/business, ecological responsibility, and appropriate aesthetics and appeal. Gold, silver, and bronze level citations are granted. The following designs received the Gold award in 1999.

For detailed descriptions, photographs, and contact information on all Gold, Silver, and Bronze winners, visit the IDSA on the Internet at *www.idsa.org/idea99/*.

IDEA99 Gold Award Winners:

Business & Industrial Equipment

Hot-Plug Hard Drive Tray
Compaq Computers Corp.

¡l.000 Multi Service Wireless Communicator, Motorola Inc.

SmartGlas™ Flat panel Display System, Product insight, Inc. and Pixel Vision Inc.

SoftBook, IDEO, Lunar Design, and SoftBook Press

V-mail Camera., Philips Electronics

WAVE Work Assist Vehicle David Smith, John F. McClusky, Ergonomic Systems Design Inc., and Crown Equipment Corp.

Consumer Products

Benwin "Executive" Multimedia Speakers, RKS Design Inc.

Craftsman Low Profile Detachable Vacuum, Emerson Tool Co.

DishDrawer (DD602), Fisher & Paykel Ltd.

EKCO Clip'n Stay Clothespin, Ancona 2 Inc.

Flexible Footwear Flexible Footwear Technologies Ltd. and Design Central

iMac, Apple Computer Inc.

OXO Good Grips Soap Pump Palm Brush, Smart Design

Tonka Joe Workshop PC Playset Klitsner Industrial Design Inc.

Triax Running Watches Astro Products Inc. and Nike Inc.

Tropicool Personal Fan Insight Product Development LLC and Holmes Products Corp.

Industrial Design Excellence Awards (IDEA) (Con't)

Design Exploration
   E-TRANS™ "The Mouse"
   GVO, Powderjet Corp., and ALZA
   Corp.

   IBM Electronic Newspaper
   Better.Design Solutions, Germany,
   and IBM Corp.

   Next Generation Reach Truck Design
   Research, Ergonomic System Design
   Inc. and Crown Equipment Corp.

   Nissan Sport Utility Truck
   Nissan Design International Inc.

   Trail Tag
   Carr & Lamb Design

Environmental Designs
   Micaela
   Eight Inc.

   Sony Electronics Comdex 98 Exhibit
   Mauk Design

   Tommy Boy Music Offices
   Turett Collaborative Architects

Furniture
   Escale
   Haworth Inc.

   Kart
   5D Studio

Medical & Scientific Products
   Hi & Dri
   Microplas Inc.

   PharmASSIST
   Steiner Design Associates and R&D
   Design

   Sovereign Medical System
   Designworks/USA

Packaging & Graphics
   New Leaf Gravity VITA BIN
   New Leaf Design Inc.

   WAVE Operator Manual
   XXL Design, A&M Graphics, and
   Crown Equipment Corp.

Student Design
   10th Mountain Patrol Pack
   University of Cincinnati

   Kidcom
   Art Center College of Design for
   Nokia Mobile Phone

   Nimbus Meteorological Park
   Art Center College Of Design

   "Vivace" Conference Chair
   Art Center College of Design

Transportation
   R 1200 C Motorcycle
   BMW AG

IDEA99 Jury:
   Chair: Katherine J. McCoy, FIDSA
   Jorge Gomez Abrams
   Aaron Betsky, IDSA
   Ayse Birsel, IDSA
   Chris Conley, IDSA
   Tom Devlin, IDSA
   Dale Fahnstrom, IDSA
   David B. Law, IDSA
   Sam Lucente, IDSA
   J. Mays, IDSA
   Glenn Polinsky, IDSA
   Adam Richardson, IDSA
   Michael Vanderbyl, IDSA
   Mitzi Vernon, IDSA
   Craig Vogel, IDSA

Source: Industrial Designers Society of America

Interior Design Competition

The Interior Design Competition is presented jointly each year by the International Interior Design Association (IIDA) and *Interior Design* magazine. The Competition was established in 1973 to recognize outstanding interior design and to foster new interior design ideas and techniques. Winning projects appear in *Interior Design* magazine; the "Best of Competition" winner receives a $5,000 cash prize.

For more information, contact IIDA at (888) 799-IIDA or visit their Web site at *www.iida.org.*

1999 Best of Competition:
An investment management firm
Chicago, Illinois
VOA Associates Inc.

1999 Award Winners:
The Associations at 1307 New York Avenue
Washington, D.C.
Greenwell Goetz Architects, PC

Matthew's Restaurant
Jacksonville, Florida
Larry Wilson Design Associates, Inc.

Palladio
Vancouver, British Columbia
Robert M. Ledingham Inc.

Cathedral of Saints Constantine & Helen
Brooklyn, New York
S. P. Papadatos Assoc. PC

Lake Orion High School
Lake Orion, Michigan
URS Greiner Woodward Clyde

1999 Jury:
Laura Barnett, IIDA
Barbara Barry
Michael Bedner
Richard Carlson, FIIDA
Judy Niedermaier
Richar, IIDA

Source: *International Interior Design Association and Interior Design magazine*

When your heart is big, you open your house to many friends. When your heart is small, you close it to be alone. To me, your design is good if it can accept so many different roles.

Andrée Putman

Interiors' Annual Design Awards

Since 1980, *Interiors* magazine has hosted its Annual Design Awards competition to honor and recognize outstanding interior design projects. Entries are judged in one of 12 categories: Large Offices (50 or more workers), Small Offices, Hotels, Restaurants, Healthcare Facilities, Sports/Fitness Facilities, Retail Projects, Educational Facilities, Public Spaces, Entertainment Venues, Showrooms/Exhibits, and Residences. A jury of design professionals selects winners based on aesthetics, design creativity, function, and achievement of client objectives. Winners are honored at an Annual Awards Breakfast in New York.

For more information, contact *Interiors* at (212) 536-5141.

1999 Award Winners:

Best Large Office
McCann-Erikson Worldwide 16th Floor Renovation; New York, New York; Resolution: 4 Architecture

Best Small Office
Serge Nivelle Studios
New York, New York
Thanhauser & Esterson Architects

Best Restaurant
Michael Jordan's – The Steak House
New York, New York; Rockwell Group

Best Healthcare Project
Galter Medical Pavilion, Swedish Covenant Hospital; Chicago, Illinois
Eva Maddox Associates

Best Retail Project
Cove Landing; Lyme, Connecticut
L.A. Morgan

Best Educational Facility
Boys Club of Sioux City; Sioux City, Iowa; Randy Brown Architects

Best Public Space
McCormick Place South Building Expansion; Chicago, Illinois

Thompson, Ventulett, Stainback & Associates

Best Showroom/Exhibit
E! Lounge; Traveling Exhibit
Architropolis

Best Residence
Fifth Avenue Apartment
New York, New York
Shelton, Mindel & Associates

Best Sports of Fitness Facility
Institut Clarins; Houston, Texas
HLW International

Best Hotel
No winner

Best Entertainment Venue
No winner

1999 Jury:
Richard Brayton
Martha Burns, NBBJ
Lovejoy Duryea
Pamela Light
John Lijewski
David Rockwell

Source: Interiors

International Design Award, Osaka

Through its biennial International Design Award, Osaka, the Japan Design Foundation honors organizations and individuals who have made a significant contribution to the promotion of industry culture and the betterment of society through their design work. The award embraces all fields of the design profession. Nominations are solicited from leading figures in design from around the world. Winners are selected by a jury of five Japanese members.

For more information, visit the Japan Design Foundation on the Internet at *www.jidpo.or.jp/japanese/jdf/html/en_index.htm* or email them at *jdf@silver.ocn.ne.jp*.

1983
Chermayeff & Geismar Associates (USA)
Maria Benktzon & Sven-Eric Juhlin (Sweden)
Paola Navone (Italy)
Pentagram (United Kingdom)
Honorary Award for the Encouragement of Design Activities: Prime Minister, Margaret Thatcher (United Kingdom)

1985
Bang & Olufsen A/S (Denmark)
Philip Johnson (USA)
Bruno Munari (Italy)
Douglas Scott (United Kingdom)
Honorary Award: Tadashi Tsukasa (Japan)

1987
Kenji Ekuan (Japan)
Norman Foster (United Kingdom)
The Netherlands PTT (Netherlands)

1989
Otl Aicher (Federal Republic of Germany)
Jens Nielsen (Denmark)
Frei Otto (Federal Republic of Germany)
Yuri Borisovitch Soloviev (U.S.S.R)

1991
Fritz Hansens Eft. A/S (Denmark)
Fumihiko Maki (Japan)
Antti Nurmesniemi and Vuokko Eskolin-Nurmesniemi (Finland)

1993
Department of Architecture and Design of the Museum of Modern Art, New York (USA)
Yusaku Kamekura (Japan)

1995
Tadao Ando (Japan)
Lawrence Halprin (USA)
Arthur J. Pulos (USA)

1997
Hans J. Wegner (Denmark)

1999
Pasqual Maragall (Spain)
Ryohin Keikaku Co., Ltd. (Japan)

Source: Japan Design Foundation

Jean Tschumi Prize

The Jean Tschumi Prize is awarded by the International Union of Architects (UIA) to individuals for their significant contribution to architectural criticism or architectural education.

For more information, visit the UIA's web site at *www.uia-architectes.org.*

1967   J.P. Vouga (Switzerland)
1969   I. Nikolaev (USSR)
        P. Ramirez Vazquez (Mexico)
1972   J.B. Vilanova Artigas (Brazil)
1975   R. Banham (U.K.)
1978   Rectory and Faculty of Architecture of the University of Lima (Peru)
1981   Neville Quarry (Australia)
        Honorary Mention:
            Jorge Glusberg (Argentina) and Tadeusz Barucki (Poland)
1984   Julius Posener (GDR)
1987   C. Norberg-Schultz (Norway)
        A. L. Huxtable (USA)

1990   Eduard Franz Sekler (Austria);
        Honorary Mention:
            Dennis Sharp (U.K.) and Claude Parent (France)
1993   Eric Kumchew Lye (Malaysia)
1996   Peter Cook (U.K.); Liangyong Wu (P.R. of China)
        Honorary Mention:
            Toshio Nakamura and the Mexican editor COMEX
1999   Juhani Pallasmaa (Finland)
        Honorary Mention:
            Jennifer Taylor (Australia)

Source: International Union of Architects

Did you know...
The first recorded restoration in America occurred in 1828 with the Touro Synagogue (1765) in Newport, Rhode Island.

Mies van der Rohe Award for European Architecture

Established in 1987 by the European Commission, the European Parliament, and the Mies van der Rohe Foundation, the Mies van der Rohe Award for European Architecture seeks to highlight notable projects within the context of contemporary European architecture. Works by European architects which are constructed in the member states of the European Union and associated European states within the two years following the granting of the previous award are eligible for the program. Winning projects are chosen for their innovative character and excellence in design and execution by an international panel of experts in the field of architecture and architectural criticism. The Award consists of a 50,000 Euro cash prize and a sculpture by Xavier Corberó, a design inspired by the Mies van der Rohe Pavilion.

For more information, visit the Mies van der Rohe Foundation's Web site at *www.miesbcn.com.*

1988
  Borges e Irmão Bank, Vila do Conde, Portugal
  Alvaro Siza Vieira

1990
  New Terminal Development, Stansted Airport, London, England
  Norman Foster & Partners

1992
  Municipal Sports Stadium, Badalona, Barcelona, Spain
  Esteve Bonell and Francesc Rius

1994
  Waterloo International Station, London, England
  Nicholas Grimshaw & Partners

1996
  Bibliotèque Nationale de France, Paris, France
  Dominique Perrault

1999
  Art Museum in Bregenz, Bregenz, Austria
  Peter Zumthor

Source: Mies van der Rohe Foundation

Mies van der Rohe Award for Latin American Architecture

A sister award to the Mies van der Rohe Award for European Architecture, this biennial award recognizes projects in Mexico, Central America, South America, Cuba, and the Dominican Republic. The Foundation created the award in 1987 to bring greater attention to contemporary Latin American architecture by honoring works of considerable conceptual, aesthetic, technical, and construction solutions. In order to be eligible, projects must have been completed within the previous two years prior to the granting of the Award and be located in a member country. The Award itself is identical to that of the European award, a cash prize of 50,000 Euros and a sculpture by Xavier Corberó inspired by the pillars of the Mies van der Rohe Pavilion in Barcelona.

For more information, visit the Mies van der Rohe Foundation's Web site at *www.miesbcn.com*.

1998
    Televisa Headquarters
    Mexico City
    TEN Architects

Source: Mies van der Rohe Foundation

Ambiguity and paradox lie at the heart of many design decisions. Indeed, design is a slippery critter. And, depending on how we perceive its inherent moral fiber and cultural value, it can either leave humanity on the doorstep or it can inspire and soar.

Scott Simpson

National Building Museum Honor Award

Since 1986 the National Building Museum has honored individuals and organizations that have made an exceptional contribution to America's built history. The award is presented each year at an elegant gala held in the Museum's Great Hall, which has often been the site of the Presidential Inaugural Ball since 1885.

For more information, contact the National Building Museum at (202) 272-2448 or visit their Web site at *www.nbm.org.*

1986 J. Irwin Miller
1988 James W. Rouse
1989 Senator Daniel Patrick Moynihan
1990 IBM
1991 The Rockefeller Family
1992 The Civic Leadership of Greater Pittsburgh
1993 J. Carter Brown
1994 James A. Johnson and Fannie Mae
1995 Lady Bird Johnson
1996 Cindy and Jay Pritzker
1997 Morris Cafritz, Charles E. Smith, Charles A. Horsky, and Oliver T. Carr, Jr.
1998 Riley P. Bechtel and Stephen D. Bechtel, Jr. of the Bechtel Group
1999 Harold and Terry McGraw and The McGraw-Hill Companies

Source: National Building Museum

National Medal of Arts

The National Medal of Arts was established by Congress in 1984 to honor individuals and organizations "who in the President's judgement are deserving of special recognition by reason of their outstanding contributions to the excellence, growth, support and availability of the arts in the United States." All categories of the arts are represented; although awards are not always granted in each category every year. No more than 12 medals may be awarded per year. Individuals and organizations nationwide may make nominations to the National Endowment for the Arts (NEA). The National Council on the Arts reviews these nominations and makes recommendations to the President of the United States for final selection of the annual medal. The following individuals received this honor for their work in the design profession.

Visit the NEA's Web site at *www.arts.endow.gov/guide/Medals99/Medalsindex.html* for additional information or nomination forms.

1988 I.M. Pei - Architect
1989 Leopold Adler - Preservationist
1990 Ian McHarg - Landscape Architect
1991 Pietro Belluschi - Architect
1992 Robert Venturi and Denise Scott Brown - Architects

1995 James Ingo Freed - Architect
1997 Daniel Urban Kiley - Landscape Architect
1998 Frank Gehry - Architect
1999 Michael Graves - Architect

Source: National Endowment for the Arts

Have nothing in your homes that you do not know to be useful and believe to be beautiful.

William Morris

P/A Awards

The P/A Awards were first handed out in 1954 by *Progressive Architecture* magazine, and are now presented annually by *Architecture* magazine. The awards are designed to "recognize design excellence in unbuilt projects." A jury of designers and architects decides winners.

For more information, see the magazine on the Internet at *www.architecturemag.com* or call (212) 536-6221.

1999 P/A Award Winners:

Piazza Isolo
Verona, Italy
Gabellini Associates

Tocker / McCormack House
Phoenix, Arizona
Wendell Burnette Architects

Jones Plaza Renovation
Houston, Texas
Willis, Bricker & Cannady, Architects

Reframing the Suburban Landscape:
    A Masterplan for the Town of
    Wayland
Wayland, Massachusetts
Office dA

Minneapolis Rowing Club Boathouse
Minneapolis, Minnesota
Vincent James Associates

1999 P/A Award Citations:

Two Scupper Houses or The Dogtrot
    and the Shotgun, Revisited
Pensacola, Florida
Andrews/LeBlanc

Museum of Sex
New York City
SHOP

Muskoka Boathouse, Lake Muskoka
Ontario, Canada
Shim-Sutcliffe Architects

Taghkanic House
Taghkanic, New York
Thomas Phifer and Partners

WRAPPER: 40 Possible City
    Surfaces for the Museum of
    Jurassic Technology
Culver City, California
Studio Works

The Toledo House
Bilbao, Spain
Office dA

University of Toronto
    Graduate/Second Entry Residence
Toronto, Canada
Morphosis

Somis Hay Barn & Stable
Somis, California
SPF:a

Stabile Hall
Brooklyn, New York
Pasanella + Klien Stolzman + Berg
    Architects

Wieden & Kennedy World
    Headquarters
Portland, Oregon

P/A Awards (Con't)

Allied Works Architecture
Module VII Chiller Plant at the
  University of Pennsylvania
Philadelphia, Pennsylvania
Leers Weinzapfel Associates

Nursing and Biomedical Sciences
  Building, Texas Medical Center
Houston, Texas
Patkau Architect

350 Madison Avenue
New York City
Skidmore, Owings & Merrill

Von Erlach House Addition
Shelter Island, New York
Cho Slade Architecture

1999 P/A Award Jury:
  Rodolío Machado
  Thomas Fisher
  Eva Jiriene
  Billie Tsien
  Mchradad Yazdani

Source: Architecture magazine

If I were asked to name the chief benefit of the house, I should say: the house shelters daydreaming.

Gaston Bachelard

Philip Johnson Award

With its Philip Johnson Award, the Society of Architectural Historians (SAH) annually recognizes an outstanding architectural exhibition catalogue. In order to be eligible for this annual recognition, the catalogue must have been published within the preceding two years.

For more information contact the SAH at (312) 573-1365 or visit their Web site at *www.sah.org/awards.html.*

1990
    Los Angeles Blueprints for Modern Living: History and Legacy of the Case Study Houses by Elizabeth A.T. Smith (The Museum of Contemporary Art and MIT Press)

1991
    Architecture and Its Image: Four Centuries of Architectural Representation, Works from the Collection of the Canadian Centre for Architecture by Eve Blau and Edward Kaufman, eds. (The Canadian Centre for Architecture and MIT Press)

1992
    no award granted

1993
    The Making of Virginia Architecture by Charles Brownell (Virginia Museum of Fine Arts and the University Press of Virginia)

    Louis Kahn: In the Realm of Architecture by David Brownlee (The Museum of Contemporary Art and Rizzoli International)

1994
    Chicago Architecture and Design 1923-1993: Reconfiguration of an American Metropolis by John Zukowsky (Prestel and Art Institute of Chicago)

1995
    The Palladian Revival: Lord Burlington, His Villa and Garden in Chiswick by John Harris (Yale University Press)

1996
    The Perspective of Anglo-American Architecture by James F. O'Gorman (The Athenaeum of Philadelphia)

    An Everyday Modernism: The Houses of William Wurster by Marc Treib (San Francisco Museum of Modern Art and the University of California Press)

1997
    Sacred Realm: The Emergence of the Synagogue in the Ancient World by Steven Fine (Yeshiva University Museum and Oxford University Press)

1998
    Building for Air Travel: Architecture and Design for Commercial Aviation by John Zukowsky (Art Institute of Chicago and Prestel)

1999
    The Work of Charles and Ray Eames: a Legacy of Invention by Donald Albrecht (The Library of Congress, Vitra Design Museum, and Abrams Publishing)

Source: Society for Architectural Historians

Opposite: Getty Center, Los Angeles, CA, Richard Meier
Photograph © J. Paul Getty Trust. Photo by Scott Frances/Esto.

Praemium Imperiale

The Praemium Imperiale is awarded by the Japan Art Association, Japan's premier cultural institution, for lifetime achievement in the fields of painting, sculpture, music, architecture, and theater/film. The following individuals received this honor for architecture which includes a commemorative medal and a 15,000,000 yen ($125,000 approx.) honorarium.

For more information visit the Japan Art Association's Web site at *www.fujisankei-g.co.jp/PI/en/index.html.*

1989 I. M. Pei (United States)
1990 James Stirling (U.K.)
1991 Gae Aulenti (Italy)
1992 Frank Gehry (United States)
1993 Kenzo Tange (Japan)
1994 Charles Correa (India)

1995 Renzo Piano (Italy)
1996 Tadao Ando (Japan)
1997 Richard Meier (United States)
1998 Alvaro Siza (Portugal)
1999 Fumihiko Maki (Japan)

Source: Japan Art Association

Did you know...
The amount of steel used in Chicago's Sears Tower (1974, Skidmore, Owings & Merrill) is enough to build 50,000 cars.

Presidential Design Awards

Established by President Ronald Reagan in 1983, the Presidential Design Awards recognize outstanding contributions to federal design by government agencies and employees and private designers in the categories of architecture, engineering, graphic design, historic preservation, interior design, landscape architecture, industrial & product design, and urban design & planning. The Presidential Design Awards are administered by the National Endowment for the Arts (NEA) and are presented every four years. The program includes two levels of awards: Federal Design Achievement Awards are merit awards given by the National Endowment for the Arts as its highest recognition of quality design; and Presidential Awards for Design Excellence are presented by the President of the United States for design of the highest quality in accordance with international standards. Works that have been sponsored, authorized, commissioned, produced or supported by the Government of the United States of America and completed in the 10 years prior to the date of the award are eligible. Projects are judged based on their purpose, leadership, cost, aesthetics and performance. For Round Four of the Presidential Design Awards in 1995, the jury selected 75 projects to receive Federal Design Achievement Awards. Of these, nine were recommended to receive Presidential Awards for Design Excellence, which are listed below.

For a detailed description of the winners from both award programs and photographs of the projects listed below, visit the NEA's Web site at *www.arts.endow.gov/pub/Design95/index.htm.*

1995 Presidential Awards for Design Excellence Recipients:

Focus: HOPE Center for Advanced Technologies
Detroit, Michigan
Smith Hinchman & Grylls Assoc., Inc.

The Byron White United States Courthouse
Denver, Colorado
Michael Barber Architecture

Presidential Design Awards (Con't)

United States Holocaust Memorial
   Museum
Washington, DC
Pei Cobb Freed & Partners

United States Holocaust Memorial
   Museum Permanent Exhibition
Washington, DC
Ralph Appelbaum Associates
   Incorporated

The Double Arch Bridge of the
   Natchez Trace Parkway
Franklin, Tennessee
Figg Engineering Group

Interstate 90 Completion Project
Seattle, Washington
Washington State Department of
   Transportation

River Relocation Project
Providence, Rhode Island
William D. Warner, Architects &
   Planners and Maguire Group, Inc.

The Cooper-Hewitt, National
   Museum of Design, Smithsonian
   Institution
New York, New York
Smithsonian Institution, Cooper-
   Hewitt, National Design Museum

FDA Food Label Design
Greenfield/Belser Ltd.

Juries:
   Donlyn Lyndon (chair)

*Architecture/Preservation and Interior
Design Jury:*
   Graham Gund (chair), Beverly
   Russell, Adèle Naudé Santos, Dr.
   Sharon E. Sutton, Jane Thompson,
   Cynthia Weese, Amy Weinstein

*Graphic Design and Product/Industrial
Design Jury:*
   Richard Saul Wurman (chair), Bryce
   Ambo, Robert Brunner, Matthew
   Carter, Nancye Green, Richard
   Poulin, Patrick Whitney, Lorraine
   Wild

*Landscape Architecture, Urban Design
and Planning Jury:*
   Everett L. Fly (chair), Michael Barker,
   Catherine Brown

Engineering Jury:
   Guy Nordenson (chair), Joseph P.
   Colaco, Virginia Fairweather, Joe
   Passonneau

*Source: U.S. General Services Administration and the
National Endowment for the Arts*

Did you know...
**The Great Pyramid at Giza
contains 2.3 million
square blocks, each of
which weighs an average
of 2.5 tons.**

Pritzker Architecture Prize

In 1979 Jay and Cindy Pritzker, through the Hyatt Foundation, established the Pritzker Architecture Prize to inspire greater creativity among the architectural profession and to generate a heightened public awareness of architecture. Today it is revered as one of the highest honors in the field of architecture. The Prize is awarded each year to a living architect whose body of work represents a longstanding, significant contribution to the built environment. Nominations are accepted every January from any interested party. Architects from all nations are eligible. Laureates of the Pritzker Prize receive a $100,000 grant, citation certificate, and, since 1987, a bronze medallion.

For additional information, visit their Web site at *www.pritzkerprize.com.*

1979	Philip Johnson (United States)	1991	Robert Venturi (United States)
1980	Luis Barragan (Mexico)	1992	Alvaro Siza (Portugal)
1981	James Stirling (U.K.)	1993	Fumihiko Maki (Japan)
1982	Kevin Roche (United States)	1994	Christian de Portzamparc (France)
1983	Ieoh Ming Pei (United States)		
1984	Richard Meier (United States)	1995	Tadao Ando (Japan)
1985	Hans Hollein (Austria)	1996	Rafael Moneo (Spain)
1986	Gottfried Boehm (Germany)	1997	Sverre Fehn (Norway)
1987	Kenzo Tange (Japan)	1998	Renzo Piano (Italy)
1988	Gordon Bunshaft (United States)	1999	Sir Norman Foster (U.K.)
	Oscar Niemeyer (Brazil)		
1989	Frank O. Gehry (United States)		*Source: The Pritzker Architecture Prize*
1990	Aldo Rossi (Italy)		

Pulitzer Prize for Architectural Criticism

As one of the many lasting contributions he made to the field of journalism, Joseph Pulitzer established the Pulitzer Prize as an incentive to excellence in journalism, music, and letters. Over the years the scope of the awards has been expanded from its original 1917 configuration. Since 1970, the Pulitzer Prize Board has awarded a prize for distinguished journalistic criticism. In the past this category has included winners in the arts, culture, and literary fields. The following individuals received this honor for their work in architectural criticism.

Visit the Pulitzer Prize's Web site at *www.pulitzer.org* for a detailed history, chronology, and archive of past winners.

1970	Ada Louise Huxtable *The New York Times*	1990	Allan Temko *San Francisco Chronicle*
1979	Paul Gapp *Chicago Tribune*	1996	Robert Campbell *The Boston Globe*
1984	Paul Goldberger *The New York Times*	1999	Blair Kamin *Chicago Tribune*

Since 1980 the Pulitzer Prize Board has also acknowledged the two finalists in each category. The following individuals were finalists for their work in architectural criticism.

1981	Allan Temko *San Francisco Chronicle*	1997	Herbert Muschamp *The New York Times*
1983	Beth Dunlop *The Miami Herald*		*Source: The Pulitzer Prize Board*
1988	Allan Temko *San Francisco Chronicle*		

Did you know...
In 1929, the White Castle building in Wichita, Kansas was the first to employ porcelain enamel on its exterior.

RAIC Gold Medal

The Royal Architectural Institute of Canada (RAIC) began its Gold Medal program in 1967 to recognize the achievements of architects or individuals related to the field and their contributions to Canada's built environment. As the RAIC Gold Medal is merit based, awards are not always granted yearly.

For more information, contact the RAIC at (613) 241-3600 or visit their Web site at *www.raic.org/awards/index.html*.

1967	Mayor Jean Drapeau
1968	The Right Honorable Vincent Massey
1970	Dr. Eric R. Arthur, FRAIC
1970	The Late John A. Russell
1973	Professor Serge Chermayeff, FRIBA
1976	Dr. Constantinos Doxiadis
1979	John C. Parkin, FRAIC
1981	Jane Jacobs
1982	Ralph Erskine
1984	Arthur Erickson, FRAIC
1985	John Bland, FRAIC
1986	Ed Zeidler, FRAIC
1989	Raymond T. Affleck, FRAIC
1991	Phyllis Lambert, FRAIC
1992	Doug Shadbolt, FRAIC
1994	Barton Myers, FRAIC
1995	Moshe Safdie, FRAIC
1997	Raymond Moriyama, FRAIC
1998	Frank O. Gehry, FAIA, Hon. FRAIC
1999	Douglas Cardinal, OC, FRAIC

Source: The Royal Architectural Institute of Canada

Beauty – the adjustment of all parts proportionately so that one cannot add or subtract or change without impairing the harmony of the whole.

Alberti

RIBA Royal Gold Medal

Presented annually for distinction in architecture, the Royal Gold Medal is presented by Her Majesty the Queen on the advice of the Royal Institute of British Architects (RIBA). Since it was first granted by Queen Victoria in 1848, the RIBA confers the Royal Gold Medal annually. For the first time in the Medal's history, the 1999 award was presented to a city – Barcelona, Spain – and not to an individual.

For additional information, visit the RIBA on the Internet at *http://st10.yahoo.net/award-schemes/*.

1848	Charles Robert Cockerell	1878	Alfred Waterhouse
1849	Luigi Canine	1879	Marquis de Vogue
1850	Sir Charles Barry	1880	John L. Peerson
1851	Thomas L. Donaldson	1881	George Godwin
1852	Leo von Klenze	1882	Baron von Ferstel
1853	Sir Robert Smirke	1883	Fras. Cranmer Penrose
1854	Philip Hardwick	1884	William Butterfield
1855	J. I. Hittorff	1885	H. Schliemann
1856	Sir William Tite	1886	Charles Garnier
1857	Owen Jones	1887	Ewan Christian
1858	August Stuler	1888	Baron von Hansen
1859	Sir G. Gilbert Scott	1889	Sir Charles T. Newton
1860	Sydney Smirke	1890	John Gibson
1861	J. B. Lesueur	1891	Sir Arthur Blomfield
1862	Rev. Robert Willis	1892	Cesar Daly
1863	Anthony Salvin	1893	Richard Morris Hunt
1864	E. Violett-le-Duc	1894	Lord Leighton
1865	Sir James Pennethorne	1895	James Brooks
1866	Sir M. Digby Wyatt	1896	Sir Ernest George
1867	Charles Texier	1897	Dr. P.J.H.Cuypers
1868	Sir Henery Layard	1898	George Aitchison
1869	C.R. Lepsius	1899	George Frederick Badley
1870	Benjamin Ferrey	1900	Rodolfo Amadeo Lancani
1871	James Fergusson	1901	*(Not awarded due to the death of Queen Victoria)*
1872	Baron von Schmidt		
1873	Thomas Henry Wyatt	1902	Thomas Edward Collcutt
1874	George Edmund Street	1903	Charles F. McKim
1875	Edmund Sharpe	1904	Auguste Choisy
1876	Joseph Louis Duc	1905	Sir Aston Webb
1877	Charles Barry	1906	Sir L. Alma-Taderna

RIBA Royal Gold Medal (Con't)

1907	John Belcher	1949	Sir Howard Robertson
1908	Honore Daumet	1950	Eliel Saarinen
1909	Sir Arthur John Evans	1951	Emanuel Vincent Harris
1910	Sir Thomas Graham Jackson Bart	1952	George Grey Wornum
		1953	Le Corbusier (C.E. Jeanneret)
1911	Wilhelm Dorpfeld	1954	Sir Arthur George Staphenson
1912	Basil Champneys	1955	John Murray Easton
1913	Sir Reginald Blomfield RA	1956	Dr. Walter Adolf Georg Gropius
1914	Jean Louis Pascal	1957	Hugo Alvar Henrik Aalto
1915	Frank Darling	1958	Robert Schofield Morris
1916	Sir Robert Rowand Anderson	1959	Ludwig Mies van der Rohe
1917	Henri Paul Nenot	1960	Pier Luigi Nervi
1918	Ernest Newton RA	1961	Lewis Mumford
1919	Leonard Stokes	1962	Sven Gottfrid Markeluis
1920	Charles Louis Girault	1963	The Lord Holford
1921	Sir Edwin Landseer Lutyens	1964	E. Maxwell Fry
1922	Thomas Hastings	1965	Kenzo Tange
1923	Sir John James Burnet	1966	Ove Arup
1924	(Not awarded)	1967	Sir Nikolaus Pevsner
1925	Sir Giles Gilbert Scott	1968	Dr. Richard Buckminster Fuller
1926	Ragnar Ostberg	1969	Jack Antonio Coia
1927	Sir Herbert Baker	1970	Sir Robert Mathew
1928	Sir Guy Dawber	1971	Hubert de Cronin Hastings
1929	Victor Alexandre Frederic Laloux	1972	Louis I. Kahn
1930	Sir Percy Scott Worthington	1973	Sir Leslie Martin
1931	Sir Edwin Cooper	1974	Powell & Moya
1932	Dr. Hendrik Petrus Berlage	1975	Michael Scott
1933	Sir Charles Reed Peers	1976	Sir John Summerson
1934	Henry Vaughan Lanchester	1977	Sir Denys Lasdun
1935	Willem Marinus Dudok	1978	Jorn Utzon
1936	Charles Henry Holden	1979	The Office of Charles and Ray Eames
1937	Sir Raymond Unwin		
1938	Ivar Tengborn	1980	James Stirling
1939	Sir Percy Thomas	1981	Sir Philip Dowson
1940	Charles Francis Annesley Voysey	1982	Berthold Lubetkin
1941	Frank Lloyd Wright	1983	Sir Norman Foster
1942	William Curtis Green	1984	Charles Correa
1943	Sir Charles Herbert Reilly	1985	Sir Richard Rogers
1944	Sir Edward Maufe	1986	Arata Isozaki
1945	Victor Vesnin	1987	Ralph Erskine
1946	Sir Patrick Abercrombie	1988	Richard Meier
1947	Sir Albert Edward Richardson	1989	Renzo Piano
1948	Auguste Perret	1990	Aldo van Eyck

RIBA Royal Gold Medal (Con't)

1991	Coin Stansfield Smith	1996	Harry Seidler
1992	Peter Rice	1997	Tadao Ando
1993	Giancarlo de Carlo	1998	Oscar Niemeyer
1994	Michael and Patty Hopkins	1999	Barcelona, Spain
1995	Colin Rowe		

Source: Royal Institute of British Architects

Opposite: Tjibaou Cultural Center, Noumea, New Caledonia, Renzo Piano
Photograph © Tim Griffith/Esto.

Rudy Bruner Award for Urban Excellence

The biennial Rudy Bruner Award for Urban Excellence is awarded to projects which approach urban problems with creative inclusion of often competing political, community, environmental, and formal considerations. Established in 1987, the Award recognizes one Gold Medal Winner and four Silver Medal winners. Any project which fosters urban excellence is eligible to apply. A multi-disciplinary Selection Committee performs an on-site evaluation of each finalist before final selections are made.

For photographs and project descriptions, visit the Bruner Foundation on the Internet at *www.brunerfoundation.org* or contact them at (617) 876-8404.

1999 Gold Medal Winner:
Yerba Buena Gardens
San Francisco, CA

1999 Silver Winners:
ARTScorpsLA, Inc.
Los Angeles, California

National Aids Memorial Grove,
Golden Gate Park
San Francisco, California

Parkside Preservation
Philadelphia, Pennsylvania

The Portland Public Market
Portland, Maine

1999 Selection Committee:
Curtis Davis, AIA
Lawrence P. Goldman
Min Kantrowitz, AICP, M. Arch
Rick Lowe, Founding Director
Frieda Molina
Hon. Tom Murphy

Source: The Bruner Foundation

Did you know...
The Hardoy Chair (more commonly known as the butterfly chair), design by Argentinean architect Jorge Ferrari-Hardoy and produced by Knoll, today i one of the most widely copied pieces of furniture.

Sir Patrick Abercrombie Prize

The International Union of Architects (UIA) grants this triennial award to an internationally renowned architect or architects for significant work in town planning and territorial development.

For more information, visit the UIA's Web site at *www.uia-architectes.org.*

1961 Town Planning Service of the City of Stockholm (S. Markelius and G. Onblahd, Sweden)

1963 G. Dioxiadis (Greece)

1965 C. Buchanan and team (United Kingdom)

T. Farkas and team (Hungary)

1967 G. De Carlo (Italy)

1969 H. Bennet and team (United Kingdom)

Honrary Mention:
Belaunde Terry (Peru)

1972 Centre for Experimentation, Research and Training (Morocco)

1975 Iosif Bronislavovitch Orlov and Nilolai Ivanovitch Simonov (USSR)

1978 The City of Louvain la Neuve (Belgium)

1981 Warsaw architects (Poland) for the reconstruction of their capital

Honorary Mention:
M. Balderiotte and team (Argentina)

1984 Hans Blumenfeld (Canada)
Lucio Costa (Brazil)

1987 AIA Regional/Urban Design Assistance Team (R/UDAT) (USA)

Honorary Mention:
Eduardo Leira (Spain)
L. Bortenreuter, K. Griebel and H.G. Tiedt for the remodeling of the city center of Gera (GDR)

1990 Famund N. Bacon (USA)

1993 Jan Gehl (Denmark)

1996 Juan Gil Elizondo (Mexico)

1999 Karl Ganser (Germany)

Honorary Mention:
Master plan of the city of Shenzhen (People's Republic of China)

Source: International Union of Architects

Most of us spend most of our time in, near or influenced by built surroundings. We spend our lives in what were once the thoughts of architects.

Christopher Day

Sir Robert Matthew Prize

The International Union of Architects (UIA) awards the Sir Robert Matthew Prize triennially to an internationally renowned architect or architects whose work has improved the quality of human settlements.

For more information, visit the UIA's web site at *www.uia-architectes.org.*

1978 John F.C. Turner (U.K.)

1981 Hassan Fathy (Egypt);
      Honorary Mention:
          Rod Hackney (U.K.) and
          Hardt Walther Hamer (GFR)

1984 Charles Correa (India)

1987 Housing Reconstruction
      Programme for the City of
      Mexico (Mexico)

1990 Department of Architecture of
      the Singapore Housing &
      Development Board
      (Singapore)

1993 Laurie Baker (U.K.)

1996 Professor Giancarlo De Carlo (Italy)
      Jury citation:
          Oberste Baubehörde (the
          German team under the guid-
          ance of architect Benno
          Brugger and led by Hans Jörg
          Nussberger)

1999 Martin Treberspurg (Austria)
      Honorary Mention:
          Development & Construction
          Branch of the Hong Kong
          Housing Department

Source: International Union of Architects (UIA)

Did you know...
The Empire State Building, Chrysler Building, and John Hancock Center are the only buildings constructed prior to 1970 which still rank among the world's 20 tallest buildings.

Spiro Kostof Book Award

The Society of Architectural Historians (SAH) grants the annual Spiro Kostof Award to a work that has made the greatest contribution to understanding the historical development of the change in urbanism and architecture.

For more information, contact the SAH at (312) 573-1365 or visit their Web site at *www.sah.org/awards.html.*

1994
: *Architecture Power and National Identity* by Lawrence J. Vale (Yale University Press)

1995
: *In the Theatre of Criminal Justice: The Palais de Justice in Second Empire Paris* by Katherine Fischer Taylor (Princeton University Press)

1996
: *The Topkapi Scroll: Geometry and Ornament in Islamic Architecture* by Gülru Necipoglu (Getty Center for the History of Art and Humanities)

1997
: *The Projective Cast: Architecture and Its Three Geometries* by Robin Evans (MIT Press)

Auschwitz: 1270 to the Present by Debórah Dwork and Robert Jan van Pelt (Norton)

1998
: *The Architects and the City* by Robert Bruegmann (University of Chicago Press)

Magnetic Los Angeles by Gregory Hise (Johns Hopkins Press)

1999
: *City Center to Regional Mall: Architecture, the Automobile and Retailing in Los Angeles, 1920-1950* by Richard Longstreth (MIT Press)

Housing Design and Society in Amsterdam: Reconfiguring Urban Order and Identity, 1900-1920 by Nancy Stieber (University of Chicago Press)

Source: Society of Architectural Historians

You employ stone, wood, and concrete, and with these materials you build houses and palaces.... But suddenly you touch my heart.... That is Architecture.

Le Corbusier

Star Award

Through its Star Award the International Interior Design Association (IIDA) recognizes individuals who have made an outstanding contribution to the interior design profession. No more than one award is granted each year. However, as this is merit based, awards are not always given each year. Although non-members are eligible for the Star Award, the IIDA Board of Directors, the selection body, only accepts nominations from IIDA Fellows, chapter presidents, and directors.

For more information about the Star Award, visit IIDA's Web site at *www.iida.org* or contact them at (888) 799-4432.

1985	Lester Dundes	1992	M. Arthur Gensler, Jr., FAIA, FIIDA
1986	William Sullivan		
1987	Orlando Diaz-Azcuy	1993	Sivon C. Reznikoff, IIDA
1988	Paul Brayton, IIDA	1994	Michael Kroelinger, FIIDA
1989	Florence Knoll Bassett	1995	Douglas R. Parker, AIA
1990	Beverly Russell	1997	Michael Wirtz, FIIDA
1991	Stanley Abercrombie, FAIA, Hon. IIDA	1998	Charles and Ray Eames
		1999	Michael Brill

Source: International Interior Designers Association

Did you know...
As the Washington Monument rises, its wall thickness tapers from 15 feet at the bottom to 18 inches at the top.

Thomas Jefferson Awards for Public Architecture

The Thomas Jefferson Awards for Public Architecture are presented annually by The American Institute of Architects (AIA) to recognize and foster the importance of design excellence in government and infrastructure projects. Awards are presented in three categories:

- Category One – Private sector architects who have amassed a portfolio of accomplished and distinguished public facilities (C1)

- Category Two – Public sector architects who produce quality projects within their agencies (C2)

- Category Three – Public officials or others who have been strong advocates for design excellence (C3)

For more information, visit the AIA on the Internet at *www.e-architect.org* or contact the AIA Honors and Awards Department at (202) 626-7586.

1992 James Ingo Freed, FAIA (C1)
George M. White, FAIA (C2)
The Honorable Patrick J. Moynihan, Hon. AIA (C3)

1993 The Honorable Jack Brooks, Hon. AIA (C3)

1994 Richard Dattner, FAIA (C1)
M.J. "Jay" Brodie, FAIA (C2)
The Honorable Joseph P. Riley Jr., Hon. AIA (C3)

1995 Herbert S. Newman, FAIA (C1)
Edward A. Feiner, FAIA (C2)
Henry G. Cisneros, Hon. AIA (C3)

1996 Thomas R. Aidala, FAIA (C2)
The Honorable Douglas P. Woodlock (C3)

1997 John Tarantino, AIA (C2)
Richard A. Kahan (C3)
Hunter Morrison (C3)

1998 Arthur Rosenblatt, FAIA (C2)

1999 Lewis Davis, FAIA (C1)
Robert Kroin (C2)

Source: American Institute of Architects

Did you know...
By the end of the twentieth-century, the number of people living in towns and cities throughout the world has grown from one out of ten in 1900 to almost 3 billion of the world's 6 billion inhabitants.

TOPAZ Medallion

The TOPAZ Medallion is jointly awarded by the American Institute of Architects (AIA) and the American Collegiate Schools of Architecture (ACSA) to honor individuals who have made an outstanding contribution to the field of architectural education. Candidates are nominated by colleagues, students and former students. Recipients have made a significant impact on the field of architecture, expanded into fields beyond their specialty, and affected a lasting impact on their students.

For additional information about this award program, visit the AIA's Web site at *www.e-architect.com.*

1976	Jean Labatut, FAIA, Princeton University
1977	Henry Kamphoefner, FAIA, North Carolina State University
1978	Lawrence Anderson, FAIA, MIT
1979	G. Holmes Perkins, FAIA, University of Pennsylvania
1980	Serge Chermayeff, Yale University
1981	Marcel Breuer, FAIA, Harvard University
1982	Joseph Esherick, FAIA, University of California, Berkeley
1983	Charles E. Burchard, FAIA, Virginia Polytechnic University
1984	Robert Geddes, FAIA, Princeton
1985	Colin Rowe, Cornell University
1986	Vincent Scully Jr., Hon. AIA, Yale University
1987	Ralph Rapson, FAIA, University of Minnesota
1988	John Hejduk, FAIA, Cooper Union
1989	Charles Moore, FAIA, University of California, Berkeley
1990	Raymond L. Kappe, FAIA, Southern California Institute of Architecture
1991	Kenneth B. Frampton, Columbia University
1992	Spiro Kostof, University of California, Berkeley*
1993	Mario Salvadori, Hon. AIA, Columbia University
1994	Harlan E. McClure, FAIA, Clemson University
1995	Henry N. Cobb, FAIA, Harvard University
1996	Denise Scott-Brown, RIBA, University of Pennsylvania
1997	Donlyn Lyndon, FAIA, University of California, Berkeley
1998	Werner Seligmann, Syracuse University
1999	W. Cecil Steward, FAIA, University of Nebraska

* honored posthumously

Source: The American Institute of Architects

Twenty-five Year Award

Awarded annually by the American Institute of Architects (AIA), the Twenty-five Year Award is presented to projects which excel under the test of time. Projects must have been completed 25 to 35 years ago by an architect licensed in the United States, though the nominated facility may be located anywhere in the world. To be eligible submissions must still be carrying out their original program and demonstrate a continued viability in their function and form.

For more information, visit the AIA on the Internet at *www.e-architect*.org or contact the AIA Honors and Awards Department at (202) 626-7586.

1969
    Rockefeller Center
    New York City, NY
    Reinhard & Hofmeister; Corbett,
        Harrison & MacMurray
1971
    The Crow Island School
    Winnetka, IL
    Perkins, Wheeler & Will; Eliel & Eero
        Saarinen
1972
    Baldwin Hills Village
    Los Angeles, CA
    Reginald D. Johnson; Wilson, Merrill
        & Alexander; Clarence S. Stein
1973
    Taliesin West
    Paradise Valley, AZ
    Frank Lloyd Wright
1974
    Johnson and Son Administration
        Building
    Racine, WI
    Frank Lloyd Wright
1975
    Philip Johnson's Residence, ("The
        Glass House")
    New Caanan, CT
    Philip Johnson

1976
    860-880 North Lakeshore Drive
        Apartments
    Chicago, IL
    Ludwig Mies van der Rohe
1977
    Christ Lutheran Church
    Minneapolis, MN
    Saarinen, Saarinen & Associates;
        Hills, Gilbertson & Hays
1978
    The Eames House
    Pacific Palisades, CA
    Charles and Ray Eames
1979
    Yale University Art Gallery
    New Haven, CT
    Louis I. Kahn, FAIA
1980
    Lever House
    New York City, NY
    Skidmore, Owings & Merrill
1981
    Farnsworth House
    Plano, IL
    Ludwig Mies van der Rohe

Twenty-five Year Award (Con't)

1982
Equitable Savings and Loan Building
Portland, OR
Pietro Belluschi, FAIA

1983
Price Tower
Bartlesville, OK
Frank Lloyd Wright

1984
Seagram Building
New York City, NY
Ludwig Mies van der Rohe

1985
General Motors Technical Center
Warren, MI
Eero Saarinen and Associates with
Smith, Hinchman & Grylls

1986
Solomon R. Guggenheim Museum
New York City, NY
Frank Lloyd Wright

1987
Bavinger House
Norman, OK
Bruce Goff

1988
Dulles International Airport
Terminal Building
Chantilly, VA
Eero Saarinen and Associates

1989
Vanna Venturi House
Chestnut Hill, PA
Robert Venturi, FAIA

1990
The Gateway Arch
St. Louis, MO
Eero Saarinen and Associates

1991
Sea Ranch Condominium I
The Sea Ranch, CA
Moore Lyndon Turnbull Whitaker

1992
The Salk Institute for Biological
Studies
La Jolla, CA
Louis I. Kahn, FAIA

1993
Deere & Company Administrative
Center
Moline, IL
Eero Saarinen and Associates

1994
The Haystack Mountain School of
Crafts
Deer Isle, ME
Edward Larrabee Barnes

1995
The Ford Foundation Headquarters
New York City, NY
Kevin Roche John Dinkeloo and
Associates

1996
The Air Force Academy Cadet Chapel
Colorado Springs, CO
Skidmore, Owings & Merrill

1997
Phillips Exeter Academy Library
Exeter, NH
Louis I. Kahn, FAIA

1998
Kimbell Art Museum
Fort Worth, TX
Louis I. Kahn, FAIA

1999
The John Hancock Center
Chicago, IL
Skidmore, Owings & Merrill

Source: American Institute of Architects

Opposite: Johnson Wax Tower, Racine, WI,
Frank Lloyd Wright
Photograph © Jeff Goldberg/Esto.

UIA Gold Medal

Every three years at the World Congress of the International Union of Architects (UIA), the UIA awards its Gold Medal to a living architect who has made an outstanding achievement to the field of architecture. This honor recognizes the recipient's lifetime of distinguished practice, contribution to the enrichment of mankind, and the promotion of the art of architecture.

For more information, visit the UIA's Web site at *www.uia-architectes.org.*

1984   Hassan Fathy (Egypt)
1987   Reima Pietila (Finland)
1990   Charles Correa (India)
1993   Fumihiko Maki (Japan)
1996   Rafael Moneo (Spain)
1999   Ricardo Legorreta (Mexico)

Source: International Union of Architects

Nothing is quite beautiful alone; nothing is beautiful but in the whole. A single object is only so far beautiful as it suggests this universal grace. The poet, the musician, the architect seek each to concentrate this radiance of the world on one point.

Ralph Waldo Emerson

Urban Land Institute Awards for Excellence

The Urban Land Institute Awards for Excellence follow the organization's mission "to provide responsible leadership in the use of land in order to enhance the environment." Considered by many the most prestigious awards within the development community, the Urban Land Institute has recognized outstanding land development projects throughout the world since 1979. Submissions are accepted from developers in the United States and Canada (except for the International Award which is worldwide in scope) and judged by a panel of experts. Winning entries represent superior design, improve the quality of the built environment, exhibit a sensitivity to the community, display financial viability, and demonstrate relevance to contemporary issues.

For more information about the awards, contact the Urban Land Institute at 800-321-5011 or visit their Web site at *www.uli.org.*

1979
   The Galleria, Houston, TX

1980
   Charles Center, Baltimore, MD

1981
   WDW/Reedy Creek, Orlando, FL

1982
   Heritage Village, Southbury, CT (large scale)

   Promontory Point, Newport Beach, CA (small scale)

1983
   Toronto Eaton Center, Toronto, Canada (large scale)

1984
   Embarcadero Center, San Francisco, CA (large scale)

   Rainbow Centre, Niagra Falls, NY (small scale)

1985
   Las Colinas, Irving, TX (large scale new community)

   Museum Tower, New York, NY (large scale residential)

   Sea Colony Condominiums, Santa Monica, CA (small scale urban mixed-use)

   Sea Pines Plantation, Hilton Head, SC (large scale recreation)

   Vista Montoya, Los Angeles, CA (small scale urban mixed-use)

1986
   2000 Pennsylvania Avenue, Washington, D.C. (small scale mixed-use)

   Downtown Costa Mesa, Costa Mesa, CA (small scale rehabilitation)

Urban Land Institute Awards for Excellence (Con't)

Inner Harbor Shoreline, Baltimore, MD (Special Award)

Kaanapali Beach Resort, Kaanapali, HI (large scale recreational)

The Landings on Skidaway Island, Savannah, GA (large scale residential)

The Purdue Frederick Company, Norwalk, CT (small scale industrial/office park)

Water Tower Place, Chicago, IL (large scale recreational)

1987
Bishop Ranch Business Park, San Ramon, CA (large scale industrial/office)

Loews Ventana Canyon Resort, Tucson, AZ (small scale commercial retail)

St. Louis Union Station, St. Louis, MO (large scale urban mixed-use)

Straw Hill, Manchester, NH (small scale residential)

The Willard Inter-Continental, Washington, D.C. (rehabilitation)

1988
Copley Place, Boston, MA (large scale urban mixed-use)

Downtown Women's Center, Los Angeles, CA (Special Award)

Northpoint, Chicago, IL (rehabilitation)

Pickleweed Apartment, Mill Valley, CA (small scale residential)

Rector Place, New York, NY (large scale residential)

The Grand Avenue, Milwaukee, WI (large scale commercial retail)

Wilshire Palisades, Santa Monica, CA (small scale office)

1989
Charleston Place, Charleston, SC (small scale urban/mixed-use)

Commonwealth Development, Boston, MA (rehabilitation)

Escondido City Hall, Escondido, CA (small scale office)

Norwest Center, Minneapolis, MN (large scale office)

Pratt-Willert Neighborhood, Buffalo, NY (Special Award)

Reston, Reston, VA (new community)

Rockefeller Center, New York, NY (Heritage Award)

Rowes Wharf, Boston, MA (large scale urban mixed-use)

1990
Carnegie Center, Princeton, NJ (large scale industrial)

Columbia Place, San Diego, CA (small scale residential)

River Run, Boise, ID (large scale residential)

Tent City, Boston, MA (Special Award)

The Boulders, Carefree, AZ (small scale commercial)

Wayne County Building, Detroit, MI (rehabilitation)

Woodlake, Richmond, VA (new community)

1991
Del Mar Plaza, Del Mar, CA (small scale commercial/retail)

Urban Land Institute Awards for Excellence (Con't)

Fashion Center at Pentagon, City, Arlington, VA (large scale urban mixed-use)

Garibaldi Square, Chicago, IL (small scale urban mixed-use)

Ghent Square, Norfolk, VA (large scale residential)

Grand Central Partnership, New York, NY (Special Award)

James R. Mills Building, San Diego, CA (small scale office)

Marina Village, Alameda, CA (rehabilitation)

Union Station, Washington, D.C. (Special Award)

1992

CoCoWalk, Miami, FL (small scale commercial retail)

Harbor Point, Boston, MA (public project)

Market Square, Washington, DC (large scale mixed-use)

Planned Community of Mission Viejo (new community)

Summit Place, St. Paul, MN (small scale residential)

The Coeur d'Alene Resort Golf Course, Coeur d'Alene, ID (Special Award)

The Delancey Street Foundation, San Francisco, CA (Special Award)

Tysons Corner Center, McLean, VA (rehabilitation)

1993

Beverly Hills Senior Housing, Beverly Hills, CA (small scale residential development)

Charlestown Navy Yard, Charlestown, MA (Special Award)

Furness House, Baltimore, MD (small scale rehabilitation)

Kapalua, Kapalua, Maui, HI (large scale recreational development)

Post Office Square at Park and Garage, Boston, MA (Special Award)

Schlitz Park, Milwaukee, WI (large scale rehabilitation)

The Country Club Plaza, Kansas City, MO (Heritage Award)

The Cypress of Hilton Head Island, Hilton Head Island, SC (large scale residential development)

The Somerset Collection, Troy, MI (small scale commercial retail)

1994

Broadgate, London, England (International Award)

Orchard Village, Chattanooga, TN (small scale residential)

Oriole Park at Camden Yards, Baltimore, MD (public project)

Phipps Plaza, Atlanta, GA (large scale rehabilitation)

Sea Pines Plantation, Hilton Head Island, SC (Heritage Award)

The Pennsylvania Avenue Plan, Washington, DC (Special Award)

The Woodlands, The Woodlands, TX (Special Award)

Washington Mutual Tower, Seattle, WA (large scale office)

Woodbridge, Irvine, CA (large scale residential)

Urban Land Institute Awards for Excellence (Con't)

1995

640 Memorial Drive, Cambridge, MA (small scale rehabilitation)

Broadway Plaza, Walnut Creek, CA (large scale commercial/ retail)

Disneyland Park, Anaheim, CA (Heritage Award)

Irvine Spectrum, Orange County, CA (large scale industrial/office park)

Little Nell Hotel and Aspen Mountain Base, Aspen, CO (area development)

Monterey Bay Aquarium, Monterey, CA (Special Award)

Pelican Bay, Naples, FL (new community)

Riverbank State Park, New York, NY (Special Award)

Strathern Park Apartments, Sun Valley, CA (small scale residential)

1996

Avenel, Potomac, MD (large scale residential)

Bryant Park, New York, NY (public project)

Comerica Tower at Detroit Center, Detroit, MI (large scale office)

The Court Home Collection at Valencia NorthPark, Valencia, CA (small scale residential)

The Forum Shops, Las Vegas, NV (small scale commercial/retail)

The Heritage on the Garden, Boston, MA (small scale mixed-use)

Kiawah Island, Kiawah Island, SC (large scale recreational)

The Scattered Site Program, Chicago, IL (Special Award)

1997

The Arizona Biltmore Resort and Villas, Phoenix, AZ (Heritage Award)

Chelsea Piers, New York City, NY (large scale rehabilitation)

A Contemporary Theatre, Seattle, WA (small scale rehabilitation)

Desert Mountain, Scottsdale, AZ (large scale recreational)

Mercado Apartments, San Diego, CA (small scale residential)

Park Meadows, Littleton, CO (large scale commercial/hotel)

The Pennsylvania Convention Center, Philadelphia, PA (Special Award)

A Safe House for Kids and Moms, Newport Beach, CA (Special Award)

Smyrna Town Center, Smyrna, GA (public project)

Stockley Park at Heathrow, Stockley Park, England, (International Award)

1998

Alliance, Fort Worth, TX (large scale business park)

American Visionary Art Museum, Baltimore, MD (Special Award)

Calakmul, Mexico City, Mexico (International Award)

Courthouse Hill, Arlington, VA (small scale residential)

Harold Washington Library Center, Chicago, IL (public project)

Richmond City Center, Richmond, CA (Special Award)

Urban Land Institute Awards for Excellence (Con't)

Twenty-Eight State Street, Boston, MA (rehabilitation)

UtiliCorp United World Headquarters/ New York Life Building, Kansas City, MO (rehabilitation)

Village Center, Beaver Creek, CO (small scale recreational)

Source: Urban Land Institute

Did you know...

When the New York legislature purchased the 1750 Hasbrouck House in 1850, General George Washington's headquarters in Newburgh, it became the nation's first historic house museum.

Veronica Rudge Green Prize in Urban Design

Established by Harvard University in 1986, the Veronica Rudge Green Prize in Urban Design awards excellence in urban design with an emphasis on projects that contribute to the public spaces in cities and improve the quality of urban life. The Prize is awarded biennially by a jury of experts in the field of architecture and urban design. Nominations are made to the Harvard Design School by a panel of critics, academics, and practitioners in the field of architecture, landscape architecture, and urban design. Eligible projects must be larger in scope than a single building and must have been constructed within the last 10 years. Winners receive a monetary award and certificate.

Additional information about the award can be found on the Internet at *www.gsd.harvard.edu/prizes/grn.html.*

1988
>   Ralph Erskine, Byker Redevelopment in Newcastle upon Tyne, U.K.
>
>   Alvaro Siza Vieira, Malagueira Quarter Housing Project in Evora, Portugal

1990
>   The City of Barcelona, Urban Public Spaces of Barcelona

1993
>   Fumihiko Maki, Hillside Terrace Complex, Tokyo, Japan
>
>   Luigi Snozzi, Master Plan and Public Buildings of Monte Carasso, Switzerland

1996
>   Mexico City, Restoration of the Historic Center of Mexico City and Ecological Restoration of the District of Xochimilco

1998
>   Sir Norman Foster and Foster and Partners, subway system in Bilbao, Spain and the development of Carré d'Art Plaza in Nîmes, France.

Source: Harvard Graduate School of Design/School of Architecture

Every facet of the design process has to maintain a relationship with the senses. When you confront an object, you've got to touch it, smell it, listen to it.

Bruno Munari

Whitney M. Young, Jr. Award

The American Institute of Architects (AIA) bestows the Whitney M. Young Jr. Award annually upon an architect or architecturally oriented organization that makes a significant contribution toward meeting the challenge set forth by Mr. Young to architects: to assume a professional responsibility toward current social issues. These issues are ever present and flexible and include such things as housing the homeless, affordable housing, minority and women participation in the profession, disability issues, and literacy.

For more information, visit the AIA on the Internet at *www.e-architect.org* or contact the AIA Honors and Awards Department at (202) 626-7586.

1972	Robert J. Nash, FAIA	1988	Habitat for Humanity
1973	Architects Workshop of Philadelphia	1989	John H. Spencer, FAIA
		1990	Harry G. Robinson III, FAIA
1974	Stephen Cram*	1991	Robert Kennard, FAIA
1975	Van B. Bruner Jr., FAIA	1992	Curtis J. Moody, AIA
1976	Wendell J. Campbell, FAIA	1993	David Castro-Blanco, FAIA
1980	Leroy M. Campbell*	1994	Ki Suh Park, FAIA
1981	Robert T. Coles, FAIA	1995	William J. Stanley, III, AIA, NOMA
1982	John S. Chase, FAIA	1996	John L. Wilson, AIA
1983	Howard Hamilton Mackey Sr., FAIA	1997	Alan Y. Taniguchi, FAIA
1984	John Louis Wilson, FAIA	1998	Leon Bridges, FAIA
1985	Milton V. Bergstedt, AIA	1999	Charles McAfee, FAIA
1986	The Rev. Richard McClure Prosse*		
1987	J. Max Bond Jr., AIA		

* Honored posthumously

Source: American Institute of Architects

Did you know...

When the Eiffel Tower was completed in 1889, it became the world's tallest man-made structure, a title it held for 40 years.

Wolf Prize for Architecture

Dr. Ricardo Wolf established the Wolf Foundation in 1976 in order to "promote science and arts for the benefit of mankind." In this vein, the Wolf prize is awarded annually to outstanding living scientists and artists in the fields of agriculture, chemistry, mathematics, medicine, physics, and the arts. The awards, an honorarium of US$100,000 and a diploma, are presented each year in Jerusalem's Chagall Hall. In the arts category, the Wolf Prize rotates annually between architecture, music, painting, and sculpture. The following individuals received this honor for their contribution to the field of architecture.

For more information about the Wolf Prize, contact the Wolf Foundation at +972 (9) 955 7120 or visit their Web site at *www.aquanet.co.il/wolf.*

1983   Ralph Erskine (Sweden)

1988   Fumihiko Maki (Japan)
       Giancarlo de Carlo (Italy)

1992   Frank O. Gehry (US)
       Jorn Utzon (Denmark)
       Sir Denys Lasdun (U.K.)

1996   Frei Otto (Germany)
       Aldo van Eyck (Holland)

Source: Wolf Foundation

Architecture as an agent of change – which is why a leader like Mahatma Gandi is called Architect of the Nation. Not the Engineer, nor the Dentist, nor the Historian. But the Architect – the generalist who speculates on how the pieces fit together in more advantageous ways, one who is concerned with what might be.

Charles Correa

Opposite: Guggenheim Bilbao, Bilbao Spain, Frank Gehry
Photograph © Jeff Goldberg/Esto.

Young Architects Award

The Young Architects Award is presented annually by The American Institute of Architects (AIA) to an architect in the early stages of his or her career who has made "significant contributions" to the profession. The competition is open to AIA members who have been licensed to practice for less than 10 years; the term "young architect" has no reference to the age of nominees.

For additional information about the Young Architects Award visit the AIA online at *www.e-architect.org* or contact the AIA Honors and Awards Department at (202) 626-7586.

1993
Design - Joan M. Soranno, AIA
Service - Vicki L. Hooper, AIA
Service - Thomas Somerville Howorth, AIA
Service - Brett Keith Laurila, AIA

1995
Design - William A. Blanski, AIA
Service - Anne Tate, AIA

1996
Design - Christopher W. Coe, AIA
Design & Service -
    George Thrush, AIA
Design - Keith Moskow, AIA

1997
Design - Robert S. Rothman, AIA
Education - William J. Carpenter, AIA
Service - Michael A. Fischer, AIA
Service - Brad Simmons, AIA

1998
Design - J. Windom Kimsey, AIA
Design - Jose Luis Palacious, AIA
Service - Karin M. Pitman, AIA
Design - Charles Rose, AIA
Design - Karl W. Stumpf, AIA
Design - David Louis Swartz, AIA
Design - Maryann Thompson, AIA
Service - Randall C. Vaughn, AIA

1999
Design - Father Terrence Curry, AIA
Service - Victoria Tama Jacobson, AIA
Design - Michael Thomas Maltzan, AIA
Design - David T. Nagahiro, AIA
Service - Peter Steinbrueck, AIA

Source: American Institute of Architects

Did you know...
Richard N. Swett, the United States' ambassador to Denmark, is the first architect-ambassador in more than a century.

ORGANIZATIONS

ORGANIZATIONS

American Architectural Foundation (AAF)

Headquartered in America's oldest museum devoted to architecture, Washington D.C.'s Octagon, the American Architectural Foundation (AAF) is dedicated to furthering the public's understanding of architecture and the human experience. The non-profit AAF sponsors education and outreach programs which foster public participation in the design process, encourages public stewardship of America's architectural heritage, and promotes alliances between architects and their communities. They are also a repository for a growing architectural archive of over 60,000 drawings, 30,000 photographs, and more.

Address:
1735 New York, Avenue NW
Washington, D.C. 20006
Telephone: (202) 626-7500
Internet: www.amerarchfoundation.com

When I am working on a problem, I never think about beauty. I think only how to solve the problem. But when I have finished, if the solution is not beautiful, I know it is wrong.

Buckminster Fuller

American Consulting Engineers Council (ACEC)

The American Consulting Engineers Council (ACEC) represents private engineering firms in the U.S. by promoting their interests and providing educational opportunities to members. Specifically, the goals of the group are to help members achieve higher business standards, ensure ethical standards are maintained, act as an information clearinghouse, advise on legislation, and to support the advancement of engineering. The ACEC was formed by the union of the American Institute of Consulting Engineers and the Consulting Engineers Council in 1973. Today it is the largest national organization of consulting engineers. Fifty-two state and regional Member Organizations represent more than 5,700 engineering firms. These firms employ more than 250,000 engineers, architects, land surveyors, scientists, technicians and other professionals who design approximately $100 billion of private and public works annually.

Address:
1015 15th St, NW, #802
Washington, DC 20005
Telephone: (202) 347-7474
Internet: www.acec.org

American Institute of Architects (AIA)

Representing the professional interests of America's architects and seeking to increase national design literacy among the public, The American Institute of Architects (AIA) provides education, government advocacy, community redevelopment and public outreach activities with and for its 62,000 members. With 305 local and state AIA organizations, the Institute monitors closely legislative and regulatory actions at all levels of government. It provides professional development opportunities, industry standard contract documents, information services, and a comprehensive awards program.

Address:
1735 New York Ave., NW
Washington, DC 20006
Telephone: (202) 626-7300
(800) AIA-3837
www.e-architect.com

Did you know...
As the John Hancock Center tapers as it rises, it decreases from 50,000 square feet per floor at the base to only 16,000 at the summit.

American Institute of Architecture Students (AIAS)

The American Institute of Architecture Students (AIAS) is a non-profit, independent, student-run organization that seeks to promote exccllence in architecture education, training and practice, as well as to organize architecture students and promote the practice of architecture. The AIAS was formed in 1956 and today serves over 7,500 undergraduate and graduate architecture students. More than 150 chapters at U.S. and Canadian colleges and universities support members with professional development seminars, community projects, curriculum advisory committees, guest speakers and many other programs.

Address:
1735 New York Avenue, NW
Washington, DC 20006
Telephone: (202) 626-7472
Internet: www.aiasnatl.org

There are three basic principles behind any well-designed product: truth, humanity, and simplicity.

Sohrab Vossoughi

American Planning Association (APA)

The American Planning Association (APA) represents 30,000 planners, officials and citizens involved with urban and rural planning issues. Sixty-five percent of APA's members are employed by state and local government agencies. The mission of the organization is to encourage planning that will contribute to public well-being by developing communities and environments that meet the needs of people and society more effectively. APA is headquartered in Washington, D.C. and has 46 regional chapters. The American Institute of Certified Planners (AICP) is APA's professional and educational arm, certifying planners who have met specific criteria and passed the certification. The group also has research, publications, conference, and education components.

Address:
1776 Massachusetts Ave., NW
Washington, D.C. 20036
Telephone: (202) 872-0611
Internet: www.planning.org

Architecture is both a matter of utility and a matter of art, its complexities exceeding our expectations for the merely useful or merely artistic.

Dora P. Crouch

American Society of Interior Designers (ASID)

The American Society of Interior Designers (ASID) was formed in 1975 with the consolidation of the American Institute of Designers (AID) and the National Society of Interior Designers (NSID). It serves over 30,000 members with continuing education, government affairs, conferences, publications, online services, and more. Members include residential and commercial designers, 3,500 manufacturers of design-related products and services, also know as Industry Partners, and 7,500 students of interior design. ASID has 49 chapters throughout the United States.

Address:
608 Massachusetts Avenue, NE
Washington, DC 20002-6006
Telephone: (202) 546-3480
Internet: www.asid.org

American Society of Landscape Architects (ASLA)

Representing the landscape architecture profession in the United States since 1899, the American Society of Landscape Architects (ASLA) currently serves over 13,000 members through 47 chapters across the country. The ASLA's goal is to advance knowledge, education, and skill in the art and science of landscape architecture. The benefits of membership include a national annual meeting, *Landscape Architecture* magazine, continuing education credits, seminars and workshops, professional interest groups, government advocacy, and award programs. In addition, the U.S. Department of Education has authorized the Landscape Architectural Accreditation Board (LAAB) of the ASLA as the accrediting agency for landscape architecture programs at U.S. colleges and universities.

Address:
636 Eye Street, NW
Washington, DC 20091-3736
Telephone: (202) 898-2444
Internet: www.asla.org

Ten acres of inner-city land is equivalent to one acre on the water.

F. L. Olmsted

Architects' Council of Europe (ACE)

Membership of the Architects' Council of Europe (ACE) is comprised of most European representative bodies of the architecture profession. Their constitution states: "The Association of member organizations shall be a non-profit association...as the Liaison Committee of the Representative Bodies of the profession of Architecture, be dedicated to the better understanding of cultural values and the promotion of the highest standards of education and practice in architecture, and shall seek to ensure and shall promote the independence and integrity of the Architectural Profession within the European Community and shall, in these matters, act as its Liaison Committee in seeking, insofar as possible, consensus among the Member Organizations; and shall, without prejudice to the right of Derogation set out at Article 11.5 of this Constitution, promote and represent the common interests of the Profession of Architect in the European Community." Currently the ACE is focusing on deregulation, sustainability issues, and continued work on opening up avenues of communication throughout Europe among politicians, developers, and members of the construction industry.

Address:
Avenue Louise 207 b. 10 1050
Brussels, Belgium
Telephone: (32-2) 645-0905

Architectural Institute of Japan (AIJ)

The Architectural Institute of Japan (AIJ) is an academic association with nearly 40,000 members. The organization, dedicated to cultivating the talents of its members and promoting architectural quality in Japan, celebrated its 100th anniversary in 1986. AIJ activities include publications, research, prizes, lectures, exhibitions, and library services. The Board of Directors consists of the President, five Vice Presidents, 18 General Directors, and nine Directors representing the nine local chapters.

Address:
26-20, Shiba 5-chome, Minato-ku
Tokyo 108-8414 Japan
Telephone: +81-3-3456-2051
Internet: www.aij.or.jp/

Construction Specifications Institute (CSI)

Headquartered in Alexandria, Virginia, the Construction Specifications Institute (CSI) represents nearly 18,000 members, including architects, engineers, specifiers, contractors, building owners, facility managers, and product manufacturers. As a professional association, CSI provides technical information, continuing education, conferences, and product shows for members. It strives to meet the industry's need for a common system of organizing and presenting construction documents, as demonstrated by its MasterFormat™ system and the new Uniform Drawing System™, which are quickly becoming an industry standard. CSI also publishes The Construction Specifier, a monthly magazine featuring articles on technologies, applications, legal issues, trends, and new products.

Address:
601 Madison Street
Alexandria, Virginia 22314-1791
Telephone: (800) 689-2900 or (703) 684-0300
Internet: www.csinet.org

Profit in business comes from repeat customers, customers that boast about your project or service, and that bring friends with them.

W. Edwards Deming

Council on Tall Buildings and Urban Habitat (CTBUH)

The Council on Tall Buildings and Urban Habitat (CTBUH) was established to study and report on all aspects of the planning, design, construction, and operation of tall buildings. The group is sponsored by architecture, engineering, and planning professionals. One of the Council's major focuses is the publication of monographs on tall buildings, as well as studying not only the technological factors related to tall buildings, but the social and cultural aspects of the structures. They maintain an extensive database of tall buildings and produce the definitive list of the world's tallest buildings. The Council Headquarters is located at Lehigh University in Bethlehem, Pennsylvania.

Address:
CTBUH – Lehigh University
11 East Packer Avenue
Bethlehem, PA
Telephone: (610) 758-3515
Internet: www.ctbuh.edu

Did you know...
Sir Norman Foster's Hong Kong and Shanghai Banking Corporation Headquarters features a computer-controlled "sun-scoop:" a mirrored panel which follows the sun and reflects its rays into the top of the central building's atrium, flooding the building with light.

Design-Build Institute of America (DBIA)

The Design-Build Institute of America (DBIA) is a voice supporting the integrated design-build project delivery method. Founded in 1993, DBIA membership includes design-builders, contractors, design professionals, subcontractors, representatives of government agencies, and other professionals. The DBIA strives to improve the level of design-build practice, to disseminate educational information, and to furnish advice and support to facility owners and users. Toward this end, the Institute's programs include dissemination and development of standard procedures and formats, promotion of design-build in public forums and with private corporations and government agencies, educational programs, and providing information support and assistance to members.

Address:
1010 Massachusetts Avenue, N.W.
Suite 350
Washington, D.C. 20001
Telephone: (202) 682-0110
Internet: www.dbia.org

I'm not sure office buildings are even architecture. They're really a mathematical calculation, just three-dimensional investments.

Gordon Bunshaft

Design Futures Council (DFC)

The Design Futures Council (DFC) is a Washington D.C. think-tank with the mission to explore trends, changes, and new opportunities in design, architecture, engineering, and building technology for the purpose of fostering innovation and improving the performance of member organizations. Participants represent a full spectrum of design, manufacturing, and service professionals. Council activities include proprietary surveys, industry focus groups, and conference facilitation. Member companies receive a host of benefits, including a seat on the Board of the Design Futures Council, which meets at least twice annually.

Address:
11921 Freedom Drive, Suite 550
Reston, VA 20190
Telephone: (800) 726-8603

Design Management Institute (DMI)

The Design Management Institute (DMI) is a professional organization that primarily serves senior design executives and other executives involved in the development of products, communications, and environments, as well as educators. Through its conferences, publications, and research, DMI strives to be the international authority and advocate on design management. Their quarterly *Design Management Journal*, the industry's only scholarly journal, emphasizes contemporary design management thinking with features from the world's leading experts in design management.

Address:
29 Temple Place
Boston, MA 02111-1350
Telephone: (617) 338-6380
Internet: www.designmgt.org

Did you know...
1964's Chesapeake Bay Bridge-Tunnel project crosses 23 miles of water with its hybrid system of four artificial islands, two tunnels, two truss bridges and more than 12 miles of low-level trestled roadways.

Industrial Designers Society of America (IDSA)

Since 1965, the Industrial Designers Society of America (IDSA) has been dedicated to communicating the value of industrial design to society, business, government, and the general public. IDSA serves its constituency through its professional journal *Innovations*, award programs, annual conference, research, networking opportunities, and promotion of the practice at all levels of government.

Address:
1142 Walker Rd
Great Falls, VA 22066
Telephone: (703) 759-0100
Internet: www.idsa.org

Did you know...
The Eames Fiberglass Chair, designed by Charles Eames and produced by Herman Miller from 1951 to 1995, was the first successfully mass-produced molded plastic chair.

Initiative for Architectural Research (IAR)

The Initiative for Architectural Research (IAR) was formed by the Association of Collegiate Schools of Architecture (ACSA), American Institute of Architects (AIA) and Architectural Research Centers Consortium (ARCC) primarily to serve as an advocate for architectural research, to serve as a clearing-house for information about architectural research, and to facilitate research efforts that address specific needs of the architectural profession. The IAR produces *A/R: Architecture/Research*, the directory of architectural research abstracts from universities, architecture firms, national laboratories, and research centers throughout the US and Canada, as well as co-producing the annual Research Awards with *Architecture* magazine.

Address:
IAR c/o ACSA
1735 New York Avenue, NW
Washington, DC 20006
Telephone: (202) 785-2324
Internet: www.architectureresearch.org

Did you know...
Boeing's 747 and 767 aircraft assembly facility in Everett, Washington, is the world's largest manufacturing plant at 291 million cubic feet, large enough to house California's Disneyland.

International Council of Societies of Industrial Design (ICSID)

The International Council of Societies of Industrial Design (ICSID) strives to advance the discipline of industrial design worldwide This non-profit, non-governmental organization was formed in 1957 and is supported by 152 organizations and societies in 53 countries. Through these groups, ICSID represents approximately 150,000 professionals. Member groups work with an Advisory Senate and Executive Board in the areas of practice, education, promotion, and development to enhance the profession.

Address:
Yrjönkatu 11 E
00120 Helsinki
Finland
Telephone: +358 9 696 22 90
Internet: www.icsid.org

International Federation of Interior Architects/Designers (IFI)

The goals of the International Federation of Interior Architects/Designers (IFI) are to promote the interior architecture and design profession, to represent its practitioners, to act as a clearinghouse for professional and cultural information, to encourage international cooperation, and to assist and serve the industry. The IFI engages in a number of activities to further these ends, such as maintaining a public relations program, lobbying for policies benefiting the practice, organizing conferences and supporting minimum standards of education and a Code of Ethics and Practice. Its membership is composed of professional interior design organizations in countries throughout the world.

Address:
P.O. Box 91640
Auckland Park
Johannesburg, 2006
South Africa
Telephone: +27 11 4772279
Internet: www.ifi.co.za

Different places on the face of the earth have different vital effluence, different vibration, different chemical exhalation, different polarity, with different stars: call it what you like. But the spirit of place is a great reality.

D. H. Lawrence

International Federation of Landscape Architects (IFLA)

The International Federation of Landscape Architects (IFLA) represents various national associations of landscape architects. The non-profit, non-governmental organization was formed in 1948 to promote the practice of landscape architecture and to establish standards of professional practice throughout the world. The IFLA is governed by a World Council with jurisdiction over regional councils. Members join IFLA through their national membership associations; although individuals from countries which do not have a national representative group may also join. The IFLA publishes a newsletter twice a year and sponsors a biennial World Conference. Other regional meetings are held on a regular basis.

Address:
4 rue Hardy, RP no 914
78009 Versailles
Cedex, France
Internet: www.ifla.kee.hu/ifla/

International Interior Design Association (IIDA)

With a mission of promoting excellence in interior design and advancing the practice through knowledge, the International Interior Design Association (IIDA) provides a variety of services and benefits for its 11,000 members. It advocates for design excellence, nurtures the interior design community worldwide, maintains educational standards, responds to trends in business and design, and provides a wealth of information about interior design and related issues. The organization maintains 9 international regions with more than 30 chapters and 64 U.S. city centers.

Address:
341 Merchandise Mart
Chicago, IL 60654
Telephone: (312) 467-1950
Internet: www.iida.org

I don't think of form as a kind of architecture. The architecture is the result of the forming. It is the kinesthetic and visual sense of position and wholeness that puts the thing into the realm of art.

Roy Lichtenstein

International Union of Architects (UIA)

Founded in 1948, the International Union of Architects (UIA) is an international, non-governmental organization dedicated to uniting the architects of the world. Through its 92 UIA Member Sections, the group represents over a million architects. The UIA's mission is to represent architects and promote the practice with other professional organizations worldwide, other non-governmental organizations, and intergovernmental institutions. The UIA General Secretariat is the Union's executive body and the administrative center for the coordination of relations between the UIA Member Sections and their activities. A personal information service is available from the General Secretariat allowing architects to keep up with UIA activities, its partners, and Member Sections.

Address:
51, rue Raynouard
75 016 Paris, France
Telephone: 33 (1) 45 24 36 88
Internet: www.uia-architectes.org

Did you know...
At 198 feet, the Cape Hatteras Lighthouse (1869, North Carolina) is the tallest lighthouse in the world.

Japan Institute of Architects (JIA)

The Japan Institute of Architects (JIA) serves to define and promote the social and legal status of professional architects in Japan and to promote their interests abroad. Currently, JIA represents over 6,300 members through 10 chapters. A member of the Architects Regional Council Asia (ARCASIA) as well as the International Union of Architects (IUA), the Japan Institute of Architects was formed in 1987 when the Japan Architects Association (JAA) and the Japan Federation of Professional Architects Association (JFPAA) united.

Address:
2-3-18, Jingumae
Shibuya-ku, Tokyo
150-0001 Japan
Telephone: +81-3-3408-7125
Internet:
http://web.jia.or.jp/jia/intro/about_e/main.htm

We, as architects, enliven people's experiences. I felt, as far as the sensitivity behind these buildings, if architects could learn from that and look at that, then we could make better buildings. To look at how people live, and not at what other designers have already conceived of, I think that's really key.

David Slovic

Joslyn Castle Institute for Sustainable Communities

Housed in Omaha, Nebraska's historic 1902 Joslyn Castle, the Joslyn Castle Institute for Sustainable Communities is a partnership among Nebraska state government, the Joslyn Art Museum, the University of Nebraska College of Architecture, and other public and private organizations. The Institute focuses on promoting sustainable development through outreach and education programs, as well as research. Its goal is to encourage communities to develop by balancing economic, social and environmental needs. The institute is one of 18 centers worldwide partnering with the United Nations Center for Human Settlement (UNCHS) in its Best Practices in Local Leadership Program (BLP).

Address:
3902 Davenport Street
Omaha, Nebraska 68131
Telephone: (402) 595-1902

Any well-designed product or experience acknowledges the user. It's that respect for the user that makes a design great.

Clement Mok

National Institute of Building Sciences (NIBS)

The National Institute of Building Sciences (NIBS) serves the public interest by promoting a rational regulatory environment for the building community, facilitating the introduction of new technology, and disseminating technical information. NIBS was established by Congress as an authoritative national source on building science and technology issues. It is a non-governmental, non-profit organization. Of its 21-member Board of Directors, 15 are elected and six are appointed by the President of the United States with the approval of the U.S. Senate. NIBS committees are integral in establishing industry-wide standards for the construction industry. They also publish many books on specific building technologies and techniques.

Address:
1090 Vermont Avenue, NW, Suite 700
Washington, DC 20005-4905
Telephone: (202) 289-7800
Internet: www.nibs.org

Design is the liberal arts of the information age.

Richard Buchanan

National Organization of Minority Architects (NOMA)

The National Organization of Minority Architects (NOMA) was formed in 1971 for the purpose of enhancing diversity in architecture. Today there are 12 NOMA chapters and 19 student chapters across the country, increasing recognition on university campuses and providing access to government policy makers. The organization works to advance minority architects, from job placement for college students to aiding member firms in securing contracts. NOMA annually holds a conference, organizes a design award program, and produces a newsletter.

Address:
Internet: www.noma.net

Our task has evolved beyond creating spaces that are aesthetically wonderful. Design is a science – the science of enhancing human interaction, connection, emotion and motion.

Gary E. Wheeler

Royal Architectural Institute of Canada (RAIC)

The Royal Architectural Institute of Canada (RAIC) "works towards a future in which Canadians will view our total environment, both natural and built, as our most important asset and the Institute's members as essential to its creation and maintenance." Established in 1907, the Institute represents more than 3,000 architects, educators, and graduates of accredited Canadian schools of architecture. The organization focuses its activities in five areas: publications, symposia and exhibitions, research, awards, and practice committees.

Address:
55 Murray Street, Suite 330
Ottawa, Ontario, K1N 5M3
Canada
Telephone: (613) 241-3600
Internet: www.raic.org

Did you know...
The fillet in the north rose window of Notre Dame in Paris supports over 1,300 square feet of glass and has only suffered minor buckling in over 700 years.

Royal Australian Institute of Architects (RAIA)

The Royal Australian Institute of Architects (RAIA) represents over 8,000 members in Australia and overseas, largely through eight state chapters. Established in 1929, the RAIA seeks to raise awareness among the public about the value of architecture and the importance of good design and to promote creativity and continuous training among its members. Their mission is to "unite architects to advance architecture." Each year the RAIA sponsors the Architecture Awards in the states and territories, culminating in a national prize. The group also publishes Australia's premier architecture magazine, *Architecture Australia*, and the highly regarded and regularly updated *Environment Design Guide*.

Address:
2a Mugga Way
Red Hill ACT 2603
Australia
Telephone: (02) 6273 1548
Internet: www.raia.com.au

Architecture is to make us know and remember who we are.

Sir Geoffrey Jellicoe

Royal Institute of British Architects (RIBA)

Founded in 1834, the Royal Institute of British Architects (RIBA) was one of the world's first architectural associations. Representing more than 32,000 members in over 100 countries, the RIBA is a worldwide organization committed to the improvement and enjoyment of the physical environment. Its mission is "the advancement of architecture and the promotion of the acquirement of the knowledge of the arts and sciences connected therewith." The organization sponsors several prestigious award programs including the Stirling Prize and the Royal Gold Medal. Their RIBA Architecture Gallery features many exhibits on architecture and design each year. Members also have access to Ribanet Conference, a global communication system connecting architects through their computers, allowing them to use electronic conferencing to exchange ideas, share files, participate in one-to-one online chats, and send and receive emails. RIBA membership is open to anyone, whether an architect or a patron of the practice. Established in 1934, RIBA's British Architectural Library is the largest and most comprehensive resource in the United Kingdom for research and information on all aspects of architecture.

Address:
66 Portland Place
London W1N 4AD UK
Telephone: 44 171 580 5533
Internet: www.riba.net

United Nations Centre for Human Settlements (Habitat)

The United Nations Centre for Human Settlements (Habitat) was established in 1978 as the lead agency for coordinating human settlements and development activities within the United Nations family, focusing on the following priority areas: shelter and social services; urban management; environment and infrastructure; and assessment, monitoring, and information. Habitat supports and works in partnership with governments, local authorities, non-governmental organizations, and the private sector. Currently, Habitat has over 200 operational programs and projects underway in 80 countries, focusing on urban management, housing, basic services, and infrastructure development. Habitat promotes sustainable human settlement development through policy formulation, capacity-building, knowledge creation, and the strengthening of partnerships between governments and civil society. In 1996, the United Nations General Assembly designated Habitat as a focal point for the implementation of the Habitat Agenda, the global plan of action adopted at the second United Nations Conference on Human Settlements.

Address:
P. O. Box 30030
Nairobi, Kenya
Tel: (254-2) 623153
Internet: www.unchs.org

Urban Land Institute (ULI)

Formed in 1936 as a research arm of the National Association of Real Estate Boards (now the National Association of Realtors), the Urban Land Institute (ULI) is an independent institution dedicated to promoting the responsible use of land to enhance the total environment. The group represents 15,000 professionals in 50 states and 52 countries. ULI activities include research, forums and task forces, awards, education, and publishing.

Address:
1025 Thomas Jefferson Street, NW
Suite 500 West
Washington, DC 20007
Telephone: (202) 624-7000
Internet: www.uli.org

> The city is a fact in nature, like a cave, a run of mackerel or an ant-heap. But it is also a conscious work of art...The dome and the spire, the open avenue and the story, not merely of different physical accommodations, but of essentially different conceptions of man's destiny...With language itself [the city] remains man's greatest work of art.
>
> *Lewis Mumford*

Vernacular Architecture Forum (VAF)

Devoted to the "ordinary" architecture of North America, the Vernacular Architecture Forum (VAF) was formed in 1980 to encourage the study and preservation of traditional structures and landscapes. These include agricultural buildings, industrial and commercial structures, twentieth-century suburban houses, settlement patterns and cultural landscapes, and areas historically overlooked by scholars. The VAF embraces multidisciplinary interaction. Historians, designers, archaeologists, folklorists, architectural historians, geographers, museum curators and historic preservationists contribute to the organization. The VAF holds its conference every May with part of the agenda focusing on the vernacular architecture of that region. Every few years papers are selected from past conferences and published in the series *Perspectives in Vernacular Architecture*. The VAF presents two annual awards: The Abbot Lowell Cummings Award for excellence in scholarly writing, and the Paul E. Buchanan Award for outstanding examples of field work, exhibits and presentations.

Address:
Internet: www.vernaculararchitecture.org.

Did you know...
Lever House, the 1952 New York landmark designed by Gordon Bunshaft of Skidmore, Owings and Merrill, is only 53 feet wide.

MUSEUMS

MUSE

MUSEUMS

Alvar Aalto Museum

Founded in 1966, Finland's Alvar Aalto Museum houses a permanent collection of the designer/architect's work, produces publications related to his work, and oversees conservation of his buildings. Additionally, the Museum arranges Aalto exhibits worldwide. The museum's architectural collection features 1,200 original models and artifacts designed by Aino and Alvar Aalto, as well as a photo archive and reproductions of Aalto's original drawings. A library featuring architecture and literature centered around Alvar Aalto is open to researchers and students by appointment.

Address:
Alvar Aallon katu 7
40600 Jyvaskyla, Finland
Telephone: +358 (0) 14 624 809
Internet: www.alvaraalto.fi/museum/index.htm

Exhibition Schedule:
Alvar Aalto. Architect
Permanent Exhibit

"Beauty in Everyday Things"
December 2, 1999 – February 6, 2000

Travelling Exhibitions:
Alvar Aalto - A Gentler Structure for Life
(check with the museum for the tour schedule)

Alvar Aalto and Red Brick: Space, Form, Surface
(check with the museum for the tour schedule)

Art Institute of Chicago

The Art Institute of Chicago encompasses The School of the Art Institute of Chicago and a museum with ten curatorial departments. Collections at the Art Institute include: African and Amerindian Art, American Art, Architecture, Asian Art, Ancient Art, European Painting, Photography, European Decorative Arts and Sculpture, Prints and Drawings, Textiles, Arms and Armor and Twentieth-Century Painting and Sculpture. The Department of Architecture at the Art Institute was established in 1981 from the architectural drawings collection within the Burnham Library of Architecture (founded in 1912) and the architectural fragments collection of the Department of American Arts. The Ernest R. Graham Study Center for Architectural Drawings houses a collection of more than 130,000 architectural sketches and drawings, largely of designs by Chicago architects, including Walter Burley Griffin, Louis Sullivan, Ludwig Mies van der Rohe and Frank Lloyd Wright. The collection also features architectural models and fragments, including a reconstruction of the Adler and Sullivan trading room from the Chicago Stock Exchange (1893-94). The Burnham Library of Architecture, one of the first organizations in the United States to collect architectural drawings, architects' papers, and primary documentary materials, is open to researchers and scholars.

Art Institute of Chicago (Con't)

Address:
111 South Michigan Avenue
Chicago, Illinois 60603
Telephone: (312) 443-3949
Internet: www.artic.edu/aic/index.html

Exhibition Schedule:
Design from the Heartland: Henry Glass, Richard Ten Eyck and John Polivaka
October 1999 – February 2000

Bilbao: The Transformation of a City
April – July 2000

Skyscrapers: The Next Millennium
August 2000 – January 2001

2001. Architecture and Design for Space. Vision and Reality
March – September 2001

Architecture is the art which so disposes and adorns the edifices raised by man, that the sight of them may contribute to his mental health, power, and pleasure.

John Ruskin

Athenaeum of Philadelphia

The Athenaeum of Philadelphia was founded in 1814 to collect and disseminate information related to American history and the "useable arts." They offer public programs, lectures and changing exhibitions, as well as administering trusts that provide awards and grants. The Athenaeum's National Historic Landmark building, designed by John Nott in 1845 near Independence Hall, is open to the public as a museum furnished with American fine and decorative arts from the first half of the nineteenth century. The member-supported library contains a vast architecture and interior design collection with an emphasis on the period 1800 to 1945. The library is open to qualified readers without charge.

Address:
219 S. Sixth Street
Philadelphia, PA 19106-3794
Telephone: (215) 925-2688
Email: athena@libertynet.org
Internet: www.libertynet.org/athena/

Exhibition Schedule:
Designing Independence
October 1999 – January 31, 2000

Treasures of the Athenaeum
(working title)
April – October 2000

Canadian Centre for Architecture (CCA)

Montréal's Canadian Centre for Architecture (CCA) is a museum and study center devoted to local, national, and international architecture and other disciplines that contribute to the built environment. The CCA occupies an award-winning 130,000 square foot building which houses exhibition galleries, the Paul Desmarais Theatre, and the CCA Bookstore, as well as the library, curatorial offices, conservation and collection storage facilities, and the Study Centre. CCA Administrative offices are located in the adjacent Shaughnessy House, built in 1874. The lower floor of the house is open to the public. Also on the property is the CCA Garden, both an urban garden and outdoor museum of architecture.

Address:
1920 Baile Street
Montréal, Québec
Canada H3H 2S6
Telephone: (514) 939-7026
Internet: www.cca.qc.ca

Exhibition Schedule:
Cedric Price: Mean Time
October 19, 1999 to February 27, 2000

En chantier: The Collections of the CCA, 1989-1999
November 24, 1999 to April 30, 2000

Visions and Views: The Architecture of Borromini in the Photographs of Edward Burtynsky
March 8 to May 7, 2000

Shaping the Great City: Modern Architecture in Central Europe, 1890-1937 (working title)
May 8 to October 15, 2000

CCA Exhibitions on Tour:
The American Lawn: Surface of Everyday Life
Florida Museum of Art, Fort Lauderdale
September 3, 1999 to January 2, 2000

Chicago Athenaeum: Museum of Architecture and Design

The only independent museum of art and design in the United States, the Chicago Athenaeum was founded in 1988 and is dedicated to the art of design in all areas of the discipline. The museum's mission is to advance public education about the value of good design. In addition to providing programs, exhibits, and educational services, the Chicago Athenaeum features a professional resource center, photographic and video/film archives, and a growing collection of architectural, industrial, and graphic items. They also award the annual GOOD DESIGN® Competition, founded in Chicago in 1950 by Charles and Ray Eames, Eero Saarinen, and Edgar Kaufman to honor innovation, form, materials, construction, concept, function, and utility in design.

Address:
6 North Michigan Avenue
Chicago, Illinois 60602
Telephone: (312) 251-0175
Internet: www.chi-athenaeum.org

Exhibition Schedule:
Landmark Chicago: The City of Modern Design
Permanent Exhibition

The GOOD DESIGN Show
October 31, 1999 – March 31, 2000

Sold, Sensible + Swiss: New Designs from Switzerland
December 1, 1999 – February 28, 2000

Design at the Millennium: Masterpieces of the 20th Century
Through 2000

Chicago Athenaeum: Museum of Architecture and Design (Con't)

Exhibition Schedule: (Con't)
MADE IN CHICAGO: Industrial Design Objects from the Museum's Permanent Collections
Through 2000

New Chicago Furniture: 10th Annual Exhibition
February 12 – May 30, 2000

The Art of Japanese Graphic
April 1 – September 2000

The EU Designs
June 14, Septebmer 21, 2000

American Architecture Awards
June 14 – October 31, 2000

Did you know...
Pisa, Italy's famed Leaning Tower, constructed during the 12th century, began to lean as soon as the first story was completed. In later years, attempts were made to compensate by building subsequent stories at an angle, altering the size of pillars, and hanging the heaviest bells in the tower on the North side. None of these proved to be successful, and the tower continues to shift.

Cooper-Hewitt, National Design Museum, Smithsonian Institution

The Cooper-Hewitt, National Design Museum, Smithsonian Institution is the only museum in the U.S. devoted exclusively to the study of historical and contemporary design. Reflecting the belief that design links individuals, societies and the natural environment, the museum's program addresses five key issues: Function, Innovation & Creativity, Communication, History & Criticism, and Context. Four curatorial departments care for and evaluate the Museum's collections: applied arts and industrial design, drawings and prints, textiles, and wallcoverings. The Museum's interests encompass graphic design, architecture, urban planning, and environmental design. The Cooper-Hewitt also maintains a large Education Department which sponsors more than 200 public programs serving over 10,000 people annually. Educators may peruse a variety of design education books, curriculum guides, and videos in the Department's Design Education Resource Library.

Address:
2 East 91st Street
New York, New York 10128
Telephone: (212) 849-8400
Internet: http://web2.si.edu/ndm/

Exhibition Schedule:
The Work of Charles and Ray Eames: A Legacy of Invention
October 12, 1999 through January 9, 2000

National Design Museum Triennial
March 7, 2000 - August 6, 2000

Cooper-Hewitt, National Design Museum, Smithsonian Institution (Con't)

Exhibition Schedule: (Con't)

Masterpieces from the Vitra Museum
October 3, 2000 - March 4, 2001

Venini: Art and Design in Glass from Venice
April 10, 2001 - September 9, 2001

Landscape and Wallcoverings
May 15, 2001 - October 14, 2001

Easier Living: Russel Wright and the Modern Domestic Environment
November 20, 2001 - March 10, 2002

Architecture presents man, literature tells you about him, painting will picture him to you. You can listen and hear him, but if you want to realize him and experience him go into his buildings, and that's where you'll find him as he is. He can't hide there from you and he can't hide from himself.

Frank Lloyd Wright

Design Museum

Located in London's South Bank area in a converted 1950s warehouse, the Design Museum is the only museum devoted exclusively to 20th century industrial design. Since its founding in 1989 by the Conran Foundation, the Museum's many changing exhibits and educational programs have offered an insight into the role of design and mass production in our everyday lives. The Museum's exhibits include the Collection Gallery, which highlights historical trends and design of the past 100 years; the Review Gallery, featuring new, innovative designs and prototypes; and many special exhibitions. The Museum's reach is further extended through it extensive educational program of contract teaching, outreach activities, teacher training courses, and resources for classroom use.

Address:
Shad Thames
London SE1 2YD
U.K.
Telephone: 0171 378 6055

Exhibition Schedule:
Design: Process: Progress: Practice
October 21, 1999 – January 30, 2000

Bauhaus Dessau
February 10, 2000 – June 4, 2000

The Life and Work of Buckminster Fuller
June 15, 2000 – October 15, 2000

Five Designs of Mr. Brunel
October 26, 2000 – February 25, 2001

Luis Barragan
March 8, 2001 – July 8, 2001

Museum of Modern Art (MoMA)

New York City's Museum of Modern Art (MoMA) encompasses six curatorial areas, including the world's first department devoted to architecture and design, established in 1932. The Department of Architecture and Design's collection includes architectural documents, drawings and photographs such as the Ludwig Mies van der Rohe Archive, as well as collections from other leading architects. It also includes over 3,000 design objects, from furniture to tools, automobiles and textiles. The graphic design collection contains over 4,000 pieces. Other curatorial areas are: Drawings, Film and Video, Painting & Sculpture, Photography, and Prints & Illustrated Books. MoMA maintain several research centers – the Library, Museum Archives and various Study Centers, including the The Lily Auchincloss Study Center for Architecture and Design which is open by appointment. The catalogs of the Library, Museum Archives and Study Centers have been combined into DAD-ABASE, an online search service on MoMA' Web site. The Museum offers many lectures programs, gallery talks and other regular events in addition to its regular exhibition schedule.

Address:
11 West 53 Street
New York, NY 10019
Telephone: (212) 708-9400
Internet: www.moma.org

Museum of Modern Art (MoMA) (Con't)	**Exhibition Schedule:** All museum galleries have been reconfigured for MoMA2000, a museum-wide, seventeen-month-long series of exhibitions to mark the millennium. MoMA2000 comprises three cycles each exploring themes, movements, and relationships between works of art from the Museum's collections.

The opening cycle of exhibitions in MoMA2000 is ModernStarts, which examines the beginnings of modernism by focusing on the years from 1880 to 1920. The exhibit's three distinct parts will open on a staggered schedule:

ModernStarts
PEOPLE
October 7, 1999 – February 1, 2000

PLACES
October 28, 1999 – March 14, 2000

THINGS
November 21, 1999 – March 14, 2000

ModernStarts is followed by Making Choices, which will deal with the period from 1920 to 1960, and Open Ends, which will examine the period from 1960 to the present.

Making Choices (1920 – 1960)
March 16 – September 12, 2000

Open Ends (1960 – 2000)
September 14, 2000 - February 13, 2001

National Building Museum

Established by an act of Congress in 1985, the National Building Museum, a private, nonprofit institution, is dedicated to exploring all facets of the built environment. From architecture, urban planning and construction to engineering and design, the Museum reveals the connections between the way we build and the way we live. The Museum is located in Washington D.C.'s historic Pension Bureau Building, constructed in 1887. The Museum's impressive Great Hall is often the site of the President's Inaugural Ball among many other gala events. Through exhibitions and education programs, the Museum is the forum for exchanging information about topical issues such as managing suburban growth, preserving landmarks, and revitalizing urban centers.

Address:
4 01 F Street NW
Washington, DC 20001
Telephone: (202) 272-2448
Internet: www.nbm.org

Exhibition Schedule:
The Corner Store
September 22, 1999 – March 6, 2000

See the USA: Roadside Travel & the American Landscape
November 18, 1999 – May 7, 2000

White House in Miniature
Spring 2000

Tools as Art VI
Spring 2000

Wood: From the Forest to the Future
Summer 2000

When Design Means Business: The American Office at the Millennium
Fall 2000

Netherlands Architecture Institute (NAI)

Located at the edge of Museumpark in the center of Rotterdam and housed in a building designed by Jo Coenen in 1993, the Netherlands Architecture Institute (NAI) is a museum and cultural institution concerned with architecture, urban design, and space planning. Through its exhibitions and other programs, the NAI strives to inform, inspire, and stimulate architects and laymen alike about the value of design. The NAI possesses one of the largest architectural collections in the world with over 15 kilometers of shelving containing drawings, sketches, models, photographs, books and periodicals, including work by virtually every important Dutch architect since 1800. This collection, as well as its 40,000 volume library, is open to researchers. Lectures, study tours, and a variety of publications are also offered by the NAI.

Address:
Museumpark 25
3015 CB Rotterdam
Netherlands
Telephone: 31 (0) 10-4401200
Internet: www.nai.nl/nai_eng.html

Exhibition schedule:
Two Centuries of Architecture in the Netherlands
Permanent Exhibition

Landscape
9+1 Young Dutch Landscape Architects
Through January 2, 2000

Silent Collisions
Morphosis: Work in Progress
September 4, 1999 - mid-January 2000

Bureau Van den Broek en Bakema 1948 - 1988
February 5 - April 24, 2000

Norwegian Museum of Architecture (NAM)

Founded by the National Association of Norwegian Architects in 1975, the Norwegian Museum of Architecture (NAM) collects, processes, and disseminates information and material concerned with architecture with a focus towards the 20th century. The Museum is housed in one of Oslo's oldest buildings, Kongens gate 4, part of which dates to 1640. The Museum boasts an archive of over 200,000 drawings and photographs which are available to researchers by appointment. In the past, museum exhibits have been concerned with various aspects of Norwegian architecture, from the work of individuals to overviews of contemporary architecture. The Museum also hosts traveling exhibitions which are typically in English.

Address:
Kongens gate 4, N-0153
Oslo, Norway
Telephone: +47-22 42 40 80
Internet: www.mnal.no/nam/NAM-eng.html

Exhibition Schedule:
History of Buildings: 1000 Years of Norwegian Architecture
Permanent Exhibit

(Contact the NAM for changing exhibits)

The Octagon

Located one block west of the White House, The Octagon was one of Washington, D.C.'s first residences and was instrumental in establishing the L'Enfant plan for the city. It was designed by Dr. William Thornton, the first architect of the U.S. Capitol, and was completed in 1801. The home was owned by John Tayloe III and his descendants until it was purchased by The American Institute of Architects (AIA) in 1902 to served as its headquarters. The American Architectural Foundation (AAF), the foundation established by the AIA in 1942, purchased the building in 1968 and opened it to the public as a museum in 1970. A National Historic Landmark, the Octagon is the oldest museum in the United States devoted to architecture and design. They offer tours of the historic house and regularly host architectural exhibits.

Address:
1799 New York Ave. NW
Washington, D.C., 20006
Telephone: (202) 638-3105
Internet: www.amerarchfoundation.com/octabout.htm

Exhibition Schedule:
A Voyage of Discovery: The Nile Journal of Richard Morris Hunt
July 30, 1999 – January 2, 2000

Ralph Rapson: Sixty Years of Modern Design
Late January – April 2000

Unlocking the Secrets of the Past (working title)
May – December 2000

RIBA Architecture Gallery

The Royal Institute of British Architects' (RIBA) Architecture Gallery (formerly known as the RIBA Architecture Centre) features both historical and contemporary architecture and design exhibitions. Through exhibitions, talks, publications, events for children and the family, the Internet, and collaborations, it provides a cultural focus for the communication and presentation of architecture and a forum for debate and the exchange of ideas. Due to the relocating of the RIBA Heinz Gallery to the Victoria and Albert Museum and reorganization of the buildings that both museums occupied, exhibits throughout 2000 are tentative.

Address:
66 Portland Square
London W1H 4AD UK
Telephone: +44 (0)171 580 5533
Internet: www.riba.net

Exhibition Schedule:
Future City
November 6 – January 15, 2000

President's Medals for Architecture –
Best Student Work
December 1, 1999 – January 22, 2000

Architecture for Humanity - Building for Kosovo
December 11, 1999 – 22 January 22, 2000

San Francisco Museum of Modern Art (SFMOMA)

Originally named the San Francisco Museum of Art when it opened in 1935, the "modern" in San Francisco Museum of Modern Art (SFMOMA) was added in 1975 to more accurately describe its mission. SFMOMA's international permanent collection consists of over 18,000 works, including 5,600 paintings, sculptures and works on paper; approximately 9,800 photographs; 3,200 architectural drawings, models and design objects, and a growing collection of works related to the media arts. In 1983, the Museum established its Department of Architecture and Design, the first museum on the West Coast to do so. The department focuses on architecture and design projects pertaining to the Bay Area, California, the American West and Pacific Rim. Their growing collection contains architecture, furniture design, product design, and graphic design from both historic and contemporary periods. The department's Architecture and Design Forum also organizes lectures, symposia, and competitions.

Address:
151 Third Street
San Francisco, CA 94103-3159
Telephone: (415) 357-4000
Internet: www.sfmoma.org

Exhibition Schedule:
Far Out: Bay Area Design, 1967-1973
November 12, 1999 – February 20, 2000

The Architecture of Graphics: Designs for SCI-Arc from the Permanent Collection of Architecture of Design
November 12, 1999 – February 20, 2000

San Francisco Museum of Modern Art (SFMOMA) (Con't)

Edge of a City: Work by Steven Holl from the Permanent Collection of Architecture and Design
November 12, 1999 – February 20, 2000

Structure and Surface: Contemporary Japanese Textiles
March 10, 2000 – June 20, 2000

Experiments: Recent Acquisitions in Architecture and Design
July 2000 – October 2000

If New York keeps on permitting the building of skyscrapers, each one having as many people every day as we used to have in a small city, disaster must overtake us.

Thomas Alva Edison, 1926

Sir John Soane's Museum

Sir John Soane's Museum in London has been open to the public since the mid-19th century. Originally the home of Sir John Soane, R.A., architect (1753 – 1837), in 1833, Soane negotiated an Act of Parliament to settle and preserve the house and his collections of art and antiques for the benefit of amateurs and students in architecture, painting, and sculpture. As a Professor of Architecture at the Royal Academy, Soane arranged his books, casts, and models so that the students might have easy access to them. He opened his house for the use of the Royal Academy students the day before and the day after each of his lectures. Today, as Soane requested, the house has, as much as possible, been left as it was over 150 years ago. The Museum's extensive research library is open to researchers by appointment. Staff is available to help with queries relating to many fields including: the restoration of authentic historic interiors, architectural history from the 17th century to the early 19th century, the conservation of drawings and works of art and methods of display, archives, and architectural models.

Address:
13 Lincoln's Inn Fields
London, WC2A 3BP
United Kingdom
Telephone: +44 (0) 171-405 2107
Internet: www.soane.org

Exhibition Schedule:
Ongoing exhibition of Sir John Soane's Home

Skyscraper Museum

The Skyscraper Museum is devoted to the study of historical, contemporary, and future high-rise buildings. Located in New York City's Wall Street financial district, the Museum was founded in 1996 as a private, not-for-profit, educational corporation. Its mission expands the traditional view of skyscrapers, viewing them as investments in real estate, sites of construction and places of work. The Museum's first exhibit, Downtown New York: The Architecture of Business/The Business of Buildings, attracted 20,000 visitors. In late 2001 the Museum will open in its permanent home in New York's Battery Park City with expanded facilities for permanent and temporary exhibits, a lecture hall, and curatorial space.

Address:
16 Wall Street
New York, NY, 10005
Telephone: (212) 766-1324
Internet: www.skyscraper.org

Exhibition Schedule:
Big Buildings
October 1, 1999 – December 31, 1999

Other exhibits in their current location are tentative due to the uncertain status of their lease. Visitors should call the museum or check their Web site prior to visiting their Wall Street location.

Swedish Museum of Architecture

Stockholm's Swedish Museum of Architecture serves as a repository of information about Swedish architecture, maintains a collection of architectural artifacts, and, through its exhibitions, educates people about the architectural heritage of Sweden. Its archives contain over 2,000,000 architectural drawings and nearly 600,000 photographs. The Museum's permanent exhibition, the History of Swedish Building, covers a period of 1,000 years of Swedish design.

Address:
Skeppsholmen, SE-111 49
Stockholm, Sweden
Telephone: 08-587 270 00
Internet: www.arkitekturmuseet.se

Exhibition Schedule:
The History of Swedish Building
Permanent Exhibit

Land for the Future
October 28, 1999 – January 9, 2000

Sweden Builds, 1995 – 1999
November 20, 1999 – February 13, 2000

Housing as Architecture
November 20, 1999 – February 13, 2000

Vitra Design Museum

Germany's Vitra Design Museum is dedicated to documenting the history and current trends in industrial furniture design. Changing exhibitions are housed in a building Frank O. Gehry designed for the Vitra Design Museum in 1989. Items from the Vitra's permanent collection are housed in the Vitra Fire Station, designed by Zaha Hadid in 1993, and may be viewed by the public on special guided tours only. In addition to its changing exhibits and expansive permanent collection, the Vitra sponsors international travelling exhibitions around the world. The Museum also conducts student workshops, publishes books on design, and manufactures special editions of objects.

Address:
Charles-Eames-Str. 1
D-79576 Weil am Rhein
Germany
Telephone: + 49 7621 702 35 78
Internet: www.design-museum.com

Exhibition Schedule:
Automobility - What Moves Us
November 6, 1999 - January 9, 2000

Verner Panton
February – December 6, 2000

Luis Barragan
June 22 – October 15, 2000

Isamu Noguchi
October 2000 – February 2001

NOTED
INDIVIDUALS

NOTED INDIVIDUALS

Fellows of the American Academy in Rome

Every year the American Academy in Rome grants fellowships to study and work in Rome at the Academy's center for independent study, advanced research, and creative work. Also known as the Rome Prize, the fellowships are granted in a broad range of fields including design, music, literature, and archaeology. The following individuals have been the recipients of the Rome Prize for design related disciplines.

Architecture:

Stanley Abercrombie, FAAR'83

Kimberly A. Ackert, FAAR'97

Anthony Ames, FAAR'84

Joseph AmIsano, FAAR'52

Amy Anderson, FAAR'81

Ross S. Anderson, FAAR'90

Richard W. Ayers, FAAR'38

Clarence Dale Badgeley, FAAR'29

Gregory S. Baldwin, FAAR'71

Marc Balet, FAAR'75

Richard Bartholomew, FAAR'72

Frederick Blehle, FAAR'87

James L. Bodnar, FAAR'80

Thomas L. Bosworth, FAAR'81

Charles G. Brickbauer, FAAR'57

Cecil C. Briggs, FAAR'31

Turner Brooks, FAAR'84

Andrea Clark Brown, FAAR'80, AIA

Theodore L. Brown, FAAR'88

William Bruder, FAAR'87

Marvin Buchanan, FAAR'76

Walker o. Cain, FAAR'48

Peter Carl, FAAR'76

Daniel Castor, FAAR'98

Judith Chafee, FAAR'77

Coleman Coker, FAAR'96

Caroline B. Constant, FAAR'79

Frederic S. Coolidge, FAAR'48

Roger Crowley, FAAR'85

Teddy Edwin Cruz, FAAR'92

Thomas V. Czarnowski, FAAR'68

Royston T. Daley, FAAR'62

Spero Daltas, FAAR'51

Douglas Darden, FAAR'89

Thomas L. Dawson, FAAR'52

Joseph De Pace, FAAR'85

Andrea o. Dean, FAAR'80

Kathryn Dean, FAAR'87

Judith Di Maio, FAAR'78

Ronald L. Dirsmith, FAAR'60

Robert Ward Evans, FAAR'73

James Favaro, FAAR'86

Ronald C. Filson, FAAR'70, FAIA

Garrett S. Finney, FAAR'95

Mark M. Foster, FAAR'84

Robert M. Golder, FAAR'63

Alexander C. Gorlin, FAAR'84

Michael Graves, FAAR'62, RAAR'78

James A. Gresham, FAAR'56

Brand Norman Griffin, FAAR'74

Olindo Grossi, FAAR'36

Michael Gruber, FAAR'96

Michael Guran, FAAR'71

Steven Harby, FAAR'00

George E. Hartman, FAAR'78, RAAR'96

John D. Heimbaugh, Jr., FAAR'70

George A. Hinds, FAAR'84

Peter Hopprier, FAAR'77

Elizabeth Humstone, FAAR'86

Sanda D. Iliescu, FAAR'95

Franklin D. Israel, FAAR'75

Erling F. Iversen

David J. Jacob, FAAR'58, RAAR'71

Allan B. Jacobs, FAAR'86, RAAR'96

Fellows of the American Academy in Rome (Con't)

James R. Jarrett, FAAR'59

E. Fay Jones, FAAR'81

Wesley Jones, FAAR'86

Wendy Evans Joseph, FAAR'84

Henri V. Jova, FAAR'51

Robert Kahn, FAAR'82

Spence Kass, FAAR'81

Stephen J. Kieran, FAAR'S 1

Grace R. Kobayaski, FAAR'90

Johannes M.P. Knoops, FAAR'00

Peter Kommers, FAAR'76

Eugene Kupper, FAAR'83

James R. Lamantia, FAAR'49

James L. Lambeth, FAAR'79

Gary Larson, FAAR'83

Thomas N. Larson, FAAR'64

John Q. Lawson, FAAR'81

David L. Leavitt, FAAR'50

Celia Ledbetter, FAAR'83

Diane Lewis, FAAR'77

Paul Lewis, FAAR'99

Roy W. Lewis, FAAR'86

George T. Licht, FAAR'37

Theodore Liebman, FAAR'66

Robert S. Livesey, FAAR'75

John H. MacFadyen, FAAR'54

Robert Mangurian, FAAR'77

Tallie B. Maule, FAAR'52

Arthur May, FAAR'76

David Mayernik, FAAR'89

John J. McDonald, FAAR'83

William G. McMinn, FAAR'82

Cameron McNall, FAAR'92

D. Blake Middleton, FAAR'82

Henry D. Mirick, FAAR'33

Robert Mittelstadt, FAAR'66

Grover E. Mouton III, FAAR'73

Vincent Mulcahy, FAAR'77

Anne Munly, FAAR'96

Theodore J. Musho, FAAR'61

Robert Myers, FAAR'54

John Naughton, FAAR'85

Stanley H. Pansky, FAAR'53

William Pedersen, FAAR'66

Charles o. Perry, FAAR'66

Warren A. Peterson, FAAR'55

Thomas M. Phifer, FAAR'96

Warren Platner, FAAR'56

Antoine S. Predock, FAAR'85, FAIA

George L. Queral, FAAR'88

Patrick J. Quinn, FAAR'80

Jason H. Ramos, FAAR'91

William Reed, FAAR'68

Walter L. Reichardt, FAAR'33

Jesse Reiser, FAAR'85

Richard Rosa, FAAR'99

Peter Miller Schmitt, FAAR'72

Thomas L. Schumacher, FAAR'69, RAAR'91

J. Michael Schwarting, FAAR'70

Frederic D. Schwartz, FAAR'85

Daniel V. Scully, FAAR'70

Catherine Seavitt, FAAR'98

Werner Seligmann, FAAR'81

Thomas Silva, FAAR'89

Jorge Silvetti, FAAR'86

Thomas G. Smith, FAAR'80

Barbara Stauffacher Solomon, FAAR'83

Friedrich St. Florian, FAAR'85

Charles Stifter, FAAR'63

James S. Stokoe, FAAR'79

John J. Stonehill, FAAR'60

Wayne Taylor, FAAR'62

Milo H. Thompson, FAAR'65

Duane Thorbeck, FAAR'64, FAIA

James Timberlake, FAAR'83

Robert H. Timme, FAAR'86

Fred Travisano, FAAR'82

William Turnbull, Jr., FAAR'80

James Velleco, FAAR'77

Robert Venturi, FAAR'56

Austris J. Vitols, FAAR'67

Peter D. Waldman, FAAR'00

Craig H. Walton, FAAR'82

Fellows of the American Academy in Rome (Con't)

Robert A. Weppner, Jr., FAAR'36

Nichole Wiedemann, FAAR'97

Charles D. Wiley, FAAR'48

Tod Williams, FAAR'83

Christian Zapatka, FAAR'91

Astra Zarina, FAAR'63

Landscape Architecture

Eric Armstrong, FAAR'61

E. Bruce Baetjer, FAAR'54

Julie Bargmann, FAAR'90

Richard C. Bell, FAAR'53, RAAR'75

Stephen F. Bochkor, FAAR'57

Elise Brewster, FAAR'98

Robert T. Buchanan, FAAR'59

Richard Burck, FAAR'82

Vincent C. Cerasi, FAAR'50

Henri E. Chabanne, FAAR'34

Linda J. Cook, FAAR'89

Joanna Dougherty, FAAR'86

F. W. Edmondson, FAAR'48 (1)

Jon S. Emerson, FAAR'67

Eric Reid Fulford, FAAR'92

Ralph E. Griswold, FAAR'23

Edgar C. Haag, FAAR'79

Robert Mitchell Hanna, FAAR'76

Stephen C. Haus, FAAR'79

Dale H. Hawkins, FAAR'52

Elizabeth Dean Hermann, FAAR'87

Gary R. Hilderbrand, FAAR'95

Walter Hood, FAAR'97

Alden Hopkins, FAAR'35

Dr. Frank D. James, FAAR'68

Dean A. Johnson, FAAR'66

Mary Margaret Jones, FAAR'98

John F. Kirkpatrick, FAAR'39

Robert S. Kitchen, FAAR'38

Albert R. Lamb, III, FAAR'70

Edward Lawson, FAAR'21

Tom Leader, FAAR'99

James M. Lister, FAAR'37

Roger B. Martin, FAAR'64

Laurel McSherry, FAAR'00

Stuart M. Mertz, FAAR'40

Stacy T. Moriarty, FAAR'84

Richard C. Murdock, FAAR'33

Norman T. Newton, FAAR'26, RAAR-67

Peter O'Shea, FAAR'96

Laurie D. Olin, FAAR'74, RAAR'90

Don H. Olson, FAAR'62

Thomas R. Oslund, FAAR'92

Nell H. Park, FAAR'33

George E. Patton, FAAR'51

Paul R. V. Pawlowski, FAAR'69

Peter M. Pollack, FAAR'71

Thomas D. Price, FAAR'32

Charles A. Rapp, FAAR'72

Michael Rapuano, FAAR'30

Peter G. Rolland, FAAR'78, FASLA

Leslie A. Ryan, FAAR'95

Peter Lindsay Schaudt, FAAR'91, ASLA

Terry Schnadelbach, FAAR'66

Seth H. Seablom, FAAR'68

Stephen Sears, FAAR'00

Charles Sullivan, FAAR'85

Jack Sullivan, FAAR'83

Charles R. Sutton, FAAR'32

Erik A. Svenson, FAAR'58

L. Azeo Torre, FAAR'76

Morris E. Trotter, FAAR'35

James R. Turner, FAAR'76

Daniel Tuttle, FAAR'88

Michael R. Van Valkenburgh, FAAR'8

E. Michael Vergason, FAAR'80

Craig P. Verzone, FAAR'99

Richard K. Webel, FAAR'29, RAAR'6

Professor James L. Wescoat, FAAR'9

Brooks E. Wigginton, FAAR'50

Gall Wittwer, FAAR'96

John L. Wong, FAAR'81

Prof. Ervin H. Zube, FAAR'61

Fellows of the American Academy in Rome (Con't)

Historic Preservation and Conservation

Elmo Baca, FAAR'00
Prof. Margaret Holben Ellis, FAAR'94
Shelley Fletcher, FAAR'98
Eric Gordon, FAAR'97
Anne Frances Maheux, FAAR'96
Pablo Ojeda-O'Neill, FAAR'96
Alice Boccia Paterakis, FAAR'00
Leslie Rainer, FAAR'99
Bettina A. Raphael, FAAR'94
Thomas C. Roby, FAAR'95
Catherine Sease, FAAR'95
Prof. Frederick Steiner, FAAR'98
Jonathan Thorton, FAAR'99
Dr. George Wheeler, FAAR'97

Design Arts

William Adair, FAAR'92
Gerald D. Adams, FAAR'68
Thomas Angotti, FAAR'90
Donald Appleyard, FAAR'75
Joseph H. Aronson, FAAR'74
Morley Baer, FAAR'80
Gordon C. Baldwin, FAAR'78
Phillip R. Baldwin, FAAR'94
Karen Bausman, FAAR'95
Ellen Beasley, FAAR'89
Anna Campbell Bliss, FAAR'84
Robert W. Braunschweiger, FAAR'74
Paul M. Bray, FAAR'97
Steven Brooke, FAAR'91
Michael B. Cadwell, FAAR'99
Heather Carson, FAAR'99
John J. Casbarian, FAAR'86, FAIA
Adele Chatfield-Taylor, FAAR'84
Walter Chatham, FAAR'89
Morison S. Cousins, FAAR'85
Russell Rowe Culp, FAAR'80
Phoebe Cutler, FAAR'89
Joseph Paul D'Urso, FAAR'88

Paul Davis, FAAR'98
Robert S. Davis, FAAR'91
Robert De Fuccio, FAAR'76
Robert Regis Dvorak, FAAR'72
Hsin-ming Fung, FAAR'92
Jeanne Giordano, FAAR'87
Miller Horns, FAAR'90
Robert Jensen, FAAR'76
June Meyer Jordan, FAAR'71
Wendy Kaplan, FAAR'00
J. Michael Kirkland, FAAR'70
Robert Kramer, FAAR'72
George Krause, FAAR'77, RAAR'80
Norman Krumholz, FAAR'87
Michael Lax, FAAR'78
Debra McCall, FAAR'89
R. Alan Melting, FAAR'70
Donald Oenslager
Donald Peting, FAAR'78
William L. Plumb, FAAR'86
William Reed, FAAR'68
Julie Riefler, FAAR'87
Mark Robbins, FAAR'97
Michael Rock, FAAR'00
Danny M. Samuels, FAAR'86
Mark Schimmenti, FAAR'98
Paul D. Schwartzman, FAAR'77
William V. Shaw, FAAR'68
Alison Sky, FAAR'78
Paul L. Steinberg, FAAR'82
Joel Sternfeld, FAAR'91
Michelle Stone, FAAR'78
Edward Marc Treib, FAAR'85
Kevin Walz, FAAR'95
Emily M. Whiteside, FAAR'82
Janet Zweig, FAAR'92

FAAR = Fellow of the American Academy in Rome
RAAR = Resident of the American Academy in Rome

Source: American Academy in Rome

Fellows of the American Academy of Arts and Sciences

Since its founding in 1780, the American Academy of Arts and Sciences has pursued its goal "To cultivate every art and science which may tend to advance the interest, honor, dignity, and happiness of a free, independent, and virtuous people." Throughout its history, the Academy's diverse membership has included the best from the arts, science, business, scholarship, and public affairs. Nominations for new members are taken from existing fellows and evaluated by panels from each discipline and the membership at large.

Design Professionals, Academics, and Writers:

Christopher Alexander '96
U. of Calif., Berkeley

Edward Larrabee Barnes '78
Edward Larrabee Barnes/
John M. Y. Lee Architects,
New York

Herbert Lawrence Block '59
Washington, D.C.

Denise Scott Brown '93
Venturi Scott Brown &
Assoc., Inc., Philadelphia

Robert Campbell '93
Cambridge, Mass.

Henry Nichols Cobb '84
Pei, Cobb, Freed & Partners,
New York

Kenneth Frampton '93
Columbia University

James Ingo Freed '94
Pei, Cobb, Freed & Partners,
New York

Frank Owen Gehry '91
Frank O. Gehry and Associates,
Santa Monica, Calif.

Lawrence Halprin '78
San Francisco, Calif.

Robert S.F. Hughes '93
Time Magazine

Ada Louise Huxtable '74
New York, N.Y.

Philip Johnson '77
Philip Johnson Architects,
New York

Gerhard Michael Kallmann '85
Kallmann, McKinnell and Wood,
Architects, Inc., Boston

(Noel) Michael McKinnell '85
Kallmann, McKinnell and Wood,
Architects, Inc., Boston

Richard Alan Meier '95
New York, NY

Henry Armand Millon '75
National Gallery of Art,
Washington, D.C.

William Mitchell '97
Massachusetts Institute of
Technology

I(eoh) M(ing) Pei '67
Pei, Cobb, Freed & Partners,
New York

Fellows of the American Academy of Arts and Sciences (Con't)

Kevin Roche '94
Hamden, Conn.

Robert Rosenblum '84
New York University

Moshe Safdie '96
Moshe Safdie & Assoc.,
Sommerville, Mass.

Vincent J. Scully '86
Yale University

Hugh Asher-Stubbins '57
Ocean Ridge, Fla.

Robert Venturi '84
Venturi Scott Brown & Assoc., Inc.,
Philadelphia

Foreign Honorary Members:

Charles Correa '93
Bombay, India

Carl Theodor Dreyer '65
Copenhagen, Denmark

Norman Robert Foster '96
Foster and Associates, London

Phyllis Lambert '95
Center Canadien d'Architecture,
Montreal, Quebec

Ricardo Legorreta '94
Mexico City, Mexico

Fumihko Maki '96
Maki and Associates, Tokyo, Japan

J. Rafael Moneo '93
Harvard University

Oscar Niemeyer '49
Rio de Janeiro, Brazil

Renzo Piano '93
London, England

Alvaro Siza '92
Porto, Portugal

Kenzo Tange '67
Tokyo, Japan

Source: American Academy of Arts and Sciences

Did you know...
**Stonehenge's lintels weigh
nearly seven tons each.**

Fellows of The American Institute of Architects

The College of Fellows of The American Institute of Architects (AIA) is composed of AIA members who have been elected to Fellowship by a jury of their peers. Fellowship is granted for significant contributions to architecture and society and for achieving a high standard of professional excellence. Architect members who have been in good standing for at least 10 years may be nominated for Fellowship. The following individuals are current active members of The American Institute of Architects' College of Fellows.

A

Carlton S. Abbott, Williamsburg, VA

J. C. Abbott Jr., Sarasota, FL

James Abell, Tempe, AZ

Jan M. Abell, Tampa, FL

Stephen N. Abend, Kansas City, MO

Bruce A. Abrahamson, Minneapolis, MN

Max Abramovitz, Pound Ridge, NY

Raymond C. Abst, Modesto, CA

Harold L. Adams, Baltimore, MD

William M. Adams, Venice, CA

William T. Adams, Dallas, TX

Michael Adlerstein, New York, NY

P. Aguirre Jr., Dallas, TX

Loren P. Ahles, Minneapolis, MN

Thomas R. Aidala, San Francisco, CA

Roula Alakiotou, Chicago, IL

Charles A Albanese, Tucson, AZ

Richard K. Albyn, Pisgah Forest, NC

N. Sue Alden, Seattle, WA

Iris S. Alex, New York, NY

Cecil A. Alexander Jr., Atlanta, GA

Earle S. Alexander, Jr., Houston, TX

Henry C. Alexander, Jr., Coral Gables, FL

James G. Alexander, Boston, MA

A. Notley Alford, Englewood, FL

Stanley N. Allan, Chicago, IL

Maurice B. Allen, Jr., Bloomfield Hills, MI

Ralph G. Allen, Chicago, IL

Rex W. Allen, Sonoma, CA

Robert E. Allen, San Francisco, CA

Robert E. Allen, Longview, TX

Gerald L. Allison, Newport Beach, CA

Killis P. Almond, Jr., San Antonio, TX

Alfred S. Alschuler, Highland Park, IL

Ronald A. Altoon, Los Angeles, CA

Jesus E. Amaral, San Juan, PR

Joseph Amisano, Atlanta, GA

Dorman D. Anderson, Seattle, WA

Harry F. Anderson, Oakbrook, IL

J. Timothy Anderson, Cambridge, MA

John D. Anderson, Denver, CO

Richard Anderson, Tucson, AZ

Samuel A. Anderson, Charlottesville, VA

William L. Anderson, Des Moines, IA

J. Philip Andrews, Pittsburgh, PA

Lavone D. Andrews, Houston, TX

Martha P. Andrews, Portland, OR

George Anselevicius, Albuquerque, NM

James H. Anstis, West Palm Beach, FL

Richard M. Archer, San Antonio, TX

Fellows of The American Institute of Architects (Con't)

Peter F. Arfaa, Philadelphia, PA

Bruce P. Arneill, Glastonbury, CT

Chris Arnold, Palo Alto, CA

Christopher C. Arnold, Commerce Township, MI

Robert V. Arrigoni, San Francisco, CA

Yvonne W. Asken, Portage, MI

Laurin B. Askew, Columbia, MD

Lee Hewlett Askew III, Memphis, TN

Neil L. Astle, Salt Lake City, UT

Louis D. Astorino, Pittsburgh, PA

Charles H. Atherton, Washington, DC

Tony Atkin, Philadelphia, PA

John L. Atkins, Research Triangle Park, NC

Eugene E. Aubry, Holmes Beach, FL

Seymour Auerbach, Chevy Chase, MD

Douglas H. Austin, San Diego, CA

Daniel Avchen, Minneapolis, MN

Donald C. Axon, Laguna Beach, CA

Alfred L. Aydelott, Carmel, CA

B

Howard J. Backen, Sausalito, CA

Edmund N. Bacon, Philadelphia, PA

David C. Baer, Houston, TX

Stuart Baesel, La Jolla, CA

Deon F. Bahr, Lincoln, NE

Ray B. Bailey, Houston, TX

William J. Bain, Jr., Seattle, WA

Royden Stanley Bair, Houston, TX

Louis J. Bakanowsky, Cambridge, MA

David Baker, San Francisco, CA

Isham O. Baker, Washington, DC

Jack Sherman Baker, Champaign, IL

James Barnes Baker, London

Gregory S. Baldwin, Portland, OR

Samuel T. Balen, Waldport, OR

Rex M. Ball, Tulsa, OK

Richard S. Banwell, Walnut Creek, CA

Shalom S. Baranes, Washington, DC

Robert A. Barclay, Cleveland, OH

Paul H. Barkley, Falls Church, VA

John M. Barley, II, Jacksonville, FL

Charles C. Barlow, Jackson, MS

Edward L. Barnes, Cambridge, MA

Linda Barnes, Portland, OR

Jay William Barnes Jr., Austin, TX

Jonathan Barnett, Washington, DC

Carol R. Barney, Chicago, IL

Howard R. Barr, Austin, TX

Raj Barr-Kumar, Washington, DC

Nolan E. Barrick, Lubbock, TX

Errol Barron, New Orleans, LA

Richard E. Barrow, Birmingham, AL

Richard W. Bartholomew, Philadelphia, PA

Armand Bartos, New York, NY

Edward C. Bassett, Mill Valley, CA

Fred Bassetti, Seattle, WA

Peter Batchelor, Raleigh, NC

Ronald J. Battaglia, Buffalo, NY

Jay S. Bauer, Newport Beach, CA

Joseph D. Bavaro, Punta Gorda, FL

John Craig Beale, Dallas, TX

Burtch W. Beall Jr., Salt Lake City, UT

Leroy E. Bean, Petaluma, CA

Alan J. Beard, Portland, OR

Lee P. Bearsch, Binghamton, NY

William H. Beaty, Memphis, TN

William B. Bechhoefer, Bethesda, MD

Lee Becker, Washington, DC

Rex L. Becker, St. Louis, MO

Herbert Beckhard, New York, NY

Robert M. Beckley, Ann Arbor, MI

Michael Bednar, Charlottesville, VA

Fellows of The American Institute of Architects (Con't)

Carmi Bee, New York, NY

David W. Beer, New York, NY

Edgar C. Beery, Springfield, VA

Ann M. Beha, Boston, MA

Byron Bell, New York, NY

M Wayne Bell, Austin, TX

John Belle, New York, NY

Ralph C. Bender, San Antonio, TX

Barry Benepe, New York, NY

Daniel D. Bennett, Fayetteville, AR

David J. Bennett, Minneapolis, MN

Frederick R. Bentel, Locust Valley, NY

Maria A. Bentel, Locust Valley, NY

Kenneth E. Bentsen, Houston, TX

Frederick J. Bentz, Minneapolis, MN

Karl A. Berg, Denver, CO

Richard R. Bergmann, New Canaan, CT

Lloyd F. Bergquist, Bloomington, MN

Robert J. Berkebile, Kansas City, MO

Marlene J. Berkoff, San Rafael, CA

Anthony N. Bernheim, San Francisco, CA

K Norman Berry, Louisville, KY

Richard J. Bertman, Boston, MA

Ronald P. Bertone, Middletown, NJ

Frederic A. Bertram, Clearwater, FL

Hobart Betts, Sag Harbor, NY

John H. Beyer, New York, NY

John H. Bickel, Louisville, KY

Frederick C. Biebesheimer, III, Old Lyme, CT

T. J. Biggs, Jackson, MS

Rebecca L. Binder, Playa Del Rey, CA

Lance L. Bird, Pasadena, CA

John R. Birge, Omaha, NE

Gunnar Birkerts, Bloomfield Hills, MI

James A. Bishop, Bellville, TX

George Bissell, Newport Beach, CA

J. Sinclair Black, Austin, TX

Walter S. Blackburn, Indianapolis, IN

Leonard D. Blackford, Sacramento, CA

Jan Gaede Blackmon, Dallas, TX

Boyd A. Blackner, Salt Lake City, UT

Peter Blake, Riverdale, NY

Frederick A. Bland, New York, NY

Wilfred E. Blessing, Oak Harbor, WA

Richard L. Blinder, New York, NY

Richard L. Bliss, Kirkwood, MO

Robert L. Bliss, Salt Lake City, UT

Ronald B. Blitch, New Orleans, LA

John D. Bloodgood, Des Moines, IA

Sigmund F. Blum, Naples, FL

Susan Blumentals, Brooklyn Center, MN

H M. Blumer, Paradise Valley, AZ

Kirk V. Blunck, Des Moines, IA

William A. Blunden, Cleveland, OH

William E. Blurock, Newport Beach, CA

L. Kirkpatrick Bobo, Memphis, TN

Michael L. Bobrow, Los Angeles, CA

William N. Bodouva, New York, NY

Joe Boehning, Albuquerque, NM

Robert J. Boerema, Gainesville, FL

Joseph Boggs, Annapolis, MD

Walter F. Bogner, Larchmont, NY

Peter Bohlin, Wilkes Barre, PA

Friedrich K.M. Bohm, Columbus, OH

Mario H. Boiardi, Washington, DC

Stanley G. Boles, Portland, OR

Michael E. Bolinger, Baltimore, MD

Robert D. Bolling, Torrance, CA

Antonio R. Bologna, Memphis, TN

Preston M. Bolton, Houston, TX

James R. Bonar, Los Angeles, CA

J. Max Bond, Jr., New York, NY

Charles Hussey Boney, Wilmington, NC

Leslie N. Boney, Jr., Wilmington, NC

Paul D. Boney, Wilmington, NC

Fellows of The American Institute of Architects (Con't)

Dwight M. Bonham, Wichita, KS

Daniel Boone, Abilene, TX

David C. Boone, Santa Cruz, CA

Laurence O. Booth, Chicago, IL

Bill C. Booziotis, Dallas, TX

L. G. Borget, Houston, TX

Bernard Bortnick, Dallas, TX

Thomas L. Bosworth, Seattle, WA

Elmer E. Botsai, Honolulu, HI

Elmer Botsai, Honolulu, HI

Gary A. Bowden, Baltimore, MD

David M. Bowen, Fishers, IN

Gary Bowen, Omaha, NE

Ronald Gene Bowen, Middleton, WI

John A. Bower, Jr., Philadelphia, PA

Paul D. Bowers, Jr., Grand Rapids, MI

William A. Bowersox, Saint Louis, MO

Chester Bowles, Jr.., San Francisco, CA

J. Donald Bowman, Bellevue, WA

John Harold Box, Austin, TX

Robert A. Boynton, Richmond, VA

John Bozalis, Oklahoma City, OK

James H. Bradburn, Denver, CO

David R. Braden, Dallas, TX

Richard H. Bradfield, Clearwater, FL

Thomas G. Bradley, Decatur, IL

Clyde A. Brady, III, Orlando, FL

Scott W. Braley, Atlanta, GA

Ronald M. Brame, Dallas, TX

Joel Brand, Houston, TX

Robert Brannen, Boston, MA

Charles S. Braun, Longwood, FL

Richard M. Brayton, San Francisco, CA

William E. Brazley, Jr., Matteson, IL

Melvin Brecher, Broomall, PA

William N. Breger, New York, NY

Simon Breines, Scarsdale, NY

John Michael Brendle, Denver, CO

Daniel R. Brents, Houston, TX

Adrienne G. Bresnan, New York, NY

Joseph Bresnan, New York, NY

Benjamin E. Brewer, Jr., Houston, TX

Leon Bridges, Baltimore, MD

Stanford R. Britt, Washington, DC

Joseph M. Brocato Sr., Alexandria, LA

Myra M. Brocchini, Berkeley, CA

Ronald G. Brocchini, Berkeley, CA

Paul Broches, New York, NY

Raymond D. Brochstein, Houston, TX

William R. Brockway, Baton Rouge, LA

M. J. Brodie, Baltimore, MD

H. Gordon Brooks, II, Lafayette, LA

John W. Broome, Tualatin, OR

Robert C. Broshar, Clear Lake, IA

David J. Brotman, Los Angeles, CA

Charles E. Broudy, Philadelphia, PA

Jennie Sue Brown, Seattle, WA

Kenneth F. Brown, Honolulu, HI

Paul B. Brown, Traverse City, MI

Robert L. Brown, Jr., Lithonia, GA

Robert F. Brown, Jr., Philadelphia, PA

Woodlief Brown, Abilene, TX

George D. Brown Jr., Peekskill, NY

C. William Brubaker, Chicago, IL

Barry B. Bruce, Bellaire, TX

Van B. Bruner, Jr., Haddonfield, NJ

Harry A. Bruno, Walnut Creek, CA

Larry S. Bruton, Portland, OR

Harvey Bryan, Belmont, MA

John H. Bryant, Stillwater, OK

Algimantas V. Bublys, Birmingham, MI

Marvin H. Buchanan, Berkeley, CA

James W. Buckley, Greensboro, GA

Michael P. Buckley, New Haven, CT

Fellows of The American Institute of Architects (Con't)

Huber H. Buehrer, Maumee, OH

John B. Buenz, Chicago, IL

Glenn A. Buff, Miami, FL

Henrik H. Bull, San Francisco, CA

Ellis W. Bullock, Jr., Pensacola, FL

Thomas A. Bullock, Sr., Brenham, TX

W. Glenn Bullock, Knoxville, TN

Franklin S. Bunch, Sugar Land, TX

Richard S. Bundy, San Diego, CA

John H. Burgee, Montecito, CA

Charles E. Burgess, Houston, TX

J. Armand Burgun, Kitty Hawk, NC

Edward M. Burke, Austin, TX

James E. Burlage, Sausalito, CA

Robert Burley, Waitsfield, VT

Arthur L. Burns, Winter Haven, FL

John A. Burns, Alexandria, VA

Norma DeCamp Burns, Raleigh, NC

Robert P. Burns, Raleigh, NC

Rodger E. Burson, Wimberley, TX

John A. Busby, Jr., Atlanta, GA

C. Joe Buskuhl, Dallas, TX

H. Kennard Bussard, Des Moines, IA

Jerome R. Butler, Chicago, IL

Theodore R. Butler, Minneapolis, MN

Fred W. Butner, Winston Salem, NC

Thomas K. Butt, Point Richmond, CA

Harold Buttrick, New York, NY

Paul S. Byard, New York, NY

Brent Byers, Austin, TX

Arne Bystrom, Seattle, WA

C

Burns Cadwalader, Oakland, CA

Harold Calhoun, Houston, TX

Robert Campbell, Cambridge, MA

Wendell J. Campbell, Chicago, IL

H. F. Candela, Coral Gables, FL

Robert H. Canizaro, Jackson, MS

William T. Cannady, Houston, TX

Jamie Cannon, Town & Country, MO

Marvin J. Cantor, Fairfax, VA

Horace S. Cantrell Jr., Indianapolis, IN

Kenneth Harvey Cardwell, Berkeley, CA

Jean P. Carlhian, Boston, MA

William A. Carlisle, Columbia, SC

DeVon M. Carlson, Boulder, CO

Donald Edwin Carlson, Seattle, WA

Clyde R. Carpenter, Lexington, KY

Jack A. Carpenter, San Diego, CA

Edwin Winford Carroll, El Paso, TX

M. E. Carroll, Chevy Chase, MD

Marley Carroll, Charlotte, NC

W. T. Carry, Atlanta, GA

Chris Carson, San Antonio, TX

Donald K. Carter, Pittsburgh, PA

Virgil R. Carter, Newtown Square, PA

David R. Cartnal, San Jose, CA

Timothy A. Casai, Bloomfield Hills, MI

John Casbarian, Houston, TX

A. Cascieri, Lexington, MA

Donald W. Caskey, Irvine, CA

Heather W. Cass, Washington, DC

Joseph W. Casserly, Chicago, IL

John J. Castellana, Bloomfield Hills, MI

Stephan Castellanos, Stockton, CA

Samuel J. Caudill, Aspen, CO

Giorgio Cavaglieri, New York, NY

W. Brooks Cavin Jr., Shelburne, VT

Lawrence Chaffin, Jr., Koloa, HI

Ann R. Chaintreuil, Rochester, NY

Alfred V. Chaix, South Pasadena, CA

Dean B. Chambliss, Denver, CO

Junius J. Champeaux, II, Lake Charles, LA

Fellows of The American Institute of Architects (Con't)

Lo-Yi Chan, Ashley Falls, MA

Wing T. Chao, Burbank, CA

L. William Chapin II, Alexandria, VA

Donald D. Chapman, Kula, HI

John S. Chase, Houston, TX

Walter F. Chatham, New York, NY

Peter Chermayeff, Boston, MA

Edith Cherry, Albuquerque, NM

Edward E. Cherry, Hamden, CT

Robert A. Chervenak, FAIA

Lugean L. Chilcote, Little Rock, AR

G. Cabell Childress, Castle Rock, CO

David M. Childs, New York, NY

Maurice F. Childs, Boston, MA

Susan Chin, New York, NY

Robert E. Chisholm, Miami, FL

Gordon H. Chong, San Francisco, CA

Frederick L. Christensen, Salinas, CA

George W. Christensen, Scottsdale, AZ

James W. Christopher, Salt Lake City, UT

Eric A. Chung, Radnor, PA

William C. Church, Portland, OR

Richard J. Chylinski, Los Angeles, CA

Mario J. Ciampi, Kentfield, CA

Robert L. Cioppa, New York, NY

Eugene D. Cizek, PhD, New Orleans, LA

George L. Claflen, Philadelphia, PA

John M. Clancy, Boston, MA

James F. Clapp, Jr., Cambridge, MA

Gerald L Clark, Havasu City, AZ

Roger H. Clark, Raleigh, NC

John P. Clarke, Trenton, NJ

Marshall F. Clarke, Greenville, SC

Fred W. Clarke III, New Haven, CT

Thomas R. Clause, Des Moines, IA

Jerry L. Clement, St. Louis, MO

Glen E. Cline, Boise, ID

Elizabeth Close, St. Paul, MN

Robert K. Clough, Chicago, IL

James A Clutts, Dallas, TX

Henry N. Cobb, New York, NY

R. F. Coffee, Austin, TX

Andrew S. Cohen, Middlebury, CT

Jack C. Cohen, Bethesda, MD

Martin H. Cohen, Armonk, NY

Stuart Cohen, Evanston, IL

Doris Cole, Concord, MA

Robert Traynham Coles, Buffalo, NY

David S. Collins, Cincinnati, OH

William T. Conklin, Washington, DC

Richard T. Conrad, Sacramento, CA

W M. Conrad, Kansas City, MO

John Conron, Santa Fe, NM

J. J. Conroy, Chicago, IL

Eugene E. Cook, Roselle, IL

Lawrence D. Cook, Falls Church, VA

Richard B. Cook, Chicago, IL

William H. Cook, Sonoita, AZ

Alexander Cooper, New York, NY

Jerome M. Cooper, Atlanta, GA

W Kent Cooper, Washington, DC

Christopher Coover, Phoenix, AZ

Gerald M. Cope, Philadelphia, PA

Lee G. Copeland, Seattle, WA

C. Jack Corgan, Dallas, TX

Jack M. Corgan, Dallas, TX

William Corlett, Berkeley, CA

Araldo A. Cossutta, New York, NY

Walter H. Costa, Lafayette, CA

Leland Cott, Cambridge, MA

John O. Cotton, Marina Del Rey, CA

C. H. Cowell, Houston, TX

Dan C. Cowling, Little Rock, AR

David C. Cox, Washington, DC

Fellows of The American Institute of Architects (Con't)

Frederic H Cox, Richmond, VA

Warren J. Cox, Washington, DC

Whitson W. Cox, Carmichael, CA

Bruce I. Crabtree, Jr., Nashville, TN

Kirk R. Craig, Greenville, SC

George M. Crandall, Portland, OR

David A. Crane Tampa, FL

Ronald O. Crawford, Roanoke, VA

Martin W. Crennen, Helena, MT

Frank W. Crimp, Milton, MA

James H. Crissman, Watertown, MA

Edwin B. Crittenden, Anchorage, AK

K. C. Crocco, Chicago, IL

Charles B. Croft, Austin, TX

Edwin B. Cromwell, Little Rock, AR

Eason Cross, Jr., Alexandria, VA

Samuel Crothers, III, Radnor, PA

R. L. Crowther, Denver, CO

Randolph R. Croxton, New York, NY

Metcalf Crump, Memphis, TN

Evan D. Cruthers, Honolulu, HI

John W. Cuningham, Minneapolis, MN

Ben Cunningham, St. Petersburg, FL

Gary M. Cunningham, Dallas, TX

Warren W. Cunningham, Philadelphia, PA

James L Cutler, Bainbridge Is, WA

Bernard J. Cywinski, Havertown, PA

D

Charles E. Dagit, Jr., Philadelphia, PA

Fernand W. Dahan, Rockville, MD

David A. Daileda, Springfield, VA

Todd Dalland, New York, NY

J. E. Dalton, Kent, OH

Leo A. Daly III, Washington, DC

Paul Damaz, E Hampton, NY

Sylvester Damianos, Pittsburgh, PA

Robert Damora, Bedford, NY

George E. Danforth, Chicago, IL

Arthur C. Danielian, Irvine, CA

George N. Daniels, Salt Lake City, UT

Stanley L. Daniels, Atlanta, GA

Doris Andrews Danna, St. Louis, MO

Robert F. Darby, Jacksonville, FL

Samuel N. Darby, Rockford, IL

Edwin S. Darden, Fresno, CA

Ben R. Darmer, Atlanta, GA

Richard Dattner, New York, NY

Theoharis L. David, New York, NY

D. G. Davidson, Washington, DC

David S. Davidson, Great Falls, MT

Robert I. Davidson, New York, NY

Albert J. Davis, Blacksburg, VA

Arthur Q. Davis, New Orleans, LA

Charles M. Davis, San Francisco, CA

Clark A. Davis, San Francisco, CA

Jerry A Davis, New York, NY

John M. Davis, Austin, TX

Lewis Davis, New York, NY

Steven M. Davis, New York, NY

W. T. Davis, Greenville, SC

Clare Henry Day, Redlands, CA

Frederic L. Day, Jr., Concord, MA

Natalie De Blois, San Antonio, TX

John Neff De Haas Jr., Bozeman, MT

Alfredo De Vido, New York, NY

Jack DeBartolo, Jr., Phoenix, AZ

Rudolph V. DeChellis, Woodland Hills, CA

Vernon DeMars, Berkeley, CA

Kenneth DeMay, Watertown, MA

Louis DeMoll, Moylan, PA

J. R. DeStefano, Chicago, IL

Panayotis E. DeVaris, South Orange, NJ

E. L. Deam, Highland Park, IL

Fellows of The American Institute of Architects (Con't)

Robert C. Dean, Boston, MA

C. M. Deasy, San Luis Obispo, CA

Howard S. Decker, Chicago, IL

Ward W. Deems, Solana Beach, CA

Allan J. Dehar, New Haven, CT

Jorge Del Rio, San Juan, PR

Homer T. Delawie, San Diego, CA

Eugene A. Delmar, Olney, MD

Sidney L. Delson, E Hampton, NY

Jos. Robert Deshayes, Caldwell, TX

Gary L. Desmond, Denver, CO

John J. Desmond, Baton Rouge, LA

Gita Dev, Woodside, CA

Suzanne Di Geronimo, Paramus, NJ

Antonio Di Mambro, Boston, MA

A P. DiBenedetto, Portland, OR

Eugene L. DiLaura, Milan, MI

Robert Diamant, Longboat Key, FL

J. J. Diamond, Jacksonville, FL

Katherine Diamond, Los Angeles, CA

Horacio Diaz, San Juan, PR

James R. Diaz, San Francisco, CA

David R. Dibner, McLean, VA

Gerald G. Diehl, Dearborn, MI

Paul E. Dietrich, Cambridge, MA

Robert H. Dietz, Apache Junction, AZ

William M. Dikis, Des Moines, IA

Frank Dimster, Los Angeles, CA

Philip Dinsmore, Tucson, AZ

David D. Dixon, Boston, MA

F. Dail Dixon, Jr., Chapel Hill, NC

John M. Dixon, Old Greenwich, CT

Michael A. Dixon, St.. Charles, IL

Lawrence S. Doane, San Francisco, CA

Jim C. Doche, Amarillo, TX

Peter H. Dodge, San Francisco, CA

George S. Dolim, San Francisco, CA

Peter Hoyt Dominick Jr., Denver, CO

Milford W. Donaldson, San Diego, CA

Janet Donelson, Seattle, WA

Richard C. Donkervoet, Baltimore, MD

Kermit P. Dorius, Newport Bch, CA

Albert A. Dorman, Los Angeles, CA

Richard L. Dorman, Santa Fe, NM

Robert W. Dorsey, Cincinnati, OH

Darwin V. Doss, Salem, OR

Betsey O. Dougherty, Costa Mesa, CA

Brian P. Dougherty, Costa Mesa, CA

Frank F. Douglas, Houston, TX

H Robert Douglass, Missouri City, TX

Gerald A. Doyle, Phoenix, AZ

Peter G. Doyle, Houston, TX

Boris Dramov, San Francisco, CA

Roy M. Drew, San Diego, CA

Albert M. Dreyfuss, Sacramento, CA

Robert W. Drummond, Gainesville, FL

Andres Duany, Miami, FL

Martin David Dubin, Highland Park, IL

George A. Dudley, Rensselaerville, NY

J. Paul Duffendack, Leawood, KS

Herbert E. Duncan, Kansas City, MO

Foster W. Dunwiddie, Henderson, NV

Eugene C. Dunwody, Macon, GA

William L. Duquette, Los Gatos, CA

Almon J. Durkee, Traverse City, MI

William R. Dutcher, Berkeley, CA

Daniel L. Dworsky, Los Angeles, CA

E

Mary Jean Eastman, New York, NY

John P. Eberhard, Alexandria, VA

Jeremiah Eck, Boston, MA

Stanton Eckstut, New York, NY

Robert N. Eddy, Bakersfield, CA

Fellows of The American Institute of Architects (Con't)

Judith Edelman, New York, NY

Jared I. Edwards, Hartford, CT

David J. Edwards Jr., Columbia, SC

Albert Efron, Staten Island, NY

David L. Eggers, West Palm Beach, FL

Ezra D. Ehrenkrantz, New York, NY

John P. Ehrig, Merritt Island, FL

Joseph Ehrlich, Menlo Park, CA

Steven D. Ehrlich, Culver City, CA

Thomas N. Eichbaum, Washington, DC

John A. Eifler, Chicago, IL

Steven L. Einhorn, Albany, NY

Peter D. Eisenman, New York, NY

Sidney H. Eisenshtat, Los Angeles, CA

Richard Karl Eisner, Oakland, CA

Barry P. Elbasani, Berkeley, CA

Joseph L. Eldredge, Vineyard Hvn, MA

Charles N. Eley, San Francisco, CA

James H. Eley, Jackson, MS

Howard F. Elkus, Boston, MA

Harry Ellenzweig, Cambridge, MA

Robin M. Ellerthorpe, Chicago, IL

Dale R. Ellickson, Great Falls, VA

Benjamin P. Elliott, Rockville, MD

Rand L. Elliott, Oklahoma City, OK

John M. Ellis, New York, NY

James E. Ellison, Washington, DC

James W. Elmore, Phoenix, AZ

Frederick E. Emmons, Bel Tiburon, CA

Terrel M. Emmons, Springfield, VA

William Eng, Champaign, IL

Douglas K. Engebretson, West Springfield, MA

Mark C. Engelbrecht, Des Moines, IA

William L. Ensign, Annapolis, MD

Lawrence Enyart, Phoenix, AZ

Herbert Epstein, Delray Beach, FL

Elizabeth S. Ericson, Boston, MA

Jerome R. Ernst, Seattle, WA

Philip A. Esocoff, Washington, DC

Harold Lionel Esten, Silver Spring, MD

A B. Etherington, Honolulu, HI

Deane M. Evans, Jr., Arlington, VA

J. Handel Evans, Camarillo, CA

Ralph F. Evans, Salt Lake City, UT

Robert J. Evans, Marshall, CA

William S. Evans, Shreveport, LA

C. Richard Everett, Houston, TX

Thomas J. Eyerman, RIBA, Chicago, IL

F

Otto Reichert Facilides, Philadelphia, PA

William H. Fain, Jr., Los Angeles, CA

James Falick, Houston, TX

Kristine K. Fallon, Chicago, IL

Jay David Farbstein, San Luis Obispo, CA

Michael Farewell, Princeton, NJ

Richard T. Faricy, Saint Paul, MN

Richard C. Farley, Denver, CO

Stephen J. Farneth, San Francisco, CA

Avery C. Faulkner, Delaplane, VA

Winthrop W. Faulkner, Chevy Chase, MD

James G. Fausett, Marietta, GA

Robert E. Fehlberg, Pleasanton, CA

Werner L. Feibes, Schenectady, NY

Daniel J. Feil, Washington, DC

Edward A. Feiner, Fairfax, VA

Jose Feito, Miami, FL

Curtis W. Fentress, Denver, CO

S. Scott Ferebee, Jr., Charlotte, NC

Franklin T. Ferguson, Salt Lake City, UT

Richard E. Fernau, Berkeley, CA

Stephanie E. Ferrell, Tampa, FL

Miguel Ferrer, Santurce, PR

Fellows of The American Institute of Architects (Con't)

Richard B. Ferrier, Arlington, TX

James D. Ferris, Michigan City, IN

Robert D. Ferris, San Diego, CA

M. L. Ferro, Weare, NH

Donald E. Ferry, Springfield, IL

Michael T. Fickel, Kansas City, MO

H. H. Field, Shirley, MA

John L. Field, San Francisco, CA

Robert A. Fielden, Las Vegas, NV

Michael M. Fieldman, New York, NY

Kenneth J. Filarski, Providence, RI

Bob G. Fillpot, Norman, OK

Ronald C. Filson, New Orleans, LA

Curtis Finch, Lake Oswego, OR

James H. Finch, Alpharetta, GA

Robert A. Findlay, Ames, IA

Maurice N. Finegold, Boston, MA

Ira S. Fink, Berkeley, CA

Jerry V. Finrow, Seattle, WA

A. Robert Fisher, Belvedere, CA

James Herschel Fisher, Dallas, TX

John L. Fisher, Marysville, CA

Hollye C. Fisk, Dallas, TX

Michael A. Fitts, Nolensville, TN

Darrell A. Fitzgerald, Atlanta, GA

James T. Fitzgerald, Cincinnati, OH

Joseph F. Fitzgerald, Chicago, IL

Richard A. Fitzgerald, Houston, TX

Joseph H. Flad, Madison, WI

Earl Robert Flansburgh, Boston, MA

Ted Flato, San Antonio, TX

Joseph L. Fleischer, New York, NY

Richard J. Fleischman, Cleveland, OH

Norman C. Fletcher, Lexington, MA

David J. Flood, Santa Monica, CA

Colden R. Florance, Washington, DC

Luis Flores-Dumont, Santurce, PR

J. Chadwick P. Floyd, Centerbrook, CT

Richard F. Floyd, Dallas, TX

W. Jeff Floyd Jr., Atlanta, GA

Ligon B. Flynn, Wilmington, NC

John W. Focke, Houston, TX

Bernd Foerster, Manhattan, KS

James Follett, Chicago, IL

Fred L. Foote, San Francisco, CA

Stephen M. Foote, Boston, MA

Peter Forbes, Boston, MA

Robert M. Ford, Starkville, MS

Russell Forester, La Jolla, CA

Bernardo Fort-Brescia, Miami, FL

James R. Foster, Fayetteville, AR

Richard Foster, Wilton, CT

Bruce S. Fowle, New York, NY

Bob J. Fowler, PE, CBO, Pasadena, CA

Marion L. Fowlkes, Nashville, TN

Sheldon Fox, Stamford, CT

Harrison Fraker, Berkeley, CA

Edward D. Francis, Detroit, MI

Jay E. Frank, Dallas, TX

Richard C. Frank, Gregory, MI

James R Franklin, San Luis Obispo, CA

Gregory Franta, Boulder, CO

Ulrich J. Franzen, New York, NY

Robert J. Frasca, Portland, OR

James I. Freed, New York, NY

Beverly L. Freeman, Charlotte, NC

William W. Freeman, Burlington, VT

Jeffrey S. French, Philadelphia, PA

Thomas K. Fridstein, Chicago, IL

Stephen Friedlaender, Cambridge, MA

Hans A. Friedman, Evanston, IL

Rodney F. Friedman, Belvedere, CA

Edward Friedrichs, Santa Monica, CA

Louis E. Fry, Jr., Washington, DC

Louis E. Fry, Washington, DC

Richard E. Fry, Ann Arbor, MI

Fellows of The American Institute of Architects (Con't)

Joseph Y. Fujikawa, Winnetka, IL

Albert B. Fuller Jr., St. Louis, MO

Frank L. Fuller, IV, Oakland, CA

Duncan T. Fulton, Dallas, TX

David F. Furman, Charlotte, NC

James E. Furr, Houston, TX

G

Robert C. Gaede, Cleveland, OH

Herbert K. Gallagher, Boston, MA

Leslie M. Gallery-Dilworth, Philadelphia, PA

Harvey B. Gantt, Charlotte, NC

Robert D. Garland Jr., El Paso, TX

Charles E. Garrison, Diamondhead, MS

Truitt B. Garrison, Granbury, TX

Alan G. Gass, Denver, CO

Fred C. Gast, Jr., Portland, OR

Kirk A. Gastinger, Kansas City, MO

Martha M. Gates, Pittsford, NY

Robert F. Gatje, New York, NY

James B. Gatton, Houston, TX

F. E. Gaulden, Greenville, SC

John C. Gaunt, Lawrence, KS

Robert Geddes, Princeton, NJ

Barbara L. Geddis, Stamford, CT

William J. Geddis, Chestnut Hill, MA

Robert J. Geering, San Francisco, CA

Frank O. Gehry, Santa Monica, CA

Carolyn D. Geise, Seattle, WA

Martin B. Gelber, Los Angeles, CA

M. Arthur Gensler, Jr., San Francisco, CA

David W. George, Southlake, TX

Frank Dan George, Stamford, CT

Reagan W. George, Willow City, TX

Robert S. George, San Bruno, CA

Stephen A. George, Pittsburgh, PA

Preston M. Geren, Fort Worth, TX

Phillip H. Gerou, Evergreen, CO

Joe P. Giattina, Jr., Birmingham, AL

Dale L. Gibbs, Lincoln, NE

Donald H. Gibbs, Long Beach, CA

Randall C. Gideon, Fort Worth, TX

Sidney P. Gilbert, New York, NY

Victor C. Gilbertson, Minnetonka, MN

Wilmot G. Gilland, Eugene, OR

Norman M. Giller, Miami Beach, FL

W. Douglas Gilpin, Charlottesville, VA

James S. Gimpel, Chicago, IL

Raymond L. Gindroz, Pittsburgh, PA

David L. Ginsberg, New York, NY

Raymond Girvigian, South Pasadena, CA

Joseph Carl Giuliani, Washington, DC

Romaldo Giurgola, Manuka ACT ,

Richard E. Glaser, Cincinnati, OH

William R. Glass, Oakland, CA

David Evan Glasser, Fayetteville, AR

E. A. Glendening, Cincinnati, OH

Val Glitsch, Houston, TX

Richard J. Gluckman, New York, NY

Harold D. Glucksman, Union, NJ

James M. Glymph, Santa Monica, CA

Ronald V. Gobbell, Nashville, TN

James Goettsch, Chicago, IL

Alan E. Goldberg, New Canaan, CT

Steven M. Goldberg, New York, NY

M. H. Goldfinger, New York, NY

Ron Goldman, Malibu, CA

Nicholas Goldsmith, New York, NY

Roger Neal Goldstein, Boston, MA

Stanley J. Goldstein, West Orange, NJ

Harmon H. Goldstone, New York, NY

Harry A. Golemon, Houston, TX

Bennie M. Gonzales, Nogales, AZ

Donald W. Y. Goo, Honolulu, HI

R. L. Good, Dallas, TX

Fellows of The American Institute of Architects (Con't)

D. B. Goodhue, Monterey, CA

Cary C. Goodman, Kansas City, MO

John P. Goodman, Manlius, NY

Michael K. Goodwin, Phoenix, AZ

Joan E. Goody, Boston, MA

Ezra Gordon, Chicago, IL

Harry T. Gordon, Washington, DC

Robert E. Gould, Kansas City, MO

Ronald Gourley, Tucson, AZ

Brian Gracey, Knoxville, TN

Bernard J. Grad, Elberon, NJ

Bruce J. Graham, Hobe Sound, FL

Gary L. Graham, Boston, MA

Roy E. Graham, Washington, DC

Robert E. Gramann, Cincinnati, OH

Warren Wolf Gran, New York, NY

Charles P. Graves, Lexington, KY

Dean W. Graves, Kansas City, MO

Michael Graves, Princeton, NJ

David Lawrence Gray, Santa Monica, CA

Thomas A. Gray, Little Rock, AR

Lyn E. Graziani, Miami, FL

Robert E. Greager, Pleasant Ridge, MI

Dennis W. Grebner, St. Paul, MN

Aaron G. Green, San Francisco, CA

Curtis H. Green, Shorewood, MN

Richard J. Green, Cambridge, MA

Thomas G. Green, Boston, MA

Aubrey J. Greenberg, Chicago, IL

James A. Greene, Oviedo, FL

Sanford R. Greenfield, Westfield, NJ

Susan Greenwald, Chicago, IL

John O. Greer, Bryan, TX

Glenn H. Gregg, New Haven, CT

Raymond Grenald, Narberth, PA

James A. Gresham, Tucson, AZ

William C. Gridley, Washington, DC

L. Duane Grieve, Knoxville, TN

James R. Grieves, Baltimore, MD

Donald I. Grinberg, Boston, MA

Edward A. Grochowiak, San Diego, CA

Olindo Grossi, Manhasset, NY

William H. Grover, Centerbrook, CT

J. C. Grube, Portland, OR

Ernest A. Grunsfeld, Chicago, IL

Jordan L. Gruzen, New York, NY

John C. Guenther, St. Louis, MO

Francis A. Guffey II, Charleston, WV

Paul J. Gumbinger, San Mateo, CA

Graham Gund, Cambridge, MA

Brooks R. Gunsul, Portland, OR

Gerald Gurland, West Orange, NJ

William R. Gustafson, Philadelphia, PA

Dean L. Gustavson, Salt Lake City, UT

Cabell Gwathmey, Harwood, MD

Charles Gwathmey, New York, NY

Willard E. Gwilliam, Hayes, VA

H

E. Keith Haag, Cuyahoga Falls, OH

Lester C. Haas, Shreveport, LA

Wallace L. Haas, Jr., Redding, CA

Donald J. Hackl, Chicago, IL

John B. Hackler, Charlotte, NC

L. R. Hahnfeld, Fort Worth, TX

Frank S. Haines, Honolulu, HI

William H. Haire, Stillwater, OK

Gaines B. Hall, Downers Grove, IL

Mark W. Hall, Toronto, ON

William A. Hall, New York, NY

Harry C. Hallenbeck, Sacramento, CA

Stanley I. Hallet, Washington, DC

Gerald Hallissy, Port Washington, NY

Anna M. Halpin, New York, NY

Frances Halsband, New York, NY

Fellows of The American Institute of Architects (Con't)

William Hamby, New York, NY

Robert L. Hamill, Jr., Boise, ID

D. K. Hamilton, Bellaire, TX

E. G Hamilton, Jr., Dallas, TX

Theodore S. Hammer, New York, NY

Gerald S. Hammond, Cincinnati, OH

John Hyatt Hammond, Greensboro, NC

W. Easley Hamner, Cambridge, MA

Mark G. Hampton, Coconut Grove, FL

John Paul C. Hanbury, Norfolk, VA

Peter H. Hand, Atlanta, GA

J. Paul Hansen, Savannah, GA

Richard F. Hansen, Sanibel, FL

Robert E. Hansen, Hendersonville, NC

Ernest H. Hara, Honolulu, HI

John M. Hara, Honolulu, HI

Dellas H. Harder, Columbus, OH

Donald L. Hardison, El Cerrito, CA

Hugh Hardy, New York, NY

John C. Harkness, Arlington, MA

Sarah P. Harkness, Lexington, MA

Frank Harmon, Raleigh, NC

Harry W. Harmon, Lake San Marcos, CA

John C. Haro, Scottsdale, AZ

Charles F. Harper, Wichita Falls, TX

David M. Harper, Coral Gables, FL

Robert L. Harper, Centerbrook, CT

James W. Harrell, Cincinnati, OH

David A. Harris, Washington, DC

Edwin F. Harris, Jr., Raleigh, NC

James Martin Harris, Tacoma, WA

Robert S. Harris, Los Angeles, CA

Robert VM Harrison, Jackson, MS

Roy P. Harrover, Memphis, TN

Craig W. Hartman, San Francisco, CA

Douglas C. Hartman, Dallas, TX

George E. Hartman, Washington, DC

Morton Hartman, Highland Park, IL

William E. Hartmann, Castine, ME

John F. Hartray Jr., Chicago, IL

Timothy Hartung, New York, NY

Wilbert R. Hasbrouck, Chicago, IL

Dennis E. Haskell, Seattle, WA

Albert L. Haskins Jr., Raleigh North, NC

Peter M. Hasselman, Orinda, CA

Sami Hassid, Pleasant Hill, CA

Herman A. Hassinger, Moorestown, NJ

George J. Hasslein, San Luis Obispo, CA

L. J. Hastings, Seattle, WA

Marvin Hatami, Denver, CO

Harold D. Hauf, Sun City, AZ

Robert O. Hausner, Santa Fe, NM

Daniel J. Havekost, Denver, CO

Perry A. Haviland, Oakland, CA

Velpeau E Hawes, Jr., Dallas, TX

H. Ralph Hawkins, Dallas, TX

Jasper Stillwell Hawkins, Phoenix, AZ

William J. Hawkins, III, Portland, OR

William R. Hawley, E Palo Alto, CA

Bruce A. Hawtin, Jackson, WY

Richard S. Hayden, New York, NY

J. F. Hayes, Cambridge, MA

John Freeman Hayes, Radnor, PA

Irving B. Haynes, Lincoln, RI

Edward H. Healey, Cedar Rapids, IA

Michael M. Hearn, San Francisco, CA

George T. Heery, Atlanta, GA

Clovis Heimsath, Austin, TX

Dan Heinfeld, Irvine, CA

John Hejduk, Bronx, NY

Margaret Helfand, New York, NY

Jeffrey Heller, San Francisco, CA

Maxwell Boone Hellmann, Cardiff by the Sea, CA

Fellows of The American Institute of Architects (Con't)

George F. Hellmuth, St. Louis, MO

A. C. Helman, Maitland, FL

David P. Helpern, New York, NY

James C. Hemphill, Jr., Charlotte, NC

Arn Henderson, Norman, OK

John D. Henderson, San Diego, CA

Philip C. Henderson, Dallas, TX

James L. Hendricks, Rockwall, TX

William R. Henry, Jackson, MS

Donald C. Hensman, Pasadena, CA

Charles Herbert, Des Moines, IA

Robert G. Herman, San Francisco, CA

William W. Herrin, Huntsville, AL

Robert G. Hershberger, Tucson, AZ

Paul A. Hesson, San Antonio, TX

Charles R. Heuer, Charlottesville, VA

D. M. Hewitt, Seattle, WA

Warren Cummings Heylman, Spokane, WA

Mason S. Hicks, Fayetteville, NC

Charles C. Hight, Charlotte, NC

Dean F. Hilfinger, Bloomington, IL

John W. Hill, Baltimore, MD

J. Robert Hillier, Princeton, NJ

Mark Hinshaw, Seattle, WA

Kem G. Hinton, Nashville, TN

Don M. Hisaka, Berkeley, CA

Gregory O. Hnedak, Memphis, TN

Paul S. Hoag, Bellevue, WA

Richard W. Hobbs, Washington, DC

Peter S. Hockaday, Seattle, WA

Murlin R. Hodgell, Norman, OK

Thomas H. Hodne, Minneapolis, MN

David C. Hoedemaker, Seattle, WA

August F. Hoenack, Bethesda, MD

David L. Hoffman, Wichita, KS

David H. Hoffman, Evant, TX

John J. Hoffmann, North Haven, CT

John A. Holabird, Chicago, IL

L. M. Holder, Austin, TX

Major L. Holland, Tuskegee, AL

Dwight E. Holmes, Tampa, FL

Jess Holmes, Henderson, NV

Nicholas H. Holmes, Jr., Mobile, AL

Harry J. Holroyd, Columbus, OH

David A. Holtz, Potomac, MD

Malcolm Holzman, New York, NY

George W. Homsey, San Francisco, CA

Bobbie S. Hood, San Francisco, CA

Van D. Hooker, Albuquerque, NM

G. N. Hoover, Houston, TX

George Hoover, Denver, CO

Ray C. Hoover III, Atlanta, GA

Frank L. Hope Jr., San Diego, CA

Gene C. Hopkins, Detroit, MI

Edward M. Hord, Baltimore, MD

Howard N. Horii, Newark, NJ

Gerald Horn, Chicago, IL

Patrick Horsbrugh, South Bend, IN

T. Horty, Minneapolis, MN

Reginald D Hough, Larchmont, NY

Marvin C. Housworth, Atlanta, GA

David C. Hovey, Winnetka, IL

J. Murray Howard, Charlottesville, VA

John Howey, Tampa, FL

Thomas S. Howorth, Oxford, MS

Charles K. Hoyt, Old Lyme, CT

Michael M. Hricak, Jr.., Venice, CA

Robert Y. Hsiung, Boston, MA

Charles A. Hubbard, Cortez, CO

Jeffrey A. Huberman, Charlotte, NC

Richard W. Huffman, Philadelphia, PA

Stephan S. Huh, Minneapolis, MN

Robert E. Hull, Seattle, WA

Charles F. Hummel, Boise, ID

Fred E. Hummel, Sacramento, CA

Fellows of The American Institute of Architects (Con't)

Harry J. Hunderman, Northbrook, IL

Frances P. Huppert, New York, NY

Sam T. Hurst, Montecito, CA

Syed V. Husain, Kensington, CA

Mary Alice Hutchins, Portland, OR

Remmert W. Huygens, Wayland, MA

Bryden B. Hyde, Jarretsville, MD

Fred J. Hynek, Parker, CO

I

Dean Illingworth, Indianapolis, IN

Elizabeth W. Ingraham, Colorado Springs, CO

William A. Isley, Bainbridge Island, WA

H. Curtis Ittner, St. Louis, MO

Robert A. Ivy, Jr., New York, NY

J

Huson Jackson, Lexington, MA

Mike Jackson, Springfield, IL

R. G. Jackson, Houston, TX

Ralph T. Jackson, Boston, MA

Bernard Jacob, Minneapolis, MN

Harry M. Jacobs, Oakland, CA

Stephen B. Jacobs, New York, NY

Hugh N. Jacobsen, Washington, DC

Phillip L. Jacobson, Seattle, WA

J. P. Jacoby, Menomonee Falls, WI

Helmut Jahn, Chicago, IL

Timm Jamieson, Roanoke, VA

Henry A. Jandl, Richmond, VA

William R. Jarratt, Ann Arbor, MI

Peter Jefferson, Highlands, NC

Jordan O. Jelks, Macon, GA

J. J. Jennewein, Tampa, FL

Richard W. Jennings, Austin, TX

Bruce H. Jensen, Salt Lake City, UT

Jon Adams Jerde, Venice, CA

John W. Jickling, Birmingham, MI

John M. Johansen, New York, NY

Anthony N. Johns, Jr., Mt. Irvine, Tobago

Arthur D. Johnson, Omaha, NE

Edwin J. Johnson, Dallas, TX

Floyd E. Johnson, Scottsville, VA

James H. Johnson, Denver, CO

Jeh V. Johnson, Wappingers Falls, NY

Marvin R. Johnson, Raleigh, NC

Philip C. Johnson, New York, NY

Ralph E. Johnson, Chicago, IL

Scott Johnson, Los Angeles, CA

Walker C. Johnson, Chicago, IL

Yandell Johnson, Little Rock, AR

Norman J. Johnston, Seattle, WA

James O. Jonassen, Seattle, WA

Arthur E. Jones, Houston, TX

Bernard I. Jones, Carbondale, IL

E. Fay Jones, Fayetteville, AR

J. Delaine Jones, PhD, Troy, NY

Jack B. Jones, Tamuning, Guam

Johnpaul Jones, Seattle, WA

Paul Duane Jones, Kailua, HI

Robert Lawton Jones, Tulsa, OK

Rudard Artaban Jones, Urbana, IL

Bendrew G. Jong, Orinda, CA

Joe J. Jordan, Philadelphia, PA

David A. Jordani, Minneapolis, MN

Roberta W. Jorgensen, Irvine, CA

H. V. Jova, Atlanta, GA

Bruce D. Judd, San Francisco, CA

Yu Sing Jung, Boston, MA

Howard H. Juster, San Diego, CA

K

Carl F. Kaelber Jr., Pittsford, NY

Richard E. Kaeyer, Mt. Kisco, NY

Fellows of The American Institute of Architects (Con't)

David T. Kahler, Milwaukee, WI

Charles H. Kahn, Chapel Hill, NC

Eino O. Kainlauri, Ames, IA

Harry Kale, Conshohocken, PA

G. M. Kallmann, Boston, MA

Stephen H. Kanner, Los Angeles, CA

Gary Y. Kaplan, Red Bank, NJ

Richard H. Kaplan, Cleveland, OH

Raymond L. Kappe, Pacific Palisades, CA

Raymond John Kaskey, Washington, DC

Kirby M. Keahey, Houston, TX

Gustave R. Keane, Bradenton, FL

Jan Keane, New York, NY

Richard C. Keating, Marina Del Rey, CA

Douglas S. Kelbaugh, Dean, Ann Arbor, MI

Duane A. Kell, St. Paul, MN

John H. Kell, San Antonio, TX

Larry J. Keller, Fairfax, VA

Frank S. Kelly, Houston, TX

F. L. Kelsey, Scottsdale, AZ

Diane Legge Kemp, Chicago, IL

William D Kendall, Houston, TX

Robert N. Kennedy, Indianapolis, IN

Gertrude L. Kerbis, Chicago, IL

Thomas L. Kerns, Arlington, VA

William H. Kessler, Detroit, MI

Herbert A. Ketcham, Minneapolis, MN

Russell V. Keune, Arlington, VA

A H. Keyes, Jr., Washington, DC

Stephen J. Kieran, Philadelphia, PA

Lee F. Kilbourn, Portland, OR

James R. Killebrew, Grapevine, TX

Edward A. Killingsworth, Long Beach, CA

Tai Soo Kim, Hartford, CT

Jong S. Kimm, Apo, AP

David R H King, Washington, DC

Dennis M. King, Huntington Woods, MI

Gordon L. King, Sacramento, CA

J. Bertram King, Asheville, NC

Leland King, Bodega Bay, CA

Sol King, Palm Beach, FL

M. Ray Kingston, Salt Lake City, UT

Paul Kinnison Jr., San Antonio, TX

Ballard H. Kirk, Columbus, OH

D. W. Kirk, Jr., Fort Worth, TX

Stephen J. Kirk, Grosse Pointe Pk, MI

John M. Kirksey, Houston, TX

Peyton E. Kirven, Westlake Village, CA

Robert S. Kitchen, Ocean Hills, CA

Henry Klein, Mount Vernon, WA

J. Arvid Klein, New York, NY

Robert M. Kliment, New York, NY

Stephen A. Kliment, New York, NY

Kenneth F. Klindtworth, Duck Key, FL

Lee B. Kline, Los Angeles, CA

Vincent G. Kling, Chester Springs, PA

James F. Knight, Gunnison, CO

Roy F. Knight, Tallahassee, FL

William H. Knight, Santa Rosa, CA

Charles M. Kober, Long Beach, CA

Carl Koch, Cambridge, MA

Steven Y. Kodama, San Francisco, CA

Edward J. Kodet Jr., Minneapolis, MN

Pierre F. Koenig, Los Angeles, CA

Alfred H. Koetter, Boston, MA

A. Eugene Kohn, New York, NY

Keith R. Kolb, Seattle, WA

Nathaniel K. Kolb Jr., Dallas, TX

S. Richard Komatsu, El Cerrito, CA

Hendrik Koning, Santa Monica, CA

Norman L. Koonce, McLean, VA

James F. Kortan, Atlanta, GA

Panos G. Koulermos, La Crescenta, CA

Alexander Kouzmanoff, Rye Brook, NY

Fellows of The American Institute of Architects (Con't)

Gerhardt Kramer, Webster Groves, MO

Robert Kramer, Brookline, MA

M. Stanley Krause, Jr., Newport News, VA

Eugene Kremer, Manhattan, KS

Jerrily R. Kress, Washington, DC

John L. Kriken, San Francisco, CA

Robert N. Kronewitter, Denver, CO

Kenneth C. Kruger, Santa Barbara, CA

James O. Kruhly, Philadelphia, PA

Rod Kruse, Des Moines, IA

Denis G. Kuhn, New York, NY

Julian E. Kulski, Orlean, VA

Ernest J. Kump, Zurich,

Moritz Kundig, Spokane, WA

Theodore E. Kurz, Cleveland, OH

Sylvia P. Kwan, San Francisco, CA

Michael Kwartler, New York, NY

L

David N. LaBau, Bloomfield, CT

Ronald J. Labinski, Kansas City, MO

John W. Lackens Jr., Minneapolis, MN

Bill N. Lacy, Purchase, NY

Thomas Laging, Lincoln, NE

Henry J. Lagorio, Orinda, CA

David C. Lake, San Antonio, TX

Charles E. Lamb, Annapolis, MD

James Lambeth, Fayetteville, AR

James I. Lammers, Chisago City, MN

Gregory W. Landahl, Chicago, IL

Peter H. Landon, Chicago, IL

D. E. Landry, Dallas, TX

Jane Landry, Dallas, TX

John M. Laping, West Amherst, NY

Arnold Les Larsen, Port Salerno, FL

Dayl A. Larson, Denver, CO

William N. Larson, Park Ridge, IL

William L. Larson, Omaha, NE

Carroll J. Lawler, West Hartford, CT

Charles E. Lawrence, Houston, TX

Jerry Lawrence, Tacoma, WA

Robert M. Lawrence, Oklahoma City, OK

David E. Lawson, Madison, WI

Elizabeth Lawson, Charlottesville, VA

William R. Lawson, Reston, VA

Franklin D. Lawyer, Houston, TX

John C. Le Bey, Savannah, GA

Robert LeMond, Fort Worth, TX

Glen S. LeRoy, Kansas City, MO

Benjamin B. Lee, Honolulu, HI

Donald R. Lee, Charlotte, NC

Elizabeth B. Lee, Lumberton, NC

M. David Lee, Boston, MA

Gene Leedy, Winter Haven, FL

James M. Leefe, Sausalito, CA

Andrea P. Leers, Boston, MA

Gillet Lefferts, Darien, CT

Spencer A. Leineweber, Honolulu, HI

Lawrence J. Leis, Louisville, KY

Richard Leitch, South Laguna, CA

Herbert Lembcke, San Francisco, CA

James T. Lendrum, Phoenix, AZ

Peter A. Lendrum, Phoenix, AZ

Eason H. Leonard, Carmel, CA

Ralph Lerner, Princeton, NJ

Nicholas Lesko, Cleveland, OH

Francis D. Lethbridge, Nantucket, MA

Brenda A. Levin, Los Angeles, CA

Richard D. Levin, Longboat Key, FL

Alan G. Levy, Philadelphia, PA

Eugene P. Levy, Little Rock, AR

Herbert W. Levy, Spring House, PA

Fellows of The American Institute of Architects (Con't)

Morton L. Levy, Houston, TX

Toby S. Levy, San Francisco, CA

Anne McCutcheon Lewis, Washington, DC

Calvin F. Lewis, Des Moines, IA

David Lewis, Homestead, PA

George B. Lewis, Oklahoma City, OK

Richard L. Lewis, Pebble Beach, CA

Roger K. Lewis, Washington, DC

Tom Lewis, Jr., Kissimmee, FL

Walter H. Lewis, Champaign, IL

Alan C. Liddle, Lakewood, WA

Frederick Liebhardt, La Jolla, CA

Theodore Liebman, New York, NY

Bernard J. Liff, Pittsburgh, PA

John H. Lind, Iowa City, IA

David Lindsey, Seattle, WA

H. Mather Lippincott Jr., Moylan, PA

William H. Liskamm, San Rafael, CA

Robert A. Little, Cleveland, OH

Stanley C. Livingston, San Diego, CA

Thomas W. Livingston, Anchorage, AK

Walter R. Livingston, Jr., Crum Lynne, PA

Peter Lizon, Knoxville, TN

W. Kirby Lockard, Tucson, AZ

James L. Loftis, Oklahoma City, , OK

Donn Logan, Berkeley, CA

Dirk Lohan, Chicago, IL

Thomas E. Lollini, Berkeley, CA

Jerrold E. Lomax, Carmel Valley, CA

J. Carson Looney, Memphis, TN

R. Nicholas Loope, Phoenix, AZ

Gabor Lorant, Phoenix, AZ

Larry Lord, Atlanta, GA

George H. Loschky, Seattle, WA

John C. Loss, Whitehall, MI

Rex Lotery, Montecito, CA

William C. Louie, New York, NY

William Love, Los Angeles, CA

Wendell H. Lovett, Seattle, WA

Frank E. Lucas, Charleston, SC

Thomas J. Lucas, Southfield, MI

Lenore M. Lucey, Washington, DC

Carl F. Luckenbach, Ann Arbor, MI

Graham B. Luhn, Houston, TX

Anthony J. Lumsden, Los Angeles, CA

Frithjof Lunde, Center Valley, PA

Phillip Lundwall, Grand Rapids, MI

Victor A. Lundy, Bellaire, TX

Donald H. Lutes, Springfield, OR

Frederic P. Lyman, Sebeka, MN

Robert Dale Lynch, Pittsburgh, PA

Robert J. Lynch, Scottsdale, AZ

Donlyn Lyndon, Berkeley, CA

Maynard Lyndon, Kuessaberg

M

Michael Maas, W. Hampton Bch, NY

Charles H. MacMahon, Deland, FL

John E. MacAllister, San Francisco, CA

Donald MacDonald, San Francisco, CA

Virginia B. MacDonald, Kaneohe, HI

H A. MacEwen, Tampa, FL

Ian MacKinlay, San Francisco, CA

Robert C. Mack, Minneapolis, MN

Eugene J. Mackey, III, St. Louis, MO

John Macsai, Chicago, IL

Robert P. Madison, Cleveland, OH

Peter E. Madsen, Boston, MA

Theodore S. Maffitt, Jr., Palestine, TX

Henry J. Magaziner, Philadelphia, PA

Gary Mahaffey, Minneapolis, MN

Victor C. Mahler, New York, NY

John E. Mahlum, Seattle, WA

C. R. Maiwald, Wilmington, NC

Fellows of The American Institute of Architects (Con't)

Marvin J. Malecha, Raleigh, NC

L. Vic Maloof, Atlanta, GA

Arthur E. Mann, Irvine, CA

Carter H. Manny Jr., Chicago, IL

Clark D. Manus, San Francisco, CA

Virginia S. March, Fairhope, AL

Roger W. Margerum, Detroit, MI

Phillip T. Markwood, Columbus, OH

Harvey V. Marmon, Jr., San Antonio, TX

Jud R. Marquardt, Seattle, WA

Clinton Marr, Jr., Riverside, CA

Mortimer M. Marshall, Jr., Reston, VA

Richard C. Marshall, San Francisco, CA

Albert C. Martin, Los Angeles, CA

Christopher C. Martin, Los Angeles, CA

David C. Martin, Los Angeles, CA

Robert E. Martin, Toledo, OH

W. Mike Martin, Berkeley, CA

Walter B. Martinez, Miami, FL

Thomas S. Marvel, San Juan, PR

Joseph V. Marzella, Wallingford, PA

Ronald L. Mason, Denver, CO

George Matsumoto, Oakland, CA

Edward H. Matthei, Chicago, IL

Robert F. Mattox, Boston, MA

Frank J. Matzke, St. Augustine, FL

John M. Maudlin-Jeronimo, Bethesda, MD

Laurie M. Maurer, Brooklyn, NY

Susan A. Maxman, Philadelphia, PA

Murvan M. Maxwell, Metairie, LA

Arthur May, New York, NY

Kenneth D. Maynard, Anchorage, AK

Charles Mc Cafferty, Saint Clair Shores, MI

Joe M. McCall, Dallas, TX

Michael A. McCarthy, New York, NY

A. S. McGaughan, Washington, DC

John M. McGinty, Houston, TX

Milton B. McGinty, Houston, TX

Richard A. McGinty, Hilton Hd Island, SC

James R. McGranahan, Lacey, WA

Herbert P. McKim, Wrightsville Beach, NC

Noel M. McKinnell, Boston, MA

H Roll McLaughlin, Carmel, IN

Charles F. McAfee, Wichita, KS

E. K. McCagg, II, Kirkland, WA

John McCartney, Washington, DC

Bruce McCarty, Knoxville, TN

Harlan E. McClure, Pendleton, SC

Wesley A. McClure, Raleigh, NC

Richard E. McCommons, Falls Church, VA

Robert E. McConnell, Tucson, AZ

Edward D. McCrary, Hillsborough, CA

M. Allen McCree, Austin, TX

Gerald M. McCue, Cambridge, MA

Grant G. McCullagh, Chicago, IL

James McCullar, New York, NY

Margaret McCurry, Chicago, IL

William A. McDonough, Charlottesville VA

Connie S. McFarland, Tulsa, OK

John W. McGough, Spokane, WA

David A. McKinley, Seattle, WA

Thomas L. McKittrick, College Station, TX

C. Andrew Andrew McLean, II, Atlanta, GA

James M. McManus, Glastonbury, CT

George A. McMath, Portland, OR

William G. McMinn, Coconut Grove, FL

E. Eean McNaughton Jr., New Orleans, LA

Carrell S. McNulty, Jr., Cincinnati, OH

E. Keith McPheeters, Auburn, AL

Fellows of The American Institute of Architects (Con't)

John M. McRae, Starkville, MS

Charles B. McReynolds, Newport News, VA

George C. Means Jr., Clemson, SC

Philip J. Meathe, Grosse Pte Farms, MI

David Meckel, San Francisco, CA

Henry G. Meier, Fishers, IN

Richard A. Meier, New York, NY

Carl R. Meinhardt, New York, NY

Lawrence P. Melillo, Louisville, KY

Roger C. Mellem, Port Republic, MD

R. A. Melting, New York, NY

John O. Merrill, Tiburon, CA

William Dickey Merrill, Carmel, CA

David R. Messersmith, Lubbock, TX

Robert C. Metcalf, Ann Arbor, MI

William H. Metcalf, McLean, VA

Andrew Metter, Evanston, IL

James H. Meyer, Richardson, TX

Kurt W. Meyer, Los Angeles, CA

Richard C. Meyer, Philadelphia, PA

Marshall D. Meyers, Pasadena, CA

Nancy A. Miao, New York, NY

Linda H. Michael, Charlottesville, VA

Constantine E. Michaelides, St. Louis, MO

Valerius Leo Michelson, Minneapolis, MN

Arnold Mikon, Detroit, MI

Juanita M. Mildenberg, Bethesda, MD

Don C. Miles, Seattle, WA

Daniel R. Millen Jr., Cherry Hill, NJ

David E. Miller, Seattle, WA

Ewing H. Miller, Port Republic, MD

George H. Miller, New York, NY

Henry F. Miller, Orange, CT

Hugh C. Miller, Richmond, VA

James W. Miller, Madison, WI

John F. Miller, Cambridge, MA

Joseph Miller, Washington, DC

L. Kirk Miller, San Francisco, CA

Leroy B. Miller, Santa Monica, CA

William C. Miller, Salt Lake City, UT

Edward I. Mills, New York, NY

Willis N. Mills, Jr., Ponte Vedra Beach, FL

Adolfo E. Miralles, Altadena, CA

Henry D. Mirick, Fairless Hills, PA

Dan S. Mitchell, St. Louis, MO

Ehrman B. Mitchell, Jr., Philadelphia, PA

Richard R. Moger, Port Washington, NY

Ronald L. Moline, Bourbonnais, IL

Robert B. Molseed, Annandale, VA

Lynn H. Molzan, Indianapolis, IN

Frank Montana, Dade City, FL

Joseph D. Monticciolo, Woodbury, NY

Curtis J. Moody, Columbus, OH

Thomas B. Moon, Rancho Santa Margarita, CA

Arthur C. Moore, Washington, DC

Barry M. Moore, Houston, TX

Gerald L. Moorhead, Houston, TX

Jesse O. Morgan, Jr., Shreveport, LA

Robert Lee Morgan, Port Townsend, WA

W. N. Morgan, Jacksonville, FL

Howard H. Morgridge, Newport Beach, CA

Lamberto G. Moris, San Francisco, CA

Seth I. Morris, Houston, TX

Lionel Morrison, Dallas, TX

John Morse, Seattle, WA

James R. Morter, Vail, CO

Allen D. Moses, Kirkland, WA

Robert Mosher, La Jolla, CA

Samuel Z. Moskowitz, Naples, FL

Eric O. Moss, Culver City, CA

G. Michael Mostoller, Princeton, NJ

Fellows of The American Institute of Architects (Con't)

Kenneth L. Motley, Roanoke, VA

John K. Mott, Alexandria, VA

Edward A. Moulthrop, Atlanta, GA

Jennifer T. Moulton, Denver, CO

Frederic D. Moyer, Northbrook, IL

Frank R. Mudano, Clearwater, FL

Theodore Mularz, Ashland, OR

Paul Muldawer, Atlanta, GA

John W. Mullen III, Dallas, TX

Rosemary F. Muller, Oakland, CA

Harold C. Munger, Toledo, OH

Frank W. Munzer, Clinton Corners, NY

Charles F. Murphy, Carefore, AZ

Frank N. Murphy, Clayton, MO

David G. Murray, Tulsa, OK

Stephen A. Muse, Washington, DC

Robert C. Mutchler, Fargo, ND

John V. Mutlow, Los Angeles, CA

Donald B. Myer, Washington, DC

John R. Myer, Tamworth, NH

Barton Myers, Beverly Hills, CA

Ralph E. Myers, Prairie Village, KS

N

Daniel J. Nacht, Fair Oaks, CA

Herbert N. Nadel, Los Angeles, CA

Chester Emil Nagel, Colorado Springs, CO

James L. Nagle, Chicago, IL

Louis Naidorf, Burbank, CA

Noboru Nakamura, Orinda, CA

C. S. Nakata, Colorado Springs, CO

Robert J. Nash, Oxon Hill, MD

Thomas M. Nathan, Memphis, TN

Kenneth H. Natkin, Esq., San Francisco, CA

James A. Neal, Greenville, SC

Paul R. Neel, San Luis Obispo, CA

Ibsen Nelsen, Vashon, WA

Edward H. Nelson, Tucson, AZ

James Richard Nelson, Wilmington, DE

John H. Nelson, Chicago, IL

T. C. Nelson, Kansas City, MO

Ede I. Nemeti, Houston, TX

Donald E. Neptune, Newport Beach, CA

John F. Nesholm, Seattle, WA

Barbara Neski, New York, NY

Julian J. Neski, New York, NY

Walter A. Netsch, Chicago, IL

Perry King Neubauer, Cambridge, MA

J. Victor Neuhaus, III, Hunt, TX

William O. Neuhaus, III, Houston, TX

David J. Neuman, Palo Alto, CA

Hans Neumann, Las Vegas, NV

S. Kenneth Neumann, Beverly Hills, MI

Peter Newlin, Chestertown, MD

Herbert S. Newman, New Haven, CT

Michael Newman, Winston-Salem, NC

Robert L. Newsom, Los Angeles, CA

Chartier C. Newton, Austin, TX

Doreve Nicholaeff, Osterville, MA

Robert Duncan Nicol, Oakland, CA

George Z. Nikolajevich, St. Louis, MO

Edward R. Niles, Malibu, CA

Ivey L. Nix, Atlanta, GA

Robert J. Nixon, Port Angeles, WA

George M. Notter Jr., Washington, DC

John M. Novack, Dallas, TX

Jimmie R. Nunn, Flagstaff, AZ

O

W. L. O'Brien, Jr., RTP, NC

L J. O'Donnell, Chicago, IL

Arthur F. O'Leary, County Louth

Paul Murff O'Neal Jr., Shreveport, LA

Fellows of The American Institute of Architects (Con't)

Charles W. Oakley, Pacific Palisades, CA

Gyo Obata, Saint Louis, MO

Jeffrey K. Ochsner, Seattle, WA

Robert A. Odermatt, Berkeley, CA

Mary L. Oehrlein, Washington, DC

Rolf H. Ohlhausen, New York, NY

Richard M. Olcott, New York, NY

Edward A. Oldziey, Wyckoff, NJ

P. S. Oles, Newton, MA

H. B. Olin, Chicago, IL

Donald E. Olsen, Berkeley, CA

Carole J. Olshavsky, Columbus, OH

James W. Olson, Seattle, WA

Herbert B. Oppenheimer, New York, NY

Edward L. Oremen, San Diego, CA

Robert E. Oringdulph, Portland, OR

Gordon D. Orr Jr., Madison, WI

David William Osler, Ann Arbor, MI

G. F. Oudens, Chevy Chase, MD

Raymond C. Ovresat, Wilmette, IL

P

C J. Paderewski III, San Diego, CA

Elizabeth Seward Padjen, Marblehead, MA

Gregory Palermo, Des Moines, IA

Joshua J. Pan, Sec Taipei, Taiwan

Solomon Pan, Tucson, AZ

Lester C. Pancoast, Miami, FL

John R. Pangrazio, Seattle, WA

Donald H. Panushka, Salt Lake City, UT

Dennis A. Paoletti, San Francisco, CA

Tician Papachristou, New York, NY

Laszlo Papp, New Canaan, CT

George C. Pappageorge, Chicago, IL

Nicholas A. Pappas, Richmond, VA

Ted P. Pappas, Jacksonville, FL

Charles J. Parise, Grosse Pointe Woods, MI

Ki Suh Park, Los Angeles, CA

Sharon C. Park, Arlington, VA

Alfred B. Parker, Gainesville, FL

Derek Parker, San Francisco, CA

Howard C. Parker, Dallas, TX

Leonard S. Parker, Minneapolis, MN

R C. Parrott, Knoxville, TN

Steven A. Parshall, Houston, TX

Giovanni Pasanella, New York, NY

C. H. Paseur, Houston, TX

Joseph Passonneau, Washington, DC

Piero Patri, San Francisco, CA

Allen L. Patrick, Columbus, OH

S. Glen Paulsen, Ann Arbor, MI

Charles Harrison Pawley, Coral Gables, FL

Thomas M. Payette, Boston, MA

H. Morse Payne, Lincoln, MA

Richard W. Payne, Houston, TX

George Clayton Pearl, Albuquerque, NM

Bryce Pearsall, Phoenix, AZ

Charles Almond Pearson Jr., Arlington, VA

J. Norman Pease, Jr., Charlotte, NC

John G. Pecsok, Indianapolis, IN

William Pedersen, Jr., New York, NY

Gerard W. Peer, Charlotte, NC

William R. Peery, Clearwater, FL

I. M. Pei, New York, NY

Maris Peika, Toluca Lake, CA

John W. Peirce, Topsfield, MA

Cesar Pelli, New Haven, CT

William M. Pena, Houston, TX

Thompson E. Penney, Charleston, SC

David L. Perkins, Lafayette, LA

G. Holmes Perkins, Philadelphia, PA

L. Bradford Perkins, New York, NY

Norman K. Perttula, Aurora, OH

Fellows of The American Institute of Architects (Con't)

Stuart K. Pertz, New York, NY

Robert W. Peters, Albuquerque, NM

Carolyn S. Peterson, San Antonio, TX

Charles E. Peterson, Philadelphia, PA

Leonard A. Peterson, Chicago, IL

Edward G. Petrazio, Spanish Fort, AL

Eleanore Pettersen, Saddle River, NJ

Jay S. Pettitt Jr., Beulah, MI

Mark A. Pfaller, Elm Grove, WI

Norman Pfeiffer, Los Angeles, CA

J. D. Pfluger, Austin, TX

Barton Phelps, Los Angeles, CA

Frederick F. Phillips, Chicago, IL

W. Irving Phillips, Jr., Houston, TX

J. Almont Pierce, Falls Church, VA

John Allen Pierce, Dallas, TX

Walter S. Pierce, Lexington, WA

Raymond A. Pigozzi, Evanston, IL

George J. Pillorge, Oxford, MD

Robert J. Piper, Winnetka, IL

Carl W. Pirscher, Windsor, ON

John W. Pitman, Santa Barbara, CA

Peter A. Piven, Philadelphia, PA

Elizabeth Plater-Zyberk, Miami, FL

Charles A. Platt, New York, NY

Kalvin J. Platt, Sausalito, CA

G. Gray Plosser, Jr., Birmingham, AL

Jan Hird Pokorny, New York, NY

Lee A. Polisano, London

William M. Polk, Seattle, WA

Wilson Pollock, Cambridge, MA

James Stewart Polshek, New York, NY

Ralph Pomerance, New York, NY

Leason F. Pomeroy, III, Santa Ana, CA

Lee H. Pomeroy, New York, NY

Lynn S. Pomeroy, Sacramento, CA

Gerrard S. Pook, Bronx, NY

Samuel D. Popkin, West Bloomfield, MI

William L. Porter, Cambridge, MA

John C. Portman, Jr., Atlanta, GA

Penny H. Posedly, Phoenix, AZ

Raymond G. Post Jr., Baton Rouge, LA

Boone Powell, San Antonio, TX

James Pratt, Dallas, TX

Antoine Predock, Albuquerque, NM

William T. Priestley, Lake Forest, IL

Arnold J. Prima, Jr., Washington, DC

Harold E. Prinz, Dallas, TX

Donald Prowler, Philadelphia, PA

Homer L. Puderbaugh, Lincoln, NE

David A. Pugh, Portland, OR

William L Pulgram, Atlanta, GA

James G. Pulliam, Pasadena, CA

Joe T. Pursell, Jackson, MS

Michael Pyatok, Oakland, CA

Q

Jerry L. Quebe, Chicago, IL

Robert W. Quigley, San Diego, CA

Marcel Quimby, Dallas, TX

Michael L. Quinn, Washington, DC

Richard W. Quinn, Avon, CT

R

Martin D. Raab, New York, NY

Bruce A. Race, Berkeley, CA

John A. Raeber, San Francisco, CA

Craig E. Rafferty, St. Paul, MN

George E. Rafferty, St. Paul, MN

Richard J. Rafferty, St. Paul, MN

Lemuel Ramos, Miami, FL

Peter A. Rand, Minneapolis, MN

Terry Rankine, Cambridge, MA

Raymond R. Rapp, Galveston, TX

Ralph Rapson, Minneapolis, MN

Howard Terry Rasco, Little Rock, AR

Peter T. Rasmussen, Tacoma, WA

Fellows of The American Institute of Architects (Con't)

John K. Rauch, Jr., Philadelphia, PA

John G. Rauma, Minneapolis, MN

William L. Rawn, Boston, MA

James T. Ream, San Francisco, CA

Charles Redmon, Cambridge, MA

Louis G. Redstone, Southfield, MI

Vernon Reed, Liberty, MO

William R. Reed, Tacoma, WA

Henry S. Reeder Jr., Cambridge, MA

Frank Blair Reeves, Gainesville, FL

I. S. K. Reeves, V, Winter Park, FL

Roscoe Reeves Jr., Chevy Chase, MD

Victor A. Regnier, Los Angeles, CA

Patrick C. Rehse, Phoenix, AZ

Pierce K. Reibsamen, Los Angeles, CA

Leonard H. Reinke, Oshkosh, WI

Ilmar Reinvald, Tacoma, WA

John Rex, Carpinteria, CA

M. Garland Reynolds Jr., Gainesville, GA

David A. Rhodes, Memphis, TN

James W. Rhodes, New York, NY

Kenneth Ricci, New York, NY

Paul J. Ricciuti, Youngstown, OH

David E. Rice, San Diego, CA

Richard L. Rice, Raleigh, NC

James W. Rich, Tulsa, OK

Lisle F. Richards, San Jose, CA

Heidi A. Richardson, Sausalito, CA

Walter J. Richardson, Newport Beach, CA

Charles H. Richter, Jr., Baltimore, MD

David R. Richter, Corpus Christi, TX

Hans Riecke, Haiku, HI

James V. Righter, Boston, MA

Jefferson B. Riley, Centerbrook, CT

Ronnette Riley, New York, NY

David N. Rinehart, La Jolla, CA

David Rinehart, Los Angeles, CA

M. Jack Rinehart, Jr., Charlottesville, VA

Mark W. Rios, Los Angeles, CA

Darrel D. Rippeteau, Delray Beach, FL

Dahlen K. Ritchey, Bradfordwoods, PA

P. Richard Rittelmann, Butler, PA

James W. Ritter, Alexandria, VA

Richard E. Ritz, Portland, OR

I. L. Roark, Lawrence, KS

Jack Robbins, Berkeley, CA

Darryl Roberson, San Francisco, CA

Jaquelin T. Robertson, New York, NY

C. David Robinson, San Francisco, CA

J. W. Robinson, Atlanta, GA

Harry G. Robinson III, Washington, DC

Kevin Roche, Hamden, CT

Garth Rockcastle, Minneapolis, MN

George T. Rockrise, AICP, ASLA, Glen Ellen, CA

Burton L. Rockwell, San Francisco, CA

Kenneth A. Rodrigues, San Jose, CA

Carl D. Roehling, Detroit, MI

Chester E. Roemer, St. Louis, MO

Ralph J. Roesling, II, San Diego, CA

R. G. Roessner, Austin, TX

Archibald C. Rogers, Baltimore, MD

James G. Rogers, III, New York, NY

John D. Rogers, Asheville, NC

John B. Rogers, Denver, CO

Craig W. Roland, Santa Rosa, CA

B. F. Romanowitz, Lexington, KY

James G. Rome, Corpus Christi, TX

Benjamin T. Rook, Charlotte, NC

Robert W. Root, Denver, CO

Richard M. Rosan, Washington, DC

William A. Rose, Jr., White Plains, NY

Alan Rosen, Palm Desert, CA

Alan R. Rosen, Lake Forest, IL

Manuel M. Rosen, La Jolla, CA

Arthur Rosenblatt, New York, NY

Norman Rosenfeld, New York, NY

Edgar B. Ross, Tiburon, CA

Fellows of The American Institute of Architects (Con't)

James S. Rossant, New York, NY

Louis A. Rossetti, Birmingham, MI

Harold Roth, New Haven, CT

Richard Roth, Jr., Freeport,

Edward N. Rothe, Edison, NJ

Martha L. Rothman, Boston, MA

Richard Rothman, Rising Fawn, GA

Bernard B. Rothschild, Atlanta, GA

Bernard Rothzeid, New York, NY

Maurice Rotival, Paris, France

Michael Rotondi, Los Angeles, CA

Lauren L. Rottet, Los Angeles, CA

Judith L. Rowe, Oakland, CA

Ralph T. Rowland, Cheshire, CT

Albert W. Rubeling, Jr., Towson, MD

John Ruble, Santa Monica, CA

J. Ronald Rucker, Tyler, TX

J. W. Rudd, Knoxville, TN

Gordon E. Ruehl, Spokane, WA

Evett J. Ruffcorn, Seattle, WA

John A. Ruffo, San Francisco, CA

Herman O. Ruhnau, Riverside, CA

Peter L. Rumpel, Saint Augustine, FL

William W. Rupe, St. Louis, MO

T. T. Russell, Miami, FL

Walter A. Rutes, Scottsdale, AZ

H. Mark Ruth, Agana, Guam

Roger N. Ryan, N. Canton, OH

James E. Rydeen, Rio Verde, AZ

Donald P. Ryder, New Rochelle, NY

S

Werner Sabo, Chicago, IL

Harold G. Sadler, San Diego, CA

Moshe Safdie, Somerville, MA

Carol S. Sakata, Honolulu, HI

Raj Saksena, Bristol, RI

F. Cuthbert Salmon, Stillwater, OK

Nathaniel W. Sample, Madison, WI

Peter Samton, New York, NY

Danny Samuels, Houston, TX

Gil A. Sanchez, Santa Cruz, CA

James J. Sanders, Seattle, WA

Linda Sanders, Walnut, CA

Donald Sandy, Jr., San Francisco, CA

Adele N. Santos, San Francisco, CA

Sanz, Santurce, PR

Charles M. Sappenfield, Sanibel, FL

Angel C. Saqui, Coral Gables, FL

Louis Sauer, Pittsburgh, PA

Louis R. Saur, Clayton, MO

Robert W. Sawyer, Wilmington, NC

Peter M. Saylor, Philadelphia, PA

Sam Scaccia, Chicago, IL

Joseph J. Scalabrin, Columbus, OH

Mario L. Schack, Baltimore, MD

K. M. Schaefer, Kirkwood, MO

Robert J. Schaefer, Wichita, KS

Walter Schamu, Baltimore, MD

David Scheatzle, Tempe, AZ

James A. Scheeler, Reston, VA

Jeffrey Allen Scherer, Minneapolis, MN

G. G. Schierle, Los Angeles, CA

Arthur A. Schiller, Manhasset, NY

Don P. Schlegel, Albuquerque, NM

Frank Schlesinger, Washington, DC

Jon R. Schleuning, Portland, OR

John I. Schlossman, Hubbard Woods, IL

Roger Schluntz, Albuquerque, NM

Mildred F. Schmertz, New York, NY

Fred C. Schmidt, Oklahoma City, OK

Wayne S. Schmidt, Indianapolis, IN

R. Christian Schmitt, Charleston, SC

Herbert W. Schneider, Scottsdale, AZ

Walter Scholer, Jr., Fort Myers, FL

John P. Schooley, Columbus, OH

Fellows of The American Institute of Architects (Con't)

Barnett P. Schorr, Seattle, WA

Charles F. Schrader, San Rafael, CA

Douglas F. Schroeder, Chicago, IL

Kenneth A. Schroeder, Chicago, IL

John H. Schruben, North Bethesda, MD

George A. D. Schuett, Glendale, WI

Van Fossen Schwab, Towson, MD

Kenneth E. Schwartz, San Luis Obispo, CA

Alan Schwartzman, Paris, France

Charles E. Schwing, Baton Rouge, LA

Alan D. Sclater, Seattle, WA

David M. Scott, Pullman, WA

William W. Scott, Taylors Falls, MN

Der Scutt, New York, NY

Jim W. Sealy, Dallas, TX

Linda Searl, Chicago, IL

Thomas J. Sedgewick, Clio, MI

Paul Segal, New York, NY

Lawrence P. Segrue, Visalia, CA

E. J. Seibert, Boca Grande, FL

Alexander Seidel, Belvedere, CA

Larry D. Self, St. Louis, MO

Theodore Seligson, Kansas City, MO

Bruce M. Sellery, Marina Del Rey, CA

Dale E. Selzer, Dallas, TX

John C. Senhauser, Cincinnati, OH

Ronald S. Senseman, Silver Spring, MD

Jerome M. Seracuse, Colorado Springs, CO

Diane Serber, Old Chatham, NY

Phillip K. Settecase, Salem, OR

Betty Lee Seydler-Hepworth, Franklin, MI

Richard S. Sharpe, Norwich, CT

John A. Sharratt, Boston, MA

James L. Shay, San Rafael, CA

Leo G. Shea, Leland, MI

John P. Sheehy, Mill Valley, CA

George C. Sheldon, Portland, OR

W. Overton Shelmire, Dallas, TX

Carol Shen, Berkeley, CA

John V. Sheoris, Grosse Pointe, MI

Herschel E. Shepard, Atlantic Beach, FL

Hugh Shepley, Manchester, MA

Patricia C. Sherman, Concord, NH

Takashi Shida, Santa Monica, CA

Roger D. Shiels, Portland, OR

Edward H. Shirley, Atlanta, GA

Philip A. Shive, Charlotte, NC

George Whiteside Shupee, Arlington, TX

Jack T. Sidener, Shatin, New Territories

Paul G. Sieben, Toledo, OH

Lloyd H. Siegel, Washington, DC

Robert H. Siegel, New York, NY

Charles M. Sieger, Miami, FL

Henry N. Silvestri, Corona Del Mar, CA

Cathy J. Simon, San Francisco, CA

Mark Simon, Centerbrook, CT

Lawrence L. Simons, Santa Rosa, CA

Donal R. Simpson, Dallas, TX

Robert T. Simpson, Jr., Berkeley, CA

Scott Simpson, Cambridge, MA

Howard F. Sims, Detroit, MI

Jerome J. Sincoff, St. Louis, MO

Donald I. Singer, Fort Lauderdale, FL

E. Crichton Singleton, Kansas City, MO

Charles S. Sink, Denver, CO

William H. Sippel, Jr., Allison Park, PA

Michael M. Sizemore, Atlanta, GA

Ronald L. Skaggs, Dallas, TX

Norma M. Sklarek, Pacific Palisades, CA

Gary Skog, Southfield, MI

Murray A. Slama, Walnut Creek, CA

Clifton M. Smart, Jr., Fayetteville, AR

Saul C. Smiley, Minnetonka, MN

Adrian D. Smith, Chicago, IL

Fellows of The American Institute of Architects (Con't)

Arthur Smith, Southfield, MI

Bill D. Smith, Dallas, TX

Bruce H. Smith, Pontiac, MI

Christopher J. Smith, Honolulu, HI

Cole Smith, Dallas, TX

Colin L. M. Smith, Cambridge, MA

Darrell L. Smith, Eugene, OR

Fleming W. Smith, Jr., Nashville, TN

Frank Folsom Smith, Sarasota, FL

Hamilton P. Smith, Garden City, NY

Harwood K. Smith, Dallas, TX

Ivan H. Smith, Jacksonville, FL

John R. Smith, Ketchum, ID

Joseph N. Smith, III, Atlanta, GA

Macon S. Smith, Raleigh, NC

Stephen B. Smith, Salt Lake City, UT

T. Clayton Smith, Baton Rouge, LA

Tyler Smith, Hartford, CT

Whitney R. Smith, Sonoma, CA

David I. Smotrich, New York, NY

Neil H. Smull, Boise, ID

Richard Snibbe, New York, NY

Julie V. Snow, Minneapolis, MN

Walter H. Sobel, Chicago, IL

Daniel Solomon, San Francisco, CA

Richard J. Solomon, Chicago, IL

Stuart B. Solomon, Watertown, MA

James Hamilton Somes Jr., Portsmouth, NH

John R. Sorrenti, Mineola, NY

Charles B. Soule, Montgomery Village, MD

Michael Southworth, Berkeley, CA

Edward A. Sovik, Northfield, MN

George S. Sowden, Fort Worth, TX

Marvin Sparn, Boulder, CO

Laurinda H. Spear, Miami, FL

Lawrence W. Speck, Austin, TX

Michael H. Spector, New Hyde Park, NY

John H. Spencer, Hampton, VA

Tomas H. Spiers, Jr., Camp Hill, PA

Pat Y. Spillman, Dallas, TX

Robert A. Spillman, Bethlehem, PA

Donald E. Sporleder, South Bend, IN

Joseph G. Sprague, Dallas, TX

Paul D. Spreiregen, Washington, DC

Bernard P. Spring, Brookline, MA

Everett G. Spurling Jr., Bethesda, MD

Dennis W. Stacy, Dallas, TX

Alfred M. Staehli, Portland, OR

Richard P. Stahl, Springfield, MO

Raymond F. Stainback, Jr., Atlanta, GA

Duffy B. Stanley, El Paso, TX

William J. Stanley, III, Atlanta, GA

Jane M. Stansfeld, Austin, TX

Michael J. Stanton, San Francisco, CA

Earl M. Starnes, Cedar Key, FL

Frank A. Stasiowski, Newton, MA

Donald J. Stastny, Portland, OR

Russell L. Stecker, Montpelier, VT

John E. Stefany, Tampa, FL

Peter Steffian, Boston, MA

Charles W. Steger Jr., Blacksburg, VA

Douglas Steidl, Akron, OH

Carl Stein, New York, NY

Goodwin B. Steinberg, San Jose, CA

Robert T. Steinberg, San Jose, CA

Ralph Steinglass, New York, NY

Henry Steinhardt, Mercer Island, WA

Douglas E. Steinman, Jr., Beaumont, TX

James A. Stenhouse, Charlotte, NC

Donald J. Stephens, Berlin, NY

Michael J. Stepner, San Diego, CA

Robert A. M. Stern, New York, NY

William F. Stern, Houston, TX

Preston Stevens, Jr., Atlanta, GA

Fellows of The American Institute of Architects (Con't)

James M. Stevenson, Highland Park, IL

W. Cecil Steward, Lincoln, NE

William W. Stewart, Clayton, MO

Sherwood Stockwell, Wolcott, CO

Claude Stoller, Berkeley, CA

Neal P Stowe Salt Lake City, UT

H. T. Stowell, Western Springs, IL

Ronald A. Straka, Denver, CO

Michael J. Stransky, Salt Lake City, UT

Frank Straub, Troy, MI

Carl A. Strauss, Cincinnati, OH

John R. Street Jr., Marietta, GA

Arthur V. Strock, Santa Ana, CA

Hugh Asher Stubbins, Jr., Cambridge, MA

Sidney W. Stubbs, Jr., Mount Pleasant, SC

Donald L. Stull, Boston, MA

Robert S. Sturgis, Weston, MA

Erik Sueberkrop, San Francisco, CA

Marvin D. Suer, Willow Grove, PA

John W. Sugden, Park City, UT

Douglas R. Suisman, Santa Monica, CA

Edward Sullam, Honolulu, HI

Patrick M. Sullivan, Claremont, CA

Gene R. Summers, Cloverdale, CA

Alan R. Sumner, Saint Louis, MO

Richard P. Sundberg, Seattle, WA

Donald R. Sunshine, Blacksburg, VA

Eugene L. Surber, Atlanta, GA

Charles R. Sutton, Honolulu, HI

Sharon E. Sutton, Seattle, WA

George Suyama, Seattle, WA

Eugene C. Swager, Peoria, IL

Robert M. Swatt, San Francisco, CA

Earl Swensson, Nashville, TN

H. H. Swinburne, Philadelphia, PA

John M. Syvertsen, Chicago, IL

T

William B. Tabler, New York, NY

Edgar Tafel, Venice, FL

Marvin Taff, Beverly Hills, CA

Ray Takata, Sacramento, CA

Francis T. Taliaferro, Santa Monica, CA

R. H. Tan, Spokane, WA

Ted Tokio Tanaka, Marina Del Rey, CA

Virginia W. Tanzmann, Pasadena, CA

Charles R. Tapley, Houston, TX

A. Anthony Anthony Tappe, Boston, MA

H. Harold Tarleton, Greenville, SC

D. Coder Taylor, Glenview, IL

Marilyn J. Taylor, New York, NY

Richard L. Taylor, Jr., Atlanta, GA

Walter Q. Taylor, Jacksonville, FL

Thomas H. Teasdale, Kirkwood, MO

Clinton C. Ternstrom, Los Angeles, CA

Roland Terry, Mt Vernon, WA

Robert L. Tessier, Yarmouth Port, MA

B C. Tharp, Montgomery, TX

Dorwin A. J. Thomas, Boston, MA

James B. Thomas, Houston, TX

James L. Thomas, Spartanburg, SC

Joseph F. Thomas, Pasadena, CA

Benjamin Thompson, Cambridge, MA

David C. Thompson, San Diego, CA

Milo H. Thompson, Minneapolis, MN

Robert L. Thompson, Portland, OR

Warren D. Thompson, Fresno, CA

Charles B. Thomsen, Houston, TX

Duane Thorbeck, Minneapolis, MN

Karl Thorne, Gainesville, FL

Oswald H. Thorson, Marco, FL

Stanley Tigerman, Chicago, IL

Patrick Tillett, Portland, OR

James H. Timberlake, Philadelphia, PA

Fellows of The American Institute of Architects (Con't)

Robert H. Timme, Los Angeles, CA

Leslie D. Tincknell, Saginaw, MI

James D. Tittle, Abilene, TX

Philip E. Tobey, Reston, VA

Calvin J. Tobin, Highland Park, IL

Logic Tobola, II, El Campo, TX

Anderson Todd, Houston, TX

David F. M. Todd, New York, NY

Thomas A. Todd, Jamestown, RI

John Tomassi, Chicago, IL

James E. Tomblinson, Flint, MI

Frank Tomsick, San Francisco, CA

Coulson Tough, The Woodlands, TX

Dennis T. Toyomura, Honolulu, HI

Jack Train, Chicago, IL

Karl E. Treffinger, Sr., West Linn, OR

Kenneth Treister, Coconut Grove, FL

David M. Trigiani, Jackson, MS

William H. Trogdon, Olga, WA

Leroy Troyer, Mishawaka, IN

Charles N. Tseckares, Boston, MA

Edward T. M. Tsoi, Arlington, MA

Seab A. Tuck, III, Nashville, TN

Jack R. Tucker Jr., Memphis, TN

Thomas B. Tucker, San Diego, CA

Richard L. Tully, Columbus, OH

Emanuel N. Turano, Boca Raton, FL

John Gordon Turnbull, San Francisco, CA

Thomas P. Turner, Jr., Charlotte, NC

Wilbur H. Tusler, Jr., Kentfield, CA

James L. Tyler, Pacific Palisades, CA

Robert Tyler, Tarzana, CA

Anne G. Tyng, Philadelphia, PA

U

Edward K. Uhlir, Chicago, IL

Kenneth A. Underwood, Philadelphia, PA

Dean F. Unger, Sacramento, CA

Denorval Unthank, Jr., Eugene, OR

Robert H. Uyeda, Los Angeles, CA

V

Joseph D. Vaccaro, Los Angeles, CA

Edward Vaivoda, Jr., Portland, OR

William E. Valentine, San Francisco, CA

Joseph M. Valerio, Chicago, IL

William L. Van Alen, Wilmington, DE

Robert Van Deusen, Grand Junction, CO

George V. Van Fossen Schwab, Baltimore, MD

Thomas Van Housen, Minneapolis, MN

Peter van Dijk, Cleveland, OH

Harold F. VanDine Jr., Birmingham, M

Johannes VanTilburg, Santa Monica, CA

Mitchell Vanbourg, Berkeley, CA

Harutun Vaporciyan, Huntington Woods, MI

Harold R. Varner, Berkley, MI

Leonard M. Veitzer, San Diego, CA

Thomas W. Ventulett, Atlanta, GA

Robert Venturi, Philadelphia, PA

Shirley J. Vernon, Philadelphia, PA

William R. Vick, Sacramento, CA

Robert L. Vickery, Charlottesville, VA

Wilmont Vickrey, Chicago, IL

Gregory D. Villanueva, Los Angeles, CA

John Vinci, Chicago, IL

Rafael Vinoly, New York, NY

Stephen Vogel, Detroit, MI

Leonard W. Volk II, Dallas, TX

A. R. Von Brock, Buchanan, VA

Robert J. Von Dohlen, W Hartford, CT

Richard L. Von Luhrte, Denver, CO

Bartholome Voorsanger, New York, NY

R. Randall Vosbeck, Vail, CO

Fellows of The American Institute of Architects (Con't)

William F. Vosbeck, Alexandria, VA

Thomas R. Vreeland, Century City, CA

R. E. Vrooman, College Station, TX

W

Hobart D. Wagener, Coronado, CA

William J. Wagner, Dallas Center, IA

John G. Waite, Albany, NY

Lawrence G. Waldron, Mercer Island, WA

Bruce M. Walker, Spokane, WA

Kenneth H. Walker, New York, NY

David A. Wallace, Philadelphia, PA

David D. Wallace, Westport, MA

Donald Q. Wallace, Lexington, KY

Les Wallach, Seattle, WA

Charles G. Walsh, Los Angeles, CA

Lloyd G. Walter Jr., Winston Salem, NC

W. G. Wandelmaier, New York, NY

Sheldon D. Wander, New York, NY

R. J. Warburton, Coral Gables, FL

G. T. Ward, Fairfax, VA

Robertson Ward Jr., Boston, MA

C. E. Ware, Rockford, IL

John Carl Warnecke, San Francisco, CA

Charles H. Warner, Jr., Nyack, NY

Clyde K. Warner, Jr., Louisville, KY

William D. Warner, Exeter, RI

Sharon F. Washburn, Bethesda, MD

Robert E. Washington, Richmond, VA

Barry L. Wasserman, Sacramento, CA

Joseph Wasserman, Southfield, MA

David H. Watkins, Bellaire, TX

Donald R. Watson, Trumbull, CT

Raymond L. Watson, Newport Beach, CA

William J. Watson, LaJolla, CA

John L. Webb, Ponchatoula, LA

P. R. Webber, Rutland, VT

Arthur M. Weber, Aiea, HI

Frederick S. Webster, Cazenovia, NY

C. R. Wedding, St. Petersburg, FL

Benjamin H. Weese, Chicago, IL

Cynthia Weese, Chicago, IL

Gary K. Weeter, Dallas, TX

Bryce Adair Weigand, Dallas, TX

Joe Neal Weilenman, Pago Pago, AS

Nicholas H. Weingarten, Chicago, IL

Amy Weinstein, Washington, DC

Edward Weinstein, Seattle, WA

Jane Weinzapfel, Boston, MA

Gerald G. Weisbach, San Francisco, CA

Sarelle T. Weisberg, New York, NY

Steven F. Weiss, Chicago, IL

Martha L. Welborne, Los Angeles, CA

Frank D. Welch, Dallas, TX

John A. Welch, Tuskegee, AL

William P. Wenzler, Milwaukee, WI

Helge Westermann, Cambridge, MA

Merle T. Westlake, Lexington, MA

Paul E. Westlake, Jr., Cleveland, OH

I. Donald Weston, Brooklyn, NY

Charles H. Wheatley, Charlotte, NC

C. Herbert Wheeler, State College, PA

Daniel H. Wheeler, Chicago, IL

James H. Wheeler Jr., Abilene, TX

Kenneth D. Wheeler, Lake Forest, IL

Richard H. Wheeler, Los Angeles, CA

Murray Whisnant, Charlotte, NC

Arthur B. White, Havertown, PA

George M. White, Bethesda, MD

Janet Rothberg White, Bethesda, MD

Norval C. White, Salisbury, CT

Samuel G. White, New York, NY

Stephen Q. Whitney, Detroit, MI

Leonard S. Wicklund, Long Grove, IL

Fellows of The American Institute of Architects (Con't)

Chester A. Widom, Santa Monica, CA

William Wiese, II, Shelburne, VT

E. D. Wilcox, Tyler, TX

Jerry Cooper Wilcox, Little Rock, AR

Gordon L. Wildermuth, Greeley, PA

James E. Wiley, Dallas, TX

Charles E. Wilkerson, Richmond, VA

Joseph A. Wilkes, Annapolis, MD

Michael B. Wilkes, San Diego, CA

Barbara E. Wilks, Baltimore, MD

Paul Willen, Yorktown Heights, NY

A. Richard Williams, Saint Ignace, MI

Allison G. Williams, San Francisco, CA

Daniel E. Williams, Coconut Grove, FL

E. Stewart Williams, Palm Springs, CA

F. Carter Williams, Raleigh, NC

Frank Williams, New York, NY

George Thomas Williams, Kitty Hawk, NC

Harold L. Williams, Los Angeles, CA

Homer L. Williams, Riverside, MO

John G. Williams, Fayetteville, AR

Lorenzo D. Williams, Minneapolis, MN

Mark F. Williams, Ambler, PA

Roger B. Williams, Seattle, WA

Terrance R. Williams, Washington, DC

Tod C. Williams, New York, NY

W. Gene Williams, The Woodlands, TX

Wayne R. Williams, Harmony, CA

Beverly A. Willis, New York, NY

Michael E. Willis, San Francisco, CA

John C. Wilmot, Damascus, MD

John L. Wilson, Boston, MA

John E. Wilson, Richmond, VA

William D. Wilson, Bridgehampton, NY

Steven R. Winkel, Berkeley, CA

Jon Peter Winkelstein, San Francisco, CA

John H. Winkler, Verbank, NY

Paul D. Winslow, Phoenix, AZ

Arch R. Winter, Mobile, AL

Steven Winter, Norwalk, CT

Marjorie M. Wintermute, Lake Oswego, OR

Norman E. Wirkler, Denver, CO

Joseph J. Wisnewski, Alexandria, VA

Gayland B. Witherspoon, Pendleton, SC

Charles Witsell, Jr., Little Rock, AR

Gordon G. Wittenberg, Little Rock, AR

Fritz Woehle, Birmingham, AL

Robert L. Wold, Hilton Head, SC

Martin F. Wolf, Wilmette, IL

Richard Wolf, San Mateo, CA

Harry C. Wolf, III, Malibu, CA

Gin D. Wong, Los Angeles, CA

Kellogg H. Wong, New York, NY

Carolina Y. Woo, San Francisco, CA

George C. Woo, Dallas, TX

Kyu S. Woo, Cambridge, MA

H. A. Wood, III, Boston, MA

John M. Woodbridge, Sonoma, CA

David Geoffrey Woodcock, College Station, TX

David Woodhouse, Chicago, IL

Robert S. Woodhurst III, Augusta, GA

Stanford Woodhurst Jr., Augusta, GA

Thomas E. Woodward, Buena Vista, CO

Evans Woollen, Indianapolis, IN

J. R. Wooten, Fort Worth, TX

John C. Worsley, Portland, OR

David H. Wright, Seattle, WA

George S. Wright, Fort Worth, TX

Henry L. Wright, Canby, OR

John L. Wright, Redmond, WA

Marcellus Wright, Jr., Richmond, VA

Rodney H. Wright, Liberty, KY

Thomas W. D. Wright, Washington, DC

Scott W. Wyatt, Seattle, WA

Fellows of The American Institute of Architects (Con't)

Y

Jack R. Yardley, Dallas, TX

John L. Yaw, Aspen, CO

Zeno Lanier Yeates, Memphis, TN

Raymond W. Yeh, Honolulu, HI

Ronald W. Yeo, Corona Del Mar, CA

David N. Yerkes, Washington, DC

William R. Yost, Portland, OR

Clayton Young, Seattle, WA

Joseph L. Young, Clemson, SC

Theodore J. Young, Greenwich, CT

Hachiro Yuasa, Orleans, CA

Robert J. Yudell, Santa Monica, CA

Z

Saul Zaik, Portland, OR

H. Alan Zeigel, Denver, CO

J. Zemanek, Houston, TX

Golden J. Zenon Jr., Omaha, NE

Robert L. Ziegelman, Birmingham, MI

Raymond Ziegler, Altadena, CA

Frank Zilm, Kansas City, MO

John J. Zils, Chicago, IL

Bernard B. Zimmerman, Los Angeles, CA

Gary V. Zimmerman, Milwaukee, WI

Thomas A. Zimmerman, Rochester, NY

Hugh M. Zimmers, Philadelphia, PA

Peter Jay Zweig, Houston, TX

Source: American Institute of Architects

Too often, we confuse
design with marketability
– a product with a label
that tries to tell us that the
product is a 'good design.'

Deborah Berke

Fellows of the American Society of Interior Designers

The American Society of Interior Designers (ASID) grants fellowship to those members who have made notable and substantial contributions to the profession and society. The following individuals are current, active fellows of the ASID.

Stanley Abercrombie
Dan Acito
Stephen W. Ackerman
Gail Adams
Joy E. Adcock
Estelle Alpert
Jerry R. Alsobrook
William F. Andrews
Ellen Angell
Robert H. Angle*
Robert A. Arehart
Warren G. Arnett
Anita Baltimore
David Barrett
Nancy Hoff Barsotti
Jeannine Bazer-Schwartz
Tamara A. Bazzle
Roy F. Beal
Marjorie A. Bedell
Frank Lee Berry
Hal F.B. Birchfield
Adriana Bitter
Edwin Bitter*
Joan Blutter
Penny Bonda
William D. Bowden
Blair S. Bowen
Susan Bradford
Bruce J. Brigham
Everett Brown
C. Dudley Brown
R. Michael Brown
Walton E. Brown*
Mary A. Bryan
Eleanor Brydone

Joyce A. Burke-Jones
David M. Butler
Rosalyn Cama
Orville V. Carr
Elizabeth M. Castleman
Juliana M. Catlin
Rita St.Clair
Carl E. Clark
John P. Conron
Loverne C. Cordes
Herbert Cordier
Jini Costello
Virginia W. Courtenay
P.A. Dale
Hortense Davis
Robert John Dean
Hon C. Doxiadis*
Dede Draper
Hilda M. East
H. Gerard Ebert
Barbara Ebstein
Garrett Eckbo*
Arlis Ede
Martin Elinoff
John Elmo
Joel M. Ergas
Sammye J. Erickson
Adele Faulkner
Jon J. Fields
John G. Ford
Thomas Frank
Charles D. Gandy
Marion Gardiner
Francis J. Geck*
Alexander Girard*

Fellows of the American Society of Interior Designers (Con't)

Judy Girod

Milton Glaser

Thomas C. Grabowski

Theodora Kim Graham

Stephen Greenberger

Roberta S. Griffin

Olga Gueft*

Rita C. Guest

David W. Hall

Lawrence Halprin*

James M. Halverson

William D. Hamilton*

A. Niolon Hampton

Patricia Harvey

Dennis Haworth

Dorothy G. Helmer

Albert E. Herbert

Fred B. Hershey

Joseph P. Horan

Elizabeth B. Howard

Nina Hughes

Dorian Hunter

H. Cliff Ivester

Barbara L. Jacobs

Sarah B. Jenkins

Connie Johannes

Wallace R. Jonason

Richard W. Jones

Henry Jordan

Henri V. Jova

Franklin S. Judson*

Janet E. Kane

Mary V. Knackstedt

Binnie Kramer

Karlyn Kuper

Anita M. Laird*

Hugh L. Latta

Dennis W. Leczinski

Robert S. Lindenthal

Boyd L. Loendorf

Michael Love

Odette Lucck

Ruth K. Lynford

William M. Manly

Helen Masoner

James E. McIntosh

James Mezrano

John Richard Miller

Thomas H. Miller

Susan I. Mole

Kathy Ford Montgomery

Mark Nelson

Roi C. Nevaril

Linda Newton

W. E. Noffke

Suzanne Patterson

Lawrence Peabody

Edward J. Perrault

BJ Peterson

H. Albert Phibbs

Dianne H. Pilgrim*

Norman Polsky*

Betty J. Purvis

Catharine G. Rawson

William Dunn Ray

Martha Garriott Rayle

Pedro Rodriguez

Agnes H. Rogers

Jack G. Ruthazer

Chester F. Sagenkahn

Barbara A. Sauerbrey

Janet S. Schirn

E. Williard Schurz

Irving D. Schwartz

Otho S. Shaw

James L. Simpson

Theodore A. Simpson

Edna A. Smith

James Merrick Smith

Sandra H. Sober

Jerrold Sonet*

Michael Sorrentino*

Fellows of the American Society of Interior Designers (Con't)

Beulah G. Spiers
Paul D. Spreiregen*
Edward H. Springs
Russell M. Stanley
Ed Starr
Karl L. Steinhauser
Deborah Steinmetz
C. Eugene Stephenson
Blanche F. Strater
Ann Sullivan
Doris Nash Upshur
Bernard Vinick
G.F. Weber

Maurice Weir
Vicki Wenger
Gary E. Wheeler
Miriam Whelan
William L. Wilkoff
Frances E. Wilson
John B. Wisner
D. C. Witte
Edmund D. Wood
Julie M. Wyatt

Honorary Fellow

Source: American Society of Interior Designers

Did you know...
A recent survey by the American Society of Interior Designers (ASID) found that 90% of respondents believe that improvements in office design can increase worker productivity.

Fellows of the American Society of Landscape Architects

Fellows of the American Society of Landscape Architects (ASLA) are landscape architects of at least ten years standing as Full Members of the ASLA, elected to Fellowship in honor of their outstanding contributions to the profession. Categories of election are: works of landscape architecture, administrative work, knowledge, and service to the profession. There have been a total of 754 Fellows elected since 1899. The list below indicates current, active Fellows of the ASLA.

Howard G. Abel
Wm. Dwayne Adams, Jr.
Marvin I. Adleman
Russell A. Adsit
John F. Ahern
J. Robert Anderson
Domenico Annese
David E. Arbegast
David S. Armbruster
Henry F. Arnold
Roy O. Ashley
D. Lyle Aten
Donald B. Austin
Ted Baker
William H. Baker
Harry J. Baldwin
Edward B. Ballard
Alton A. Barnes, Jr.
Milton Baron
Cheryl Barton
James H. Bassett
Kenneth E. Bassett
Anthony M. Bauer
Clarence W. Baughman
Howard R. Baumgarten
Eldon W. Beck
Yoshiro Befu
Arthur G. Beggs
William A. Behnke

James R. Bell
Richard C. Bell
Vincent Bellafiore
Armand Benedek
Claire R. Bennett
Shary Page Berg
Charles A. Birnbaum
Calvin T. Bishop
David H. Blau
Kerry Blind
Lloyd M. Bond
Norman K. Booth
W. Frank Brandt
Theodore W. Brickman, Jr.
Samuel W. Bridgers
Donald Carl Brinkerhoff
Mark K. Brinkley
Robert F. Bristol
Joseph E. Brown
Jeffrey L. Bruce
Jackie Karl Bubenik
Alexander Budrevics
Robert S. Budz
Dennis R. Buettner
Wayne L. Buggenhagen
Frank Burggraf, Jr.
Arthur E. Bye, Jr.
Willard C. Byrd
Raymond F. Cain

Fellows of the American Society of Landscape Architects (Con't)

Robert A. Callans
William B. Callaway
Craig S. Campbell
Paschall Campbell
Robert R. Cardoza
Charles Cares
Bryan D. Carlson
Dennis B. Carmichael
Derr A. Carpenter
Jot D. Carpenter
David B. Carruth
Donald R. Carter
Eugene H. Carter
Anthony B. Casendino
Carlos J. Cashio
James E. Christman
Ann Christoph
Alan B. Clarke
Lewis J. Clarke
Roger D. Clemence
Franklin C. Clements
Jon Charles Coe
Beatriz de Winthuysen Coffin
Laurence E. Coffin, Jr.
John F. Collins
George Glenn Cook
Fred J. Correale
Kenneth R. Coulter
Van L. Cox
H. Kenneth Crasco
George E. Creed
Samuel G. Crozier
Joseph H. Crystal
George W. Curry
John E. Cutler
Jack R. Daft
Edward L. Daugherty
Stuart O. Dawson
Francis H. Dean
Neil J. Dean
Roy H. DeBoer

Richard K. Dee
Robert B. Deering
Bruce Dees
C. Christopher Degenhardt
Roger DeWeese
P. Woodward Dike
F. Christopher Dimond
Nicholas T. Dines
Carlton T. Dodge
Dan W. Donelin
Thomas R. Dunbar
Robert W. Dyas
Robert P. Ealy
Garrett Eckbo
Allen R. Edmonson
Donald H. Ensign
Morgan Evans
L. Susan Everett
Julius Gy. Fabos
Barbara Faga
Oliver M. Fanning
Damon Farber
David Fasser
Rudy J. Favretti
Barbara V. Fealy
Bruce K. Ferguson
Donald L. Ferlow
Phillip E. Flores
William L. Flournoy, Jr.
Everett L. Fly
George E. Fogg
Donald Mark Fox
Kathleen M. Fox
Mark Francis
Carol L. Franklin
Robert L. Frazer
Jere S. French
John W. Frey
M. Paul Friedberg
John F. Furlong
Emily J. Gabel-Luddy

Fellows of the American Society of Landscape Architects (Con't)

Paul Gardescu

Harry L. Garnham

Benjamin W. Gary, Jr.

George G. Gentile

Richard George Gibbons

James E. Glavin

D. Newton Glick

Donald H. Godi

James B. Godwin

Robert E. Goetz

Philip H. Graham, Jr.

Leonard Grassli

Bradford M. Greene

Isabelle Clara Greene

E. Robert Gregan

John N. Grissim

Clare A. Gunn

Anthony M. Guzzardo

Richard Haag

Frederick Edward Halback

Lawrence Halprin

Calvin S. Hamilton

Asa Hanamoto

Byron R. Hanke

Richard E. Hanson

Nancy M. Hardesty

George Hargreaves

Terence G. Harkness

Charles W. Harris

Robert R. Harvey

Richard G. Hautau

William H. Havens

Robert Graham Heilig

Kenneth I. Helphand

Edith H. Henderson

Glenn O. Hendrix

Donald F. Hilderbrandt

Arthur W. Hills

Allen W. Hixon, Jr.

Leonard J. Hopper

Perry Howard

Donovan E. Hower

Joseph Hudak

Sam L. Huddleston

Mark B. Hunner

Alice R. Ireys

Wayne D. Iverson

Ronald M. Izumita

H. Rowland Jackson

Peter D. A. Jacobs

Susan L.B. Jacobson

Dale G.M. Jaeger

Frederick D. Jarvis

Leerie T. Jenkins, Jr.

Linda Lee Jewell

Carl D. Johnson

Carol R. Johnson

Dean A. Johnson

Mark W. Johnson

William J. Johnson

Grant R. Jones

Ilze Jones

Robert Trent Jones

Warren D. Jones

Dirk Jongejan

Gary E. Karner

Joseph P. Karr

Jean Stephans Kavanagh

Frank H. Kawasaki

James E. Keeter

Walter H. Kehm

J. Timothy Keller

Leslie A. Kerr

Gary B. Kesler

Masao Kinoshita

Charles L. Knight

Ken R. Krabbenhoft

Brian S. Kubota

William B. Kuhl

Bruce G. Kulik

Ray O. Kusche

Joseph J. Lalli

Fellows of the American Society of Landscape Architects (Con't)

Joe W. Langran
Lucille Chenery Lanier
Mary Ann Lasch
Warren E. Lauesen
Michael M. Laurie
Dennis L. Law
Richard K. Law
Jack E. Leaman
Donald F. Lederer
Donald W. Leslie
Aaron Levine
Philip H. Lewis, Jr.
J. Roland Lieber
Mark S. Lindhult
Karl Linn
J. Mack Little
Susan P. Little
R. Burton Litton, Jr.
Thomas A. Lockett
Nimrod W. E. Long, III
David O. Lose
Eldridge Lovelace
Paul C. K. Lu
J. Douglas Macy
Michael H. Malyn
Cameron R. J. Man
Lane L. Marshall
Richard K. Marshall
Edward C. Martin, Jr.
Roger B. Martin
Steve Martino
Robert E. Marvin
Robert M. Mattson
Lewis T. May
Richard E. Mayer
Carol Mayer-Reed
Earl Byron McCulley
Vincent C. McDermott
Roger B. McErlane
Ian McHarg
Kathryn E. McKnight-Thalden

David A. McNeal
Gary W. Meisner
Robert Melnick
Vincent N. Merrill
Stuart M. Mertz
Richard J. Meyers
Luciano Miceli
E. Lynn Miller
Patrick A. Miller
Ann Milovsoroff
Debra L. Mitchell
Michael T. Miyabara
Lawrence R. Moline
Donald J. Molnar
Lynn A. Moore
Patrick C. Moore
Richard A. Moore
Paul F. Morris
Darrel G. Morrison
Mark K. Morrison
Robert H. Mortensen
Robert K. Murase
Thomas A. Musiak
Kenneth S. Nakaba
Kenichi Nakano
Joan I. Nassauer
Darwina L. Neal
John A. Nelson
William R. Nelson, Jr.
Joseph N. Nevius
Thomas J. Nieman
Satoru Nishita
Robert L. O'Boyle
Patricia M. O'Donnell
William A. O'Leary
Cornelia A. Oberlander
Warren J. Oblinger
Neil Odenwald
Wolfgang W. Oehme
Laurie D. Olin
Peter J. Olin

Fellows of the American Society of Landscape Architects (Con't)

Edward J. Olinger

Don H. Olson

Brian Orland

Theodore Osmundson

Dennis Y. Otsuji

J. Steve Ownby

Michael Painter

Meade Palmer

Thomas P. Papandrew

Cary M. Parker

John G. Parsons

Tito Patri

Gerald D. Patten

Courtland P. Paul

Merlyn J. Paulson

Robert Perron

Robert C Perry, Jr.

Owen H. Peters

Karen A. Phillips

Robert W. Pierson

T. Edward Pinckney

Marjorie E. Pitz

Kenneth J. Polakowski

Peter M. Pollack

Harry W. Porter

Joe A. Porter

Neil H. Porterfield

Marion Pressley

William Pressley

Rae L. Price

Paul N. Procopio

Edward L. Pryce

Helen M. Quackenbush

Nicholas Quennell

F. Truitt Rabun, Jr.

David C. Racker

John Rahenkamp

Robert S. Reich

Robert G. Reimann

John J. Reynolds

Artemas P. Richardson

Donald Richardson

Jane S. Ries

Robert B. Riley

William H. Roberts

Gary O. Robinette

Richard H. Rogers

Peter G. Rolland

Clarence Roy

Robert N. Royston

Harvey M. Rubenstein

Robert H. Rucker

Virginia Lockett Russell

Terry Warriner Ryan

Paul M. Saito

Margaret Sand

William D. Sanders

Hideo Sasaki

George L. Sass

Terry W. Savage

William Scatchard

Herbert R. Schaal

Horst Schach

Janice C. Schach

Sally Schauman

Mario G. Schjetnan

Arno S. Schmid

Helmut Schmitz

Gunter A. Schoch

Ollie Schrickel

Bradford G. Sears

Jonathan G. Seymour

Bruce Sharky

Juanita D. Shearer-Swink

Ruth P. Shellhorn

J. Kipp Shrack

Jeffrey L. Siegel

Kenneth B. Simmons, Jr.

John Ormsbee Simonds

John B. Slater

Herrick H. Smith

Jerrold Soesbe

Fellows of the American Society of Landscape Architects (Con't)

Stanley V. Specht

James C. Stansbury

Barry W. Starke

Richard G. Stauffer

Robert Steenhagen

John Goddfrey Stoddart

Edward D. Stone, Jr.

Edward H. Stone, II

Allen D. Stovall

William G. Swain

Rodney L. Swink

Leslee A. Temple

Barry R. Thalden

Robert Thayer, Jr.

Michael Theilacker

J. William Thompson

William H. Tishler

Donald H. Tompkins

L. Azeo Torre

Shavaun Towers

Roger T. Trancik

Howard E. Troller

Peter J. Trowbridge

Stephen J. Trudnak

James R. Turner

Jerry Mitchell Turner

Ronald W. Tuttle

Raymond L. Uecker

James R. Urban

James Van Sweden

Michael R. Van Valkenburgh

Albert R. Veri

John Wacker

Lawrence L. Walker

Peter E. Walker

Theodore D. Walker

Victor J. Walker

Thomas H. Wallis

Ronald M. Walters

Barry J. Warner

Kent E. Watson

Dwight W. Weatherford

E. Neal Weatherly, Jr.

Richard K. Webel

Scott S. Weinberg

V. Michael Weinmayr

Roger Wells

William E. Wenk

Robert A. Weygand

James K. Wheat

Morgan Dix Wheelock

Robert F. White

George W. Wickstead

Richard A. Wilson

Theodore J. Wirth

Robert L. Woerner

J. Daniel Wojcik

David G. Wright

Patrick H. Wyss

Joseph Y. Yamada

Mark J. Zarillo

Floyd W. Zimmerman

Robert L. Zion

Robert W. Zolomij

Ervin H. Zube

Laurence W. Zuelke

Source: American Society of Landscape Architects

Fellows of the Construction Specifications Institute

Fellowship in the Construction Specifications Institute (CSI) is the highest honor granted to its members. Fellows are chosen by their peers from those who have been members in good standing for at least five years and who have demonstrated extraordinary service to CSI and notably contributed to the advancement of construction technology, the improvement of construction specifications, and education in the construction profession. The following individuals are current, active Fellows of the CSI.

Jerome H. Alciatore
Joel R. Aftland
John C. Anderson
Stephen John Andros
John C. Arant
Robert E. Armitage
Robert L. Ashbrook
Livingston E. Atkins. Jr.
R. Stanley Bair
Jane D. Baker
Frank L. Barsotti
Richard P. Bastyr
Gary A. Betts
Walter F. Bishop
S. Steve Blumenthal
H. Maynard Blumer
J. Steven Bonner
J. Gregg Borchelt
James C. Bort
William Calvin Bowne, Jr.
Charles Chief Boyd
William M. Brenan
William R. Brightbill
Wayne C. Brock
Larry Brooks
A. Larry Brown
Robert G. Burkhardt
Scott Campbell
Charles R. Carroll, Jr.

Michael D. Chambers
S. Elmer Chambers
James A. Chaney
Gary D. Church
Donald G. Clark
Thomas L. Clarke, Jr.
Melvin G. Cole
Pamela J. Cole
Lynton B. Cooper, Jr.
Eugene H. Cortrell
Frank L. Couch
John Milton Creamer
Wrenn M. Creel
Ray E. Cumrine
Douglas W. Day
Larry Craig Dean
Christopher G. Delgado
Charles M. Denisac, Jr.
James N. De Serio
Wesley J. Dolginoff
Jo Drummond
William P. Dunne
Jerry W. Durham
R. Grant Easterling
Paul Edlund
Richard C. Ehmann
Donald G. Engelhard
Rodney E. Erickson
Richard A. Eustis

Fellows of the Construction Specifications Institute (Con't)

Dell R. Ewing

Larry G. Fisher

John C. Fleck

Glenn G. Frazier

Elliot H. Gage

Woodward Garber

George S. George

Michael F. Gibbons

William Goudeket, Jr.

Jorgen Graugaard

Alana S. Griffith

Benjamin M. Gruzen

Kenneth E. Guthrie

Diana M. Hamilton

Craig K. Haney

James B. Hardin

Robert W. Harrington

Robert V.M. Harrison

Douglas C. Hartman

Betty C. Hays

Paul Heineman

Marshall A. Hildebrand, Jr.

Robert C. Hockaday

Robert W. Holstein

Herman R. Hoyer

Gilman K.M. Hu

Thomas D. Hubbard

Clarence Huettenrauch

Mary A. Hutchins

Harry F. Iram

Sheldon B. Israel

R. Graham Jackson

Seth Jackson

W.L. Jacobsen

Martin J. Janka

Edwin J. Johnson

Harry L. Johnson, Jr.

Robert W. Johnson

Wilbur L. Johnson

Joseph H. Kasimer

Walter R. Kaye

Lee F. Kilbourn

Clarence H. King, Jr.

Michael J. King

Frederick J. Klemeyer, Jr.

Norman Kruchkow

John William Kuremsky

Ralph G. Lane

Grant Alvin Larsen

Curtis H. Lee

Thomas E. Lewis

William T. Lohmann

David E. Lorenzini

Lendall W. Mains

Donald W. Manley

Dr. Oscar E. Marsch

Mortimer M. Marshall, Jr.

Marvin Martin

Robert Kipp Mayer

Charles E. McGuire

Joseph J. McGuire

Robert L. McManus

Hans W. Meier

Donald D. Meisel

Arthur J Miller

Mori Mitsui

Robert B. Moleseed

Thomas D. Montero

Peter J. Monterose

Kenneth J. Moore

Robert J. Morin

Lee C. Murray

Robert William Myers

Kenneth T. Nagie

Weldon W. Nash, Jr.

Ronald R. Nattress

R. James Noone

Robert W. Nordstrom

Arthur A. Nording

Roger A. Nourse

Harold L. Olsen

Jerome I. Orland

Fellows of the Construction Specifications Institute (Con't)

Edwin T. Pairo

Dennis M. Pelletier

Herbert F. Pendleton

Daniel A. Perkins

Richard C. Perrell

Robert L. Petterson

Milton C. Potee

James Owen Power

Manuel Press

Terry W. Preston

Katherine S. Proctor

Andrew D. Rae

John A. Raeber

Vincent G. Raney

Raymond R. Rieger

William F. Riesberg

James M. Robertson

Harold J. Rosen

Bernard B. Rothschild

Kelsey Y. Saint

Louis H. Sams

Maxwell L. Saul

Kenneth M. Schaefer

Lawrence E. Schwietz

Kenneth L. Searl

Alice Elizabeth Shelly

Paul W. Simonsen

Robert E. Simpson

Edward F. Smith

William A. Skoglund

Roscoe D. Smith

Tom F. Sneary

Edward L. Soenke

Richard B. Solomon

Michael L. Spence

Ross Spiegel

Everett G. Spurling, Jr.

Norbert R. Steeber

Joel E. Stegall, Jr.

J. Stewart Stein

Howard R. Steinmann

Terry J. Strong

Albert E. Taylor

David E. Thomas

Paul H. Tiffin

David F.M. Todd

Philip J. Todisco

Knox H. Tumlin

Albert R. Vallin

Donald P. Van Court

George A. Van Niel

William P. Vickers

Terry M. Wadsworth

Edith S. Washington

Wayne N. Watson

E. Ernest Waymon

Richard T. Weatherby

Roger T. Welcome

Raymond Whalley

George F. White, Jr.

Thomas I. Young

Werner Edwin Zarnikow

Source: Construction Specifications Institute

A great design has nothing more than it needs to do the job.

Davin Stowell

Fellows of the Industrial Designers Society of America

Membership in the Industrial Designers Society of America's (IDSA) Academy of Fellows is conferred by a two-thirds majority vote of its Board of Directors. Fellows must be Society members in good standing who have earned the special respect and affection of the membership through distinguished service to the Society and to the profession as a whole. The following individuals are the current, active fellows of the IDSA.

James M. Alexander
Wallace H. Appel
Alfons Bach
Alexander Bally
George Beck
Nathaniel Becker
Arthur N. BecVar
Melvin H. Best
Robert I. Blaich
Alfred M. Blumenfeld
Eugene Bordinat
William Bullock
Peter Bresseler
Joseph Carriero
Arthur H. Crapsey
Donald E. Dailey
Thomas David
Niels Diffrient
Jay Doblin
H. Creston Doner
Henry Dreyfuss
Arden Farey
Vincent M. Foote
James F. Fulton
Roger Funk
Walter Furlani
Carroll M. Gantz
Franceco Gianninoto
Henry P. Glass
William Goldsmith

John S. Griswold
Robert Gruen
Olle E. Haggstrom
James G. Hansen
Jon W. Hauser
Stephen G. Hauser
Richard Hollerith
Robert H. Hose
James L. Hvale
Marnie Jones
Belle Kogan
George Kosmak
Rowena Reed Kostellow
Rudolph W. Krolopp
David Kusuma
LeRoy LaCelle
Richard S. Latham
Raymond Loewy
Peter E. Lowe
Paul MacAlister
Tucker P. Madawick
Joseph R. Mango
Katherine J. McCoy
Donald McFarland
Leon Gordon Miller
Dana W. Mox
Peter Müller-Munk
C. Stowe Myers
George Nelson
Joseph M. Parriott

Fellows of the Industrial Designers Society of America (Con't)

Lee Payne
Charles Pelly
Nancy Perkins
James J. Pirkl
William L. Plumb
Arthur J. Pulos
Robert E. Redmann
Jean Otis Reinecke
Harold Reynolds
Deane W. Richardson
James Ryan
Clair A. Samhammer
Kenneth Schory
F. Eugene Smith
Robert G. Smith
Paul B. Specht
Raymond Spilman
Darrell S. Staley

Budd Steinhilber
Brooks Stevens
Philip H. Stevens
Ernest L. Swarts
Sharyn Thompson
David D. Tompkins
Herbert H. Tyrnauer
John Vassos
Read Viemeister
Tucker Viemeister
Noland Vogt
Sandor Weisz
Arnold Wolf
Peter Wooding
Cooper C. Woodring
Edward J. Zagorski

Source: Industrial Designers Society of America

Fellows of the International Interior Design Association

Professional members of the International Interior Design Association (IIDA) are inducted into the College of Fellows by a two-thirds vote by their Board of Directors. This honor recognizes members who have demonstrated outstanding service to the IIDA, the community, and the interior design profession. The following individuals are current, active fellows of the IIDA.

Laura Bailey

Jeanne Baldwin

Claude Berube

Charles Blumberg

Dan Bouligny

Michael Bourque

Rus Calder

Richard Carlson

Particia Gutierrez Castellanos

Amarjeet Chatrath

Susan Coleman

David Cooke

Eleanor Corkle

Christine Dandan

Eugene Daniels

Carol Disrud

Jacqueline Duncan

Cheryl Duvall

Hilda East

Marilyn Farrow

James Ferguson II

Dorothy Fowles

Neil Frankel

Angela Frey

Gerald Gelsomino

M. Arthur Gensler Jr.

Carol S. Graham

Karen Guenther

Beth Harmon-Vaughan

Judith Hastings

Jo Heinz

Edna Henner

John Herron

Frederick Hutchirs

David Immenschuh

Christina Johnson

Carol Jones

Margo Jones

Robert Kennedy

Tessa Kennedy

Sooz Klinkhamer

Lili Kray

Marjorie Kriebel

Michael Kroelinger

Robert Ledingham

Fola Lerncr-Miller

Jack Levin

Neville Lewis

Charles Littleton

Ronald Lubben

Hiroko Machida

Candace MacKenzie

Richard Mazzucotelli

Jose Medrano

Ruth Mellergaard

Kenneth Muller

Donald Parker

Janie Petkus

Paul Petrie

Carole Price Shanis

Sandra Ragan

Charles Raymond

Patti Richards

Wayne Ruga

Fellows of the International Interior Design Association (Con't)

Joyce Saunders
Donald Sherman
Rayne Sherman
Gail Shiel
Bernard Soep
Andre Staffelbach
Andrew Stafford
William Stankiewicz
Janice Stevenor Dale
Donald Thomas
Joann Thompson
Betty Treanor
Marcia Troyan

Robert Valentine
Margaret Velardo
Roen Viscovich
Ron Whitney-Whyte
Glenda Wilcox
Frances Wilson
M. Judith Wilson
D. Geary Winstead
Michael Wirtz
Susan Wood
Minoru Yokoyama
Janice Young

Source: International Interior Design Association

Did you know...
The 1859 Vienna Café Chair designed by German cabinet maker Michael Thornet was virtually unknown until Le Corbusier used it in his innovative housing exhibit L'Espirit Nouveau at the Paris Exposition Internationale in 1925. By 1930, over 50 million chairs had been sold.

15 Leading Women Architects and Designers of the 20th Century

Suzana Antonakakis

Greek. Born Suzana-Maria Kolokytha in Athens, June 25, 1935. Antonakakis studied at the National Technical University, School of Architecture, in Athens, 1954-59, and established a partnership with her husband Dimitris in 1958. Suzana Antonakakis worked as an architect/consultant for the Archaeological and Restoration Service of Athens and has lectured internationally. Her firm has been influenced by Modernism and the rich historical environment of Greece. Her architecture demonstrates a creative use of space. Geometry, materials, and socio-cultural values are combined in a rational yet complex structure.

Gae(tana) Aulenti

Italian. Born in Palazolo dello Stella (Udine), December 4, 1927. Aulenti received her Dip. Arch. from the Milan Polytechnic's School of Architecture in 1954. She has been in private practice in Milan as an exhibition and industrial designer since 1954. She has also taught in Venice, Milan, Barcelona, and Stockholm. Her other professional involvements include being a member of the editorial staff of *Casabella-Continuità* from 1955-65 and of the Board of Directors of Lotus International in Venice in 1974. Gae Aulenti has won many prestigious industrial design and architectural prizes. Aulenti's work evolved in the Milanese architecture scene, and she has become one of its major exponents. Her body of work includes exhibition design, interiors as well as architecture.

Her most famous work to date is her conversion of the Gare d'Orsay in Paris into the highly successful Museum d'Orsay.

Sylvia Crowe

British. Born in Barnbury, Oxfordshire, September 15, 1901. Crowe studied at Swanley Horticultural College in Kent, 1920-22, and has been in private practice as a landscape architect in London since 1945. Crowe was President of the Institute of Landscape Architects in London from 1957-61. She also won the Woman of the Year Award from London's *Architects' Journal* in 1970. Sylvia Crowe holds Honorary Doctorates from the University of Newcastle, Heriot–Watt University in Edinburgh, University of Sussex, and University of Brighton. She was also made an Honorary Fellow of the Royal Institute of British Architects in 1969. Although Crowe was first recognized for her domestic garden designs, her career was largely served with postwar architects and town planners. Through her professional work and books, Crowe has dedicated her career to the interest of landscape as a whole.

Jane Beverly Drew

British. Born in Thornton Heath, Surrey, March 24, 1911. Drew received her diploma from London's Architectural Association, School of Architecture in 1934. She worked with her husband, E. Maxwell Fry, from 1945-77 in Fry Drew and Partners, London. She also served as the joint editor of the *Architects Yearbook* from 194

15 Leading Women Architects and Designers of the 20th Century (Con't)

62. Drew has taught at the Massachusetts Institute of Technology and Harvard University. Among her awards are Honorary Doctorates from the University of Ibadan, Nigeria; Open University, Milton Keynes, Buckinghamshire; University of Newcastle; and Witwaterstrand University, Johannesburg. Much of Drew's work has been in tropical countries in Africa and on the Indian continent. Her architecture is characterized by a functional adaptation of the modern idiom to tropical buildings. Some of her best earlier work was in conjunction with Le Corbusier, Pierre Jeanneret and Maxwell Fry in Chandigarh, India.

Joan Edelman Goody

American. Born Joan Edelman in New York City, December 1, 1935. Goody studied at the University of Paris from 1954-55, received her B.A from Cornell University in 1956, and earned a M. Arch. degree from the Harvard Graduate School of Design in 1960. She has been a principal at Goody, Clancy and Associates in Boston since 1961. She received *Progressive Architecture's* Urban Planing Award in 1983 and has won numerous awards from The American Institute of Architects, the Boston Society of Architects, and the American Planning Association. Much of Good's work is contextual and demonstrates sensitivity to community, scale, and regional building traditions.

Eileen Gray

Irish. Born at Brownswood, Enniscorthy, County Wexford, Ireland,

August 9, 1879. Gray studied at the Slate School of Art in London from 1898-1902. She worked as an architect in France from 1926 until her death in 1976. She was awarded the Honorary Royal Designer for Industry from the Royal Society of Arts, London, in 1972 and was made a Fellow of the Royal Institute of Irish Architects, Dublin, in 1973. Eileen Gray was a furniture designer who designed a small number of buildings and interiors. Her architecture reflected the close affinity between furniture and building. She also brought humanity to modernism. Although small in number, her architectural work is as original and skillful as anything by the great masters. Her house, E. 1027, was sometimes attributed to Le Corbusier or to the architect and critic Jean Badovici who assisted Gray on the house. Her gender has led to her work being overlooked and underrated.

Zaha Hadid

Iraqi. Born in Baghdad in 1950. Hadid studied at the American University in Beirut and under Rem Koolhaas at the Architectural Association, School of Architecture in London, from which she graduated in 1977. She was a Unit Master at the Architectural Association from 1977-87 and a visiting professor at Harvard and Columbia University in 1986 and 1987. Hadid received the British Architectural Awards' Gold Medal in 1982. Although she won numerous first prizes in international building competitions during the 1980s, Hadid actually built little during that period. Generally known as a

15 Leading Women Architects and Designers of the 20th Century (Con't)

Deconstructivist, Hadid has been classified in this group since the 1988 MoMA exhibition entitled "Deconstructive Architecture." Her recent work, such as the Vitra Fire Station and her garden pavilion, both in Weil am Rhein, Germany, displays a mastery of form and technology. She is one of the most famous avant-garde architects of the 1990s.

Käpy Paavilainen
Finish. Born in Vaasa, June 1944. Paavilainen studied at the Helsinki University of Technology where she received a Dip. Arch. in 1975. Since 1982 she has been a visiting lecturer at the Helsinki University of Technology. She also has been a visiting lecturer in Barcelona and Berlin. In 1977 she established a partnership with her husband in Helsinki. Paavilainen won the Architectural Prize, Tiili, in 1983 and the State Award for Architecture and Community Planning. Most of her work is in Finland. Her architecture is minimal yet has important classical influences and is characterized by close attention to place with materials that provide a contextual richness.

Patricia Patkau
Canadian. Born in Winnipeg, Manitoba 1950. She received a BA in 1973 from the University of Manitoba and a MA from Yale University in 1978. Since 1992 she has been an associate professor at the School of Architecture, University of British Columbia. In 1978 she established a partnership with her husband John in Edmonton, which in 1984 moved to Vancouver, British Columbia. The firm has won numerous awards of excellence and many first prizes in competitions. Patricia Patkau describes her work as focusing on the particular in an effort to balance the tendency towards generalization which is increasingly dominant in Western culture.

Charlotte Perriand
French. Born in Paris, October 24, 1903. Perriand studied design at the Ecole de l'Union Centrale des Arts Décoratifs in Paris from 1920-25. She has been in private practice in Paris since 1927 when she established her own studio in the Place Saint Suplice, 1927-30, and in the Boulevard de Montparnasse, 1930-37. She also served as the associate in charge of furniture and fittings in the studio of Le Corbusier from 1927-37. From 1937-40 she worked with Jean Prouvé, Pierre Jeanneret, and Georges Blanchon in Paris. She also began an office for prefabricated building research in Paris in 1940. Throughout her career she worked frequently in Tokyo, Rio de Janeiro as well as Latin America. She served as a member of the editorial board for *Architecture d'aujourd'hui* in Paris, 1930-74. Perriand received national and international recognition. During her long and highly successful career, Charlotte Perriand designed interiors as well as their furnishings.

Denise Scott Brown
American. Born Denise Lakofskiin Nkana in Zambia, October 3, 1931. She

15 Leading Women Architects and Designers of the 20th Century (Con't)

emigrated to the United States in 1958 and was naturalized in 1967. Scott Brown studied at the University of the Witwaterstrand, Johannesburg from 1948-51 and at the Architectural Association, School of Architecture in London, 1952-55, where she received an AA Diploma and Certificate in Tropical Architecture in 1956. She also studied at the University of Pennsylvania under Louis I. Kahn, 1958-60, and earned a Masters in City Planning in 1960. She has been the principal in charge of urban planning and design at Venturi, Scott Brown and Associates since 1989. Denise Scott Brown has taught at a number of Universities including Yale, University of Pennsylvania, Harvard, and MIT. Her work has received national and international recognition. Along with her husband, Robert Venturi, Scott Brown's built work and books such as *Learning from Las Vegas* ushered in Post-Modernism and influenced an entire generation of architects.

Alison Smithson

British. Born Alison Margaret Gill in Sheffield, June 22, 1928. Smithson studied architecture at the University of Durham, 1944-49. In 1950 she formed a partnership with her husband Peter. She was a founding member of Independent Group and was associated with Team 10 throughout her career. She also served as a lecturer at the Architectural Association, School of Architecture in London. Smithson died in 1993. Alison Smithson practiced, taught, and also wrote a number of books. With her husband-partner, she formed a team whose architectural influence extended beyond England. Their work has been described as a "Gentle Cultural Accommodation." Through their teaching at the Architectural Association they influenced generations of students throughout the world, among these Denise Scott-Brown.

Laurinda Spear

American. Born 1951. Spear studied Fine Arts at Brown University, receiving her BA in 1972. She also earned a MA from Columbia University in 1975. She won the Rome Prize in Architecture in 1978 and awards from *Progressive Architecture* in 1978 and 1980. Spear is the principal and co-founder of Arquitectonica, which she formed in 1977 with her husband Barnardo Fort-Brescia. Their work is characterized by sculpted intersecting geometric forms and bright colors and is recognized as being stylistically appropriate for Miami.

Helena Syrkus

Polish. Born Helena Niemirowska in Warsaw, May 14, 1900. Syrkus studied architecture at Warsaw's Institute of Technology from 1918-23 and humanities and philosophy at the University of Warsaw from 1923-25. Helena Syrkus combined practice with teaching for much of her career, lecturing at the Institute of Architecture and Town Planning in Warsaw. She established a partnership with her husband in 1962 until her death in 1982. She won many national awards for both her architectural work and her writings. The life and work of Helena and her husband

15 Leading Women Architects and Designers of the 20th Century (Con't)

Szymon Syrkus are linked to international avant-garde architectural thought. The fundamental principle of their long partnership is that social co-operation is more rewarding than competition and rivalry.

Susana Torre

American. Born in Puan, Buenos Aires, Argentina, November 2, 1944 and later emigrated to the United States. Torre studied at the Universidad de La Plata, 1961-63 and received her Dipl. Arch. from the Universidad de Buenos Aires in 1967. Torre also did postgrduate studies at Columbia University. She has been a principal of Susana Torre and Associates in New York since 1988. Torre has lectured and has been a visiting critic at Columbia University, Yale University, Cooper Union, Carnegie Mellon and Syracuse University. She was a member of the editorial board for the *Journal of Architectural Education* from 1983-85. She has received awards from *Architectural Record* and the National Endowment for the Arts. Her work is interesting for its recognition of groups who have experienced displacement (i.e. new immigrants) and its critical feminist consciousness. Urban memory plays an important role in her designs.

Eva Vecsei

Canadian. Born Eva Hollo in Vienna, Austria, August 21, 1930, and emigrated to Canada in 1957 where she was naturalized in 1962. Vecsei studied at the University of Technical Sciences, School of Architecture in Budapest from 1948-52 where she earned a BA in 1952. She has been in partnership with Andrew Vescei at Vescei Architects since 1984. Eva Vecsei has received 5 Massey Architecture Awards and an Award of Excellence from *Canadian Architect*. In her 30s, she became the head designer for one of the largest buildings in the world, the Place Bonaventure in Montreal. Her second mammoth project was La Cité, Montreal's first large-scale mixed-use downtown development. No woman architect has ever before had such broad responsibility for the design and construction of projects of this magnitude and excellence.

Source: Pauline Morin

Honorary Fellows of The American Institute of Architects

The American Institute of Architects (AIA) grants Honorary Fellowship status to non-members, both architects and non-architects, who have made substantial contributions to the field of architecture. The following individuals are current Honorary Fellows of the AIA.

Kurt h.c. Ackermann, Munich, Germany

Gunnel Adlercreutz, Helsinki, Finland

O J. Aguilar, Lima, Peru

Hisham Albakri, Kuala Lumpur, Malaysia

William A. Allen, London, England

Alfred V. Alvares, Vancouver, Canada

Jose Alvarez, Lima, Peru

Mario R. Alvarez, Buenos Aires, Argentina

Tadao Ando, Osaka, Japan

John H. Andrews, Australia

Carlos D. Arguelles, Manila, Philippines

Gordon R. Arnott, Regina, Canada

Carl Aubock, Austria

George G. Baines, England

W D. Baldwin, Sterling, VA

W. K. Banadayga, Sterling, VA

Essy Baniassad, Halifax, Canada

Nikolai B. Baranov, Moscow, Russia

Geoffrey M. Bawa, Columbo, Sri Lanka

Eugene Beaudouin, France

Gerard Benoit, Paris, France

Jai R. Bhalla, New Delhi, India

Jacob Blegvad, Aalborg, Denmark

Richard L. Bofill, Barcelona, Spain

Oriol Bohigas, Barcelona, Spain

Irving D. Boigon, Richmond Hill, Canada

Ferenc Callmeyer, Telki, Hungary

Santiago A. Calvo, Lima, Peru

Felix Candela, Raleigh, North Carolina

Rifat Chadirji, Surrey, England

Suk-Woong Chang, Seoul, Korea

Te L. Chang, Taipei, Taiwan

Bill Chomik, Calgary, Canada

Adolf Ciborowski, Warsaw, Poland

E. Gresley Cohen, Dalkeith, Australia

Charles M. Correa, Bombay, India

Philip S. Cox, Sydney, Australia

Charles H. Cullum, Newfoundland, Canada

Carlos E. Da Silva, Rizal, Philippines

John M. Davidson, Richmond, Australia

David Y. Davies, Surrey, England

Sara T. De Grinberg, Mexico

Rafael De La Hoz, Spain

S D. De La Tour, Durville, France

Eduardo De Mello, Braga, Portugal

Costantin N. Decavalla, Greece

Ignacio M. Delmonte, Mexico City, Mexico

A J. Diamond, Toronto, Canada

Ignacio Diaz-Morales, Jalisco, Mexico

Balkrishna V. Doshi, Ahmedabad , India

Philip Dowson, London, England

Kiril Doytchev, Sofia, Bulgaria

G M. Dubois, Toronto, Canada

Honorary Fellows of The American Institute of Architects (Con't)

Allan F. Duffus, Halifax, Canada

Werner Duttman, Lindenalle, Germany

David W. Edwards, Regina, Canada

Yehya M. Eid, Cairo, Egypt

Abdel W. El Wakil, Kent, England

Arthur C. Erickson, Vancouver, Canada

Lord Esher, England

Inger Exner, Denmark

Johannes Exner, Denmark

Tobias Faber, Copenhagen, Denmark

Francisco B. Fajardo, Philippines

Hassan Fathy, Egypt

Sverre Fehn, Oslo, Norway

Bernard M. Feilden, Norfolk, England

Ji Z. Feng, Shanghai, People's Republic Of China

Angelina Munoz Fernandez de Madrid, Sonora, Mexico

A. I. Ferrier, Red Hill, Australia

Jozsef Finta, Budapest, Hungary

Antonio F. Flores, Mexico

Cesar X. Flores, Mexico D.F., Mexico

Norman Foster, London, England

Charles A. Fowler, Canada

Juan Gonzalez, Spain

Roderick P. Hackney, Cheshire, England

H. H. Hallen, Australia

Shoji Hayashi, Tokyo, Japan

Tao Ho, North Point, Hong Kong

Barry J. Hobin, Ottawa, Canada

Hans Hollein, Vienna, Austria

Wilhelm Holzbauer, Vienna, Austria

Sir Michael Hopkins, London, England

Lady Patricia Hopkins, London, England

Thomas Howarth, Toronto, Canada

Arata Isozaki, Tokyo, Japan

Toyo Ito, Tokyo, Japan

Daryl Jackson, Melbourne, Australia

R. D. Jackson, Sydney, Australia

P. N. Johnson, Australia

Vladimir Karfik, Brno, Czech Republic

Kiyonori Kikutake, Tokyo, Japan

Reiichiro Kitadai, Tokyo, Japan

Azusa Kito, Tokyo, Japan

Josef P. Kleihues, Berlin, Germany

Rob Krier, Berlin, Germany

Dogan Kuban, Istanbul, Colombia

Alexandr P. Kudryavtsev, Moscow, Russia

Kisho Kurokawa, Tokyo, Japan

Colin Laird, Port of Spain, Trinidad and Tobago

Jean L. Lalonde, Canada

Henning Larsen, Denmark

Denys L. Lasdun, London, England

Kwang-Ro Lee, Seoul Korea, Korea

Juha Ilmari Leiviska, Helsinki, Finland

Jaime Lerner, Parana, Brazil

Wu Liang Yong, Beijing, People's Republic Of China

Kington Loo, Kuala Lumpur, Malaysia

Aldana E. Lorenzo, San Jeronimo, Mexico

Serapio P. Loza, Jalisco, Mexico

Kjell Lund, Oslo, Norway

Olufemi Majekodunmi, Gaborone, Botswana

Fumihiko Maki, Tokyo, Japan

Matti K. Makinen, Finland

Rutilo Malacara, Mexico D F, Mexico

Motlatsi Peter Malefane, Johannesburg, South Africa

Albert Mangones, Port Au Prince, Haiti

Honorary Fellows of The American Institute of Architects (Con't)

Yendo Masayoshi, New York, New York

Robert Peter McIntyre, Victoria, Australia

Rodrigo Mejia-Andrion, Panama

Hector Mestre, Mexico, D.F., Mexico

Jose Raphael Moneo, Madrid, Spain

Padraig Murray, Dublin, Ireland

Toshio Nakamura, Tokyo, Japan

Nikola I. Nikolov, Sofia, Bulgaria

Juan Bassegoda Nonell, Barcelona, Spain

Rafael Norma, Mexico City, Mexico

Jean Nouvel, Paris, France

Jorge Nu Ex Verdugo, Mexico

Carl J.A. Nyren, Stockhlm, Sweden

ShinIchi Okada, Tokyo, Japan

Oluwole O. Olumyiwa, Lagos, Nigeria

Georgui M. Orlov, Moscow, Russia

Juhani Pallasmaa, Helsinki, Finland

Gustav Peichl, Wein, Austria

Raili Pietila, Helsinki, Finland

Methodi A. Pissarski, Sofia, Bulgaria

Ernst A. Plischke, Wien, Austria

Ivor C. Prinsloo, Rondebosch, South Africa

Victor M. Prus, Montreal, Canada

Luis M. Quesada, Lima, Peru

Hector M. Restat, Santiago, Chile

Jose F. Reygadas, Mexico City, Mexico

Philippe Robert, Paris, France

Derry Menzies Robertson, Picton, Canada

Juan J. Rocco, Montevideo, Uruguay

Xavier Cortes Rocha, Coyoacan, Mexico

Aldo A. Rossi, Milano, Italy

Witold Rybczynski, Philadelphia, PA

Thomas J. Sanabria, Miami, FL

Alberto Sartoris, Cossonay Ville, Switzerland

Helmut C. Schulitz, Braunschweig Gem, Germany

Michael Scott, Ireland

Harry Seidler, Australia

Peter F. Shepheard, Philadelphia, PA

Dr. Tsutomu Shigemura, Kobe, Japan

Kazuo Shinohara, Yokohama, Japan

Brian Sim, Vancouver, Canada

Antonio S. Sindiong, Rizal, Philippines

Heikki Siren, Helsinki, Finland

Kaija Siren, Helsinki, Finland

Nils Slaatto, Oslo, Norway

Vladimir Slapeta, Praha, Czech Republic

Inette L. Smith, Cornwall, England

J. M. Smith, Cornwall, England

Gin Su, Bethesda, Maryland,

Minoru Takeyama, Littleton, Colorado,

Yoshio Taniguchi, Tokyo, Japan

German Tellez, Bogota, Colombia

Anders Tengbom, Sweden

Paul-Andre Tetreault, FIRAC, Montreal, Canada

Alexandros N. Tombazis, Athens, Greece

Luben N. Tonev, Bulgaria

Marion Tournon-Branly, Paris, France

Shozo Uchii, Tokyo, Japan

Lennart Uhlin, Stockholm, Sweden

Jorn Utzon, Denmark

Pierre Vago, Noisy, France

Gino Valle, Udine, Italy

Marcelo E. Vargas, Lima, Peru

Pedro R. Vasquez, Mexico City, Mexico

Eva Vecsei, Montreal, Canada

Jorge N. Verdugo, Mexico City, Mexico

Honorary Fellows of The American Institute of Architects (Con't)

Tomas R. Vicuna, Santiago, Chile

Ricardo L. Vilchis, Mexico City, Mexico

Eduardo O. Villacortaq, Lima, Peru

William Whitefield, London, England

Terence J. Williams, Victoria, Canada

Roy W. Willwerth, Halifax, Canada

C A. Wnderlich, Guatemala City, Guatemala

Bernard Wood, Ottawa, Canada

Rutang Ye, Beijing, People's Republic Of China

Richard Young, Sterling, VA

Abraham Zabludovsky, Codesa, Mexico

Jose M. Zaragoza, Philippines

Eberhard Heinrich Zeidler, Toronto, Canada

Jorge Gamboa de Buen, Mexico DF, Mexico

Alvaro Joaquim de Meio Siza, Porto, Portugal

Christian de Portzamparc, Paris, France

Source: The American Institute of Architects

Ah, to build, to build!
That is the noblest art of
all the arts.
Painting and sculpture are
but images,
Are merely shadows cast
by outward things
On stone or canvas,
having in themselves
No separate existence.
Architecture,
Existing in itself, and not
in seeming
A something it is not,
surpasses them
As substance shadow.

Henry Wadsworth Longfellow

Honorary Members of The American Institute of Architects

The American Institute of Architects (AIA) grants honorary membership to individuals outside the architecture profession who are not otherwise eligible for membership in the Institute. They are chosen for their distinguished service to architecture or the allied arts and sciences. Nominations may be submitted by the national AIA Board of Directors or a component PIA. National and component staff with 10 years or more of service are also eligible for Honorary Membership. The following individuals are Honorary Members of the AIA.

Ava J. Abramowitz, Chevy Chase, MD

Joseph F. Addonizio, New Rochelle, NY

His Highness The Aga Khan

Joseph Ahearn, Littleton, CO

Michael L. Ainslie, New York, NY

R. Mayne Albright, Charlotte, NC

George A. Allen, CAE, Tallahassee, FL

Trudy Aron

Ludd Ashley, Washington, DC

Janice Axon, Laguna Niguel, CA

Mariana Barthold

Augustus Baxter, Sr., Philadelphia, PA

Stephen M. Bennett, Columbus, OH

Elaine Bergman

James Biddle, Andalusia, PA,

J. Bidwill, Chicago, IL,

Sherry Birk, Washington, DC

The Honorable Sherwood L. Boehlert

Oriol Bohigas, Barcelona, Spain

Sara H. Boutelle, Santa Cruz, CA

A. S. Boyd, Washington, DC

Ann Marie Boyden, Arlington, VA

Eleanor K. Brassel, Bethesda, MD

John W. Braymer, Ph.D., CAE, Richmond, VA

David Brinkley, Chevy Chase, MD

Jack Brooks, Washington, DC

A. B. Brown, Providence, RI

J. N. Brown, Providence, RI

William A. Brown Sr., Washington, DC

John M. Bryan, Columbia, SC

Muriel Campaglia, Washington, DC

Donald Canty, Seattle, WA

Joan Capelin, New York, NY

Edward Carlough

Charles M. Cawley, Wilmington, DE

Henry C. Chambers, Beaufort, SC

Mary Chapman-Smith, Mancelona, MI

William W. Chase, Alexandria, VA

Henry Cisneros, San Antonio, TX

F. J. Clark, Washington, DC

Grady Clay Jr., Louisville, KY

Ernest A. Connalley, Alexandria, VA

S. B. Conroy, Washington, DC

Rolaine V. Copeland, Seattle, WA

Weld Coxe, Block Island, RI

Lois Craig, Cambridge, MA,

James P. Cramer, Norcross, GA

Alfonse M. D'Amato, Washington, DC

Kathleen L. Daileda, Washington, DC

Ann Davidson, North Canton, OH

Joan K. Davidson, New York, NY

Mabel S. Day, Alexandria, VA

Fred R. Deluca, Washington, DC

Honorary Members of The American Institute of Architects (Con't)

Deborah Dietsch, Washington, DC

Carlos Diniz

Rae Dumke, Detroit, MI

M. Durning, Seattle, WA

J. Sprigg Duvall

Linda J. Ebitz, Oakland, PA

Judy A. Edwards, New Haven, CT

M. D. Egan, Anderson, SC

James R. Ellis, Seattle, WA,

John D. Entenza, Santa Monica, CA

Marie L. Farrell, Belvedere, CA

Alan M. Fern, Chevy Chase, MD

Angelina Munoz Fernandez de Madrid, Sonora, Mexico

L. A. Ferre, San Juan, PR

David W. Field, CAE, Columbus, OH

Harold B. Finger, Washington, DC

James M. Fitch, New York, NY

J. D. Forbes, Charlottesville, VA,

William S. Fort, Eugene, OR

Arthur J. Fox Jr., New York, NY

Doris C. Freedman, New York, NY

Mildred Friedman, New York, NY

Patsy L. Frost, SDA/C, Columbus, OH

Ruth Fuller, Houston, TX

Paul Gapp, Chicago, IL

D. E. Gardner, Delaware, OH

Paul Genecki, Kensington, MD

C. D. Gibson, Ogden, UT

Brendan Gill, New York, NY

Jorge Glusberg, Buenos Aires, Argentina

Alfred Goldberg, Belvedere Tiburo, CA

Howard G. Goldberg, Esq.

Paul Goldberger, New York, NY

Douglas E. Gordon

H. B. Gores, Alpharetta, GA

D. R. Graham, Tallahassee, FL

Ginny W. Graves, Prairie Village, KS,

Barbara Gray, Takoma Park, MD

Roberta Gratz

Cecil H. Green, Dallas, TX

Thomas Griffith, New York, NY

Roberta J. Guffey, Charleston, WV

Robert Gutman, Princeton, NJ

Richard Hagg

Donald J. Hall, Kansas City, MO

Donalee Hallenbeck, Sacramento, CA

P. Hammer, Beverley Beach, MD

Marga Rose Hancock, Seattle, WA

Partrick K. Harrison, London, England

Dr. F. Otto Hass

Arthur A. Hart, Boise, ID

Dianne Hart

Beverly E. Hauschild-Baron, Minneapolis, MN

A. Hecksher, New York, NY

Andrew Heiskell, New York, NY

Amy Hershfang

Gerald D. Hines, Houston, TX

Charles L. Hite

William Houseman, Portland, ME

Thomas P. Hoving, New York, NY

Philip A. Hutchinson, Harwood, MD

Ada L. Huxtable, New York, NY

J. Michael Huey, Esq.

Donald G. Iselin, Santa Barbara, CA

Kathy C. Jackson, CAE, Jackson, MS

J. B. Johnson, Watertown, NY

Dr. Joseph E. Johnson, Ed.D

Lady B. Johnson, Austin, TX

Elaine Sewell Jones

Gerre Jones, Albuquerque, NM

V. Jordan, Jr., New York, NY

H. A. Judd, Beaverton, OR

Lloyd Kaiser, Oakmont, PA

Shelly Kappe

Robert J. Kapsch, Gaithersburg, MD

Suzanne Keller, Princeton, NJ

Honorary Members of The American Institute of Architects (Con't)

Dorothy Kender

Roger G. Kennedy, Alexandria, VA

Jonathan King, Houston, TX

R. Lawrence Kirkegaard, Downers Grove, IL

Lee E. Koppelman, Stonybrook, NY

Peter H. Kostmayer, Washington, DC

Mabel Krank, Oklahoma City, OK

Florence C. Ladd, Cambridge, MA

Anita M. Laird, Cape May, NJ

George Latimer, St. Paul, MN

William J. Le Messurier, Cambridge, MA,

Aaron Levine, Menlo Park, CA

E. H. Levitas, Washington, DC

Lawrence Lewis Jr.

Weiming Lu, St. Paul, MN

Major General Eugene a. Lupia

Jane Maas, New York, NY

Diane Maddox

Randell Lee Makinson

Stanley Marcus, Dallas, TX

Louis L. Marines, Corte Madera, CA

Judy Marks, Washington, DC

Albert R. Marschall, Alexandria, VA

Maureen Marx, Springfield, VA

Mary Tyler Cheek McClenaham

F M. McConihe, Potomac, MD

Terrence M. McDermott, Chicago, IL

Evelyn B. McGrath, Holiday, FL

Ian L. McHarg, Philadelphia, PA

Eleanor McNamara

Paul Mellon, Upperville, VA

Betty H. Meyer

E. P. Mickel, Bethesda, MD

J. I. Miller, Columbus, IN

Martha P. Miller, Portland, OR

R. Miller, Sherman Oaks, CA

Richard B. Miller, Elmsford, NY

Roger Milliken, Spartanburg, SC

Hermine Mitchell, Philadelphia, PA

Martha Barber Montgomery, Ph.D.

William B. Moore Jr., Kilmarnock, VA

John W. Morris, Arlington, VA

Philip A. Morris, Birmingham, AL

Terry B. Morton, Chevy Chase, MD

Woolridge Brown Morton III

Jean G. Muntz, Omaha, NE

Martha Murphree

Maria Murray, Kensington, MD

Betty J. Musselman, Accokeek, MD

Raymond D. Nasher

Doreen Nelson, Los Angeles, CA

Shirley J. Norvell, Springfield, IL

Laurie D. Olin, Philadelphia, PA

Mary E. Osman, Columbia, SC

Ronald J. Panciera, Bradenton, FL

R. B. Pease, Pittsburgh, PA

C. Ford Peatross, Washington, DC

Robert A. Peck, Esq, Washington, DC,

Claiborne Pell, Washington, DC,

David Perdue, Silver Spring, MD

Honorable Pete Wilson, Washington, DC

G. E. Pettengill, Arlington, VA

Janet D. Pike

Philip W. Pillsbury Jr., Washington, DC

Walter F. Pritchard II, Costa Mesa, CA

Jay A. Pritzker, Chicago, IL

Jody Proppe, Portland, OR

Sidney A. Rand, Minneapolis, MN

David P. Reynolds, Richmond, VA

William G. Reynolds Jr., Richmond, VA

Brenda Richards

Carolyn Richie

Raymond P. Rhinehart, Washington, DC

Joseph P. Riley, Charleston, SC

J. P. Robin, Pittsburgh, PA

Laurance Rockefeller, New York, NY

Barbara J. Rodriguez, Albany, NY

Honorary Members of The American Institute of Architects (Con't)

Gini Rountree, Sacramento, CA

Mario G. Salvadori, New York, NY

Carl M. Sapers, Boston, MA

William D. Schaefer

Martin Schaum, Garden City, NY

Paul Schell, Seattle, WA

Vincent C. Schoemehl Jr., Clayton, MO

Philip Schreiner, Washington, DC

Rosemary Schroeder, Dallas, TX

Susan E. Schur

Frederick D. Schwengel

Suzanne K. Schwengels, CAE, Des Moines, IA

Rex Scouten, Washington, DC

B. Sebastian, San Francisco, CA

James H. Semans, Durham, NC

Julian B. Serrill, Des Moines, IA

Elaine K. Sewell Jones, Los Angeles, CA

Polly E. Shackleton, Washington, DC

Julius Shulman, Los Angeles, CA

Betty W. Silver, Raleigh, NC

Alice Sinkevitch

John B. Skilling, Seattle, WA

W. L. Slayton, Washington, DC

Eleanor McNamara Smith, Somerset, WI

Nancy Somerville, Washington, DC

S. Spencer, Washington, DC

Ann Stacy, Baltimore, MD

S. Steinborn, Seattle, WA

Saundra Stevens, Portland, OR

P. D. Stitt, Yreka, CA

Deborah Sussman, Culver City, CA

Pipsan S. Swanson, Bloomfield, MI

G. B. Tatum, Chester, CT

Anne Taylor

Richard Thevenot, Baton Rouge, LA

J. S. Thurmond, Washington, DC

Carolyn H. Toft, St. Louis, MO

Bernard Tomson, Voorheesville, NY

W. F. Traendly, Thetford Center, VT

R. E. Train, Washington, DC

Pierre Vago, Noisy, France

Mariana L. Verga, Edmond, OK

Wolf Von Eckardt, Washington, DC

Connie C. Wallace, CAE, Nashville, TN

Paul Weidlinger, New York, NY

Paul W. Welch, Jr. Sacramento, CA

Emmet L. Wemple, Los Angeles, CA

Katie Westby, Tulsa, OK

Frank J. Whalen Jr., Cheverly, MD

Richard Guy Wilson, Charlottesville, VA

Arol Wolford, Norcross, GA

Marilyn Wood, Santa Fe, NM

Tony P. Wrenn, Fredricksburg, VA

Honorable Sidney Yates, Washington, DC

Jill D. Yeomans, Santa Barbara, CA

John Zukowsky, Chicago, IL

Source: The American Institute of Architects

Did you know...
At a rate of 1,800 feet a minute, the elevators in the John Hancock Building in Chicago ascend its 100 stories in less than a minute.

Honorary Members of the American Society of Landscape Architects

Honorary Membership is granted by the American Society of Landscape Architects' (ASLA) Board of Directors, to persons, other than landscape architects, who have performed notable service to the profession of landscape architecture. The following individuals are current, active Honorary Members of the ASLA.

Edward H. Able, Jr.
Hon. Douglas Bereuter
Hon. Dale Bumpers
Pres. James Earl Carter, Jr.
Grady Clay
Russell E. Dickenson
Walter L. Doty
Marvin Durning
Carolyn B. Etter
Don D. Etter
Albert Fein
Charles E. Fraser
Marshall M. Fredericks
Gwen Frostic
Donald M. Harris
George B. Hartzog, Jr.
Vance R. Hood
Patrick Horsbrugh
Thomas Hylton
Lyndon B. Johnson
Dr. Harley Jolley
Hon. Edward M. Kennedy
Balthazar Korab
Balthazar Korab, Ltd.

Norbert Kraich
Prof. Walter H. Lewis, FAIA
Dr. Binyi Liu
John A. Love
Lee MacDonald
Prof. E. Bruce MacDougall
Charles C. McLaughlin
Hugh C. Miller
Philip A. Morris
Frederick L. Noland
Gyo Obata
Ross D. Pallay
R. Max Peterson
William Phelps
Richard Pope, Sr.
Gen. Colin Powell
Peter H. Raven
Hon. Joseph P. Riley, Jr.
L. S. Rockefeller
Martin J. Rosen
John Seiberling
Ron Taven
Dr. Ralph J. Warburton

Source: American Society of Landscape Architects

Honorary Members of the Industrial Designers Society of America

The Board of Directors of the Industrial Designers Society of America (IDSA) grants honorary membership to individuals whose relationship to, involvement with, or special efforts on behalf of the design profession merit the recognition and gratitude of the Society. Honorary membership is awarded by a three-quarters majority vote by the Board of Directors.

1965 R. Buckminster Fuller	1983 Ralph Caplan
1965 Edgar Kaufmann, Jr.	1988 Brian J. Wynne
1981 Ray Eames	1998 Bruce Nussbaum
1982 Florence Knoll Bassett	

Source: Industrial Designers Society of America

It is often thought that heaviness is synonymous with strength. In my opinion it is just the opposite.

Mies van der Rohe

Honorary Members of the International Interior Design Association

The International Interior Design Association (IIDA) grants honorary membership to individuals who, although they are not interior designers, have made substantial contributions to the interior design profession. The following individuals are current Honorary Members of the IIDA.

Stanley Abercrombie
Clarellen Adams
George Baer
Shirley Black
Charles Blumberg
Chilton Brown
Margaret Buckingham
Len Corlin
Christine Cralle
James P. Cramer
Tom Cramer
Lori Graham
Dianne Jackman
Cynthia Leibrock

Paul Leonard
Viscount David Linley
Chris McKellar
Doug Parker
Norman Polsky
Lois Powers
John Sample
Thomas Sutton, Jr.
Dean Thompson
Jan Toft
Jill Vanderfleet-Scott
John West

Source: International Interior Design Association

Past Presidents of the American Institute of Architects

1900-1	Robert S. Peabody	1968	Robert L. Durham
1902-3	Charles F. McKim	1969	George E. Kassabaum
1904-5	William S. Eames	1970	Rex W. Allen
1906-7	Frank M. Day	1971	Robert F. Hastings
1908-9	Cass Gilbert	1972	Max O. Urbahn
1910-11	Irving K. Pond	1973	S. Scott Ferebee Jr.
1912-3	Walter Cook	1974	Archibald C. Rogers
1914-5	R. Clipston Sturgis	1975	William "Chick" Marshall Jr.
1916-8	John L. Mauran	1976	Louis DeMoll
1919-20	Thomas R. Kimball	1977	John M. McGinty
1921-2	Henry H. Kendall	1978	Elmer E. Botsai
1923-4	William B. Faville	1979	Ehrman B. Mitchell Jr.
1925-6	Dan E. Waid	1980	Charles E. Schwing
1927-8	Milton B. Medary	1981	R. Randall Vosbeck
1929-30	Charles H. Hammond	1982	Robert M. Lawrence
1931-2	Robert D. Kohn	1983	Robert C. Broshar
1933-4	Earnest J. Russell	1984	George M. Notter Jr.
1935-6	Stephen F. Voorhees	1985	R. Bruce Patty
1937-8	Charles D. Maginnis	1986	John A Busby Jr.
1939-40	Edwin Bergstrom	1987	Donald J. Hackl
1941-2	Richmond H. Shreve	1988	Ted P. Pappas
1943-4	Raymond J. Ashton	1989	Benjamin E. Brewer Jr.
1945-6	James R. Edmunds Jr.	1990	Sylvester Damianos
1947-8	Douglas W. Orr	1991	C. James Lawler
1949-50	Ralph T. Walker	1992	W. Cecil Steward
1951-2	A. Glenn Stanton	1993	Susan A. Maxman
1953-4	Clair W. Ditchy	1994	L. William Chapin Jr.
1955-6	George B. Cummings	1995	Chester A. Widom
1957-8	Leon Chatelain Jr.	1996	Raymond G. "Skipper" Post Jr.
1959-60	John Noble Richards	1997	Raj Barr-Kumar
1961-2	Philip Will Jr.	1998	Ronald A. Altoon
1963	Henry L. Wright	1999	Michael J. Stanton
1964	J. Roy Carroll Jr.	2000	Ronald Skaggs
1965	A. Gould Odell Jr.		
1966	Morris Ketchum Jr.		
1967	Charles M. Nes Jr.		

Source: American Institute of Architects

Past Presidents of the American Institute of Architecture Students

1956-57	James R. Barry, Rice Univ.	1975-76	Ella Hall, North Carolina State Univ.
1957-58	Robert Harris, Princeton Univ.	1976-77	Jerry Compton, Southern California Inst. of Arch.
1958-59	Paul Ricciutti, Case Western Reserve Univ.	1977-78	Charles Guerin, Univ. of Houston
1959-60	Charles Jones, Univ. of Arizona	1978-79	John Maudlin-Jeronimo, Univ. of Miami
1960-61	Ray Gaio, Univ. of Notre Dame	1979-80	Richard Martini, Boston Architectural Center
1961-62	Donald Williams, Univ. of Illinois at Urbana-Champaign	1980-81	Alejandro Barbarena, Univ. of Houston
1962-63	Carl Schubert, California State Polytechnic Univ.	1981-82	Bill Plimpton, Univ. of California at Berkeley
1964-65	Joseph Morse, Howard Univ.	1982-83	Robert Klancher, Univ. of Cincinnati
1965-66	Kenneth Alexander, Pratt Institute	1983-84	Robert Fox, Temple Univ.
1966-67	Jack Worth III, Georgia Institute of Technology	1984-85	Thomas Fowler IV, NYIT–Old Westbury
1967-68	Morten Awes, Univ. of Idaho	1985-86	Scott Norberg, Univ. of Nebraska
1968-69	Edward Mathes, Univ. of Southwestern Louisiana	1986-87	Scott Norberg, Univ. of Nebraska
1969-70	Taylor Culver, Howard Univ.	1987-88	Kent Davidson, Univ. of Nebraska
1970-71	Michael Interbartolo, Boston Architectural Center	1988-89	Matthew W. Gilbertson, Univ. of Minnesota
1971-72	Joseph Siff, Rice Univ.	1989-90	Douglas A. Bailey, Montana State Univ.
1972-73	Fay D'Avignon, Boston Architectural Center	1990-91	Alan D.S. Paradis, Roger Williams College
1973-74	Fay D'Avignon, Boston Architectural Center	1991-92	Lynn N. Simon, Univ. of Washington
1974-75	Patric Davis, Boston Architectural Center	1992-93	Courtney E. Miller, Univ. of Maryland
		1993-94	Garen D. Miller, Drury College
		1994-95	Dee Christy Briggs, City College of New York

Past Presidents of the American Institute of Architecture Students (Con't)

1995-96	Robert J. Rowan, Washington State Univ.	1998-99	Jay M. Palu, Univ. of Nebraska
1996-97	Raymond H. Dehn, Univ. of Minnesota	1999-2000	Melissa Mileff, Univ. of Oklahoma
1997-98	Robert L. Morgan, Clemson Univ.		

Source: American Institute of Architects Students

Did you know...

At a time when buildings usually contained no mor than 50% glass, the Hallidie Building (Willis Polk, San Francisco) was unprecedented for its all-glass façade in 1918.

Past Presidents of the American Society of Interior Designers

1974-75	Norman DeHann		1989-90	Elizabeth Howard
1974-76	Richard Jones		1990-91	Robert John Dean
1977-78	H. Albert Phibbs		1991-92	Raymond Kennedy
1978-79	Irving Schwartz		1992-93	Martha G. Rayle
1979-80	Rita St. Clair		1993-94	BJ Peterson
1980-81	Wallace Jonason		1994-95	Gary Wheeler
1981-82	Jack Lowery		1995-96	Peggy Bonda
1982-83	Martin Ellinoff		1996-97	Kathy Ford Montgomery
1984-85	William Richard Waley		1997-98	Joyce Burke Jonas
1985-86	Gail Adams		1998-99	Rosalyn Cama
1986-87	Janet Schirm			
1987-88	Joy Adcock			
1988-89	Charles Gandy			

Source: American Society of Interior Designers

The intuitive mind is a sacred gift and the rational mind is a faithful servant. We have created a society that honours the servant and has forgotten the gift.

Albert Einstein

Past Presidents of the American Society of Landscape Architects

1899-1901	John C. Olmsted*	1974-1975	Owen H. Peters
1902	Samuel Parsons, Jr.*	1975-1976	Edward H. Stone, II
1903	Nathan F. Barrett*	1976-1977	Benjamin W. Gary, Jr.
1904-1905	John C. Olmsted*	1977-1978	Lane L. Marshall
1906-1907	Samuel Parsons, Jr.*	1978-1979	Jot Carpenter
1908-1909	Frederick Law Olmsted, Jr.*	1979-1980	Robert L. Woerner
1910-1911	Charles N. Lowrie*	1980-1981	William A. Behnke
1912	Harold A. Caparn	1981-1982	Calvin T. Bishop
1913	Ossian C. Simonds*	1982-1983	Theodore J. Wirth
1914	Warren H. Manning*	1983-1984	Darwina L. Neal
1915-1918	James Sturgis Pray	1984-1985	Robert H. Mortensen
1919-1922	Frederick Law Olmsted, Jr.*	1985-1986	John Wacker
1923-1927	James L. Greenleaf	1986-1987	Roger B. Martin
1927-1931	Arthur A. Shurcliff	1987-1988	Cheryl L. Barton
1931-1935	Henry Vincent Hubbard	1988-1989	Brain S. Kubota
1935-1941	Albert D. Taylor	1989-1990	Gerald D. Patten
1941-1945	S. Herbert Hare	1990-1991	Claire R. Bennett
1945-1949	Markley Stevenson	1991-1992	Cameron R.J. Man
1949-1951	Gilmore D. Clarke	1992-1993	Debra L. Mitchell
1951-1953	Lawrence G. Linnard	1993-1994	Thomas Papandrew
1953-1957	Leon Zach	1994-1995	Dennis Y. Otsuji
1957-1961	Norman T. Newton	1995-1996	Vincent Bellafiore
1961-1963	John I. Rogers	1996-1997	Donald W. Leslie
1963-1965	John Ormsbee Simonds	1997-1998	Thomas R. Dunbar
1965-1967	Hubert B. Owens	1998-1999	Barry W. Starke
1967-1969	Theodore Osmundson		
1969-1971	Campbell E. Miller		
1971-1973	Raymond L. Freeman		
1973-1974	William G. Swain		

*Charter Member

Source: American Society of Landscape Architects

Past Presidents of the Association of Collegiate Schools of Architecture

1912-21	Warren Laird, Univ. of Pennsylvania	1959-61	Harlan McClure, Clemson College
1921-23	Emil Lorch, Univ. of Michigan	1961-63	Olindo Grossi, Pratt Institute
1923-25	William Emerson, Massachusetts Institute of Technology	1963-65	Henry Kamphoefner, North Carolina St. College
1925-27	Francke Bosworth, Jr., Cornell Univ.	1965-67	Walter Sanders, Univ. of Michigan
1927-29	Goldwin Goldsmith, Univ. of Kansas	1967-69	Robert Bliss, Univ. of Utah
1929-31	Everett Meeks, Yale Univ.	1969-71	Charles Burchard, Virginia Polytechnic
1931-34	Ellis Lawrence, Univ. of Oregon	1971-72	Alan Taniguchi, Rice Univ. & Univ. of Texas, Austin
1934-36	Roy Childs Jones, Univ. of Minnesota	1972-73	Robert Harris, Univ. of Oregon
1936-38	Sherely Morgan, Princeton Univ.	1973-74	Sanford Greenfield, Boston Arch. Center
1938-40	George Young, Jr., Cornell Univ.	1974-75	Don Schlegal, Univ. of New Mexico
1940-42	Leopold Arnaud, Columbia Univ.	1975-76	Bertram Berenson, Univ. of Illinois at Chicago
1942-45	Wells Bennett, Univ. of Michigan	1976-77	Donlyn Lyndon, Massachusetts Institute of Technology
1945-47	Loring Provine, Univ. of Illinois	1977-78	Dwayne Nuzum, Univ. of Colorado, Boulder
1947-49	Paul Weigel, Kansas State College	1978-79	William Turner, Tulane Univ.
1949-51	B. Kenneth Johnstone, Carnegie Institute	1979-80	Robert Burns, North Carolina State Univ.
1951-53	Thomas FitzPatrick, Iowa State College	1980-81	Richard Peters, Univ. of California, Berkeley
1953-55	Lawrence Anderson, Massachusetts Institute of Technology	1981-82	Eugene Kremer, Kansas State Univ.
1955-57	Elliott Whitaker, Ohio State Univ.	1982-83	O. Jack Mitchell, Rice Univ.
1957-59	Buford Pickens, Washington Univ.	1983-84	Charles Hight, Univ. of North Carolina, Charlotte

Past Presidents of the Association of Collegiate Schools of Architecture (Con't)

1984-85	Wilmot Gilland, Univ. of Oregon	1992-93	James Barker, Clemson Univ.
1985-86	George Anselevicius, Univ. of New Mexico	1993-94	Kent Hubbell, Cornell Univ.
1986-87	Blanche Lemco van Ginkel, Univ. of Toronto	1994-95	Diane Ghirardo, Univ. of Southern California
1987-88	J. Thomas Regan, Univ. of Miami	1995-96	Robert Greenstreet, Univ. of Wisconsin-Milwaukee
1988-89	Robert Beckley, Univ. of Michigan	1996-97	Linda W. Sanders, Calif. State Polytechnic Univ.
1989-90	Marvin Malecha, Cal. State Poly. Univ., Pomona	1997-98	John M. McRae, Mississippi State Univ.
1990-91	John Meunier, Arizona State Univ.	1998-99	R. Wayne Drummond, Univ. of Florida
1991-92	Patrick Quinn, Rensselaer Polytechnic Institute		

Source: Association of Collegiate Schools of Architecture

Good spaces can help us all live more fully.

Horace Havemeyer III

Past Presidents of the Construction Specifications Institute

948-49	James B. Moore		1975-76	Larry C. Dean
949-50	James B. Moore		1976-77	Philip J. Todisco
950-51	Francis R. Wragg		1977-78	Louis H. Sams
951-52	Carl J. Ebert		1978-79	R. Stanley Bair
952-53	Carl J. Ebert		1979-80	Howard R. Steinmann
953-54	Lester T. Burn		1980-81	George S. George
954-55	Lester t. Burn		1981-82	Robert J. Schmidt
955-56	Joseph A. McGinnis		1982-83	Terry J. Strong
956-57	J. Norman Hunter		1983-84	Donald D. Meisel
957-58	J. Norman Hunter		1984-85	Terry M. Wadsworth
958-59	J. Stewart Stein		1985-86	Richard B. Solomon
959-60	J. Stewart Stein		1986-87	Charles Chief Boyd
960-61	Glen H. Abplanalp		1987-88	Robert L. McManus
961-62	James C. Bort		1988-89	Weldon W. Nash, Jr.
962-63	Edwin T. Pairo		1989-90	S. Steve Blumenthal
963-64	Jack R. Lewis		1990-91	Robert W. Johnson
964-65	Terrell R. Harper		1991-92	Sheldon B. Israel
965-66	Henry B. Baume		1992-93	Thomas I. Young
966-67	Henry B. Baume		1993-94	Jerome H. Alciatore
967-68	John C. Anderson		1994-95	William F. Riesberg
968-69	Kelsey Y. Saint		1995-96	Jane D. Baker
969-70	Arthur W. Brown		1996-97	Richard A. Eustis
970-71	Ben F. Greenwood		1997-98	Robert R. Molseed
971-72	Arthur J. Miller		1998-99	Kenneth E. Guthrie
972-73	John C. Fleck			
973-74	Robert E. Vansant			
974-75	Larry C. Dean			

Source: Construction Specification Institute

Did you know...
The faces on South Dakota's Mount Rushmore, the world's largest sculpture, have noses 20 feet long, mouths 18 feet wide and eyes 11 feet across.

Past Presidents of the Industrial Designers Society of America

1965	Henry Dreyfuss	1983-84	Katherine J. McCoy
1966	Joseph M. Parriott	1985-86	Cooper C. Woodring
1967-68	Robert Hose	1987-88	Peter H. Wooding
1969-70	Tucker Madawick	1989-90	Peter W. Bressler
1971-72	William Goldsmith	1991-92	Charles Pelly
1973-74	Arthur Pulos	1993-94	David Tompkins
1975-76	James Fulton	1995-96	James Ryan
1977 78	Richard Hollerith	1997-98	Craig Vogel
1979-80	Carroll M. Gantz	1999-00	Mark Dziersk
1981-82	Robert G. Smith		

Source: Industrial Designers Society of America

Above all, an object must function well and efficien
ly – and getting that part right requires a good deal of time and attention.

Sir Terence Conran

Past Presidents of the International Interior Design Association

1994-1995 Marilyn Farrow
1995-1996 Judith Hastings
1996-1997 Beth Harmon-Vaughan
1997-1998 Karen Guenther

1998-1999 Neil Frankel
1999-2000 Carol Jones

Source: International Interior Design Association

The job of buildings is to improve human relations: architecture must ease them, not make them worse.

Ralph Erskine

Past Presidents of the National Council for Architectural Registration Boards

1920-22	Emil Loch	1972	Daniel Boone
1923-24	Arthur Peabody	1973	Thomas J. Sedgewick
1925	Miller I. Kast	1974	E.G. Hamilton
1926-27	W.H. Lord	1975	John (Mel) O'Brien, Jr.
1928	George D. Mason	1976	William C. Muchow
1929-30	Clarence W. Brazer	1977	Charles A. Blondheim, Jr.
1931-32	James M. White	1978	Paul H. Graven
1933	A.L. Brockway	1979	Lorenzo D. Williams
1933	A.M. Edelman	1980	John R. Ross
1934-35	Joseph W. Holman	1981	Dwight M. Bonham
1936	Charles Butler	1982	Thomas H. Flesher, Jr.
1938-39	William Perkins	1983	Sid Frier
1940-41	Mellen C. Greeley	1984	Ballard H.T. Kirk
1942-44	Louis J. Gill	1985	Robert E. Oringdulph
1945-46	Solis Seiferth	1986	Theodore L. Mularz
1947-49	Warren D. Miller	1987	Robert L. Tessier
1950	Clinton H. Cowgill	1988	Walter T. Carry
1951	Roger C. Kirchoff	1989	George B. Terrien
1952-52	Charles E. Firestone	1990	Herbert P. McKim
1954-55	Fred L. Markham	1991	Charles E. Garrison
1956-58	Edgar H. Berners	1992	Robert H. Burke, Jr.
1959-60	Walter F. Martens	1993	Harry G. Robinson, III
1961	A. Reinhold Melander		William Wiese, II (Honorary
1962	Chandler C. Cohagen		Past President)
1963	Paul W. Drake	1994	Robert A. Fielden
1964	Ralph O. Mott	1995	Homer L. Williams
1965	C.J. "Pat" Paderewski	1996	Richard W. Quinn
1966	Earl L. Mathes	1997	Darrell L. Smith
1967	George F. Schatz	1998	Ann R. Chaintreuil
1968-69	Howard T. Blanchard	1999	Susan May Allen, AIA
1970	Dean L. Gustavson	2000	Joseph P. Giattina, Jr.
1971	William J. Geddis		

Source: National Council for Architectural Registration

Past Presidents of the Royal Institute of British Architects

1835-59	Earl de Grey	1935-37	Sir Percy Thomas
1860	Charles Robert Cockerell	1937-39	H.S. Goodhart-Rendel
1861-63	Sir William Tite	1939-40	E. Stanley Hall
1863-65	Thomas L. Donaldson	1940-43	W.H. Ansell
1865-67	A.J.B. Beresford Hope	1943-46	Sir Percy Thomas
1867-70	Sir William Tite	1946-48	Sir Lancelot Keay
1870-73	Thomas Henry Wyatt	1948-50	Michael T. Waterhouse
1873-76	Sir Gilbert G. Scott	1950-52	A. Graham Henderson
1876-79	Charles Barry	1952-54	Sir Howard Robertson
1879-81	John Whichcord	1954-56	C.H.Aslin
1881	George Edmund Street	1956-58	Kenneth M.B. Cross
1882-84	Sir Horace Jones	1958-60	Sir Basil Spence
1884-86	Ewan Christian	1960-62	The Lord Holford
1886-87	Edward l'Anson	1962-64	Sir Robert Matthew
1888-91	Alfred Watershouse	1964-65	Sir Donald Gibson
1891-94	J. Macvicar Anderson	1965-67	The Viscount Esher
1884-96	Francis C. Penrose	1967-69	Sir Hugh Wilson
1896-99	George Aitchison	1969-71	Sir Peter Shepheard
1899-1902	Sir William Emerson	1971-73	Sir Alex Gordon
1902-04	Sir Aston Webb	1973-75	F.B.Pooley
1904-06	John Belcher	1975-77	Eric Lyons
1906-08	Thomas Edward Collcut	1977-79	Gordon Graham
1908-10	Sir Ernest George	1979-81	Bryan Jefferson
1910-12	Leonard Stokes	1981-83	Owen Luder
1912-14	Sir Reginald Blomfield	1983-85	Michael Manser
1914-17	Ernest Newton	1985-87	Larry Rolland
1917-19	Henry Thomas Hare	1987-89	Rod Hackney
1919-21	Sir John William Simpson	1989-91	Max Hutchinson
1921-23	Paul Waterhouse	1991-93	Richard C. MacCormac
1923-25	J. Alfred Gotch	1993-95	Frank Duffy
1925-27	Sir Guy Dawber	1995-97	Owen Luder
1927-29	Sir Walter Tapper	1997-99	David Rock
1929-31	Sir Banister Fletcher	1999-	Marco Goldschmied
1931-33	Sir Raymond Unwin		
1933-35	Sir Giles Gilbert Scott		

Source: Royal Institute of British Architects

Past Presidents of the Society of Architectural Historians

1941-42	Turpin C. Bannister	1970-71	James F. O'Gorman
1943-44	Rexford Newcomb	1972-74	Alan W. Gowans
1945-47	Kenneth John Conant	1975-76	Spiro Kostof
1948-49	Carroll L.V. Meeks	1976-78	Marian C. Donnelly
1950	Buford L. Pickens	1978-80	Adolph K. Placzek
1951	Charles E. Peterson	1982-84	Damie Stillman
1952-53	Henry-Russell Hitchcock	1984-86	Carol Herselle Krinsky
1954	Agnes Addison Gilchrist	1986-88	Osmund Overby
1955-56	James G. Van Derpool	1988-90	Richard J. Betts
1957-58	Carroll L. V. Meeks	1990-93	Elisabeth Blair MacDougall
1959	Walter L. Creese	1993-94	Franklin Toker
1960-61	Barbara Wriston	1994-96	Keith N. Morgan
1962-63	John D. Forbes	1996-98	Patricia Waddy
1964-65	H. Allen Brooks	1998-2000	Richard Longstreth
1966-67	George B. Tatum		
1968-69	Henry A. Millon		

Source: Society of Architectural Historians

Architecture is inhabited sculpture.

Constantin Brancusi

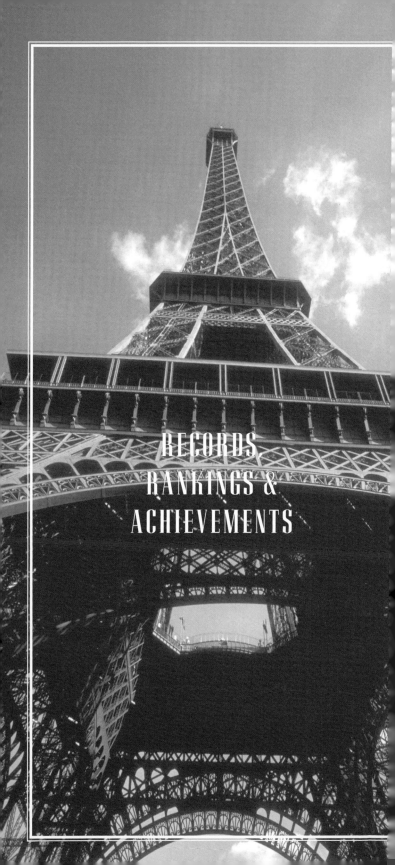

RECORDS, RANKINGS & ACHIEVEMENTS

RECORDS, RANKINGS & ACHIEVEMENTS

Century's Top 10 Construction Achievements

The Top 10 Construction Achievements of the 20th Century were chosen from a list of over a 100 international nominations which included such diverse projects as bridges, dams, highways, roads, tunnels, buildings, stadiums, commercial centers, and transportation facilities. Besides requiring that the projects be entirely developed during the 20th century, the selection criterion also included integrity in construction and design, contribution to improving the quality of life, technological progressiveness, and positive economic impact. This program was established to promote the construction industry's increased contribution to the advancement of our society. The final judging occurred at the triennial CONEXPO-CON/AGG exposition in March 1999 in Las Vegas by a panel of editors and executives from the construction and construction materials industry.

1. The Channel Tunnel between Dover, England and Calais, France

2. The Golden Gate Bridge, San Francisco

3. The U.S. Interstate Highway System

4. The Empire State Building, New York City

5. Hoover Dam, Nevada and Arizona

6. The Panama Canal

7. Sydney Opera House, Sydney, Australia

8. Aswan High Dam, Egypt

9. The World Trade Center, New York City

10. Chek Lap Kok Airport, Hong Kong

Source: Architecture magazine and CONEXPO-CON/AGG

Opposite: Sydney Opera House, Sydney, Australia, Jørn Utzon
Photograph © Brad Simmons/Esto.

Construction Costs – 25 Least Expensive Cities

These cities are currently the least expensive locales in the United States and Canada to construct a building according to R.S. Means, the country's leading construction costing company. This ranking is based on 1999 square foot costs for a 2-4 story office building of average construction type. Costs include labor, materials, and professional design fees.

1. Fayetteville, Arkansas
2. Alliance, Nebraska
3. Columbia, South Carolina
4. Provo, Utah
4. El Paso, Texas
4. Charleston, South Carolina
4. Asheville, North Carolina
4. Charlotte, North Carolina
9. Martinsburg, West Virginia
9. Durham, North Carolina
9. Raleigh, North Carolina
9. Winston-Salem, North Carolina
9. Greensboro, North Carolina
14. Abilene, Texas
14. McAllen, Texas
14. Rapid City, South Dakota
14. Jackson, Mississippi
14. Columbus, Georgia
19. Corpus Christi, Texas
19. Laredo, Texas
19. Dallas, Texas
19. Aberdeen, South Dakota
19. Tallahassee, Florida
19. Little Rock, Arkansas
19. Montgomery, Alabama

Source: R.S. Means

Did you know...
In 1840, Richard Morris Hunt became the first American to receive the French Ecole des Beaux Arts' certificate.

Construction Costs – 25 Most Expensive Cities

These cities are currently the most expensive locales in the United States and Canada to construct a building according to R.S. Means, the country's leading construction costing company. This ranking is based on 1999 square foot costs for a 2-4 story office building of average construction type. Costs include labor, materials, and professional design fees.

1. New York, New York
2. Anchorage, Alaska
3. Fairbanks, Alaska
4. San Francisco, California
4. Brooklyn, New York
6. Honolulu, Hawaii
7. Yonkers, New York
8. San Jose, California
9. Oakland, California
9. Berkeley, California
9. Santa Rosa, California
12. Boston, Massachusetts
13. Palo Alto, California
13. Vallejo, California

15. Toronto, Canada
16. Salinas, California
16. Newark, New Jersey
16. Paterson, New Jersey
16. Albuquerque, New Mexico
16. Philadelphia, Pennsylvania
21. Los Angeles, California
21. Sacramento, California
21. Chicago, Illinois
21. Jersey City, New Jersey
21. Trenton, New Jersey

Source: R.S. Means

Fastest Growing Firms

Over 650 design firms in major U.S. cities were surveyed to determine which had experienced the greatest growth in the preceding year. In the case of firms with multiple offices, only information from the respective city offices was considered; no corporate-wide statistics were used. The following rankings are based on the percentage of growth experienced by the firms between 1998 and 1999.

Atlanta
1. Gensler
2. Godwin Associates
3. Sizemore Floyd Architects, Inc.
4. Hellmuth, Obata + Kassabaum, Inc.
5. Leo A. Daly

Boston
1. Koetter Kim & Associates
2. Cubellis Associates, Inc.
3. Einhorn Yaffee Prescott Architecture & Engineering, PC
4. CBT/Childs Bertman Tsechares Inc.
5. Symmes Maini & McKee Associates/ SMMA

Chicago
1. HDR Architecture, Inc.
1. Teng & Associates, Inc.
3. Hellmuth, Obata + Kassabaum, Inc.
4. Mekus Studios Ltd.
5. Skidmore, Owings & Merrill, LLP

Cleveland
1. ASD
2. Dorsky Hodgson + Partners, Inc.
3. HWH Architects Engineers Planners Inc.
4. Design Collective Incorporated
5. Richard Fleischman Architects Inc.

Dallas
1. Gensler
2. Croft Compton Co., Inc.
3. Hodges & Associates
3. IA – Dallas
4. Urban Architects

Denver
1. Barker Rinker Seacat Architects
2. Anderson Mason Dale Architects
3. Fentress Bradburn Architects
4. Humphries Poli Architects, PC
5. RNL Design, PC

Detroit
1. Gensler
2. Marco Design Group
3. Ford & Earl Associates, Inc.
4. Scarcello Associates, Inc.
5. BEI Associates, Inc.
5. TMP Associates, Inc.
5. The Argos Group

Florida
1. Arquitectonica
2. IA – Fort Lauderdale
3. Forum Architecture and Interior Design, Inc.
3. SCHENKELSHULTZ
3. Perkins & Will

Fastest Growing Firms (Con't)

Houston

1. John S. Chase, Architects, Inc.
2. PBK Architects, Inc.
3. Popham Walter Architects & Engineers
4. Hellmuth, Obata + Kassabaum, Inc.
5. FKP Architects, Inc.
5. Hunter-Moody Architects
5. Leo A. Daly

Indianapolis

1. Steed Hammond Paul Inc.
2. BSA Design
3. SCHENKELSHULTZ
4. Ratio Architects, Inc.
5. Architectural Alliance, Inc.

Los Angeles

1. Wirt Design Group
2. Johnson Fain Partners
3. McLarand Vasquez & Partners
4. LPA
5. Perkins & Will

Minneapolis

1. Shea Architects, Inc.
2. Meyer, Scherer & Rockcastle, Ltd.
3. DLR Group
4. Tushie-Montgomery & Associates, Inc.
5. BWBR Architects, Inc.
5. BDH & Young Space Design, Inc.

New York

1. Perkins Eastmand Architects, PC
2. Highland Associates, PC
3. HLW International, LLP
4. Davis Brody Bond, LLP
5. The Hillier Group

Philadelphia

1. Partridge Tackett Architects
2. Ballinger
2. BLM Group
4. Granary Associates
5. Raytheon Architects, Ltd.

San Francisco

1. Ellerbe Becket
2. Mancini Duffy
3. Brayton & Hughes
4. Barrett Quezada Architecture
4. NBBJ

Seattle

1. GGLO P.L.L.C.
2. The Retail Group
3. JPC Architects
4. Zimmer Gunsul Frasca Partnership
5. Northwest Architectural Company

St. Louis

1. Gray Design Group, Inc.
2. William B. Ittner, Inc.
3. Directions in Design, Inc.
4. Davis Mason & Associates, Inc.
5. Cannon

Washington, D.C.

1. KCF/SHG
2. The Hillier Group/WHDA
3. Gensler & Associates
4. Heery International
5. Models, Inc.

Source: Counsel House Research/Greenway Group

Did you know...
Worldwide, IBM procures over $100 million in professional design fees each year.

Firm Anniversaries

The following currently practicing architecture firms were founded in 1900, 1925, 1950, and 1975 respectively.

Firms Celebrating their 100th Anniversary

DLR Group Architecture & Planning, Portland, OR

Hamme Associates Architects & Engineers, York, PA

JMGR Inc., Memphis, TN

Mead & Hunt, Madison, WI

Nikken Sekki Ltd., Tokyo, Japan

Steed Hammond Paul Inc., Hamilton, OH

Firms Celebrating their 75th Anniversary

Castro-Buchel Architects & Planners, Inc., Chicago, IL

Colvig Architects PC, Des Moines, IA

Giffels Associates, Inc., Southfield, MI

Loebl Schlossman & Hackl/Hague Richards, Chicago, IL

Scholer Corporation, Lafayette, IN

Smiley Glotter Nyberg Architects, Inc. Architects/Planners/Interior Designers, Minneapolis, MN

Firms Celebrating their 50th Anniversary

Alderman & MacNeish Architects, West Springfield, MA

Argus Supply Company, Roseville, MI

Barron Heinberg & Brocato, Alexandria, LA

Becker and Becker Associates, Inc., New Canaan, CT

Jack Beers – Architects/Engineers, Lincoln NE

Casazza Peetz & Hancock Architects & Planners, Reno, NV

Celli-Flynn and Associates, Pittsburgh, PA

Chipman Adams Ltd., Park Ridge, IL

Community Tectonics, Inc., Knoxville, TN

Daniels & Zermack Associates, Inc., Ann Arbor, MI

Dreyfuss & Blackford Architects, Sacramento, CA

The Harmon Group Architects / Clubhouse Designs, Potomac, MD

Hollis & Miller Group, Inc., Prairie Village, KS & Lee's Summit, MO

Jackson-Jackson & Associates, Inc., Omaha, NE

Oglesby-Greene Inc., Dallas, TX

Perkins Pryde Kennedy & Steevensz Architects, Ltd., Glen Ellyn, IL

Willis Regier, AIA, Architect, Inc., Bellevue, NE

Ruhnau Ruhnau Associates, Inc, Riverside, CA

L.K. Sorensen Associates, Inc., Salt Lake City, UT

Thompson Professional Group, Inc., Houston, TX

VBN Architects, Oakland, CA

Zaugg & Zaugg Architects, Mansfield, OH

Firms Celebrating their 25th Anniversary

Allegretti Architects, St. Joseph, MI

Alpha Design Group Inc., Raleigh, NC

Aldo Altobelli, AIA, West Springfield, MA

Anthony Ames, Architect, Atlanta, GA

Anderson Mason Dale PC, Denver, CO

Firm Anniversaries (Con't)

Andropogon Associates Ltd., Philadelphia, PA

Archeon Inc, Memphis, TN

Architectural Design Group Inc., Oklahoma City, OK

The Architectural Partnership, Lincoln, NE

Architecture/Artistry/Interiors/Inc., Traverse City, MI

The Architecture Company, Tucson, AZ

Ard-Wood Architects Inc., Greenville, SC

Askew Nixon Ferguson Architects Inc., Memphis, TN

Giorgio Balli, AIA, Architect, Miami, FL

Barker, Rinker Seacat and Partners, Architects, PC, Denver, CO

Barun Basu Associates, New London, CT

The Blackstone Partnership, Houston, TX

Blitz Architectural Group, PC, Philadelphia, PA

Reuben E. Bohnert, AIA, Fredericksburg, TX

Boland Associates, St. Louis, MO

Niles Bolton Associates Inc., Atlanta, GA

Bowles, Kendrick & Lemanski, Architects, San Francisco, CA

Breakaway Architects, San Francisco, CA

Brinkley Sargent Architects, Dallas, TX

D. R. Brooks Architects Inc., Cincinnati, OH

BSA Design, Indianapolis, IN

Burt Taggart and Associates/ Architects, North Little Rock, AZ

Callison Architecture, Seattle, WA

W. S. Carson Architect, Hilton Head Island, SC

CDG Architects, Ltd., Tucson, AX

Cedar Corporation, Menomonie, WI

Centerbrook Architects and Planners, LLC, Essex, CT

Timothy Trevor Clark, Architect, Dorset, VT

Addison Clipson Associate Architects Inc., Cincinnati, OH

Joseph A. Courter Jr., AIA, Tuckerton, NJ

Richard L. Crowther, FAIA, Denver, CO

Curts Gaines Hall Architects Planners Inc., Tampa, FL

Daimwood Derryberry Pavelchak Architects PA, Longwood, FL

Dassa/Richardi Architects, West Paterson, NJ

Davis Associates Architects & Consultants, Inc., Chicago, IL

Degenshein Architects – Planners, Nyack, NY

Aramis Del Pino Architects, Coral Gables, FL

Denker & Bodnar PC, Nyack, NY

Dewberry & Davis, Marion, VA

Eck/Architect Inc., Boston, MA

EN Associates Inc., Culver City, CA

Nelson Fay, AIA, Inc., Encino, CA

FCM Corporation, Inc., Madison, WI

Warren Freedenfeld & Associates Inc., Boston, MA

Stanley J. French, AIA, Architect, Ruidoso, NM

Gibbons Heidtmann & Salvador Architects & Planners PC, Mount Kisco, NY

Peter Gisolfi Associates, Hastings-on-Hudson, NY

Christopher G. Green & Associates, St. Thomas, Virgin Islands

Groupdesigners, Lafayette, CA

Steven F. Haas, Architect, Alford, MA

Habermann Builders Inc, Old Greenwich, CT

Haldemann Powell & Partners, Dallas, TX

Hall Hurley Deutsch, Santa Maria, CA

Arthur Manns Harden, AIA, Architects, Mantoloking, NJ

Firm Anniversaries (Con't)

Helman Hurley Charvat Peacock/ Architects, Inc., Maitland, FL

Hilbert Architecture, Mercer Island, WA

The Hill Partnership, Inc., Newport Beach, CA

Hodges/Marvin, Architects, Inc., Dillon, CO

John Hueser Associates, Kansas City, MO

Huitt-Zollars Inc., Fort Worth, TX

Robert Jackson Architects, Austin, TX

M. S. James III AIA Architects Inc., PS, Olympia, WA

JDM Associates-Architects/Planners, San Antonio, TX

Jensen . Hayes . Shropshire Architects, PA, Pocatello, ID

Johnson + Bailey Architects PC, Mufreesboro, TN

Bendrew G. Jong, AIA, Orinda, CA

JRA Architects Inc., Tallahassee, FL

Stanley B. Kalb . Associates, Lawrence, NY

Rolf Karl, Architect, PC, New York, NY

The Keimig Associates, Architects/ Planners, Auburn, WA

Killefer Flammang Purtill Architects, Santa Monica, CA

Klick Inter Arch Design, Ltd., Anoka, MN

Bruce Knutson Architects Inc., Minneapolis, MN

Joseph J. Kobylecky, AIA, PC, Charlotte, NC

Lauri J. Kurki Jr. AIA, Southampton, PA

Labunski Associates Architects, Harlingen, TX

Richard Landau Architects & Planners, Blairsville, GA

G. Franklin Lee, AIA, Abington, PA

Leifeste/Belanger & Associates, Houston, TX

Lew & Patnaude Inc., Fresno, CA

Jack Lindeman-Specifications Consultant, Minneapolis, MN

Lindsay Ponder Brayfield & Associates Inc., Lawrenceville, GA

Livingston Slone, Inc., Anchorage, AK

Lumpkin & Associates Architects, Ardmore, OK

Eva Maddox Associates, Inc., Chicago, I

Peter Marino & Associates Architects, New York, NY

James D. Marshall Jr., AIA, Architect, Prairie Village, KS

McCall & Associates, Inc., Valdosta, GA

F. Xavier McGeady, AIA PE, Architect & Engineer, Severna Park, MD

Darryl Charles McMillen Architect, PA, Sun Valley, ID

Meister Architects, West Reading, PA

Walter B. Melvin, AIA, Architects, New York, NY

The Merit Design Group, Pasadena, CA

Moore II Architects, West Tisbury, MA

Morter Architects, Vail, CO

Myers/Anderson Architects, Pocatello, II

Barton Myers Associates, Inc., Beverly Hills, CA

Ellis Myers Architect, Inc., Atlanta, GA

R. G. Myers & Associates, Inc., Plymouth, MI

Mylan Architectural Group, Verona, NJ

Chartier Newton & Associates, Austin, T.

Nicoloff and Associates Inc., San Diego CA

O'Brien/Atkins Associates, Research Triangle Park, NC

Omni Architects, Lexington, KY

Howard Oxley Associates, La Jolla, CA

Parkhill, Smith & Cooper Architecture Division, Lubbock, TX

Parsons Brinckerhoff Quade & Dougla: Inc., Orange, CA

L. P. Perfido Associates, Pittsburgh, PA

Firm Anniversaries (Con't)

Dan Peterson & Associates Inc., Point Richmond CA

Peterson/Raeder Incorporated Architects, Akron, OH

PFDA Inc, Chicago, IL

Bert S. Pincolini Architect, Reno, NV

Planning Design Research Corporation, Houston, TX

Plaseied & Associates, Vienna, VA

Pat M. Pulitano, AIA, PC, Greenwich, CT

Rees Associates, Inc., Oklahoma City, OK

Glenn Ritter, NCARB, Kulpsville, PA

J. J. Rose & Associates, Fayetteville, NC

Michael Rosenfeld Inc., Architect, Acton, MA

George Cooper Rudolph III Architects, New York, NY

Ruprecht Schroeder Hoffman Architects Pittsburgh, PA

Salemi Associates Architects, Inc., Saugus, MA

Jaime Schapiro, AIA, and Associates Architects Planners Inc, North Miami Beach, FL

Scheer, Tanaka, Dennehy Architects Inc., Irvine, CA

J. S. Schultz Architect and Associates, Coral Springs, FL

Steven B. Schwortz, AIA, Architect PA, North Miami Beach, FL

Seaver Franks Architects, Tucson, AZ

Joseph D. Sekely III, Architect, Dellroy, OH

Robert K. Seymour Architect, South Lyon, MI

Burton L. Shatz AIA Architect, Darien, CT

Sheehan Van Woert Architects, Reno, NV

Sheriff & Associates, Los Angeles, CA

Franz Joseph Shropa, AIA, Architects & Planners, Inc., Plantation, FL

Roy Skarl, Jr., AIA, Architect, Huntington, WV

Gray Smith's Office, Philadelphia, PA

Charles A. Spitz, AIA, Architect, West Long Branch, NJ

The Stichler Design Group, Inc., Phoenix, AZ

Frank J. Stiene Group, PA, Ridgewood, NJ

Patrick Sullivan Associates, Claremont, CA

Swatt Architects, San Francisco, CA

Swilley Curtis Mundy Associates Architects, Lakeland, FL

Tate Hill Jacobs Architects, Lexington, KY

Tetra Design Inc., Los Angeles, CA

Ronald Thurber & Associates, Boise, ID

J. Stuart Todd Architects, Dallas, TX

Ullman & Fill/Architects, Chicago, IL

Urban Design Group Inc., Tulsa, OK

Frederick J. Voytko, AIAA, PA, West Long Branch, NJ

Washington Architectural Group, PA, Morristown, NJ

The Watry Design Group, San Mateo, CA

D. E. Weatherby & Associates, Inc., Gahanna, OH

Widseth Smith Nolting, Crookston, MN

Thomas Williamson, Architect, San Diego, CA

R. G. Wood & Associates Ltd., Honolulu, HI

WRS, Inc, Kansas City, MO

Yielding, Wakeford & McGee, Architects, PC, Albany, GA

David Carl Zimmermann-Architect, Scarsdale, NY

Source: Counsel House Research/Greenway Group

Largest Architecture and Design Firms

Over 650 design firms in major U.S. cities were surveyed to measure how their staff is allocated. In the case of firms with multiple offices, only information from the respective city offices was considered; no corporate-wide statistics were used. The following rankings are based on the number of design professionals - architects, interior designers, design engineers, and landscape architects - the firms reported they currently employ.

Atlanta

1. Thompson, Ventulett, Stainback & Associates
2. Niles Bolton Associates, Inc.
3. Cooper Carry, Inc.
4. Perkins & Will
5. Heery International

Boston

1. Griswold Heckel & Kelly Associates, Inc.
2. Sasaki Associates, Inc.
3. Shepley Bulfinch Richardson and Abbott
4. CBT/Childs Bertman Tsechares Inc.
5. Elkus/Manfredi Architects, Ltd.

Chicago

1. Skidmore, Owings, Merrill, LLP
2. O'Donnell Wicklund Pigozzi & Peterson
3. The Environments Group
4. Perkins & Will
5. Loebl Schlossman & Hackl/Hague Richards

Cleveland

1. Van Dijk, Pace, Westlake & Partners
2. Dorsky Hodgson + Partners, Inc.
3. Collins Gordon Bostwick Architects
3. KA, Inc. Architecture
5. Spice Costantino Architects, Inc.

Dallas

1. HKS Inc,
2. Corgan Associates, Inc.
3. SHW Group, Inc.
4. RTKL
5. Gromatzky Dupree and Associates
5. Robert Young Associates

Denver

1. RNL Design, PC
2. Ohlson Lavoie Corporation
3. H & L Architecture, Ltd.
3. Klipp Colussy Jenks DuBois Architecture, Interiors, Planning
5. Fentress Bradburn Architects

Detroit

1. TMP Associates, Inc.
2. Giffels Associates
3. SmithGroup, Inc.
4. Ford & Earl Associates, Inc.
4. Ghafari Associates

Florida

1. The Haskell Company
2. Pavlik Design Team
3. HOK
4. Arquitectonica
5. Forum Architecture and Interior Design, Inc.

Largest Design Firms (Con't)

Houston

1. Hermes Reed Architects
2. Kirksey and Partners Architects
3. Gensler
3. Pierce Goodwin Alexander & Linville
4. FKP Architects, Inc.

Indianapolis

1. Schmidt Associates, Inc.
2. BSA Design
2. CSO Architects, Engineers & Interiors
4. HNTB
5. Browning Day Mullins Dierdorf, Inc.

Los Angeles

1. DMJM
2. RTKL
3. HOK – Santa Monica
4. The Jerde Partnership International Inc.
5. Lee Burkhart Liu Inc.

Minneapolis

1. Ellerbe Becket
2. Hammel Green and Abrahamson, Inc.
3. Setter, Leach & Lindstrom
4. BWBR Architects, Inc.
5. Cunningham Group
5. Elness Swenson Graham Architects Inc.

New York

1. Gensler
2. Perkins Eastman Architects, PC
3. Skidmore Owings & Merrill, LLP
4. Mancini Duffy
5. The Phillips Group

Philadelphia

1. Ewing Cole Cherry Brott
2. Kling Lindquist
3. Ballinger
4. Granary Associates
5. Vitetta Group

San Francisco

1. Gensler
2. Hellmuth, Obata + Kassabaum, Inc.
3. Kaplan/McLauglin/Diaz
4. Backen Arrigoni & Ross, Inc.
5. RMW Architecture + Design

Seattle

1. NBBJ Architects
2. Callison Architects
3. Mithun Partners
4. LMN Architects
5. Northwest Architectural Company

St. Louis

1. Hellmuth, Obata + Kassabaum, Inc.
2. Christner, Inc.
3. Peckham Guyton Albers & Viets, Inc.
4. Cannon
4. Sverdrup Facilities, Inc.

Washington, D.C

1. Gensler & Associates
2. CUH2A, Inc.
3. Einhorn Yaffee Prescott Architecture
4. Hellmuth, Obata + Kassabaum, Inc.
5. AI
5. KCF/SHG
5. Leo A. Daly

Source: Counsel House Research/Greenway Group

Longest Covered Bridges in the World

Covered bridges still survive throughout the world from many periods of history. Bridges are also being resorted and rebuilt by covered bridge enthusiasts. The following list contains the 30 longest covered bridges in the world.

For additional information about covered bridges, contact the National Society for the Preservation of Covered Bridges at *dickroych1@juno.com*, or visit *www.atawalk.com* on the Web for covered bridge items of interest from around the world.

Rank	Bridge	Feet	Location	Truss Type	# spans	Year built
1	Hartland Bridge	1282	Carleton County, New Brunswick, Canada	Howe	7	1921
2	Reinbrücke	673	Between Stein, Switzerland and Sackingen, Germany	Multiple Queen (overlapping)	7	1803
3	Kapellbrücke	656	Luzern, Switzerland	1 multiple King span, 25 stringers	26	1333
4	St. Nicholas River Bridge	504	Kent County, New Brunswick, Canada	Howe	3+	1919
5	Marchand Bridge	499	Pontiac County, Quebec, Canada	Town lattice & Queen	6	1898
6	Perrault Bridge	495	Beauce County, Quebec, Canada	Town lattice variation	4	1928
7	Sevelen/Vaduz Bridge	480	Liechtenstein-Canton of St. Gallen, Switzerland	Howe (double X)	6	1901
8	Cornish-Windsor Bridge	460	Sullivan County, New Hampshire & Windsor County, Vermont	Timber Notch Lattice	2	1866
9	Rosenstein Park Footbridge	449	Baden-Wurrtemberg State, Germany	Ext. Queen & Ext. Steel Queen	2	1977
10	Medora Bridge	434	Jackson County, Indiana	Burr Arch	3	1875
11	unknown	410	Heilbronn-Kochendorf, Germany	Stringer	6	1976
12	Ashnola River Road Bridge	400	Similkameen Division, British-Columbia, Canada	Howe	3	1923

Longest Covered Bridges in the World (Con't)

Rank	Bridge	Feet	Location	Truss Type	# spans	Year built
13	Williams Bridge	376	Lawrence County, Indiana	Howe	2	1884
13	Bath Bridge	376	Grafton County, New-Hampshire	Multiple King Post	4	1832
15	Degussa Footbridge	369	Baden-Wurtemberg State, Germany	Stringer	7	1979
16	Schwäbisch-Hall's Stadtwerke footbridge	362	Schwabisch-Hall, Germany	Inverted Multiple King	6	1981
17	Cesky-Krumov Footbridge	361	Southern Bohemia, Czech Republic	unknown		
17	Betlemska-Kaple Bridge	361	Central Bohemia, Czech Republic	unknown		
19	Medno Footbridge	348	Mendo, Slovenia	Suspension	1	1934
20	Moscow Bridge	334	Rush County, Indiana	Burr Arch	2	1886
21	Shieldstown Bridge	331	Jackson County, Indiana	Burr Arch	2	1876
22	Bell's Ford Bridge	330	Jackson County, Indiana	Post	2	1869
22	Kasernenbrücke	330	Bern Canton, Switzerland	Ext. King	5	1549
22	Knights Ferry Bridge	330	Stanislaus County, California	Pratt	4	1864
25	Swann or Joy Bridge	320	Blount County, Alabama	Town lattice	3	1933
26	West Union Bridge	315	Parke County, Indiana	Burr Arch	2	1876
27	Academia/ Pomeroy	305	Juniata County, Pennsylvania	Burr Arch	2	1901
27	Eschikofen-Bonau Bridge	305	Thurgau Canton, Switzerland	Multiple Queen	5	1837
29	Philippi Bridge	304	Barbour County, West Virginia	Burr Arch variation	2	1852
30	St-Edgar Bridge	293	Bonaventure County, Quebec, Canada	Town lattice variation	2	1938

Source: National Society for the Preservation of Covered Bridges, Inc.

Oldest Practicing Architecture Firms in the United States

The following currently operating firms were all founded prior to 1900 (their specific founding dates indicated below).

1832
Lockwood Greene
Spartanburg, SC

1853
KCF/SHG, Inc.
Washington, D.C.

1853
Luckett & Farley Architects,
Engineers and Construction
Managers, Inc.,
Louisville, KY

1853
SHG Incorporated
Detroit, MI

1868
Jensen and Halstead Ltd.
Chicago, IL

1868
King & King Architects
Manlius, NY

1870
Harriman Associates
Auburn, ME

1871
Scholtz-Gowey-Gere-Marolf
Architects & Interior Designers, PC
Davenport, IA

1873
Graham Anderson Probst & White
Chicago, IL

1874
Chandler, Palmer & King
Norwich, CT

1874
Shepley Bulfinch Richardson and
Abbott Inc.
Boston, MA

1878
The Austin Company
Kansas City, MO

1878
Ballinger
Philadelphia, PA

1880
Beatty Harvey & Associates,
Architects
New York, NY

1880
Holabird & Root LLP
Chicago, IL

1880
Zeidler Roberts Partnership, Inc.
Toronto, Canada

1883
Ritterbush-Ellig-Hulsing PC,
Bismarck, ND

1885
Cromwell Architects Engineers,
Little Rock, AR

1885
HLW International LLP
New York, NY

1888
Reid & Stuhldreher, Inc.
Pittsburgh, PA

Oldest Practicing Architecture Firms in the United States (Con't)

1889
CSHQA Architects/Engineers/ Planners
Boise, ID

1889
MacLachlan, Cornelius & Filoni, Inc.
Pittsburgh, PA

1890
Kendall, Taylor & Company, Inc.
Billerica, MA

1890
The Mathes Group PC
New Orleans, LA

1891
Shive/Spinelli/Perantoni & Assoc.
Somerville, NJ

1891
Wilkins Wood Goforth Mace Assoc. Ltd.
Florence, SC

1892
Bauer Stark + Lashbrook, Inc.
Toledo, OH

1892
FreemanWhite, Inc.
Charlotte, NC

1893
Foor & Associates
Elmira, NY

1893
Wright, Porteous & Lowe/Bonar
Indianapolis, IN

1895
Albert Kahn Associates, Inc.
Detroit, MI

1896
Hummel Architects, PA
Boise, ID

1896
Lehman Architectural Partnership
Roseland, NJ

1897
Baskervill & Son
Richmond, VA

1897
L_H_R_S Architects, Inc.
Huntington, IN

1898
Beardsley Design Associates
Auburn, NY

1898
Berners/Schober Associates, Inc.
Green Bay, WI

1898
Bottelli Associates
Summit, NJ

1898
Burns & McDonnell
Kansas City, MO

1898
The Eckles Company Architects
New Castle, PA

1898
Emery Roth Associates
New York, NY

1898
Foss Associates
Fargo, ND & Moorhead, MN

1898
Page Southerland Page
Austin, TX

1899
William B. Ittner, Inc.
St. Louis, MO

Source: Counsel House Research/Greenway Group

Tallest Buildings in the World

The following list ranks the 100 tallest buildings in the world. Each building's architect, number of stories, height, location, and completion year are also provided. (Buildings which are under construction are deemed eligible and are indicated with a 'UC' in the year category.)

For additional resources about tall buildings, visit the Council on Tall Buildings and Urban Habitat on the Internet at *www.ctbuh.org* or *www.worldstallest.com*.

#	Building	Year	City/Country	Feet/Meters	Stories	Architect
1	Petronas Tower 1	1998	Kuala Lumpur, Malaysia	1483/452	88	Cesar Pelli & Associates
2	Petronas Tower 2	1998	Kuala Lumpur, Malaysia	1483/452	88	Cesar Pelli & Associates
3	Sears Tower	1974	Chicago, USA	1450/442	110	Skidmore, Owings & Merrill
4	Jin Mao Building	1999	Shanghai, China	1381/421	88	Skidmore, Owings & Merrill
5	World Trade Center One	1972	New York, USA	1368/417	110	M. Yamasaki, Emery Roth & Sons
6	World Trade Center Two	1973	New York, USA	1362/415	110	M. Yamasaki, Emery Roth & Sons
7	Citic Plaza	1996	Guangzhou, China	1283/391	80	Dennis Lau & Ng Chun Man
8	Shun Hing Square	1996	Shenzhen, China	1260/384	69	K.Y. Cheung Design Associates
9	Empire State Building	1931	New York, USA	1250/381	102	Shreve, Lamb & Harmon
10	Central Plaza	1992	Hong Kong, China	1227/374	78	Ng Chun Man & Associates
11	Bank of China Tower	1989	Hong Kong, China	1209/369	70	I.M. Pei & Partners
12	Emirates Tower One	UC99	Dubai, U.A.E	1165/355	55	NORR Group Consultants

Tallest Buildings in the World (Con't)

#	Building	Year	City/Country	Feet/Meters	Stories	Architect
13	The Centre	1998	Hong Kong, China	1148/350	79	Dennis Lau & Ng Chun Man
14	T & C Tower	1997	Kaohsiung, Taiwan	1140/348	85	C.Y. Lee/Hellmuth, Obata & Kassabaum
15	Amoco Building	1973	Chicago, USA	1136/346	80	Edward D. Stone
16	John Hancock Center	1969	Chicago, USA	1127/343	100	Skidmore, Owings & Merrill
17	Burj al Arab Hotel	UC99	Dubai, U.A.E.	1053/321	60	W. S. Atkins & Partners
18	Baiyoke Tower II	1997	Bangkok, Thailand	1050/320	90	Plan Architects Co.
19	Chrysler Building	1930	New York, USA	1046/319	77	William van Alen
20	NationsBank Tower	1993	Atlanta, USA	1023/312	55	Kevin Roche, John Dinkeloo & Associates
21	Library Tower	1990	Los Angeles, USA	1018/310	75	Pei Cobb Freed & Partners
22	Telekom Malaysia Headquarters	1999	Kuala Lumpur, Malaysia	1017/310	55	Daewoo & Partners
23	AT&T Corporate Center	1989	Chicago, USA	1007/307	61	Skidmore, Owings & Merrill
24	Chase Tower	1982	Houston, USA	1000/305	75	I. M. Pei & Partners
25	Emirates Tower Two	UC99	Dubai, U.A.E	1000/305	52	NORR Group Consultants
26	Two Prudential Plaza	1990	Chicago, USA	995/303	64	Leobl Schlossman Dart & Hackl
27	Ryugyong Hotel	1995	Pyongyang, N. Korea	984/300	105	Baikdoosan Architects & Engineers
28	Commerzbank Tower	1997	Frankfurt, Germany	981/299	56	Sir Norman Foster & Partners
29	Wells Fargo Plaza	1983	Houston, USA	972/296	71	Skidmore, Owings & Merrill

Tallest Buildings in the World (Con't)

#	Building	Year	City/ Country	Feet/ Meters	Stories	Architect
30	Landmark Tower	1993	Yokohama, Japan	971/296	70	Stubbins Associates
31	311 S. Wacker Drive	1990	Chicago, USA	961/293	65	Kohn Pedersen Fox Associates
32	American International Building	1932	New York, USA	952/290	67	Clinton & Russell
33	First Canadian Place	1975	Toronto, Canada	951/290	72	Bregman + Hamann Architects
34	Cheunh Kong Centre	1990	Hong Kong, China	951/290	70	Cesar Pelli & Associates, Leo A. Daly
35	Key Tower	1991	Cleveland, USA	950/290	57	Cesar Pelli & Associates
36	One Liberty Place	1987	Philadelphia, USA	945/287	61	Murphy/Jahn
37	Columbia Seafirst Center	1985	Seattle, USA	943/287	76	Chester Lindsey Architects
38	The Trump Building	1930	New York, USA	927/283	72	H. Craig Severance
39	NationsBank Plaza	1985	Dallas, USA	921/281	72	JPJ Architects
40	Overseas Union Bank Center	1986	Singapore	919/280	66	Kenzo Tange Associates
41	United Overseas Bank Plaza	1992	Singapore	919/280	66	Kenzo Tange Associates
42	Republic Plaza	1995	Singapore	919/280	66	Kisho Kurakawa
43	Citicorp Center	1977	New York, USA	915/279	59	Stubbins Associates
44	Scotia Plaza	1989	Toronto, Canada	902/275	68	The Webb Zerafa Menkes Housden Partnership
45	Williams Tower	1983	Houston, USA	901/275	64	Johnson/Burgee Architects
46	Renaissance Tower	1975	Dallas, USA	886/270	56	Skidmore, Owings & Merrill

Tallest Buildings in the World (Con't)

#	Building	Year	City/Country	Feet/Meters	Stories	Architect
47	900 N. Michigan Ave.	1989	Chicago, USA	871/265	66	Kohn Pederson Fox Associates
48	NationsBank Corporate Center	1992	Charlotte, USA	871/265	60	Cesar Pelli & Associates
49	Sun Trust Plaza	1992	Atlanta, USA	871/265	60	John Portman & Associates
50	BEC Place-Canada Trust Tower	1990	Toronto, Canada	863/263	51	Skidmore, Owings & Merrill, Bregman + Hamann
51	Water Tower Place	1976	Chicago, USA	859/262	74	Loebl Schlossman Dart & Hackl
52	First Interstate Bank	1974	Los Angeles, USA	858/262	62	Charles Luckman & Associates
53	Transamerica Pyramid Headquarters	1972	San Francisco, USA	853/260	48	William Pereira
54	G. E. Building/Rockefeller Center	1933	New York, USA	850/259	70	Raymond Hood
55	First National Plaza	1969	Chicago, USA	850/259	60	C.F. Murphy
56	Two Liberty Place	1990	Philadelphia, USA	848/258	58	Murphy/Jahn
57	Messeturm	1990	Frankfurt, Germany	843/257	63	Murphy/Jahn
58	USX Tower	1970	Pittsburgh, USA	841/256	64	Harrison & Abramovitz
59	Rinku Gate Tower	1996	Osaka, Japan	840/256	56	Nikken Sekkei
60	Osaka World Trade Center	1995	Osaka, Japan	827/252	55	Nikken Sekkei
61	One Atlantic Center	1988	Atlanta, USA	820/250	50	Johnson/Burgee Architects
62	BNI City Tower	1995	Jakarta, Indonesia	820/250	46	Zeidler Roberts Partnership w/DP Architects
63	Korea Life Insurance Co.	1985	Seoul, South Korea	817/249	60	C.M. Park w/S.O.M.

Tallest Buildings in the World (Con't)

#	Building	Year	City/Country	Feet/Meters	Stories	Architect
64	CitySpire	1989	New York, USA	814/248	75	Murphy/Jahn
65	Rialto Towers	1985	Melbourne, Australia	814/248	63	Gerard de Preu & Partners
66	Chase Manhattan Plaza	1961	New York, USA	813/248	60	Skidmore, Owings & Merrill
67	MetLife	1963	New York, USA	808/246	59	Emery Roth & Sons, Pietro Belluschi
68	JR Central Tower	UC00	Nagoya, Japan	804/245	51	
69	Shin Kong Life Tower	1993	Taipei, Taiwan	801/244	51	K.M.G. Architects & Engineers
70	Malayan Bank	1988	Kuala Lumpur, Malaysia	799/244	50	Hijjas Kasturi Associates
71	Tokyo City Hall	1991	Tokyo, Japan	797/243	48	Kenzo Tange Associates
72	Woolworth Building	1913	New York, USA	792/241	57	Cass Gilbert
73	Mellon Bank Center	1991	Philadelphia, USA	792/241	54	Kohn Pedersen Fox Associates
74	John Hancock Tower	1976	Boston, USA	788/240	60	I. M. Pei & Partners
75	Bank One Center	1987	Dallas, USA	787/240	60	Johnson/Burgee Architects
76	Commerce Court West	1973	Toronto, Canada	784/239	57	Page & Steele, I. M. Pei & Partners
77	Moscow State University	1953	Moscow, Russia	784/239	26	L. Roudnev, P. Abrossimov, A. Khariakov
78	Empire Tower	1994	Kuala Lumpur, Malaysia	781/238	62	
79	NationsBank Center	1983	Houston, USA	780/238	56	Johnson/Burgee Architects
80	Bank of America Center	1969	San Francisco, USA	779/237	52	Skidmore, Owings & Merrill

Tallest Buildings in the World (Con't)

#	Building	Year	City/Country	Feet/Meters	Stories	Architect
81	Worldwide Plaza	1989	New York, USA	778/237	47	Skidmore, Owings & Merrill
82	One Canada Square	1991	London, UK	777/237	50	Cesar Pelli & Associates
83	IDS Center	1973	Minneapolis, USA	775/236	52	Johnson/Burgee Architects
84	First Bank Place	1992	Minneapolis, USA	774/236	58	Pei Cobb Freed & Partners
85	Norwest Center	1988	Minneapolis, USA	773/235	57	Cesar Pelli & Associates
86	Treasury Building	1986	Singapore	770/235	52	Stubbins Associates
87	191 Peachtree Tower	1991	Atlanta, USA	770/235	50	Johnson/Burgee Architects
88	Opera City Tower	1997	Tokyo, Japan	768/234	54	
89	Shinjuku Park Tower	1994	Tokyo, Japan	764/233	52	Kenzo Tange Associates
90	Heritage Plaza	1987	Houston, USA	762/232	52	M. Nasr & Partners
91	Kompleks Tun Abdul Razak Building	1985	Penang, Malaysia	760/232	65	International Sdn./Jurubena Bertiga Intnl. Sdn.
92	Palace of Culture and Science	1955	Warsaw, Poland	758/231	42	L. W. Rudinev
93	Carnegie Hall Tower	1991	New York, USA	757/231	60	Cesar Pelli & Associates
94	Three First National Plaza	1981	Chicago, USA	753/230	57	Skidmore, Owings & Merrill
95	Equitable Center	1986	New York, USA	752/229	51	Edward Larrabee Barnes Associates
96	MLC Center	1978	Sydney, Australia	751/229	65	Harry Seidler & Associates
97	One Penn Plaza	1972	New York, USA	750/229	57	Kahn & Jacobs

Tallest Buildings in the World (Con't)

#	Building	Year	City/Country	Feet/Meters	Stories	Architect
98	1251 Ave. of Americas	1972	New York, USA	750/229	54	Harrison, Abramovitz & Harris
99	Prudential Center	1964	Boston, USA	750/229	52	Charles Luckman & Associates
100	Two California Plaza	1992	Los Angeles, USA	750/229	52	Arthur Erickson Architects

Source: Council on Tall Buildings and Urban Habitat, Lehigh University

Opposite: Petronas Towers, Kuala Lumpur, Malaysia, Cesar Pelli
Photograph © Jeff Goldberg/Esto.

29 Best Buildings of the 20th Century

The following 29 buildings were judged by a panel of industry experts to be the Best Buildings of the 20th Century. Buildings designed and constructed during the 20th century, regardless of location, were deemed eligible. Buildings were judged based on the following: their influence on the course of 20th century architecture, significant aesthetic contribution, promotion of design principles which have had a positive impact on the built environment, and/or a lasting impact on the history of the 20th century. The buildings below are listed alphabetically and are not ranked in any order.

Air Force Academy Chapel,
Colorado Springs, CO
SOM

Chrysler Building
New York, NY
William Van Allen

Dulles Airport
Chantilly, VA
Eero Saarinen

East Wing of the National Gallery
Washington, D.C.
I.M. Pei

Fallingwater
Bear Run, PA
Frank Lloyd Wright

Flatiron Building
New York, NY
Daniel Burnham

Gambel House
Pasadena, CA
Greene and Greene

Getty Center
Los Angeles, CA
Richard Meier

Glass House
New Canaan, CT
Philip Johnson

Guggenheim Museum
Bilbao, Spain
Frank Gehry

Hearst Castle
San Simeon, CA
Julia Morgan

Hong Kong and Shanghai Bank
Hong Kong SAR
Norman Foster

Opposite: Chrysler Building, New York, NY,
William Van Alen
Photograph © Peter Mauss/Esto.

29 Best Buildings of the 20th Century (Con't)

Il Palazzo Hotel
Fukuota, Japan
Aldo Rossi

Seagram Building
New York, NY
Mies van der Rohe

John Deere Headquarters
Moline, IL
Eero Saarinen

Stockholm City Hall
Stockholm, Sweden
Ragnar Ostburg

John Hancock Building
Chicago, IL
SOM

Sydney Opera House
Sydney, Australia
Jorn Utzon

Johnson Wax Building
Racine, WI
Frank Lloyd Wright

Thorncrown Chapel
Eureka Springs, AR
Fay Jones

Kimball Art Musuem
Fort Worth, TX
Louis Kahn

Tokyo City Hall
Tokyo, Japan
Kenzo Tange

La Sagrada Familia
Barcelona, Spain
Antonio Gaudi

Villa Savoye
Poissy, France
Le Corbusier

National Farmers' Bank
Owatonna, MN
Louis Sullivan

Woolworth Building
New York, NY
Cass Gilbert

Nebraska State Capitol
Lincoln, NE
Bertram Goodhue

Source: Council House Research/Greenway Group

Notre Dame-du-Haut
Ronchamp, France
Le Corbusier

Salk Institute
La Jolla, CA
Louis Kahn

Did you know...
In 1970, the Time Life Building in Chicago became the first tall building to employ the use of double-decker elevators.

World's Best Skylines

The list on the following pages ranks the world's cities according to the density and height of the skyscrapers in their skylines. Each building over 151 meters (495 feet) tall contributes points to its home city's score equal to the number of meters by which it exceeds this benchmark height. This list also provides the name of the tallest buildings in each city along with their heights and world rankings.

For more information sources about skyscrapers worldwide, visit Egbert Gramsbergen's Web site (the compiler of this list) at *www.library.tudelft.nl/~egram/skylines.htm* and *www.worldstallest.com*.

Ranking	Points	City	Country	# bldgs. >151m	Highest Building
1	6207	New York	USA	159	One World Trade Center (417m, #5)
2	2891	Chicago	USA	69	Sears Tower (442m, #3)
3	1858	Hong Kong	China	41	Central Plaza (374m, #8)
4	1395	Houston	USA	27	Texas Commerce Tower (305m, #22)
5	1061	Singapore	Singapore	25	Overseas Union Bank (280m, #36)
6	1039	Los Angeles	USA	21	Library Tower (310m, #20)
7	951	Kuala Lumpur	Malaysia	8	Petronas Tower I (452m, #1)
8	876	Dallas	USA	18	NationsBank Plaza (281m, #35)
9	838	Tokyo	Japan	20	Tokyo City hall (243m,#66)
10	776	Atlanta	USA	11	NationsBank Tower (312m, #19)
11	677	Toronto	Canada	10	First Canadian Place (290m, #30)
12	623	Shanghai	China	18	Jin Mao Bldg. (421m, #4)
13	580	Melbourne	Australia	16	Rialto Towers (242m, #61)

World's Best Skylines (Con't)

Ranking	Points	City	Country	# bldgs. >151m	Highest Building
14	544	Philadelphia	USA	9	One Liberty Place (288m, #32)
15	493	San Francisco	USA	16	Transamerica Corporate Headquarters (260m, #49)
16	458	Seattle	USA	10	Columbia Seafirst Center (288m, #33)
17	409	Kaoshiung	Taiwan	7	T & C Tower (348m, #01)
18	380	Frankfurt	Germany	8	Commerzbank Tower (299m, #25)
19	372	Sydney	Australia	11	M. L. C. Center (228m, #91)
20	366	Minneapolis	USA	7	Norwest Center (236m, #78)
21	351	Boston	USA	13	John Hancock Tower (240m, #69)
22	341	Pittsburgh	USA	9	USX Tower (256m, #54)
23	341	Bangkok	Thailand	6	Baiyoke Tower II (320m, #17)
24	287	Osaka	Japan	5	Rinku Gate Tower (256m, #55)
25	264	Cleveland	USA	4	Society Tower (290m, #31)
26	241	Shenzhen	China	2	Shun Hing Square (325m, #14)
27	223	Denver	USA	6	Republic Plaza (218m, #142)
28	213	Montreal	Canada	6	1000 Rue de la Gauchetiere (204m, #202)
29	209	Guangzhou	China	2	CITIC Plaza (322m, #15)
30	199	Paris	France	6	Tour Maine Montparnasse (209m, #182)
31	179	Moscow	Russia	4	Moscow State University (239m, #72)
32	175	Detroit	USA	7	Westin Hotel (221m #124)
33	175	Seoul	South Korea	2	Korea Life Insurance Co. (249m, #59)
34	174	Perth	Australia	3	Central Park Tower (223m, #119)
35	171	Dubai	U.A.E.	2	Chicago Beach Hotel Tower (321m, #16)

World's Best Skylines (Con't)

Ranking	Points	City	Country	# bldgs. >151m	Highest Building
36	161	Calgary	Canada	8	Petro Canada Tower (210m, #175)
37	161	New Orleans	USA	5	One Shell Square (212m, #164)
38	149	Pyongyang	North Korea	1	Ryugyong Hotel (300m, #24)
39	145	Yokohama	Japan	1	Landmark Tower (296m, #27)
40	144	Charlotte	USA	3	NationsBank Corporate Center (265m, #44)
41	142	Miami	USA	5	First Union Financial Center (225m, #115)
42	140	Caracas	Venezuela	2	Parque Central Torre Officinas II (221m, #127)
43	127	Mexico City	Mexico	4	Petrolaos Mexicanos (214m, #153)
44	125	London	U.K.	2	1 Canada Square (244m, #77)
45	121	Taipei	Taiwan	3	Shin Kong Life Tower (244m, #64)
46	114	Taichung	Taiwan	2	Chang Tower (224m, #117)
47	109	Tulsa	USA	4	Bank of Oklahoma Tower (203m, #204)
48	99	Jakarta	Indonesia	1	BNI City Tower (250m, #58)
49	94	Bogota	Columbia	4	Colpatria Tower (192m, #252)
50	94	Warsaw	Poland	2	Palace of Culture and Science (231m, #87)
51	84	St. Louis	USA	3	Metropolitan Square Tower (181m, #337)
52	81	Penang	Malaysia	1	Tun Abdul Rasak Bldg. (232m, #86)
53	80	Johannesburg	South Africa	2	Carlton Centre (222m, #122)
54	76	Indianapolis	USA	3	Bank One Tower (213m, #157)
55	75	Columbus	USA	5	State Office Tower (190m, #273)
56	73	Tampa	USA	4	100 N. Tampa (177m, #384)
57	72	Kansas City	USA	3	One Kansas City Place (191, #262)

World's Best Skylines (Con't)

Ranking	Points	City	Country	# bldgs. >151m	Highest Building
58	64	Manila	Philippines	3	Petron MegaPlaza, Makati (210m, #177)
59	62	Sao Paulo	Brazil	2	Edifico Italia (194m, #241)
60	61	Hamamastsu	Japan	1	Act Tower (212m, #168)
61	57	Beijing	China	1	Jing Guang Bldg. (208m, #188)
62	56	Milwaukee	USA	2	Firstar Center (191m, #270)
63	54	Tangerang	Indonesia	2	Amartapura (198m, #225)
64	53	Jacksonville	USA	2	Barnett Tower (192m, #249)
65	52	Tel Aviv	Israel	2	*Azrieli Center Circular Tower (187m, #299)
66	49	Hefei	China	1	Anhui Internatioal Trade Center (200m, #214)
67	43	Fort Worth	USA	3	Burnett Plaza (170m, #449)
68	41	Dunwoody, Ga	USA	2	Concourse Tower #5 (174m, #418)
69	41	Des Moines	USA	1	Principal Financial Group (192m, #254)
70	37	Nashville	USA	1	South Central Bell Bldg. (188m, #288)
71	34	Brisbane	Australia	2	Central Plaza One (174m, #399)
72	31	Portland	USA	3	US West Tower (166m, #493)
73	30	Hartford	USA	3	City Place (163m, #535)
74	30	Chiba	Japan	1	Makuhari Prince Hotel (181m, #336)
75	29	Albany	USA	1	Erastus Corning II Tower (180m, #354)
76	24	Medellin	Colombia	1	Coltejer (175m, #401)
77	24	Cincinnati	USA	1	Carew Tower (175m, #398)
78	21	Louisville	USA	2	Providian Center (167m, #486)
79	17	Cape Canaveral	USA	1	Vehicle Assembly Bldg. (168m, #469)

World's Best Skylines (Con't)

Ranking	Points	City	Country	# bldgs. >151m	Highest Building
80	15	San Antonio	USA	1	Marriott Rivercenter (166m, #495)
81	15	Little Rock	USA	1	TCBY Towers (166m, #494)
82	14	Baltimore	USA	2	U. S. F. & G. Co. (161m, #565)
83	14	Lyons	France	1	Tour de Credit Lyonnais (165m, #505)
84	13	Rio de Janeiro	Brazil	1	Rio Sul Center (164m, #524)
85	12	Macau	Macau	1	Bank of China (163m #583)
86	10	Buffalo	USA	1	Marine Midland Center (161m, #564)
87	9	Cali	Colombia	1	Torre de Cali (160m, #543)
88	9	Las Vegas	USA	1	New York, New York Hotel and Casino (160m, #580)
89	7	Makuhari	Japan	1	World Business Garden (158m, #628)
90	7	Kobe	Japan	1	Shin-Kobe Oriental Hotel (158m, #625)
91	7	Panama City	Panama	1	Platinum Tower (158m, #615)
92	6	Barcelona	Spain	2	Mapfre Tower (154m, #681)
93	6	Madrid	Spain	1	Plaza Picasso (157m, #632)
94	2	Leipzig	Germany	1	Karl Marx Univ. (153m, #695)
95	2	Damascus	Syria	1	Assad Tower (153m, #693)
96	1	San Diego	USA	1	One American Plaza (152m, #714)
97	1	Oklahoma City	USA	1	Liberty Tower (152m, #713)
98	1	Colombo	Sri Lanka	1	World Trade Center (2 Bldgs.) (152m, #709)

Source: Egbert Gramsbergen

America's 11 Most Endangered Historic Places

Every June the National Trust for Historic Preservation (NTHP) compiles a list of the eleven most threatened historic sites in the United States. Since 1988 this list has served to bring a broader awareness to the country's diminishing historic resources and to generate local support for the preservation efforts of the 11 endangered sites. While being listed does not guarantee protection or financial support, in the past the attention generated for the Endangered Historic Places has aided in many successful preservation efforts.

For additional information, contact the National Trust for Historic Preservation at (800) 944-6847 or visit their Web site at *www.nationaltrust.org/main/endangered/heritage.html.*

The Corner of Main and Main, Nationwide

Richard H. Allen Auditorium, Sitka, Alaska

Angel Island Immigration Station, San Francisco Bay, California

Country Estates of River Road, Louisville, Kentucky

Four National Historic Landmark Hospitals, New York State

Hulett Ore Unloaders, Cleveland, Ohio Lancaster County, Pennsylvania

Pullman Administration Building and Factory Complex, Chicago, Illinois

Traveler's Rest, Lolo, Montana
San Diego Arts and Warehouse District, San Diego, California

West Side of Downtown Baltimore, Baltimore, Maryland

Source: National Trust for Historic Preservation

Antoinette Forrester Downing Award

The Society for Architectural Historians annually grants the Antoinette Forrester Downing Award to an author for an outstanding publication in the field of historic preservation. Works published in the two years prior to the award are eligible.

For more information contact the SAH at 312-573-1365 or visit their web site at *www.sah.org/awards.html*.

1987
Providence, A Citywide Survey of Historic Resources by William McKenzie Woodward and Edward F. Sanderson (Rhode Island Historic Preservation Commission)

1990
East Cambridge: A Survey of Architectural History in Cambridge by Susan E. Maycock (MIT Press)

1991
Somerset: An Architectural History by Paul Touart (Maryland Historical Trust and Somerset County Historical Trust)

1994
The Buried Past: An Archaeological History of Philadelphia by John L. Cotter (University of Pennsylvania Press)

1995
Along the Seaboard Side: the Architectural History of Worcester County, Maryland by Paul Baker Touart (Worcester County)

1996
The Historic Architecture of Wake County, North Carolina by Kelly A. Lally (Wake County Government)

1997
A Guide to the National Road and The National Road by Karl B. Raitz (Johns Hopkins University Press)

1998
A Guide to the Historic Architecture of Eastern North Carolina by Catherine W. Bishir & Michael T. Southern (Chapel Hill University of N.C. Press)

1999
no award granted

Source: Society for Architectural Historians

Crowninshield Award

The National Trust for Historic Preservation's highest honor, the Louise Du Pont Crowninshield Award, each year recognizes an individual or organization who has demonstrated extraordinary lifetime achievement in the preservation of America's heritage. Winners are selected by the Preservation Committee of the National Trust's Board of Trustees.

For more information contact the National Trust at (800) 944-6847 or visit their Web site at *www.nationaltrust.org*.

1960	The Mount Vernon Ladies Association
1961	Henry Francis Dupont
1962	Katherine Prentis Murphy
1963	Martha Gilmore Robinson
1964	Mr. and Mrs. Bertram R. Little
1965	Charles E. Peterson
1966	Ima Hogg
	Mary Gordon Latham Kellenberger
1967	no award granted
1968	St. Clair Wright
1969	Mr. and Mrs. Henry N. Flynt
1970	Frank L. Horton
1971	Frances R. Edmunds
1972	Alice Winchester
1973	Dr. Ricardo E. Alegria
1974	Mr. and Mrs. Jacob H. Morrison
1975	no award granted
1976	Katherine U. Warren
1977	San Antonio Conservation Society
1978	Helen Duprey Bullock
1979	Old Post Office Landmark Committee
1980	William J. Murtagh
	Ernest Allen Connally
1981	Gordon C. Gray
1982	Helen Abell
1983	Historic American Buildings Survey (HABS) of the National Park Service, U.S. Department of the Interior, in cooperation with the American Institute of Architects and the Library of Congress, Washington, D.C.
1984	Leopold Adler II
1985	James Marston Fitch
1986	Antoinette Downing
1987	Blair Reeves
1988	Robert Stipe
1989	Fred Rath
	Association of Junior Leagues
1990	Frederick Gutheim
1991	Robert Garvey
1992	Joan Bacchus Maynard
1993	Carl B. Westmoreland
	Arthur P. Ziegler, Jr.
1994	Walter Beinecke, Jr.
1995	Dana Crawford
1996	Richard H. Jenrette
1997	Marguerite Neel Williams
1998	Frederick Williamson
	Anice Barber Read
1999	Senator Daniel Patrick Moynihan

Source: National Trust for Historic Preservation

DOCOMOMO International

DOCOMOMO (Documentation and Conservation of Buildings, Sites and Neighborhoods of the Modern Movement) International is headquartered in Eindhoven, Holland, with working parties in 33 countries. Membership consists of architects, engineers, historians, and others dedicated to preserving the architectural heritage of the Modern Movement through documentation and conservation. Founded in 1990, the group has six specialist committees concentrating on registers, technology, education, urbanism, landscapes and gardens, and publications. They also produce the *DOCOMOMO Journal*, published twice a year, with thematic articles and news from the individual chapters. Their technical publications focus on conservation issues related to modern structures.

Address:
Delft University of Technology, Faculty
of Architecture
Berlageweg 1
2628 CR Delft
Netherlands
Telephone: 31-15-2788755
Internet:
www.ooo.nl/docomomo/home.htm

Design is not beautification. It's a thought process – a non-linear, spatial way of thinking in which connections are made between seemingly unrelated things.

Sohrab Vossoughi

Great American Main Street Awards

Each year the National Trust for Historic Preservation's National Main Street Center selects five communities that have shown considerable success at preservation based revitalization. These towns have all generated broad based support from its residents and business leaders, drawn support from both public and private sources, and have created innovative solutions to their unique situations. Winners each receive $5000 to be used towards further revitalization efforts, a bronze plaque, road signs, and a certificate. Since its inception, the Main Street Center has helped over 1400 communities which has resulted in an average of $35 in new downtown investments for every dollar spent on the revitalization effort.

For more information, visit the Main Street Center's Web site at *www.mainst.org* or contact them at (202) 588-6219.

1995
  Clarksville, MO
  Dubuque, IA
  Franklin, TN
  Sheboygan Falls, WI
  Old Pasadena, CA

1996
  Bonaparte, IA
  Chippewa Falls, WI
  East Carson Street Business District,
    Pittsburgh, PA
  Saratoga Springs, NY
  Wooster, OH

1997
  Burlington, VT
  DeLand, FL
  Georgetown, TX
  Holland, MI
  Libertyville, IL

1998
  Corning, IA
  Lanesboro, MN
  Morgantown, WV
  Thomasville, GA
  York, PA

1999
  Bay City, MI
  Cordell, OK
  Denton, TX
  Lafayette, IN
  San Luis Obispo, CA

Source: The National Trust Main Street Center

Did you know...
The Split Rock Light House in Two Harbors, MN receives over 125,000 visitors each year.

Historic American Buildings Survey (HABS)

The Historic American Buildings Survey (HABS) operates as part of the National Park Service and is dedicated to recording America's historic buildings through measured drawings, written histories, and large-format photographs. The program was started in 1933 as a Civil Works Administration project using unemployed architects to make permanent records of historic American architecture. Following a drop-off in activity after World War II, the program was restored in the early 1950's with student architects providing the research, a practice that continues to the present day. In 1969, the Historic American Engineering Record (HAER) was established as a companion program focusing on America's technological heritage. Records of the over 32,000 recorded historic structures and sites are available to the public through the Prints and Photographs Division of the Library of Congress.

Address:
National Park Service
HABS/HAER Division
1849 "C" Street, NW, Room NC300
Washington, D.C. 20240
Telephone: (202) 343-9625
Internet: www.cr.nps.gov/habshaer/

For information on HABS and HAER archives, contact:

Prints and Photographs Reading Room
Library of Congress
James Madison Building, Room LM-337
Washington, DC 20540-4730
Telephone: (301) 713-6800
Internet: http://lcweb.gov/rr/print

International Centre for the Study of the Preservation and Restoration of Cultural Property (ICCROM)

Founded by the United Nations' Educational, Scientific and Cultural Organization (UNESCO) in 1956, the International Centre for the Study of the Preservation and Restoration of Cultural Property (ICCROM) is an intergovernmental organization dedicated to the conservation of heritage of all types. It is funded by contributions from its 95 Member States, plus donors and sponsors. ICCROM provides members with information, publications and training; offers technical assistance and sponsors workshops; performs ongoing research and archives findings; and serves as an advocate for preservation. The group maintains one of the largest conservation libraries in the world.

Address:
13, Via di San Michele
I-00153 Rome, Italy
Telephone: (+39-06) 585 531
Internet: www.iccrom.org

Good design is good business.

Stuart Lipton

International Council on Monuments and Sites (ICOMOS)

Dedicated to the conservation of the world's historic monuments and sites, the International Council on Monuments and Sites (ICOMOS) is an international, non-governmental organization with National Committees in over 90 countries. The group is the United Nations Educational, Scientific and Cultural Organization's (UNESCO) principal advisor in matters concerning the conservation of monuments and sites. With the World Conservation Union (IUCN), ICOMOS advises the World Heritage Committee and UNESCO on the nomination of new sites to the World Heritage List. The group also works to establish international standards for the preservation, restoration and management of the cultural environment. ICOMOS members are professional architects, archaeologists, urban planners, engineers, heritage administrators, art historians, and archivists. All members join ICOMOS through the National Committee of their respective countries.

Address:
49-51 rue de la Fédération
75015 Paris, France
Telephone: +33 (0) 1 45 67 67 70
Internet: www.icomos.org

Did you know...
During his 72-year career, Frank Lloyd Wright completed approximately 500 buildings and also designed roughly that many unbuilt projects.

Most Visited Historic House Museums

The following historic house museums, ranked in order of popularity, are the most visited in the United States.

1. Mount Vernon
   Mount Vernon, VA
   George Washington, 1785-86

2. Newport Mansions
   Newport, RI*
   various architects

3. Biltmore Estate
   Asheville, NC
   Richard Morris Hunt, 1895

4. Hearst Castle
   San Simeon, CA
   Julia Morgan, 1927-1947

5. Graceland
   Memphis, TN
   Architect unknown, 1939

6. Monticello
   Charlottesville, VA
   Thomas Jefferson, 1768-79, 1793-1809

7. Arlington House, The Robert E. Lee Memorial
   Arlington, VA
   George Hadfield, 1817

8. Lincoln Home
   Springfield, IL
   Architect unknown, 1839

9. Maymont
   Richmond, VA
   Edgeton Rogers, 1893

10. Martin Luther King Jr. Birth Home
    Atlanta, GA
    Architect unknown, c. 1893

11. Betsy Ross House
    Philadelphia, PA
    Architect unknown, 1740

12. Paul Revere House
    Boston, MA
    Architect unknown, c.1680

13. Bellingrath House
    Theodore, AL
    George B. Rogers, 1935

14. Carter's Grove
    Williamsburg, VA
    John Wheatley, c. 1750-55

15. The Hermitage: Home of President Andrew Jackson
    Hermitage, TN
    Architect unknown, 1819

16. Olana State Historic Site
    Hudson, NY
    Frederick Church, 1876

17. Viscaya
    Miami, FL
    Burrall Hoffman, 1916

18. Magnolia Plantation
    Charleston, SC
    Architect unknown, 1730

19. House of the Seven Gables
    Salem, MA
    Architect unknown, 1668

20. Beehive House
    Salt Lake City, Utah
    Truman Angel, 1854

21. Fallingwater
    Mill Run, PA
    Frank Lloyd Wright, 1939

22. Franklin D. Roosevelt Home
    Hyde Park, NY
    Architect unknown, 1826

Most Visited Historic House Museums (Con't)

23. Little White House
    Warm Springs, GA
    Henry Toombs, 1932

24. George Eastman House
    Rochester, NY
    J. Foster Warner, 1905

25. Vanderbilt Mansion
    Hyde Park, NY
    McKim, Mead, and White, 1898

* The Newport Mansions consists of The Breakers, Marble House, Chateau-sur-Mer, Rosecliff, The Elms, Issac Bell House, Hunter House, Green Animals, Chepstow, Kingcote, and The Breakers Stable & Coach House. They are owned and operated by the Preservation Society of Newport County.

Source: Council House Research/Greenway Group

National Preservation Honor Awards

The National Preservation Honor Awards are the National Trust for Historic Preservation's (NTHP) annual program to recognize projects which demonstrate a high level of dedication and support of the ideals and benefits of historic preservation. A jury of preservation professionals and representatives selects winning projects based on their positive effect on the community, pioneering nature, quality, and degree of difficulty. Special interest is placed on those undertakings which utilize historic preservation as a method of revitalization.

For more information, contact the National Trust at 1-800-944-6847 or visit their Web site at *www.nationaltrust.org*.

NTHP's 1999 National Preservation Honor Award Winners:

The Boston Custom House, Boston, Massachusetts

Buffalo Historical Society, Inc., Buffalo, North Dakota

Edith Bingham, Glenview, Kentucky

General Services Administration - National Capital Region

Grand Central Terminal, New York City, New York

Historic Restoration, Inc., New Orleans, Louisiana

Idaho Heritage Trust, Bellevue, Idaho

Jeanne Jackson, CEO and President of Banana Republic, New York City, New York

Maryland Department of Natural Resources – Program Open Space and Rural Legacy

Ralph Sr. and Sunny Wilson House, Temple, Texas

Salve Regina University, Newport, Rhode Island

San Francisco City Hall, San Francisco, California

University of Washington-Tacoma, Tacoma, Washington

Walter Payton's Roundhouse Complex and City of Aurora, Illinois

Wilbur M. Feltner, Chairman of F&M Bank, Winchester, Virginia

Source: National Trust for Historic Preservation

National Preservation Institute (NPI)

The National Preservation Institute (NPI) is a non-profit organization dedicated to the management, development, and preservation of historic, cultural, and environmental resources. Toward this end, NPI offers specialized information, continuing education, and, upon request, professional training tailored to the sponsor's needs. Many preservation-related services are available from NPI, including authentication of historic reproductions and historic real estate. NPI is also registered with the American Institute of Architects Continuing Education System.

Address:
P.O. Box 1702
Alexandria, VA 22313
Telephone: (703) 765-0100
Internet: www.npi.org

Did you know...
From its beginning in 1946, Knoll has produced furniture designed by many notable architects, including: Mies van der Rohe (Barcelona, Bruno, and Weissenhof chairs); Eero Saarinen (Pedestal and Womb chair); Marcel Breuer (Cesca chair); Ralph Rapson (Rapson Rocker); and Frank Gehry (Bentwood chair).

National Trust for Historic Preservation

Since its founding in 1949, the National Trust for Historic Preservation (NTHP) has worked to preserve historic buildings and neighborhoods. Through educational programs, publications, financial assistance and government advocacy, the National Trust has been successful in revitalizing communities across the country. This private, non-profit organization operates six regional offices, 20 historic sites, publishes the award winning *Preservation* magazine, hosts the nation's largest preservation conference every year, and works with thousands of local community groups nationwide, through such programs as Main Street, to preserve their history and buildings.

Address:
1785 Massachusetts Avenue, NW
Washington, DC 20036
Telephone: (202) 588-6000
www.nationaltrust.org

> Architecture is the handwriting of man.... When you enter his domain you know...his dreams.
>
> *Bernard Maybeck*

National Trust Historic Hotels of America

The properties listed on the National Trust for Historic Preservation's Historic Hotels of America are a compilation of some of the country's most noteworthy historic hotels, resorts, and inns. Each of the properties are fifty years or older. In addition, they are either eligible for or listed on the National Register of Historic Places or of locally recognized historic significance.

For more information, contact the National Trust for Historic Preservation at 1-800-944-6847 or visit the Historic Hotels of America on the Web at *www.nationaltrust.org/main/hotels/hotelsmain.htm.*

Alabama
  Radisson Admiral Semmes Hotel, Mobile

Arizona
  Arizona Inn, Tucson
  Hotel San Carlos, Phoenix

California
  El Encanto Hotel and Garden Villas, Santa Barbara
  The Eureka Inn, Eureka
  Furnace Creek Inn, Death Valley
  The Georgian Hotel, Santa Monica
  Hotel del Coronado, San Diego
  Hyatt Sainte Claire, San Jose
  La Playa Hotel, Carmel
  La Quinta Resort & Club, La Quinta
  La Valencia Hotel, La Jolla
  Hotel La Rose, Santa Rosa
  Mendocino Hotel and Garden Suites, Mendocino
  Mission Inn, Riverside
  Ojai Valley Inn & Spa, Ojai
  Regal Biltmore Hotel, Los Angeles

Colorado
  The Brown Palace Hotel, Denver
  Historic Strater Hotel, Durango
  Hotel Boulderado, Boulder
  Hotel Jerome, Aspen
  The Oxford Hotel, Denver
  The Redstone Inn, Redstone

Connecticut
  The Lighthouse Inn, New London

Delaware
  Hotel du Pont, Wilmington
  The Inn at Montchanin Village, Montchanin

Florida
  The Biltmore Hotel, Coral Gables
  The Colony Hotel & Cabaña Club, Del Ray Beach
  The Don CeSar Beach Resort and Spa, St. Pete Beach
  Lakeside Inn, Mount Dora
  The Park Central Hotel, Miami Beach
  Renaissance Vinoy Resort, St. Petersburg
  Ritz Plaza Hotel, Miami Beach
  The Tiffany Hotel, Miami Beach

Georgia
  Jekyll Island Club Hotel, Jekyll Island

National Trust Historic Hotels of America (Con't)

The King and Prince Beach & Golf
Resort, St. Simons Island
The Partridge Inn, Augusta
River Street Inn, Savannah
Windsor Hotel, Americus

Illinois
Hotel Baker, St. Charles
Deer Path Inn, Lake Forest
Omni Ambassador East, Chicago
Regal Knickerbocker Hotel, Chicago
Whitehall Hotel, Chicago

Iowa
Hotel Fort Des Moines, Des Moines

Kentucky
Boone Tavern Hotel of Berea College,
Berea

Louisiana
Radisson Hotel Bentley, Alexandria
The Delta Queen Steamboat Co.,
New Orleans
Le Pavillon Hotel, New Orleans
Hotel Monteleone, New Orleans
Hotel Maison de Ville and The
Audubon Cottages, New Orleans

Maine
Asticou Inn, Northeast Harbor
Black Point Inn, Prouts Neck,
Scarborough
The Colony Hotel, Kennebunkport
Portland Regency Hotel, Portland

Maryland
Admiral Fell Inn, Baltimore
Historic Inns of Annapolis,
Annapolis
Kent Manor Inn, Stevensville

Massachusetts
Boston Park Plaza Hotel, Boston
Chatham Bars Inn, Chatham, Cape
Cod

The Fairmont Copley, Plaza Boston
Hawthorne Hotel, Salem
Harbor View Hotel, Martha's
Vineyard, Edgartown
The Hotel Northampton,
Northampton
The Red Lion Inn, Stockbridge

Michigan
The Landmark Inn, Marquette

Minnesota
The Saint Paul Hotel, St. Paul
St. James Hotel, Red Wing

Mississippi
Monmouth Plantation, Natchez
Natchez Eola Hotel, Natchez

Missouri
Hyatt Regency St. Louis at Union
Station, St. Louis

Montana
The Pollard, Red Lodge
New Hampshire
The BALSAMS Grand Resort Hotel,
Dixville Notch
Eagle Mountain House, Jackson

New Mexico
The Bishop's Lodge, Santa Fe
Hotel St. Francis, Santa Fe
La Fonda, Santa Fe

New York
Hotel Saranac of Paul Smith's
College, Saranac Lake
The Hotel Syracuse, Syracuse
Mohonk Mountain House, New Palt
The Otesaga, Cooperstown
The Plaza, New York City
The Sagamore, Bolton Landing,
Adirondacks/Lake George

National Trust Historic Hotels of America (Con't)

North Carolina

The Carolina Inn, Chapel Hill

The Dunhill Hotel, Charlotte

Lake Lure Inn, Lake Lure

The Lords Proprietors' Inn, Edenton

Pinehurst Resort & Country Club
Village of Pinehurst

Radisson Prince Charles Hotel and
Suites, Fayetteville

Ohio

The Cincinnatian Hotel, Cincinnati

The Lafayette, Marietta

Omni Netherland Plaza, Cincinnati

Renaissance Cleveland Hotel Tower
City Center, Cleveland

Oregon

The Governor Hotel, Portland

The Heathman Hotel, Portland

Pennsylvania

The Hotel Hershey, Hershey

Puerto Rico

Hotel El Convento, Old San Juan

Rhode Island

The Hotel Viking, Newport

South Carolina

John Rutledge House Inn,
Charleston

Kings Courtyard Inn, Charleston

The Westin Francis Marion Hotel,
Charleston

Tennessee

The Peabody, Memphis

The Westin Hermitage Suite Hotel,
Nashville

Texas

The Driskill, Austin

The Menger Hotel, San Antonio

The Stoneleigh Hotel, Dallas

Utah

Historic Radisson Suite Hotel,
Ogden

Vermont

Basin Harbor Club, Vergennes

The Equinox, Manchester Village

Green Mountain Inn, Stowe

The Old Tavern at Grafton, Grafton

The Middlebury Inn, Middlebury

Virginia

The Homestead, Hot Springs

The Jefferson, Richmond

Linden Row Inn, Richmond

The Wayside Inn, Middletown

Williamsburg Inn, Williamsburg

Washington

Mayflower Park Hotel, Seattle

National Park Inn, Mt. Rainier
National Park, Ashford

Paradise Inn, Mr. Rainier National
Park, Ashford

Rosario Resort, Eastsound

Washington, D.C.

The Hay-Adams Hotel

The Henley Park Hotel

Morrison-Clark Inn

Renaissance Mayflower Hotel

The Jefferson

West Virginia

Historic Blennerhassett Hotel,
Parkersburg

The Greenbrier, White Sulphur
Springs

Wisconsin

The American Club, Kohler

The Pfister, Milwaukee

Source: The National Trust for Historic Preservation

Secretary of the Interior's Standards for Rehabilitation

The Secretary of the Interior's Standards for Rehabilitation were developed to help protect our nation's irreplaceable cultural resources by promoting consistent preservation practices. The Standards recognize the need to alter or add to a historic property in order to meet continuing or changing uses. Following the Standards helps to preserve the distinctive character of a historic building and its site while accommodating new uses. The Standards (36 CFR Part 67) apply to historic buildings of all periods, styles, types, materials, and sizes. They apply to both the exterior and the interior of historic buildings. The Standards also encompass related landscape features and the building's site and environment as well as attached, adjacent, or related new construction. In addition, in order for a rehabilitation project to be eligible for the 20% rehabilitation tax credit, the Standards must be followed.

For more information about how to apply these Standards and tax credits, visit the National Park Service's Web site at *www2.cr.nps.gov/tps/tax/*.

1. A property shall be used for its historic purpose or be placed in a new use that requires minimal change to the defining characteristics of the building and its site and environment.

2. The historic character of a property shall be retained and preserved. The removal of historic materials or alteration of features and spaces that characterize a property shall be avoided.

3. Each property shall be recognized as a physical record of its time, place, and use. Changes that create a false sense of historical development, such as adding conjectural features or architectural elements from other buildings, shall not be undertaken.

4. Most properties change over time; those changes that have acquired historic significance in their own right shall be retained and preserved.

5. Distinctive features, finishes, and construction techniques or examples of craftsmanship that characterize a historic property shall be preserved.

Secretary of the Interior's Standards for Rehabilitation (Con't)

6. Deteriorated historic features shall be repaired rather than replaced. Where the severity of deterioration requires replacement of a distinctive feature, the new feature shall match the old in design, color, texture, and other visual qualities and, where possible, materials. Replacement of missing features shall be substantiated by documentary, physical, or pictorial evidence.

7. Chemical or physical treatments, such as sandblasting, that cause damage to historic materials shall not be used. The surface cleaning of structures, if appropriate, shall be undertaken using the gentlest means possible.

8. Significant archeological resources affected by a project shall be protected and preserved. If such resources must be disturbed, mitigation measures shall be undertaken.

9. New additions, exterior alterations, or related new construction shall not destroy historic materials that characterize the property. The new work shall be differentiated from the old and shall be compatible with the massing, size, scale, and architectural features to protect the historic integrity of the property and its environment.

10. New additions and adjacent or related new construction shall be undertaken in such a manner that if removed in the future, the essential form and integrity of the historic property and its environment would be unimpaired.

Source: *Department of the Interior, National Park Service*

Did you know...
In 1928, the 21-story Milam Building in San Antonio, Texas, marked a milestone in building technology as the first fully air conditioned office building.

Threatened National Historic Landmarks

National Historic Landmarks are buildings, sites, districts, structures, and objects which the Secretary of the Interior determines possess national significance in American history and culture. These landmarks have been identified as being an exceptional representation of the heritage of the United States and worthy of preservation. Each year out of these over 2,100 entries, the National Park Service compiles a list of Landmarks which are in eminent danger of destruction due to deterioration, incompatible new construction, demolition, erosion, vandalism, and looting. The purpose of this list is to alert the Federal government and the American people of this potential loss of their heritage.

For additional information about the National Historic Landmarks program or the Threatened List, visit the National Park's web site at *www2.cr.nps.gov/nhl/index.htm* or contact Heritage Preservation Services at 202-343-9583.

1998 Threatened National Historic Landmarks – Buildings and Historic Districts

Alaska
Adak Army Base and Adak Naval Operating Base
Fort William H. Seward
Holy Assumption Orthodox Church
Japanese Occupation Site, Kiska Island
Seal Island Historic District

American Samoa
Government House

Arizona
Fort Huachuca

California
Alcatraz Island
C.A. Thayer (Schooner)
Las Flores Adobe
Locke Historic District
Mare Island Naval Shipyard
Presidio of San Franciso
Warner's Ranch

Colorado
Central City/Black Hawk Historic District
Cripple Creek Historic District

Connecticut
Huntington (Samuel) Birthplace

District of Columbia
Terrell (Mary Church) House

Illinois
Adler Planetarium
Old Stone Gate, Chicago Union Stockyards
Orchestra Hall
Pullman Historic District
Room 405, George Herbert Jones Laboratory, University of Chicago

Threatened National Historic Landmarks (Con't)

Indiana
Bailly (Joseph) Homestead
Cannelton Cotton Mill
Eleutherian College Classroom and
    Chapel Building

Iowa
Fort Des Moines Provisional Army
    Officer Training School
Hepburn (William P.) House

Kansas
Fort Leavenworth
Nicodemus Historic District

Louisiana
Courthouse (The) and Lawyer's Row
Fort St. Philip

Maryland
Chestertown Historic District
Resurrection Manor

Massachusetts
Boston Naval Shipyard
Fenway Studio

Michigan
Calumet Historic District
Quincy Mining Company Historic
    District

Minnesota
Fort Snelling
Washburn A Mill Complex

Mississippi
Montgomery (I.T.) House
Pemberton's Headquarters

Montana
Great Northern Railway Buildings

Nevada
Fort Ruby
Virginia City Historic District

New Jersey
Abbott Farm Historic District
Cape May Historic District
Fort Hancock and Sandy Hook
    Proving Ground Historic District
Great Falls of the Passaic Society for
    Universal Manufacturing Historic
    District
Lucy, the Margate Elephant

New York
Governors Island
Hudson River State Hospital, Main
    Building
Mount Lebanon Shaker Village
Niagara Reservation

Ohio
Hotel Breakers
Kettering (Charles F.) House
S Bridge, National Road

Oklahoma
101 Ranch Historic District

Pennsylvania
Bedford Springs Hotel Historic
    District
Bomberger's Distillery
Cambria Iron Company
Dudley (Charles B.) House
East Broad Top Railroad
Eastern State Penitentiary
Gallatin (Albert) House
Harrisburg Station and Train Shed
Meason (Isaac) House
Philadelphia Savings Fund Society
    (PSFS) Building
United States Naval Asylum
Woodlands

Rhode Island
Fort Adams

Threatened National Historic Landmarks (Con't)

South Carolina
    Chapelle Administration Building
    Fort Hill (John C. Calhoun House)

South Dakota
    Frawley Ranch Historic District

Tennessee
    The Hermitage

Texas
    Fort Brown
    Fort Sam Houston
    Garner (John Nance) House

Virginia
    Jackson Ward Historic District

Washington
    Seattle Electric Company
        Georgetown Steam Plant

West Virginia
    Elkins Coal and Coke

Wisconsin
    Dousman Hotel
    Greene (Thomas A.) Memorial
    Namur Historic District
    Taliesin East

Wyoming
    Sun (Tom) Ranch
    Swan Land and Cattle Company
        Headquarters

Source: National Park Service

World Heritage List

Since 1972 the World Heritage Committee has inscribed 582 properties on the World Heritage List (445 cultural, 117 natural and 20 mixed properties in 114 States Parties). The World Heritage List was established under terms of The Convention Concerning the Protection of the World Cultural and Natural Heritage, adopted in November 1972 at the 17th General Conference of the United Nations Educational, Scientific, and Cultural Organization (UNESCO). The Convention states that a World Heritage Committee "will establish, keep up-to-date and publish" a World Heritage List of cultural and natural properties, submitted by the States Parties and considered to be of outstanding universal value. One of the main responsibilities of this Committee is to provide technical cooperation under the World Heritage Fund for the safeguarding of World Heritage properties to States Parties whose resources are insufficient. Other assistance with the nomination process, training, grants, and loans are also available. The following list contains all the cultural properties which are representative of architectural or technological advances of man.

For a complete listing of all the World Heritage properties with detailed descriptions and photographs of each, visit their Web site at *www.unesco.org/whc/nwhc/pages/sites/ main.htm*.

Algeria:
- M'Zab Valley
- Djémila
- Tipasa
- Timgad
- Kasbah of Algiers

Argentina and Brazil:
- Jesuit Missions of the Guaranis: San Ignacio Mini, Santa Ana, Nuestra Señora de Loreto and Santa Maria Mayor (Argentina), Ruins of Sao Miguel das Missoes (Brazil)

Armenia:
- Monastery of Haghpat

Austria:
- Historic Centre of the City of Salzburg
- Palace and Gardens of Schönbrunn
- Hallstatt-Dachstein Salzkammergut Cultural Landscape
- Semmering Railway

Bangladesh:
- Historic Mosque City of Bagerhat
- Ruins of the Buddhist Vihara at Paharpur

World Heritage List (Con't)

Belgium:
Flemish Béguinages
The Four Lifts on the Canal du
    Centre and their Environs, La
    Louvière and Le Roeulx (Hainault)
Grand-Place, Brussels

Benin:
Royal Palaces of Abomey*

Bolivia:
City of Potosi
Jesuit Missions of the Chiquitos
Historic City of Sucre
El Fuerte de Samaipata

Brazil:
Historic Town of Ouro Preto
Historic Centre of the Town of Olinda
Historic Centre of Salvador de Bahia
Sanctuary of Bom Jesus do Congonhas
Brasilia
Historic Centre of São Luis

Bulgaria:
Boyana Church
Rock-hewn Churches of Ivanovo
Thracian Tomb of Kazanlak
Ancient City of Nessebar
Rila Monastery
Thracian tomb of Sveshtari

Cambodia:
Angkor*

Canada:
Quebec (Historic Area)
Lunenburg Old Town

China:
The Great Wall
Mount Taishan
Imperial Palace of the Ming and
    Qing Dynasties
Mausoleum of the First Qin Emperor
The Mountain Resort and its
    Outlying Temples, Chengde
Temple and Cemetery of Confucius,
    and the Kong Family Mansion in
    Qufu
Ancient Building Complex in the
    Wudang Mountains
Potala Palace, Lhasa
Lushan National Park
Mount Emei and Leshan Giant
    Buddha
Old Town of Lijiang
Ancient City of Ping Yao
Classical Gardens of Suzhou
Summer Palace, an Imperial Garden
    in Beijing
Temple of Heaven -- an Imperial
    Sacrificial Altar in Beijing

Colombia:
Port, Fortresses and Group of
    Monuments, Cartagena
Historic Centre of Santa Cruz de
    Mompox

Croatia:
Old City of Dubrovnik
Historic Complex of Split with the
    Palace of Diocletian
Episcopal Complex of the
    Euphrasian Basilica in the
    Historic Centre of Porec
Historic City of Trogir

Cuba:
Old Havana and its Fortifications
Trinidad and the Valley de los Ingenic
San Pedro de la Roca Castle,
    Santiago de Cuba

Cyprus:
Paphos
Painted Churches in the Troodos
    Region
Choirokoitia

World Heritage List (Con't)

Czech Republic:
Historic Centre of Prague
Historic Centre of Cesky Krumlov
Historic Centre of Telc
Pilgrimage Church of St. John of
    Nepomuk at Zelena Hora
Kutná Hora: Historical Town Centre
    with the Church of Saint Barbara
    and the Cathedral of our Lady at
    Sedlec
Lednice-Valtice Cultural Landscape
Holasovice Historical Village
    Reservation
Gardens and Castle at Kromeríz

Denmark:
Roskilde Cathedral

Dominican Republic:
Colonial City of Santo Domingo

Ecuador:
City of Quito

Egypt:
Memphis and its Necropolis - the
    Pyramid Fields from Giza to
    Dahshur
Ancient Thebes with its Necropolis
Nubian Monuments from Abu
    Simbel to Philae
Islamic Cairo
Abu Mena

Estonia:
The Historic Centre (Old Town) of
    Tallinn

Eithiopia:
Rock-hewn Churches, Lalibela
Fasil Ghebbi, Gondar Region
Aksum

Finland:
Old Rauma
Fortress of Suomenlinna

Petäjävesi Old Church
Verla Groundwood and Board Mill

Former Yugoslav Rep. of Macedonia
Ohrid Region, including its cultural
    and historic aspects, and its natur-
    al environment

France:
Mont-Saint-Michel and its Bay
Chartres Cathedral
Palace and Park of Versailles
Vézelay, Church and Hill
Palace and Park of Fontainebleau
Chateau and Estate of Chambord
Amiens Cathedral
Roman Theatre and its Surroundings
    and the "Triumphal Arch" of Orange
Roman and Romanesque
    Monuments of Arles
Cistercian Abbey of Fontenay
Royal Saltworks of Arc-et-Senans
Place Stanislas, Place de la Carrière,
    and Place d'Alliance in Nancy
Church of Saint-Savin sur Gartempe
Pont du Gard (Roman Aqueduct)
Strasbourg-Grande îsle
Paris, Banks of the Seine
Cathedral of Notre-Dame, Former
    Abbey of Saint-Remi and Palace of
    Tau, Reims
Bourges Cathedral
Historic Centre of Avignon
Canal du Midi
Historic Fortified City of Carcassonne
Routes of Santiago de Compostela in
    France
Historic Site of Lyons

Georgia:
City-Museum Reserve of Mtskheta
Bagrati Cathedral and Gelati
    Monastery
Upper Svaneti

World Heritage List (Con't)

Germany:
Aachen Cathedral
Speyer Cathedral
Würzburg Residence, with the Court
Gardens and Residence Square
Pilgrimage Church of Wies
The Castles of Augustusburg and
Falkenlust at Brühl
St. Mary's Cathedral and St.
Michael's Church at Hildesheim
Roman Monuments, Cathedral and
Liebfrauen-Church in Trier
Hanseatic City of Lübeck
Palaces and Parks of Potsdam and
Berlin
Abbey and Altenmünster of Lorsch
Mines of Rammelsberg and Historic
Town of Goslar
Town of Bamberg
Maulbronn Monastery Complex
Collegiate Church, Castle, and old
Town of Quedlinburg
Völklingen Ironworks
Cologne Cathedral
Bauhaus and its sites in Weimar and
Dessau
Luther Memorials in Eisleben and
Wittenberg
Classical Weimar

Ghana:
Forts and Castles, Volta Greater
Accra, Central and Western
Regions
Ashanti Traditional Buildings

Greece:
Temple of Apollo Epicurius at Bassae
Archaeological Site of Delphi
Acropolis, Athens
Mount Athos
Meteora
Paleochristian and Byzantine
Monuments of Thessalonika
Archaeological Site of Epidaurus
Medieval City of Rhodes
Mystras
Archaeological Site of Olympia
Delos
Monasteries of Daphni, Hossios
Luckas and Nea Moni of Chios
Pythagoreion and Heraion of Samos

Guatemala:
Antigua Guatemala

Haiti:
National Historic Park – Citadel,
Sans, Souci, Ramiers

Holy See:
Vatican City

Honduras:
Mayan Site of Copan

Hungary:
Budapest, the Banks of the Danube
and the Buda Castle Quarter
Hollokö
Millenary Benedictine Monastery of
Pannonhalma and its Natural
Environment

India:
Ajanta Caves
Ellora Caves
Agra Fort
Taj Mahal
Sun Temple, Konarak
Group of Monuments at
Mahabalipuram
Churches and Convents of Goa
Khajuraho Group of Monuments
Group of Monuments at Hampi
Fatehpur Sikri
Group of Monuments at Pattadakal
Brihadisvara Temple, Thanjavur
Buddhist Monuments at Sanchi
Humayun's Tomb, Delhi

World Heritage List (Con't)

Qutb Minar and its Monuments, Delhi

Indonesia:
Borobudur Temple Compounds
Prambanan Temple Compounds

Iran:
Tchogha Zanbil
Persepolis
Meidan Emam, Esfahan

Iraq:
Hatra

Ireland:
Skellig Michael

Italy:
The Church and Dominican Convent of Santa Maria delle Grazie with "The Last Supper" by Leonardo da Vinci
Historic Centre of Florence
Venice and its Lagoon
Piazza del Duomo, Pisa
Historic Centre of San Gimignano
I Sassi di Matera
City of Vicenza and the Palladian Villas of the Veneto
Historic Centre of Siena
Historic Centre of Naples
Crespi d'Adda
Ferrara: City of the Renaissance
Castel del Monte
The trulli of Alberobello
Early Christian Monuments of Ravenna
Historic Centre of the City of Pienza
18th-Century Royal Palace at Caserta with the Park, the Aqueduct of Vanvitelli and the San Leucio Complex
Residences of the Royal House of Savoy

Botanical Garden (Orto Botanico), Padua
Portovenere, Cinque Terre, and the Islands (Palmaria, Tino and Tinetto)
Cathedral, Torre Civica and Piazza Grande, Modena
Archaeological Areas of Pompei, Herulaneum, and Torre Annuziata
Costiera Amalfitana
Villa Romana del Casale
Archaeological Areas of Agrigento
Su Nuraxi di Barumini
Archaeological Area and the Patriarchal Basilica of Aquileia
Cilento and Vallo di Diano National Park with the Archeological sites of Paestum and Velia, and the Certosa di Padula
Historic Centre of Urbino

Italy/Holy See:
Historic centre of Rome, the Properties of the Holy See in that City Enjoying Extraterritorial Rights, and San Paolo Fuori le Mura

Japan:
Buddhist Monuments in the Horyu-ji Area
Himeji-jo
Historic Monuments of Ancient Kyoto (Kyoto, Uji and Otsu Cities)
Historic Villages of Shirakawa-go and Gokayama
Itsukushima Shinto Shrine
Historic Monuments of Ancient Nara

Jerusalem:
Old City of Jerusalem and its Walls*

World Heritage List (Con't)

Jordan:
- Petra
- Quseir Amra

Lao People's Democratic Republic:
- Town of Luang Prabang

Latvia:
- Historic Centre of Riga

Lebanon:
- Anjar
- Baalbek
- Byblos
- Tyre
- Ouadi Qadisha (the Holy Valley) and the Forest of the Cedars of God (Horsh Arz el-Rab)

Libyan Arab Jamahiriya:
- Archaeological Site of Leptis Magna
- Archaeological Site of Sabratha
- Archaeological Site of Cyrene
- Old Town of Ghadames

Lithuania:
- Vilnius Historic Centre

Luxembourg:
- City of Luxemburg: its Old Quarters and Fortifications

Mali:
- Old Towns of Djenné
- Timbuktu*

Malta:
- City of Valetta
- Megalithic Temples of Malta

Mauritania:
- Ancient Ksour of Ouadane, Chinguetti, Tichitt and Oualata

Mexico:
- Pre-Hispanic City and National Park of Palenque
- Historic Centre of Mexico City and Xochimilco
- Pre-Hispanic City of Teotihuacan
- Historic Centre of Oaxaca and Archaeological Site of Monte Alban
- Historic Centre of Puebla
- Historic Town of Guanajuato and Adjacent Mines
- Pre-Hispanic City of Chichen-Itza
- Historic Centre of Morelia
- El Tajin, Pre-Hispanic City
- Historic Centre of Zacatecas
- Earliest 16th-Century Monasteries on the Slopes of Popocatepetl
- Pre-Hispanic Town of Uxmal
- Historic Monuments Zone of Querétaro
- Hospicio Cabañas, Guadalajara
- Archaeological Zone of Paquimé, Casas Grandes
- Historic Monuments Zone of Tlacotalpan

Morocco:
- Medina of Fez
- Medina of Marrakesh
- Ksar of Aït-Ben-Haddou
- Historic City of Meknes
- The Medina of Tétouan (formerly known as Titawin)

Mozambique:
- Island of Mozambique

Nepal:
- Kathmandu Valley
- Lumbini, the Birthplace of the Lord Buddha

Netherlands:
- Schokland and Surroundings
- Defense Line of Amsterdam
- Mill Network at Kinderdijk-Elshout

World Heritage List (Con't)

Historic Area of Willemstad, Inner
City, and Harbour, the
Netherlands Antilles

Ir.D.F. Woudagemaal (D.F. Wouda
Steam Pumping Station)

Norway:

Urnes Stave Church

Bryggen

Røros

Oman:

Bahla Fort*

Pakistan:

Archaeological Ruins at Moenjodaro

Taxila

Buddhist Ruins of Takht-i-Bahi and
Neighbouring City Remains at
Sahi-i-Bahlol

Historic Monuments of Thatta

Fort and Shalamar Gardens in Lahore

Rohtas Fort

Panama:

Fortifications on the Caribbean side
of Panama: Portobelo-San Lorenzo

The Historic District of Panamá,
with the Salón Bolivar

Paraguay:

Jesuit Missions of La Santisima
Trinidad de Parana and Jesus de
Tavarangue

Peru:

City of Cuzco

Historic Sanctuary of Machu Picchu

Chavin

Chan Chan Archaeological Zone*

Historic Centre of Lima

Philippines:

Baroque Churches of the Philippines

Poland:

Cracow's Historic Centre

Wieliczka Salt Mine

Historic Centre of Warsaw

Old City of Zamosc

The Medieval Town of Torun

Castle of the Teutonic Order in Malbork

Portugal:

Central Zone of the Town of Angra
do Heroismo in the Azores

Monastery of the Hieronymites and
Tower of Belem in Lisbon

Monastery of Batalha

Convent of Christ in Tomar

Historic Centre of Evora

Monastery of Alcobaça

Cultural Landscape of Sintra

Historic Centre of Oporto

Republic of Korea:

Sokkuram Buddhist Grotto

Haiensa Temple Changgyong
P'ango, the Depositories for the
Tripitaka Koreana Woodblocks

Chongmyo Shrine

Ch'angdokkung Palace Complex

Hwasong Fortress

Romania:

Biertan and its Fortified Church

Monastery of Horezu

Churches of Moldavia

Russian Federation:

Historic Centre of St. Petersburg and
Related Groups of Monuments

Kizhi Pogost

Kremlin and Red Square, Moscow

Historic Monuments of Novgorod
and Surroundings

Cultural and Historic Ensemble of
the Solovetsky Islands

White Monuments of Vladimir and
Suzdal

Architectural Ensemble of the Trinity
Sergius Lavra in Sergiev Posad

World Heritage List (Con't)

Church of the Ascension,
Kolomenskoye

Senegal:
Island of Gorée

Slovakia:
Vlkolinec
Banska Stiavnica
Spissky Hrad and its Associated
Cultural Monuments

Spain:
Historic Centre of Cordoba
Alhambra, Generalife and Albayzin,
Granada
Burgos Cathedral
Monastery and Site of the Escurial,
Madrid
Parque Güell, Palacio Güell and Casa
Mila in Barcelona
Old Town of Segovia and its Aqueduct
Monuments of Oviedo and the
Kingdom of the Asturias
Santiago de Compostela (Old town)
Old Town of Avila, with its Extra-
Muros churches
Mudejar Architecture of Teruel
Historic City of Toledo
Old Town of Caceres
Cathedral, Alcazar and Archivo de
Indias in Seville
Old City of Salamanca
Poblet Monastery
Archaeological Ensemble of Mérida
Royal Monastery of Santa Maria de
Guadalupe
Route of Santiago de Compostela
Historic Walled Town of Cuenca
La Lonja de la Seda de Valencia
Las Médulas
The Palau de la Música Catalana and
the Hospital de Sant Pau, Barcelona
San Millán Yuso and Suso Monasteries
University and Historic Precinct of
Alcalá de Henares

Sri Lanka:
Sacred City of Anuradhapura
Ancient City of Polonnaruva
Ancient City of Sigiriya
Sacred City of Kandy
Old Town of Galle and its Fortifications
Golden Temple of Dambulla

Sweden:
Royal Domain of Drottningholm
Birka and Hovgården
Engelsberg Ironworks
Skogskyrkogården
Hanseatic Town of Visby
Church Village of Gammelstad, Luleå
Naval Port of Karlskrona

Switzerland:
Convent of St. Gall
Benedictine Convent of St. John at
Müstair
Old City of Berne

Syrian Arab Republic:
Ancient City of Damascus
Ancient City of Bosra
Site of Palmyra
Ancient City of Aleppo

Thailand:
Historic Town of Sukhothai and
Associated Historic Towns
Historic City of Ayutthaya and
Associated Historic Towns

Tunisia:
Medina of Tunis
Site of Carthage
Amphitheatre of El Jem
Punic Town of Kerkuane and its
Necropolis
Medina of Sousse
Kairouan
Dougga/Thugga

World Heritage List (Con't)

Turkey:
Historic Areas of Istanbul
Göreme National Park and the Rock
   Sites of Cappadocia
Great Mosque and Hospital of Divrigi
Hattusha
Nemrut Dag
Xanthos-Letoon
Hierapolis-Pamukkale
City of Safranbolu
Archaeological Site of Troy

Ukraine:
Kiev: Saint-Sophia Cathedral and
   Related Monastic Buildings, Kiev-
   Pechersk Lavra
L'viv - the Ensemble of the Historic
   Centre

United Kingdom:
Durham Castle and Cathedral
Ironbridge Gorge
Studley Royal Park, including the
   Ruins of Fountains Abbey
Stonehenge, Avebury and Associated
   Sites
Castles and Town Walls of King
   Edward in Gwynedd
St. Kilda
Blenheim Palace
City of Bath
Hadrian's Wall
Westminster Palace, Westminster
   Abbey, and Saint Margaret's
   Church
Tower of London
Canterbury Cathedral, St. Augustine's
   Abbey and St. Martin's Church
Old and New Towns of Edinburgh
Maritime Greenwich

United Republic of Tanzania:
Ruins of Kilwa Kisiwani and Ruins
   of Songo Mnara

United States of America:
Independence Hall
La Fortaleza and San Juan Historic
   Site in Puerto Rico
The Statue of Liberty
Monticello, and University of
   Virginia in Charlottesville
Pueblos de Taos

Uruguay:
Historic Quarter of the City of
   Colonia del Sacramento

Uzbekistan:
Itchan Kala
Historic Centre of Bukhara

Venezuela:
Coro and its Port

Viet Nam:
Complex of Hué Monuments

Yemen:
Old Walled City of Shibam
Old City of Sana'a
Historic Town of Zabid

Yugoslavia:
Stari Ras and Sopocani
Natural and Culturo-Historical
   Region of Kotor*
Studenica Monastery

Zimbabwe:
Khami Ruins National Monument

* *Indicates the site is also on the List of*
World Heritage in Danger as deter-
mined by the World Heritage
Committee.

Source: World Heritage Committee, UNESCO

World's 100 Most Endangered Sites

The World Monuments Fund's biennial List of 100 Most Endangered Sites designates those cultural sites most in danger of destruction, either by natural or man-made causes. Initial nominations for the list are solicited annually from governments, heritage conservation organizations, and concerned individuals. Each nominated site must have the support of a sponsoring institution, substantial cultural significance, an urgent need for intervention, and a viable intervention plan. The final selection committee is comprised of a panel of international experts. Limited financial support is also available from the World Monuments Watch Fund and is awarded on a competitive basis to selected sites on the list. The World Monuments Fund is a private, non-profit organization created in 1965 with the purpose of fostering a greater awareness of the world's cultural, artistic, and historic resources; facilitating preservation and conservation efforts; and generating private financial assistance.

For more information or to find out how to nominate a site, visit the World Monuments Fund's Web site at *www.worldmonuments.org* or contact them at 212-517-9367.

Albania
Butrint Archaeological Site, Sarande

Algeria
Tipasa Archaeological Park, Tipasa

Belgium
Tour and Taxis (transport hub), Brussels

Bosnia and Herzegovina
Mostar Historic Center, Mostar

Brazil
Santo Antonio do Paraguaçu, São Francisco do Paraguaça, Bahia
Vila de Paranapiacaba, Santo André, São Paulo

Bulgaria
Ivanovo Rock Chapels, Rousse Region

Cambodia
Banteay Chhmar Temple of Jayavarman VII, Thmar Puok

Chile
Orongo Ceremonial Site, Easter Island

China
Dulan County Tibetan Royal Tomb Group, Reshuixiang-Xuewei, Dulan
Palpung Monastery, Babang Village, Sichuan

World's 100 Most Endangered Sites (Con't)

Temple of Agriculture
(Xiannongtan), Beijing
Xuanjian Tower, Yuci City, Shanxi

Croatia
Vukovar City, Center Vukovar

Cuba
National Art Schools, Cubanacán,
Havana
San Isidro de los Destiladeros, Valle
de los Ingenios, Trinidad
Santa Teresa de Jesús Cloisters,
Havana

Czech Republic
Kuks Forest Sculptures, Kuks

Dominican Republic
Puerto Plata Lighthouse, Puerto Plata

Egypt
Khasekhemwy at Hierakonpolis,
Edfu, Kom el Ahmar
Sultan Qa'itbay Complex, Cairo
Valley of the Kings, Thebes, Luxor

El Salvador
Suchitoto City, Cuscatlán

Ethiopia
Mentewab-Qwesqwam Palace,
Gondar

France
Saint Pierre Cathedral, Beauvais

Georgia
Ikorta Church of the Archangel,
Zemo Artsevi Village
Tbilisi Historic District, Tbilisi

Germany
Gartenreich Dessau-Wörlitz, Dessau
Thomaskirche, Leipzig

Greece
Kahal Shalom Synagogue, Rhodes

India
Basgo Gompa (Maitreya Temples),
Ladakh, Leh
Champaner Archaeological Site,
Panchmahal, Gujarat
Jaisalmer Fort, Rajasthan
Metropolitan Building, Calcutta
Saint Anne Church, Talaulim, Goa

Indonesia
Omo Hada (Royal Palace Complex),
Nias, North Sumatra
Tanah Lot Temple, Tabanan, Bali

Iraq
Erbil Citadel, Kurdish Autonomous
Region

Ireland
Saint Brendan's Cathedral, Clonfert,
County Galway

Israel
Tel-Dan Canaanite Gate, near
Kibbutz Dan, Upper Galilee
Ramle White Mosque Archaeological
Site, Ramle

Italy
Ancient Pompeii, Naples
Bridge of Chains, Bagni di Lucca
Cinque Terre, Liguria
Santi Quattro Coronati Cloister,
Rome

Jamaica
Falmouth Historic Town, Trelawny
Parish

Jordan
Petra Archaeological Site, Wadi
Mousa

Kenya
Thimlich Ohinga Cultural
Landscape, Migori

World's 100 Most Endangered Sites (Con't)

Lebanon

Enfeh Archaeological Site, Enfeh, near Tripoli

Malaysia

George Town Historic Enclave, Penang State

Kampung Cina River Frontage, Kuala Terengganu

Malta

Mnajdra Prehistoric Temples, Mnajdra

Mexico

Madera Cave Dwellings, Madera, Chihuahua

San Juan de Ulúa Fort, Veracruz

Santa Prisca Parish Church, Taxco de Alarcón, Guerrero

Teotihuacán Archaeological Site, San Juan Teotihuacán

Yaxchilán Archaeological Zone, Cuenca del Usumacinta, Chiapas

Mongolia

Bogd Khaan Palace Museum, Ulaanbaatar

Nepal

Itum Monastery, Kathmandu

Teku Thapatali Monument Zone, Kathmandu

Niger

Giraffe Rock Art Site

Pakistan

Uch Monument Complex, Bahawalpur, Punjab

Panama

San Lorenzo Castle and San Gerónimo Fort, Colón and Portobelo

Peru

Cusco Historic Center, Cusco

Los Pinchudos Archaeological Site, Rio Abiseo National Park

Machu Picchu, Urubamba, Cusco

Philippines

Rice Terraces of the Cordilleros, Ifugao

Poland

Vistulamouth Fortress, Gdansk

Romania

Bánffy Castle, Bontida

Russia

Arkhangelskoye State Museum, Moscow

Irkoutsk Historic Center, Irkoutsk

Oranienbaum State Museum, Lomonosov

Paanajärvi Village, Kemi Province

Rostov Veliky Historic Center, Rostov Veliky

Russakov Club, Moscow

Viipuri Library, Vyborg

Slovakia

Basil the Great Church, Krajné Cierno

Sudan

Gebel Barkal Archaeological Site, Karima

Suriname

Jodensavanne Archaeological Site, Redi Doti

Turkey

Ani Archaeological Site, Ocarli Köyü, Kars

Çatalhöyük, Çumra, Konya

Mount Nemrut Archaeological Site, Kâhta

Zeyrek Mosque, Istanbul

World's 100 Most Endangered Sites (Con't)

Turkmenistan
  Merv Archaeological Site, Bairam Ali

Ukraine
  Kamyanets Podilsky Castle Bridge,
    Kamyanets Podilsky
  Zhovkva Synagogue, Zhovkva

United Kingdom
  Abbey Farmstead, Faversham, Kent,
    England
  Saint Francis Church and Monastery,
    East Manchester, England

U.S.A.
  Eastern State Penitentiary,
    Philadelphia, Pennsylvania
  Lancaster County, Lancaster County,
    Pennsylvania
  Seventh Regiment Armory, New
    York, New York
  Tree Studios and Medinah Temple,
    Chicago, Illinois
  VDL Research House II, Los
    Angeles, California

Uzbekistan
  Abdulazizkhan Complex, Bukhara

Venezuela
  San Francisco Church, Coro, Falcón

Vietnam
  Minh Mang Tomb, Hue
  My Son Temple Complex, Duy
    Xuyen, Quang Nam

Yemen
  Tarim Historic City, Wadi
    Hadhramaut

Yugoslavia
  Subotica Synagogue, Subotica

Zimbabwe
  Khami National Monument,
    Bulawayo

Source: World Monuments Fund

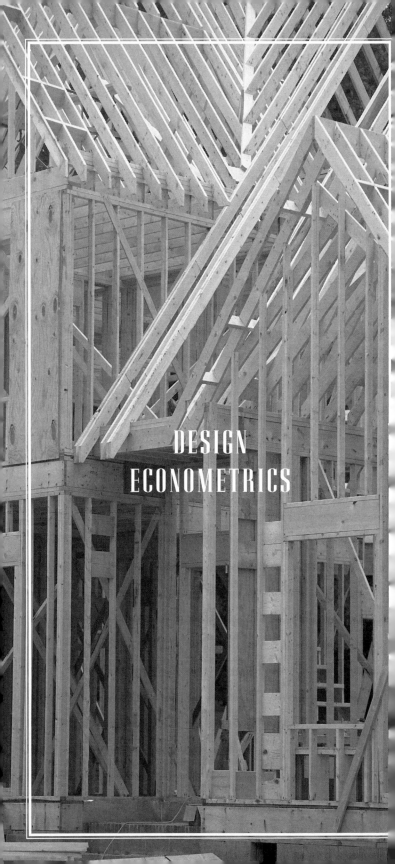

DESIGN
ECONOMETRICS

DESIGN ECONOMETRICS

Annual Value of Construction Put in Place: 1994-1998

Type of construction	Constant (1992) dollars (in millions)				
	1994	1995	1996	1997	1998
Total construction	480,620	478,069	506,655	520,117	538,399
Private construction	367,247	360,040	385,967	395,321	417,273
Residential buildings	218,005	201,677	220,017	221,546	242,378
New housing units	153,250	142,413	153,966	156,038	173,109
1 unit	140,416	126,773	136,516	137,156	153,170
2 units or more	12,833	15,640	17,450	18,882	19,939
Improvements	64,755	59,264	66,052	65,508	(N/A)
Nonresidential buildings	111,416	120,627	131,188	139,067	139,380
Industrial	26,803	29,043	28,503	26,440	24,743
Office	20,553	22,891	24,329	27,631	31,185
Hotels, motels	4,308	6,351	9,521	10,741	11,653
Other commercial	34,756	38,098	42,042	42,748	40,723
Religious	3,584	3,864	3,955	4,951	5,222
Educational	4,471	4,908	5,880	7,101	7,473
Hospital and institutional	11,377	10,051	10,280	11,576	10,939
Miscellaneous [1]	5,565	5,421	6,677	7,880	7,441
Farm nonresidential	2,990	2,692	3,319	3,329	(N/A)
Public utilities	32,074	32,401	29,286	29,448	(N/A)
Telecommunications	9,785	10,073	10,245	9,918	10,271
Other public utilities	22,289	22,328	19,041	19,529	(N/A)
Railroads	3,186	3,201	3,894	4,321	(N/A)
Electric light and power	13,877	12,656	9,914	10,545	(N/A)
Gas	4,308	5,637	4,330	3,820	(N/A)
Petroleum pipelines	918	834	903	843	(N/A)
All other private [2]	2,763	2,643	2,156	1,931	2,105
Public construction	113,373	118,029	120,688	124,796	121,125
Buildings	45,728	49,683	51,119	53,515	52,269
Housing and redevelop.	3,495	3,928	3,958	4,055	3,712
Industrial	1,358	1,348	1,214	842	811
Educational	18,838	20,800	21,035	22,786	22,398
Hospital	3,663	3,871	4,050	4,247	3,175
Other [3]	18,373	19,737	20,863	21,585	22,173

Annual Value of Construction: 1994-1998 (Con't)

Type of construction	Constant (1992) dollars (in millions)				
	1994	1995	1996	1997	1998
Highways and streets	36,219	35,303	36,483	38,605	37,345
Military facilities	2,196	2,728	2,317	2,223	2,250
Conservation and develop.	5,996	5,779	5,335	4,841	4,717
Sewer systems	8,199	8,557	9,260	8,951	8,835
Water supply facilities	4,237	4,695	5,187	5,393	5,586
Miscellaneous public 4	10,799	11,284	10,987	11,267	10,124

/A - Not available, but estimates are included in totals.

Includes amusement and recreational buildings, bus and airline terminals, animal hospitals and shelters, etc.

Includes privately owned streets and bridges, parking areas, sewer and water facilities, parks and playgrounds, golf courses, airfields, etc.

Includes general administrative buildings, prisons, police and fire stations, courthouses, civic centers, passenger terminals, space facilities, postal facilities, etc.

Includes open amusement and recreational facilities, power generating facilities, transit systems, airfields, open parking facilities, etc.

Source: U.S. Census Bureau

Architecture Student Demographics

Based on a study conducted by the National Architectural Accrediting Board (NAAB), the following information outlines demographic information about NAAB accredited architecture degree programs at U.S. colleges and universities.

	1993/94	1994/95	1995/96	1996/97	1997/98
Pre-professional Undergrad. Programs					
Full-time students	10,420	10,790	9,655	12,130	11,789
Part-time students	1,504	1,577	1,494	1,602	1,524
Women students	3,419	3,895	3,432	4,317	4,419
African-American students	635	723	496	660	682
American Indian students	59	59	80	62	67
Asian/Pacific Isle students	929	1,010	807	1,112	1,065
Hispanic students	1,144	967	750	991	955
Total Graduates	2,260	2,369	2,154	2,324	2,199
Women graduates	662	708	603	746	807
African-American graduates	105	75	74	83	81
American Indian graduates	7	7	6	10	9
Asian/Pacific Isle graduates	238	219	198	225	233
Hispanic graduates	149	147	101	157	162
Accredited B. Arch Programs					
Full-time students	16,899	16,500	16,424	16,025	16,423
Part-time students	1,924	1,500	1,364	1,178	1,377
Women students	5,007	5,107	5,155	5,046	5,413
African-American students	1,252	1,174	1,247	1,122	1,165
American Indian students	101	143	195	163	138
Asian/Pacific Isle students	1,699	1,735	1,665	1,591	1,497
Hispanic students	1,473	1,466	1,436	1,340	1,249
Total Graduates	3,206	2,837	2,948	3,028	2,710
Women graduates	832	775	742	849	762
African-American graduates	152	144	148	131	111
American Indian graduates	20	16	14	14	8
Asian/Pacific Isle graduates	282	277	276	307	294
Hispanic graduates	188	185	215	223	222

Architecture Student Demographics (Con't)

	1993/94	1994/95	1995/96	1996/97	1997/98
Accredited M. Arch Programs					
Full-time students	4,812	4,664	5,196	5,252	5,461
Part-time students	537	491	724	533	677
Women students	1,855	1,883	2,164	2,143	2,273
African-American students	117	121	142	133	133
American Indian students	18	11	21	17	20
Asian/Pacific Isle students	521	508	540	522	550
Hispanic students	260	235	267	302	301
Total Graduates	1,654	1,629	1,676	1,645	1,799
Women graduates	541	580	558	580	747
African-American graduates	28	28	26	45	32
American Indian graduates	1	3	5	3	9
Asian/Pacific Isle graduates	158	169	140	156	164
Hispanic graduates	75	87	83	82	92

Source: National Architectural Accrediting Board

Did you know...

The Empire State Building contains 200,000 cubic feet of Indiana limestone and granite, 10 million bricks, and 730 tons of aluminum and steel.

Commercial Building Characteristics: 1995 (in thousands)

Building Characteristics	All Buildings	Buildings by Size			
		1,001 to 5,000 Square Feet	5,001 to 10,000 Square Feet	10,001 to 25,000 Square Feet	25,001 to 50,000 Square Feet
All Buildings	4,579	2,399	1,035	745	213
Principal Building Activity					
Education	309	100	60	62	49
Food Sales	137	108	Q	Q	Q
Food Service	285	210	52	Q	Q
Health Care	105	57	Q	16	5
Lodging	158	46	40	43	14
Mercantile and Service	1,289	736	295	195	33
Office	705	405	131	94	35
Public Assembly	326	128	110	64	13
Public Order and Safety	87	Q	Q	23	Q
Religious Worship	269	92	84	78	11
Warehouse and Storage	580	2B6	135	95	34
Other	67	Q	Q	Q	Q
Vacant	261	149	68	34	4
Year Constructed					
1919 or Before	353	175	92	65	11
1920 to 1945	562	309	145	70	17
1946 to 1959	867	461	222	123	34
1960 to 1969	718	343	159	135	45
1970 to 1979	813	428	174	137	38
1980 to 1989	846	422	151	186	46
1990 to 1992	218	132	50	16	11
1993 to 1995	202	129	43	13	9
Floors					
One	3,018	1,894	618	358	90
Two	1,002	378	283	236	62
Three	399	123	97	115	37
Four to Nine	148	Q	37	35	24
Ten or More	12	Q	Q	Q	Q

Buildings by Size				Building Characteristics
50,001 to 100,000 Square Feet	100,001 to 200,000 Square Feet	200,001 to 500,000 Square Feet	Over 500,000 Square Feet	
115	48	19	6	**All Buildings**
				Principal Building Activity
26	9	3	Q	Education
Q	Q	Q	Q	Food Sales
Q	Q	0	Q	Food Service
2	Q	2	1	Health Care
9	4	2	Q	Lodging
18	8	2	2	Mercantile and Service
22	10	5	1	Office
7	2	1	Q	Public Assembly
Q	Q	Q	Q	Public Order and Safety
Q	Q	Q	Q	Religious Worship
17	9	3	1	Warehouse and Storage
Q	Q	Q	Q	Other
3	Q	Q	Q	Vacant
				Year Constructed
6	2	Q	Q	1919 or Before
11	6	2	1	1920 to 1945
19	5	3	*	1946 to 1959
21	12	3	1	1960 to 1969
20	9	4	1	1970 to 1979
26	9	4	1	1980 to 1989
6	3	1	*	1990 to 1992
6	Q	*	*	1993 to 1995
				Floors
37	16	4	1	One
32	8	2	1	Two
18	7	2	*	Three
26	14	7	1	Four to Nine
Q	3	4	2	Ten or More

Commercial Building Characteristics: 1995 (Con't)

Building Characteristics	All Buildings	Buildings by Size			
		1,001 to 5,000 Square Feet	5,001 to 10,000 Square Feet	10,001 to 25,000 Square Feet	25,001 to 50,000 Square Feet
Census Region					
Northeast	725	351	162	139	38
Midwest	1,139	638	224	181	48
South	1,750	953	380	276	74
West	964	457	269	149	53
Ownership and Occupancy					
Nongovernment Owned	4,025	2,176	909	646	158
Owner Occupied	3,158	1,746	704	503	109
Nonowner Occupied	698	325	163	126	47
Unoccupied	170	105	Q	Q	Q
Government Owned	553	223	125	98	55
Predominant Ext. Wall Material					
Masonry	3,061	1,454	749	545	170
Siding or Shingles	639	465	116	50	5
Metal Panels	662	390	146	97	18
Concrete Panels	106	Q	10	30	14
Window Glass	46	Q	Q	Q	4
Other	50	Q	Q	Q	Q
No One Major Type	15	Q	Q	Q	Q
Predominant Roof Material					
Built-up	1,369	591	331	258	97
Shingles (Not Wood)	1,486	915	331	191	29
Metal Surfacing	908	512	192	158	29
Synthetic or Rubber	351	133	62	71	40
Slate or Tile	202	105	60	21	10
Wooden Materials	152	72	50	Q	Q
Concrete	58	Q	Q	Q	Q
Other	36	Q	Q	Q	Q
No One Major Type	Q	Q	Q	Q	Q

Q: Data withheld because the Relative Standard Error (RSE) was greater than 50 percent, or fewer than 20 buildings were sampled.
* = Value rounds to zero in the units displayed.

Buildings by Size				Building Characteristics
50,001 to 100,000 Square Feet	100,001 to 200,000 Square Feet	200,001 to 500,000 Square Feet	Over 500,000 Square Feet	
				Census Region
20	10	5	2	Northeast
28	14	5	1	Midwest
42	17	6	1	South
24	8	3	1	West
				Ownership and Occupancy
83	35	13	4	Nongovernment Owned
58	24	10	4	Owner Occupied
24	10	3	*	Nonowner Occupied
Q	Q	Q	Q	Unoccupied
32	13	6	1	Government Owned
				Predominant Ext. Wall Material
91	35	14	4	Masonry
Q	Q	Q	Q	Siding or Shingles
7	2	Q	*	Metal Panels
12	6	2	*	Concrete Panels
3	2	1	1	Window Glass
Q	Q	*	Q	Other
Q	Q	Q	Q	No One Major Type
				Predominant Roof Material
54	25	10	3	Built-up
14	4	1	*	Shingles (Not Wood)
13	3	1	Q	Metal Surfacing
25	13	5	2	Synthetic or Rubber
4	Q	Q	Q	Slate or Tile
Q	Q	Q	Q	Wooden Materials
Q	Q	Q	*	Concrete
Q	0	Q	Q	Other
Q	Q	Q	Q	No One Major Type

ource: Energy Information Administration, Office of Energy Markets and End Use,1995 Commercial Buildings Energy Consumption Survey

Construction Costs by City (in dollars per square foot)

Location	CCI	Apartment, 1 Story	Church	College Clsrm., 2-3 Story	College Dorm, 2-3 Story	Fire Station, 1 Story	Hospital, 4-8 Story	Hotel, 8-24 Story
National Average		88.35	102.40	85.40	86.70	88.10	109.30	86.2c
ALABAMA								
Birmingham	0.87	76.86	89.09	74.30	75.43	76.65	95.09	74.99
Huntsville	0.83	73.33	84.99	70.88	71.96	73.12	90.72	71.5
Mobile	0.83	73.33	84.99	70.88	71.96	73.12	90.72	71.5
Montgomery	0.80	70.68	81.92	68.32	69.36	70.48	87.44	68.9(
ALASKA								
Anchorage	1.26	111.32	129.02	107.60	109.24	111.01	137.72	108.6
Fairbanks	1.25	110.44	128.00	106.75	108.38	110.13	136.63	107.7
ARIZONA								
Mesa/Tempe	0.86	75.98	88.06	73.44	74.56	75.77	94.00	74.1
Phoenix	0.90	79.52	92.16	76.86	78.03	79.29	98.37	77.5
Tuscon	0.89	78.63	91.14	76.01	77.16	78.41	97.28	76.7
ARKANSAS								
Fayetteville	0.67	59.19	68.61	57.22	58.09	59.03	73.23	57.7
Little Rock	0.80	70.68	81.92	68.32	69.36	70.48	87.44	68.9
CALIFORNIA								
Anaheim	1.10	97.19	112.64	93.94	95.37	96.91	120.23	94.8
Bakersfield	1.06	93.65	108.54	90.52	91.90	93.39	115.86	91.3
Berkeley	1.18	104.25	120.83	100.77	102.31	103.96	128.97	101.7
Fresno	1.09	96.30	111.62	93.09	94.50	96.03	119.14	93.9
Inglewood	1.08	95.42	110.59	92.23	93.64	95.15	118.04	93.1
Long Beach	1.08	95.42	110.59	92.23	93.64	95.15	118.04	93.1
Los Angeles	1.11	98.07	113.66	94.79	96.24	97.79	121.32	95.6
Modesto	1.10	97.19	112.64	93.94	95.37	96.91	120.23	94.8
Oakland	1.18	104.25	120.83	100.77	102.31	103.96	128.97	101.7
Oxnard	1.09	96.30	111.62	93.09	94.50	96.03	119.14	93.9
Palo Alto	1.16	102.49	118.78	99.06	100.57	102.20	126.79	99.9
Pasadena	1.07	94.53	109.57	91.38	92.77	94.27	116.95	92.2
Riverside	1.09	96.30	111.62	93.09	94.50	96.03	119.14	93.9
Sacramento	1.11	98.07	113.66	94.79	96.24	97.79	121.32	95.6
Salinas	1.12	98.95	114.69	95.65	97.10	98.67	122.42	96.5
San Bernardino	1.06	93.65	108.54	90.52	91.90	93.39	115.86	91.3

Library	Nursing Home	Office, 2-4 Story	Office, 11-20 Story	Post Office	School, Elementary	School, High 2-3 Story	Store, Dept., 3 Story	Location
90.35	79.80	69.80	92.20	73.40	75.95	78.70	70.30	**National Average**
								ALABAMA
78.60	69.43	60.73	80.21	63.86	66.08	68.47	61.16	Birmingham
74.99	66.23	57.93	76.53	60.92	63.04	65.32	58.35	Huntsville
74.99	66.23	57.93	76.53	60.92	63.04	65.32	58.35	Mobile
72.28	63.84	55.84	73.76	58.72	60.76	62.96	56.24	Montgomery
								ALASKA
113.84	100.55	87.95	116.17	92.48	95.70	99.16	88.58	Anchorage
112.94	99.75	87.25	115.25	91.75	94.94	98.38	87.88	Fairbanks
								ARIZONA
77.70	68.63	60.03	79.29	63.12	65.32	67.68	60.46	Mesa/Tempe
81.32	71.82	62.82	82.98	66.06	68.36	70.83	63.27	Phoenix
80.41	71.02	62.12	82.06	65.33	67.60	70.04	62.57	Tuscon
								ARKANSAS
60.53	53.47	46.77	61.77	49.18	50.89	52.73	47.10	Fayetteville
72.28	63.84	55.84	73.76	58.72	60.76	62.96	56.24	Little Rock
								CALIFORNIA
99.39	87.78	76.78	101.42	80.74	83.55	86.57	77.33	Anaheim
95.77	84.59	73.99	97.73	77.80	80.51	83.42	74.52	Bakersfield
106.61	94.16	82.36	108.80	86.61	89.62	92.87	82.95	Berkeley
98.48	86.98	76.08	100.50	80.01	82.79	85.78	76.63	Fresno
97.58	86.18	75.38	99.58	79.27	82.03	85.00	75.92	Inglewood
97.58	86.18	75.38	99.58	79.27	82.03	85.00	75.92	Long Beach
100.29	88.58	77.48	102.34	81.47	84.30	87.36	78.03	Los Angeles
99.39	87.78	76.78	101.42	80.74	83.55	86.57	77.33	Modesto
106.61	94.16	82.36	108.80	86.61	89.62	92.87	82.95	Oakland
98.48	86.98	76.08	100.50	80.01	82.79	85.78	76.63	Oxnard
104.81	92.57	80.97	106.95	85.14	88.10	91.29	81.55	Palo Alto
96.67	85.39	74.69	98.65	78.54	81.27	84.21	75.22	Pasadena
98.48	86.98	76.08	100.50	80.01	82.79	85.78	76.63	Riverside
100.29	88.58	77.48	102.34	81.47	84.30	87.36	78.03	Sacramento
101.19	89.38	78.18	103.26	82.21	85.06	88.14	78.74	Salinas
95.77	84.59	73.99	97.73	77.80	80.51	83.42	74.52	San Bernardino

Construction Costs by City (Con't)

Location	CCI	Apartment, 1 Story	Church	College Clsrm., 2-3 Story	College Dorm, 2-3 Story	Fire Station, 1 Story	Hospital, 4-8 Story	Hotel, 8-24 Story
San Diego	1.07	94.53	109.57	91.38	92.77	94.27	116.95	92.23
San Francisco	1.24	109.55	126.98	105.90	107.51	109.24	135.53	106.89
San Jose	1.20	106.02	122.88	102.48	104.04	105.72	131.16	103.44
Santa Ana	1.07	94.53	109.57	91.38	92.77	94.27	116.95	92.23
Santa Barbara	1.09	96.30	111.62	93.09	94.50	96.03	119.14	93.96
Santa Rosa	1.18	104.25	120.83	100.77	102.31	103.96	128.97	101.72
Stockton	1.09	96.30	111.62	93.09	94.50	96.03	119.14	93.96
Vallejo	1.16	102.49	118.78	99.06	100.57	102.20	126.79	99.99
COLORADO								
Colorado Springs	0.91	80.40	93.18	77.71	78.90	80.17	99.46	78.44
Denver	0.94	83.05	96.26	80.28	81.50	82.81	102.74	81.03
Fort Collins	0.91	80.40	93.18	77.71	78.90	80.17	99.46	78.44
CONNECTICUT								
Bridgeport	1.03	91.00	105.47	87.96	89.30	90.74	112.58	88.79
Hartford	1.04	91.88	106.50	88.82	90.17	91.62	113.67	89.65
New Haven	1.04	91.88	106.50	88.82	90.17	91.62	113.67	89.65
Stamford	1.05	92.77	107.52	89.67	91.04	92.51	114.77	90.51
Waterbury	1.04	91.88	106.50	88.82	90.17	91.62	113.67	89.65
D.C.								
Washington	0.96	84.82	98.30	81.98	83.23	84.58	104.93	82.75
DELAWARE								
Wilmington	0.98	86.58	100.35	83.69	84.97	86.34	107.11	84.48
FLORIDA								
Fort Lauderdale	0.87	76.86	89.09	74.30	75.43	76.65	95.09	74.99
Jacksonville	0.84	74.21	86.02	71.74	72.83	74.00	91.81	72.41
Miami	0.87	76.86	89.09	74.30	75.43	76.65	95.09	74.99
Orlando	0.86	75.98	88.06	73.44	74.56	75.77	94.00	74.13
St. Petersburg	0.85	75.10	87.04	72.59	73.70	74.89	92.91	73.27
Tallahassee	0.80	70.68	81.92	68.32	69.36	70.48	87.44	68.96
Tampa	0.84	74.21	86.02	71.74	72.83	74.00	91.81	72.41
GEORGIA								
Atlanta	0.88	77.75	90.11	75.15	76.30	77.53	96.18	75.86
Columbus	0.79	69.80	80.90	67.47	68.49	69.60	86.35	68.10

Library	Nursing Home	Office, 2-4 Story	Office, 11-20 Story	Post Office	School, Elementary	School, High 2-3 Story	Store, Dept., 3 Story	Location
96.67	85.39	74.69	98.65	78.54	81.27	84.21	75.22	San Diego
112.03	98.95	86.55	114.33	91.02	94.18	97.59	87.17	San Francisco
108.42	95.76	83.76	110.64	88.08	91.14	94.44	84.36	San Jose
96.67	85.39	74.69	98.65	78.54	81.27	84.21	75.22	Santa Ana
98.48	86.98	76.08	100.50	80.01	82.79	85.78	76.63	Santa Barbara
106.61	94.16	82.36	108.80	86.61	89.62	92.87	82.95	Santa Rosa
98.48	86.98	76.08	100.50	80.01	82.79	85.78	76.63	Stockton
104.81	92.57	80.97	106.95	85.14	88.10	91.29	81.55	Vallejo
								COLORADO
82.22	72.62	63.52	83.90	66.79	69.11	71.62	63.97	Colorado Springs
84.93	75.01	65.61	86.67	69.00	71.39	73.98	66.08	Denver
82.22	72.62	63.52	83.90	66.79	69.11	71.62	63.97	Fort Collins
								CONNECTICUT
93.06	82.19	71.89	94.97	75.60	78.23	81.06	72.41	Bridgeport
93.96	82.99	72.59	95.89	76.34	78.99	81.85	73.11	Hartford
93.96	82.99	72.59	95.89	76.34	78.99	81.85	73.11	New Haven
94.87	83.79	73.29	96.81	77.07	79.75	82.64	73.82	Stamford
93.96	82.99	72.59	95.89	76.34	78.99	81.85	73.11	Waterbury
								D.C.
86.74	76.61	67.01	88.51	70.46	72.91	75.55	67.49	Washington
								DELAWARE
88.54	78.20	68.40	90.36	71.93	74.43	77.13	68.89	Wilmington
								FLORIDA
78.60	69.43	60.73	80.21	63.86	66.08	68.47	61.16	Fort Lauderdale
75.89	67.03	58.63	77.45	61.66	63.80	66.11	59.05	Jacksonville
78.60	69.43	60.73	80.21	63.86	66.08	68.47	61.16	Miami
77.70	68.63	60.03	79.29	63.12	65.32	67.68	60.46	Orlando
76.80	67.83	59.33	78.37	62.39	64.56	66.90	59.76	St. Petersburg
72.28	63.84	55.84	73.76	58.72	60.76	62.96	56.24	Tallahassee
75.89	67.03	58.63	77.45	61.66	63.80	66.11	59.05	Tampa
								GEORGIA
79.51	70.22	61.42	81.14	64.59	66.84	69.26	61.86	Atlanta
71.38	63.04	55.14	72.84	57.99	60.00	62.17	55.54	Columbus

Construction Costs by City (Con't)

Location	CCI	Apartment, 1 Story	Church	College Clsrm., 2-3 Story	College Dorm, 2-3 Story	Fire Station, 1 Story	Hospital, 4-8 Story	Hotel, 8-24 Story
Macon	0.82	72.45	83.97	70.03	71.09	72.24	89.63	70.68
Savannah	0.82	72.45	83.97	70.03	71.09	72.24	89.63	70.68
HAWAII								
Honolulu	1.23	108.67	125.95	105.04	106.64	108.36	134.44	106.03
IDAHO								
Boise	0.94	83.05	96.26	80.28	81.50	82.81	102.74	81.03
ILLINOIS								
Bloomington	0.99	87.47	101.38	84.55	85.83	87.22	108.21	85.34
Champaign	1.00	88.35	102.40	85.40	86.70	88.10	109.30	86.20
Chicago	1.11	98.07	113.66	94.79	96.24	97.79	121.32	95.68
North Suburban	1.08	95.42	110.59	92.23	93.64	95.15	118.04	93.10
Peoria	1.01	89.23	103.42	86.25	87.57	88.98	110.39	87.06
Rockford	1.04	91.88	106.50	88.82	90.17	91.62	113.67	89.65
South Suburban	1.08	95.42	110.59	92.23	93.64	95.15	118.04	93.10
Springfield	0.98	86.58	100.35	83.69	84.97	86.34	107.11	84.48
INDIANA								
Bloomington	0.92	81.28	94.21	78.57	79.76	81.05	100.56	79.30
Columbus	0.92	81.28	94.21	78.57	79.76	81.05	100.56	79.30
Evansville	0.94	83.05	96.26	80.28	81.50	82.81	102.74	81.03
Fort Wayne	0.92	81.28	94.21	78.57	79.76	81.05	100.56	79.30
Gary	0.97	85.70	99.33	82.84	84.10	85.46	106.02	83.61
Indianapolis	0.95	83.93	97.28	81.13	82.37	83.70	103.84	81.89
South Bend	0.90	79.52	92.16	76.86	78.03	79.29	98.37	77.58
IOWA								
Cedar Rapids	0.90	79.52	92.16	76.86	78.03	79.29	98.37	77.58
Des Moines	0.91	80.40	93.18	77.71	78.90	80.17	99.46	78.44
Dubuque	0.86	75.98	88.06	73.44	74.56	75.77	94.00	74.12
KANSAS								
Kansas City	0.92	81.28	94.21	78.57	79.76	81.05	100.56	79.30
Topeka	0.85	75.10	87.04	72.59	73.70	74.89	92.91	73.27
Wichita	0.85	75.10	87.04	72.59	73.70	74.89	92.91	73.27
KENTUCKY								
Frankfort	0.88	77.75	90.11	75.15	76.30	77.53	96.18	75.86

Library	Nursing Home	Office, 2-4 Story	Office, 11-20 Story	Post Office	School, Elementary	School, High 2-3 Story	Store, Dept., 3 Story	Location
74.09	65.44	57.24	75.60	60.19	62.28	64.53	57.65	Macon
74.09	65.44	57.24	75.60	60.19	62.28	64.53	57.65	Savannah
								HAWAII
111.13	98.15	85.85	113.41	90.28	93.42	96.80	86.47	Honolulu
								IDAHO
84.93	75.01	65.61	86.67	69.00	71.39	73.98	66.08	Boise
								ILLINOIS
89.45	79.00	69.10	91.28	72.67	75.19	77.91	69.60	Bloomington
90.35	79.80	69.80	92.20	73.40	75.95	78.70	70.30	Champaign
100.29	88.58	77.48	102.34	81.47	84.30	87.36	78.03	Chicago
97.58	86.18	75.38	99.58	79.27	82.03	85.00	75.92	North Suburban
91.25	80.60	70.50	93.12	74.13	76.71	79.49	71.00	Peoria
93.96	82.99	72.59	95.89	76.34	78.99	81.85	73.11	Rockford
97.58	86.18	75.38	99.58	79.27	82.03	85.00	75.92	South Suburban
88.54	78.20	68.40	90.36	71.93	74.43	77.13	68.89	Springfield
								INDIANA
83.12	73.42	64.22	84.82	67.53	69.87	72.40	64.68	Bloomington
83.12	73.42	64.22	84.82	67.53	69.87	72.40	64.68	Columbus
84.93	75.01	65.61	86.67	69.00	71.39	73.98	66.08	Evansville
83.12	73.42	64.22	84.82	67.53	69.87	72.40	64.68	Fort Wayne
87.64	77.41	67.71	89.43	71.20	73.67	76.34	68.19	Gary
85.83	75.81	66.31	87.59	69.73	72.15	74.77	66.79	Indianapolis
81.32	71.82	62.82	82.98	66.06	68.36	70.83	63.27	South Bend
								IOWA
81.32	71.82	62.82	82.98	66.06	68.36	70.83	63.27	Cedar Rapids
82.22	72.62	63.52	83.90	66.79	69.11	71.62	63.97	Des Moines
77.70	68.63	60.03	79.29	63.12	65.32	67.68	60.46	Dubuque
								KANSAS
83.12	73.42	64.22	84.82	67.53	69.87	72.40	64.68	Kansas City
76.80	67.83	59.33	78.37	62.39	64.56	66.90	59.76	Topeka
76.80	67.83	59.33	78.37	62.39	64.56	66.90	59.76	Wichita
								KENTUCKY
79.51	70.22	61.42	81.14	64.59	66.84	69.26	61.86	Frankfort

Construction Costs by City (Con't)

Location	CCI	Apartment, 1 Story	Church	College Clsrm., 2-3 Story	College Dorm, 2-3 Story	Fire Station, 1 Story	Hospital, 4-8 Story	Hotel, 8-24 Story
Lexington	0.85	75.10	87.04	72.59	73.70	74.89	92.91	73.27
Louisville	0.91	80.40	93.18	77.71	78.90	80.17	99.46	78.44
LOUISIANA								
Baton Rouge	0.83	73.33	84.99	70.88	71.96	73.12	90.72	71.55
Lafayette	0.83	73.33	84.99	70.88	71.96	73.12	90.72	71.55
New Orleans	0.85	75.10	87.04	72.59	73.70	74.89	92.91	73.27
Shreveport	0.81	71.56	82.94	69.17	70.23	71.36	88.53	69.82
MAINE								
Bangor	0.92	81.28	94.21	78.57	79.76	81.05	100.56	79.30
Portland	0.90	79.52	92.16	76.86	78.03	79.29	98.37	77.58
MARYLAND								
Annapolis	0.90	79.52	92.16	76.86	78.03	79.29	98.37	77.58
Baltimore	0.92	81.28	94.21	78.57	79.76	81.05	100.56	79.30
MASSACHUSETTS								
Boston	1.17	103.37	119.81	99.92	101.44	103.08	127.88	100.81
Lowell	1.09	96.30	111.62	93.09	94.50	96.03	119.14	93.90
Springfield	1.02	90.12	104.45	87.11	88.43	89.86	111.49	87.92
Worcester	1.07	94.53	109.57	91.38	92.77	94.27	116.95	92.2
MICHIGAN								
Ann Arbor	1.01	89.23	103.42	86.25	87.57	88.98	110.39	87.00
Detroit	1.04	91.88	106.50	88.82	90.17	91.62	113.67	89.6
Flint	0.98	86.58	100.35	83.69	84.97	86.34	107.11	84.40
Grand Rapids	0.87	76.86	89.09	74.30	75.43	76.65	95.09	74.90
Lansing	0.96	84.82	98.30	81.98	83.23	84.58	104.93	82.7
MINNESOTA								
Bemidji	0.98	86.58	100.35	83.69	84.97	86.34	107.11	84.4
Duluth	1.04	91.88	106.50	88.82	90.17	91.62	113.67	89.6
Minneapolis	1.09	96.30	111.62	93.09	94.50	96.03	119.14	93.90
Rochester	1.01	89.23	103.42	86.25	87.57	88.98	110.39	87.00
St. Paul	1.06	93.65	108.54	90.52	91.90	93.39	115.86	91.3
MISSISSIPPI								
Biloxi	0.81	71.56	82.94	69.17	70.23	71.36	88.53	69.8
Jackson	0.79	69.80	80.90	67.47	68.49	69.60	86.35	68.1

Library	Nursing Home	Office, 2-4 Story	Office, 11-20 Story	Post Office	School, Elementary	School, High 2-3 Story	Store, Dept., 3 Story	Location
76.80	67.83	59.33	78.37	62.39	64.56	66.90	59.76	Lexington
82.22	72.62	63.52	83.90	66.79	69.11	71.62	63.97	Louisville
								LOUISIANA
74.99	66.23	57.93	76.53	60.92	63.04	65.32	58.35	Baton Rouge
74.99	66.23	57.93	76.53	60.92	63.04	65.32	58.35	Lafayette
76.80	67.83	59.33	78.37	62.39	64.56	66.90	59.76	New Orleans
73.18	64.64	56.54	74.68	59.45	61.52	63.75	56.94	Shreveport
								MAINE
83.12	73.42	64.22	84.82	67.53	69.87	72.40	64.68	Bangor
81.32	71.82	62.82	82.98	66.06	68.36	70.83	63.27	Portland
								MARYLAND
81.32	71.82	62.82	82.98	66.06	68.36	70.83	63.27	Annapolis
83.12	73.42	64.22	84.82	67.53	69.87	72.40	64.68	Baltimore
								MASSACHUSETTS
105.71	93.37	81.67	107.87	85.88	88.86	92.08	82.25	Boston
98.48	86.98	76.08	100.50	80.01	82.79	85.78	76.63	Lowell
92.16	81.40	71.20	94.04	74.87	77.47	80.27	71.71	Springfield
96.67	85.39	74.69	98.65	78.54	81.27	84.21	75.22	Worcester
								MICHIGAN
91.25	80.60	70.50	93.12	74.13	76.71	79.49	71.00	Ann Arbor
93.96	82.99	72.59	95.89	76.34	78.99	81.85	73.11	Detroit
88.54	78.20	68.40	90.36	71.93	74.43	77.13	68.89	Flint
78.60	69.43	60.73	80.21	63.86	66.08	68.47	61.16	Grand Rapids
86.74	76.61	67.01	88.51	70.46	72.91	75.55	67.49	Lansing
								MINNESOTA
88.54	78.20	68.40	90.36	71.93	74.43	77.13	68.89	Bemidji
93.96	82.99	72.59	95.89	76.34	78.99	81.85	73.11	Duluth
98.48	86.98	76.08	100.50	80.01	82.79	85.78	76.63	Minneapolis
91.25	80.60	70.50	93.12	74.13	76.71	79.49	71.00	Rochester
95.77	84.59	73.99	97.73	77.80	80.51	83.42	74.52	St. Paul
								MISSISSIPPI
73.18	64.64	56.54	74.68	59.45	61.52	63.75	56.94	Biloxi
71.38	63.04	55.14	72.84	57.99	60.00	62.17	55.54	Jackson

Construction Costs by City (Con't)

Location	CCI	Apartment, 1 Story	Church	College Clsrm., 2-3 Story	College Dorm, 2-3 Story	Fire Station, 1 Story	Hospital, 4-8 Story	Hotel, 8-24 Story
MISSOURI								
St. Louis	1.03	91.00	105.47	87.96	89.30	90.74	112.58	88.79
Kansas City	0.99	87.47	101.38	84.55	85.83	87.22	108.21	85.34
Springfield	0.87	76.86	89.09	74.30	75.43	76.65	95.09	74.99
MONTANA								
Billings	0.96	84.82	98.30	81.98	83.23	84.58	104.93	82.75
Great Falls	0.95	83.93	97.28	81.13	82.37	83.70	103.84	81.89
NEBRASKA								
Alliance	0.73	64.50	74.75	62.34	63.29	64.31	79.79	62.93
Lincoln	0.83	73.33	84.99	70.88	71.96	73.12	90.72	71.55
Omaha	0.88	77.75	90.11	75.15	76.30	77.53	96.18	75.86
NEVADA								
Las Vegas	1.04	91.88	106.50	88.82	90.17	91.62	113.67	89.65
Reno	0.99	87.47	101.38	84.55	85.83	87.22	108.21	85.34
NEW HAMPSHIRE								
Manchester	0.95	83.93	97.28	81.13	82.37	83.70	103.84	81.89
Portsmouth	0.92	81.28	94.21	78.57	79.76	81.05	100.56	79.30
NEW JERSEY								
Elizabeth	1.08	95.42	110.59	92.23	93.64	95.15	118.04	93.10
Jersey City	1.11	98.07	113.66	94.79	96.24	97.79	121.32	95.68
Newark	1.12	98.95	114.69	95.65	97.10	98.67	122.42	96.54
Paterson	1.12	98.95	114.69	95.65	97.10	98.67	122.42	96.54
Trenton	1.11	98.07	113.66	94.79	96.24	97.79	121.32	95.68
NEW MEXICO								
Albuquerque	1.12	98.95	114.69	95.65	97.10	98.67	122.42	96.54
Santa Fe	1.00	88.35	102.40	85.40	86.70	88.10	109.30	86.20
NEW YORK								
Albany	0.97	85.70	99.33	82.84	84.10	85.46	106.02	83.61
Brooklyn	1.24	109.55	126.98	105.90	107.51	109.24	135.53	106.89
Buffalo	1.02	90.12	104.45	87.11	88.43	89.86	111.49	87.92
New York	1.34	118.39	137.22	114.44	116.18	118.05	146.46	115.51
Rochester	1.01	89.23	103.42	86.25	87.57	88.98	110.39	87.06

Library	Nursing Home	Office, 2-4 Story	Office, 11-20 Story	Post Office	School, Elementary	School, High 2-3 Story	Store, Dept., 3 Story	Location
								MISSOURI
93.06	82.19	71.89	94.97	75.60	78.23	81.06	72.41	St. Louis
89.45	79.00	69.10	91.28	72.67	75.19	77.91	69.60	Kansas City
78.60	69.43	60.73	80.21	63.86	66.08	68.47	61.16	Springfield
								MONTANA
86.74	76.61	67.01	88.51	70.46	72.91	75.55	67.49	Billings
85.83	75.81	66.31	87.59	69.73	72.15	74.77	66.79	Great Falls
								NEBRASKA
65.96	58.25	50.95	67.31	53.58	55.44	57.45	51.32	Alliance
74.99	66.23	57.93	76.53	60.92	63.04	65.32	58.35	Lincoln
79.51	70.22	61.42	81.14	64.59	66.84	69.26	61.86	Omaha
								NEVADA
93.96	82.99	72.59	95.89	76.34	78.99	81.85	73.11	Las Vegas
89.45	79.00	69.10	91.28	72.67	75.19	77.91	69.60	Reno
								NEW HAMPSHIRE
85.83	75.81	66.31	87.59	69.73	72.15	74.77	66.79	Manchester
83.12	73.42	64.22	84.82	67.53	69.87	72.40	64.68	Portsmouth
								NEW JERSEY
97.58	86.18	75.38	99.58	79.27	82.03	85.00	75.92	Elizabeth
100.29	88.58	77.48	102.34	81.47	84.30	87.36	78.03	Jersey City
101.19	89.38	78.18	103.26	82.21	85.06	88.14	78.74	Newark
101.19	89.38	78.18	103.26	82.21	85.06	88.14	78.74	Paterson
100.29	88.58	77.48	102.34	81.47	84.30	87.36	78.03	Trenton
								NEW MEXICO
101.19	89.38	78.18	103.26	82.21	85.06	88.14	78.74	Albuquerque
90.35	79.80	69.80	92.20	73.40	75.95	78.70	70.30	Santa Fe
								NEW YORK
87.64	77.41	67.71	89.43	71.20	73.67	76.34	68.19	Albany
112.03	98.95	86.55	114.33	91.02	94.18	97.59	87.17	Brooklyn
92.16	81.40	71.20	94.04	74.87	77.47	80.27	71.71	Buffalo
121.07	106.93	93.53	123.55	98.36	101.77	105.46	94.20	New York
91.25	80.60	70.50	93.12	74.13	76.71	79.49	71.00	Rochester

Construction Costs by City (Con't)

Location	CCI	Apartment, 1 Story	Church	College Clsrm., 2-3 Story	College Dorm, 2-3 Story	Fire Station, 1 Story	Hospital, 4-8 Story	Hotel, 8-24 Story
Syracuse	0.98	86.58	100.35	83.69	84.97	86.34	107.11	84.48
Yonkers	1.22	107.79	124.93	104.19	105.77	107.48	133.35	105.16
NORTH CAROLINA								
Asheville	0.77	68.03	78.85	65.76	66.76	67.84	84.16	66.37
Charlotte	0.77	68.03	78.85	65.76	66.76	67.84	84.16	66.37
Durham	0.78	68.91	79.87	66.61	67.63	68.72	85.25	67.24
Greensboro	0.78	68.91	79.87	66.61	67.63	68.72	85.25	67.24
Raleigh	0.78	68.91	79.87	66.61	67.63	68.72	85.25	67.24
Winston-Salem	0.78	68.91	79.87	66.61	67.63	68.72	85.25	67.24
NORTH DAKOTA								
Bismark	0.85	75.10	87.04	72.59	73.70	74.89	92.91	73.27
Fargo	0.83	73.33	84.99	70.88	71.96	73.12	90.72	71.51
Grand Forks	0.83	73.33	84.99	70.88	71.96	73.12	90.72	71.51
OHIO								
Akron	1.00	88.35	102.40	85.40	86.70	88.10	109.30	86.26
Cincinnati	0.93	82.17	95.23	79.42	80.63	81.93	101.65	80.11
Cleveland	1.02	90.12	101.15	87.11	88.43	89.86	111.49	87.91
Columbus	0.94	83.05	96.26	80.28	81.50	82.81	102.74	81.0
Dayton	0.92	81.28	94.21	78.57	79.76	81.05	100.56	79.36
Toledo	0.98	86.58	100.35	83.69	84.97	86.34	107.11	84.4
OKLAHOMA								
Oklahoma City	0.83	73.33	84.99	70.88	71.96	73.12	90.72	71.5
Tulsa	0.83	73.33	84.99	70.88	71.96	73.12	90.72	71.5
OREGON								
Eugene	1.03	91.00	105.47	87.96	89.30	90.74	112.58	88.7
Portland	1.05	92.77	107.52	89.67	91.04	92.51	114.77	90.5
Salem	1.03	91.00	105.47	87.96	89.30	90.74	112.58	88.7
PENNSYLVANIA								
Allentown	1.01	89.23	103.42	86.25	87.57	88.98	110.39	87.0
Erie	0.96	84.82	98.30	81.98	83.23	84.58	104.93	82.7
Philadelphia	1.12	98.95	114.69	95.65	97.10	98.67	122.42	96.5
Pittsburg	1.03	91.00	105.47	87.96	89.30	90.74	112.58	88.7

Library	Nursing Home	Office, 2-4 Story	Office, 11-20 Story	Post Office	School, Elementary	School, High 2-3 Story	Store, Dept., 3 Story	Location
88.54	78.20	68.40	90.36	71.93	74.43	77.13	68.89	Syracuse
110.23	97.36	85.16	112.48	89.55	92.66	96.01	85.77	Yonkers
								NORTH CAROLINA
69.57	61.45	53.75	70.99	56.52	58.48	60.60	54.13	Asheville
69.57	61.45	53.75	70.99	56.52	58.48	60.60	54.13	Charlotte
70.47	62.24	54.44	71.92	57.25	59.24	61.39	54.83	Durham
70.47	62.24	54.44	71.92	57.25	59.24	61.39	54.83	Greensboro
70.47	62.24	54.44	71.92	57.25	59.24	61.39	54.83	Raleigh
70.47	62.24	54.44	71.92	57.25	59.24	61.39	54.83	Winston-Salem
								NORTH DAKOTA
76.80	67.83	59.33	78.37	62.39	64.56	66.90	59.76	Bismark
74.99	66.23	57.93	76.53	60.92	63.04	65.32	58.35	Fargo
74.99	66.23	57.93	76.53	60.92	63.04	65.32	58.35	Grand Forks
								OHIO
90.35	79.80	69.80	92.20	73.40	75.95	78.70	70.30	Akron
84.03	74.21	64.91	85.75	68.26	70.63	73.19	65.38	Cincinnati
92.16	81.40	71.20	94.04	74.87	77.47	80.27	71.71	Cleveland
84.93	75.01	65.61	86.67	69.00	71.39	73.98	66.08	Columbus
83.12	73.42	64.22	84.82	67.53	69.87	72.40	64.68	Dayton
88.54	78.20	68.40	90.36	71.93	74.43	77.13	68.89	Toledo
								OKLAHOMA
74.99	66.23	57.93	76.53	60.92	63.04	65.32	58.35	Oklahoma City
74.99	66.23	57.93	76.53	60.92	63.04	65.32	58.35	Tulsa
								OREGON
93.06	82.19	71.89	94.97	75.60	78.23	81.06	72.41	Eugene
94.87	83.79	73.29	96.81	77.07	79.75	82.64	73.82	Portland
93.06	82.19	71.89	94.97	75.60	78.23	81.06	72.41	Salem
								PENNSYLVANIA
91.25	80.60	70.50	93.12	74.13	76.71	79.49	71.00	Allentown
86.74	76.61	67.01	88.51	70.46	72.91	75.55	67.49	Erie
101.19	89.38	78.18	103.26	82.21	85.06	88.14	78.74	Philadelphia
93.06	82.19	71.89	94.97	75.60	78.23	81.06	72.41	Pittsburg

Construction Costs by City (Con't)

Location	CCI	Apartment, 1 Story	Church	College Clsrm, 2-3 Story	College Dorm, 2-3 Story	Fire Station, 1 Story	Hospital, 4-8 Story	Hotel, 8-24 Story
RHODE ISLAND								
Providence	1.05	92.77	107.52	89.67	91.04	92.51	114.77	90.51
SOUTH CAROLINA								
Charleston	0.77	68.03	78.85	65.76	66.76	67.84	84.16	66.37
Columbia	0.76	67.15	77.82	64.90	65.89	66.96	83.07	65.51
SOUTH DAKOTA								
Aberdeen	0.80	70.68	81.92	68.32	69.36	70.48	87.44	68.96
Rapid City	0.79	69.80	80.90	67.47	68.49	69.60	86.35	68.10
Sioux Falls	0.81	71.56	82.94	69.17	70.23	71.36	88.53	69.82
TENNESSE								
Chattanooga	0.83	73.33	84.99	70.88	71.96	73.12	90.72	71.55
Knoxville	0.86	75.98	88.06	73.44	74.56	75.77	94.00	74.13
Memphis	0.83	73.33	84.99	70.88	71.96	73.12	90.72	71.55
Nashville	0.85	75.10	87.04	72.59	73.70	74.89	92.91	73.27
TEXAS								
Abilene	0.79	69.80	80.90	67.47	68.49	69.60	86.35	68.10
Amarillo	0.81	71.56	82.94	69.17	70.23	71.36	88.53	69.82
Austin	0.83	73.33	84.99	70.88	71.96	73.12	90.72	71.55
Beaumont	0.86	75.98	88.06	73.44	74.56	75.77	94.00	74.13
Corpus Christi	0.80	70.68	81.92	68.32	69.36	70.48	87.44	68.96
Dallas	0.80	70.68	81.92	68.32	69.36	70.48	87.44	68.96
El Paso	0.77	68.03	78.85	65.76	66.76	67.84	84.16	66.37
Fort Worth	0.87	76.86	89.09	74.30	75.43	76.65	95.09	74.99
Houston	0.89	78.63	91.14	76.01	77.16	78.41	97.28	76.72
Laredo	0.80	70.68	81.92	68.32	69.36	70.48	87.44	68.96
Lubbock	0.82	72.45	83.97	70.03	71.09	72.24	89.63	70.68
McAllen	0.79	69.80	80.90	67.47	68.49	69.60	86.35	68.10
San Antonio	0.84	74.21	86.02	71.74	72.83	74.00	91.81	72.4
Waco	0.81	71.56	82.94	69.17	70.23	71.36	88.53	69.8
Wichita Falls	0.84	74.21	86.02	71.74	72.83	74.00	91.81	72.4
UTAH								
Provo	0.77	68.03	78.85	65.76	66.76	67.84	84.16	66.3
Salt Lake City	0.88	77.75	90.11	75.15	76.30	77.53	96.18	75.8

Library	Nursing Home	Office, 2-4 Story	Office, 11-20 Story	Post Office	School, Elementary	School, High 2-3 Story	Store, Dept., 3 Story	Location
								RHODE ISLAND
94.87	83.79	73.29	96.81	77.07	79.75	82.64	73.82	Providence
								SOUTH CAROLINA
69.57	61.45	53.75	70.99	56.52	58.48	60.60	54.13	Charleston
68.67	60.65	53.05	70.07	55.78	57.72	59.81	53.43	Columbia
								SOUTH DAKOTA
72.28	63.84	55.84	73.76	58.72	60.76	62.96	56.24	Aberdeen
71.38	63.04	55.14	72.84	57.99	60.00	62.17	55.54	Rapid City
73.18	64.64	56.54	74.68	59.45	61.52	63.75	56.94	Sioux Falls
								TENNESSE
74.99	66.23	57.93	76.53	60.92	63.04	65.32	58.35	Chattanooga
77.70	68.63	60.03	79.29	63.12	65.32	67.68	60.46	Knoxville
74.99	66.23	57.93	76.53	60.92	63.04	65.32	58.35	Memphis
76.80	67.83	59.33	78.37	62.39	64.56	66.90	59.76	Nashville
								TEXAS
71.38	63.04	55.14	72.84	57.99	60.00	62.17	55.54	Abilene
73.18	64.64	56.54	74.68	59.45	61.52	63.75	56.94	Amarillo
74.99	66.23	57.93	76.53	60.92	63.04	65.32	58.35	Austin
77.70	68.63	60.03	79.29	63.12	65.32	67.68	60.46	Beaumont
72.28	63.84	55.84	73.76	58.72	60.76	62.96	56.24	Corpus Christi
72.28	63.84	55.84	73.76	58.72	60.76	62.96	56.24	Dallas
69.57	61.45	53.75	70.99	56.52	58.48	60.60	54.13	El Paso
78.60	69.43	60.73	80.21	63.86	66.08	68.47	61.16	Fort Worth
80.41	71.02	62.12	82.06	65.33	67.60	70.04	62.57	Houston
72.28	63.84	55.84	73.76	58.72	60.76	62.96	56.24	Laredo
74.09	65.44	57.24	75.60	60.19	62.28	64.53	57.65	Lubbock
71.38	63.04	55.14	72.84	57.99	60.00	62.17	55.54	McAllen
75.89	67.03	58.63	77.45	61.66	63.80	66.11	59.05	San Antonio
73.18	64.64	56.54	74.68	59.45	61.52	63.75	56.94	Waco
75.89	67.03	58.63	77.45	61.66	63.80	66.11	59.05	Wichita Falls
								UTAH
69.57	61.45	53.75	70.99	56.52	58.48	60.60	54.13	Provo
79.51	70.22	61.42	81.14	64.59	66.84	69.26	61.86	Salt Lake City

Construction Costs by City (Con't)

Location	CCI	Apartment, 1 Story	Church	College Clsrm., 2-3 Story	College Dorm, 2-3 Story	Fire Station, 1 Story	Hospital, 4-8 Story	Hotel, 8-24 Story
VERMONT								
Burlington	0.85	75.10	87.04	72.59	73.70	74.89	92.91	73.2
Montpelier	0.83	73.33	84.99	70.88	71.96	73.12	90.72	71.5
VIRGINIA								
Alexandria	0.90	79.52	92.16	76.86	78.03	79.29	98.37	77.5
Arlington	0.89	78.63	91.14	76.01	77.16	78.41	97.28	76.7
Fairfax	0.88	77.75	90.11	75.15	76.30	77.53	96.18	75.8
Fredericksburg	0.91	80.40	93.18	77.71	78.90	80.17	99.46	78.4
Newport News	0.82	72.45	83.97	70.03	71.09	72.24	89.63	70.6
Portsmouth	0.82	72.45	83.97	70.03	71.09	72.24	89.63	70.6
Richmond	0.85	75.10	87.04	72.59	73.70	74.89	92.91	73.2
WASHINGTON								
Seattle	1.05	92.77	107.52	89.67	91.04	92.51	114.77	90.9
Spokane	1.00	88.35	102.40	85.40	86.70	88.10	109.30	86.2
Tacoma	1.03	91.00	105.47	87.96	89.30	90.74	112.58	88.7
WEST VIRGINIA								
Charleston	0.93	82.17	95.23	79.42	80.63	81.93	101.65	80.
Martinsburg	0.78	68.91	79.87	66.61	67.63	68.72	85.25	67.2
Morgantown	0.93	82.17	95.23	79.42	80.63	81.93	101.65	80.
WISCONSIN								
Green Bay	0.97	85.70	99.33	82.84	84.10	85.46	106.02	83.
Madison	0.99	87.47	101.38	84.55	85.83	87.22	108.21	85.
Milwaukee	1.01	89.23	103.42	86.25	87.57	88.98	110.39	87.0
WYOMING								
Casper	0.84	74.21	86.02	71.74	72.83	74.00	91.81	72.
Cheyenne	0.83	73.33	84.99	70.88	71.96	73.12	90.72	71.
CANADA								
Calgary	0.99	87.47	101.38	84.55	85.83	87.22	108.21	85.
Charlottetown	0.92	81.28	94.21	78.57	79.76	81.05	100.56	79.
Edmondton	0.99	87.47	101.38	84.55	85.83	87.22	108.21	85.
Halifax	0.97	85.70	99.33	82.84	84.10	85.46	106.02	83.
Moncton	0.93	82.17	95.23	79.42	80.63	81.93	101.65	80.

Library	Nursing Home	Office, 2-4 Story	Office, 11-20 Story	Post Office	School, Elementary	School, High 2-3 Story	Store, Dept., 3 Story	Location
								VERMONT
76.80	67.83	59.33	78.37	62.39	64.56	66.90	59.76	Burlington
74.99	66.23	57.93	76.53	60.92	63.04	65.32	58.35	Montpelier
								VIRGINIA
81.32	71.82	62.82	82.98	66.06	68.36	70.83	63.27	Alexandria
80.41	71.02	62.12	82.06	65.33	67.60	70.04	62.57	Arlington
79.51	70.22	61.42	81.14	64.59	66.84	69.26	61.86	Fairfax
82.22	72.62	63.52	83.90	66.79	69.11	71.62	63.97	Fredericksburg
74.09	65.44	57.24	75.60	60.19	62.28	64.53	57.65	Newport News
74.09	65.44	57.24	75.60	60.19	62.28	64.53	57.65	Portsmouth
76.80	67.83	59.33	78.37	62.39	64.56	66.90	59.76	Richmond
								WASHINGTON
94.87	83.79	73.29	96.81	77.07	79.75	82.64	73.82	Seattle
90.35	79.80	69.80	92.20	73.40	75.95	78.70	70.30	Spokane
93.06	82.19	71.89	94.97	75.60	78.23	81.06	72.41	Tacoma
								WEST VIRGINIA
84.03	74.21	64.91	85.75	68.26	70.63	73.19	65.38	Charleston
70.47	62.24	54.44	71.92	57.25	59.24	61.39	54.83	Martinsburg
84.03	74.21	64.91	85.75	68.26	70.63	73.19	65.38	Morgantown
								WISCONSIN
87.64	77.41	67.71	89.43	71.20	73.67	76.34	68.19	Green Bay
89.45	79.00	69.10	91.28	72.67	75.19	77.91	69.60	Madison
91.25	80.60	70.50	93.12	74.13	76.71	79.49	71.00	Milwaukee
								WYOMING
75.89	67.03	58.63	77.45	61.66	63.80	66.11	59.05	Casper
74.99	66.23	57.93	76.53	60.92	63.04	65.32	58.35	Cheyenne
								CANADA
89.45	79.00	69.10	91.28	72.67	75.19	77.91	69.60	Calgary
83.12	73.42	64.22	84.82	67.53	69.87	72.40	64.68	Charlottetown
89.45	79.00	69.10	91.28	72.67	75.19	77.91	69.60	Edmondton
87.64	77.41	67.71	89.43	71.20	73.67	76.34	68.19	Halifax
84.03	74.21	64.91	85.75	68.26	70.63	73.19	65.38	Moncton

Construction Costs by City (Con't)

Location	CCI	Apartment, 1 Story	Church	College Clsrm., 2-3 Story	College Dorm, 2-3 Story	Fire Station, 1 Story	Hospital 4-8 Story	Hotel, 8-24 Story
Montreal	1.04	91.88	106.50	88.82	90.17	91.62	113.67	89.6
Ottawa	1.09	96.30	111.62	93.09	94.50	96.03	119.14	93.9
Quebec	1.05	92.77	107.52	89.67	91.04	92.51	114.77	90.9
Regina	0.94	83.05	96.26	80.28	81.50	82.81	102.74	81.0
Saint John	0.96	84.82	98.30	81.98	83.23	84.58	104.93	82.7
Saskatoon	0.94	83.05	96.26	80.28	81.50	82.81	102.74	81.0
St. John's	0.96	84.82	98.30	81.98	83.23	84.58	104.93	82.7
Thunder Bay	1.05	92.77	107.52	89.67	91.04	92.51	114.77	90.
Toronto	1.13	99.84	115.71	96.50	97.97	99.55	123.51	97.4
Vancouver	1.08	95.42	110.59	92.23	93.64	95.15	118.04	93.
Victoria	1.08	95.42	110.59	92.23	93.64	95.15	118.04	93.
Winnipeg	0.99	87.47	101.38	84.55	85.83	87.22	108.21	85.

Did you know...

When the San Francisco International Airport's new International Terminal is completed in mid-2000, it will be 2,000,000 square feet, equivalent to 35 football fields.

Library	Nursing Home	Office, 2-4 Story	Office, 11-20 Story	Post Office	School, Elementary	School, High 2-3 Story	Store, Dept., 3 Story	Location
93.96	82.99	72.59	95.89	76.34	78.99	81.85	73.11	Montreal
98.48	86.98	76.08	100.50	80.01	82.79	85.78	76.63	Ottawa
94.87	83.79	73.29	96.81	77.07	79.75	82.64	73.82	Quebec
84.93	75.01	65.61	86.67	69.00	71.39	73.98	66.08	Regina
86.74	76.61	67.01	88.51	70.46	72.91	75.55	67.49	Saint John
84.93	75.01	65.61	86.67	69.00	71.39	73.98	66.08	Saskatoon
86.74	76.61	67.01	88.51	70.46	72.91	75.55	67.49	St. John's
94.87	83.79	73.29	96.81	77.07	79.75	82.64	73.82	Thunder Bay
102.10	90.17	78.87	104.19	82.94	85.82	88.93	79.44	Toronto
97.58	86.18	75.38	99.58	79.27	82.03	85.00	75.92	Vancouver
97.58	86.18	75.38	99.58	79.27	82.03	85.00	75.92	Victoria
89.45	79.00	69.10	91.28	72.67	75.19	77.91	69.60	Winnipeg

Source: R.S. Means

The most successful leader of all is one who sees another picture not yet actualized.

Mary Parker Follett

Expenditures to Owner-Occupied Residential Properties: 1993 to 1998 (Millions of dollars)

Type of job [1]	1993	1994	1995	1996	1997	1998
Total	72,882	81,737	78,583	80,070	85,305	90,209
Additions	11,519	8,793	6,576	10,276	8,838	8,805
Decks and porches	1,856	1,618	2,419	2,356	2,792	1,658
Attached garages	2,290	1,618	1,688	1,312	460	1,690
Rooms	7,372	5,556	2,468	6,608	5,587	5,458
Alterations	18,514	22,996	19,176	21,667	23,817	24,818
Plumbing	877	658	1,050	771	1,547	649
HVAC	955	1,591	1,232	1,940	1,902	1,683
Electrical	528	796	485	720	542	474
Flooring	1,791	2,202	2,000	2,952	2,508	3,213
Kitchen remodeling	1,564	1,379	1,716	2,038	3,141	2,593
Bathroom remodeling	2,246	3,643	2,501	2,609	3,675	4,749
Kitchen and bathroom remodeling	630	1,470	608	845	167	927
Finishing space	967	709	1,146	1,196	1,185	1,037
Interior restructuring	1,275	2,855	2,249	3,318	3,187	2,993
Siding	977	1,245	550	685	1,134	673
Windows and doors	848	703	359	538	605	473
Other alterations	5,858	5,746	5,280	4,055	4,224	5,356
Outside Additions and Alterations	6,516	8,904	8,221	8,387	8,424	9,072
Detached buildings	577	1,895	1,271	1,868	2,038	2,335
Patios and terraces	520	775	484	983	1,323	668
Driveways and walkways	818	468	814	497	1,209	1,313
Fences	1,176	1,280	1,447	1,419	1,524	1,585
Other outside additions and alterations	3,427	4,486	4,204	3,621	2,329	3,171
Major Replacements	14,200	15,869	18,348	18,053	17,600	21,517
Plumbing	1,655	1,811	1,997	1,312	1,516	1,128
HVAC	3,331	2,815	5,014	3,719	4,487	4,027
Siding	1,169	978	1,056	1,849	1,077	1,555
Roofing	3,006	4,030	4,176	5,212	5,312	6,443
Driveways and walkways	760	875	438	457	537	1,138
Windows	1,838	2,487	2,435	3,030	2,739	3,904
Doors	958	1,157	1,020	986	982	1,068
Other major replacements	1,484	1,716	2,213	1,489	950	2,254

Expenditures to Owner-Occupied Residential Properties: 1993 to 1998 (Con't)

Type of job	1993	1994	1995	1996	1997	1998
Maintenance and Repairs	22,133	25,175	26,262	21,687	26,626	25,998
Painting and papering	6,833	6,669	6,660	7,247	7,748	8,641
Plumbing	2,002	2,945	2,281	2,285	2,618	2,240
HVAC	1,680	1,687	1,692	2,044	1,375	1,845
Electrical	483	551	615	418	503	493
Siding	584	497	587	241	706	298
Roofing	2,707	2,439	2,902	1,670	2,666	2,297
Flooring	774	1,490	1,417	1,093	1,638	826
Windows and doors	351	855	726	515	853	797
Materials to have on hand	1,965	2,270	1,990	2,650	2,726	3,234
Other maintenance and repairs	4,752	5,771	7,392	3,523	5,793	5,326

Note: Components may not add to totals because of rounding.

N/A: Not applicable

The expenditures given for each specified type of job consist of those outlays which have been identified as being primarily of the specified type. Thus, expenditures for one type of job done incidental to another type are included under the latter classification. For example, the relatively minor cost of painting done in conjunction with a roofing job is included in the roofing category.

Source U.S. Census Bureau

Did you know...
North Americans cultivate more than 32 million acres of lawn, which occupies more land than any single crop including corn, wheat, or tobacco.

Homeownership Rates (percentage)

	1900	1910	1920	1930	1940
US total	**46.50**	**45.90**	**45.60**	**47.80**	**43.60**
Alabama	34.40	35.10	35.00	34.20	33.60
Alaska	(N/A)	(N/A)	(N/A)	(N/A)	(N/A)
Arizona	57.50	49.20	42.80	44.80	47.90
Arkansas	47.70	46.60	45.10	40.10	39.70
California	46.30	49.50	43.70	46.10	43.40
Colorado	46.60	51.50	51.60	50.70	46.30
Connecticut	39.00	37.30	37.60	44.50	40.50
Delaware	36.30	40.70	44.70	52.10	47.10
District of Columbia	24.00	25.20	30.30	38.60	29.90
Florida	46.80	44.20	42.50	42.00	43.60
Georgia	30.60	30.50	30.90	30.60	30.80
Hawaii	(N/A)	(N/A)	(N/A)	(N/A)	(N/A)
Idaho	71.60	68.10	60.90	57.00	57.90
Illinois	45.00	44.10	43.80	46.50	40.30
Indiana	56.10	54.80	54.80	57.30	53.10
Iowa	60.50	58.40	58.10	54.70	51.50
Kansas	58.10	59.10	56.90	56.00	51.00
Kentucky	51.50	51.60	51.60	51.30	48.00
Louisiana	31.40	32.20	33.70	35.00	36.90
Maine	64.80	62.50	59.60	61.70	57.30
Maryland	40.00	44.00	49.90	55.20	47.40
Massachusetts	35.00	33.10	34.80	43.50	38.10
Michigan	62.30	61.70	58.90	59.00	55.40
Minnesota	63.50	61.90	60.70	58.90	55.20
Mississippi	34.50	34.00	34.00	32.50	33.30
Missouri	50.90	51.10	49.50	49.90	44.30
Montana	56.60	60.00	60.50	54.50	52.00
Nebraska	56.80	59.10	57.40	54.30	47.10
Nevada	66.20	53.40	47.60	47.10	46.10
New Hampshire	59.30	51.20	49.80	55.00	51.70
New Jersey	34.30	35.00	38.30	48.40	39.40
New Mexico	68.50	70.60	59.40	57.40	57.30
New York	33.20	31.00	30.70	37.10	30.30
North Carolina	46.60	47.30	47.40	44.50	42.40
North Dakota	80.00	75.70	65.30	58.60	49.80

1950	1960	1970	1980	1990	
55.00	61.90	62.90	64.40	64.20	US total
49.40	59.70	66.70	70.10	70.50	Alabama
54.50	48.30	50.30	58.30	56.10	Alaska
56.40	63.90	65.30	68.30	64.20	Arizona
54.50	61.40	66.70	70.50	69.60	Arkansas
54.50	61.40	54.90	55.90	55.60	California
58.10	63.80	63.40	64.50	62.20	Colorado
51.10	61.90	62.50	63.90	65.60	Connecticut
58.90	66.90	68.00	69.10	70.20	Delaware
32.30	30.00	28.20	35.50	38.90	District of Columbia
57.60	67.50	68.60	68.30	67.20	Florida
46.50	56.20	61.10	65.00	64.90	Georgia
33.00	41.10	46.90	51.70	53.90	Hawaii
65.50	70.50	70.10	72.00	70.10	Idaho
50.10	57.80	59.40	62.60	64.20	Illinois
65.50	71.10	71.70	71.70	70.20	Indiana
63.40	69.10	71.70	71.80	70.00	Iowa
63.90	68.90	69.10	70.20	67.90	Kansas
58.70	64.30	66.90	70.00	69.60	Kentucky
50.30	59.00	63.10	65.50	65.90	Louisiana
62.80	66.50	70.10	70.90	70.50	Maine
56.30	64.50	58.80	62.00	65.00	Maryland
47.90	55.90	57.50	57.50	59.30	Massachusetts
67.50	74.40	74.40	72.70	71.00	Michigan
66.40	72.10	71.50	71.70	71.80	Minnesota
47.80	57.70	66.30	71.00	71.50	Mississippi
57.70	64.30	67.20	69.90	68.80	Missouri
60.30	64.00	65.70	68.60	67.30	Montana
60.60	64.80	66.40	68.40	66.50	Nebraska
48.70	56.30	58.50	59.60	54.80	Nevada
58.10	65.10	68.20	67.60	68.20	New Hampshire
53.10	61.30	60.90	62.00	64.90	New Jersey
58.80	65.30	66.40	68.10	67.40	New Mexico
37.90	44.80	47.30	48.60	52.20	New York
53.30	60.10	65.40	68.40	68.00	North Carolina
66.20	68.40	68.40	68.70	65.60	North Dakota

Homeownership Rates (Con't)

	1900	1910	1920	1930	1940
Ohio	52.50	51.30	51.60	54.40	50.00
Oklahoma	54.20	45.40	45.50	41.30	42.80
Oregon	58.70	60.10	54.80	59.10	55.40
Pennsylvania	41.20	41.60	45.20	54.40	45.90
Rhode Island	28.60	28.30	31.10	41.20	37.40
South Carolina	30.60	30.80	32.20	30.90	30.60
South Dakota	71.20	68.20	61.50	53.10	45.00
Tennessee	46.30	47.00	47.70	46.20	44.10
Texas	46.50	45.10	42.80	41.70	42.80
Utah	67.80	64.80	60.00	60.90	61.10
Vermont	60.40	58.50	57.50	59.80	55.90
Virginia	48.80	51.50	51.10	52.40	48.90
Washington	54.50	57.30	54.70	59.40	57.00
West Virginia	54.60	49.50	46.80	45.90	43.70
Wisconsin	66.40	64.60	63.60	63.20	54.40
Wyoming	55.20	54.50	51.90	48.30	48.60

1950	1960	1970	1980	1990	
61.10	67.40	67.70	68.40	67.50	Ohio
60.00	67.00	69.20	70.70	68.10	Oklahoma
65.30	69.30	66.10	65.10	63.10	Oregon
59.70	68.30	68.80	69.90	70.60	Pennsylvania
45.30	54.50	57.90	58.80	59.50	Rhode Island
45.10	57.30	66.10	70.20	69.80	South Carolina
62.20	67.20	69.60	69.30	66.10	South Dakota
56.50	63.70	66.70	68.60	68.00	Tennessee
56.70	64.80	64.70	64.30	60.90	Texas
65.30	71.70	69.30	70.70	68.10	Utah
61.30	66.00	69.10	68.70	69.00	Vermont
55.10	61.30	62.00	65.60	66.30	Virginia
65.00	68.50	66.80	65.60	62.60	Washington
55.00	64.30	68.90	73.90	74.10	West Virginia
63.50	68.60	69.10	68.20	66.70	Wisconsin
54.00	62.20	66.40	69.20	67.80	Wyoming

Note: Alaska and Hawaii are NOT included in the 1950 US total.

Source: U.S. Census Bureau

Did you know...

The recently completed Vontz Center for Molecular Studies at the University of Cincinnati is the first building designed by Frank Gehry which utilizes brick throughout its entire facade.

Housing Characteristics: 1997 (percentage)

Housing Unit Characteristics	Total	Census Region			
		Northeast	Midwest	South	West
Total	100.0	100.0	100.0	100.0	100.0
Census Region and Division					
Northeast	19.4	100.0	-	-	-
New England	5.2	26.9	-	-	-
Middle Atlantic	14.2	73.1	-	-	-
Midwest	23.7	-	100.0	-	-
East North Central	16.7	-	70.3	-	-
West North Central	7.0	-	29.7	-	-
South	35.4	-	-	100.0	-
South Atlantic	18.4	-	-	52.1	-
East South Central	6.3	-	-	17.7	-
West South Central	10.7	-	-	30.2	-
West	21.5	-	-	-	100.0
Mountain	6.1	-	-	-	28.3
Pacific	15.4	-	-	-	71.7
Urban Status					
Urban	77.5	82.5	73.9	70.6	88.4
Central City	36.2	30.3	36.2	34.0	45.5
Suburban	41.2	52.2	37.7	36.6	42.9
Rural	22.5	17.5	26.1	29.4	11.6
Estimated Floorspace [1] (in square feet)					
Fewer than 600	7.8	9.7	6.9	5.7	10.3
600 to 900	21.2	22.4	21.3	19.0	23.4
1000 to 1,599	29.9	25.8	28.8	32.8	30.0
1,600 to 1,999	15.1	12.2	17.5	15.8	13.7
2,000 to 2,399	7.8	6.9	7.6	8.3	7.9
2,400 to 2,999	5.3	4.9	5.8	5.0	5.3
3,000 or more	4.1	3.4	4.1	5.1	3.0
No estimate provided	9.0	14.8	7.9	8.2	6.3

Housing Characteristics: 1997 (Con't)

Housing Unit Characteristics	Total	Census Region			
		Northeast	Midwest	South	West
Ownership of Unit					
Owned	67.4	64.6	71.8	70.7	59.8
Rented	32.6	35.4	28.2	29.3	40.2
Type and Ownership of Housing Unit					
Single-Family Detached	62.8	54.0	69.1	66.6	57.7
Owned	54.8	49.9	61.7	57.6	46.9
Rented	8.0	4.1	7.4	9.0	10.7
Single-Family Attached	9.8	15.6	7.6	7.7	10.6
Owned	5.4	9.7	3.9	4.8	4.2
Rented	4.4	5.9	3.7	2.8	6.4
Multifamily (2 to 4 units)	5.5	8.6	7.1	3.9	3.7
Owned	0.9	1.7	1.7	Q	Q
Rented	4.6	6.9	5.4	3.6	3.5
Multifamily (5 or more units)	15.6	19.3	11.7	13.4	20.1
Owned	1.1	1.5	Q	1.0	1.7
Rented	14.4	17.8	11.1	12.4	18.3
Mobile Home	6.2	2.5	4.6	8.3	8.0
Owned	5.2	1.8	4.0	6.9	6.7
Rented	1.0	Q	0.5	1.5	1.3
Year of Construction					
1939 or before	18.4	32.2	30.0	8.6	9.5
1940 to 1949	9.1	9.8	8.7	7.9	10.7
1950 to 1959	12.4	13.7	11.3	11.7	13.4
1960 to 1969	14.3	13.2	13.2	14.2	16.5
1970 to 1979	19.3	13.4	16.7	21.8	23.4
1980 to 1989	17.1	11.9	12.0	22.8	17.8
1990 to 1997 [2]	9.6	5.9	8.2	12.9	8.8
Observed Location of Household					
City	47.5	34.8	47.3	45.8	62.1
Town	17.9	26.2	18.8	14.8	14.8

Housing Characteristics: 1997 (Con't)

Housing Unit Characteristics	Total	Census Region			
		Northeast	Midwest	South	West
Suburbs	18.3	21.8	18.7	19.3	13.1
Rural or Open Country	16.2	17.2	15.1	20.1	10.0
Total Number of Rooms (Excluding Bathrooms)					
1 or 2	3.0	3.2	2.3	1.7	5.8
3	9.0	11.3	6.2	7.9	12.0
4	18.0	18.1	17.8	16.2	21.2
5	20.9	17.3	20.1	24.2	19.9
6	19.7	19.8	20.1	20.7	17.8
7	14.0	14.1	15.0	15.0	11.3
8	8.2	8.7	10.7	7.6	6.2
9 or more	6.9	7.4	7.8	6.8	5.8
Bedrooms					
None or 1	13.0	16.6	11.4	9.7	16.9
2	28.4	28.2	27.7	27.4	30.9
3	40.3	36.1	40.6	46.1	34.5
4 or More	18.3	19.1	20.4	16.8	17.7
Other Rooms (Excluding Bathrooms)					
None or 1	5.0	5.0	3.1	3.6	9.3
2	38.1	35.4	34.8	38.1	43.9
3	30.5	31.8	30.5	31.3	28.2
4	17.3	18.5	20.1	18.2	11.7
5 or More	9.1	9.3	11.5	8.1	6.9
Full Bathrooms					
None or 1	58.5	71.9	64.5	50.6	52.8
2	35.4	25.4	30.2	42.4	38.9
3 or More	6.1	2.7	5.4	7.0	8.3
Half Bathrooms					
None	72.0	66.4	68.7	74.0	77.2
1	26.1	30.9	28.9	24.5	21.5
2 or More	Q	Q	Q	Q	Q

Housing Characteristics: 1997 (Con't)

Housing Unit Characteristics	Total	Census Region			
		Northeast	Midwest	South	West
Number of Stories					
Single-Family Homes	72.7	69.7	76.7	74.3	68.2
1 Story	40.5	19.3	33.7	53.0	46.5
2 Stories	26.5	42.8	34.6	17.4	18.1
3 Stories	3.2	5.7	3.6	2.3	1.9
Split-Level	2.4	1.6	4.7	1.6	1.7
Other	Q	Q	Q	Q	Q
Mobile Homes	6.2	2.5	4.6	8.3	8.0
Foundation/Basement of Single-Family Homes (More than one may apply)					
Basement	32.7	57.1	58.6	13.7	13.3
Crawlspace	22.2	7.2	16.1	30.1	29.3
Concrete Slab	22.6	9.8	9.5	34.2	29.7
Not Asked (Mobile Homes and Multi-Family Units)	27.3	30.3	23.3	25.7	31.8
Garage/Carport					
Yes	53.7	47.4	62.1	48.3	58.9
1-Car Garage	16.0	22.9	17.3	13.0	13.3
2-Car Garage	29.2	21.5	38.0	24.2	34.7
3-Car Garage	2.7	1.9	4.6	1.2	3.8
Covered Carport	6.3	1.4	2.3	10.9	7.8
No	25.2	24.7	19.1	34.3	17.3
Not Asked (Apartments)	21.1	27.9	18.8	17.4	23.8
Main Heating Fuel					
Natural Gas	52.4	46.7	73.4	38.4	57.5
Electricity	29.6	12.2	12.4	48.7	33.0
Fuel Oil	9.2	35.0	4.3	3.2	1.0
LPG	4.4	1.2	7.1	5.5	2.6
Wood	2.2	2.2	1.9	1.9	3.1
Kerosene	0.9	1.9	Q	1.2	Q
Solar	Q	Q	Q	Q	Q
Other/None	0.3	0.7	Q	Q	Q

Estimated based on heated floorspace area.

Does not include all new construction for 1997.

Q: Data withheld either because the Relative Standard Error (RSE) was greater than 50 percent or fewer than 10 households were sampled.

Source: *Energy Information Administration, Office of Energy Markets and End Use, 1997 Residential Energy Consumption Survey*

Housing Density: 1940 to 1990

	Total Housing Units	Total Land Area (in square miles)	Housing Density (per square mile)	Total Population	Population Density (per square mile)
1990	102,263,678	3,536,338	28.9	248,709,873	70.3
1980	88,410,627	3,539,289	25.0	226,542,199	64.0
1970	68,704,315	3,536,855	19.4	203,302,031	57.5
1960	58,326,357	3,540,911	16.5	179,323,175	50.6
1950	46,137,076	3,550,206	13.0	151,325,798	42.6
1940	37,438,714	3,554,608	10.5	132,164,569	37.2

Source: US Census Bureau

Number of Licensed Landscape Architects by State

The number of licensed landscape architects in a state is determined by both the number of registered landscape architects who are residents and those who are registered as reciprocal or out-of-state registrants. Based on current population levels, the chart below also provides the number of resident landscape architects per 100,000 of population in each state.

State	Resident	Non-Resident	Total	Population [1]	# Resident Arch. Per 100,000
Alabama	104	97	201	4,351,999	2
Alaska	253	364	617	614,010	41
Arizona	253	364	617	4,668,361	5
Arkansas	484	778	1,262	2,538,303	19
California	16,415	4,476	20,891	32,666,550	50
Colorado	2,603	3,135	5,738	3,970,971	66
Connecticut	1,391	7,879	9,270	3,274,069	42
Delaware	120	1,009	1,129	743,603	16
D.C.	546	2,632	3,178	523,124	104
Florida	4,477	3,526	8,003	14,915,980	30
Georgia	2,232	2,665	4,897	7,642,207	29
Hawaii	977	814	1,791	1,193,001	82
Idaho	490	1,312	1,802	1,228,684	40
Illinois	5,475	3,686	9,161	12,045,326	45
Indiana	1,095	3,248	4,343	5,899,195	19
Iowa	419	1,018	1,437	2,862,447	15
Kansas	980	1,496	2,476	2,629,067	37
Kentucky	701	1,757	2,458	3,936,499	18
Louisiana	1,123	1,509	2,632	4,368,967	26
Maine	327	796	1,123	1,244,250	26
Maryland	1,658	2,826	4,484	5,134,808	32
Massachusetts	3,290	2,698	5,988	6,147,132	54
Michigan	2,472	2,378	4,850	9,817,242	25
Minnesota	1,762	1,445	3,207	4,725,419	37
Mississippi	271	973	1,244	2,752,092	10
Missouri	1,854	2,374	4,228	5,438,559	34

Number of Licensed Landscape Architects by State (Con't)

State	Resident	Non-Resident	Total	Population [1]	# Resident Arch. Per 100,000
Montana	349	655	1,004	880,453	40
Nebraska	546	944	1,490	1,662,719	33
Nevada	446	1,928	2,374	1,746,898	26
New Hampshire	252	764	1,016	1,185,048	21
New Jersey	2,400	4,600	7,000	8,115,011	30
New Mexico	725	1,291	2,016	1,736,931	42
New York	8,000	5,000	13,000	18,175,301	44
North Carolina	1,860	2,626	4,486	7,546,493	25
North Dakota	125	375	500	638,244	20
Ohio	3,521	2,881	6,402	11,209,493	31
Oklahoma	749	1,240	1,989	3,346,713	22
Oregon	1,399	1,150	2,549	3,281,974	43
Pennsylvania	3,595	3,536	7,131	12,001,451	30
Rhode Island	257	1,011	1,268	988,480	26
South Carolina	950	2,038	2,988	3,835,962	25
South Dakota	111	559	670	738,171	15
Tennessee	1,600	1,590	3,190	5,430,621	29
Texas	6,825	3,187	10,012	19,759,614	35
Utah	837	800	1,637	2,099,758	40
Vermont	294	524	818	590,883	50
Virginia	2,306	3,121	5,427	6,791,345	34
Washington	3,290	1,627	4,917	5,689,263	58
West Virginia	130	920	1,050	1,811,156	7
Wisconsin	1,502	2,815	4,317	5,223,500	29
Wyoming	112	724	836	480,907	23
Totals	**96,966**	**105,466**	**202,432**	**270,298,254**	

[1] 1998 Population Estimate from the U.S. Census Bureau

Source: Council of Landscape Architectural Registration Boards

Number of Months From Start to Completion of New One-Family Houses (Average)

Year	United States	Region				Construction purpose		
		Northeast	Midwest	South	West	Built for Sale	Contractor	Owner
1989	6.4	9.3	5.8	5.6	6.5	5.9	5.3	10.2
1990	6.4	9.3	5.6	5.7	6.9	5.9	5.3	10.3
1991	6.3	8.9	5.6	5.5	6.9	5.6	5.1	10.2
1992	5.8	7.6	5.6	5.1	6.1	5.0	5.0	9.5
1993	5.6	7.2	5.5	5.2	6.0	4.9	5.4	9.0
1994	5.6	7.1	5.7	5.3	5.6	4.9	5.3	9.1
1995	5.9	7.4	6.0	5.4	6.0	5.2	5.8	9.5
1996	6.0	8.2	6.1	5.6	5.6	5.2	5.8	9.9
1997	6.0	7.3	6.2	5.6	5.8	5.2	5.9	9.8
1998	6.0	7.1	6.2	5.5	6.1	5.4	6.0	9.5

Source: US Census Bureau

Number of New Privately Owned Housing Units Completed (in thousands of units)

Period	Total	In structures with-			
		1 unit	2 units	3 and 4	5 units
1989	1,422.8	1,026.3	24.1	34.6	337.9
1990	1,308.0	966.0	16.5	28.2	297.3
1991	1,090.8	837.6	16.9	19.7	216.6
1992	1,157.5	963.6	15.1	20.8	158.0
1993	1,192.7	1,039.4	9.5	16.7	127.1
1994	1,346.9	1,160.3	12.1	19.5	154.9
1995	1,312.6	1,065.5	14.8	19.8	212.4
1996	1,412.9	1,128.5	13.6	19.5	251.3
1997	1,400.5	1,116.4	13.6	23.4	247.1
1998	1,474.2	1,159.7	16.2	24.4	273.9

Did you know...
The average house size has increased from 1,500 to 2,200 square feet in the past 30 years, whereas the average family size has dropped from 3.16 to 2.7 people.

Period	Inside MSAS [1]	Outside MSAS [1]	Northeast	Midwest	South	West
1989	1,181.2	241.7	218.8	267.1	549.4	387.5
1990	1,060.2	247.7	157.7	263.3	510.7	376.3
1991	862.1	228.7	120.1	240.4	438.9	291.3
1992	909.5	248.0	136.4	268.4	462.4	290.3
1993	943.0	249.8	117.6	273.3	512.0	290.0
1994	1,086.3	260.6	123.4	307.1	580.9	335.5
1995	1,065.0	247.6	126.9	287.9	581.1	316.7
1996	1,163.4	249.4	125.1	304.5	637.1	346.2
1997	1,152.8	247.7	134.0	295.9	634.1	336.4
1998	1,228.5	245.7	137.3	305.1	671.6	360.2

Note: Detail may not add to total because of rounding.

N/A: Not available.

[1] Metropolitan statistical areas.

Source: U.S. Census Bureau

Number of Registered Architects by State

Registered architects in each state can be divided into two categories - those who are residents and reciprocal or out-of-state registrants. Based on current population levels, the chart below also calculates the number of resident architects per 100,000 of population in each state.

State	Resident Architects	Reciprocal Registrations	Total	Population [1]	# Resident Architects per 100,000 Population
Alabama	718	979	1,697	4,351,999	16
Alaska	300	204	504	614,010	49
Arizona	1,975	3,300	5,275	4,668,361	42
Arkansas	484	778	1,262	2,538,303	19
California	16,415	4,476	20,891	32,666,550	50
Colorado	2,603	3,135	5,738	3,970,971	66
Connecticut	1,391	7,879	9,270	3,274,069	42
Delaware	120	1,009	1,129	743,603	16
D.C.	546	2,632	3,178	523,124	104
Florida	4,477	3,526	8,003	14,915,980	30
Georgia	2,232	2,665	4,897	7,642,207	29
Hawaii	977	814	1,791	1,193,001	82
Idaho	490	1,312	1,802	1,228,684	40
Illinois	5,475	3,686	9,161	12,045,326	45
Indiana	1,095	3,248	4,343	5,899,195	19
Iowa	419	1,018	1,437	2,862,447	15
Kansas	980	1,496	2,476	2,629,067	37
Kentucky	701	1,757	2,458	3,936,499	18
Louisiana	1,123	1,509	2,632	4,368,967	26
Maine	327	796	1,123	1,244,250	26
Maryland	1,658	2,826	4,484	5,134,808	32
Massachusetts	3,290	2,698	5,988	6,147,132	54
Michigan	2,472	2,378	4,850	9,817,242	25
Minnesota	1,762	1,445	3,207	4,725,419	37
Mississippi	271	973	1,244	2,752,092	10
Missouri	1,854	2,374	4,228	5,438,559	34
Montana	349	655	1,004	880,453	40
Nebraska	546	944	1,490	1,662,719	33
Nevada	446	1,928	2,374	1,746,898	26

Number of Registered Architects by State (Con't)

State	Resident Architects	Reciprocal Registrations	Total	Population [1]	# Resident Architects per 100,000 Population
New Hampshire	252	764	1,016	1,185,048	21
New Jersey	2,400	4,600	7,000	8,115,011	30
New Mexico	725	1,291	2,016	1,736,931	42
New York	8,000	5,000	13,000	18,175,301	44
North Carolina	1,860	2,626	4,486	7,546,493	25
North Dakota	125	375	500	638,244	20
Ohio	3,521	2,881	6,402	11,209,493	31
Oklahoma	749	1,240	1,989	3,346,713	22
Oregon	1,399	1,150	2,549	3,281,974	43
Pennsylvania	3,595	3,536	7,131	12,001,451	30
Rhode Island	257	1,011	1,268	988,480	26
South Carolina	950	2,038	2,988	3,835,962	25
South Dakota	111	559	670	738,171	15
Tennessee	1,600	1,590	3,190	5,430,621	29
Texas	6,825	3,187	10,012	19,759,614	35
Utah	837	800	1,637	2,099,758	40
Vermont	294	524	818	590,883	50
Virginia	2,306	3,121	5,427	6,791,345	34
Washington	3,290	1,627	4,917	5,689,263	58
West Virginia	130	920	1,050	1,811,156	7
Wisconsin	1,502	2,815	4,317	5,223,500	29
Wyoming	112	724	836	480,907	23
Totals	**96,336**	**104,819**	**201,155**	**270,298,254**	

[1] 1998 Population Estimate from the U.S. Census Bureau

Source: National Council of Architectural Registration Boards

Office Building Vacancy Rates: 1980 to 1997

	1980	1985	1989	1990	1991	1992
Total [1]	4.6	16.9	19.5	20.0	20.2	20.5
Atlanta, GA	10.0	21.0	19.9	19.1	19.5	19.4
Baltimore, MD	7.2	11.5	16.4	20.0	21.0	20.6
Boston, MA	3.8	13.1	15.3	19.6	19.1	17.5
Charlotte, NC	(N/A)	16.7	14.3	16.5	19.4	(N/A)
Cincinnati, OH	(N/A)	(N/A)	16.6	(N/A)	(N/A)	19.4
Dallas, TX	8.6	23.0	26.9	25.8	26.0	31.3
Denver, CO	6.6	24.7	26.1	24.8	23.0	21.5
Detroit, M I	(N/A)	(N/A)	(N/A)	(N/A)	(N/A)	(N/A)
Fort Lauderdale, FL	(N/A)	(N/A)	26.3	23.0	24.9	22.9
Houston, TX	4.0	27.6	27.5	24.9	27.3	27.0
Indianapolis, IN	(N/A)	(N/A)	20.0	21.2	21.4	22.4
Las Vegas, NV	(N/A)	(N/A)	(N/A)	(N/A)	(N/A)	(N/A)
Los Angeles, CA	0.9	15.3	19.7	16.8	20.2	21.2
Memphis, TN	(N/A)	(N/A)	(N/A)	(N/A)	(N/A)	(N/A)
Miami, FL	2.4	20.9	22.0	23.4	22.6	18.5
Minneapolis, MN	(N/A)	(N/A)	20.2	(N/A)	18.9	19.9
Nashville, TN	(N/A)	(N/A)	(N/A)	25.1	18.4	(N/A)
New Jersey (Central)	(N/A)	(N/A)	(N/A)	(N/A)	(N/A)	(N/A)
New Jersey (North)	(N/A)	(N/A)	(N/A)	(N/A)	(N/A)	(N/A)
Orlando, FL	(N/A)	(N/A)	(N/A)	(N/A)	(N/A)	(N/A)
Philadelphia, PA	6.3	14.5	16.3	18.2	17.3	19.0
Phoenix, AZ	(N/A)	(N/A)	(N/A)	27.6	24.8	24.4
Pittsburgh, PA	1.2	(N/A)	16.3	16.3	14.2	(N/A)
Portland, OR	(N/A)	(N/A)	(N/A)	(N/A)	(N/A)	14.5
Richmond, VA		(N/A)	(N/A)	(N/A)	(N/A)	(N/A)
Sacramento, CA		(N/A)	(N/A)	(N/A)	(N/A)	(N/A)
San Diego, CA	(N/A)	24.7	17.6	19.5	23,7	23.8
San Francisco, CA	0.3	13.7	15.7	14.7	13.3	12.5
Seattle, WA	(N/A)	(N/A)	12.4	12.3	12.8	15.9
Silicon Valley, CA	(N/A)	(N/A)	(N/A)	(N/A)	(N/A)	(N/A)
St. Louis, MO	(N/A)	(N/A)	22.6	21.0	20.5	21.8
St Paul, MN	(N/A)	(N/A)	(N/A)	(N/A)	19.7	18.5
Tampa/St. Petersburg, FL	(N/A)	(N/A)	(N/A)	(N/A)	(N/A)	(N/A)
Washington, DC	2.5	9.0	14.4	19.0	17.6	15.4
West Palm Beach, CA	(N/A)	(N/A)	(N/A)	(N/A)	(N/A)	(N/A)
Wilmington, DE	(N/A)	(N/A)	12.4	20.3	21.0	19.8
Winston-Salem/Greensboro, NC	(N/A)	(N/A)	(N/A)	(N/A)	(N/A)	(N/A)

N/A - Not available

[1] Includes other North American markets not shown separately. In 1997, 41 markets were covered.

1993	1994	1995	1996	1997	
19.4	**16.2**	**14.3**	**12.4**	**10.4**	Total [1]
16.8	13.0	10.4	9.2	10.5	Atlanta, GA
17.3	15.5	17.0	14.3	11.6	Baltimore, MD
17.7	13.3	10.4	6.2	4.4	Boston, MA
(N/A)	10.0	8.9	8.2	7.1	Charlotte, NC
(N/A)	15.3	(N/A)	13.1	11.5	Cincinnati, OH
29.5	21.7	18.7	16.2	14.7	Dallas, TX
15.9	12.8	12.1	10.8	9.3	Denver, CO
21.4	19.7	16.9	11.1	8.5	Detroit, M I
(N/A)	10.8	(N/A)	10.5	10.4	Fort Lauderdale, FL
25.1	24.7	21.9	17.5	12.1	Houston, TX
18.8	18.4	14.3	(N/A)	14.2	Indianapolis, IN
(N/A)	8.7	(N/A)	10.5	11.8	Las Vegas, NV
21.0	19.6	23.2	22.1	13.8	Los Angeles, CA
(N/A)	(N/A)	(N/A)	13.6	12.0	Memphis, TN
19.0	15.4	13.8	12.4	11.2	Miami, FL
(N/A)	8.2	(N/A)	6.5	6.2	Minneapolis, MN
(N/A)	7.5	(N/A)	6.9	6.0	Nashville, TN
(N/A)	20.7	(N/A)	16.0	11.2	New Jersey (Central)
(N/A)	16.5	(N/A)	14.5	11.9	New Jersey (North)
(N/A)	12.1	(N/A)	6.5	6.4	Orlando, FL
17.8	16.3	16.2	13.7	10.9	Philadelphia, PA
(N/A)	11.8	(N/A)	11.5	9.3	Phoenix, AZ
17.0	15.8	14.5	(N/A)	15.4	Pittsburgh, PA
(N/A)	9.4	(N/A)	5.8	5.6	Portland, OR
(N/A)	11.9	(N/A)	9.7	9.7	Richmond, VA
(N/A)	14.1	(N/A)	12.4	12.3	Sacramento, CA
22.1	18.8	17.4	14.1	10.1	San Diego, CA
13 7	11.7	10.2	5.4	4.0	San Francisco, CA
17.6	14.7	7.1	5.3	4.5	Seattle, WA
(N/A)	12.7	(N/A)	8.7	5.8	Silicon Valley, CA
19.1	18.1	12.7	13.4	12.3	St. Louis, MO
(N/A)	15.2	(N/A)	12.5	9.9	St Paul, MN
(N/A)	(N/A)	(N/A)	13.0	9.1	Tampa/St. Petersburg, FL
14.1	13.4	10.8	9.3	8.0	Washington, DC
(N/A)	16.8	(N/A)	12.0	12.3	West Palm Beach, CA
(N/A)	16.7	(N/A)	9.5	9.7	Wilmington, DE
(N/A)	13.2	(N/A)	14.1	12.3	Winston-Salem/Greensboro, NC

Source: ONCOR International, Houston, TX, 1980 and 1985, National Ofice Market Report, semi-annual; 1989-1990, International Office Market Report, semi-annual; thereafter, Year-End (year) Market Data Book, annual (copyright).

Salary and Compensation Guide

Each year the Greenway Group, management consultants to the design professions, tracks the hiring of design professionals and reviews compensation packages for marketplace competitiveness. The following compensation figures reflect cash compensation including any bonuses for 1999. This information reflects positions filled within the last twelve months in four cities in each category based on Greenway's experience. Average information is supplied by the professional associations or, in some cases, by Greenway. When limited data is available no national averages are provided.

For further information, contact Greenway Group at (770) 209-3770, The American Institute of Architects at (202) 626-7300, the International Interior Design Association at (312) 467-1950, and the Industrial Designers Society of America at (703) 759-0100.

Intern Architects

Hawaii	$41,000
San Francisco	$31,000
Minneapolis	$28,500
New York City	$35,350
National Average	$35,200

Architect – Five Years Experience

Seattle	$41,350
Phoenix	$43,500
Duluth	$37,450
Boston	$43,200
National Average	$42,000

Architect – 10 Years Experience

Detroit	$45,000
Miami	$51,000
Dallas	$46,500
Sacramento	$49,000
National Average	$50,400

Architect – 15 Years Experience

Chicago	$72,000
Kansas City	$68,000
Washington DC	$77,000
Las Vegas	$64,350
Est. National Average	$64,800

Architect – Principal – Owner – Small Sole Proprietorship

Des Moines	$102,000
Los Angeles	$99,500
Miami	$74,000
Chicago	$135,000
National Average	$95,000

Interior Designer – 10 – 15 Years Experience

New York City	$77,500
Chicago	$62,800
San Francisco	$71,000
Minneapolis	$58,000
Est. National Average	$49,000

Salary and Compensation Guide (Con't)

Interior Designer - Principal

New York City	$220,000
Chicago	$148,500
Dallas	$85,000
Phoenix	$102,000
Est. National Average	$89,000

Technology Manager - Design Firm

Lexington	$47,500
Fort Worth	$55,000
Madison	$65,000
Washington DC	$73,000
Est. National Average	$50,000

Industrial Designer/Product Designer in Private Practice

Chicago	$64,300
Palo Alto	$73,000
San Francisco	$77,000
New York City	$82,500
National Average	$70,000

Industrial Design/Product Designer Principal/Owner/President

Chicago	$136,500
New York	$500,000
Philadelphia	$95,800
Houston	$115,000
National Average	$126,320

Landscape Architect - 10 - 15 Years Experience

Des Moines	$48,000
Denver	$37,800
Chicago	$44,500
Boston	$54,000
National Average	$48,000

Principal - Boutique Small Firm – Architecture

Sioux Falls	$71,000
Chicago	$145,000
Portland	$104,000
Charlotte	$95,000

Principal - Medium Size Full Service Firm A/E/D

Nashville	$130,000
Atlanta	$145,000
Denver	$115,000
New York City	$184,000

Principal - Large Firm

New York City (A/E)	$350,000
San Francisco (A/D)	$195,000
Salt Lake City (A)	$135,000
Omaha (A/E)	$115,000

CEO - Large Firm Multidiscipline

Washington DC (A)	$285,000
New York City (A/E)	$750,000
Boston (A)	$220,000
Minneapolis (A/D/E/P)	$345,000
National Average	$225,000

Architecture and Design Faculty Cash Compensation Est. for 1999

Professor	$71,000
Associate Professor	$52,400
Assistant Professor	$42,500
Instructor	$32,500
Adjunct Professor	Honorarium

Average Faculty Salaries 1998-99

Architecture and Related Fields

Public	$56,876
Private	$59,551

Civil Engineering

Public	$66,382
Private	$67,743

Engineering Related Technologies

Public	$50,998
Private	$45,668

(A=Architect, E=Engineer, D=Designer, P=Planner)

Source: Counsel House Research, Greenway Group, The American Institute of Architects, International Interior Design Association, Industrial Designers Society of America, Chronicle of Higher Education

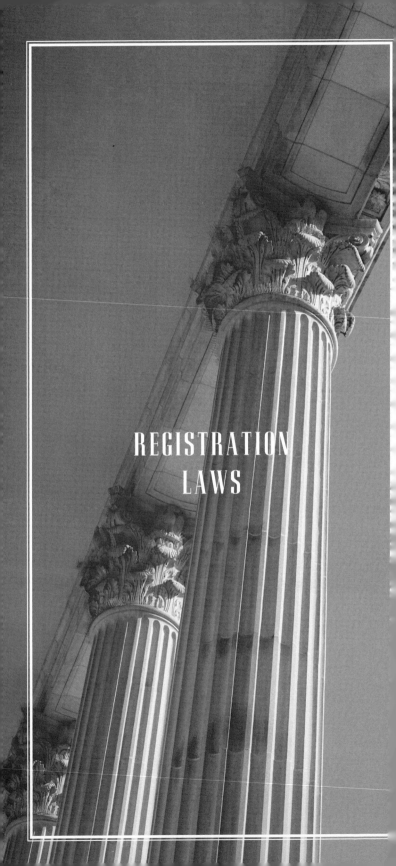

REGISTRATION
LAWS

REGISTRATION LAWS

pp

Architecture Registration Laws

The following information provides a brief overview of the major components of initial licensure for architects including work experience, degree requirements, and the Architectural Registration Exam (ARE). Complete information regarding registration requirements, renewal procedures, interstate registration, and corporate practice guidelines is available from the individual state boards at the phone numbers listed below. Due to the complex and changing nature of the requirements, it is recommended that the state licensing board(s) be contacted to receive the most up-to-date information. The National Council of Architectural Registration Boards (NCARB) also maintains information about registration on their Web site at *www.ncarb.org/stateboards/index.html.*

States and State Boards	Type of Law		Initial Requirements			Ongoing Requir.
	Title Act	Practice Act	College Degree Req'd	Internship Req'd	ARE Exam Req'd	Cont. Ed. Req'd
Alabama (334) 242-4179	X	X	X	X	X	X
Alaska (907) 465-1676	X	X	X	X	X	
Arizona (602) 255-4053	X	X			X	
Arkansas (501) 682-3171	X	X	X	X	X	X
California (916) 445-3394	X	X			X	
Colorado (303) 894-7794	X	X		X	X	
Connecticut (860) 713-6135	X	X	X	X	X	
Delaware (302) 739-4522	X	X	X	X	X	P
D.C. (202) 442-4461	X	X	X	X	X	P
Florida (850) 488-6685	X	X	X	X	X	X
Georgia (404) 656-2281	X	X	X	X	X	

Architecture Registration Laws (Con't)

States and State Boards	Type of Law		Initial Requirements			Ongoing Requir.
	Title Act	Practice Act	College Degree Req'd	Internship Req'd	ARE Exam Req'd	Cont. Ed. Req'd
Hawaii (808) 586-2702	X	X		P	X	
Idaho (208) 334-3233	X	X		X	X	
Illinois (217) 785-0877	X	X		X	X	
Indiana (317) 233-6223	X	X	X	X	X	
Iowa (515) 281-7362	X	X		X	X	X
Kansas (785) 296-3053	X	X	X	X	X	X
Kentucky (606) 246-2069	X	X		X	X	X
Louisiana (225) 925-4802	X	X	X	X	X	X
Maine (207) 624-8603	X	X		X	X	
Maryland (410) 333-6322	X	X		X	X	
Massachusetts (617) 727-3072	X	X	X	X	X	
Michigan (517) 241-9253	X	X	X	X	X	P
Minnesota (651) 297-3096	X	X	X	X	X	P
Mississippi (601) 359-6020	X	X	X	X	X	
Missouri (573) 751-0047	X	X			X	
Montana (406) 444-3745	X	X	X	X	X	P
Nebraska (402) 471-2021	X	X	X	X	X	P
Nevada (702) 486-7300	X	X	X	X	X	P
New Hampshire (603) 271-2219	X	X		X	X	
New Jersey (973) 504-6385	X	X	X	X	X	P
New Mexico (505) 827-6375	X	X	X	X	X	

Architecture Registration Laws (Con't)

States and State Boards	Type of Law		Initial Requirements			Ongoing Requir.
	Title Act	Practice Act	College Degree Req'd	Internship Req'd	ARE Exam Req'd	Cont. Ed. Req'd
New York (518) 474-3930	X	X		X	X	
North Carolina (919) 733-9544	X	X	X	X	X	X
North Dakota (701) 223-3184	X	X	X	X	X	
Ohio (614) 466-2316	X	X	X	X	X	
Oklahoma (405) 751-6512	X	X	X		X	X
Oregon (503) 378-4270	X	X	X	X	X	
Pennsylvania (717) 783-3397	X	X	X	X	X	
Rhode Island (401) 222-2565	X	X	X	X	X	
South Carolina (803) 896-4408	X	X	X	X	X	
South Dakota (605) 394-2510	X	X	X	X	X	X
Tennessee (615) 741-3221	X	X		X	X	X
Texas (512) 305-9000	X	X		X	X	P
Utah (801) 530-6621	X	X	X	X	X	P
Vermont (802) 828-2373	X	X		X	X	X
Virginia (804) 367-8514	X	X	X		X	
Washington (360) 664-1386	X	X		P	X	
West Virginia (304) 528-5825	X	X	X	X	X	X
Wisconsin (608) 266-5511	X	X		X	X	
Wyoming (307) 777-7788	X	X	X	X	X	P

P = There is current legislation pending regarding this requirement.

Source: National Council of Architectural Registration Boards

Global Architecture Practice Standards

The following guidelines outline the major requirements for U.S. architects and architecture firms to practice in other countries. This information is meant to be an overview and should not be used as a substitute for or synthesis of the complex and changing stipulations. Architects should always contact the appropriate agency in each country (indicated below) prior to beginning a project in order to obtain the most up-to-date requirements. U.S Embassies in each country may also be helpful in understanding and fulfilling requirements.

Country	License or Reg. Required for Indigenous Arch.	License or Reg. Required for Foreign Arch.	Local Rep. Required	Local Participation Required	English Official Language	Metric System Standard	Official Licensing Body
Australia	X	X			X	X	Architects Registration Boards in each state
Austria	X	3	X	X		X	Federal Ministry of Economic Affairs +43 (1) 71-1000
Belgium	X	X			4	X	Orde Van Architecten, Nationale Raad
Bermuda	X	X	X	X	X	X	Architects Registration Council (809) 297-7705
Brazil	X	X		X	4	X	Regional Council of Engineering, Architecture, and Agronomy in each state
Canada	X	X	X	X	X	X	Professional bodies in each province
China	X	X	X		4	X	National Administrative Board of Architectural Registration +86 (1) 839-4250
Colombia	X	X	X	X		X	Consejo Profesional Nacional de Ingenieria y Arquitectura

Global Architecture Practice Standards (Con't)

Country	License or Reg. Required for Indigenous Arch.	License or Reg. Required for Foreign Arch.	Local Rep. Required	Local Participation Required	English Official Language	Metric System Standard	Official Licensing Body
Czech Republic	X		X	X		X	Czech Chamber of Architects +42 (2) 2451-0112
Denmark	X					X	None
Egypt	X	X	X	X	4	X	Egyptian Engineering Syndicate +20 (2) 74-0092
El Salvador	X	X		X		X	Registro Nacional de Arquitectos e Ingenieros
Finland	I	2		X	4	X	None
France	I	X				X	Ministere de l'Equipment, des Transports et du Tourisme
Germany	X	X				X	Chamber of Architects in each state
Greece	X	X	X		4	X	Technical Chamber of Greece +30 (I) 325-4590
Guatemala	X		X	X		X	Colegio de Arquitectos +50 (2) 69-3672
Honduras	X	X	X	U		X	National Autonomous University of Honduras & Colegio de Arquitectos de Honduras +504 38-5385
Hungary	X	X			4	X	Registration Board of Ministry of Environmental Protection & Regional Development
Iceland	X	X			4	X	Ministry of Industry +354 (I) 60-9420

Global Architecture Practice Standards (Con't)

Country	License or Reg. Required for Indigenous Arch.	License or Reg. Required for Foreign Arch.	Local Rep. Required	Local Participation Required	English Official Language	Metric System Standard	Official Licensing Body
India	X	X			X	X	Council of Architecture +91 (11) 331-5757
Indonesia	X	X	X	U	X	X	Ministry of Internal Affairs
Ireland					X	X	None
Israel	X	X	X	U	4	X	Architects and Engineers Registrar
Italy	X	X	X		4	X	Consiglio Nazionale Architetti
Jamaica	X	X	X		4	X	Architects Registration Board
Japan	X	X	X			X	Ministry of Construction +81 (3) 3580-4311
Jordon	X	X	X	X	X	X	Jordon Engineers Association +926 (6) 607-616
Kenya	X	X	X	X	X	X	Board of Registration of Architects and Quantity Surveyors +254 (2) 72-0438
Korea	X	X	X	U		X	Ministry of Construction +82 (2) 503-7357
Lebanon	X	X	X		4	X	Order of Engineers +961 (1) 83-0286
Luxembourg	X	X	U	U		X	Ordre des Architectes et des Ingenieurs Conseils +352 42-2406

Global Architecture Practice Standards (Con't)

Country	License or Reg. Required for Indigenous Arch.	License or Reg. Required for Foreign Arch.	Local Rep. Required	Local Participation Required	English Official Language	Metric System Standard	Official Licensing Body
Malaysia	X	X	X	X	4	X	Lembaga Arkitek Malaysia +60 (3) 298-8733
Mexico	X	X	X	U		X	Direccion General de Professiones en Mexico +52 (5) 550-9000
Netherlands						X	Stichting Bureau Architectenregister +31 (70) 360-7020
New Zealand					X	X	Architects Education and Registration Board
Nicaragua	X	X	X				Asociacion Nicarguense de Arquitectos Camara de La Construcion + 505 (2) 43-796
Norway						X	None
Panama	X		X	U		X	Junta Tecnica de Ingenieri y Arquitectura +507 23-7851
Peru	1	2	X			X	Colegio de Arquitectos del Peru +51 (41) 71-3778
Philippines	X	3	X	X	X	X	Professional Regulation Commission +63 (2) 741-6076
Poland	X	X		X		X	Government Offices in each province
Portugal	1	2				X	Associaçao dos Arquitecto Portugueses +351 (1) 343-2454
Romania	X	X	X		4	X	Union of Romanian Architects +40 (1) 312-0956

Global Architecture Practice Standards (Con't)

Country	License or Reg. Required for Indigenous Arch.	License or Reg. Required for Foreign Arch.	Local Rep. Required	Local Participation Required	English Official Language	Metric System Standard	Official Licensing Body
Russia	X	3	X	X		X	Russian License Architectural Centre
Saudi Arabia	X	X	X	X		X	Ministry of Commerce +966 (1) 401-2222
Singapore	X	X			X	X	Board of Architects +65 222-5295
South Africa	X	X			X	X	South African Council for Architects +27 (11) 486-1683
Spain	X	X	U	U	4	X	Colegios de Arquitectos in each region
Sweden						X	None
Switzerland	X	U			4	X	Schweizerisches Register der Ingenieure, Architekten und Techniker +41 (1) 252-3222
Taiwan	X	X	X	X		X	Construction & Planning Administration , MOI +886 (4) 328-1560
Turkey	X	X			4	X	Turkiye Mimarlar Odasi +90 (4) 417-3727
United Kingdom	U	X			X	X	Architects Registration Council of the United Kingdom +44 (71)580-5861
Venezuela	X	X				X	Colegio de Ingenieros, Arquitectos y Profesiones Afines de Venezuela +58 (2) 241-8007

U Specific requirements are unclear. The local agency should be contacted.
1 A license or registration is not required for indigenous architects; however, there are other stipulations which must be met in order for indigenous persons to practice architecture.
2 A license or registration is not required for foreign architects; however, there are other stipulations which must be met in order for a foreign architect to practice architecture.
3 Generally US architects may not practice in the country independently.
4 Although not the official language, English is commonly used in the commercial arena.
Source: National Council of Architectural Registration Boards

Interior Design Registration Laws

The following information provides a brief overview of the major components of initial registration for interior designers including work experience, degree requirements and the National Council for Interior Design Qualification (NCIDQ) exam. More specific information about these requirements is available from the individual state board phone numbers listed below. Due to the complex and changing nature of the requirements, it is recommended that the state licensing board(s) be contacted to receive the most up to date information. The American Society of Interior Designers (ASID) also maintains information about registration on their Web site at *www.asid.org/ethics/factsheet.htm.*

| States and State Board Phone Numbers | Type of Law | | Initial Requirements | | | Ongoing Req. |
	Title Act	Practice Act	Post-HS Education Req.	Work Experience Req.	NCIDQ Exam Req.	Continuing Education Req.
Alabama (256) 340-9003	X		X		X	
Arkansas (501) 664-3008	X		X	X	X	X
California (760) 761-4734	I			X	X	X
Connecticut (860) 713-6135	X	X	X	X	X	
Florida (850) 488-6685	X	X	X	X	X	X
Georgia (404) 656-3941	X		X		X	X
Illinois (217) 785-0813	X		X	X	X	
Louisiana (225) 925-3921	X		X	X	X	X
Maine (207) 624-8603	X		X	X	X	
Maryland (410) 333-6322	X		X	X	X	X
Minnesota (651) 296-2388	X		X	X	X	
Missouri (573) 522-4683	X		X	X	X	X

Interior Design Registration Laws (Con't)

States and State Board Phone Numbers	Type of Law		Initial Requirements			Ongoing Req.
	Title Act	Practice Act	Post-HS Education Req.	Work Experience Req.	NCIDQ Exam Req.	Continuing Education Req.
Nevada (702) 486-7300	X	X	X	X	X	
New Mexico (505) 476-7077	X		X	X	X	X
New York (518) 474-3846	X		X	X	X	
Tennessee (615) 741-3221	X		X	X	X	X
Texas (512) 305-8539	X		X	X	X	
Virginia (804) 367-8514	X		X	X	X	
Washington, D.C. (202) 442-4330	X	X	X	X	X	X
Wisconsin (608) 266-5439	X		X	X	X	X

[1] Self-Certification Act

Source: American Society of Interior Designers

Did you know...
The Secretariat Building of New York's United Nations, designed by an international board of architects supervised by Walter K. Harrison and completed in 1950, was the first building constructed in New York City utilizing a glass curtain wall.

Landscape Architecture Licensure Laws

The following information provides a brief overview of the major components of initial licensure for landscape architects. Complete information regarding licensing requirements, renewal procedures, and reciprocity is available from the individual state boards, at the phone numbers listed below. It is recommended that the state licensing board(s) be contacted to receive the most up to date information. The Council of Landscape Architectural Registration Boards (CLARB) also maintains information about licensure on their Web site at *www.clarb.org*.

States & State Board Phone Numbers	Type of Law		Initial Requirements			Ongoing Req.
	Title Act	Practice Act	College Degree Req'd.	Work Experience Req'd	LARE Exam Req'd	Continuing Education Req'd
Alabama (334) 262-1351	X	X		X	X	X
Arizona (602) 255-4053	X	X		X	X	
Arkansas* (501) 682-3171						
California (916) 445-4954	X	X	2	X	X	
Connecticut (860) 566-5130		X	X	X	X	X
Delaware (302) 739-4522	X		X	3	X	X
Florida (850) 488-6685 ext. 2		X		X	X	
Georgia (404) 656-3941	X	X	X	X	X	X
Hawaii (808) 586-2702	X	X		X	X	
Idaho (208) 334-3233	X			3	X	
Illinois* (217) 785-0800						
Indiana (317) 232-2980	X			3	X	
Iowa (515) 281-5596	X			X	X	X

Landscape Architecture Licensure Laws (Con't)

States & State Board Phone Numbers	Type of Law		Initial Requirements			Ongoing Req.
	Title Act	Practice Act	College Degree Req'd.	Work Experience Req'd	LARE Exam Req'd	Continuing Education Req'd
Kansas (913) 296-3053	X	X	X	X	X	X
Kentucky (502) 573-6687	X	X	X	X	X	X
Louisiana (504) 925-7772	X	X	X	X	X	
Maine (207) 624-8522	X		X	X	X	
Maryland (410) 333-6322	X	X		1	X	
Massachusetts (617) 727-3072	X		X	X	X	
Michigan (517) 241-9253	X			X	X	
Minnesota (651) 296-2388	X	X		X	X	
Mississippi (601) 359-6020	X			3	X	
Missouri (573) 751-0039	X		X	X	X	
Montana (406) 444-5924	X				X	
Nebraska (402) 344-8711	X	X		X	X	X
Nevada (702) 359-8110	X	X	X	X	X	
New Jersey (973) 504-6385	X		X	X	X	X
New Mexico (505) 476-7077	X	X	X	X	X	X
New York (518) 474-3430	X	X		X	X	
North Carolina (919) 850-9088		X		X	X	X
Ohio (614) 466-2316	X	X		X	X	
Oklahoma (405) 751-6512	X		X	X	X	X
Oregon (503) 589-0093	X		X	3	X	
Pennsylvania (717) 772-8528	X	X		X	X	X

Landscape Architecture Licensure Laws (Con't)

States & State Board Phone Numbers	Type of Law		Initial Requirements			Ongoing Req.
	Title Act	Pracice Act	College Degree Req'd.	Work Experience Req'd	LARE Exam Req'd	Continuing Education Req'd
Rhode Island (401) 222-2565	X	X	X	X	X	
South Carolina (803) 734-9131	X	X	2	X	X	
South Dakota (605) 394-2510	X	X		X	X	X
Tennessee (615) 741-3221	X	X	X	X	X	X
Texas (512) 305-8539	X			3	X	
Utah (801) 530-6632	X	X		3	X	
Virginia (804) 367-8514	X			3	X	
Washington (360) 753-6967	X			X	X	
West Virginia (304) 293-2141 ext. 4490	X		X	X	X	
Wisconsin[1] (608) 266-3423						
Wyoming (307) 777-7788	X	X	X	X	X	

1 Information from these state licensing boards was not available.
2 Some post-high school course work is required.
3 No experience is required with a Landscape Architectural Accreditation Board (LAAB) accredited Landscape Architecture degree; however, other degree types may require experience.
+ Also referred to as Professional Development Hours (PDH).

Note:
Alaska, Colorado, Washington, D.C., North Dakota, and Vermont currently do not have a Landscape Architecture licensure program.

Source: Council of Landscape Architectural Registration Boards

LEADING U.S.
FIRMS

250 Leading U.S. Based Architecture Firms

Each year the Greenway Group charts the size, growth rates, awards, and significant contributions of architecture firms in the United States and abroad. The following is their 1999 list of the 250 leading U.S. based firms who have achieved distinction for their resources, accomplishments, and service record. The Greenway Group conducts an annual survey of firms in the United States in order to make judgements as to their list of 250. There are numerous other firms who have achieved regional recognition or are notable for their project and type of work which are beyond the scope of this list. Firms wishing to be surveyed are invited to fill out the information form in the back of the Almanac and forward it to the Greenway Group.

For additional information about U.S. architecture firms, we recommend that readers refer to *ProFile: The Architects Sourcebook* published by CMD Group in cooperation with The American Institute of Architects. This annual publication includes approximately 18,000 architecture firms based in the United States. Numerous state AIA chapters also maintain updated firm directories. Readers are reminded to use the resources of the many associations listed in this Almanac for their directories of design talent.

3D/International
Houston, Texas
Tel: (713) 877-0000
www.3di.com

Ai
Washington, D.C
Tel: (202) 737-1021
www.ellstreet.com

AC Martin Partners
Los Angeles, California
Tel: (213) 683-1900
www.acmartin.com

ADD Inc.
Cambridge, Massachusetts
Tel: (617) 234-3100
www.addarch.com

ADP Marshall, Inc.
Phoenix, Arizona
Tel: (602) 230-9660
www.adpmarshall.com

Aguirre Corporation
Dallas, Texas
Tel: (972) 788-1508
www.aquirre.com

250 Leading U.S. Based Architecture Firms (Con't)

Albert Kahn Associates, Inc.
Detroit, Michigan
Tel: (313) 202-7000
www.albertkahn.com

Altoon + Porter Architects
Los Angeles, California
Tel: (323) 939-1900
www.altoonporter.com

AM Partners, Inc.
Honolulu, Hawaii
Tel: (808) 526-2828

Ankrom Moisan Associated Architects
Portland, Oregon
Tel: (503) 245-7100
www.amaa.com

Anshen + Allen
San Francisco, California
Tel: (415) 882-9500
www.anshen.com

Arbuckle Costic Architects Inc.
Salem, Oregon
Tel: (503) 584114
www.arbucklecostic.com

Architects Hawaii Limited
Honolulu, Hawaii
Tel: (808) 523-9636
www.architects-hawaii.com

Architectural Resources Cambridge, Inc.
Cambridge, Massachusetts
Tel: (617) 547-2200
www.arcusa.com

Arquitectonica
Miami, Florida
Tel: (305) 372-1812
www.arqintl.com

Arrowstreet, Inc.
Somerville, Massachusetts
Tel: (617) 623-5555
www.arrowstreet.com

Ballinger
Philadelphia, Pennsylvania
Tel: (215) 665-0900
www.ballinger-ae.com

Beck Group - Beck Architecture LTD
Dallas, Texas
Tel: (214) 965-1211
www.beckgroup.com

The Benham Group
Oklahoma City, Oklahoma
Tel: (405) 478-5353
www.benham.com

Bentz Thompson Reitow
Minneapolis, Minnesota
Tel: (612) 332-1234
www.btr-architect.com

Bergmeyer Associates
Boston, Massachusetts
Tel: (617) 542-1025
www.bergmeyer.com

Beyer Blinder Belle
New York, New York
Tel: (212) 777-7800

BLM Group
Bala Cynwyd, Pennsylvania
Tel: (610) 667-8877
www.theblmgroup

Bohlin Cywinski Jackson
Wilkes-Barre, Pennsylvania
Tel: (717) 825.8756
www.bcj.com

BOORA Architects, Inc.
Portland, Oregon
Tel: (503) 226-1575
www.boora.com

Brennan Beer Gorman/Architects
New York, New York
Tel: (212) 888-7663
www.bbg-bbgm.com

250 Leading U.S. Based Architecture Firms (Con't)

Brown McDaniel Bhandari Inc.
San Francisco, California
Tel: (415) 397-9500

BSA Design
Indianapolis, Indiana
Tel: (317) 819-7878
www.bsadesign.com

BSW International
Tulsa, Oklahoma
Tel: (918) 582-8771
www.bswintl.com

Bumgardner
Seattle, Washington
Tel: (206) 223-1361
www.bumgardnerseattle.com

Burt Hill Kosar Rittelmann Associates
Butler, Pennsylvania
Tel: (724) 285-4761
www.burthill.com

Butler Rogers Baskett Architects PC
New York, New York
Tel: (212) 792-4600
www.brb.com

BWBR Architects, Inc.
St Paul, Minnesota
Tel: (612) 222-3701
www.bwbr.com

Callison Architecture, Inc.
Seattle, Washington
Tel: (206) 623-4646
www.callison.com

Cannon
Grand Island, New York
Tel: (716) 773-6800
www.cannondesign.com

Carter & Burgess Inc.
Fort Worth, Texas
Tel: (817) 735-6800
www.c-b.com

Casco Corporation
St Louis, Missouri
Tel: (314) 821-1000
www.cascocorp.com

Castro-Blanco Piscioneri and Associates, Architects, PC
New York, New York
Tel: (212) 254-2700

Centerbrook Architects
Essex, Connecticut
Tel: (860) 767-0175

Cesar Pelli & Associates
New Haven, Connecticut
Tel: (203) 777-2515
www.cesar-pelli.com

Chapman Griffin Lanier Sussenbach Architects, Inc.
Atlanta, Georgia
Tel: (404)733-5493
www.cglsarch.com

Cooper Carry, Inc.
Atlanta, Georgia
Tel: (404) 237-2000
www.coopercarry.com

Cooper, Robertson & Partners
New York, New York
Tel: (212) 247-1717
www.cooperrobertson.com

Corgan Associates, Inc.
Dallas, Texas
Tel: (214) 748-2000
www.corgan.com

Cornoyer-Hedrick, Inc.
Phoenix, Arizona
Tel: (602) 381-4848
www.cornoyerhedrick.com

Cromwell Truemper Levy Thompson Woodsmall, Inc.
Little Rock, Arkansas
Tel: (501) 372-2900
www.cromwell.com

250 Leading U.S. Based Architecture Firms (Con't)

CSO Architects, Inc.
Indianapolis, Indiana
Tel: (317) 848-7800
www.csoarchitects.com

Cunningham Group
Minneapolis, Minnesota
Tel: (612) 379-6854

Leo A. Daly
Omaha, Nebraska
Tel: (402) 391-8111
www.leodaly.com

Damianos+Anthony Architects
Pittsburgh, Pennsylvania
Tel: (412) 683-7000

Richard Dattner Architect, P.C.
New York, New York
Tel. (212) 247-2660
www.dattner.com

David Evans and Associates Inc.
Portland, Oregon
Tel: (503) 223-6663
www.deainc.com

The DeWolff Partnership, Architects
Rochester, New York
Tel: (716) 454 5860
www.dewolff.com

Development Design Group, Inc.
Baltimore, Maryland
Tel: (410) 962-0505
www.ddg-usa.com

Dewberry & Davis
Fairfax, Virginia
Tel: (703) 849-0100
www.dewberry.com

DLR Group
Omaha, Nebraska
Tel: (402) 393-4100
www.dlrgroup.com

Dorsky Hodgson + Partners, Inc.
Cleveland, Ohio
Tel: (216) 464-8600

Dougherty + Dougherty
Costa Mesa, California
Tel: (714) 427-0277
www.ddaia.com/history.html

Duany Plater ~ Zyberk & Company
Miami, Florida
Tel: (305) 644-1023
www.dpz.com

Durrant Group, Inc., The
Dubuque, Iowa
Tel: (604) 535-9801
www.durrant.com

Earl R. Flansburgh Associates
Boston, Massachusetts
Tel: (617) 367-3970
www.erfa.com

Ehrlich-Rominger+HDR
Los Altos, California
Tel: (650) 949-1300
www.erarch.com

Einhorn Yaffee Prescott
Albany, New York
Tel: (518) 431-3300
www.eypae.com

Eisenman Architects
New York, New York
(212) 645-1400

Elkus/Manfredi Architects Ltd
Boston, Massachusetts
Tel: (617) 426-1300
www.tiac.net.users.bdr.elkus.elkustop.html

Ellenzweig Associates, Inc.
Cambridge Massachusetts
Tel: (617) 491-5575

250 Leading U.S. Based Architecture Firms (Con't)

Ellerbe Becket
Minneapolis, Minnesota
Tel: (612) 376-2000
www.ellerbebecket.com

Epstein A. & Sons International Inc.
Chicago, Illinois
Tel: (312) 454-9100
www.epstein-isi.com

Ewing Cole Cherry Brott
Philadelphia, Pennsylvania
Tel: (215) 923-2020
www.ewingcole.com

Fanning/Howey Associates, Inc.
Celina, Ohio
Tel: (419) 586-7771
www.fhai.com

Farnsworth & Wylie, Inc.
Bloomington, IL
Tel: (309) 686-5100
www.f-w.com

Ferris, Roger & Partners
Westport, Connecticut
Tel: (203)222-4848
www.ferrisarch.com

Flad & Associates
Madison, Wisconsin
Tel: (608) 238-2661
www.flad.com

Fletcher Farr Ayotte PC
Portland, Oregon
Tel: (503) 222-1661
www.ffadesign.com

Fox & Fowle Architects, P.C.
New York, New York
Tel: (212) 627-1700
www.foxfowle.com

FRCH Design Worldwide
Cincinnati, Ohio
Tel: (513) 241-3000
www.frch.com

Freeman White, Inc.
Charlotte, North Carolina
Tel: (704)523-2230
www.freemanwhite.com

G2 Architecture/Mulvanny Architects
Seattle, Washington
Tel: (206) 621-7572
www.g2architecture.com

GBD Architects Incorporated
Portland, Oregon
Tel: (503) 224-9656
www.gbdarchitects.com

Frank O. Gehry and Associates, Inc.
Santa Monica, CA 90404
Tel: (310) 828-6088

Gensler
San Francisco, California
Tel: (415) 433-3700
www.gensler.com

Giffels Associates, Inc.
Southfield, Michigan
Tel: (248) 936-8300
www.giffels-usa.com

Richard Gluckman Architects
New York, New York
Tel: (212) 925-1713

Godwin Associates
Atlanta, Georgia
(707) 804-1280
www.godwinassociates.com

Goody, Clancy & Associates
Boston, Massachusetts
Tel: 617-262-2760
www.gcassoc.com

250 Leading U.S. Based Architecture Firms (Con't)

Gossen Livingston Associates, Inc.
Wichita, Kansas
Tel: (316) 265-9367
www.gossenlivingston.com

Graeber, Simmons & Cowan
Austin, Texas
Tel: (512) 477-9417
www.gsc-inc.com

Graham Gund Architects, Inc.
Cambridge, Massachusetts
Tel: (617) 577-9600
www.grahamgund.com

Michael Graves & Associates, Inc.
Princeton, New Jersey
Tel: (609) 924-6409
www.michaelgraves.com

Gresham Smith & Partners
Nashville, Tennessee
Tel: (615) 770-8100
www.gspnet.com

Griswold, Heckel & Kelly Associates, Inc.
Chicago, Illinois
Tel: (312) 263-6605

Group Mackenzie
Portland, Oregon
Tel: (503) 224-9560
www.europa.com/~grpmack.com

Gruzen Samton Architects Planners Interior Designers LLP
New York, New York
Tel: (212) 477-0900
www.gruzensamton.com

Gwathmey Siegel & Associates Architects
New York, New York
Tel: (212) 947-1240
www.gwathmey-siegel.com

Hammel, Green and Abrahamson, Inc.
Minneapolis, Minnesota
Tel: (612) 337-4100
www.hga.com

Hammond Beeby Rupert Ainge
Chicago, Illinois
Tel: (312) 527-3200

Hardy Holzmann Pfeiffer Associates
New York, New York
Tel: (212) 677-6030
www.hhpa.com

Harley Ellington Design
Southfield, Michigan
Tel: (248) 262-1500
www.hedesign.com

Hartman-Cox Architects
Washington, DC
Tel: (202) 333-6446

Harvard Jolly Clee Toppe Architects, PA
St. Petersburg, Florida
Tel: (813) 896-4611
www.hjct.com

Hayes, Seay, Mattern & Mattern, Inc.
Roanoke, Virginia
Tel: (540) 857-3100
www.hsmm.com

HDR Architecture, Inc.
Omaha, Nebraska
Tel: (402) 399-1000
www.hdrinc.com

Heery International, Inc.
Atlanta, Georgia
Tel: (404) 881-9880
www.heeery.com

Hellmuth, Obata Kassabaum, Inc.
St. Louis, Missouri
Tel: (314) 421-2000
www.hok.com

Herbert Lewis Kruse Blunck Architects
Des Moines, Iowa
Tel: (515) 288-9536

250 Leading U.S. Based Architecture Firms (Con't)

Hill Glazier Architects, Inc.
Palo Alto, California
Tel: (650) 617-0366
www.hillglazier.com

Hillier Group, The
Princeton, New Jersey
Tel: (609) 452-8888
www.hillier.com

HKS Inc.
Dallas, Texas
Tel: (214) 969-5599
www.hksinc.com

HLM Design
Charlotte, North Carolina
Tel: (704) 358-0779
www.hlmdesign.com

HLW International, LLP
New York, New York
Tel: (212) 353-4600
www.hlw.com

HMC Group
Ontario, California
Tel: (909) 989-9979
www.hmcgroup.com

HNTB Corporation
Kansas City, Missouri
Tel: (816) 472-1201
www.hntb.com

Holabird & Root
Chicago, Illinois
Tel: (312) 726-5960
www.holabird.com

Steven Holl Architects
New York, New York
Tel: (212) 989-0918

Holmes & Narver
Orange, California
Tel: (714) 567-2691
www.hninc.com

Hornberger Worstell, Inc.
San Francisco, California
Tel: (415) 391-1080
www.hornbergerworstell.com

Hugh Newell Jacobsen
Washington, D.C.
Tel: (202) 337-5200
www.home.earthlink.net/~jacobsenarch

The Jerde Partnership International
Venice, California
(310) 399-1987
www.jerde.com

Jung/Brannen Associates, Inc.
Boston , Massachusetts
Tel: (617) 482-2299
www.jb2000.com

KA Inc., Architecture
Cleveland, Ohio
Tel: (216) 781-9144
www.kainc.com

Kahler Slater
Milwuakee, Wisconsin
Tel: (404) 272-2000

Kallmann McKinnell & Wood Architects
Boston, Massachusetts
Tel: (617) 267-0808
www.kmwarch.com

Kaplan McLaughlin Diaz
San Francisco, California
Tel: (415) 398-5191
www.kmd-arch.com

Karlsberger Companies
Columbus, Ohio
Tel: (614) 461-9500
www.karlsberger.com

Kimball, L. Robert and Associates, Inc.
Ebensburg, Pennsylvania
Tel: (814) 472-7700
www.lrkimball.com

250 Leading U.S. Based Architecture Firms (Con't)

Kirksey and Partners Architects
Houston, Texas
Tel: (713) 850-9600

KKE Architects
Minneapolis, Minnesota
Tel: (612) 339-4200

Kling Lindquist
Philadelphia, Pennsylvania
Tel: (215) 569-2900
www.tklp.com

Koetter Kim & Associates
Boston, Massachusetts
Tel: (617) 536-8560
www.koetterkim.com

Kohn Pedersen Fox Associates
New York, New York
Tel: (212) 777-6500
www.kpf.com

Langdon Wilson
Los Angeles, California
Tel: (213) 250-1186
www.langdonwilson.com

C. J. Lawler Associates
West Hartford, Connecticut
Tel: (860) 233-8526

Lee Harris Pomeroy Associates, PC
New York, New York
Tel: (212) 334-2600
www.lhparch.com

Lee, Burkhart, Liu, Inc.
Santa Monica, California
Tel: (310) 829-2249
www.lblarch.com

Legat Architects, Inc.
Waukegan, Illinois
Tel: (847) 263-3535
www.legat.com

Leonard Parker Associates Architects (Durrant)
Minneapolis, Minnesota
Tel: (612) 871-6864
www.parkerarch.com

LMN Architects
Seattle, Washington
Tel: (206) 682-3460
www.lmnarchitects.com

Lockwood Greene
Spartanburg, South Carolina
Tel: (864) 578-2000
www.lg.com

Loebl Schlossman & Hackl
Chicago, Illinois
Tel: (312) 565-1800
www.lshdesign.com

Lohan Associates, Inc.
Chicago, Illinois
Tel: (312) 938-4455
www.lohan.com

Looney Ricks Kiss
Memphis, Tennessee
Tel: (905) 521-1440
www.homeplans.lrk.com

LRS Architects
Portland, Oregon
Tel: (503) 221-1121

Luckett & Farley Architects, Engineers and Construction Managers, Inc.
Louisville, Kentucky
Tel: (502) 585-4181
www.luckett-farley.com

M.Kliment & Frances Halsband Architects
New York, New York
Tel: (212) 243-7400
www.kliment-halsband.com

250 Leading U.S. Based Architecture Firms (Con't)

Machado and Silvetti Associates, Inc.
Boston, Massachusetts
Tel: (617) 426-7070
www.machado-silvetti.com

Mahlum Architects
Seattle, Washington
Tel: (206) 441-4151

MCG Architecture
Pasadena, California
Tel: (626) 793-9119

William McDonough & Partners
Charlottesville, Virginia
Tel: (804) 979-1111
www.mcdonough.com

Merrick & Co.
Denver, Colorado
Tel: (303) 751-0741
www.merrick.com

Meyer, Scherer and Rockcastle Architects
Minneapolis, Minnesota
Tel: (612) 375-0336
www.msrltd.com

Michael Baker, Corp.
Pittsburgh, Pennsylvania
Tel: (412) 269-6300
www.mbakercorp.com

Miller Cook Architects, PC
Portland, Oregon
Tel: (503) 226-0622

Mitchell/Giurgola Architects LLP
New York, New York
Tel: (212) 663-4000

Mithun Partners, Inc.
Seattle, Washington
Tel: (206) 623-3344
www.mithun.com

MMM Design Group
Norfolk, Virginia
Tel: (757) 623-1641
www.mmmdesign.com

Moore Ruble Yudell Architects & Planners
Santa Monica, California
Tel: (310) 450-1400

Morris Architects
Houston, Texas
Tel: (713) 622-1180
www.morrisarchitects.com

Moshe Safdie Architects Limited
Sommerville, Massachusetts
Tel: (617) 629-2100
www.msafdie.com

Murphy/Jahn, Inc.
Chicago, Illinois
Tel: (312) 427-7300

NADEL Architects, Inc
Los Angeles, California
Tel: (310) 826-2100
www.nadelarchitects.com

Nave, Newell & Stampfl, Ltd.
King of Prussia, Pennsylvania
Tel: (610) 265-8323
www.nnsonesource.com

NBBJ
Seattle, Washington
Tel: (206) 223-5555
www.nbbj.com

Niles Bolton Associates, Inc.
Atlanta, Georgia
Tel: (404) 365-7600
www.nilesbolton.com

Northwest Architectural Company, P.S.
Spokane, Washington
Tel: (509) 838-8240
www.nwarchco.com

NTD Architects
Pasadena, California
Tel: (626) 963-1401
www.ntd.com

250 Leading U.S. Based Architecture Firms (Con't)

Odell Associates Inc.
Charlotte, North Carolina
Tel: (704) 377-5941
www.odell.com

O'Donnell Wicklund Pigozzi & Peterson
Chicago, Illinois
Tel: (312) 332-9600
www.owpp.com

Olson/Sundberg Architects Inc.
Seattle, Washington
Tel: (206) 624-5670
www.olsonsundberg.com

Onyx Group, The
Alexandria, Virginia
Tel: (703) 548-6699
www.onyxgroup.com

Page Southerland Page
Austin, Texas
Tel: (512) 472-6721
www.psp.com

Parsons Brinckerhoff Inc.
New York, New York
Tel: (212) 465-5000
www.pbworld.com

Payette Associates, Inc.
Boston, Massachusetts
Tel: (617) 342-8200
www.payette.com

Pei Cobb Freed & Partners Architects LLP
New York, New York
Tel: (212) 751-3122
www.pcfandp.com

Perkins & Will Group Ltd., The
Chicago, Illinois
Tel: (312) 755-0770
www.perkinswill.com

Perkins Eastman Architects PC
New York, New York
Tel: (212) 353-7291
www.peapc.com

Perry Dean Rogers & Partners Architects
Boston, Massachusetts
Tel: (617) 423-0100
www.perrydean.com

Phillips Group Architects, PC, The
New York, New York
Tel: (212) 768-0800
www.thephillipsgroup.com

Phillips Swager Associates
Peoria, Illinois
Tel: (309) 688-9511
www.psa-ae.com

Pieper O'Brien Herr
Alpharetta, Georgia
Tel: (770) 569-1706
www.pohatlanta.com

Pierce Goodwin Alexander & Linville
Houston, Texas
Tel: (713) 622-1444
www.pgal.com

Polshek & Partners Architects LLP
New York, New York
Tel: (212) 807-7171
www.polshek.com

John Portman and Associates, Inc.
Atlanta, Georgia
Tel: (404) 614-5555

Antoine Predock
Albuquerque, New Mexico
Tel: (505) 843-7390
www.predock.com

Renaissance Design Group
Des Moines, Iowa
(515) 288-3141
www.rdgusa.com

Reynolds, Smith and Hills, Inc.
Jacksonville, Florida
Tel: (904) 296-2000
www.rsandh.com

250 Leading U.S. Based Architecture Firms (Con't)

Richard Meier & Partners
New York, New York
Tel: (212) 967-6060
www.richardmeier.com

RMW Architecture & Design
San Francisco, California
Tel: (415) 781-9800
www.rmw.com

RNL Design
Denver, Colorado
Tel: (303) 295-1717
www.rnldesign.com

Kevin Roche John Dinkeloo & Assoc.
Hamden, Connecticut
Tel: (203) 777-7251

Rochlin Baran & Balbona, Inc.
Los Angeles, California
Tel: (310) 473-3555
www.rbbinc.com

Rosser International, Inc.
Atlanta, Georgia
Tel: (404) 876-3800
www.rosser.com

RTKL International, Inc.
Baltimore, Maryland
Tel: (410) 528-8600
www.rtkl.com

S/L/A/M Collaborative, The
Glastonbury, Connecticut
Tel: (860) 657-8077
www.slamcoll.com

Sasaki Associates, Inc.
Watertown, Massachusetts
Tel: (617) 926-3300
www.sasaki.com

Schenkel & Schultz, Inc.
Fort Wayne, Indiana
Tel: (219) 424-9080
www.schenkelshultz.com

Scogin Elam Bray
Atlanta, Georgia
Tel: (404) 525-6869

Scott Partnership Architecture, Inc. The
Orlando, Florida
Tel: (407) 660.2766
www.scottarchitects.com

Shepley Bulfinch Richardson & Abbott
Boston, Massachusetts
Tel: (617) 423-1700
www.sbra.com

Sienna Architecture
Portland, Oregon
Tel: (503) 227-5616
www.archsienna.com

Skidmore, Owing & Merrill LLP (SOM)
Chicago, Illinois
Tel: (312) 554-9090
www.som.com

Smallwood, Reynolds, Stewart, Stewart Associates, Inc.
Atlanta, Georgia
Tel: (404) 233-5453
www.srssa.com

Smith Group Incorporated
Detroit, Michigan
Tel: (313) 983-3600
www.smithgroup.com

Smith - Miller + Hawkinson
New York, New York
Tel: (212) 966-3875
www.smharch.com

Soderstrom Architects, PC
Portland, Oregon
Tel: (503) 228-5617
www.sdra.com

250 Leading U.S. Based Architecture Firms (Con't)

Spector Group
North Hills, New York
Tel: (516) 365-4240
www.spectorgroup.com

Spencer Magee
Los Angeles, California
Tel: (310) 820-4376

Spillis Candela & Partners, Inc.
Coral Gables, Florida
Tel: (305) 447-3536
www.scpmiami.com

SSOE Inc.
Toledo, Ohio
Tel: (419) 255-3830
www.ssoe.com

Robert A. M. Stern Architects
New York, New York
Tel: (212) 967-5100

Stubbins Associates, Inc., The
Cambridge, Massachusetts
Tel: (617) 491-6450
www.tsa-arch.com

Studios Architecture
San Francisco, California
Tel: (415) 398-7575
www.studiosarch.com

Sverdrup Corporation
Maryland Heights, Missouri
Tel: (314) 436-7600
www.sverdrup.com

Swanke Hayden Connell Architects
New York, New York
Tel: (212) 226-9696
www.shca.com

Symmes Maini & McKee Associates
Cambridge, Massachusetts
Tel: (617) 547-5400
www.smma.com

Taliesen Architects
Scottsdale, Arizona
Tel: (480) 860-2700

TAMS Consultants, Inc.
New York, New York
Tel: (212) 867-1777
www.tamsconsultants.com

Teng & Associates
Chicago, Illinois
Tel: (312) 616-0000
www.teng.com

Thomas Associates Architects Engineers PC
Ithaca, New York
Tel: (617) 277-7100
www.thomasamerica.com

Thomas Hacker and Associates
Portland, Oregon
Tel: (503) 227-1254
www.thomashacker.com

Thompson Vaivoda & Associates Architects
Portland, Oregon
Tel: (503) 220-0668

Thompson, Ventulett, Stainback & Associates, Inc.
Atlanta, Georgia
Tel: (404) 888-6600
www.tvsa.com

Tigerman McCurry Architects
Chicago, Illinois
Tel: (312) 644-5880
www.tigerman-mccurry.com

Tod Williams Billie Tsien and Associates
New York, New York
Tel: (212) 582-2385

Torti Gallas & Partners/CHK, Inc.
Silver Spring, Maryland
Tel: (301) 588-4800

250 Leading U.S. Based Architecture Firms (Con't)

TRO/The Ritchie Organization
Newton, Massachusetts
Tel: (617) 969-9400
www.troarch.com

Tsoi/Kobus & Associates
Boston, Massachusetts
Tel: (617) 491-3067
www.tka-architects.com

URS Greiner Woodward-Clyde
San Francisco, California
Tel: (415) 774-2700
www.ursgreiner.com

Venturi, Scott Brown and Associates
Philadelphia, Pennsylvania
Tel: (215) 487-0400
www.vsba.com

Rafael Viñoly Architects PC
New York, New York
Tel: (212) 924-5060
www.rvapc.com

Vitetta Group
Philadelphia, Pennsylvania
Tel: (215) 235-3500
www.vitetta.com

VOA Associates Incorporated
Chicago, Illinois
Tel: (312) 554-1400

Wallace Roberts and Todd
Philadelphia, Pennsylvania
Tel: (215) 732-5215
www.wrtdesign.com

Wallace, Floyd Associates, Inc.
Boston, Massachusetts
Tel: (617) 350-7400
www.wfa.com

Watkins Hamilton Ross Architects, Inc.
Bellaire, Texas
Tel: (713) 665-5665

Weinstein Associates Architects
Washington, DC
Tel: (202) 232-2400

Wimberly Allison Tong & Goo
Honolulu, Hawaii
Tel: (808) 521-8888
www.watg.com

Wold Architects and Engineers
St. Paul, Minnesota
Tel: (651) 227-7773
www.woldae.com

Wolfberg Alvarez and Partners
Miami, Florida
Tel: (305) 666-5474

WTW Architects
Pittsburgh, Pennsylvania
Tel: (412) 321-0550

Zimmer Gunsul Frasca Partnership
Portland, Oregon
Tel: (503) 224-3860
www.zgf.com

Zimmerman Design Group, The
Milwaukee, Wisconsin
Tel: (414) 476-9500
www.zdg.com

Source: Counsel House Research/Greenway Group

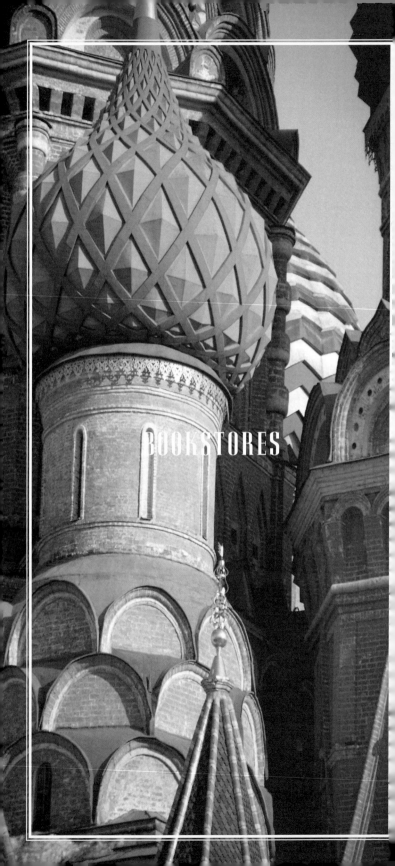

BOOKSTORES

Architecture & Design Bookstores

In additional to the ubiquitous Borders, Barnes and Noble, and Amazon.com, the following list outlines the specialty bookstores of architecture and design throughout the United States. This information also includes antiquarian book dealers which specialize in design titles.

ABI Books
11 E. De Lax Guerra St.
Santa Barbara, CA 93101
(805) 262-5893

Acanthus Books
48 W. 22nd St., No. 4
New York, NY 10011
(212) 463-0750

AIA Bookstore, American Institute of Architects
1735 New York Ave. NW
Washington, DC 20006
(202) 626-7475

Amphion Antiquarian Books
1069 Beacon St.
Bookline, MA 02146
(617) 566-3425

Anchor & Dophin Books
30 Franklin St., P.O. Box 823
Newport, RI 02840
(401) 846-6890

ArchiCenter Bookstore
330 S. Dearborn
Chicago, IL 60604
(312) 922-3431

Archiectural Book Center
231 Peachtree St. NE
Atlanta, GA 30303
(404) 222-9920

Architectural Center Bookstore
Indiana Society of Architects
47 S. Pennsylvania St.
Indianapolis, IN 46204
(317) 634-3871

Archivia: The Decorative Arts Bookshop
944 Madison Ave.
New York, NY 10021
(212) 439-9194

Argosy Bookstore
116 E. 59th St.
New York, NY 10022
(212) 753-4455

Ars Libri
560 Harrison Ave.
Boston, MA 02118
(617) 357-5212

Arthur H. Minters Booksellers
96 Fulton
New York, NY 10038
(212) 587-4014

Builder's Book
7943 Canoga Ave.
Canoga Park, CA 91304
(818) 887-7828

Builders Booksource
1817 Fourth St.
Berkeley, CA 94710
(510) 845-6874

Architecture & Design Bookstores (Con't)

Builders Booksource
300 Deharo St.
San Francisco, CA 94103
(415) 575-3980

Building News Books
3055 Overland Ave.
Los Angeles, CA 90034
(310) 202-7775

Building News Bookstore
77 Wexford St.
Needham Heights, MA 02194
(617) 455-1466

Cambridge Architectural Books
12 Bow St.
Cambridge, MA 02138
(617) 354-5300

Charles B. Wood III Antiquarian Booksellers
P.O. Box 2369
Cambridge, MA 02238
(617) 868-1711

Chicago Architecture Foundation Bookstore
224 S. Michigan Ave.
Chicago, IL 60604
(312) 922-3432

Chicago Architecture Foundation Bookstore
875 N. Michigan Ave.
Chicago, IL 60611
(312) 751-1380

Coliseum Books
1771 Broadway
New York, NY 10012
(212) 757-8381

Colorado Historical Society Museum Store
1300 Broadway
Denver, CO 80203
(303) 866-4993

Construction Bookstore
1830 NE 2nd St., P.O. Box 2959
Gainesville, FL 32602
(904) 378-9784

Contract Design Center Bookshop
11-111 Merchandise Mart, P.O. Box 3442
Chicago, IL 60654
(312) 527-3509

F.A. Bernett
2001 Palmer Ave.
Larchmont, NY 10538
(914) 834-3026

Franz Bader Bookstore
1911 I St. NW
Washington, DC 20006
(202) 337-5440

Hacker Art Books
45 W. 57th St.
New York, NY 10019
(212) 688-7600

Did you know...
The Louisiana Superdome was built to withstand winds of over 150 mph and gusts up to 200 mph – the level of a Class V hurricane.

Architecture & Design Bookstores (Con't)

Hennessey & Ingalls Art and Architecture Books
1254 3rd St. Promenade
Santa Monica, CA 90401
(310) 458-9074

J.B. Muns Fine Arts Books
1162 Shattuck Ave.
Berkeley, CA 94707
(510) 525-2420

Jaap Rietman
134 Spring St.
New York, NY 10012
(212) 966-8044

James Hodgson
710 County St.
New Bedford, MA 02740
(508) 992-7260

McGraw-Hill Bookstore
1221 Avenue of the Americas
New York, NY 10020
(212) 512-4100

Michael Shamansky, Bookseller
P.O. Box 3904
Kingston, KY 12401
(914) 331-8519

Moe's Art & Antiquarian Books
2476 Telegraph Ave.
Berkeley, CA 94704
(510) 849-2133

National Building Museum Shop
Pension Building
Judiciary Square
Washington, DC 20001
(202) 272-7706

Peter Miller Architecture and Design Books
1930 First Ave.
Seattle, WA 98101
(206) 441-4114

Prairie Avenue Bookshop
711 S. Dearborn St.
Chicago, IL 60605
(312) 922-8311

Preservation Bookshop National Trust for Historic Preservation
1600 H St. NW
Washington, DC 20006
(202) 842-1856

Rizzoli Bookstore
31 W. 57th St.
New York, NY 10019
(212) 759-2424
(800) 522-6657

Strand Book Store
828 Broadway
New York, NY 10003
(212) 473-1452

Stubbs Books & Prints
153 E. 70th
New York, NY 10021
(212) 772-3120

Urban Center Books Villard Houses
457 Madison Ave.
New York, NY 10022
(212) 935-3592

William Stout Architectural Books
804 Montgomery St.
San Francisco, CA 94133
(415) 391-6757

JOURNALS
&
MAGAZINES

Architecture & Design Journals & Magazines

The following is a list of major architecture and design journals, magazines, and newsletters, ranging from the most popular to cutting edge publications. Whether looking for periodicals which take a less traditional approach, or searching for newsletters which deal with management and communication issues, it is hoped this list will provide an opportunity to explore new ideas and perspectives about design and expand knowledge about the profession.

4dfile
81 Sukhumvit 26
Bangkok 10110, Thailand
(662) 259-3863-4, 259-7707
http://www.4dfile.com/
Published 2 times a year by Corporation 4d Ltd.

a+u magazine
31-2, Yushima 2-chome, Bunkyo-ku
Tokyo 113, Japan
(03) 816-2935
http://www.japanarchitect.co.jp/au/index.htm
Montly bilingual magazine published by A&U Publishing Co., Ltd.

Abitare
Corso Monforte 15
Milano 20122, Italy
39 027 6090211
www.abitare.it
Monthly magazine in Italian and English

AD (Architectural Design)
Academy Editions
42 Leinster Gardens
London W@3AN, U.K.
011 44 71 402 2141
Bimonthly; Pub. by Academy Editions

AJ (Architects' Journal)
EMAP Architecture
33 39 Bowling Green Lane
London EC1R 0DA, U.K.
011 44 71 837 1212
Published by EMAP Architecture

APA Journal
122 S. Michigan Ave.
Suite 1600
Chicago, IL 60603-6107
(312) 431-9100
www.planning.org
Journal of the American Planning Assoc.

Archis
Elsevier Bedrijfsinformatie bv
PO Box 4
BA Doetinchem 7000, The Netherlands
+31(0)314-349888
www.archis.org
Montly bilingual magazine published by the Netherlands Architecture Institute (NAI) in collaboration with Elsevier Business Information BV.

Architectural Digest
4 Times Square
New York, NY 10036
(212) 286-2500
www.archdigest.com
Published monthly by Conde Nast Publications, Inc.

Architecture & Design Journals & Magazines (Con't)

**Architectural History: The Journal of
the Society of Architectural Historians
of Great Britain**
4 Woodland's Ave, Finchley
London N3 2NR, U.K.
081 346 5139

Architectural Record
2 Penn Plaza
9th Floor
New York, NY 10121-2298
(212) 904-2594
www.archrecord.com
Published monthly by The McGraw-Hill
Companies; the magazine of the AIA

Architectural Review
EMAP Architecture
33 39 Bowling Green Lane
London EC1R 0DA, U.K.
011 44 71 837 1212
Published by EMAP Architecture

Architecture
1515 Broadway
New York, NY 10036
(212) 536-6221
www.architecturemag.com
Published monthly by BPI
Communications

Architecture Australia
4 Princes Street
3rd Floor
Port Melbourne
Victoria 3207, Australia
+613 9646 4760
http://www.archmedia.com.au/aa/aa.htm
Official magazine of the RAIA

Arkitektur
P.O. Box 1742
Stockholm S-111 87, Sweden
08 679 6105
Published eight times yearly; with
English summaries

Art News
48 W. 38th St.
New York, NY 10018
212-398-1690
www.artnewsonline.com
Published monthly except August

Australian Building News
Suite 303, 64-76 Kippax Street
Surry Hills
NSW 2010, Australia
+61 (02) 9211 0125
http://www.abn.com.au/

Blueprint
26 Cramer St.
London W1M 3HE, U.K.
Published monthly except August, by
Aspen Publishing

Canadian Architect
1450 Don Mills Road
Don Mills
ON M3B 2X7, Canada
(416) 442-3390
www.cdnarchitect.com
Southam Magazine Group Limited

Did you know...
**Construction of the Great
Wall of China took nearly
2,000 years.**

Architecture & Design Journals & Magazines (Con't)

Casabella
Via Manzoni 12
Rozzano
Milan 20089, Italy
011 39 2 57512575
Published by Agenzia Italiana di
Esportazione

CMD AEC Magazine
30 Technology Pkwy. South
Suite 100
Norcross. GA 30092
(770) 417-4163
Published quarterly by CMD Group

Communication Arts
410 Sherman Ave.
P.O. Box 10300
Palo Alto, CA 94303

Daidalos: architektur kunst kultur
Postfach 120
Gutersloh D-33311, Germany
011 49 5241 80
Quarterly in English and German; pub-
lished by Bertelsmann Fachzeitschriften
GmbH

Design Book Review
c/o Cathy Ho
1418 Spring Way
Berkely, CA 94708
Triennial

Design Intelligence
Two Fountain Square
11921 Freedom Drive, Ste. 550
Reston, VA 20190
(703) 904-8065
www.di.net
Published by the Greenway Group

*Design: The Journal of the Design
Council*
Haymarket House
1 Oxenden Street
London SW1Y 4EE, U.K.
0171 208 2121
Quarterly

Domus
Via Grandi 5-7
Rozzano
Milan 20089, Italy
02 824 72527
http://domus.edidomus.it/domus_eng/
home.htm
Published 11 times a year in Italian and
English

Engineering News Record
2 Penn Plaza, 9th Floor
New York, NY 10121
www.enr.com
Published by McGraw-Hill Construction
Information Group

Fine Homebuilding
63 S. Main St.
Newtown, CT 06470-5506
(203) 426-8171
http://www.taunton.com/fh/index.htm
Published monthly by Taunton Press

GA Architect
3-12-14 Sendagaya
Shibuya-ku
Tokyo 151, Japan
Published by ADA Edita Tokyo Co. Ltd.

Harvard Design Magazine
48 Quincy St.
Cambridge, MA 02138
(617) 495-7814
www.harvard.edu/hdm
Published quarterly by Harvard
University's Graduate School of Design

Architecture & Design Journals & Magazines (Con't)

Hinge
17/F, Queen's centre. Queen's Road east
Wanchai, Hong Kong
(852) 2520 2468
http://www.hingenet.com/hinge/hinge.htm
Published monthly

I.D.
116 East 27th St. Floor 6
New York. NY 10106
(212) 447-1400
www.idonline.com
Published 8 times per year

Innovation
1142 Walker Rd.
Great Falls, VA 22066
(703) 759-0100
www.idsa.org
Quarterly Journal of the IDSA

Interior Design
345 Hudson St.
New York, NY 10014
(212) 519-7265
Published monthly by Cahners
Publishing Co.

Interiors
1515 Broadway
New York, NY 10036
(212) 536-5193
Published monthly by BPI
Communications

Japan Architect
31-2 Yshima 2-chome
Bunkyo-ku
Tokyo 113, Japan
(03) 816-2935
Quarterly

Journal of Architectural Education (JAE)
55 Haywood St.
Cambridge, MA 02142
(617) 625-8481
Published quarterly by MIT Press

Journal of Architecture
Routledge Customer Service
7625 Empire Drive
Florence, KY 41042
(800) 634-7064
http://st11.yahoo.com/riba-journals/
Published four times a year by
Routledge for RIBA and E & FN Spon

Journal of Urban Design
Rankine Road
Basingstoke, Hants RG24 8PR, U.K.
+44 (0)1256 813000
www.carfax.co.uk
Carfax Publishing Limited

JSAH (Journal of the Society of Architectural Historians)
1365 N. Astor St.
Chicago, IL 60610
(215) 735-0224
Published quarterly by the Society of
Architectural Historians

Landscape Architecture
636 Eye St. NW
Washington, DC 20001-3736
(800) 787-LAMS
www.asla.org
Published monthly by the American
Society of Landscape Architects

Metropolis
61 W. 23rd St.
New York, NY 10010
(212) 627-9177
www.metropolismag.com

Architecture & Design Journals & Magazines (Con't)

Old House Journal
2 Main St.
Gloucester, MA 01930
(508) 281-8803
Published bimonthly

**Perspective: The International
Magazine of the IIDA**
341 Merchandise Mart
Chicago, IL 60654
(312) 467-1950
www.iida.org
Published quarterly by IIDA

Places
55 Haywood St.
Cambridge, MA 02142
(617) 253-2889
Published quarterly by MIT Press

Planning Perspectives
Routledge Customer Service
7625 Empire Drive
Florence, KY 41042
(800) 634-7064
http://www.journals.routledge.com/pp.html
Published by Routledge/E&FN Spon

Preservation
1785 Massachucetts Ave. NW
Washington, DC 20036
(202) 673-4000
Published bimonthly by the National
Trust for Historic Preservation

Principal's Report
29 W. 35th St., 5th Floor
New York, NY 10001-2299
(212) 244-0630
www.ioma.com
Published monthly by the Institute of
Management & Administration

Rassegna
Via Stalingrado 97-2
Bologna 40128, Italy
39-51-4199211
www.compositori.it
Published quarterly in Italian and
English by Editrice Compositori srl

RIBA Journal
39 Moreland St.
London EC1V 8BB, U.K.
071 251 0791
http://st11.yahoo.com/riba-journals/
Published monthly by the Builder
Group for RIBA Members in the U.K.

The Zweig Letter
600 Worchester St.
Natick, MA 01760
(508) 651-1559
www.zwa.com
Published weekly by Zweig, White &
Associates, Inc.

World Architecture
Exchange Tower
2 Harbour Exchange Square
London E14 9GE, U.K.
44 (0) 171 560 4120
Published by the Builder Group

Source: Counsel House Research/Greenway Group

Did you know...
**The lily-pad tops of the
columns in Frank Lloyd
Wright's Johnson Wax
Building are 18 feet across
and are constructed of
poured concrete over wire
mesh.**

COLLEGES
&
UNIVERSITIES

COLLEGES & UNIVERSITIES

Architecture Degree Programs

The following architecture degree programs are accredited by the National Architectural Accrediting Board (NAAB). Through a sequence of steps including a site visit, programs must demonstrate compliance with NAAB's twelve accreditation conditions. The NAAB accredits both undergraduate and graduate programs. As the following information is subject to change often, individual schools should be consulted for the most up to date details.

ANDREWS UNIVERSITY
www.andrews.edu/ARCH
The Division of Architecture
Berrien Springs, MI 49104-0450
(616) 471-6003
B. Arch

ARIZONA STATE UNIVERSITY
www.asu.edu/caed/Architecture
School of Architecture
P.O. Box 871605
Tempe, AZ 85287-1605
(602) 965-3536
M. Arch

AUBURN UNIVERSITY
www.auburn.edu/academic/architec-
ture/au.architecture.html
College of Architecture, Design and
Construction
202 Dudley Commons
Auburn University, AL 36849-5313
(334) 844-4524
B. Arch

BALL STATE UNIVERSITY
www.bsu.edu/cap
Department of Architecture
College of Architecture and Planning
Muncie, IN 47306-0305
(765) 285-5861
B. Arch

BOSTON ARCHITECTURAL CENTER
www.the-bac.edu
320 Newbury Street
Boston, MA 02115
(617) 262-5000, ext. 221
B. Arch

CALIFORNIA COLLEGE OF ART AND
CRAFTS
www.ccac-art.edu
School of Arch. Studies/Dept. of Arch.
450 Irwin Street
San Francisco, CA 94107
(415) 703-9516
B. Arch

CALIFORNIA POLYTECHNIC STATE
UNIVERSITY, SAN LUIS OBISPO
www.calpoly.edu/~arch
Architecture Department
College of Arch. & Environ. Design
San Luis Obispo, CA 93407
(805) 756-1316
B. Arch

CALIFORNIA STATE POLYTECHNIC
UNIVERSITY, POMONA
www.csupomona.edu/-arc
Department of Architecture
College of Environmental Design
3801 W. Temple Avenue
Pomona, CA 91768
(909) 869-2683
B. Arch, M. Arch

Architecture Degree Programs (Con't)

CARNEGIE MELLON UNIVERSITY
www.arc.cmu.edu
School of Architecture
College of Fine Arts, Room 201
Carnegie Mellon University
Pittsburgh, PA 15213
(412) 268-2355
B. Arch

CATHOLIC UNIVERSITY OF
AMERICA
www.cua.edu/www/apu/index.htm
School of Architecture and Planning
Crough Center for Architectural Studies
Washington, DC 20064
(202) 319-5188
B. Arch, M. Arch

CITY COLLEGE OF THE CITY
UNIVERSITY OF NEW YORK
www.ccny.cuny.edu
School of Arch. & Environ. Studies
Convent Avenue at 138th Street
New York, NY 10031
(212) 650-6889
B. Arch

CLEMSON UNIVERSITY
http://hubcap.clemson.edu/aah
College of Arch., Arts and Humanities
Box 340503, 145 Lee Hall
Clemson, SC 29634
(864) 656-3898
M. Arch

COLUMBIA UNIVERSITY
www.arch.columbia.edu
Graduate School of Architecture,
Planning and Preservation
400 Avery Hall
1172 Amsterdam Avenue
New York, NY 10027
(212) 854-3510
M. Arch

COOPER UNION
www.cooper.edu/architecture/arch.text.html
Irwin S. Chanin School of Architecture
Cooper Square - 7 East 7 Street
New York, NY 10003
(212) 353-4220
B. Arch

CORNELL UNIVERSITY
www.aap.cornell.edu/index.htm
Department of Architecture
College of Arch., Art and Planning
143 East Sibley Hall
Ithaca, NY 14853-6701
(607) 255-5236
B. Arch

DREXEL UNIVERSITY
www.coda.drexel.edu/departments/architecture
Department of Architecture
Nesbitt College of Design Arts
Philadelphia, PA 19104
(215) 895-2409
B. Arch

DRURY COLLEGE
www.drury.edu/info/academic/depart/arch.html
Hammons School of Architecture
900 North Benton Avenue
Springfield, MO 65802
(417) 873-7288
B. Arch

FLORIDA A&M UNIVERSITY
www.168.223.36.3/acad/college/soa
School of Architecture
1936 S. Martin Luther King Blvd.
Tallahassee, FL 32307
(850) 599-3244
B. Arch, M. Arch

Did you know...
Jorn Utzon's Sydney Opera House has 1,000 rooms, 60 of which are dressing rooms.

Architecture Degree Programs (Con't)

FLORIDA ATLANTIC UNIVERSITY
www.fau.edu/dividept/cupa
School of Architecture
Reubin O'D. Askew Tower Room 616M
220 SE 2nd Avenue
Fort Lauderdale, FL 33301
(954) 762-5654
Candidate for B. Arch

FLORIDA INTERNATIONAL UNIV,
www.flu.edu/index.htm
School of Architecture
Miami, FL 33199-0001
(305) 348-3181
M. Arch

FRANK LLOYD WRIGHT SCHOOL
OF ARCHITECTURE
www.taliesin.edu
Taliesin West
Scottsdale, AZ 85261-4430
(602) 860-2700
M. Arch

GEORGIA INST. OF TECHNOLOGY
www.arch.gatech.edu
College of Arch./Arch. Program
247 4th Street, NW
Atlanta, GA 30332-0155
(404) 894-4053
M. Arch

HAMPTON UNIVERSITY
www.hampton.edu
School of Engineering and Technology
Department of Architecture
Hampton, VA 23668
(757) 727-5440
B. Arch

HARVARD UNIVERSITY
www.gsd.harvard.edu
Graduate School of Design
48 Quincy Street
Cambridge, MA 02138
(617) 495-2591
M. Arch

HOWARD UNIVERSITY
www.imappt.org/CEACS/Departments/
Architecture/index.htm
School of Architecture and Planning
2366 Sixth Street NW
Washington, DC 20059
(202) 806-7420
B. Arch

ILLINOIS INST. OF TECHNOLOGY
www.iit.edu/~arch
College of Architecture/S.R. Crown Hall
3360 S. State Street
Chicago, IL 69616
(312) 567-3230
B. Arch, M. Arch

IOWA STATE UNIVERSITY
www.public.iastate.edu/design/arch/
index.html
Department of Architecture
156 College of Design
Ames, IA 50011-3093
(515) 294-4717
B. Arch, M. Arch

KANSAS STATE UNIVERSITY
www.ksu.edu/archdos
College of Arch., Planning and Design
Department of Architecture
211 Seaton Hall
Manhattan, KS 66506-2901
(913) 532-5953
B. Arch

KENT STATE UNIVERSITY
www.saed.kent.edu/SAED
School of Arch. and Environ. Design
200 Taylor Hall
Kent, OH 44240
(330) 672-2917
B. Arch

Architecture Degree Programs (Con't)

LAWRENCE TECHNOLOGICAL UNIV.
www.ltu.edu/architecture
College of Architecture and Design
21000 West Ten Mile Road
Southfield, MI 48075-1058
(810) 204-2805
B. Arch, M. Arch

LOUISIANA STATE UNIVERSITY
www.cadgis.lsu.edu/design/index.html
School of Arch./College of Design
136 Atkinson Hall
Baton Rouge, LA 70803
(225) 388-6885
B. Arch

LOUISIANA TECH UNIVERSITY
www.LaTech.edu/tech/arch
School of Architecture
P.O. Box 3147
Ruston, LA 71272
(318) 257-2816
B. Arch

MASSACHUSETTS INST. OF TECH.
http://sap.mit.edu
School of Architecture and Planning
Department of Architecture
Room 7-337, 77 Massachusetts Avenue
Cambridge, MA 02139-4307
(617) 253-7791
M. Arch

MIAMI UNIVERSITY
www.fna.muohio.edu
Department of Architecture
101 Alumni Hall
Oxford, OH 45056
513) 529-7210
M. Arch

MISSISSIPPI STATE UNIVERSITY
www.sarc.msstate.edu
School of Architecture
P.O. Box AQ
Mississippi State, MS 39762-5541
601) 325-2202
B. Arch

MONTANA STATE UNIVERSITY
www.montana.edu/wwwarch
School of Architecture
Cheever 160
Bozeman, MT 59717-3760
(406) 994-4256
B. Arch, M. Arch

MORGAN STATE UNIVERSITY
www.morgan.edu/acadmic/schools/arch
it/archit.htm
Institute of Architecture & Planning
Jenkins 334
1700 E. Cold Spring Lane
Baltimore, MD 21239
(410) 319-3225
M. Arch

NEW JERSEY INST. OF TECH.
www.njit.edu/Directory/Academic/SOA
School of Architecture
University Heights
Newark, NJ 07102-1982
(973) 596-3080
B. Arch, M. Arch

NEW YORK INST. OF TECH.
www.nyit.edu
School of Architecture and Design
Education Hall
Old Westbury, NY 11568-8000
(516) 686-7593
B. Arch

NEWSCHOOL OF ARCHITECTURE
www.newschoolarch.edu
1249 F Street
San Diego, CA 92101
(619) 235-4100 ext. 101
B. Arch, M. Arch

Did you know...
**Gordon Bunshaft won 12
AIA Honor Awards while a
design principal at SOM.**

Architecture Degree Programs (Con't)

NORTH CAROLINA STATE UNIV.
www.ncsu.edu/design
Architecture Dept./School of Design
NCSU Box 7701
Raleigh, NC 27695-7701
(919) 515- 8350
B. Arch, M. Arch

NORTH DAKOTA STATE UNIV.
www.ndsu.nodak.edu/arch
Dept. of Arch. and Landscape Arch.
Fargo, ND 58105-5285
(701) 231-8614
B. Arch

NORWICH UNIVERSITY
www.norwich.edu
Division of Architecture and Art
Northfield, VT 05663
(802) 485-2620
B. Arch, M. Arch

OHIO STATE UNIVERSITY
http://arch.ohio-state.edu
Austin E. Knowlton School of Arch.
105 Brown hall
190 W. 17th Avenue
Columbus, OH 43210-1368
(614) 292-1012
M. Arch

OKLAHOMA STATE UNIVERSITY
http://master.ceat.okstate.edu
School of Architecture
101 Architecture
Stillwater, OK 74078-5051
(405) 744-6043
B. Arch

PARSONS SCHOOL OF DESIGN
www.parsons.edu
A Div. of the New School for Social
Research
Department of Arch. & Environ. Design
66 Fifth Avenue
New York, NY 10011
(212) 229-8955
M. Arch

PENNSYLVANIA STATE UNIVERSITY
www.arch.psu.edu
Department of Architecture
College of Arts and Architecture
206 Engineering Unit C
University Park, PA 16802
(814) 865-9535
B. Arch

PHILADELPHIA COLLEGE OF
TEXTILES AND SCIENCE
www.philacol.edu/archdes/ad.htm
Architecture Program
School of Architecture and Design
School House Lane and Henry Avenue
Philadelphia, PA 19144-5497
(215) 951-2896
B. Arch

POLYTECHNIC UNIV. OF PUERTO
RICO
http://pupr.edu/arch
Architecture Program
Box 192017
San Juan, PR 00919-8000
(787) 754-8000 EXT. 451
Candidate for B. Arch

PRAIRIE VIEW A& M UNIVERSITY
http://www.pvamu.edu
Department of Architecture
P.O. Box 397
Prairie View, TX 77446
(409) 857-2014
B. Arch

PRATT INSTITUTE
www.pratt.edu/arch/index.html
School of Architecture
200 Willoughby Avenue
Brooklyn, NY 11205
(718) 399-4304
B. Arch

Architecture Degree Programs (Con't)

PRINCETON UNIVERSITY
www.princeton.odu:80/-soa
School of Architecture
Princeton, NJ 08544
(609) 258-3741
M. Arch

RENSSELAER POLYTECHNIC INST.
www.rpi.odu/dept/arch
School of Architecture
Greene Building
Troy, NY 12180
(518) 276-6460
B. Arch, M. Arch

RHODE ISLAND SCHOOL OF
DESIGN
www.risd.edu/arch.html
Division of Architecture & Design
2 College Street
Providence, RI 02903
(401) 454-6281
B. Arch, M. Arch

RICE UNIVERSITY
www.arch.rice.edu
School of Architecture
P.O. Box 1892
Houston, TX 77251-1892
(713) 527-4044
B. Arch, M. Arch

ROGER WILLIAMS UNIVERSITY
www.rwu.edu
School of Architecture
One Old Ferry Road
Bristol, RI 02809-2921
(401) 254-3605
B. Arch

SAVANNAH COLLEGE OF ART AND
DESIGN
www.scad.edu
Department of Architecture
342 Bull Street
P.O. Box 3146
Savannah, GA 31402-3146
(912) 238-2450
B. Arch

SOUTHERN CALIFORNIA
INSTITUTE OF ARCHITECTURE
www.sciarc.edu
SCI-Arc
5454 Beethoven Street
Los Angeles, CA 90066
(310) 574-1123 ext. 318
B. Arch, M. Arch

SOUTHERN POLYTECHNIC STATE
UNIVERSITY
www2.spsuedu/architecture/index.htm
School of Architecture
1100 South Marietta Parkway
Marietta, GA 30060-2896
(770) 528-7253
B. Arch

SOUTHERN UNIV. & A&M COLLEGE
www.subr.edu
School of Architecture
P.O. Box 11947
Baton Rouge, LA 70813
(225) 771-3015
B. Arch

SYRACUSE UNIVERSITY
http://mirror.syr.edu/soa.html
School of Architecture
103 Slocum Hall
Syracuse, NY 13244-1250
(315) 443-2256
B. Arch, M. Arch

Architecture Degree Programs (Con't)

TEMPLE UNIVERSITY
www.temple.edu/architecture
Architecture, Landscape Architecture,
and Horticulture Program
12th and Norris Streets
Philadelphia, PA 19122
(215) 204-8813
B. Arch

TEXAS A&M UNIVERSITY
http://archone.tamu.edu
Department of Architecture
College of Architecture
College Station, TX 77843-3137
(409) 845-0129
M. Arch

TULANE UNIVERSITY
www.tulane.edu/~tsahome
School of Architecture
New Orleans, LA 70118-5671
(504) 865-5389
B. Arch, M. Arch

TUSKEGEE UNIVERSITY
http://ceaps.tusk.edu
Department of Architecture
Tuskegee, AL 36088
(334) 727-8329
B. Arch

UNIVERSITY OF ARIZONA
www.architecture.arizona.edu
College of Architecture
Tucson, AZ 85721
(520) 621-6754
B. Arch

UNIVERSITY OF ARKANSAS
www.uark.edu/~archhome/school.html
School of Architecture
Vol Walker Hall 120
Fayetteville, AR 72701
(501) 575-4945
B. Arch

UNIVERSITY OF BUFFALO
www.arch.buffalo.edu/architecture/programs
(716) 829-3483 ext. 106
M. Arch

UNIV. OF CALIFORNIA AT BERKELEY
www.ced.berkeley.edu:80/arch
Department of Architecture
College of Environmental Design
Berkeley, CA 94720-1800
(510) 642-4942
M. Arch

UNIV. OF CALIFORNIA AT LOS
ANGELES
www.aud.ucla.edu
Department of Arch. and Urban Design
School of the Arts and Architecture
1317 Perloff Hall
Los Angeles, CA 90095-1467
(310) 825-7857
M. Arch

UNIVERSITY OF CINCINNATI
www.daap.uc.edu
School of Arch. and Interior Design
College of Design, Arch., Art & Planning
P.O. Box 210016
Cincinnati, OH 45221-0016
(513) 556-6426
B. Arch

UNIV. OF COLORADO AT DENVER/
BOULDER
www.cudenvor.edu/public/AandP
College of Architecture and Planning
Campus Box 126
P.O. Box 173364
Denver, CO 80217-3364
(303) 556-3382
M. Arch

Architecture, of all the arts, is the one which acts the most slowly, but the most surely, on the soul.

Ernest Dimnet

Architecture Degree Programs (Con't)

UNIVERSITY OF DETROIT MERCY
www.arch.udmercy.edu
School of Architecture
4001 W. McNichols
P.O. Box 19900
Detroit, MI 48219-0900
(313) 993-1532
B. Arch

UNIVERSITY OF FLORIDA
www.arch.ufl.edu
Department of Architecture
231 ARCH, PO Box 115702
Gainesville, FL 32611-5702
(352) 392-0205
M. Arch

UNIV. OF HAWAII AT MANOA
http://web1.arch.hawaii.edu
School of Architecture
2410 Campus Road
Honolulu, HI 96822
(808) 956-7225
B. Arch, M. Arch

UNIVERSITY OF HOUSTON
www.arch.uh.edu
Gerald D. Hines College of Architecture
4800 Calhoun
Houston, TX 77204-4431
(713) 743-2400
B. Arch, M. Arch

UNIVERSITY OF IDAHO
www.aa.uidaho.edu/arch
Department of Architecture
College of Art and Architecture
Moscow, ID 83844-2451
(208) 885-6781
B. Arch, M. Arch

UNIV. OF ILLINOIS AT CHICAGO
www.uic.edu:80/depts/arch/homepage.html
School of Architecture (m/c 030)
845 W. Harrison, Rm. 3100
Chicago, IL 60(607) 7024
(312) 996-3355
B. Arch, M. Arch

UNIVERSITY OF ILLINOIS AT
URBANA-CHAMPAIGN
www.arch.uluc.edu
School of Architecture
117 Temple Hoyne Buell Hall
611 Taft Drive
Champaign, IL 61820-6921
(217) 333-1330
M. Arch

UNIVERSITY OF KANSAS
http://arce.ukans.edu/scharch/scharch.htm
School of Arch. and Urban Design
206 Marvin Hall
Lawrence, KS 66045-2250
(785) 864-4281
B. Arch, M. Arch

UNIVERSITY OF KENTUCKY
www.uky.edu/Architecture
College of Architecture
117 Pence Hall
Lexington, KY 40506-0041
(606) 257-7619
B. Arch

UNIVERSITY OF MARYLAND
www.inform.umd.edu/ARCH
School of Architecture
College Park, MD 20742-1411
(301) 405-6284
M. Arch

Did you know...
In 1811, London was the
first city in modern history
to reach 1 million people.

Architecture Degree Programs (Con't)

UNIVERSITY OF MIAMI
www.arc.miami.edu
School of Architecture
1223 Dickinson Drive
P.O. Box 249178
Coral Gables, FL 33124-5010
(305) 284-5000
B. Arch, M. Arch

UNIVERSITY OF MICHIGAN
www.caup.umich.edu
College of Arch. and Urban Planning
2000 Bonisteel Blvd.
Ann Arbor, MI 48109-2069
(734) 763-1300
M. Arch

UNIVERSITY OF MINNESOTA
http://gumby.arch.umn.edu
Department of Architecture
College of Arch. and Landscape Arch.
110 Architecture, 89 Church Street SE
Minneapolis, MN 55455
(612) 624-7866
B. Arch, M. Arch

UNIVERSITY OF NEBRASKA
www.unl.edu/archcoll/index.htm
College of Architecture
210 Architecture Hall
Lincoln, NE 68588-0106
(402) 472-9212
M. Arch

UNIV. OF NEVADA, LAS VEGAS
www.nscee.edu/unlv/Colleges/Fine
Arts/Architecture
School of Architecture
4905 Maryland Parkway
Box 454018
Las Vegas, NV 89154
(702) 895-3031
M. Arch

UNIVERSITY OF NEW MEXICO
www.unm.edu/~saap
School of Architecture and Planning
2414 Central Avenue, SE
Albuquerque, NM 87131
(505) 277-3133
M. Arch

UNIVERSITY OF NORTH CAROLINA
AT CHARLOTTE
www.coa.uncc.edu
College of Architecture
9201 University City Boulevard
Charlotte, NC 28223-0001
(704) 547-2358
B. Arch

UNIVERSITY OF NOTRE DAME
www.nd.edu/~arch
School of Architecture
110 Bond Hall
Notre Dame, IN 46556-5652
(219) 631-6137
B. Arch, M. Arch

UNIVERSITY OF OKLAHOMA
www.ou.edu/architecturo/darch
Division of Architecture
Gould Hall, Room 162
830 Van Vleet Oval
Norman, OK 73019-0265
(405) 325-3990
B. Arch, M. Arch

UNIVERSITY OF OREGON
http://architecture.uoregon.edu/windex.html
Department of Architecture
School of Architecture and Allied Arts
1206 University of Oregon
Eugene, OR 97403-1206
(541) 346-3656
B. Arch, M. Arch

Architecture Degree Programs (Con't)

UNIVERSITY OF PENNSYLVANIA
www.upenn.edu/gsfa
Department of Architecture
Graduate School of Fine Arts
207 Meyerson Hall
Philadelphia, PA 19104-6311
(215) 898-5728
M. Arch

UNIVERSITY OF PUERTO RICO
Escuela de Arquitectura
P.O. Box 21909, UPR Station
San Juan, PR 00931
(787) 250-8581
M. Arch

UNIVERSITY OF SOUTH FLORIDA
www.arch.usf.edu
School of Arch. & Community Design
3702 Spectrum Blvd., Suite 180
Tampa, FL 33612
(813) 974-4031
M. Arch

UNIV. OF SOUTHERN CALIFORNIA
www.usc.edu/dept/architecture
School of Architecture
Los Angeles, CA 90089-0291
(213) 740-2723
B. Arch

UNIVERSITY OF SOUTHWESTERN
LOUISIANA
http://scholar5.usl.edu/architecture/index
.html
School of Architecture
College of the Arts
Lafayette, LA 70504-3850
(318) 482-6225
B. Arch

UNIV. OF TENNESSEE, KNOXVILLE
http://www.arch.utk.edu
School of Architecture
1715 Volunteer Boulevard
Knoxville, TN 37996-2400
(423) 974-5265
B. Arch, M. Arch

UNIV. OF TEXAS AT ARLINGTON
www.uta.edu/architecture
School of Architecture
Arlington, TX 76019-0108
(817) 272-2801
M. Arch

UNIVERSITY OF TEXAS AT AUSTIN
www.ar.utexas.edu
School of Architecture
Goldsmith Hall
Austin, TX 78712
(512) 471-1922
B. Arch, M. Arch

UNIV. OF TEXAS AT SAN ANTONIO
http://www.utsa.edu/Academics/COFA
H/DAID/index.html
Division of Arch. & Interior Design
6900 North Loop 1604 West
San Antonio, TX 78249-0642
(210) 458-4299
Candidate for M. Arch

UNIVERSITY OF UTAH
www.arch.utah.edu
Graduate School of Architecture
Salt Lake City, UT 84112
(801) 581-8254
M. Arch

UNIVERSITY OF VIRGINIA
www.virginia.edu/~arch
School of Architecture
Campbell Hall
Charlottesville, VA 22903
(804) 924-3715
M. Arch

Did you know...
No building of the Empire State Building's magnitude has been able to match its 1930-1 construction speed of 410 days.

Architecture Degree Programs (Con't)

UNIVERSITY OF WASHINGTON
www.arch.washington.edu/HTML/ARCH
Department of Architecture
Box 355720
Seattle, WA 98195-5720
(206) 543-4180
M. Arch

UNIV. OF WISCONSIN-MILWAUKEE
www.sarup.uwm.edu
School of Arch. & Urban Planning
P.O. Box 413
Milwaukee, WI 53201
(414) 229-4016
M. Arch

VIRGINIA POLYTECHNIC
INSTITUTE AND STATE UNIVERSITY
www.caus.vt.edu
College of Arch. & Urban Studies
202 Cowgill Hall
Blacksburg, VA 24061-0205
(540) 231-6416
B. Arch, M. Arch

WASHINGTON STATE UNIVERSITY
www.arch.wsu.edu
School of Architecture
PO Box 642220
Pullman, WA 99164-2220
(509) 335-5539
B. Arch

WASHINGTON UNIVERSITY
www.arch.wustl.edu
School of Architecture
Campus Box 1079
#1 Brookings Drive
St. Louis, MO 63130-4899
(314) 935-6200
M. Arch

WENTWORTH INST. OF TECH.
www.wit.edu
Department of Architecture
550 Huntington Avenue
Boston, MA 02115
(617) 989-4450
B. Arch

WOODBURY UNIVERSITY
www.woodburyu.edu
Architecture Department
School of Architecture & Design
7500 Glenoaks Boulevard
Burbank, CA 91510-7846
(818) 767-0888
B. Arch

YALE UNIVERSITY
http://130.132.126.39/default.html
School of Architecture
180 York Street
New Haven, CT 06520
(203) 432-2288
M. Arch

Source: National Architectural Accrediting Board

Did you know...
**Ideas for a tunnel under
the English Channel have
been bounced around for
nearly 200 years, but were
rejected by Britain for
national security reasons.
Digging on tunnel projects
began in the 1870s, 1880s,
and 1973 before work on
the Chunnel began in the
late 1980s.**

Architecture History Degree Programs

The following schools offer graduate degree programs in Architecture History with their specific areas of concentration indicated in parenthesis. No accreditation board exists for Architecture History. However, the following schools are subject to state and regional accreditation procedures. Consult the individual schools for their current accreditation status.

BOSTON UNIVERSITY
http://www.bu.edu/AH
Department of Art History
College of Liberal Arts
725 Commonwealth Avenue
Boston, MA 02215
(617) 353-2520
M.A., Ph.D. in Art History
(Ancient, Medieval, Renaissance, 19th Century, European, Modern, American, Asian, Historic Preservation, Museum Studies)

BROWN UNIVERSITY
www.brown.edu
Graduate Program in Art History
Dept. of History of Art and Architecture
64 College Street, Box 1855
Providence, RI 02912
(401) 863-1174
M.A., Ph.D. in Art History
(Classical, Medieval, Renaissance, Baroque, 19th and 20th Century American)

CITY UNIVERSITY OF NEW YORK
http://web.gc.cuny.edu/dept/arthi/arthist.htm
Graduate School and University Center
Department of Art History
33 West 42nd Street
New York, NY 10036
(212) 642-2865
Ph.D. in Art History
(17th to 20th Century European, American)

COLUMBIA UNIVERSITY
www.columbia.edu/
Graduate School of Architecture, Planning, and Preservation
400 Avery Hall
New York, NY 10027
(212) 854-3414
M.Phil., Ph.D. in Arch. Hist. and Theory
(Architecture and Urbanism, with particular emphasis on the period from 1850 to the present)

COLUMBIA UNIVERSITY
www.columbia.edu/
Dept. of Art History and Archaeology
Graduate School of Arts and Sciences
826 Schermerhorn Hall
New York, NY 10027
(212) 854-4505
M.A., M.Phil., Ph.D. in Art History
(Ancient Near East, Classical, Medieval, Renaissance, Baroque, 19th and 20th Century, American, Far Eastern, Pre-Columbian, Oceanic, Native American)

A chair is a very difficult object. A skyscraper is almost easier. That is why Chippendale is famous.

Mies van der Rohe

Architecture History Degree Programs (Con't)

CORNELL UNIVERSITY
www.cornell.edu
Graduate Field of Architecture
History of Architecture and Urbanism
College of Arch., Art, and Planning
140 East Sibley Hall
Ithaca, NY 14853
(607) 255-7439
M.A., Ph.D. in History of Arch. and
Urbanism (Ancient, Medieval,
Renaissance, Baroque, 18th-20th
Century European, American, Theory
and Criticism, Methodology,
Historiography, European and
American Landscape)

FLORIDA STATE UNIVERSITY
www.fsu.edu
Department of Art History
220-D Fine Arts Building
Tallahassee, FL 32306-1151
(850) 644-1250
M.A., Ph.D. in Art History
(Ancient, Byzantine, Medieval,
Renaissance, Baroque, Modern,
American, and Far Eastern)

GEORGE WASHINTON UNIVERSITY
www.gwu.edu
Dept. of American Studies
2108 G Street NW
Washington, DC 20052
202.994.6070
M.A., Ph.D.
(Architecture, Urban History, Folklife,
Historic Preservation, Decorative Arts,
Material Culture)

GEORGIA INSTITUTE OF TECH.
www.arch.gatech.edu/
College of Architecture
Atlanta, GA 30332-0155
(404) 894-3476
M.S., Ph.D.
(History, Theory, and Criticism)

HARVARD UNIVERSITY
www.harvard.edu
Department of Fine Arts
Sackler Museum
Cambridge, MA 02138
(617) 495-2377
Ph.D. in Art History
(Ancient (Classical and Near East),
Byzantine, Medieval, Renaissance,
Baroque, Modern, American, Islamic,
Indian, Chinese, Japanese, African)

HARVARD UNIVERSITY
www.harvard.edu
Graduate School of Design
48 Quincy Street
Cambridge, MA 02138
(617) 495-2337
Ph.D. in Architecture, Landscape
Architecture, and Urban Planning
(History and Theory of Modern
Architecture and Urbanism; Medieval,
Renaissance, and Baroque)

MASSACHUSETTS INSTITUTE OF
TECHNOLOGY
http://web.mit.edu/htc/www/
School of Architecture and Planning
Department of Architecture
History, Theory and Criticism Section
77 Massachusetts Avenue
Buildings 10-303 and 3-303/3-305
Cambridge, MA 02139-4307
(617) 258-8438, (617) 258-8439
Ph.D., S.M.Arch.S.
(History, Theory and Criticism of Art,
Architecture and Urban Form;
Renaissance and Baroque-Modern
International; Islamic)

Architecture History Degree Programs (Con't)

MCGILL UNIVERSITY
www.mcgill.ca/arch/
School of Architecture
815 Sherbrooke Street West
Montreal, Quebec
Canada H3A 2K6
(514) 398-6700
M.Arch., and Ph.D. (ad hoc)
(Within the graduate program in
Housing, the Domestic Environments
option includes the history of housing,
material culture of home, and vernacular architecture studies.)

NEW YORK UNIVERSITY
www.nyu.edu/gsas/dept/fineart/
Institute of Fine Arts
1 East 78th Street
New York, NY 10021
(212) 772-5800
M.A., Ph.D. in Art History
(Ancient, Medieval, Renaissance,
Baroque, Modern American)

NORTHWESTERN UNIVERSITY
www.cas.nwu.edu/ug/intro/arthist.html
Department of Art History
254 Kresge Hall
1859 Sheridan Road
Evanston, IL 60208-2208
(847) 491-3230
Ph.D. in Art History (Medieval,
Renaissance, Baroque, 19th Century
European and American, 20th Century
European and American, African, Asian)

OHIO STATE UNIVERSITY
http://vrl3.arts.ohio-state.edu/history_of_art/
Department of Art History
College of the Arts
100 Hayes Hall
108 North Oval Mall
Columbus, OH 43210
(614) 292-7481
M.A., Ph.D. in Art History
(Ancient, Medieval, Islamic)

PENNSYLVANIA STATE UNIVERSITY
www.psu.edu/dept/arthistory/
Department of Art History
College of Arts And Architecture
229 Arts Building
University Park, PA 16802
(814) 865-6326
M.A., Ph.D. in Art History
(Ancient, Medieval, Renaissance,
Baroque, Modern, American)

PRINCETON UNIVERSITY
http://www.princeton.edu/~artarch/
Department of Art and Archaeology
Princeton, NJ 08544
(609) 258-3781
Ph.D. in Art History
(Ancient, Medieval, Byzantine,
Renaissance, Baroque, 19th and 20th
Century European and American)

PRINCETON UNIVERSITY
http://www.princeton.edu/~soa
School of Architecture/Architecture Bldg.
Princeton, NJ 08544
(609) 258-3741
Ph.D. in Architecture
(History, Theory and Criticism of
Architecture, Urbanism, Landscape and
Building Technology)

Did you know...
**I.M. Pei's Phase II addi-
tion to the Louvre muse-
um in Paris included
development of an innova-
tive skylight system which
filters out UV light while
directing natural light to
the walls.**

Architecture History Degree Programs (Con't)

RUTGERS UNIVERSITY
http://arthistory.rutgers.edu/index.html
Dept. of Art History
Voorhees Hall
71 Hamilton Street
New Brunswick, NJ 08903
(732) 932.7041
M.A., Ph.D. in Art History
(Ancient, Medieval, Renaissance,
Baroque, Modern, Non-Western)

SAVANNAH COLLEGE OF ART
AND DESIGN
www.scad.edu
Department of Architectural History
P.O. Box 3146
Savannah, GA 31402-3146
(912) 525-6055
M.A., M.F.A. in Architectural History
(Modern, American, Vernacular,
Medieval, Renaissance, Islamic, History
of Architectural Theory, History of
Urbanism)

STANFORD UNIVERSITY
www.stanford.edu/dept/art
Art History Division/Art Department
Stanford, CA 94305-2018
(415) 723-3404
Ph.D. in Art History (Ancient,
Medieval, Renaissance-Baroque,
Modern, American, Asian, European,
Russian, Photography, Film Studies)

STATE UNIVERSITY OF NEW YORK
AT BINGHAMTON
http://arthist.binghamton.edu/
Department of Art and Art History
Binghamton, NY 13901
(607) 777-2111
M.A., Ph.D. in History and Theory of
Art and Architecture
(Medieval, Renaissance, Baroque,
Modern, American, Colonialism and
Urban Development)

SYRACUSE UNIVERSITY
www.hl.syr.edu/depts/fia.html
Department of Fine Arts in cooperation
with the School of Architecture
College of Arts and Sciences
308 Bowne Hall
Syracuse, NY 13244-1200
(315) 443-4184
M.A. in Art History (Medieval,
Renaissance, Baroque, American)

UNIVERSITY OF CALIFORNIA AT
BERKELEY
www.ced.berkeley.edu/arch
Department of Architecture
College of Environmental Design
232 Wurster Hall
Berkeley, CA 94720-1800
(510) 642-5577
M.S. and Ph.D. in Architecture
(Renaissance, Baroque, Islamic, Meso-
American, American, Vernacular, 19th
and 20th Centuries, Housing,
Urbanism, and Cultural Landscapes)

UNIVERSITY OF CALIFORNIA AT
LOS ANGELES
www.aud.ucla.edu
Department of Arch. and Urban Design
School of the Arts and Architecture
1317 Perloff Hall
Box 951467
Los Angeles, CA 90095-1465
(310) 825-7857
M.A., Ph.D. in Architecture
(Ancient, Medieval, Renaissance,
Baroque, 19th and 20th Century
Western, American, Near Eastern
(Islamic), Contemporary Theory)

Architecture History Degree Programs (Con't)

UNIVERSITY OF CALIFORNIA AT
SANTA BARBARA
www.arthistory.ucsb.edu/
History of Art and Architecture
College of Letters and Science
Santa Barbara, CA 93106-7080
(805) 893-2454
M.A., Ph.D. in Art History and
Architecture (Ancient, Pre-Columbian,
Medieval, Renaissance, Baroque,
Modern, American, Islamic, African,
North American Indian, Indonesian,
Oceanic, Asian, Theory)

UNIVERSITY OF CHICAGO
http://humanities.uchicago.edu/art/
Department of Art History
Cochrane-Woods Art Center
5540 South Greenwood Avenue
Chicago, IL 60637
(773) 702-0278
M.A., Ph.D. in Art History
(Asian, Classical, Medieval,
Renaissance, Baroque, Modern, Theory,
Criticism and Historiography)

UNIVERSITY OF DELAWARE
http://Seurat.art.udel.edu/ArtHistHP.HTML
Department of Art History
318 Old College
Newark, DE 19716
(302) 831-8415
M.A., Ph.D. in Art History
(Ancient, Medieval, Renaissance,
Baroque, 18th and 19th Century,
Modern, American)

UNIVERSITY OF COLORADO AT
DENVER
www.cudenver.edu/public/AandP
Department of Architecture and
Department of Planning and Design
College of Architecture and Planning
Boulder, CO 80309
Boulder site: (303) 492-7711
Denver site: (303) 556-4866
M.Arch., M.U.R.P., M.L.A., Ph.D.
(History, Theory, and Criticism of the
Built Environment; Design and
Planning Processes and Practices; Land
Use and Environmental Planning and
Design)

UNIVERSITY OF ILLINOIS AT
CHICAGO
www.uic.edu
Department of Art History
College of Architecture and the Arts
935 West Harrison St., M/C 201
Chicago, IL 60680
(312) 996-3303
M.A. in Art History
(Pre-Columbian, Native American,
Asian, Medieval, Renaissance, Baroque,
18th-Century European, Modern,
American, Urbanism, Theory & Criticism)

UNIVERSITY OF ILLINOIS AT
URBANA-CHAMPAIGN
www.arch.uiuc.edu/
School of Architecture
Division of Arch. History and Pres.
611 East Lorado Taft Drive
Champaign, IL 61820-6921
(217) 333-1330
M.Arch.

Architecture History Degree Programs (Con't)

UNIVERSITY OF ILLINOIS AT
URBANA-CHAMPAIGN
www.art.uiuc.edu/
Art History Program
School of Art And Design
408 East Peabody Drive
Champaign, IL 61820-6921
(217) 333-1255
M.A., Ph.D.
(Ancient, Byzantine, Medieval,
Renaissance, Baroque, 19th Century
European, Modern, American, Urban
History)

UNIVERSITY OF IOWA
www.uiowa.edu/~art/
School of Art and Art History
Iowa City, IA 52242
(319) 335-1771
M.A., Ph.D. in Art History
(Ancient, Medieval, Renaissance,
Baroque, 19th Century European,
American, Oriental, Pre-Columbian
Mexico, Modern, African)

UNIVERSITY OF LOUISVILLE
www.louisville.edu/a-s/finearts/
Allen R. Hite Art Institute
Fine Arts Department
Louisville, KY 40292
(502) 852-5914/6794
M.A., Ph.D. in Art History
(Ancient, Medieval, Renaissance,
Baroque, Modern, American, Historic
Preservation)

UNIVERSITY OF MARYLAND
www.inform.umd.edu/ARTH
Department of Art History and
Archaeology
College Park, MD 20742
(301) 405-1487
M.A. and Ph.D

UNIVERSITY OF MARYLAND
www.inform.umd.edu/ARCH
School of Architecture
College Park, MD 20742
(301) 405-6284
M.Arch
(Greek, Roman, Byzantine, Latin
American, Italian Renaissance, Modern,
American)

UNIVERSITY OF MISSOURI-
COLUMBIA
www.missouri.edu/~ahawww/
Department of Art Hist. & Archaeology
109 Pickard Hall
Columbia, MO 65211
(573) 882-6711
M.A. and Ph.D. in Art History and
Archaeology
(Greek Art and Archaeology, Roman Art
and Archaeology, Medieval Art and
Archaeology, Renaissance Art, Europe
and American in the 17th through 20th
Centuries, American Material Culture,
Architectural History, Cultural Heritage
Studies and Historic Preservation)

UNIVERSITY OF NEW MEXICO
www.unm.edu/~finearts/
Department of Art and Art History
Albuquerque, NM 87131-1401
(505) 277-5861
M.A., M.F.A., Ph.D.
(Arts of the Americas, Arts of the
Modern Age)

Did you know...
**The Malpas tunnel in
Southwest France, com-
pleted in 1681, was the
first canal tunnel ever
built.**

Architecture History Degree Programs (Con't)

UNIVERSITY OF OREGON
http://aaa.uoregon.edu/~arthist/
Department of Art History
School of Architecture and Allied Arts
Eugene, OR 97405
(541) 346-3675
M.A., Ph.D. in Art History
(Ancient, Medieval, Renaissance,
Baroque, 19th Century European,
Modern, American, Preservation)

UNIVERSITY OF PENNSYLVANIA
www.arth.upenn.edu/arth
History of Art
3405 Woodland Walk
Philadelphia, PA 19104-6208
(215) 573-9702
M.A., Ph.D. in Art History
(Ancient Near East and Egypt, Greek,
Roman, Etruscan, Early Christian and
Byzantine, Medieval, Islamic, South
Asian, Italian Renaissance, Italian 17th
and 18th Centuries, Northern
Renaissance and Baroque, 19th and
20th Centuries, American)

UNIVERSITY OF PITTSBURGH
www.pitt.edu/~arthome/
Department of History of Art and Arch.
Faculty of Arts and Sciences
104 Frick Fine Arts Building
Pittsburgh, PA 15260
(412) 648-2400
M.A., Ph.D. in Art History
(Medieval, Renaissance, 19th-Century
European, Modern, American, Asian)

UNIVERSITY OF TEXAS AT AUSTIN
www.utexas.edu
Department of Art and Art History
College of Fine Arts
Austin, TX 78712
(512) 471-7757
M.A., Ph.D. in Art History; M.F.A. in
Studio Arts
(Pre-Columbian, Asian, Ancient,
Medieval, Renaissance, Baroque, 19th
and 20th Century European, American)

UNIVERSITY OF TEXAS AT AUSTIN
www.ar.utexas.edu/
School of Architecture
Goldsmith Hall, Room 2.308
Austin, TX 78712
(512) 471-1922
M.S.A.S. in History/Theory, Ph.D. in
Architecture
(Urban Design, Design, Historical
Preservation, Design with Climate,
History and Theory)

UNIVERSITY OF VIRGINIA
www.virginia.edu
Department of Architectural History
School of Architecture
Campbell Hall
Charlottesville, VA 22903
(804) 924-1428
M. of Architectural History, Ph.D. in
Architectural History
(Ancient, Renaissance, Baroque,
Modern, American, Chinese,
Preservation, Architectural Theory)

Did you know...
**For every 10 pounds of
metal produced today, nine
pounds are steel.**

Architecture History Degree Programs (Con't)

UNIVERSITY OF WASHINGTON
http://net.art.washington.edu/
Departments of Art History and Arch.
Box 353440
Seattle, WA 98195
(206) 543-4876
M.Arch. (Department of Architecture)
M.A. and Ph.D., Architectural History
(Division of Art History);
(Medieval, Classical, African, Oceanic,
East Asian, 18th-, 19th- and 20th-
Century European and American,
Washington State Architecture,
Baroque, Theory and Criticism, Historic
Preservation, Landscape Architecture,
Urban Design)

UNIVERSITY OF WISCONSIN-
MADISON
www.wisc.edu
Department of Art History
232 Elvehjem Museum
Madison, WI 53706
(608) 263-2340
M.A., Ph.D. in Art History
(Ancient, Medieval, Modern American)

VIRGINIA COMMONWEALTH
UNIVERSITY
www.vcu.edu/artweb/History
Department of Art History
School of the Arts, Box 843046
922 West Franklin Street
Richmond, VA 23284-3046
(804) 828-2784
M.A., Ph.D. in Art History
(Renaissance, Baroque, 19th and 20th
Centuries, Latin American)

YALE UNIVERSITY
www.yale.edu
Department of Art History
Box 2009, 56 High Street
New Haven, CT 06520
(203) 432-2667
Ph.D. in Art History
(Chinese, Japanese, Medieval, Baroque,
Architecture, Renaissance, African-
American, Roman, Modern, Pre-
Columbian)

Source: Society of Architectural Historians

Did you know...
Congress originally founded the Army Corps of Engineers in 1795 for the purpose of planning and building defensive projects. West Point quickly developed as a top engineering school, and by the 1820's the Corps' duties had significantly expanded

Historic Preservation Degree Programs

The following schools offer a variety of degree programs in historic preservation at the certificate, associate, undergraduate, and graduate levels. The diversity of the programs ranges between rural and urban preservation, restoration and administration, archaeology and architecture history, and many others. In addition, some schools only offer allied degrees with a specialization in or a program emphasis on historic preservation. For additional information about each program, contact the individual schools.

ARMSTRONG ATLANTIC STATE
UNIVERSITY
www.armstrong.edu
Public History Program
Savannah, GA 31419
Telephone: (800) 633-2349 or
(912) 927-5277
M.A. History w/specialization in Public
History

BALL STATE UNIVERSITY
www.bsu.edu/cap/arch/arch.html
Historic Preservation Program
College of Architecture and Planning
Muncie, IN 47306-0350
Telephone: (765) 285-1920
M.S. in Historic Preservation

BELMONT TECHNICAL COLLEGE
Building Preservation Technology
120 Fox-Shannon Place
St. Clairsville, OH 43950-9766
Telephone: (614) 695-9500 ext. 48
A.A.S. in Building Preservation
Technology

BOSTON UNIVERSITY
http://web.bu.edu/psp/
Preservation Studies Program
226 Bay State Road
Boston, MA 02215
Telephone: (617) 353-2000
M.A. in Historic Preservation

BUCKS COUNTY COMMUNITY
COLLEGE
www.bucks.edu/catalog/3127.html
Historic Preservation Program
Newton, PA 18940
Telephone: (215) 968-8286
Historic Preservation Certificate

COLLEGE OF THE REDWOODS
www.redwoods.cc.ca.us/
Business & Applied Techonology
7351 Thompkins Hill Road
Eureaka, CA 95501
Telephone: (707) 445-6900
Historic Pres. and Restoration Certificate

COLORADO STATE UNIVERSITY
www.colostate.edu/Depts/Hist/
Department of History
Fort Collins, CO 80523
Telephone: (970) 491-6334
M.A. in History w/ HP specialization

Historic Preservation Degree Programs (Con't)

COLUMBIA UNIVERSITY
www.columbia.edu
Graduate School of Arch & Planning
Historic Preservation Program
400 Avery Hall
New York, NY 10027
Telephone: (212) 854-3518
M.S. in Historic Preservation

CORNELL UNIVERSITY
www.cornell.edu
Graduate Program in HP Planning
106 W. Sibley Hall
Ithaca, NY 14853
Telephone: (607) 255-7261
M.A. and Ph.D. in Historic Preservation
Planning

EASTERN MICHIGAN UNIVERSITY
www.emich.edu
Historic Preservation Program
Dept. of Geography & Geology
233 Strong Hall
Ypsilanti, MI 48197
Telephone: (734) 487-0232
M.S. in Historic Preservation
w/Certificate in HP Studies

GEORGE WASHINGTON UNIVERSITY
www.gwu.edu/~csas/amcv.html
Graduate Program in Hist. Preservation
American Studies Program
Washington, D.C. 20052
Telephone: (202) 994-1000
M.A. and Ph.D. History/Amer. Civ.

GEORGIA STATE UNIVERSITY
www.gsu.edu
College of Arts & Sciences
Department of History
Heritage Preservation Program
Atlanta, GA 30303
Telephone: (404) 651-2250
M. in Heritage Preservation

GOUCHER COLLEGE
www.goucher.edu
Historic Preservation Program
Baltimore, MD 21204
Telephone: (410) 337-6200
B.A and M.A. in Historic Preservation

HARRISBURG AREA COMMUNITY
COLLEGE
www.hacc.edu
Technical Institute
One HACC Drive
Harrisburg, PA 17110
Telephone: (717) 780-2300
Historic Preservation Diploma

KANSAS STATE UNIVERSITY
www.ksu.edu
Dept. of Architecture
211 Seaton Hall
Manhattan, KS 66506
Telephone: (913) 532-1103
M.Arch., M.L.A., and M.R.C.P. w/HP
specialization

KENT STATE UNIVERSITY
www.saed.kent.edu
School of Architecture and Design
Kent, OH 44242
Telephone: (330) 672-2789
M.Arch w/HP specialization

LOUISIANA STATE UNIVERSITY
www.lsu.edu
136 Atkinson Hall
Baton Rouge, LA 70803
Telephone: (504) 388-6885
M. Arch. w/HP specialization

The sun never knew how great it was until it struck the side of a building.

Louis Kahn

Historic Preservation Degree Programs (Con't)

MARY WASHINGTON COLLEGE
www.mwc.edu
Dept. of Historic Preservation
Fredericksburg, VA 22401
Telephone: (540) 654-1000
B.A. in Historic Preservation

MICHIGAN STATE UNIVERSITY
www.msu.edu
Dept. of Human Environment and
Design
204 Human Ecology
East Lansing, MI 48824
Telephone: (517) 353-5232
M.A. Interior Design and Facilities
Mgmt. w/ HP specialization

MICHIGAN STATE UNIVERSITY
www.msu.edu
Urban and Regional Planning Program
201 UPLA Bldg.
East Lansing, MI 48824
Telephone: (517) 353-9054
M.U.R.P. w/HP specialization

MICHIGAN TECHNOLOGICAL
UNIVERSITY
www.mtu.edu
Department of Social Sciences
1400 Townsend Drive
Houghton, MI 49931
Telephone: (906) 487-2070
M.S. Industrial Archaeology

MIDDLE TENNESSEE STATE
UNIVERSITY
www.mtsu.edu/~history/pubhist.htm
Public History/Pres. History Prog.
Murfreesboro, TN 37132
Telephone: (615) 898-2300
M.A. and D.A. in Historic Preservation

NORTHERN ARIZONA UNIVERSITY
www.nau.edu
Department of Anthropology
Flagstaff, AZ 86001
Telephone: (520) 523-9011
M. A. Anthropology

OHIO STATE UNIVERSITY
www.arch.ohio-state.edu/
Department of Architecture
190 W. 17th Avenue
Columbus, OH 43210
Telephone: (614) 292-OHIO
M.Arch

OKLAHOMA STATE UNIVERSITY
http://history.okstate.edu/
Applied History Program
501-H Life Sciences W. Building
Stillwater, OK 74078-0611
Telephone: (405) 744-5678
M.A. in History w/HP specialization

PRATT INSTITUTE
www.pratt.edu/arch/gcpe/index.html
Center for Planning and the
Environment
200 Willoughby Avenue
Brooklyn, NY 11205
Telephone: (718) 399-4391
M.S. City and Regional Planning w/ HP
Planning Certificate

Did you know...
The 1697 Frankford Avenue Bridge, which crosses Pennypack Creek in Philadelphia, is the oldest U.S. bridge in continuous use.

Historic Preservation Degree Programs (Con't)

ROGER WILLIAMS UNIVERSITY
www.rwu.edu
Center for Hist. Preservation
Bristol, RI 02809
Telephone: (401) 253-1040
B.S. in Historic Preservation

SAVANNAH COLLEGE OF ART AND
DESIGN
www.scad.edu/
Historic Preservation Dept.
Savannah, GA 31401
Telephone: (912) 238-2400
B.F.A., M.F.A.

SCHOOL OF THE ART INSTITUTE
OF CHICAGO
www.artic.edu
Historic Preservation Program
37 S. Wabash Ave.
Chicago, IL 60603
Telephone: (312) 629-6500
M.S.H.P

SHELDON STATE COMMUNITY
COLLEGE
202 Skyland Blvd.
Tuscaloosa, AL 35405
Historic Preservation Certificate

S.E. MISSOURI STATE UNIVERSITY
www.semo.edu
HP Program. Dept. of History
One University Plaza
Cape Girardeau, MO 63701
Telephone: (573) 651-2831
B.S. in Historic Preservation
M.A. in History w/ HP emphasis

TEXAS A&M UNIVERSITY
http://archone.tamu.edu/
College of Architecture
College Station, TX 77843-3137
Telephone: (409) 845-3211
M.Arch, M.Land Arch., M.U.P, M.S.

TEXAS TECH UNIVERSITY
www.ttu.edu
School of Architecture
Box 42091
Lubbock, TX 79409-2091
Telephone: (806) 742-3136
M.S. in Architecture

UNIVERSITY OF ARKANSAS
www.uair.edu
Department of History
Public History Program
Little Rock, AK 72202-1099
Telephone: (501) 569-8395
M.A. in History w/ HP specialization

UNIVERSITY OF CALIFORNIA
www.ucracl.ucr.edu
History Department
Riverside, CA 92521
Telephone: (909) 787-5401 x1437
M.A in History w/HP specialization

UNIVERSITY OF CALIFORNIA
www.arthistory.ucsb.edu/
Department of History
Public History Program
Santa Barbara, CA 93106
Telephone: (805) 893-8710
M.A., Ph.D. in Public History

UNIVERSITY OF CINCINNATI
www.geography.uc.edu/
Department of Geography
Cincinnati, OH 45221-0131
Telephone: (513) 556-6000
B.A., M.A., Ph.D. w/ HP specialization

UNIVERSITY OF DELAWARE
www.udel.edu
Center for Historic Arch. and Design
Newark, DE 19711
Telephone: (302) 831-1050
M.A., Ph.D. w/HP specialization

Historic Preservation Degree Programs (Con't)

UNIVERSITY OF FLORIDA
www.arch.ufl.edu/
Dept. of Architecture
Gainesville, Fl 32611
Telephone: (352) 392-3261
M.Arch

UNIVERSITY OF GEORGIA
www.uga.edu
Graduate Studies in Hist. Pres.
Caldwell Hall
Athens, GA 30602
Telephone: (706) 542-3000
M. in Historic Preservation
Certificate in Historic Pres.
J.D/M.H.P

UNIVERSITY OF HAWAII, MANOA
www.hawaii.edu
Historic Preservation Program
Dept. of American Studies
1890 East West Road
Honolulu, HI 96822
Telephone: (808) 956-9546
M.A. and Ph.D. in American Studies
w/HP Certificate

UNIVERSITY OF ILLINOIS
www.urban.uiuc.edu/
Urban and Regional Planning
611 Taft Drive
Champaign, IL 61820
Telephone: (217) 333-3890
B.A.U.P., M.A.U.P., Ph.D. w/HP
Certificate

UNIVERSITY OF KENTUCKY
www.uky.edu/Architecture/
M.A. in Historic Preservation
Graduate Program in Hist. Pres.
Lexington, KY 40506-0041
Telephone: (606) 257-7372
M.A. in HP

UNIVERSITY OF MARYLAND
www.inform.umd.edu/arch/
HISP Program
School of Architecture
College Park, MD 20742
Telephone: (310) 405-1000
HP Certificate

UNIVERSITY OF MISSOURI
www.missouri.edu
Dept. of Art and Archaeology
Columbia, OH 65211
Telephone: (573) 882-0176
M.A. in Art History, History,
Environmental Design

UNIVERSITY OF NEVADA
www.unr.edu
Historic Preservation Program
Reno, NV 89557
Telephone: (573) 882-2121
B.A. and M.A. w/HP specialization

UNIVERSITY OF NEW ORLEANS
www.uno.edu
College of Urban and Public Affairs
New Orleans, LA 70148
Telephone: (504) 280-6277
M.U.R.P., M.S., M.P.A, Ph.D. in Urban
Studies w/HP Certificate

Did you know...
The Massachusetts Institute of Technology (1865), University of Illinois (1867), and Cornell University (1871) were the first three universities in America to teach architecture.

Historic Preservation Degree Programs (Con't)

UNIVERSITY OF OREGON
http://darkwing.uoregon.edu/~uopubs/
bulletin/aaa/index.html
Historic Preservation Program
Eugene, OR 97403
Telephone: (541) 346-3631
M.S. in Historic Preservation

UNIVERSITY OF PENNSYLVANIA
www.upenn.edu/
Grad. Program in Hist. Pres.
115 Meyerson Hall
Philadelphia, PA 19104
Telephone: (215) 898-5000
M.S. w/ Hist. Pres. Certificate
Ph.D. Arch/City Planning

UNIVERSITY OF SOUTH CAROLINA
www.sc.edu
Applied History Program
Dept. of History
Columbia, SC 29208
Telephone: (803) 777-7000
M.A. in Applied History
Ph.D. in History

UNIVERSITY OF TENNESSEE
www.arch.utk.edu/
College of Arch. and Planning
1715 Volunteer Blvd.
Knoxville, TN 37996
Telephone: (423) 974-3272
B. Arch., B. Interior Design, M. Comm.
Planning

UNIVERSITY OF TEXAS
www.ar.utexas.edu/
School of Architecture
Historic Preservation
Austin, TX 78713
Telephone: (512) 471-1922
M. Arch., M.S. Arch., M. Urban
Planning

UNIVERSITY OF UTAH
www.utah.edu
Graduate School of Architecture
Rm 235 AAC
Salt Lake City, UT 84112
Telephone: (801) 581-7200
M.S. in Historic Preservation

UNIVERSITY OF VERMONT
www.uvm.edu/~histpres
Historic Preservation Program
213 Wheeler House
Burlington, VT 05405
Telephone: (802) 656-3180
M.S. in Historic Preservation

UNIVERSITY OF VIRGINIA
http://minerva.acc.virginia.edu/~arch/
Historic Preservation Program
School of Architecture
Charlottesville, VA 22903
Telephone: (804) 924-3715
M.A. Arch. History, M.U.P., M.L.A., M.
Arch. w/HP Certificate

UNIVERSITY OF WASHINGTON
www.u.washington.edu
Pres. Planning and Design Program
Box 355740
Seattle, WA 98195
Telephone: (206) 543-2100
M. Arch., M.L.A., M.U.P., Ph.D., Pres.
Planning & Design Certificate

WESTERN KENTUCKY UNIVERSITY
www.wku.edu
Programs in Fold Studies
Bowling Green, KY 42101
Telephone: (502) 745-5898
M.A. in Folk Studies w/HP specialization

Historic Preservation Degree Programs (Con't)

UNIVERSITY OF WISCONSIN
www.wisc.edu/grad/gs/programs/majors
/594.html
Dept of Landscape Architecture
25 Agricultural Hall
Madison, WI 53703
Telephone: (608) 263-7301
M.S. and M.A. in Land. Arch.

UNIVERSITY OF WISCONSIN
www.uwm.edu
Preservation Studies Program
School of Architecure
Milwaukee, WI 53201
Telephone: (414) 229-6385
M. of Architecture w/HP Certificate

YOUNGSTOWN STATE UNIVERSITY
www.ysu.edu
Historic Preservation Program
Dept. of History
Youngstown, OH 44555
Telephone: (330) 742-3452
B.A. w. HP Certificate
M. in History w/ HP Certificate

*Source: National Council for Preservation Education/
National Trust for Historic Preservation*

Did you know...
**In 1998, the National
Trust for Historic
Preservation provided
$3.35 million in financial
assistance to 178 preserva-
tion projects in 41 states.**

Industrial Design Degree Programs

The following schools offer degree programs in Industrial Design. Although no specific accrediting body exists for Industrial Design, those schools marked with an asterisk (*) have been evaluated and accredited using the standards and guidelines adopted by the National Association of Schools of Art & Design (NASAD) and formalized by the 1984 IDSA/ NASAD agreement. In addition, all of the schools listed here are subject to regional accreditation procedures and have been accredited by a body sanctioned by the U.S. Department of Education to confer a Bachelors or higher degree. As this information is constantly changing, checking with the individual schools is strongly encouraged.

ARIZONA STATE UNIVERSITY
www.asu.edu/caed/
School of Design
Tempe, AZ 85287-2105
(602) 965-4135
BS, MS, Ph.D.

ART CENTER COLLEGE OF DESIGN*
www.artcenter.edu
1700 Lida St. Box 7197
Pasadena, CA 91103-7197
(626) 396-2200
BS, MS

ART INSTITUTE OF FORT LAUDERDALE*
www.aifl.aii.edu
1799 SE 17th Street
Fort Lauderdale, FL 33316-3000
(954) 463-3000
BS

AUBURN UNIVERSITY*
www.auburn.edu/ind/
Dept. of Industrial Design
103 Smith Hall
Auburn, AL 36849-5125
(334) 844-2364
BID, MID

BRIGHAM YOUNG UNIVERSITY*
www.byu.edu
210 BRMD, P.O. Box 22500
Provo, UT 84602-2500
(801) 378-2064
BFA

CALIFORNIA COLLEGE OF ARTS & CRAFTS*
www.ccacsf.edu
450 Irwin Stree at Wisconsin
San Francisco, CA 94103
(415)703-9500
BFA

CALIFORNIA STATE UNIVERSITY - LONG BEACH*
www.csulb.edu/~design/
Dept of Design-1250 Bellflower
Long Beach, CA 90840-3501
(562) 985-5089
BS, MA

CALIFORNIA STATE UNIVERSITY - NORTHRIDGE*
www.csulb.edu/~design/
Dept of Visual Arts/I.D.
18111 Nordhoff St.
Northridge, CA 91330-8300
(818) 677-2242
BS

Industrial Design Degree Programs (Con't)

CARNEGIE-MELLON UNIVERSITY*
www.csun.cdu
School of Design
110 Margaret Morrison
Pittsburgh, PA 15213-3890
(412) 268-1641
BFA, MDes

CENTER FOR CREATIVE STUDIES*
www.ccscad.edu/ccs/departments/deptid.html
245 East Kirby, Detroit, MI 48202-4034
(313) 664-7400
BFA

CLEVELAND INSTITUTE OF ART*
www.cia.edu/industrialdesign.html
11141 East Blvd.
Cleveland, OH 44106
(216) 421-7000
BFA

COLUMBUS COLLEGE OF
ART & DESIGN*
www.ccad.edu
107 N. Ninth St.,
Columbus, OH 43215-1758
(614) 224-9101 ext.3231
BFA

CRANBROOK ACADEMY OF ART*
www.cranbrookart.edu/index.cfm
P.O. Box 801,
1221 Woodward Ave.
Bloomfield Hills, MI 48303-0801
(248) 645-3300
MFA

GEORGIA INSTITUTE OF
TECHNOLOGY
www.arch.gatech.edu.id
School of Architecture
Industrial Design Program
Atlanta, GA 30332-0155
(404) 894-4874
BS, MS

ILLINOIS INSTITUTE OF
TECHNOLOGY
www.id.iit.edu
Institute of Design
350 North LaSalle St.
Chicago, IL 60616
(312) 595-4900
MDes

ITT TECHNICAL INSTITUTE
www.itttech.edu/teach/list/id/html
920 W. Levoy Drive
Murray, UT 84123
(801) 263-3313
BAS

ITT TECHNICAL INSTITUTE
www.itttech.edu/teach/list/id/html
630 East Brier Drive, Sta 150
San Bernardino,CA 92408
(909) 889-3800
BAS

ITT TECHNICAL INSTITUTE
www.itttech.edu/teach/list/id/html
4919 Coldwater Road
Fort Wayne, IN 47715-2340
(219) 484-4107
BAS

KANSAS CITY ART INSTITUTE*
www.kcai.edu
Design Department
4415 Warwick Blvd.
Kansas City, MO 64111-1874
(816) 472-4852
BFA

KENDALL COLLEGE OF ART &
DESIGN*
www.kcad.edu
111 N. Division
Grand Rapids, MI 49503-3102
(800) 676-2787
BFA

Industrial Design Degree Programs (Con't)

MASSACHUSETTS COLLEGE OF ART*
www.massart.edu
621 Huntington
Boston, MA 02115-5882
(617) 232-1550
BFA, MFA

METROPOLITAN STATE COLLEGE
OF DENVER
http://engrtec2.mscd.edu/its/
Campus Box 90, PO Box 173362
Denver, CO 80217-3362
(303) 556-3219
BA

MILWAUKEE INSTITUTE OF ART &
DESIGN*
www.miad.edu
273 E Erie St.
Milwaukee, WI 53202-6003
(414) 291-7889
BFA

NORTH CAROLINA STATE
UNIVERSITY
www.design.ncsu.edu
School of Design, Box 7701
Raleigh, NC 27695-7701
(919) 515-8322
BID, MID

OHIO STATE UNIVERSITY*
www.arts.ohio-state.edu/design/
Hopkins Hall, Room 380
128 North Oval Mall,
Columbus, OH 43210
(614) 292-6746
BS, MA

PARSONS SCHOOL OF DESIGN-
NEW YORK*
www.parsons.edu
2 W. 13th St., 3rd Floor
New York, NY 10011
(212) 229-5885
BFA

PRATT INSTITUTE*
www.pratt.edu
Industrial Design Dept.
200 Willoughby
Brooklyn, NY 11205
(718) 636-3631
BID, MID

PURDUE UNIVERSITY
www.sla.purdue.edu/academic/vpa/
Creative Arts Bldg #1
West Lafayette, IN 47907
(765) 494-2295
BA, MA

RHODE ISLAND SCHOOL OF
DESIGN*
www.risd.edu
2 College St.
Providence, RI 02903
(401) 454-6160
BFA, BID, MFA, MID

ROCHESTER INSTITUTE OF
TECHNOLOGY*
www/rit.edu/~651www/
Dept of Industrial Design,
James Booth Bldg.
P.O. Box 9887
Rochester, NY 14623-5603
(716) 475-2668
BFA, MFA

Did you know...
Carl Otto won a Medallion Award from the Industrial Designers Institute in 1951 for his design of the Schick "20" electric razor.

Industrial Design Degree Programs (Con't)

SAN FRANCISCO STATE
UNIVERSITY*
www.dia.sfsu.edu/dia_test/welcome.htm
Dept. of Design
1600 Holloway
San Francisco, CA 94132
(415) 338-2229
BA, MA, MFA

SAN JOSE STATE UNIVERSITY*
www.sjsu.edu/depts/art_design/
School of Art & Design
One Washington Sq.,
San Jose, CA 95192-0089
(408) 924-4343
BS, MA

SAVANNAH COLLEGE OF ART &
DESIGN
www.scad.edu
P.O. Box 3146
Savannah, GA 31402-3146
(912) 238-2402
BFA, MFA, MA

SOUTHERN ILLINOIS UNIVERSITY*
www.siu.edu/~artdesn/
School of Art & Design
Carbondale, IL 62901
(618) 453-4313
BA, BFA

STANFORD UNIVERSITY
www.stanford.edu
Design Dept., School of Art
Design Div. Terman 551
Stanford, CA 94305-4021
(415) 723-4288
BS, MS, MFA

SYRACUSE UNIVERSITY*
www.syr.edu
334 Smith Hall
Syracuse, NY 13210
(315) 443-2455
BID, MID

UNIVERSITY OF THE ARTS*
www.uarts.edu/colprog/pcad.id.html
ID Dept., 320 S. Broad St.,
Philadelphia, PA19102
(215) 875-1040
BS, MID

UNIVERSITY OF BRIDGEPORT*
www.bridgeport.edu
Dept. of Industrial Design
600 University Ave.,
Bridgeport, CT 06601
(203) 576-4222
BS

UNIVERSITY OF CINCINNATI*
www.daap.uc.edu/design/default.html
Dept of Industrial Design
PO Box 210016
Cincinnati, OH 45221-0016
(513) 556-6928
BS, MDes

UNIVERSITY OF ILLINOIS-CHICAGO*
www.uic.edu/aa/artd/id.html
106 Jefferson Hall
Chicago, IL 60607-7038
(312) 996-3337
BFA

UNIV. OF ILLINOIS-URBANA
CHAMPAIGN*
www.art.uiuc.edu/A&D/id.html
School of Art & Design
408 E. Peabody Dr.,
Champaign, IL 61820
(217) 333-6632
BFA, MFA

Industrial Design Degree Programs (Con't)

UNIVERSITY OF KANSAS*
www.ukans.edu/~sfa/html/department_
of_design.html
Art & Design Building #300
Lawrence, KS 66045
(913) 864-4401
BFA, MFA

UNIVERSITY OF MICHIGAN*
www.umich.edu/~inddes/
2000 Bonisteel Blvd.
Ann Arbor, MI 48105
(734) 764-0397
BFA, MFA, MA

UNIVERSITY OF NOTRE DAME
www.nd.edu/~art/departments/Design.html
Dept. Art, Art History & Design
Notre Dame, IN 46556
(219) 631-7602
BA, BFA, MFA

UNIVERSITY OF SOUTHWEST
LOUISIANA
www.asl.edu
P.O. Box 43850, Industrial Design
Program,
Lafayette, LA 70504-3850
(318) 482-6225
BID

UNIVERSITY OF WASHINGTON
http://net.art.washington.edu/
School of Art, Box 35-3440
Seattle, WA 98195-3440
(206) 543-0907
BFA, MFA

UNIVERSITY OF WISCONSIN-
STOUT*
www.uwstout.edu/admissions/artdes.html
Dept of Art & Design
Applied Arts Bldg.
Menomonie, WI 54751-0790
(715) 232-1097
BFA

VIRGINIA POLYTECHNIC
INSTITUTE
www.vt.edu
Industrial Design Program
Cowgill Hall
Blacksburg, VA 24061-0205
(540) 231-6386
BS

WENTWORTH INSTITUTE OF
TECHNOLOGY
www.wit.edu/Academics/catalog/Catalog
_INC.html
Design & Facilities/ I.D. Program
550 Huntington Ave.
Boston, MA 02115-5901
(617) 989-4590
BS

WESTERN MICHIGAN UNIVERSITY
www.wmich.edu
1201 Oliver St., Dept. CMD/ID
Kalamazoo, MI 49008-5064
(616) 387-6515
BS

WESTERN WASHINGTON
UNIVERSITY
www.wwu.edu
Dept of Tech
516 High St ET204
Bellingham, WA 98225
(360) 650-3425
BS

Source: Industrial Designers Society of America

Did you know...

Over 2.5 million rivets lock 12,000 individual pieces in place to form the Eiffel Tower.

Interior Design Degree Programs

The following schools offer accredited degree programs in Interior Design. The Foundation for Interior Design Education Research (FIDER) is the official accrediting body for higher education Interior Design programs. It is dedicated to advancing the profession by ensuring a consistently high level of quality in education for those entering the field. Accreditation status is an ongoing process and the below information is subject to change. To ensure accurate information consult the individual schools.

ACADEMY OF ART COLLEGE
Interior Architecture and Design
79 New Montgomery Street 6th Floor
San Francisco, CA 94105
(415) 274-2209
www.academyart.edu
Bachelor of Fine Arts, Interior Design

ALEXANDRIA TECHNICAL COLLEGE
Interior Design Program
Marketing Education
1601 Jefferson Street
Alexandria, MN 56308-3799
(320) 762-4497
http://alextech.org
Associate of Applied Science

AMERICAN INTERCONTINENTAL
UNIVERSITY
Interior Design Department
1651 Westwood Boulevard
Los Angeles, CA 90024
(310) 470-2000
www.aiuniv.edu
Bachelor of Fine Arts

AMERICAN INTERCONTINENTAL
UNIVERSITY
Interior Design Program
3330 Peachtree Road NE
Atlanta, GA 30326
(404) 231-9000
www.aiuniv.edu
Bachelor of Fine Arts in Interior Design

ARIZONA STATE UNIVERSITY
Interior Design Program
School of Design
College of Architecture and
Environmental Design
Tempe, AZ 85287-2105
(602) 965-4135
www.asu.edu
Bachelor of Science in Design

ART INSTITUTE OF ATLANTA
Interior Design Program
School of Design
6600 Peachtree Dunwoody Rd.
100 Embassy Row
Atlanta, Georgia 30328
(770) 394-8300
www.aia.aii.edu
Bachelor of Fine Arts in Interior Design

ATLANTA COLLEGE OF ART
Interior Design Program
1280 Peachtree Street NE
Atlanta, GA 30309
(404) 733-5160
www.aca.edu
Bachelor of Fine Arts in Interior Design

Did you know...
Women comprise 81% of all interior design professionals.

Interior Design Degree Programs (Con't)

AUBURN UNIVERSITY
Interior Design Program
School of Architecture
College of Arch., Design, & Const.
104 Dudley Hall
Auburn, AL 36849
(334) 844-4516
www.auburn.edu
Bachelor of Interior Design

AUBURN UNIVERSITY
Interior Environments Program
Department of Consumer Affairs
School of Human Sciences
160 Spidle Hall
Auburn, AL 36849
(334) 844-1334
www.auburn.edu
Bachelor of Science, Interior
Environments

BAUDER COLLEGE
Interior Design Department
3500 Peachtree Road NE
Atlanta, GA 30326
(404) 237-7573
www.bauder.edu
Associate of Arts in Interior Design

BERKELEY COLLEGE/BERGEN CAMPUS
Interior Design Program
100 West Prospect Street
Waldwick, NJ 07463
(201) 652-0388
www.berkeleycollege.edu
Associate in Applied Science

BRENAU UNIVERSITY
Interior Design Program
Department of Visual Arts
College of Arts and Sciences
One Centennial Circle
Gainesville, GA (305) 01
(770) 534-6240
www.brenau.edu
Bachelor of Fine Arts

BROOKS COLLEGE
Interior Design Program
4825 East Pacific Coast Highway
Long Beach, CA 90804
(562) 597-6611
www.brookscollege.edu
Associate of Arts in Interior Design

CALIFORNIA COLLEGE OF ARTS
AND CRAFTS
Interior Architecture Program
School of Architectural Studies
450 Irwin Street
San Francisco, CA 94107
(415) 703-9518
www.ccac-art.edu
BFA in Interior Design

CALIFORNIA STATE UNIVERSITY,
FRESNO
Interior Design Program
Department of Art and Design
5225 N Backer Avenue, Mail Stop 65
Fresno, CA 93740-8001
(209) 278-2516
www.csufresno.edu
Bachelor of Arts in Interior Design

CALIFORNIA STATE UNIVERSITY,
NORTHRIDGE
Dept. of Family Environmental Sciences
18111 Nordhoff Street – FES
Northridge, CA 91331-8308
(818) 677-3051
www.csun.edu
Bachelor of Science

CALIFORNIA STATE UNIVERSITY,
SACRAMENTO
Interior Design
Program of Design
School of Arts and Letters
6000 J Street
Sacramento, CA 95819
(916) 278-6375
www.csus.edu
Bachelor of Arts Interior Design

Interior Design Degree Programs (Con't)

THE COLLEGE OF NEW JERSEY
Interior Design Program
Art Department
P.O. Box 7718
Ewing, NJ 08628-0718
(609) 771-2320
www.tcnj.edu
Bachelor of Fine Arts/Interior Design

COLORADO STATE UNIVERSITY
Interior Design Program
Department of Design, Merchandising
& Consumer Sciences
College of Applied Human Sciences
154 Aylesworth S.E.
Fort Collins, CO 80523-1575
(970) 491-7890
www.colostate.edu
Bachelor of Science

CORNELL UNIVERSITY
Interior Design Program
Design and Environmental Analysis
College of Human Ecology
E106 Van Rensselaer Hall
Ithaca, NY 14853-4401
(607) 255-2168
www.cornell.edu
Bachelor of Science

DAKOTA COUNTY TECHNICAL
COLLEGE
Interior Design and Sales Program
1300 145th Street East
Rosemount, MN 55068
(612) 423-8414
www.dctc.mnscu.edu
Diploma

DESIGN INSTITUTE OF SAN DIEGO
Interior Design Program
8555 Commerce Avenue
San Diego, CA 92121
(619) 566-1200
www.disd.edu/index.html
Bachelor of Fine Arts in Interior Design

DREXEL UNIVERSITY
Interior Design Program
Department of Design
Nesbitt College of Design Arts
33rd and Market Streets
Philadelphia, PA 19104
(215) 895-2390
www.drexel.edu
Bachelor of Science

EAST CAROLINA UNIVERSITY
Interior Design Program
Department of Apparel, Merchandising,
and Interior Design
Greenville, NC 27858
(252) 328-6929
www.ecu.edu
Bachelor of Science

EASTERN MICHIGAN UNIVERSITY
Interior Design Program
Department of Human Environmental
and Consumer Resources
College of Health and Human Services
206 Roosevelt Hall
Ypsilanti, MI 48197
(313) 487-2490
www.emich.edu
Bachelor of Science in Interior Design

EL CENTRO COLLEGE
Interior Design Department
Fine & Applied Arts Division
Main at Lamar Streets
Dallas, TX 75202
(214) 860-2338
www.ecc.dcccd.edu
Certificate in Interior Design

ENDICOTT COLLEGE
Interior Design Program
Design Department
376 Hale Street
Beverly, MA 01915
(978) 927-0585
www-endicott.edu
Bachelor of Science Interior Design

Interior Design Degree Programs (Con't)

FASHION INSTITUTE OF DESIGN
AND MERCHANDISING
Interior Design Program
919 South Grand Avenue
Los Angeles, CA 90015-1421
(213) 624-1200
www.fidm.com
Associate of Arts

FASHION INSTITUTE OF
TECHNOLOGY STATE UNIVERSITY
OF NEW YORK
Department of Interior Design D-314
Seventh Avenue at West 27th Street
New York, NY 10001-5992
(212) 217-7800
www.fitnyc.suny.edu/admission/3.0html
Associate in Applied Science

FLORIDA STATE UNIVERSITY
Department of Interior Design
School of Visual Arts and Dance
105 Fine Arts Annex
Tallahassee, FL 32306-1130
(904) 644-1436
www.fsu.edu
B.S. and B.A. Interior Design

HARRINGTON INSTITUTE OF
INTERIOR DESIGN
410 S Michigan Avenue
Chicago, IL 60605-1496
(312) 939-4975
www.interiordesign.edu/
Bachelor of Fine Arts in Interior Design

HOUSTON COMMUNITY COLLEGE
SYSTEM/CENTRAL COLLEGE
Interior Design Program
1300 Holman MC 1229PO Box 7849
Houston, TX 77270-7849
(713) 718-6152
http://ccollege.hccs.cc.tx.us/
Associate of Applied Science

INDIANA UNIVERSITY
Interior Design Program
Apparel Merchandising & Interior Design
College of Arts & Sciences
232 Memorial Hall East
Bloomington, IN 47405
(812) 855-5223
www.indiana.edu/iub/
Bachelor of Science in Interior Design

ILLINOIS INSTITUTE OF ART AT
SCHAUMBURG
Interior Design Department
1000 N. Plaza Drive #100
Schaumburg, IL 60173-4913
(847) 619-3450
www.ilia.aii.edu/
Bachelor of Fine Arts in Interior Design

INTERIOR DESIGNERS INSTITUTE
Interior Design Program
1061 Camelback Road
Newport Beach, CA 92660
(949) 675-4451
Bachelor of Arts Degree in Interior
Design

INTERNATIONAL ACADEMY OF
DESIGN
Interior Design Program
5225 Memorial Highway
Tampa, FL 33634
(813) 881-0007
http://www.iaod.com/
Bachelor of Fine Arts in Interior Design

Architecture is the printing-press of all ages, and gives a history of the state of the society in which it was erected.

Lady Marion Sydney

Interior Design Degree Programs (Con't)

INTERNATIONAL ACADEMY OF
MERCHANDISING AND DESIGN,
CHICAGO
Interior Design Department
One N State Street, Suite 400
Chicago, IL 60602
(312) 541-3910
www.iamd.edu/
Bachelor of Fine Arts in Interior Design

INTERNATIONAL FINE ARTS COLLEGE
Interior Design Department
1737 N Bayshore Drive
Miami, FL 33132
(305) 995-5000
www.ifac.edu/
Associate of Arts in Interior Design

IOWA STATE UNIVERSITY OF
SCIENCE AND TECHNOLOGY
Interior Design Program
Department of Art and Design
158 College of Design
Ames, IA 50011-3092
(515) 294-0677
www.iastate.edu/
Bachelor of Fine Arts in Interior Design

JAMES MADISON UNIVERSITY
Interior Design Program
Harrisonburg, VA 22807
(540) 568-6216
www.jmu.edu/
Bachelor of Fine Arts

KANSAS STATE UNIVERSITY
Department of Interior Architecture
College of Architecture, Planning &
Design
208 Seaton Hall
Manhattan, KS 66506-2912
(913) 532-5992
www.ksu.edu
Bachelor of Interior Architecture

KANSAS STATE UNIVERSITY
Interior Design Program
Department of Clothing, Textiles and
Interior Design
College of Human Ecology
Justin Hall
Manhattan, KS 66506
(785) 532-6993
www.ksu.edu
Bachelor of Science in Interior Design

KENDALL COLLEGE OF ART AND
DESIGN
Interior Design Program
Design Studios
111 Division Avenue North
Grand Rapids, MI 49503
(616) 451-2787
www.kcad.edu
Bachelor of Fine Arts in Interior Design

KENT STATE UNIVERSITY
Interior Design Program
School of Family and Consumer Studies
College of Fine and Professional Arts
100 Nixson Hall
Kent, OH 44242-0001
(330) 672-2197
www.kent.edu/
Bachelor of Arts in Interior Design

LA ROCHE COLLEGE
Interior Design Department
Div. of Graphics, Design and Communication
9000 Babcock Boulevard
Pittsburgh, PA 15237-5898
(412) 536-1024
www.laroche.edu/
Bachelor of Science in Interior Design

Interior Design Degree Programs (Con't)

LAWRENCE TECHNOLOGICAL UNIV.
Interior Architecture/Design
Department of Art & Design
College of Architecture and Design
21000 West Ten Mile Road
Southfield, MI 48075
(810) 204-2848
www.ltu.edu/
B.S. Interior Architecture/Design

LOUISIANA STATE UNIVERSITY
Department of Interior Design
College of Design
402 Design Building
Baton Rouge, LA 70803-7030
(225) 388-8422
www.lsu.edu/
Bachelor of Interior Design

LOUISIANA TECH UNIVERSITY
Interior Design Program
School of Architecture
PO Box 3175 Tech Station
Ruston, LA 71272
(318) 257-2816
www.latech.edu/
Bachelor of Interior Design

MARYLAND INST., COLLEGE OF ART
Interior Architecture & Design
1300 West Mount Royal Avenue
Baltimore, MD 21217
(410) 225-2240
www.mica.edu/
Bachelor of Fine Arts

MARYMOUNT UNIVERSITY
Interior Design Department
School of Arts and Sciences
2807 North Glebe Road
Arlington, VA 22207-4299
(703) 284-1560
www.marymount.edu/admis/
Bachelor of Arts

MARYVILLE UNIV. OF ST. LOUIS
Interior Design Program
Art and Design Department
13550 Conway Road
St. Louis, MO 63141-7299
(314) 529-9300
www.maryvillestl.edu/
Bachelor of Fine Arts in Interior Design

MEREDITH COLLEGE
Interior Design Program
Dept. of Human Environmental Sciences
3800 Hillsborough Street
Raleigh, NC 27607-5298
(919) 760-8395
www.meredith.edu
Bachelor of Science

MICHIGAN STATE UNIVERSITY
Interior Design Program
Dept. of Human Environment & Design
College of Human Ecology
204 Human Ecology
East Lansing, MI 48824-1030
(517) 353-3052
www.msu.edu
Bachelor of Arts

MIDDLE TENNESSEE STATE UNIV.
Interior Design Program
Department of Human Sciences
Box 86
Murfreesboro, TN 37132
(615) 898-2884
www.mtsu.edu/
Bachelor of Science

MISSISSIPPI STATE UNIVERSITY
Interior Design Program
School of Human Sciences
128 Lloyd-Ricks
PO Box 9745
Mississippi State, MS 39762
(601) 325-2950
www.msstate.edu/
Bachelor of Science

Interior Design Degree Programs (Con't)

MOORE COLLEGE OF ART & DESIGN
Interior Design Department
The Parkway at Twentieth Street
Philadelphia, PA 19103
(215) 568-4515
www.moore.edu/
Bachelor of Fine Arts

MOUNT IDA COLLEGE
Interior Design Program
The Chamberlayne School of Design
and Merchandising
777 Dedham Street
Newton, MA 02159
(617) 928-4500
www.mountida.edu
Bachelor of Science

MOUNT MARY COLLEGE
Interior Design Program
Art Department
2900 North Menomonee River Parkway
Milwaukee, WI 53222
(414) 256-1213
www.mtmary.edu/
Bachelor of Arts/Interior Design

NEW ENGLAND SCHOOL OF ART &
DESIGN AT SUFFOLK UNIV.
Interior Design Program
81 Arlington Street
Boston, MA 02116-3904
(617) 536-0383
www.suffolk.edu/nesad
Diploma and Bachelor of Fine Arts,
Interior Design

NEWBURY COLLEGE
Interior Design Program
Design and Merchandising Department
129 Fisher Avenue
Brookline, MA 02146
(617) 730-7049
www.newbury.edu
Associate of Science

NEW YORK INSTITUTE OF
TECHNOLOGY OLD WESTBURY
Interior Design Department
School of Architecture and Design
Midge Karr Art and Design Center
Old Westbury, NY 11568
(516) 686-7786
www.nyit.edu
Bachelor of Fine Arts in Interior Design

NEW YORK SCHOOL OF INTERIOR
DESIGN
Interior Design Program
170 East 70th Street
New York, NY 10021-5110
(212) 472-1500
www.nysid.edu/
Bachelor of Fine Arts

NORTH DAKOTA STATE UNIVERSITY
Dept. of Apparel, Textiles & Interior Design
College of Human Development & Ed.
EML 178
Fargo, ND 58105-5057
(701) 231-8604
www.ndsu.nodak.edu/
Bachelor of Arts or Bachelor of Science
in Interior Design

OHIO STATE UNIVERSITY
Interior Design
Department of Industrial, Interior and
Visual Communication Design
380 Hopkins Hall
128 North Oval Mall
Columbus, OH 43210-1318
(614) 292-6746
www.osu.edu
Bachelor of Science in Ind. Design

Inhabited space transcends geometrical space.

Gaston Bachelard

Interior Design Degree Programs (Con't)

OHIO UNIVERSITY
Interior Design Program
School of Human & Consumer Sciences
College of Health and Human Services
108 Tupper Hall
Athens, OH 45701-2979
(740) 593-2870
www.ohiou.edu/
Bachelor of Science

OKLAHOMA STATE UNIVERSITY
Interior Design Program
Design, Housing and Merchandising
College of Human Environ. Sciences
431 Human Environmental Sciences
Stillwater, OK 74078-6142
(405) 744-5035
http://osu.okstate.edu/
Bachelor of Science

O'MORE COLLEGE OF DESIGN
Interior Design Program
PO Box 908
Franklin, TN 37065
(615) 794-4254
www.omorecollege.edu/
Bachelor of Interior Design

PHILADELPHIA UNIVERSITY
(FORMERLY PHILADELPHIA
COLLEGE OF TEXTILES & SCIENCE)
Interior Design Program
School of Architecture and Design
School House Lane & Henry Avenue
Philadelphia, PA 19144
(215) 951-2896
www.philacol.edu/
Bachelor of Science in Interior Design

PRATT INSTITUTE
Interior Design Department
School of Art and Design
200 Willoughby Avenue
Brooklyn, NY 11205
(718) 636-3630
www.pratt.edu/
Bachelor of Fine Arts Interior Design

PURDUE UNIVERSITY
Interior Design Program
Department of Visual & Performing Arts
Division of Art and Design
1352 Creative Arts Building #1
West Lafayette, IN 47907
(765) 494-3058
www.purdue.edu
Bachelor of Arts

RINGLING SCHOOL OF ART AND
DESIGN
Interior Design Department
2700 North Tamiami Trail
Sarasota, FL 34234
(941) 351-5100
www.rsad.edu/
Bachelor of Fine Arts, Interior Design

RICKS COLLEGE
Interior Design Program
Home Economics
Clarke Building 244
Rexburg, ID 83460-0615
(208) 356-1340
www.ricks.edu
Three-Year Professional Degree in
Interior Design

ROCHESTER INSTITUTE OF
TECHNOLOGY
Professional Level Program
Department of Ind. and Interior Design
School of Design
College of Imaging Arts and Sciences
73 Lomb Memorial Drive
Rochester, NY 14623-6357
(716) 475-6357
www.rit.edu/index1.shtml
Bachelor of Fine Arts

Interior Design Degree Programs (Con't)

SAN DIEGO MESA COLLEGE
Interior Design Program
Architecture & Environ. Design Dept.
7250 Mesa College Drive
San Diego, CA 92111
(619) 627-2941
http://intergate.sdmesa.sdccd.cc.ca.us
Associate of Science Degree

SAN DIEGO STATE UNIVERSITY
Interior Design Program
School of Art, Design & Art History
College of Prof. Studies & Fine Arts
5300 Campanile Drive MC 4805
San Diego, CA 92182
(619) 594-6511
www.sdsu.edu
Bachelor of Arts in Applied Arts &
Sciences

SCHOOL OF VISUAL ARTS
Interior Design Department
209 East 23rd Street
New York, NY 10010
(212) 592-2572
www.sva.edu
Bachelor of Fine Arts in Interior Design

SEMINOLE COMMUNITY COLLEGE
Interior Design Technology
Career Programs
100 Weldon Boulevard
Sanford, FL 32773
(407) 328-2267
www.seminole.cc.fl.us/
Associate in Science in Interior Design
Technology

SOUTHERN COLLEGE
Interior Design Program
Department of Interior Design
1600 Lake Underhill Road
Orlando, FL 32807
(407) 273-1000
Four-Year Int. Design Assoc. in Science

SOUTHERN ILLINOIS UNIVERSITY
AT CARBONDALE
Interior Design Program
Department of Applied Arts
College of Applied Sciences and Arts
410 Quigley Hall
Carbondale, IL 62901-4337
(618) 453-3734
www.siu.edu/siuc/
Bachelor of Science in Interior Design

SOUTHWEST TEXAS STATE UNIV.
Interior Design Program
Dept. of Family & Consumer Sciences
Applied Arts & Technology
Corner Sessom & Academy
San Marcos, TX 78666
(512) 245-2155
www.swt.edu/
Bachelor of Science

STEPHEN F. AUSTIN STATE UNIV.
Interior Design Program
Department of Human Sciences
PO Box 13014 SFA Station
Nacogdoches, TX 75962
(409) 468-4502
www.sfasu.edu/
Bachelor of Science

SUFFOLK COUNTY COMM. COLLEGE
Interior Design Program
121 Speonk Riverhead Road
Riverhead, NY 11901-3499
(516) 548-2588
www.sunysuffolk.edu
Associate of Applied Science

Did you know...
The 1636 Fairbanks House in Dedham, Massachusetts, is the oldest wood frame house in America.

Interior Design Degree Programs (Con't)

SYRACUSE UNIVERSITY
Environmental Design/Interiors
Environ. Arts, Cons. Studies, & Retailing
College for Human Development
224 Slocum Hall
Syracuse, NY 13244
(315) 443-4275
www.syr.edu/
Bachelor of Environ. Design/Interiors

SYRACUSE UNIVERSITY
Interior Design Program
School of Art and Design
College of Visual & Performing Arts
334 Smith Hall
Syracuse, NY 13244-1180
(315) 443-2455
www.syr.edu/
Bachelor of Fine Arts in Interior Design

TEXAS CHRISTIAN UNIVERSITY
Interior Design Program
Dept. of Design, Merch. & Textiles
Addran College of Arts and Sciences
PO Box 298630
Fort Worth, TX 76129
(817) 257-7499
www.tcu.edu
Bachelor of Science

TEXAS TECH UNIVERSITY
Interior Design Program
College of Human Sciences
Box 41162
Lubbock, TX 79409-1162
(806) 742-3050
www.texastech.edu/
Bachelor of Interior Design

UCLA EXTENSION
Interior & Environ. Design Program
Department of the Arts
10995 Le Conte Avenue #414
Los Angeles, CA 90024
(310) 825-9061
www.unex.ucla.edu/index.htm
Prof. Designation in Int. & Env. Design

UNIVERSITY OF AKRON
Interior Design Studies
School of Home Econ. & Family Ecology
College of Fine and Applied Arts
215 Schrank Hall South
Akron, OH 44325-6103
(330) 972-7864
www.uakron.edu/
Bachelor of Arts in Interior Design

UNIVERSITY OF ALABAMA
Interior Design Program
Clothing, Textiles and Interior Design
Human Environmental Sciences
Box 870158
Tuscaloosa, AL 35487-0158
(205) 348-6176
www.ua.edu/
Bachelor of Science-Human
Environmental Sciences

UNIVERSITY OF ARKANSAS
Interior Design Program
School of Human Environ. Sciences
118 HOEC Building
Fayetteville, AR 72701-1201
(501) 575-2578
www.uark.edu/
Bachelor of Science, Human Environ.
Sciences

UNIVERSITY OF CALIFORNIA,
BERKELEY EXTENSION
Interior Design and Interior Arch.
Department of Arts, Letters & Sciences
1995 University Avenue
Berkeley, CA 94720-7002
(510) 643-6827
www.berkeley.edu/
Certificate in Interior Design and
Interior Architecture

Interior Design Degree Programs (Con't)

UNIVERSITY OF CINCINNATI
School of Arch. and Interior Design
Department of Interior Design
College of Design, Arch., Art & Planning
PO Box 210016
Cincinnati, OH 45221-0016
(513) 556-0222
http://www.uc.edu/
Bachelor of Science in Design, Interior
Design

UNIVERSITY OF FLORIDA
Department of Interior Design
College of Architecture
PO Box 115705
Gainesville, FL 32611-5705
(352) 392-0252
www.ufl.edu/
Bachelor of Design

UNIVERSITY OF GEORGIA
Interior Design Program
School of Art
Franklin College of Arts & Sciences
Jackson Street
Athens, GA 30602
(706) 542-1511
www.uga.edu/
Bachelor of Fine Arts/Interior Design

UNIVERSITY OF KENTUCKY
Interior Design Program
Department of Interior Design,
Merchandising, and Textiles
College of Human Environ. Sciences
113 Funkhouser Building
Lexington, KY 40506-0054
(606) 257-3106
www.uky.edu/
Bachelor of Arts in Interior Design

UNIVERSITY OF LOUISVILLE
Interior Design Program
Len R. Hite Fine Arts Department
College of Arts and Sciences
Schneider Hall
2301 S. Third Street
Louisville, KY 40292
(502) 852-6794
www.louisville.edu/
Bachelor of Science in Interior Design

UNIVERSITY OF
MASSACHUSETTS/AMHERST
Architectural Studies Option
Interior Design Option
Design Area
Fine Arts Centre 361
Amherst, MA 01003
(413) 545-6955
www.umass.edu/
Bachelor of Fine Arts

UNIVERSITY OF MINNESOTA
Interior Design Program
Dept. of Design, Housing, and Apparel
College of Human Ecology
240 McNeal Hall
1985 Buford Avenue
St. Paul, MN 55108
(612) 624-9700
www.umn.edu/
Bachelor of Science

You cannot make a building unless you are joyously engaged.

Louis Kahn

Interior Design Degree Programs (Con't)

UNIVERSITY OF MISSOURI,
COLUMBIA
Interior Design Program
Department of Environmental Design
Human Environmental Sciences
137 Stanley Hall
Columbia, MO 65211
(573) 882-7224
www.missouri.edu/
Bachelor of Science

UNIVERSITY OF NEBRASKA
Interior Design Program
Department of Architecture
College of Architecture
232 Arch Hall
Lincoln, NE 68588-0107
(402) 472-9245
www.unl.edu/
BS Architectural Studies ID Option

UNIVERSITY OF NEVADA,
LAS VEGAS
Interior Arch. and Design Program
College of Fine Arts
School of Architecture
4505 Maryland Parkway; Box 454018
Las Vegas, NV 89154-4018
(702) 895-3031
www.unlv.edu
Bachelor of Science in Interior
Architecture

UNIVERSITY OF NORTH CAROLINA
AT GREENSBORO
Dept. of Housing and Interior Design
School of Human Environ. Sciences
259 Stone Building
P.O. Box 26170
Greensboro, NC 27402-6170
(336) 334-5000
www.uncg.edu/
Bachelor of Science in Interior Design

UNIVERSITY OF NORTH TEXAS
Interior Design Program
School of Visual Arts
PO Box 305100
Denton, TX 76203-5100
(940) 565-4010
www.unt.edu/
Bachelor of Fine Arts

UNIVERSITY OF OKLAHOMA
Interior Design Division
College of Architecture
830 Van Vleet Oval, Room 162
Norman, OK 73019-0265
(405) 325-6764
www.ou.edu/
Bachelor of Interior Design

UNIVERSITY OF OREGON
Interior Architecture Program
Department of Architecture
210 Lawrence Hall
1206 University of Oregon
Eugene, OR 97403-1206
(541) 346-3656
www.uoregon.edu/
Bachelor or Master of Int. Architecture

UNIVERSITY OF SOUTHERN
MISSISSIPPI
Interior Design Program
School of Family and Cons. Sciences
Box 5035
Hattiesburg, MS 39406-5035
(601) 266-4679
www.usm.edu/
Bachelor of Science

UNIVERSITY OF SOUTHWESTERN
LOUISIANA
Interior Design Program
School of Arch./College of the Arts
PO Box 43850
LaFayette, LA 70504-3850
(318) 482-6225
www.usl.edu/
Bachelor of Interior Design

Interior Design Degree Programs (Con't)

UNIVERSITY OF TENNESSEE
Interior Design Program
College of Architecture and Planning
217 Art & Architecture Building
Knoxville, TN 37996-2400
(423) 974-3269
www.utk.edu/
Bachelor of Science in Interior Design

UNIV. OF TEXAS AT ARLINGTON
Interior Design Program
School of Architecture
PO Box 19108
Arlington, TX 76019-0108
(817) 272-2801
www.uta.edu/
Bachelor of Science in Interior Design

UNIVERSITY OF TEXAS AT AUSTIN
Interior Design Program
School of Architecture
115 Gearing Hall
Austin, TX 78712
(512) 471-6249
www.utexas.edu/
Bachelor of Science in Interior Design

UNIV. OF WISCONSIN, MADISON
Interior Design Major
Environment, Textiles and Design Dept.
School of Human Ecology
1300 Linden Drive
Madison, WI 53706
(608) 262-2651
www.wisc.edu/
B.S. Environment Textiles & Design-
Interior Design

UNIVERSITY OF WISCONSIN –
STEVENS POINT
Interior Architecture Program
Division of Interior Architecture and
Retail Studies
101 College of Professional Studies
Stevens Point, WI 54481
(715) 346-4600
www.uwsp.edu/
Bachelor of Science & Bachelor of Arts

UTAH STATE UNIVERSITY
Interior Design Program
Human Environments Department
Family Life College
Logan, UT 84322-2910
(435) 797-1558
www.usu.edu/
BS and BA in Interior Design

VILLA MARIA COLLEGE OF BUFFALO
Interior Design Program
Art Department
240 Pine Ridge Road
Buffalo, NY 14225-3999
(716) 896-0700
www.villa.edu/
Associate in Applied Science

VIRGINIA COMMONWEALTH UNIV.
Department of Interior Design
School of the Arts
325 North Harrison Street
Richmond, VA 23284-2519
(804) 828-1713
www.vcu.edu/
Bachelor of Fine Arts

VIRGINIA POLYTECHNIC
INSTITUTE AND STATE UNIVERSITY
Department of Near Environments (0410)
College of Human Resources & Ed.
101 Wallace Hall
Blacksburg, VA 24061-0410
(540) 231-6164
www.vt.edu/
Bachelor of Science

Interior Design Degree Programs (Con't)

WATKINS INSTITUTE COLLEGE OF
ART & DESIGN
Division of Interior Design
601 Church Street
Nashville, TN 37219-2390
(615) 242-1851
www.watkinsinstitute.org/
Associate of Fine Art in Interior Design

WASHINGTON STATE UNIVERSITY
Interior Design Program
Apparel, Merch., and Interior Design
Agriculture and Home Economics
White Hall 202, PO Box 642020
Pullman, WA 99164-2020
(509) 335-7949
www.wsu.edu/
Bachelor of Arts in Interior Design

WENTWORTH INST. OF TECHNOLOGY
Interior Design Program
Department of Design & Facilities
50 Huntington Avenue
Boston, MA 02115
(617) 989-4046
www.wit.edu/
Bachelor of Science-Interior Design

WESTERN CAROLINA UNIVERSITY
Interior Design Program
College of Applied Sciences
Human Environmental Sciences
Belk Building
Cullowhee, NC 28723
(828) 277-7272
www.wcu.edu/
Bachelor of Science

WESTERN MICHIGAN UNIVERSITY
Interior Design Program
Family and Consumer Sciences
Kalamazoo, MI 49008
(616) 387-3704
www.wmich.edu/
Bachelor of Science

WEST VALLEY COLLEGE
Interior Design Department
14000 Fruitvale Avenue
Saratoga, CA 95070
(408) 741-2406
www.wvmccd.cc.ca.us/wvc/fd/
Advanced Certificate

WEST VIRGINIA UNIVERSITY
Interior Design
Div. of Family & Consumer Sciences
College of Agriculture, Forestry &
Consumer Sciences
704-L Allen Hall
PO Box 6124
Morgantown, WV 26506-6124
(304) 293-3402
www.wvu.edu/
Bachelor of Science in Family &
Consumer Sciences/Interior Design

WINTHROP UNIVERSITY
Interior Design Program
Department of Art and Design
College of Visual and Performing Arts
Rock Hill, SC 29733
(803) 323-2126
www.winthrop.edu/
Bachelor of Fine Arts in Interior Design

WOODBURY UNIVERSITY
Department of Interior Architecture
School of Architecture and Design
7500 Glenoaks Boulevard
Burbank, CA 91510-7846
(818) 767-0888
www.woodburyu.edu/
Bachelor of Science

Source: Foundation for Interior Design Education Research

Landscape Architecture Degree Programs

The Landscape Architectural Accreditation Board (LAAB) of the American Society of Landscape Architects (ASLA) is the official accrediting agency for first-professional baccalaureate and master's degree programs in landscape architecture in the United States. ASLA accreditation evaluates each program on the basis of its stated objectives and compliance to externally mandated minimum standards. Accreditation status is an ongoing process and the below information is subject to change. To ensure accurate information consult the individual schools.

ARIZONA STATE UNIVERSITY
http://www.asu.edu/caed/Planning/PL-bsla.html
Landscape Architecture Program
School of Planning and Landscape Architecture
Arizona State University
Tempe, AZ 85287-2005
(602)-965-7167
BSLA

UNIVERSITY OF ARIZONA
http://www.architecture.arizona.edu/landscape
School of Landscape Architecture
University of Arizona
P.O. Box 210075, Room 104
Tucson, AZ 85721-0075
(520)-621-1004
BLA

UNIVERSITY OF ARKANSAS
Department of Landscape Architecture
School of Architecture
University of Arkansas
230 Memorial Hall
Fayetteville, AR 72701
(501) 575-4907
BLA

AUBURN UNIVERSITY
http://www.auburn.edu/academic/architecture/arch/index.html
School of Architecture
104 Dudley Hall
Auburn University
Auburn, AL 36849-5316
(334) 844-4516
BLA

BALL STATE UNIVERSITY
http://www.bsu.edu/cap/landscape/landscape.html
Department of Landscape Architecture
College of Architecture and Planning
Ball State University
Muncie, IN 47306
(765)285-1971
BLA, MLA

Did you know...
Frederick Law Olmsted established the first professional training course in Landscape Architecture at Harvard University in 1899.

Landscape Architecture Degree Programs (Con't)

CALIFORNIA POLYTECHNIC STATE
UNIVERSITY
http://www.calpoly.edu/~wbremer
Department of Landscape Architecture
College of Architecture and
Environmental Design
California Polytechnic State University
San Luis Obispo, CA 93407
(805) 756-1319
BSLA

CALIFORNIA STATE POLYTECHNIC
UNIVERSITY
http://www.csupomona.edu/~la
Department of Landscape Architecture
College of Environmental Design
California State Polytechnic University
3801 West Temple Avenue
Pomona, CA 91768
(909) 869-2673
BSLA, MLA

UNIVERSITY OF CALIFORNIA AT
BERKELEY
http://www.ced.berkeley.edu:80/landscape/
Department of Landscape Architecture
College of Environmental Design
University of California at Berkeley
202 Wurster Hall
Berkeley, CA 94720-2000
(510) 642-4023
MLA

UNIVERSITY OF CALIFORNIA AT
DAVIS
http://lda.ucdavis.edu
Landscape Architecture Program
Department of Environmental Design
College of Agricultural and
Environmental Sciences
University of California at Davis
One Shields Ave.
Davis, CA 95616-8585
(916) 752-3907
BSLA

CITY COLLEGE OF NEW YORK
http://www.ccny.cuny.edu
Urban Landscape Architecture Program
School of Architecture and
Environmental Studies
City College of New York
138th Street and Convent Avenue
New York, NY 10031
(212) 650-8732 or 8733
BS in LA

CLEMSON UNIVERSITY
http://hubcap.clemson.edu/aah/pla/
Dept. of Planning and Landscape
Architecture
121 Lee Hall, P.O. Box 340511
College of Architecture
Clemson University
Clemson, SC 29634-0511
(864) 656-3926
BLA

COLORADO STATE UNIVERSITY
http://www.colostate.edu/Depts/LArch
Program in Landscape Architecture
Department of Horticulture and
Landscape Architecture
College of Agricultural Sciences
Colorado State University
Fort Collins, CO 80523
(970) 491-7018
BSLA

UNIVERSITY OF COLORADO AT
DENVER
http://cudenver.edu/public/AandP/
Landscape Architecture Program
College of Architecture and Planning
University of Colorado at Denver
Campus Box 126
P.O. Box 173364
Denver, CO 80217-3364
(303) 556-4866
MLA

Landscape Architecture Degree Programs (Con't)

UNIVERSITY OF CONNECTICUT
http://canr.uconn.edu/degree.html#Hor
   ticulture/
Landscape Architecture Program
Dept. of Plant Science
College of Ag. and Natural Resources
University of Connecticut
1376 Storrs Road, U-67
Storrs, CT 06269-4067
(860) 486-2928
BSLA

CORNELL UNIVERSITY
http://www.cornell.edu/
Landscape Architecture Department
Cornell University
440 Kennedy Hall
Ithaca, NY 14853
(607) 255-9552
BS, MLA

UNIVERSITY OF FLORIDA
http://www.arch.ufl.edu/landscape/index.html
Department of Landscape Architecture
College of Architecture
University of Florida
331 Architecture Building
Gainesville, FL 32611
(904) 392-6098
BLA, MLA

FLORIDA INTERNATIONAL
UNIVERSITY
http://www.fiu.edu/~soa/
School of Architecture
University Park Campus
Florida International University
Miami, FL 33199
(305)348-3181
MLA

UNIVERSITY OF GEORGIA
http://cyclops.sed.uga.edu/
Program in Landscape Architecture
School of Environmental Design
University of Georgia
609 Caldwell Hall
Athens, GA 30602-1845
(706) 542-4725 BLA, (706) 542-4720 or
542-4704 MLA
BLA, MLA

HARVARD UNIVERSITY
http://www.gsd.harvard.edu/GSDdep.html
Department of Landscape Architecture
Graduate School of Design
Harvard University
409 Gund Hall, 48 Quincy Street
Cambridge, MA 02138
(617) 495-2573
MLA

UNIVERSITY OF IDAHO
http://www.uidaho.edu/larch/
Landscape Architecture Department
College of Art and Architecture
University of Idaho
Moscow, ID 83844-2481
(208) 885-7448
BLA

UNIVERSITY OF ILLINOIS
http://www.uiuc.edu/admin_manual/P
   oS/majors/LA.html
Department of Landscape Architecture
College of Fine and Applied Arts
University of Illinois
101 Buell Hall MC 620, 611 Taft Dr.
Champaign, IL 61820
(217) 333-0176
BLA, MLA

Landscape Architecture Degree Programs (Con't)

IOWA STATE UNIVERSITY
http://www.public.iastate.edu/~land_arch
  /homepage.html
Department of Landscape Architecture
Iowa State University
College of Design, Room 146
Ames, IA 50011
(515) 294-5676
BLA

KANSAS STATE UNIVERSITY
http://www.ksu.edu/archdes/lar/
Department of Landscape
Architecture/Regional and Community
Planning
College of Arch., Planning and Design
Kansas State University
302 Seaton Hall
Manhattan, KS 66506-2909
(785) 532-5961
BLA, MLA

UNIVERSITY OF KENTUCKY
http://www.uky.edu/Agriculture/LA/
Landscape Architecture Program
University of Kentucky
Agriculture Science Center North -
Rm N318
Lexington, KY 40546
(606) 257-3485
BSLA

LOUISIANA STATE UNIVERSITY
http://www.cadgis.lsu.edu/design/LA_
  HM.html
School of Landscape Architecture
Louisiana State University
College of Design Building
Baton Rouge, LA 70803-7020
(225) 388-1434
BLA, MLA

UNIVERSITY OF MARYLAND
http://www.larch.umd.edu
Landscape Architecture Program
Dept. of Natural Resource Sciences and
Landscape Architecture
2146 Plant Sciences Building
University of Maryland
College Park, MD 20742
(301) 405-4359
BLA

UNIVERSITY OF MASSACHUSETTS
http://www-unix.oit.umass.edu/~larp/
Department of Landscape Architecture
and Regional Planning
University of Massachusetts
Hills North 109
Amherst, MA 01003
(413) 545-2255
BSLA, MLA

MICHIGAN STATE UNIVERSITY
http://www.ssc.msu.edu/~la/
Landscape Architecture Program
Department of Geography
Michigan State University
East Lansing, MI 48824-1221
(517) 353-7880
BLA

Environment...can provide nourishment, support and balance for the human spirit as much as it can starve, oppress and pervert it.

Christopher Day

Landscape Architecture Degree Programs (Con't)

UNIVERSITY OF MICHIGAN
http://www-personal.umich.edu/~swissmis/la/
Landscape Architecture
School of Natural Resources and
Environment
University of Michigan
Dana Building, 430 East University
Ann Arbor, MI 48109-1115
(734) 763-4457
MLA

UNIVERSITY OF MINNESOTA
http://gumby.arch.umn.edu/land-
    scape_architecture/landscape.html
Department of Landscape Architecture
125 Architecture
University of Minnesota
89 Church Street, S.E.
Minneapolis, MN 55455
(612) 625-6860
MLA

MISSISSIPPI STATE UNIVERSITY
http://www.msstate.edu/Dept/LA/pub-
    lic/la_page.html
Department of Landscape Architecture
College of Agriculture and Life Sciences
Mississippi State University
P.O. Box 9725
Montgomery Hall, Room 100
Mississippi State, MS 39762-9725
(601) 325-3012
BLA

MORGAN STATE UNIVERSITY
http://www.morgan.edu/CATALOG/GR
    ADUATE/PROGRAMS/Larcmast.htm
Graduate Program in Landscape
Architecture
Institute of Architecture and Planning
Jenkins Building, Room 334
Baltimore, MD 21251
(410) 319-3312
MLA

UNIVERSITY OF NEVADA,
LAS VEGAS
http://www.nscee.edu/unlv/Colleges/Fi
    ne_Arts/Architecture
School of Architecture
University of Nevada, Las Vegas
4505 Maryland Parkway
Las Vegas, NV 89154-4018
(702) 895-4880
BLA

NORTH CAROLINA A &T STATE
UNIVERSITY
http://moore.ncat.edu/NatRes/landarch
Landscape Architecture Program
231 Carver Hall
North Carolina A & T State University
Greensboro, NC 27411
(910) 334-7520
BSLA

NORTH CAROLINA STATE
UNIVERSITY
http://www2.ncsu.edu/ncsu/design/sod4
    /Departments/Landscape/index.html
Landscape Architecture Department
School of Design
North Carolina State University
P.O. Box 7701
Raleigh, NC 27695-7701
(919) 515-8340
MLA

Did you know...
Boston's useable land is composed of the largest amount of fill of any city in North America.

Landscape Architecture Degree Programs (Con't)

NORTH DAKOTA STATE UNIVERSITY
http://www.ndsu.nodak.edu/instruct/dc
   ollito/larchprogram.html
Department of Architecture and
Landscape Architecture
North Dakota State University
P.O. Box 5285 S.U. Station
Fargo, ND 58105-5285
(701) 231-8614
BLA

OHIO STATE UNIVERSITY
http://web1.eng.ohio-state.edu/sar/index.html
Section of Landscape Architecture
Austin E. Knowlton School of
Architecture
Ohio State University
136C Brown Hall, 190 West 17th Ave.
Columbus, OH 43210-1368
(614) 292-1012
BSLA, MLA

OKLAHOMA STATE UNIVERSITY
http://www.okstate.edu/OSU_Ag/index.html
Landscape Architecture Program -
360 AGH
Oklahoma State University
Stillwater, OK 74078-6027
(405) 744-5420
BLA

UNIVERSITY OF OKLAHOMA
http://www.uoknor.edu/architecture/dla
   /idland.htm
Landscape Architecture Program
Gould Hall, Room 162
University of Oklahoma
Norman, OK 73019-0265
405-325-0358
MLA

UNIVERSITY OF OREGON
http://lazarus.uoregon.edu/~landar/LAd
   ept.html
Department of Landscape Architecture
School of Architecture and Allied Arts
University of Oregon
Eugene, OR 97403-5234
(541) 346-3634
BLA

UNIVERSITY OF PENNSYLVANIA
http://dolphin.upenn.edu/~gsfa/larp/index.html
Department of Landscape Architecture
and Regional Planning
Graduate School of Fine Arts
University of Pennsylvania
119 Myerson Hall, 210 South 34th
Street
Philadelphia, PA 19104-6311
(215) 898-6591
MLA

PENNSYLVANIA STATE UNIVERSITY
http://www.larch.psu.edu
Department of Landscape Architecture
College of Arts and Architecture
Pennsylvania State University
210 Engineering Unit D
University Park, PA 16802
(814) 865-9511
BLA

PURDUE UNIVERSITY
http://www.hort.purdue.edu/hort/landarch
Landscape Architecture Program
Horticulture Department
Purdue University
1165 Horticulture Building
West Lafayette, IN 47907-1165
(317) 494-1326
BSLA

Landscape Architecture Degree Programs (Con't)

UNIVERSITY OF RHODE ISLAND
http://www.uri.edu/cels/lar/
Landscape Architecture Program
6 Greenhouse Road, Room 208
University of Rhode Island
Kingston, RI 02881
(401) 874-4549
BLA

RHODE ISLAND SCHOOL OF
DESIGN
http://www.risd.edu
Department of Landscape Architecture
Division of Architecture and Design
Rhode Island School of Design
2 College Street
Providence, RI 02903
(401) 454-6282
BLA

RUTGERS - THE STATE UNIVERSITY
OF NEW JERSEY
http://aesop.rutgers.edu/landarch/
Department of Landscape Architecture
Rutgers - The State University of New
Jersey
Blake Hall
Cook College, Box 231
New Brunswick, NJ 08903
(732) 932-9317
BS

STATE UNIVERSITY OF NEW YORK
http://fla.esf.edu
State University of New York
College of Environmental Science and
Forestry
1 Forestry Drive
Syracuse, NY 13210-2787
(315) 470-6541
BLA, MLA

TEMPLE UNIVERSITY
http://www.temple.edu/ALAH/
Department of Landscape Architecture
and Horticulture
Temple University
580 Meetinghouse Road
Ambler, PA 19002-3994
(215) 283-1292
BSLA

TEXAS A & M UNIVERSITY
http://archone.tamu.edu/neweb/main-
    frame2.html
Department of Landscape Architecture
and Urban Planning
College of Architecture
311 Langford Architecture Center
Texas A & M University
College Station, TX 77843-3137
(409) 845-1019
BLA, MLA

TEXAS TECH UNIVERSITY
http://www.ttu.edu/~casnr/landscape/in
    dex.html
Department of Landscape Architecture
College of Agricultural Sciences and
Natural Resources
Texas Tech University
Box 42121
Lubbock, TX 79409-2121
(806) 742-2858
BLA

UNIVERSITY OF TEXAS -
ARLINGTON
http://www.uta.edu/architecture/
P.O. Box 19108
University of Texas-Arlington
Arlington, TX 76019-0108
(817) 273-5091
MLA

Landscape Architecture Degree Programs (Con't)

UTAH STATE UNIVERSITY
http://www.usu.edu/~laep/
Department of Landscape Architecture
and Environmental Planning
College of Humanities, Arts and Social
Sciences
Utah State University
Logan, UT 84322-4005
(801) 797-0500
BLA, MLA

VIRGINIA POLYTECHNIC
INSTITUTE & STATE UNIVERSITY
http://www.lar.arch.vt.edu/
Landscape Architecture Department
College of Arch. and Urban Studies
Virginia Polytechnic Institute and State
University
202 Architecture Annex
Blacksburg, VA 24061-0113
(540) 231-5583
BLA, MLA

UNIVERSITY OF VIRGINIA
http://minerva.acc.Virginia.EDU/~arch/
Department of Landscape Architecture
School of Architecture
University of Virginia
Campbell Hall
Charlottesville, VA 22903
(804) 924-3285
MLA

WASHINGTON STATE UNIVERSITY
http://coopext.cahe.wsu.edu/~hortla/
Department of Horticulture and
Landscape Architecture
College of Agriculture and Home
Economics
Washington State University
Johnson Hall 149
Pullman, WA 99164-6414
(509) 335-9502
BSLA

UNIVERSITY OF WASHINGTON
http://www.caup.washington.edu/HTML
/LARCH/
Department of Landscape Architecture
College of Architecture and Urban
Planning
University of Washington
348 Gould Hall, Box 355734
Seattle, WA 98195-5734
(206) 543-9240
BLA, MLA

WEST VIRGINIA UNIVERSITY
http://www.caf.wvu.edu/resm/la/index.html
Division of Resource Management
College of Agriculture and Forestry
West Virginia University
P.O. Box 6108
1140 Agricultural Sciences Building
Morgantown, WV 26506-6108
(304) 293-2141/2 ext. 4491
BSLA

UNIVERSITY OF WISCONSIN
http://www.wisc.edu/la/index/htm
Department of Landscape Architecture
School of Natural Resources
College of Ag. and Life Sciences
University of Wisconsin
Room 1, Agriculture Hall
1450 Linden Drive
Madison, WI 53706
(608) 263-7300
BSLA

Source: American Society of Landscape Architects

Did you know...
It took nearly five decades to complete the Washington Monument (1848-1884).

OBITUARIES

OBITUARIES (OCTOBER 1998 THROUGH SEPTEMBER 1999)

Ned H. Abrams, 83

Precast concrete pioneer Ned H. Abrams, FAIA, died February 2, 1999. He was licensed to practice in 28 states within eight years of completing his studies at the University of Pennsylvania. He designed California's first precast concrete structure and the Ridbath Hotel in Spokane, Washington, the first all-welded high rise structure west of the Mississippi River. In addition to his Sunnyvale, California practice, Abrams had been a frequent lecturer on timesaving methods for producing construction documents.

Davis Allen, 82

Davis Allen, an interior and furniture designer who spent forty years at the firm of Skidmore, Owings & Merrill, died May 13, 1999. He had been the senior interior designer for over fifty projects in the firm's New York, Chicago, and San Francisco offices. These included the Inland Steel Company headquarters in Chicago, the Mauna Kea Beach Hotel in Hawaii, and the Lyndon Baines Johnson Library in Austin, Texas. He is credited with pioneering the idea of total design in interior corporate spaces which united art, furniture, and decorative objects. Allen also designed furniture for corporate interiors. His Andover chair, a slat-back beechwood chair, and Bridgehampton chair, an updated Shaker slat-back chair, continue to be widely utilized today. In 1985, he was one of the first fifteen inductees of the Interior Design Hall of Fame.

Alfons Bach, 95

Industrial designer and architect Alfons Bach, FIDSA, died August 19, 1999. A cofounder and past National President of the American Designers Institute (now the Industrial Designers Institute of America), Bach studied architecture in Berlin before relocating to New York in 1932 and opening the design firm of Alfons Bach and Associates on Fifth Avenue. His many projects included one of the nation's first shopping malls, the Ridgeway Center in Stamford, Connecticut. He also designed the interior of Howard Hughes' legendary Constellation aircraft and other work for Hughes' TWA Airlines. Though perhaps most famous for the tubular furniture he designed for Lloyd Manufacturing of Michigan, Bach's modern works were carried by a number of other companies including Heywood Wakefield (furniture), Bigelow-Sanford (carpets), Keystone Silver (metalware), Pacific Mills (linens), General Electric, and Philco (radios). Many of those objects were displayed in a 1934 exhibition at the Metropolitan Museum of Art. When the American Designers Institute merged with the Industrial Design Society of America in 1965, Bach was named a Fellow. Bach's drawings and papers are archived at the Cooper-Hewitt National Design Museum of the Smithsonian Institution.

Edward Charles Bassett, 77

San Francisco architect Edward Charles "Chuck" Bassett, FAIA, a retired partner of Skidmore, Owings & Merrill (SOM), died August 28, 1999. The design partner for SOM's San Francisco office for 21 years, Bassett's many San Francisco projects include the Louise M. Davies Symphony Hall, the Bank of America World Headquarters building, and the Oakland Coliseum. Bassett worked all over the world, designing such landmarks as the Royal Dutch Shell Headquarters in The Hague and the Australian Mutual Provident Society complex in Melbourne. Throughout his career, Bassett remained a Modernist. He graduated from the Cranbrook School of Art and worked under Eero Saarinen at the beginning of his career. In 1955, while in his thirties, he became the chief designer at SOM in San Francisco. Bassett received the Brunner Prize in Architecture from the National Institute of Arts and Letters and the Maybeck Award from the California Council of the American Institute of Architects.

Elisabeth Benjamin, 90

Modernist architect Elisabeth Benjamin died in April 1999, in the United Kingdom. She achieved fame there as one of the few renowned British female architects in the 1930s and as an exponent of the Modern Movement. After leaving the Architectural Association, Benjamin worked in Sir Edwin Lutyens' office for a year before beginning her own practice. Most of her designs consisted of modernist residences, a body of work which has recently been rediscovered by the Twentieth Century Society. This has lead to a television documentary about her Gerrards Cross house, Eastwall, an early example of Modern architecture which she designed with Godfrey Samuels in 1935.

Wayne Berg, 52

Manhattan architect Wayne Berg, AIA, died February 25, 1999. His modern designs were widely praised for their sensuality and humanness. Berg was the partner in charge of design with Pasanella, Klein, Stolzman & Berg. He had previously worked for Robert A.M. Stern Architects from 1974 to 1978 and operated his own practice from 1978 to 1986. In 1986, he was selected to participate in the Emerging Voices series sponsored by the Architectural League of New York. He received a posthumous 1999 Progressive Architecture design award for his entry of the design for Stabile Hall at the Pratt Institute in Brooklyn. Berg was also an adjunct professor of architecture at Columbia University and was the Vice President of the New York chapter of The American Institute of Architects in 1992.

Eugene D. Birnbaum, 83

Self-taught structural engineer Eugene D. Birnbaum, SASE, died May 30, 1999. An innovator in the field, Birnbaum helped design more than 20,000 homes, commercial, and industrial buildings on the West Coast during his 50-year career. He was the first to use computer modeling to study post-elastic behavior in high-rise buildings. Birmbaum was a past president of the Society of American Structural Engineers and a fellow of the Society for Advancement of Science and Engineering. He was also a member of the UCLA Extension faculty from 1953 to 1985 and provided scholarships at UCLA and Cal State through the Eugene Birnbaum Foundation.

Sara Holmes Boutelle, 90

Architectural historian Sara Holmes Boutelle died May 13, 1999. Her book Julia Morgan, Architect (Abbeville Press, 1988) rekindled interest in Morgan's career, giving her the notoriety her work deserved. As one of the profession's first successful female practitioners and one of the most prolific architects of the 20th century, Morgan's output of nearly 800 works rivals that of Frank Lloyd Wright. Before Boutelle's book, little had been known about Morgan (1872–1957) aside from her role as designer of William Randolph Hearst's California castle, San Simeon. In 1989 Boutelle won the California Book Award Silver Medal for her biography, and in 1991 she was made an honorary member of The American Institute of Architects. Previously, she had been a teacher of art and architecture at Brearley School in New York.

William Brown, 89

William Brown, a former architectural administrator with Skidmore, Owings & Merrill (SOM), died April 4, 1999. The landmark projects he supervised for the firm included the design and construction of the Lever House in New York City. He was also instrumental in the building of the City of Oak Ridge, Tennessee, which was designed as a fully functioning city to instantly accommodate the 80,000 people working on the U.S. atomic weapons program. He was named a partner at SOM in 1949 and retired in 1969 after helping to guide the firm through decades of explosive growth.

Sir Hugh Maxwell Casson, 89

Architect, journalist, educator, and painter Sir Hugh Casson died August 15, 1999. A former president of the Royal Academy of Art in Britain, vice president of the Royal Institute of British Architects, and president of the Architectural Association, Casson was best known for his work as a good-natured coalition builder and architectural enthusiast. As director of the 1951 Festival of Britain, Casson encouraged a large group of architects to work together, resulting in a highly successful event. For this work he received a knighthood. He was a founding partner of the firm Casson, Conder & Partners and had been chairman of the architecture department at the Royal College of Art from 1953 until 1975. Following retirement, Casson had been one of the Prince of Wales' watercolor instructors. He illustrated several books and had been a contributing writer for several architectural magazines.

Henry Cohen, 76

Urban planner, educator, and former New York City official Henry Cohen died January 14, 1999. He had been the founding dean of what is now the Milano Graduate School of Management and Urban Policy at the New School for Social Research in New York. He began his career at the school in 1968 as director and then dean of the Center for New York City Affairs. He was an advocate of "new urban professions," including urban policy analysis and management, human resources management, health management and policy, and nonprofit management. Previously, Cohen served as First Deputy Administrator and Acting

Administrator of the Human Resources Administration for the City of New York. He started with the city in 1950, where he organized and then directed the research division in the Department of City Planning. He also conducted research for the New York Regional Plan Association and lectured on urban studies at Columbia University's School of General Studies and School of Social Work.

John D. Cordwell, 78

John D. Cordwell, architect and former Director of Planning in Chicago under Mayor Martin Kennelly, died February 4, 1999. In the 1960s he was one of the chief architects of Chicago's Carl Sandburg Village, a 2,600 unit, middle-class urban renewal project. Cordwell's other Chicago work included the large-scale Presidential Towers, South Commons, and the renovation of the Chicago Hilton and Towers. He was a founding partner of the firm Solomon, Cordwell and Buenz.

Elsie Krummeck Crawford, 86

Industrial designer Elsie Krummeck Crawford died June 3, 1999. Crawford attended the Parsons School of Design and began her career designing exhibits for the 1939 New York World's Fair. Her creations included furniture, toys, sculpture, and the original planters used at Los Angeles International Airport in 1960. Some of her designs had recently been exhibited in shows at the Pacific Design Center, the Pasadena Art Museum, New York's Pratt Institute, and have been added to the permanent collection of the Los Angeles County Museum of Art.

Carroll Cooper Curtice, 75

Washington D.C. architect Carroll Cooper Curtice died April 4, 1999. Curtice had been the architect of record for the Lyceum meeting house and museum in Alexandria, Virginia. He also developed plans for the restoration of Alexandria's Lloyd House. Curtice's other restoration projects included Ford's Theatre in Washington D.C. and the James Monroe Library in Fredericksburg, Virginia. He received his architectural registration through an apprenticeship with the Washington, D.C. firm of Macomber & Peter. Curtice later practiced with Macomber and eventually founded the firm of Curtice and Pavlovich.

Joseph Druffel, 60

Joseph Druffel, an architect of low-income housing projects in New York City for 25 years, died June 11, 1999. The majority of his career was dedicated to providing shelter for New York's poor in the South Bronx, East Harlem, and the West Side of Manhattan. His projects included the Msgr. Robert Fox Memorial Shelter for St. Paul's Roman Catholic Church and Pueblo En Marcha in the Bronx for the New York City Department of Housing Preservation and Development's Urban Homesteading Program. Druffel also worked with such organizations as the Clinton Housing Corporation, Hope Community Inc., and Project Green Hope to design, build, and renovate shelters and housing.

Harold Edelman, 75

Harold Edelman, FAIA, New York City architect, teacher, and preservationist died December 21, 1998. Edelman was a founding partner of the Greenwich Village firm Edelman and Salzman Architects (now the Edelman Partnership/Architects) with his wife, Judith, and Stanley Salzman. Edelman was especially active in the preservation and restoration of several key projects, including St. Mark's in the Bowery, one of New York's oldest churches. Unfortunately, the church burned when its renovation was nearly complete in 1978 and had yet to be redesigned by the architect. Edelman was also instrumental in saving the Jefferson Market Courthouse in Greenwich Village and served on the committee of architects that redesigned Washington Square Park. He had been a teacher at the Pratt Institute in Brooklyn from 1952 to 1962.

Joseph Esherick, 83

Joseph Esherick, FAIA, winner of the 1989 American Institute of Architects Gold Medal, died December 17, 1998. The San Francisco Bay-area architect, renown for his subtle, functional aesthetic and great personal humility, served on the faculty of the University of California at Berkley since 1952. A professor emeritus at the university, Esherick had been chairman of the architecture department there from 1977 to 1981. His projects included the 1967 renovation of the Cannery near Fisherman's Wharf, the Monterey Bay Aquarium, which opened in 1984, Wurster Hall for the College of

Environmental Design at the University of California at Berkley, and the demonstration homes at Sea Ranch on the Northern California coast. He was a founding partner of the firm Esherick Homsey Dodge & Davis Architecture, winner of the 1976 AIA Architecture Firm Award.

Edward H. Fickett, 83

California architect Edward H. Fickett, FAIA, died in May 1999. He was known as an innovator and pioneer in the field. Fickett designed one of the earliest prefab manufactured homes, the first hotel with private kitchenettes and patios, and the first open kitchen integrated with a living or family room. A designer of over 40,000 homes, Fickett's other projects included the original Sands Hotel in Las Vegas, the La Costa Resort near San Diego, and the Los Angeles Harbor Passenger and Cargo Terminals. During the 1950s, he was President Dwight D. Eisenhower's architectural advisor, and from 1977 to 1986 he was the architectural commissioner for the City of Beverly Hills. Fickett was honored with the Presidential Merit of Honor Award as well as awards from The American Institute of Architects, the National Association of Homebuilders, American Home magazine, Parents magazine and the cities of Los Angeles, Beverly Hills, Reno, and Seattle.

James J. Foley, 76

Ohio architect James J. Foley, FAIA, died January 2, 1999. He founded the Columbus firm Kellam & Foley in 1953 and, throughout his career, had been active in The American Institute of Architects (AIA) in their chapter, state, and national levels. In 1980, he received the AIA Ohio Gold Medal. Foley was also one of fourteen architects to travel to the People's Republic of China in 1974 as part of the first official AIA delegation.

Albert Frey, 95

Albert Frey, acclaimed modernist architect and one-time member of Le Corbusier's atelier, died November 14, 1998. Born in Zurich, Frey worked with Le Corbusier for ten months detailing the Villa Savoy in Poissy, France. He came to the United States in 1930 and worked in New York where his most famous design was the 1931 Aluminaire House with Lawrence Kocher. The house is now owned by the New York Institute of Technology and is being reconstructed on their West Islip, New Jersey campus. Frey moved to Palm Springs in 1939 and was pivotal in developing that city's signature American modern aesthetic. His projects there included the Palm Springs City Hall, in collaboration with John Porter Clark and Robson Chambers; the Raymond Loewy house, with Clark; and the Tramway Valley Station and Gas Station with Chambers. His own homes, Frey 1 and Frey 2, are featured in the recent book, Albert Frey Houses 1 + 2, published by Princeton Architectural Press.

Sir Alexander John Gordon, 82

Sir Alexander John Gordon, a former president of the Royal Institute of British Architects (RIBA), died July 23, 1999. His firm, Alex Gordon and Partners, received numerous awards and commendations, eventually branching from Wales to London, York, and Carmarthen. Throughout his career, he was actively involved with the RIBA. As its president in 1971-3, he drew much media attention to the practice of architecture over his outspoken concerns with concrete housing and their social failure. Largely through his efforts, redevelopment schemes were curtailed in favor of renovating existing properties. He continued to practice following his RIBA presidency and was knighted in 1988. In private practice, his numerous projects included the Sherman Theatre in Cardiff, Theatr y Werin at Aberystwyth, extentions to the National Museum of Wales, the Welsh Office, various university buildings, and numerous bridges.

Barbara Gray, 89

Innovative architectural researcher and Hollywood writer Barbara Gray, Hon. AIA, died November 3, 1998. She worked for more than thirty years as Vice President and Director of Research for architect William Pereira & Associates. She studied design concepts and architectural theories for Pereira which helped him create his designs. Her research was integral to his designs for UC Irvine, UC San Diego, and the master plan for USC. She was also integral in his design for the Los Angeles County Museum of Art for which she produced a preliminary study, 'What Is a Museum?' to prepare Pereira for this project. In 1961, she was named a Times Woman of the Year, and in 1986 The American Institute of Architects granted her an honorary membership. During her movie career as a story analyst and writer, Gray worked on a number of films including None But the Lonely Heart and Moon and Sixpence. She also wrote the screenplay for Istanbul, staring Errol Flynn.

Robert Gruen, 86

Industrial and packaging designer Robert Gruen died June 7, 1999. He began his career as a stage designer in New York in 1934. In 1935, he apprenticed under Norman Bel Geddes and the following year went on to become a draftsman for 20th Century Fox in Hollywood. In 1940, he returned to New York and opened Robert Gruen Associates, designers of furniture and glassware. A line of glassware which he designed for The Sweden House in Rockefeller Center was exhibited in an American Industrial Art exhibition at the Metropolitan Museum of Art. As national executive vice president of the Industrial Designers Institute (IDI), Gruen initiated discussions with the Society of Industrial Designers (SID) to merge the two organizations (now the Industrial Designers Society of America). The merger took place in 1965 when Gruen was president of IDI. Later, Gruen was vice president and director of the National Screen Service Corporation and served as an officer of the Continental Lithograph Corporation. He wrote a number of design articles for Modern Plastics, Modern Packaging, and Architectural Record.

Erwin Conrad Hock, 91

Erwin Conrad Hock, AIA, CSI, a longtime architect with the U.S. government, died September 3, 1999. During the course of his career, Hock was responsible for the construction of many residences, courthouses, post offices, schools and churches. Hock had worked as an architect, a site engineer, contractor and construction analyst for the Renewal Project Administration of the Department of Housing and Urban Development, the Public Buildings Service of the General Services Administration and the National Capital Housing Authority. Before retiring, Hock also worked in the Washington D.C. office of Perkins and Will.

Leopold H. Just, 95

Leopold H. Just, an engineer and draftsman involved in many of New York and New Jersey's most ambitious and complicated bridge construction projects, died February 25, 1999. He was a partner in the consulting engineer firm of Ammann & Whitney. Previously he held the positions of structural engineer, chief draftsman, and chief engineer at the firm. Working independently and with Ammann & Whitney, Just was involved in the design of the George Washington Bridge and Lincoln Tunnel in New York City; the Pennsylvania Turnpike; the Walt Whitman Bridge in Philadelphia; the Throgs Neck Bridge linking the Bronx and Queens; and the Verrazano-Narrows Bridge linking Staten Island with Brooklyn, the world's longest suspension bridge at the time it was built. From 1964 until retiring in 1970, Just served as Ammann & Whitney's partner in charge of international operations.

Tibor Kalman, 49

Tibor Kalman, graphic design innovator and activist, died May 2, 1999. A rule-breaker and critic of unambitious design, Kalman called upon his profession and his clients to take responsibility for their actions. He promoted environmentalism and economic equality through his work and opposed designs which are harmful to the makers and users. His New York design firm, M&Co, created graphics, exhibitions, books, magazines and film titles for progressive clients. He also founded M&Co Labs which designs clocks, watches, and other objects. His term as editor of Colors, a magazine published by the clothing company Benetton which focused on social issues, served as an outlet for his ideas and probably was his most meaningful job. Previously, Kalman provided editing and creative direction for the magazines Art Forum and Interview. As his final work, he designed the exhibition "Tiborocity," a retrospective of his work and influences which was displayed posthumously at the San Francisco Museum of Modern Art.

Rita Milaw Lawrence, 80

Rita Milaw Lawrence, founder and president of the contemporary furniture company, Architectural Pottery/Architectural Fiberglass and Group Artec, died January 22, 1999, in Los Angeles. Her life-long work as a design executive won her the National Home Furnishing League's Trailblazer Award in 1956 and UCLA's Professional Achievement Award in 1972. Lawrence graduated from UCLA and subsequently became active in the school, serving on a number of boards and committees, including the Dean's Council of the School of Architecture and Urban Planning. She was also on the boards of the Folk Art Museum of Los Angeles, California Design, Action for a Better Los Angeles, and Los Angeles Beautiful.

Michael Lax, 69

Michael Lax, a sculptor and industrial designer of household items, died May 28, 1999. Among his best-known designs are a cast-iron teakettle for Copco in 1962 and a small, high-intensity lamp created for Lightolier in 1964, now displayed in New York's Museum of Modern Art. Throughout his career, Lax designed for Mikasa, Tupperware, American Cynamid Company, Dansk, Rosenthal, Salton, Dunbar Glass, and Metaal. Winner of a Fulbright Fellowship to Finland in the early 1950's, the Scandinavian modern influence was evident in his body of work.

Charles Luckman, 89

Business leader and architect Charles Luckman died January 25, 1999. A graduate of the University of Illinois School of Architecture, Luckman went into sales during the Depression and quickly ascended to the top management level of Lever Brothers. As president of the company, Luckman shepherded the creation of Lever House, the company's 1952 modern landmark corporate headquarters on Park Avenue in New York, designed by Gordon Bunshaft of Skidmore, Owings and Merrill. In 1950, he left Lever Brothers and formed his own architectural business, the Luckman Partnership. As a practicing architect, Luckman made bottom-line considerations his primary design criteria, to the chagrin of many architecture critics and practitioners. His most famous project, New York's Madison Square Garden, called for the razing of Penn Station. This outraged preservationists and sparked the debate over saving older buildings in the United States. His other projects include Aloha Stadium in Honolulu and the original master plan for the Kennedy Space Center in Cape Canaveral, Florida. For his work as director of the Freedom Train, part of President Harry Truman's plan for rebuilding Europe following World War II, Luckman was awarded France's Legion of Honor, England's Order of St. John, and Italy's Star of Solidarity.

Harry B. Mahler, 70

Harry B. Mahler, FAIA, CEO of Grad Associates P.A. of Newark, New Jersey, died November 27, 1998. He had been with the firm 42 years, starting as a junior designer. Mahler had worked on many projects in New Jersey, including the headquarters of Nabisco in East Hanover and the headquarters of Mercedes-Benz of North America, Inc., in Montvale. A past president of AIA Newark and Suburban, Mahler was an adjunct professor at Pratt Institute and New Jersey Institute of Technology and was an instructor at Columbia University.

P. Scott Makela, 39

Groundbreaking graphic designer P. Scott Makela died May 7, 1999. His work, which included catalogs for the Minneapolis College of Art and Design (MCAD), the title sequence for the movie Fight Club, and many advertisements, was pioneering in its use and representation of technology and the digital age. It combined traditional print design and topography with multi-media applications, resulting in a sometimes frantic, layered aesthetic that rejected conventions of legibility. With his wife Laurie, Makela was a chairman of the design department at the Cranbrook Academy of Art in Bloomfield, Michigan. They also founded a design studio called Makela (originally Words + Pictures for Business + Culture), specializing in print and technology projects for corporate and cultural clients. In 1996, the Makelas authored a book and Web site entitled "Whereishere" with Lewis Blackwell that surveyed contemporary digital design.

Paul Mellon, 91

Philanthropist and architectural patron Paul Mellon, Hon. AIA, died February 1, 1999. The son of industrialist Andrew Mellon who founded the National Gallery of Art, Paul Mellon supervised the construction of the museum's first building in 1941. He later commissioned I.M. Pei to design the museum's East Wing, which opened in 1978. He also turned to Pei to design an arts center for his beloved preparatory school, Choate School in Wallingford, Connecticut. As an active alumnus of Yale University, Mellon commissioned architect Louis Kahn to design the Yale Center for British Art and British Studies, which he bequeathed to the university. During his lifetime he gifted the National Gallery nearly 1,000 works. He was president and chief executive of the National Gallery from 1963 until 1979 and chairman of its board of trustees from 1979 to 1985. For his lifelong commitment to and patronage of architecture, The American Institute of Architects granted him honorary membership in their organization.

Bruno Munari, 90

Italian designer Bruno Munari died in December 1998. Perhaps best known for his pursuit of "useless" designs, Munari went on to become one of Italy's leading designers. Although he later broke with that aesthetic, he began his career as an avowed Futurist. Munari's projects included sculpture, painting, industrial and graphic design, furniture design, and more. Throughout his life and work he continued to explore the relationship between art, craft, science, and technology. For over 40 years his graphic design was utilized by the publishing house Einaudi, and he often designed for Olivetti and Campari. His 1957 melamine cube ashtray for Danesi was a success, and his espresso machines and television designs became classics. One of Munari's most popular "useless" design was his "illegible books" which consisted of papers of varying color, material, and design with no print.

Erik Nitsche, 90

Modernist graphic designer Erik Nitsche died November 10, 1998. He was perhaps best known for his posters, advertisements and book designs; although, his work covered a broad spectrum of projects and media. Between 1955 and 1960 Nitsche developed an information design system for the General Dynamics Company, the producer of the first nuclear-powered submarine. He devised a symbolic system based on the concept "Atoms for Peace" to introduce the submarine to the public and to express the company's regard for peace. He also created a series of symbolic and abstract posters in six languages, which are now modern classics. During his career, Nitsche had made illustrations for German magazines Querschnitt and Simplicissimus, designed alphabets for the French type foundry Deberny & Peignot, and illustrated covers for many U.S. magazines. He produced several hundred record covers for the Decca label in the U.S., designed posters for Universal Pictures and 20th Century Fox, acted as a consultant to the Museum of Modern Art's Department of Design and to Standard Oil, and designed advertising campaigns for Saks Fifth Avenue and Ohrbach's department stores. His book projects included "Dynamic America," the General Dynamics company history, a 12-volume history of science and technology and a five-volume history of the 20th century.

John E. Nunemaker, 60

John E. Nunemaker, a senior vice-president of the Chicago architectural firm of Perkins & Will, died May 18, 1999. His specialty was medical research facilities. Nunemaker was instrumental in starting the firm's laboratory design group. His many projects included facilities for Northwestern University, University of Pennsylvania, Thomas Jefferson University, and the University of Minnesota. His other notable projects included the First National Bank of Chicago, the Sears Merchandise Group headquarters in Hoffman Estates, Illinois, and Abbott Laboratories in Deerfield, Illinois. Nunemaker received an undergraduate degree in architecture and a master's degree in structural engineering from University of Illinois where he was an adjunct professor.

Verner Panton, 72

Famed Danish postwar designer and architect Verner Panton died September 5, 1998. He was most famous for his 1960s curved and cantilevered plastic stacking chair, also known as the Panton chair. Manufactured by Vitra since 1967, the Panton chair is credited with being the first single-piece molded plastic chair to succeed in production. The Museum of Modern Art added it to their permanent collection in 1969. His other designs included boldly colored textiles and lighting made of plastic and metal, materials more akin to contemporary Italian design than Scandinavian. Panton worked for Arne Jacobsen in Denmark from 1950 to 1952, before opening his own office which he eventually moved to Binningen, Switzerland. Besides the MoMA, Panton's designs are also found in the design collections of the Georges Pompidou Center in Paris, the Denver Museum of Art, and the Industrial Art Museum in Copenhagen.

R. Bruce Patty, 63

Former American Institute of Architects' President, R. Bruce Patty, FAIA, died December 16, 1998. He practiced architecture in his hometown of Kansas City for many years where he was known for his efforts in civic improvements. After earning an architecture degree from the University of Kansas, he joined the firm of Kivett & Myers. He also worked in the firms of Patty Berkebile Nelson Immenschuh and Patty Archer Architects. In 1994 he joined Burns & McDonnell, an international engineering and architecture firm, as Vice President of Marketing and Architecture. During his career, Patty's projects included the design of the Kansas City International Airport, One Kansas City Place, the city's tallest building, and the Bartle Hall Concert Center.

Clair Leverett Peck, Jr., 78

Clair L. Peck Jr., a Southern California contractor responsible for building many Los Angeles landmarks, died December 14, 1998. His firm, C.L. Peck Contractor, founded by his father in 1918, constructed over 1,200 buildings in Los Angeles, including the Crystal Cathedral, the Capitol Records building, and the Forum in Inglewood. He also built the 73-story First Interstate Bank World Center, the tallest building west of the Mississippi River. Peck retired in 1987 after merging his company with Jones Brothers Construction Corporation.

Jay A. Pritzker, 76

Hyatt Hotel's mogul and founder of the Pritzker Prize, Jay A. Pritzker, died January 23, 1999. Through his Hyatt Foundation, Pritzker supported educational, religious, social welfare, scientific, and cultural activities through a variety of philanthropic endeavors in his home city of Chicago and throughout the world. Widely regarded as one of architecture's most prestigious awards, the Pritzker Architecture Prize was established in 1979 and awards $100,000 annually to each of its Laureates. Pritzker's son Thomas, who now heads the Hyatt Foundation, recalls the origins of the Prize: "In 1967, we acquired an unfinished building which was to become the Hyatt Regency Atlanta. Its soaring atrium was wildly successful and became the signature piece of our hotels around the world. It was immediately apparent that this design had a pronounced effect on the mood of our guests and attitude of our employees...So in 1978, when we were approached with the idea of honoring living architects, we were responsive."

John D. Randall, 79

Famed architectural preservationist John D. Randall died January 12, 1999. The son of prominent Chicago architect Frank Randall, John helped save several historic skyscrapers from demolition. Randall studied under Ludwig Mies van der Rohe at the Illinois Institute of Technology and spent most of his life lobbying to preserve some of America's great buildings through letter writing, booklets, direct mailings, newspaper editorials, and courting politicians and business leaders. Randall was appointed to the advisory committee of the Chicago Commission of Architectural Landmarks in 1959 and worked through the 1960s to preserve Louis Sullivan's buildings. Though he was unsuccessful at keeping Adler and Sullivan's Garrick Building in Chicago from the wrecking ball, he was instrumental in later saving their 1891 St. Louis skyscraper, the Wainwright, and their Guaranty Building in Buffalo, New York. During this period he had been an associate architect at Southern Illinois University and later went on to become an architectural associate in the office of facilities planning at the State University of New York at Buffalo.

S. Richard Rio, 87

S. Richard Rio, 87, a longtime Annandale, Virginia-based architect, died July 29, 1999. He had been a principal of the firm Beery, Rio and Associates from 1961 to 1981, during which time he designed university buildings, shopping centers, high schools, hospitals and more. He served as a consultant to the Federal National Mortgage Association on new housing design concepts and had been chief air base planner for the Department of the Air Force from 1947 to 1960.

Alexander Rotchegov, 81

Alexander Rotchegov, a leader and innovator in Russian architecture, died December 2, 1998. He was President of the Russian Academy of Architecture and Construction Sciences and founder and past president of the Union of Architects of Russia Federation. Rotchegov served as head deputy of the Architectural Department at the Hydroproject Institute, creative leader of the Architectural Workshop No. 20 at the Department Mosproject-1 for the Moscow Central Architectural Planning Board, and chief of the Department Mosproject-1. During the 1960s, he designed many residential areas in Moscow. He was also noted for utilizing the method of Arranging Volumetric-Planning Elements (AVPE), which created optimum conditions for installation and allowed for varied house heights.

Werner Seligmann

Werner Seligmann, FAIA, Dean of Syracuse University's School of Architecture from 1976 to 1990, died November 12, 1998. An educator for nearly 40 years at institutions such as Harvard, Yale, and Cornell, Seligmann won the 1998 Topaz Medallion for Excellence in Architectural Education from the Association of Collegiate Schools of Architecture and The American Institute of Architects. Seligmann had written and lectured extensively on the work of Frank Lloyd Wright, Le Corbusier, and Modern Architecture. He started his own practice in 1961, Werner Seligmann and Associates, Architects and Urban Designers. In 1963, he won a P/A Award for his work on the Beth David Synagogue in Binghampton, New York.

William L. Slayton, 82

Urban renewal leader William L. Slayton, Hon. AIA, of Washington, D.C., died August 7, 1999. He served as commissioner of the Urban Renewal Administration in the Housing and Home Finance Agency under Presidents Kennedy and Johnson, prior to the creation of the Department of Housing and Urban Development (HUD). During his tenure, Slayton instituted regulations regarding the availability of relocation housing, combating racial discrimination in relocation housing and rules to make building enforcement codes in urban renewal agencies more stringent. Previously, Slayton played a key role in the redevelopment of Southwest Washington, D.C. as vice president for planning and redevelopment for Webb and Knapp, a primary builder in that area. He had also served as the planning partner in the architectural firm of I.M. Pei, whose redevelopment projects included Society Hill in Philadelphia and Hyde Park-Kenwood in Chicago. Following his departure from the Urban Renewal Administration, Slayton became executive vice president of Urban American, creator of the National Urban Coalition. He had also been Executive Vice-

President/CEO of The American Institute of Architects
and oversaw the creation of its Washington, D.C. headquarters. Toward the end of his career, Slayton acted as
Deputy Assistant Secretary of State in charge of the
Office of Foreign Buildings, responsible for the design
and construction of embassies and federal facilities
worldwide.

Joel Spaeth, 61

Joel Spaeth, a principal with The Hillier Group,
Architects, of Princeton, N.J., died June 8, 1999. He
had been with The Hillier Group for 29 years, most
recently as its master planning specialist. The winner
of several design awards, Spaeth's many projects
included a master plan for the U.S. Military Academy
at West Point, numerous corporate architectural projects, and many university projects, including more
than a dozen international schools.

Calvin Straub, 78

Calvin Straub, FAIA, a professor of architecture for
over 40 years, died in November 1998. A 1987 recipient of the Architect of the Year award from AIA
Arizona, Straub began a 27-year tenure with Arizona
State University's School of Architecture and
Environmental Design in 1961. He is most widely
known for his work in Southern California during the
1940s and 1950s, both as a professor of architecture at
the University of Southern California and for his residential designs while at Buff, Straub & Hensman in
Los Angeles. His work was published in the Los
Angeles Times and Sunset magazine.

Michael D. Tatum, 59

Michael Tatum, IIDA, a leader in the interior design
profession and principal of Michael Tatum Consulting,
died December 17, 1998. In 1963, Tatum formed the
interiors group at Hellmuth, Obata & Kassabaum
(HOK). He had also worked with BOSTI Associates
and the Lauck Group, both of Dallas. During his
career, Tatum served on the International Interior
Design Association (IIDA) advisory board and was one
of the founders of The American Institute of
Architects' Interiors Committee. From 1988 to 1996
Tatum was the chairman of the interior design department at the University of Texas, Arlington.

Crombie Taylor, 85

Louis Sullivan enthusiast and preservationist Crombie Taylor, FAIA, died May 24. A teacher and former director of the Chicago Institute of Design, Taylor lobbied to save Chicago's architectural gems, primarily those designed by Louis Sullivan, from the wrecking ball. He is credited with saving the Auditorium Theater at Roosevelt University and reinvigorating enthusiasm for Sullivan's work. Taylor recently completed a book about Sullivan, which will be published by Harry N. Abrams in 2000. He had also been a teacher for several years at Georgia Institute of Technology and University of Southern California.

S. Goodluck Tembunkiart, 44

S. Goodluck Tembunkiart, AIA, a vice president of RTKL in Washington, D.C., died September 21, 1998. For the past several years he had been principal designer of the U.S. Capitol Center. He was also a contributing author to Why Design? Activities and Projects from the National Building Museum. Tembunkiart had been involved with many D.C. area projects, including the Pavilion at Reston Towncenter in VIrginia, an entry for the Silver Spring Redevelopment plan in Maryland, and the Washington Center office building and restoration of the Ariel Rios building in the Federal Triangle.

Fred C. Trump, 93

Although more recognized in his later years as the father of Donald than for his real estate acumen, Fred C. Trump had been a major builder and developer of multi-family housing for many years in New York. He died June 25, 1999. Mr. Trump built more than 27,000 apartments and row houses for the middle class, including Shore Haven in Bensonhurst, Beach Haven near Coney Island, and Trump Village in Coney Island. His post-war apartment towers significantly altered the landscapes of those areas as well as Sheepshead Bay, Flatbush and Brighton Beach in Brooklyn and Flushing and Jamaica Estates in Queens. Over the years, Trump also donated a number of properties to New York hospitals and other charitable organizations.

| **Lennart Uhlin** | Swedish architect Lennart Uhlin, Hon. FAIA, died in February 1999. He had been an expert in architectural preservation and had renovated several historic seventeenth-century palaces in Stockholm. In 1952, he formed a firm with Lars Malm in Stockholm. |

| **Aldo van Eyck, 80** | Former 1990 Denmark Royal Gold Medal for Architecture winner Aldo van Eyck died January 14, 1999. He had been a strong voice against the prevailing modern architecture of the 1950s and its functionalist abstraction. He specifically objected to the deadening alienation of the modern urban environment. His work was known for emphasizing the human side of building. His most famous project was the 1959 design for the state orphanage in Amsterdam. Throughout his career he taught at the School of Architecture of the Technical University at Delft and was the founder of the Netherlands' School of Structural Realism. |

| **John O. Van Koert, 86** | John O. Van Koert, modern furniture design leader, died October 11, 1998 in his home city of Santa Fe, New Mexico. In the 1950s, Van Koert designed flatware for Towle. One of his designs, the sleek "Contour," was chosen to represent modernism in a 1951 exhibition organized by the Walter Art Center of Minneapolis. In 1954, he was exhibition director of "Design in Scandinavia," a show that traveled for three years introducing Americans to Scandinavian modern design. His furniture designs in the 1950s were manufactured by Drexel and displayed in major department stores across the country. He subsequently worked for Serried Ltd. of North Carolina designing traditional home furnishings for over 20 years. |

H. Bradley Ver Bryck, 70

Architect and designer H. Bradley Ver Bryck died May 8, 1999. He had been president of the commercial interior design firm ISD, Inc. for many years. While with ISD, Ver Bryck's projects included the redesign of the Chicago Tribune newsroom in the late 1970s and the interior design of a new palace for King Hussein of Jordan. Before moving to Chicago, Ver Bryck worked with the New Canaan, Connecticut firm of Elliott Noyes and Associates as the associate in charge of design for Mobil Oil. During his tenure there, he succeeded in standardizing the design of gas stations worldwide.

Harry Weese, 83

Washington D.C. Metro system designer Harry Weese, FAIA, died November 29, 1998, in Manteno, Illinois. A Chicago architect widely known for his historic preservation work and modernist designs, Weese's firm, Harry Weese Associates, won the contract to design the 100-mile Metro system in 1967. It is widely considered to be one of the finest projects of its kind in the world. In Chicago, Weese designed the Time & Life Building and the Metropolitan Correctional Center. His preservation projects there included Adler and Sullivan's Auditorium Theater, the Field Museum of Natural History and Orchestra Hall. Weese developed the 1982 master plan for Washington D.C.'s Federal Triangle, restored Union Station, and designed that city's Arena Stage Theater. Before starting his own firm, Weese worked with Eero Saarinen at Michigan's Cranbook Academy and spent several years at Skidmore, Owings & Merrill in Chicago. Harry Weese Associates received the AIA Firm Award in 1978.

Paul Weidlinger, 84

Paul Weidlinger, an innovative structural engineer and former apprentice of Le Corbusier, died September 5, 1999. A native of Hungary, Weidlinger also apprenticed with Hungarian architect and artist Laszlo Moholy-Nagy before emigrating to the U.S. In 1949, Weidlinger formed his own firm, Weidlinger Associates, Inc., and proceeded to work with some of the world's top architects. He co-designed the Reader's Digest Building in Tokyo with Antonin Raymond and helped Gordon Bunshaft design the Banque Lambert in Brussels and One Liberty Street in New York City. During his career, he had also worked with Marcel Breuer and José Luis Sert. A pioneer in the use of materials such as high-strength concrete and fabric roofing, Weidlinger had also been the structural engineer on environmental sculptures for Picasso, Dubuffet, and Noguchi.

William H. Whyte Jr., 81

William Hollingsworth "Holly" Whyte died January 12, 1999. A former assistant managing editor of Forbes Magazine, White began a second career in the mid-1950s as an urban planner, scholar, and educator. His most famous book, The Organization Man (1956), rallied against corporate homogenization and the inherent dangers of suburban flight. He was also the author of Cluster Development (1963), The Last Landscape (1968), The Social Life of Urban Spaces (1980) and City (1989). A planning consultant, Whyte edited New York City's Master Plan in 1969, was a Distinguished Professor at Hunter College of the City University of New York, and was instrumental in the redevelopment of New York City's Bryant Park.

Marguerite Neel Williams, 82

Marguerite Neel Williams, a Georgia-based preservation activist, died May 11, 1999. Throughout her lifetime, Williams was an active promoter and supporter of preservation and initiated many important preservation programs. In 1971, she proposed the formation of the Georgia Trust for Historic Preservation and was instrumental in its launching. She also served as a board member for the National Trust for Historic Preservation during the 1980s and as the first chairman of Heritage Associates (later Heritage Society), an organization for National Trust members who contribute more than $1000. During the four year period she served in that capacity, membership tripled and $3 million was raised. In recognition of her efforts, Williams received the Trust's Louis du Pont Crowninshield Award in 1997. Williams is also credited with leading the restoration efforts in her hometown of Thomasville, Georgia.

INDEX

A

A&M Graphics, 81

Aalto, Alvar, 5, 36, 101, 164

Abbott Lowell Cummings Award, 29, 45, 160

Abbott, Carlton S., 196

Abbott, J. C., Jr., 196

Abdelhalim, Abdelhalim Ibrahim, 33

Abel, Howard G., 231

Abell, Helen, 314

Abell, James, 196

Abell, Jan M., 196

Abend, Stephen N., 196

Abercrombie, Sir Patrick, 36, 101, 105

Abercrombie, Stanley, 108, 190, 228, 259

Able, Edward H., 257

Abplanalp, Glen H., 267

Abrahamson, Bruce A., 196

Abramovitz, Max, 196

Abramowitz, Ava J., 253

Abrams, Ned H., 494

Abrossimov, A., 296

Abst, Raymond C., 196

AC Martin Partners, 413

Acito, Dan, 228

Ackerman, James, 41, 44

Ackerman, Stephen W., 228

Ackert, Kimberly A., 190

ACSA, see Association of Collegiate Schools of Architecture

Adair, William, 193

Adams, Clarellen, 259

Adams, Gail, 228, 263

Adams, Gerald D., 193

Adams, Harold L., 68, 196

Adams, William M., 196

Adams, William T., 196

Adams, Wm. Dwayne, 231

Adcock, Joy, 228, 263

ADD Inc., 413

Addison Clipson Associate Architects Inc., 283

Addonizio, Joseph F., 253

Adleman, Marvin I., 231

Adler, Leopold, 89, 314

Adlercreutz, Gunnel, 249

Adler-Schnee, Ruth, 72

Adlerstein, Michael, 196

ADP Marshall, 413

Adsit, Russell A., 231

Advanced Media Design, 77

Aéroports de Paris, 34

Affleck, Raymond T., 99

Aftland, Joel R., 237

Aga Kahn Award for Architecture, 30-35

Aguilar, O J., 249

Aguirre Corporation, 413

Aguirre, P., Jr., 196

Ahearn, Joseph, 253

Ahern, John F., 231

Ahles, Loren P., 196

Ai, 287, 413

AIA Gold Medal, 36

AIA Honor Awards, 18, 36-39, 441

AIA Honors for Collaborative Achievement, 20, 40-43

AIA, see American Institute of Architects

Aicher, Otl, 84

Aidala, Thomas R., 109, 196

Ainslie, Michael L., 253

Aitchison, George, 100, 271

Alakiotou, Roula, 196

Albakri, Hisham, 249

Albanese, Charles A, 196

Albert Kahn Associates, 52, 291, 414

Albrecht, Donald, 92

Albright, R. Mayne, 253

Albyn, Richard K., 196

Alciatore, Jerome H., 237, 267

Alden, N. Sue, 196

Alderman & MacNeish Architects, 282

Aldridge, Peter, 72

Alegria, Dr. Ricardo E., 314

Alen, William L. Van, 224

Alex, Iris S., 196

Alexander Gorlin Architect, 51

Alexander, Blake, 66

Alexander, Cecil A., Jr., 196

Alexander, Christopher, 65, 194

Alexander, Earle S., 196

Alexander, Henry C., 196

Alexander, James G., 196

Alexander, James M., 240

Alexander, Kenneth, 261

Alford, A. Notley, 196

Alice Davis Hitchcock Book Award, 18, 44-46

Allan, Stanley N., 196

Allegretti Architects, 282

Allen, Davis, 494

Allen, George A., 253, 272

Allen, Maurice B., 196

Allen, Ralph G., 196

Allen, Rex W., 196, 260

Allen, Robert E., 196, 260

Allen, Susan May, 270

Allen, William A., 249

Allen, William Van, 303

Allied Works Architecture, 91

Allison, Gerald L., 196

Alma-Taderna, Sir L., 100

Almond, Killis P., 196

Alpert, Estelle, 228

Alpha Design Group Inc., 282

Alschuler, Alfred S., 196

Alsobrook, Jerry R., 228

Altobelli, Aldo, 282

Altoon + Porter Architects, 414

Altoon, Ronald A., 196, 260

Alvar Aalto Museum, 164

Alvares, Alfred V., 249

Alvarez, Jose, 249

Alvarez, Mario R., 249

ALZA Corp., 81

AM Partners, 414

Amaral, Jesus E., 196

American Academy in Rome, 190-193

American Academy of Arts & Sciences, 193-194

American Academy of Arts and Letters Academy Awards, 47

American Academy of Arts and Letters Gold Medal for Architecture, 49

American Architectural Foundation, 128, 179

American Architecture Awards, 50-51, 170

American Consulting Engineers Council, 69-70, 129

American Institute of Architects, 4, 10, 16, 18, 20, 36, 37-39, 40-43, 52, 59, 68, 109, 110, 111-112, 121, 124, 130, 143, 179, 196-227, 249-252, 253-256, 260, 394-395, 427

American Institute of Architecture Students, 14, 24, 131, 261-262

American Planning Association, 132

American Society of Architectural Perspectivists, 43, 77

American Society of Interior Designers, 64, 133, 228-230, 263,

American Society of Landscape Architects, 20, 55, 56-57, 134, 231-236, 257, 264

Ames, Anthony, 190, 282

Amisano, Joseph, 190, 196

Anderson Design, 73-74

Anderson Mason Dale Architects, 280, 282

Anderson, Amy, 190

Anderson, Dorman D., 196

Anderson, Harry F., 196

Anderson, J. Macvicar, 271

Anderson, J. Robert, 231

Anderson, J. Timothy, 196

Anderson, John C., 237, 267

Anderson, John D., 196

Anderson, Lawrence, 110, 265

Anderson, Richard, 190, 196

Anderson, Ross S., 190

Anderson, Samuel A., 196

Anderson, Sir Robert Rowand, 101

Anderson, William L., 196

Ando, Tadao, 21, 54, 61, 84, 94, 97, 102, 249

Andreu, Paul, 34

Andrews, J. Philip, 196

Andrews, John H., 249

Andrews, John, 54, 249

Andrews, Lavone D., 196

Andrews, Martha P., 196

Andrews, William F., 228

Andropogon Associates, 283

Andros, Stephen John, 237

Angell, Ellen, 228

Angle, Robert H., 228

Angotti, Thomas, 193

Ankrom Moisan Associated Architects, 414

Anmahian Winton Associates, 37

Annese, Domenico, 231

Anselevicius, George, 66, 196, 266

Ansell, W.H., 271

Anshen + Allen, 414

Anstis, James H., 196

Antoinette Forrester Downing Award, 18, 41, 313

Antonakakis, Suzana, 244

Appel, Wallace H., 240

Apple Computer Inc., 80

Apple Design Group, 78

Appleyard, Donald, 193

Aramis Del Pino Architects, 283

Arant, John C., 237

Arbegast, David E., 231

Arbuckle Costic Architects Inc., 414

Archeon Inc, 283

Archer Engineers, 70

Archer, Richard M., 196

Architects Collaborative, The, 52, 81

Architects Hawaii Limited, 414

Architects' Council of Europe, 135

Architectural Alliance, 281

Architectural Design Group Inc., 283

Architectural Partnership, 281, 283, 291

Architectural Record, 248, 432

Architectural Resources Cambridge, 414

Architecture Company, 41, 283

Architecture Firm Award, 10, 52

Architecture Institute of Japan, 135, 148

Architecture Resource Center, 43

Architecture Studio, 33, 60

Architecture/Artistry/Interiors/Inc., 283

Architropolis, 83

Ard-Wood Architects Inc., 283

Arehart, Robert A., 228

Arfaa, Peter F., 197

Argos Group, 280

Arguelles, Carlos D., 249

Argus Supply Company, 282

Armajani, Siah, 42

Armbruster, David S., 231

Armitage, Robert E., 237

Armstrong, Eric, 192

Arnaud, Leopold, 265

Arneill, Bruce P., 197

Arnett, Warren G., 228

Arnold W. Brunner Memorial Prize, 54

Arnold, Christopher C., 197

Arnold, Henry F., 231

Arnott, Gordon R., 249

Aron, Trudy, 253

Aronson, Joseph H., 193

Arquitectonica, 247, 280, 286, 414

Arrigoni, Robert V., 197

Arrowstreet, 414

Art Institute of Chicago, 165-166

Arthur Manns Harden, 283

Arthur, Dr. Eric R., 99

Artigas, Joao Baptista Vilanova, 58, 85

Arup, Ove, 42, 76, 101

Ashbrook, Robert L., 237

Asher-Stubbins, Hugh, 195

Ashley, Ludd, 253

Ashley, Roy O., 231

Ashton, Raymond J., 260

ASID, see American Society of Interior Designers

Asken, Yvonne W., 197

Askew Nixon Ferguson Architects, 283

Askew, Laurin B., 197

Askew, Lee Hewlett, III, 197

ASLA Medal, 55

ASLA Professional Award, 56-57

ASLA, see American Society of Landscape Architects

Aslin, C.H., 271

Association of Collegiate Schools of Architecture, 6, 12, 59, 65-66, 143, 265-266

Astle, Neil L., 197

Astorino, Louis D., 197

Astro Products Inc., 80

Atelier Enam Architects, 32

Aten, D. Lyle, 231

Athenaeum of Philadelphia, 167

Atherton, Charles H., 197

Atkin, Tony, 197

Atkins, John L., 197

Atkins, W. S., & Partners, 293

Aubock, Carl, 249

Aubry, Eugene E., 197

Audi AG, 78

Auerbach, Seymour, 197

Auguste Perret Prize, 58

Aulenti, Gae, 94, 244

Austin Company, 290

Austin, Donald B., 231

Austin, Douglas H., 197

Avchen, Daniel, 197

Awards for Architectural Research, 59

Awes, Morten, 261

Awwad, Isam, 32

Axon, Donald C., 197

Axon, Janice, 253

Aydelott, Alfred L., 197

Ayers, Richard W., 190

B

Baca, Elmo, 193

Bach, Alfons, 240, 494

Backen Arrigoni & Ross, 287

Backen, Howard J., 197

Bacon, Edmund N., 40, 105, 197

Bacon, Henry, 36

Badgeley, Clarence Dale, 190

Badley, George Frederick, 100

Badovici, Jean, 245

Badran, Rasem, 34

Baer, David C., 68, 197

Baer, George, 259

Baer, Morley, 193

Baesel, Stuart, 197

Baetjer, E. Bruce, 192

Bahr, Deon F., 197

Baikdoosan Architects & Engineers, 293

Bailey Architects, 284

Bailey, Douglas A., 261

Bailey, Laura, 242

Bailey, Ray B., 197

Bain, William J., 197

Baines, George G., 249

Bair, R. Stanley, 197, 237, 267

Bakanowsky, Louis J., 197

Baker, David, 197

Baker, Isham O., 197

Baker, Jack Sherman, 197

Baker, James Barnes, 197

Baker, Jane D., 237, 267

Baker, Laurie, 106

Baker, Sir Herbert, 101

Baker, Ted, 231

Baker, William H., 231

Balderiotte, M., 105

Baldwin, Gordon C., 193

Baldwin, Gregory S., 190, 197

Baldwin, Harry J., 231

Baldwin, Jeanne, 242

Baldwin, Phillip R., 193

Baldwin, W D., 249

Balen, Samuel T., 197

Balet, Marc, 190

Ball, Rex M., 197

Ballard, Edward B., 231

Balli, Giorgio, 283

Ballinger, 281, 287, 290, 414

Ballon, Hilary, 46

Bally, Alexander, 240

Baltimore, Anita, 228

Banadayga, W. K., 249

Bang & Olufsen, 84

Banham, Reyner, 41, 85

Baniassad, Essy, 249

Bank, Red, 211

Bannister, Turpin C., 68, 272

Banwell, Richard S., 197

Baranes, Shalom S., 197

Baranov, Nikolai B., 249

Barbarena, Alejandro, 261

Barber, Michael, Architecture, 95

Barclay, Robert A., 197

Bargmann, Julie, 192

Barker, James, 66, 266

Barker, Rinker Seacat and Partners Architects, 280, 283

Barkley, Paul H., 197

Barley, John M., 197

Barlow, Charles C., 197

Barmou, Falké, 32

Barnes, Alton A., 231

Barnes, Edward Larrabee, 52, 54, 112, 194, 197, 297

Barnes, Jay William, Jr., 197

Barnes, Linda, 197

Barnett, Jonathan, 197

Barney, Carol R., 197

Baron, Milton, 231

Barr, Howard R., 197

Barragan, Luis, 97, 173, 186

Barre, Wilkes, 198

Barrett Quezada Architecture, 281

Barrett, David, 228

Barrett, Nathan F., 264

Barrick, Nolan E., 197

Barr-Kumar, Raj, 197, 260

Barron Heinberg & Brocato, 282

Barron, Errol, 197

Barrow, Richard E., 197

Barry, Charles, 100, 271

Barry, James R., 261

Barsotti, Frank L., 237

Barsotti, Nancy Hoff, 228

Bart, Sir Thomas Graham Jackson, 101

Barthold, Mariana, 253

Bartholomew, Richard, 190, 197

Bartlett, Jennifer, 41

Barton Myers Associates, 284

Barton, Cheryl, 231, 264

Bartos, Armand, 197

Barucki, Tadeusz, 85

Barun Basu Associates, 283

Baskervill & Son, 291

Bassett, Edward C., 54, 197, , 495

Bassett, Florence Knoll, 108, 258

Bassett, James H., 231

Bassett, Kenneth E., 231

Bassetti, Fred, 197

Bastyr, Richard P., 237

Batchelor, Peter, 197

Battaglia, Ronald J., 197

Bauer Stark, 291

Bauer, Anthony M., 231

Bauer, Jay S., 197

Baughman, Clarence W., 231

Baum, Joseph H., 42

Baume, Henry B., 267

Baumgarten, Howard R., 231

Bausman, Karen, 193

Bavaro, Joseph D., 197

Bawa, Geoffrey M., 249

Baxter, Augustus, 253

Bay, Bodega, 211

Bazer-Schwartz, Jeannine, 228

Bazzle, Tamara A., 228

BDH & Young Space Design, 281

Beach, Beverley, 254

Beach, Holmes, 197

Beach, Solana, 203

Beal, Roy F., 228

Beale, John Craig, 197

Beall, Burtch W., Jr., 197

Bean, Leroy E., 197

Beard, Alan J., 197

Beardsley Design Associates, 291

Bearsch, Lee P., 197

Beasley, Ellen, 193

Beatty Harvey & Associates, 290

Beaty, William H., 197

Beaudouin, Eugene, 249

Bechhoefer, William B., 197

Bechtel Group, 88

Bechtel, Riley P., 88

Bechtel, Stephen D., 88

Beck Group, 414

Beck, Eldon W., 231

Beck, George, 240

Becker Associates, 282

Becker, Lee, 197

Becker, Nathaniel, 240

Becker, Rex L., 197

Beckhard, Herbert, 197

Beckley, Robert, 197, 266

BecVar, Arthur N., 240

Bedell, Marjorie A., 228

Bednar, Michael, 197

Bee, Carmi, 198

Beeah Group Consultants, 33

Beer, David W., 198

Beery, Edgar C., 198

Befu, Yoshiro, 231

Beggs, Arthur G., 231

Beha, Ann M., 198

Behesht, Hasht, 31

Behnke, William A., 231, 264

BEI Associates, 280

Beinecke, Walter, 314

Belcher, John, 101, 271

Bell, Byron, 198

Bell, James R., 231

Bell, M Wayne, 198

Bell, Richard C., 192, 231

Bellafiore, Vincent, 231, 264

Belle, Beyer Blinder, 52, 76, 414

Belle, John, 198

Bellini, Mario, 72

Belluschi, Pietro, 36, 89, 112

Bender, Ralph C., 198

Benedek, Armand, 231

Benepe, Barry, 198

Benham Group, 414

Benisch, G., 58

Benjamin Thompson & Associates, 52

Benjamin, Elisabeth, 495

Benktzon, Maria, 84

Bennet, H., 105

Bennett, Claire R., 231, 264

Bennett, Daniel D., 198

Bennett, David J., 198

Bennett, Ralph, 66

Bennett, Stephen M., 253

Bennett, Ward, 41

Bennett, Wells, 265

Benoit, Gerard, 249

Benson, John, 41

Bentel, Frederick R., 198

Bentel, Maria A., 198

Bentsen, Kenneth E., 198

Bentz Thompson Reitow, 414

Bentz, Frederick J., 198

Berenson, Bertram, 265

Bereuter, Douglas, 257

Berg Architects, 90

Berg, Karl A., 198

Berg, Shary Page, 231

Berg, Wayne, 496

Bergman, Elaine, 253

Bergmann, Richard R., 198

Bergmeyer Associates, 414

Bergquist, Lloyd F., 198

Bergstedt, Milton V., 121

Bergstrom, Edwin, 260

Berkebile, Robert J., 198

Berkoff, Marlene J., 198

Berlage, Dr. Hendrik Petrus, 101

Berners, Edgar H., 270

Berners/Schober Associates, 291

Bernheim, Anthony N., 198

Berry, Frank Lee, 228

Berry, K. Norman, 198

Bersikutu, Arkitek, 31

Bertman, Richard J., 198

Bertone, Ronald P., 198

Bertram, Frederic A., 198

Berube, Claude, 242

Best, Melvin H., 240

Better.Design Solutions, 81

Betts, Gary A., 237

Betts, Hobart, 198

Betts, Richard J., 272

Bey, John C. Le, 212

Beyer Blinder Belle, 52, 76, 414

Beyer, John H., 198

Bhalla, Jai R., 249

Bickel, John H., 198

Biddle, James, 253

Bidwill, J., 253

Biebesheimer, Frederick C., 198

Big Design, 71

Biggs, T. J., 198

Binder, Rebecca L., 198

Birchfield, Hal F.B., 228

Bird, Lance L., 198

Birge, John R., 198

Birk, Sherry, 253

Birkerts, Gunnar, 54, 65, 198

Birnbaum, Charles A., 231

Birnbaum, Eugene D., 496

Bishir, Catherine W., 28, 313

Bishop, Calvin T., 231, 264

Bishop, James A., 198

Bishop, Walter F., 237

Bissell, George, 198

Bitter, Adriana, 228

Bitter, Edwin, 228

Black, J. Sinclair, 198

Black, Shirley, 259

Blackburn, Walter S., 198

Blackford, Leonard D., 198

Blackmar, Elizabeth, 28-29

Blackmon, Jan Gaede, 198

Blackner, Boyd A., 198

Blackstone Partnership, 283

Blackwood, Michael, 42

Blaich, Robert I., 240

Blake, Peter, 198

Blanc, Luis, 77

Blanchard, Howard T., 270

Blanchon, Georges, 246

Bland, Frederick A., 198

Bland, John, 99

Blanski, William A., 124

Blau, David H., 231

Blau, Eve, 92

Blegvad, Jacob, 249

Blehle, Frederick, 190

Blessing, Charles A., 40

Blessing, Wilfred E., 198

Blind, Kerry, 231

Blinder, Richard L., 198

Bliss, Anna Campbell, 193

Bliss, Richard L., 198

Bliss, Robert, 193, 198, 265

Blitch, Ronald B., 198

Blitz Architectural Group, 283

BLM Group, 281, 414

Block, Herbert Lawrence, 194

Blois, Natalie De, 202

Blomfield, Sir Arthur, 100

Blomfield, Sir Reginald, 101, 271

Blondheim, Charles A., 270

Bloodgood, John D., 198

Blum, Sigmund F., 198

Blumberg, Charles, 242, 259

Blumenfeld, Alfred M., 240

Blumenfeld, Hans, 105

Blumentals, Susan, 198

Blumenthal, S. Steve, 237, 267

Blumer, H. M., 198, 237

Blunck, Kirk V., 198

Blunden, William A., 198

Blurock, William E., 198

Blutter, Joan, 228

BMW Motorcycle Design Team, 73

Bobo, L. Kirkpatrick, 198

Bobrow, Michael L., 198

Bochkor, Stephen F., 192

Bödeker, Boyer, Wagenfeld and Partners, 33

Bodnar, James L., 190

Bodouva, William N., 198

Boehlert, Honorable Sherwood L., 253

Boehm, Gottfried, 97

Boehning, Joe, 198

Boerema, Robert J., 198

Bofill, Richardo L., 249

Boggs, Joseph, 198

Bogner, Walter F., 198

Bohigas, Oriol, 249, 253

Bohlin Cywinski Jackson, 37, 52, 75, 414

Bohlin, Peter, 198

Bohm, Friedrich K.M., 198

Bohnert, Reuben E., 283

Boiardi, Mario H., 198

Boigon, Irving D., 249

Boland Associates, 283

Boles, Stanley G., 198

Bolinger, Michael E., 198

Bolling, Robert D., 198

Bologna, Antonio R., 198

Bolt Beranek & Newman, 41

Bolton, Preston M., 198

Bonar, James R., 198

Bond, J. Max, Jr., 121, 198

Bond, Lloyd M., 231

Bonda, Peggy, 263

Bonda, Penny, 228

Bonell, Esteve, 86

Boney, Charles Hussey, 198

Boney, Jules, Jr., 68

Boney, Leslie N., 68, 198

Boney, Paul D., 198

Bonham, Dwight M., 199, 270

Bonner, J. Steven, 237

Boone, Daniel, 199, 270

Boone, David C., 199

BOORA Architects, 75, 414

Booth Hansen Associates, 60

Booth, Laurence O., 199

Booth, Norman K., 231

Booziotis, Bill C., 199

Borchelt, J. Gregg, 237

Bordinat, Eugene, 240

Borget, L. G., 199

Bort, James C., 237, 267

Bortenreuter, L., 105

Bortnick, Bernard, 199

Bosworth, Francke, 265

Bosworth, Thomas L., 190, 199

Botsai, Elmer E., 199, 260

Bottelli Associates, 291

Boucher, Jack E., 41

Bouligny, Dan, 242

Bourque, Michael, 242

Boutelle, Sara Holmes, 253, 496

Bowden, William D., 228

Bowen, Blair S., 228

Bowen, David M., 199

Bowen, Gary, 199

Bowen, Ronald Gene, 199

Bower, John A., 199

Bowers, Paul D., 199

Bowersox, William A., 199

Bowles, Chester, 199

Bowles, Kendrick & Lemanski, Architects,199, 283

Bowman, J. Donald, 199

Bowne, William Calvin, 237

Box, Hal, 66

Box, John Harold, 199

Boyd, A. S., 253

Boyd, Charles Chief, 237, 267

Boyden, Ann Marie, 253

Boynton, Robert A., 199

Bozalis, John, 199

Bradburn, James H., 199

Braden, David R., 199

Bradfield, Richard H., 199

Bradford, Susan, 228

Bradley, Carl L., 68

Bradley, Thomas G., 199

Brady, Clyde A., 199

Braley, Scott W., 199

Brame, Ronald M., 199

Brand, Joel, 199

Brandston, Howard, 43

Brandt, W. Frank, 231

Brannen, Robert, 199

Branner, Robert, 44

Brassel, Eleanor K., 253

Brassil, John, 73

Braun, Charles S., 199

Braunschweiger, Robert W., 193

Bray, Paul M., 193

Braymer, John W., 253

Brayton & Hughes, 281

Brayton, Paul, 108

Brayton, Richard M., 199

Brazer, Clarence W., 270

Brazley, William E., 199

Breakaway Architects, 283

Brecher, Melvin, 199

Breger, William N., 199

Bregman + Hamann Architects, 294, 295

Breines, Simon, 199

Brenan, William M., 237

Brendle, John Michael, 199

Brennan Beer Gorman/Architects, 414

Brenner, Barbara, 72

Brents, Daniel R., 199

Bresnan, Adrienne G., 199

Bresnan, Joseph, 199

Bresseler, Peter, 240, 268

Bresslergroup, 73

Breuer, Marcel, 36, 79, 110, 323, 516

Brewer, Benjamin E., Jr., 199, 260

Brewster, Elise, 192

Brickbauer, Charles G., 190

Bricker & Cannady, 90

Brickman, Theodore W., 231

Bridgers, Samuel W., 231

Bridges, Leon, 121, 199

Brien Herr, 422

Brien/Atkins Associates, 284

Briggs, Cecil C., 190

Briggs, Dee Christy, 261

Brigham, Bruce J., 228

Brightbill, William R., 237

Brill, Michael, 108

Brinkerhoff, Donald Carl, 231

Brinkley Sargent Architects, 283

Brinkley, David, 253

Brinkley, Mark K., 231

Bristol, Robert F., 231

Britt, Stanford R., 199

Brocato, Joseph M., Sr.,199

Brocchini, Myra M., 199

Brocchini, Ronald G., 199

Broches, Paul, 199

Brochstein, Raymond D., 199

Brock, A. R. Von, 224

Brock, Wayne C., 237

Brockway, A.L., 270

Brockway, William R., 199

Brodie, M. J., 199

Brody, Samuel, 54

Brook, Rye, 211

Brooke, Steven, 41, 193

Brooks, H. Allen, 45, 272

Brooks, H. Gordon, 199

Brooks, Jack, 109, 253

Brooks, James, 100, 192

Brooks, Larry, 237

Brooks, Turner, 190

Broome, John W., 199

Broshar, Robert C., 199, 260

Brotman, David J., 199

Broudy, Charles E., 199

Brown McDaniel Bhandari Inc., 415

Brown, A. B., 253

Brown, A. Larry, 237

Brown, Andrea Clark, 190

Brown, Arthur W., 267

Brown, C. Dudley, 228

Brown, Charlotte, 28

Brown, Chilton, 259

Brown, Denise Scott, 63, 66, 89, 194, 246-247

Brown, Everett, 64, 228

Brown, George D., Jr., 199

Brown, J. Carter, 88

Brown, J. N., 253

Brown, Jennie Sue, 199

Brown, Joseph E., 231

Brown, Julian, 73

Brown, Kenneth F., 199

Brown, Paul B., 199

Brown, R. Michael, 228

Brown, Robert F., 199

Brown, Robert L., 199

Brown, Theodore L., 190

Brown, Walton E., 228

Brown, William A., Sr., 253

Brown, William, 64, 190, 199, 253, 497

Brown, Woodlief, 199

Brownell, Charles, 92

Browning Day Mullins Dierdorf, 287

Brownlee, David, 46, 92

Brubaker, C. William, 199

Bruce Knutson Architects Inc., 284

Bruce, Barry B., 199

Bruce, Jeffrey L., 231

Bruder, William, 190

Bruegmann, Robert, 107

Bruner, Van B., Jr., 121, 199

Bruno, Harry A., 199

Bruno, San, 41, 206

Bruton, Larry S., 199

Bryan, Harvey, 199

Bryan, John M., 253

Bryan, Mary A., 228

Bryant, John H., 199

Bryck, H. Bradley Ver, 515

Brydone, Eleanor, 228

Brynildsen, Per Christian, 35

BSA Design, 281, 283, 287, 415

BSW International, 415

Bubenik, Jackie Karl, 231

Bublys, Algimantas V., 199

Buchanan, C., 105

Buchanan, Marvin, 190, 199

Buchanan, Robert T., 192

Büchele, Peter A., 74

Buckingham, Margaret, 259

Buckland & Taylor, 70

Buckley, James W., 199

Buckley, Michael P., 199

Budrevics, Alexander, 231

Budz, Robert S., 231

Buehrer, Huber H., 200

Buen, Jorge Gamboa de, 252

Buenz, John B., 200

Buettner, Dennis R., 231

Buff, Glenn A., 200

Buggenhagen, Wayne L., 231

Bull, Henrik H., 200

Bullock, Ellis W., 200

Bullock, Helen Duprey, 314

Bullock, Thomas A., 200

Bullock, W. Glenn, 200

Bullock, William, 240

Bumgardner, 415

Bumpers, Hon. Dale, 257

Bunch, Franklin S., 200

Bundy, Richard S., 200

Bunshaft, Gordon, 49, 54, 97, 160, 441, 505, 515

Burchard, Charles E., 110, 265

Burck, Richard, 192

Burgee, John H., 200

Burgess, Charles E., 200

Burggraf, Frank, 231

Burgun, J. Armand, 200

Burke, Edward M., 200

Burke, Robert H., 270

Burke-Jones, Joyce A., 228

Burkhardt, Robert G., 237

Burlage, James E., 200

Burley, Robert, 200

Burn, Lester T., 267

Burnet, Sir John James, 101

Burnham, Daniel, 303

Burns & McDonnell, 291, 508

Burns, Arthur L., 200

Burns, John A., 200

Burns, Norma DeCamp, 200

Burns, Robert, 66, 200, 265

Burson, Rodger E., 200

Burt Hill Kosar Rittelmann Associates, 415

Burt Taggart, 283

Busby, John A., 200

Business Week/Architectural Record Awards, 8, 59-60

Buskuhl, C. Joe, 200

Bussard, H. Kennard, 200

Butler Rogers Baskett Architects PC, 415

Butler, Charles, 270

Butler, David M., 228

Butler, Jerome R., 200

Butler, Theodore R., 200

Butner, Fred W., 200

Butt, Thomas K., 200

Butterfield, William, 100

Buttrick, Harold, 200

BWBR Architects, 281, 287, 415

Byard, Paul S., 200

Bye, Arthur E., 231

Byers, Brent, 200

Byrd, Willard C., 231

Bystrom, Arne, 200

C

C. J. Lawler Associates, 420

C. T. Male Associates, 70

Cadwalader, Burns, 200

Cadwell, Michael B., 193

Cafritz, Morris, 88

Cahan & Associates, 74

Cain, Raymond F., 231

Çakirhan, Nail, 31

Çakirlar, Ertan, 30

Calatrava, Santiago, 58

Calder, Rus, 242

Caskey, Donald W., 200

Cass, Heather W., 200

Casserly, Joseph W., 200

Casson, Sir Hugh Maxwell, 497

Castellana, John J., 200

Castellanos, Particia Gutierrez, 242

Castellanos, Stephan, 200

Castleman, Elizabeth M., 228

Castor, Daniel, 190

Castro-Blanco Piscioneri, 415

Castro-Blanco, David, 121

Castro-Buchel Architects & Planners, 282

Catlin, Juliana M., 228

Caudill, Samuel J., 200

Caudill, William Wayne, 36

Cavaglieri, Giorgio, 200

Cavin, W. Brooks, Jr., 200

Cawley, Charles M., 253

CBT/Childs Bertman Tsechares Inc., 280, 286

CDG Architects, 283

Cedar Corporation, 283

Celli-Flynn and Associates, 282

Cerasi, Vincent C., 192

Cesar Pelli & Associates, 52, 415

Cesaroni Design Associates, 71

Chabanne, Henri E., 192

Chadirji, Rifat, 35, 249

Chafee, Judith, 190

Chaffin, Lawrence, 200

Chaintreuil, Ann R., 200, 270

Chaix, Alfred V., 200

Chambers, Henry C., 253

Chambers, Michael D., 237

Chambers, S. Elmer, 237

Chambliss, Dean B., 200

Champeaux, Junius J., 200

Champneys, Basil, 101

Chan, Lo-Yi, 201

Chaney, James A., 237

Chang, Suk-Woong, 249

Chang, Te L., 249

Chao, Wing T., 201

Chapin, L. William, 201, 260

Chapman Griffin Lanier Sussenbach
    Architects, 415

Chapman, Donald D., 201

Chapman-Smith, Mary, 253

Charai, Abderrahim, 32

Chartier Newton & Associates, 284

Chase, John S., 121, 201, 281

Chase, William W., 253

Chase-Riboud, Barbara, 76

Chatelain, Leon, Jr., 260

Chatfield-Taylor, Adele, 193

Chatham, Walter, 193, 201

Chatrath, Amarjeet, 242

Chermayeff & Geismar Associates, 84

Chermayeff, Peter, 201

Chermayeff, Serge, 99, 110

Cherry, Edith, 201

Cherry, Edward E., 201

Chervenak, Robert A., 201

Chester Lindsey Architects, 294

Chicago Athenaeum, 50-51, 71, 74, 169-170

Chilcote, Lugean L., 201

Childress, G. Cabell, 201

Childs, David M., 201

Childs, Maurice F., 201

Chin, Susan, 39, 201

Chipman Adams Ltd., 282

Chisholm, Robert E., 201

Cho Slade Architecture, 91

Choisy, Auguste, 100

Chomik, Bill, 249

Chong, Gordon H., 201

Christensen, Frederick L., 201

Christensen, George W., 201

Christian, Ewan, 100, 271

Christman, James E., 232

Christner, 287

Christoph, Ann, 232

Christopher G. Green & Associates, 283

Christopher, James W., 201

Christovich, Mary Louise, 45

Chung, Eric A., 201

Church, Gary D., 237

Church, Thomas, 50, 55, 237

Cook, Walter, 260

Cook, William H., 201

Cooke, David, 242

Coolidge, Frederic S., 190

Cooper Carry, 286, 415

Cooper, Alexander, 201

Cooper, Jerome M., 201

Cooper, Lynton B., 237

Cooper, Sir Edwin, 101

Cooper, W. Kent, 201

Cooper-Hewitt Museum, 41, 96, 171-172, 495

Coover, Christopher, 201

Cope, Gerald M., 201

Copeland, Lee G., 201

Copeland, Rolaine V., 253

Corbusier, Le, 21, 36, 101, 243, 245-246, 304,
    501, 511, 515

Cordes, Loverne C., 228

Cordier, Herbert, 228

Cordwell, John D., 498

Corgan Associates, 286, 415

Corgan, C. Jack, 201

Corgan, Jack M., 201

Corkle, Eleanor, 242

Corlett, William, 201

Corlin, Len, 259

Corners, Clinton, 216

Cornoyer-Hedrick, 415

Correa, Charles, 35, 94, 101, 106, 114, 195,
    249

Correale, Fred J., 232

Cortrell, Eugene H., 237

Cossutta, Araldo A., 201

Costa, Lucio, 105

Costa, Walter H., 201

Costello, Jini, 228

Cott, Leland, 201

Cotter, John L., 313

Cotton, John O., 201

Couch, Frank L., 237

Coulter, Kenneth R., 232

Council on Tall Buildings and Urban Habit,
    138

Court, Donald P. Van, 239

Courtenay, Virginia W., 228

Courter, Joseph A., Jr., 283

Cousins, Morison S., 193

Cowell, C. H., 201

Cowgill, Clinton H., 270

Cowling, Dan C., 201

Cox, David C., 201

Cox, Frederic H, 202

Cox, Philip S., 249

Cox, Van L., 232

Cox, Warren J., 202

Cox, Whitson W., 202

Coxe, Weld, 253

Coyle, Stephen, 42

Crabtree, Bruce I., 202

Craig, Kirk R., 202

Craig, Lois, 253

Cralle, Christine, 259

Cram, Stephen, 121

Cramer, James P., 253, 259

Cramer, Tom, 259

Crandall, George M., 202

Crapsey, Arthur H., 240

Crasco, H. Kenneth, 232

Crawford, Dana, 314

Crawford, Elsie Krummeck, 498

Crawford, Ronald O., 202

Crawley, Stanley W., 66

Creamer, John Milton, 237

Creed, George E., 232

Creel, Wrenn M., 237

Creer, Philip D., 68

Creese, Walter L., 272

Crennen, Martin W., 202

Cret, Paul Philippe, 21, 36

Crimp, Frank W., 202

Crinion Associates, 78

Crissman, James H., 202

Crittenden, Edwin B., 202

Crocco, K. C., 202

Croft Compton Co., 280

Croft, Charles B., 202

Cromley, Elizabeth, 29

Cromwell Architects Engineers, 290

Cromwell Truemper Levy Thompson
    Woodsmall, 415

D

Darden, Edwin S., 202

Darling, Frank, 101

Darmer, Ben R., 202

Darryl Charles McMillen Architect, 284

Dassa/Richardi Architects, 283

Dattner, Richard, 109, 202, 416

Daugherty, Edward L., 232

Daumet, Honore, 101

David Carl Zimmermann-Architect, 285

David Evans and Associates, 416

David Ryan and Associates, 72

David Wisdom and Associates, 33

David, Theoharis L., 202

David, Thomas, 124, 209, 214, 239-240

Davidson, Ann, 253

Davidson, Colin H., 66

Davidson, D. G., 202

Davidson, David S., 202

Davidson, Joan K., 253

Davidson, John M., 249

Davidson, Kent, 261

Davidson, Robert I., 202

Davies, David Y., 249

Davis Associates Architects & Consultants, 283

Davis Brody Bond, 50, 75, 281

Davis Mason & Associates, 281

Davis, Albert J., 202

Davis, Arthur Q., 202

Davis, Brody & Associates, 52

Davis, Charles M., 202

Davis, Clark A., 202

Davis, Esherick Homsey Dodge &, 52, 500

Davis, Hortense, 228

Davis, Jerry A, 202

Davis, John M., 202

Davis, Lewis, 54, 109, 202

Davis, Patric, 261

Davis, Paul, 193

Davis, Robert S., 193

Davis, Steven M., 202

Davis, W. T., 202

Dawber, Sir Guy, 101, 271

Dawson, Stuart C., 55

Dawson, Stuart O., 232

Dawson, Thomas L., 190

Day, Clare Henry, 202

Day, Douglas W., 237

Day, Frank M., 260

Day, Frederic L., 202

Day, Mabel S., 253

DAZ Architects, 32

De Haas, John Neff, Jr., 202

Deam, E. L., 202

Dean, Francis H., 232

Dean, Kathryn, 190

Dean, Larry C., 237, 267

Dean, Neil J., 232

Dean, Robert C., 203, 228

Dean, Robert John, 228, 263

Dean/Wolf Architects, 38

Deasy, C. M., 203

DeBartolo, Jack, 202

DeBoer, Roy H., 232

Decaux, JC, 73

Decavalla, Costantin N., 249

DeChellis, Rudolph V., 202

Decker, Howard S., 203

Dee, Richard K., 232

Deems, Ward W., 203

Deering, Robert B., 232

Dees, Bruce, 232

Degenhardt, C. Christopher, 232

Degenkolb Engineers, 70

Degenshein Architects - Planners, 283

DeHann, Norman, 64, 263

Dehar, Allan J., 203

Dehn, Raymond H., 262

Delano, William Adams, 36, 49

Delawie, Homer T., 203

Delgado, Christopher G., 237

Delmar, Eugene A., 203

Delmonte, Ignacio M., 249

Delson, Sidney L., 203

Deluca, Fred R., 253

DeMars, Vernon, 202

DeMay, Kenneth, 202

Demmer, Erik, 72

DeMoll, Louis, 202, 260

Denisac, Charles M., 237

Denker & Bodnar, 283

Derpool, James G. Van, 272

Deshayes, Jos. Robert, 203

Design Alliance, 60

Design Central, 52, 80

Design Collective Incorporated, 280

Design Continuum Italia, 73

Design for Transportation Awards, 61-63

Design Futures Council, 139-140

Design Management Institute, 20, 140-141

Design Museum, 173

Design-Build Institute of America, 138-139

Designer of Distinction Award, 64

Designframe Incorporated, 74

Designworks/USA, 81

Desmond, Gary L., 203

Desmond, John J., 203

DeStefano, J. R., 51, 202

Deusen, Robert Van, 224

Dev, Gita, 203

DeVaris, Panayotis E., 202

Development Design Group, 416

Dewberry & Davis, 283, 416

DeWeese, Roger, 232

DeWolff Partnership, 416

Diamant, Robert, 203

Diamond, J., 203, 249

Diamond, Katherine, 203

Diaz, Horacio, 203

Diaz, James R., 203

Diaz-Azcuy, Orlando, 108

Diaz-Morales, Ignacio, 249

DiBenedetto, P., 203

Dibner, David R., 203

Dickenson, Russell E., 257

Diehl, Gerald G., 203

Dietrich, Paul E., 203

Dietsch, Deborah, 254

Dietz, Robert H., 203

Diffrient, Niels, 42, 78, 240

Dike, P. Woodward, 232

Dikis, William M., 203

DiLaura, Eugene L., 203

Dimond, F. Christopher, 232

Dimster, Frank, 203

Dines, Nicholas T., 232

Diniz, Carlos, 254

Dinsmore, Philip, 203

Dioxiadis, G., 105

Dirsmith, Ronald L., 190

Disrud, Carol, 242

Distinguished Professor Award, 65-66

Ditchy, Clair W., 260

Dixon, David D., 203

Dixon, F. Dail, 203

Dixon, John M., 203

Dixon, Michael A., 203

DLR Group, 281, 282, 416

DMJM, 287

Doane, Lawrence S., 203

Doblin, Jay, 240

Doche, Jim C., 203

DOCOMOMO, 18, 315

Dodge, Carlton T., 232

Dodge, Peter H., 203

Dohlen, Robert J. Von, 224

Dolginoff, Wesley J., 237

Dolim, George S., 203

Dominick, Peter Hoyt, Jr., 203

Donaldson, Milford W., 203

Donaldson, Thomas L., 100, 271

Donelin, Dan W., 232

Donelson, Janet, 203

Doner, H. Creston, 240

Donkervoet, Richard C., 203

Donnell Wicklund Pigozzi & Peterson, 286, 422

Donnell, William S., 43

Donnelly, Marian C., 272

Dorius, Kermit P., 203

Dorman, Albert A., 203

Dorman, Richard L., 203

Dorpfeld, Wilhelm, 101

Dorsey, Robert W., 203

Dorsky Hodgson, 280, 286, 416

Doshi, Balkrishna V., 34, 249

Doss, Darwin V., 203

Doty, Walter L., 257

Dougherty, Betsey O., 203

Dougherty, Brian P., 203

Ferguson, Bruce K., 232

Ferguson, Franklin T., 204

Ferguson, James, II, 242

Fergusson, James, 100

Ferlow, Donald L., 232

Fern, Alan M., 254

Fernandez-Norall, Manuel, 39

Fernau, Richard E., 204

Ferrara, Jackie, 42

Ferre, L. A., 254

Ferrell, Stephanie E., 204

Ferrer, Miguel, 204

Ferrey, Benjamin, 100

Ferrier, A. I., 250

Ferrier, Richard B., 205

Ferris, James D., 205

Ferris, Robert D., 205

Ferro, M. L., 205

Ferry, Donald E., 205

Fickel, Michael T., 205

Fickett, Edward H., 500

Field, David W., 254

Field, H. H., 205

Field, John L., 205

Fielden, Robert A., 205, 270

Fieldman, Michael M., 205

Fields, Jon J., 228

Figg Engineering Group, 96

Filarski, Kenneth J., 205

Fillpot, Bob G., 205

Filson, Ronald C., 190, 205

Finch, Curtis, 205

Finch, James H., 205

Findlay, Robert A., 205

Fine, Steven, 92

Finegold, Maurice N., 205

Finger, Harold B., 254

Fink, Ira S., 205

Finney, Garrett S., 190

Finrow, Jerry V., 205

Finta, Jozsef, 250

Firestone, Charles E., 270

Fischer, Katherine, 107

Fischer, Michael A., 124

Fisher & Paul Marantz, 41

Fisher & Paykel Ltd., 80

Fisher, A. Robert, 205

Fisher, James Herschel, 205

Fisher, John L., 205

Fisher, Larry G., 238

Fisk, Hollye C., 205

Fitch, James M., 40, 65, 254, 314

Fitch, James Marston,

Fitts, Michael A., 205

Fitzgerald, Darrell A., 205

Fitzgerald, James T., 205

Fitzgerald, Joseph F., 205

Fitzgerald, Richard A., 205

FitzPatrick, Thomas, 265

FKP Architects, 281, 287

Flad & Associates, 417

Flad, Joseph H., 205

Flansburgh, Earl Robert, 205

Flato, Ted, 205

Fleck, John C., 238, 267

Fleischer, Joseph L., 205

Fleischman, Richard J., 205

Flesher, Thomas H., 270

Fletcher Farr Ayotte PC, 417

Fletcher, Norman C., 205

Fletcher, Shelley, 193

Fletcher, Sir Banister, 271

Flex Development, 73

Flood, David J., 205

Florance, Colden R., 205

Flores, Antonio F., 250

Flores, Cesar X., 250

Flores, Phillip E., 232

Flores-Dumont, Luis, 205

Flournoy, William L., 232

Floyd Associates, 280, 425

Floyd, J. Chadwick P., 205

Floyd, Richard F., 205

Floyd, W. Jeff, Jr., 205

Fly, Everett L., 96, 232

Flynn, Ligon B., 205

Flynt, Mrs. Henry N., 314

Focke, John W., 205

Foerster, Bernd, 65, 205

Fogg, George E., 232

Foley, James J., 500

Follett, James, 205

Foor & Associates, 291

Foote, Fred L., 205

Foote, Stephen M., 205

Foote, Vincent M., 240

Forbes, J. D., 254, 272

Forbes, Peter, 50, 205

Ford & Earl Associates, 280, 286

Ford, John G., 228

Ford, Robert M., 205

Forester, Russell, 205

Forgey, Benjamin, 42

Fort, William S., 254

Fort-Brescia, Bernardo, 205

Foss Associates, 291

Foster, James R., 205

Foster, Mark M., 190

Foster, Richard, 205

Foster, Sir Norman, 13, 36, 39, 47, 54, 84, 86, 97, 101, 120, 138, 195, 250, 293, 303

Fowle, Bruce S., 205

Fowler, Bob J., 205

Fowler, Charles A., 250

Fowler, Thomas, IV, , 261

Fowles, Dorothy, 242

Fowlkes, Marion L., 205

Fox & Fowle Architects, 417

Fox, Arthur J., Jr., 254

Fox, Donald Mark, 232

Fox, Kathleen M., 232

Fox, Robert, 261, 499

Fox, Sheldon, 205

Fraker, Harrison, 39, 205

Frampton, Kenneth, 41, 110, 194

Frances Halsband Architects, 52, 75, 420

Francis, Edward D., 205

Francis, Mark, 57, 232

François de Menil Architects P.C., 37

Frank J. Stiene Group, 285

Frank, Jay E., 205

Frank, Richard C., 205, 271

Frankel, Neil, 242, 269

Franklin, Carol L., 232

Franklin, James R, 68, 205

Franta, Gregory, 205

Franz Joseph Shropa, 285

Franzen, Ulrich, 54, 205

Frasca, Robert J., 38, 205

Fraser, Charles E., 257

Frazer, Robert L., 232

Frazier, Glenn G., 238

FRCH Design Worldwide, 417

Fredericks, Marshall M., 257

Freed, James Ingo, 54, 89, 109, 194, 205

Freedman, Doris C., 254

Freeman White Inc., 291, 417

Freeman, Beverly L., 205

Freeman, Raymond L., 55, 264

Freeman, William W., 205

French, Jeffrey S., 205

French, Jere S., 232

French, Stanley J., 283

Frey, Albert, 501

Frey, Angela, 242

Frey, John W., 232

Fridstein, Thomas K., 205

Friedberg, M. Paul, 41, 232

Friedlaender, Stephen, 205

Friedman, David, 46

Friedman, Hans A., 205

Friedman, Mildred, 42, 254

Friedman, Rodney F., 205

Friedrichs, Edward, 205

Frier, Sid, 270

Frost, Patsy L., 254

Frostic, Gwen, 257

Fry, Lord Holford E. Maxwell, 101, 244

Fry, Louis E., 205

Fry, Richard E., 205

Fuccio, Robert De, 193

Fujikawa, Joseph Y., 206

Fulford, Eric Reid, 192

Fuller, Albert B., Jr., 206

Fuller, Frank L., 206

Fuller, R. Buckminster, 15, 36, 49, 101, 258

Fuller, Ruth, 254

Fulton, Duncan T., 206

Fulton, James, 240, 268

Fung, Hsin-ming, 47, 193

Gowans, Alan, 44, 272

Grabowski, Thomas C., 229

Gracey, Brian, 207

Grad, Bernard J., 207

Graham Anderson Probst & White, 290

Graham Gund Architects, 418

Graham, Bruce J., 207

Graham, Carol S., 242

Graham, D. R., 254

Graham, Gary L., 207

Graham, Gordon, 271

Graham, Lori, 259

Graham, Philip H., 233

Graham, Roy E., 207

Graham, Theodora Kim, 229

Gramann, Robert E., 207

Gran, Warren Wolf, 207

Granary Associates, 281, 287

Grassli, Leonard, 233

Gratz, Roberta, 254

Graugaard, Jorgen, 238

Graven, Paul H., 270

Graves, Charles P., 207

Graves, Dean W., 207

Graves, Ginny W., 254

Graves, Michael, 15, 38, 50, 54, 72, 89, 190, 207, 418

Gray Design Group, 281

Gray, Ann E., 43

Gray, Barbara, 254, 502

Gray, David Lawrence, 207

Gray, Eileen, 245

Gray, Gordon C., 314

Gray, Thomas A., 207

Graziani, Lyn E., 207

Greager, Robert E., 207

Great American Main Street Awards, 316

Grebner, Dennis W., 207

Greeley, Mellen C., 270

Green, Aaron G., 207

Green, Cecil H., 254

Green, Curtis H., 207

Green, Richard J., 207

Green, Thomas G., 207, 283

Green, William Curtis, 101

Greenberg, Aubrey J., 207

Greenberger, Stephen, 229

Greene, Bradford M., 233

Greene, Isabelle Clara, 233

Greene, James A., 207

Greenfield, Sanford, 207, 265

Greenfield/Belser Ltd., 96

Greenleaf, James L., 264

Greenstreet, Robert, 66, 266

Greenwald, Susan, 207

Greenwell Goetz Architects, 82

Greenwood, Ben F., 267

Greer, John O., 207

Gregan, E. Robert, 233

Gregg, Glenn H., 207

Grenald, Raymond, 207

Gresham Smith & Partners, 418

Gresham, James A., 190, 207

Grey, Earl de, 271

Gridley, William C., 207

Griebel, K., 105

Grieve, L. Duane, 207

Grieves, James R., 207

Griffin, Brand Norman, 190

Griffin, Roberta S., 229

Griffith, Alana S., 238

Griffith, Thomas, 254

Grinberg, Donald I., 207

Grinberg, Sara T. De, 249

Grissim, John N., 233

Griswold Heckel & Kelly Associates, 286

Griswold, John S., 240

Griswold, Ralph E., 192

Griyantara Architects, 32

Grochowiak, Edward A., 207

Gromatzky Dupree, 286

Gropius, Walter, 11, 36, 79, 101

Grossi, Olindo, 190, 207, 265

Groth, Paul, 29

Group Mackenzie, 418

Groupdesigners, 283

Grover, William H., 207

Groves, Webster, 212

Grube, J. C., 207

Gruber, Michael, 190

Hammer, P., 254

Hammer, Theodore S., 208

Hammond Beeby Rupert Ainge, 418

Hammond, Charles H., 260

Hammond, Gerald S., 208

Hammond, John Hyatt, 208

Hanner, W. Easley, 208

Hampton, A. Niolon, 229

Hampton, E, 202-203

Hampton, Mark G., 208

Hamzah, T.R., 34

Hanamoto, Asa, 233

Hanbury, John Paul C., 208

Hancock, Marga Rose, 254

Hand, Peter H., 208

Haney, Craig K., 238

Hanke, Byron R., 233

Hanna, Robert Mitchell, 192

Hansen, J. Paul, 208

Hansen, James G., 240

Hansen, Richard F., 208

Hansen, Robert E., 208

Hansens, Fritz, 84

Hansjerg Maier-Aichen, 72

Hanson, Richard E., 233

Hara, Ernest H., 208

Hara, John M., 208

Harbor, Oak, 198

Harbor, Sag, 198

Harby, Steven, 190

Harder, Dellas H., 208

Hardesty, Nancy M., 233

Hardin, James B., 238

Hardison, Donald L., 208

Hardwick, Philip, 100

Hardy Holzman Pfeiffer Associates, 52, 418

Hardy, Hugh, 54, 208

Hare, Henry Thomas, 271

Hare, S. Herbert, 264

Hargreaves Associates Cascade Crest, 56

Hargreaves, George, 233

Harkness, John C., 208

Harkness, Sarah P., 208

Harkness, Terence G., 233

Harley Ellington Design, 418

Harmon Group Architects, 282

Harmon, Frank, 208

Harmon, Harry, 68, 208

Harmon-Vaughan, Beth, 242, 269

Haro, John C., 208

Harper, Charles F., 208

Harper, David M., 208

Harper, Robert L., 208

Harper, Terrell R., 267

Harrell, James W., 208

Harriman Associates, 290

Harrington, Robert W., 238

Harris, Charles W., 233

Harris, Cyril M., 41

Harris, David A., 208

Harris, Donald M., 257

Harris, Edwin F., 208

Harris, Emanuel Vincent, 101

Harris, Harwell Hamilton, 65

Harris, James Martin, 208

Harris, John, 92

Harris, Richard, 29, 233

Harris, Robert, 41, 65, 208, 233, 261, 265

Harrison & Abramovitz, 295

Harrison & MacMurray, 111

Harrison, Abramovitz, & Harris, 298

Harrison, Partrick K., 254

Harrison, Robert V.M., 238

Harrison, Robert VM, 208

Harrison, Wallace K., 36

Harrover, Roy P., 208

Harry Weese & Associates, 52, 515

Hart, Arthur A., 254

Hart, Dianne, 254

Hartman, Craig W., 208

Hartman, Douglas C., 208, 238

Hartman, George E., 190, 208

Hartman, Morton, 208

Hartman-Cox Architects, 52, 418

Hartmann, William E., 208

Hartray, John F., Jr., 68, 208

Hartung, Timothy, 208

Hartzog, George B., 257

Harvard Jolly Clee Toppe Architects, 418

Harvey, Patricia, 229

Harvey, Robert R., 233

Hasbrouck, Wilbert R., 208

Haskell Company, 286

Haskell, Dennis E., 208

Haskell, Douglas, 40

Haskins, Albert L., Jr., 208

Hass, Dr. F. Otto, 254

Hasselman, Peter M., 208

Hassid, Sami, 208

Hassinger, Herman A., 208

Hasslein, George J., 208

Hastings, Hubert de Cronin, 101

Hastings, Judith, 242, 269

Hastings, L. J., 208

Hastings, Robert F., 260

Hastings, Thomas, 7, 101

Hatami, Marvin, 208

Hauf, Harold D., 208

Haus, Stephen C., 192

Hauschild-Baron, Beverly E., 254

Hauser Inc., 71

Hauser, Jon W., 240

Hauser, Stephen G., 240

Hausner, Robert O., 208

Hautau, Richard G., 233

Havekost, Daniel J., 208

Havens, William H., 233

Haviland, David S., 42

Haviland, Perry A., 208

Hawes, Velpeau E., 208

Hawkins, Dale H., 192

Hawkins, H. Ralph, 208

Hawkins, Jasper Stillwell, 208

Hawkins, William J., 208

Hawley, William R., 208

Haworth, Dennis, 229

Hawtin, Bruce A., 208

Hayashi, Shoji, 250

Hayden, Richard S., 208

Hayes, John Freeman, 208

Haynes, Irving B., 208

Hays, Betty C., 238

Hazelhurst, Franklin Hamilton, 45

HDR Architecture, 280, 418

Healey, Edward H., 208

Hearn, Michael M., 208

Heath, Thornton, 244

Heatly, Bob E., 66

Heck, Robert, 66

Heckel & Kelly Associates, 286, 418

Hecksher, A., 254

Heery International, 281, 286, 418

Heery, George T., 208

Heights, Yorktown, 226

Heilig, Robert Graham, 233

Heimbaugh, John D., 190

Heimsath, Clovis, 208

Heine/Lenz/Zizka, 74

Heineman, Paul, 238

Heinfeld, Dan, 208

Heinz, Jo, 242

Heiskell, Andrew, 254

Hejduk, John, 15, 54, 110, 208

Helfand, Margaret, 208

Heller, Jeffrey, 208

Hellmann, Maxwell Boone, 208

Hellmuth Obata + Kassabaum, 76, 209, 217, 257, 260, 280, 281, 286, 287, 293, 418, 512

Hellmuth, George F., 209

Helman, A. C., 209

Helmer, Dorothy G., 229

Helpern, David P., 209

Helphand, Kenneth I., 233

Hemphill, James C., 209

Henderson, 54, 203, 209, 233, 271

Henderson, A. Graham, 271

Henderson, Arn, 209

Henderson, Edith H., 233

Henderson, John D., 209

Henderson, Philip C., 209

Henderson, Richard, 54

Hendricks, James L., 209

Hendrix, Glenn O., 233

Henner, Edna, 242

Henry, William R., 209-210, 219, 260

Hensman, Donald C., 209

Herbert Lewis Kruse Blunck Architects, 38, 418

Herbert, Albert E., 229

Herbert, Charles, 101, 209, 270
Herbst LaZar Bell Inc., 73, 79
Herman Miller Inc., 41
Herman, Bernard, 28-29
Herman, Robert G., 209
Hermann, Elizabeth Dean, 192
Hermes Reed Architects, 287
Herrin, William W., 209
Herron, John, 242
Hershberger, Robert G., 209
Hershey, Fred B., 229
Hershfang, Amy, 254
Herzog, Thomas, 58
Hesson, Paul A., 209
Heuer, Charles R., 209
Hewitt, D. M., 209
Heylman, Warren Cummings, 209
Hicks, Mason S., 209
Highland Associates, 281
Hight, Charles, 209, 265
Hijjas Kasturi Associates, 296
Hilbert Architecture, 284
Hildebrand, Marshall A., 238
Hilderbrand, Gary R., 192
Hilderbrandt, Donald F., 233
Hilfinger, Dean F., 68, 209
Hill Glazier Architects, 419
Hill Partnership, 284
Hill, John W., 209
Hillier Group, 281, 419, 512
Hillier, J. Robert, 209
Hills, Arthur W., 233
Hilversum, William Marinus Dudok, 36
Hinchman & Grylls, 95, 112
Hinds, George A., 190
Hines, Gerald D., 254, 445
Hinshaw, Mark, 209
Hinton, Kem G., 209
Hisaka, Don M., 209
Hise, Gregory, 107
Historic American Buildings Survey, 40, 314, 317
Hitchcock, Henry-Russell, 44, 272
Hite, Charles L., 254
Hittorff, J. I., 100

Hixon, Allen W., 233
HKS Inc., 51, 286, 419
HLM Design, 419
HLW International, 83, 281, 290, 419
HMC Group, 419
Hnedak, Gregory O., 209
HNTB, 287, 419
Ho, Mui, 66
Ho, Tao, 250
Hoag, Paul S., 209
Hobbs, Richard W., 209
Hobin, Barry J., 250
Hock, Erwin Conrad, 503
Hockaday, Peter S., 209
Hockaday, Robert C., 238
Hodgell, Murlin R., 209
Hodges & Associates, 280
Hodges/Marvin, 284
Hodgetts, Craig, 47
Hodne, Thomas H., 209
Hoedemaker, David C., 209
Hoenack, August F., 209
Hoffman, David H., 209
Hoffman, David L., 209
Hoffmann, John J., 209
Hogg, Ima, 314
Holabird & Root, 52, 290, 419
Holabird, John A., 209
Holden, Charles Henry, 101
Holder, L. M., 209
Holford, The Lord, 101, 271
Holl, Steven, 37, 54, 182, 419
Holland, Major L., 209
Hollein, Hans, 97, 250
Hollerith, Richard, 240, 268
Hollis & Miller Group, 282
Hollo, Canadian. Born Eva, 248
Holman, Joseph W., 270
Holmes & Narver, 419
Holmes Products Corp., 80
Holmes, Dwight E., 209
Holmes, Jess, 209
Holmes, Nicholas H., 209
Holroyd, Harry J., 209
Holstein, Robert W., 238

Holtz, David A., 209

Holzbauer, Wilhelm, 250

Holzman, Malcolm, 54, 209

Homestead, 213, 327, 331

Homsey, George W., 209

Hood, Bobbie S., 209

Hood, Raymond, 295

Hood, Vance R., 257

Hood, Walter, 192

Hooker, Van D., 209

Hooper, Vicki L., 124

Hoover, G. N., 209

Hoover, George, 209

Hoover, Ray C., III, 209

Hope, A.J.B. Beresford, 271

Hope, Frank L., Jr., 209

Hopkins, Alden, 192

Hopkins, Gene C., 209

Hopkins, Lady Patricia, 250

Hopkins, Patty, 102

Hopkins, Sir Michael, 250

Hopper, Leonard J., 233

Hopprier, Peter, 190

Horan, Joseph P., 229

Hord, Edward M., 209

Horii, Howard N., 209

Horn, Gerald, 209

Hornall Anderson Design Works, 74

Hornberger Worstell, 419

Horns, Miller, 193

Horsbrugh, Patrick, 209, 257

Horsky, Charles A., 88

Horton, Frank L., 314

Horty, T., 209

Hose, Robert, 240, 268

Hough, Reginald D, 209

Houseman, William, 254

Housworth, Marvin C., 209

Hovey, David C., 209

Hoving, Thomas P., 254

Howard Oxley Associates, 284

Howard, Elizabeth, 229, 263

Howard, J. Murray, 209

Howard, Perry, 233

Howard/Stein-Hudson Associates, 70

Howarth, Thomas, 44, 250

Hower, Donovan E., 233

Howey, John, 209

Howorth, Thomas Somerville, 124, 209

Hoyer, Herman R., 238

Hoyt, Charles K., 209

Hoz, Rafael De La, 249

Hricak, Michael M., 209

Hsiung, Robert Y., 209

Hu, Gilman K.M., 238

Hubbard, Charles A., 209

Hubbard, Henry Vincent, 264

Hubbard, Thomas D., 238

Hubbell, Kent, 266

Huberman, Jeffrey A., 209

Hudak, Joseph, 233

Huddleston, Sam L., 233

Huettenrauch, Clarence, 238

Huey, J. Michael, 254

Huffman, Richard W., 209

Hugh Ferris Memorial Prize, 77

Hugh Stubbins & Associates, 52

Hughes, Nina, 229

Hughes, Robert S.F., 194

Huh, Stephan S., 209

Huitt-Zollars Inc., 284

Hull, Robert E., 209

Human Factors Industrial Design, 72

Hummel Architects, 291

Hummel, Charles F., 209

Hummel, Fred E., 209

Humphries Poli Architects, 280

Humstone, Elizabeth, 190

Hunderman, Harry J., 210

Hunner, Mark B., 233

Hunt, Richard Morris, 55, 100, 179, 278, 320

Hunter, Dorian, 229

Hunter, J. Norman, 267

Hunter-Moody Architects, 281

Huppert, Frances P., 210

Hursley, Timothy, 42

Hurst, Sam T., 210

Husain, Syed V., 210

Hutchins, Mary Alice, 210, 238

Hutchinson, Max, 271

Hutchinson, Philip A., 254

Hutchirs, Frederick, 242

Huxtable, Ada Louise, 85, 98, 194, 254

Huygens, Remmert W., 210

Hvale, James L., 240

HWH Architects Engineers Planners Inc., 280

Hyde, Bryden B., 210

Hylton, Thomas, 257

Hynek, Fred J., 210

I

I.D. Annual Design Review, 78-79

IBM Corp., 79, 81, 88, 281

ICCROM, see International Centre for the Study of Preservation and Restoration of Cultural Property

ICOMOS, see International Council on Monuments and Sites

IDEA Award, see Industrial Design Excellence Awards

IDSA, see Industrial Designers Society of America

IIDA, see International Interior Design Association

Iliescu, Sanda D., 190

Illingworth, Dean, 210

Imaginary Forces Design, 78

Immenschuh, David, 242

Independent Group, 247

Industrial Design Excellence Awards, 80-81

Industrial Designers Society of America, 18, 81, 142, 240-241, 258, 268, 394-395

Ingraham, Elizabeth W., 210

Initiative for Architectural Research, 143

Insight Product Development, 80

Interbartolo, Michael, 261

Interior Design Competition, 81-82

Interiors' Annual Design Awards, 83

International Centre for the Study of Preservation and Restoration of Cultural Property, 318

International Council of Societies of Industrial Design, 144

International Council on Monuments and Sites, 319

International Design Award, Osaka 66, 83, 84, 108

International Federation of Interior Architects/Designers, 145

International Federation of Landscape Architects, 16, 146

International Interior Design Association, 82, 108, 147, 242-243, 259, 269, 394-395

International Union of Architects, 58, 85, 105, 106, 114, 148

Iram, Harry F., 238

Ireys, Alice R., 233

Is, Bainbridge, 202

Iselin, Donald G., 254

Isley, William A., 210

Isozaki, Arata, 54, 101, 250

Israel, Franklin D., 47, 190

Israel, Sheldon B., 238, 267

ITO Design, 72

Ito, Toyo, 250

Ittner, H. Curtis, 210

Iversen, Erling F., 190

Iverson, Wayne D., 233

Ivester, H. Cliff, 229

Ivy, Robert A., 210

Izumita, Ronald M., 233

J

J. J. Rose & Associates, 285

J. S. Schultz Architect, 285

J. Stuart Todd Architects, 285

Jack Beers - Architects/Engineers, 282

Jack Lindeman-Specifications Consultant, 284

Jackman, Dianne, 259

Jackson, Chris, 39

Jackson, Daryl, 250

Jackson, H. Rowland, 233

Jackson, Huson, 210

Jackson, John B., 41

Jackson, Kathy C., 254

Jackson, Mike, 210

Jackson, R. D., 250

Levy, Herbert W., 212

Levy, Morton L., 213

Levy, Toby S., 213

Lew & Patnaude Inc., 284

Lewis, Anne McCutcheon, 213

Lewis, Calvin F., 213

Lewis, David, 68, 213, 238

Lewis, Diane, 191

Lewis, George B., 213

Lewis, Jack R., 267

Lewis, Lawrence, Jr., 255

Lewis, Michael J., 46

Lewis, Neville, 242

Lewis, Paul, 191, 255

Lewis, Philip H., 55, 234

Lewis, Richard L., 213

Lewis, Roger K., 213

Lewis, Roy W., 191

Lewis, Thomas E., 238

Lewis, Tom, 213

Lewis, Walter H., 213, 257

LeWitt, Sol, 41

Lezénés, Gilbert, 33

Li, Wei, 77

Libeskind, Daniel, 47

Licht, George T., 191

Liddle, Alan C., 213

Lieber, J. Roland, 234

Liebhardt, Frederick, 213

Liebman, Theodore, 191, 213

Liff, Bernard J., 213

Likovni Studio, 74

Lim, Jimmy C.S., 35

Lin, Maya, 47, 72

Lin, T.Y., 41

Lind, John H., 213

Linden, Olavi, 73

Lindenthal, Robert S., 229

Lindhult, Mark S., 234

Lindsay Ponder Brayfield & Associates Inc., 284

Lindsey, David, 213

Lindström, Joe, 31

Lindström, Sune, 31

Linley, Viscount David, 259

Linn, Karl, 224, 234

Linn, West, 224

Linnard, Lawrence G., 264

Lippincott, H. Mather, Jr., 213

Liskarim, William H., 213

Lister, James M., 192

Little, J. Mack, 234

Little, Mrs. Bertram R., 314

Little, Robert A., 213

Little, Susan P., 234

Littleton, Charles, 242

Litton, R. Burton, 234

Liu, Dr. Binyi, 257

Livesey, Robert S., 191

Livingston Slone, 284

Livingston, Stanley C., 213

Livingston, Thomas W., 213

Livingston, Walter R., 213

Lizon, Peter, 213

LMN Architects, 287, 420

Loch, Emil, 270

Lockard, W. Kirby, 213

Lockett, Thomas A., 234

Lockwood Greene, 290, 420

Lodsworth, Baroness Jackson of, 40

Loebl Schlossman & Hackl/Hague Richards, 282, 286, 420

Loebl Schlossman Dart & Hackl, 293, 295

Loendorf, Boyd L., 229

Loew, Christopher, 71

Loewy, Raymond, 64, 240, 501

Loftis, James L., 213

Logan, Donn, 213

Lohan Associates, 420

Lohan, Dirk, 213

Lohmann, William T., 238

Lollini, Thomas E., 213

Lomax, Jerrold E., 213

Long, Nimrod W. E., 234

Longstreth, Richard, 29, 107, 272

Loo, Kington, 250

Looney Ricks Kiss, 420

Looney, J. Carson, 213

Loope, R. Nicholas, 213

Lorant, Gabor, 213

Lorch, Emil, 265

Lord, Larry, 213

Lord, W.H., 270

Lorenzini, David E., 238

Lorenzo, Aldana E., 250

Loschky Marquardt & Nesholm, 39

Loschky, George H., 213

Lose, David O., 234

Loss, John C., 213

Lotery, Rex, 213

Louie, William C., 213

Lounsbury, Carl, 28-29

Louth, County, 216

Love, John A., 257

Love, Michael, 229

Love, William, 213

Lovelace, Eldridge, 234

Lovelace, Richard, 77

Lovett, Wendell H., 213

Lowe, Peter E., 240

Lowery, Jack, 263

Lowrie, Charles N., 264

Loza, Serapio P., 250

LPA, 281

LRS Architects, 420

Lu, Paul C. K., 234

Lu, Weiming, 255

Lubben, Ronald, 242

Lubetkin, Berthold, 101

Lucas, Frank E., 213

Lucas, Thomas J., 213

Lucey, Lenore M., 213

Luckenbach, Carl F., 213

Luckett & Farley Architects, 290, 420

Luckman, Charles, 295, 298, 505

Luder, Owen, 271

Lueck, Odette, 229

Luhn, Graham B., 213

Luhrte, Richard L. Von, 224

Lukova, Luba, 74

Lumpkin & Associates Architects, 284

Lumsden, Anthony J., 213

Lunar Design, 73, 80

Lund, Kjell, 250

Lunde, Frithjof, 213

Lunden, Samuel E., 68

Lundwall, Phillip, 213

Lundy, Victor A., 213

Lupia, Major General Eugene, 255

Lutes, Donald H., 213

Lutyens, Sir Edwin Landseer, 36, 101

Lye, Eric Kumchew, 85

Lyle, John, 55

Lyman, Frederic P., 213

Lynch, Robert Dale, 213

Lynch, Robert J., 213

Lyndon, Donlyn, 96, 110, 213, 265

Lyndon, Maynard, 213

Lynford, Ruth K., 229

Lynne, Crum, 213

Lyons, Eric, 271

M

M & Co, 39

M. Nasr & Partners, 297

M.Kliment & Frances Halsband Architects, 420

Maas, Jane, 255

Maas, Michael, 213

MacAlister, Paul, 240

MacAllister, John E., 213

Macaulay, David A., 40

MacCormac, Richard C., 271

MacDonald, Donald, 213

MacDonald, Lee, 257

MacDonald, Virginia B., 213

MacDonald, William J., 46

MacDougall, Elisabeth Blair, 272

MacDougall, Prof. E. Bruce, 257

MacEwen, H A., 213

MacFadyen, John H., 191

Machado, Rodolfo, 47

Machado, Silvetti Associates, 421

Machida, Hiroko, 242

Mack, Robert C., 213

MacKenzie, Candace, 242

Mackey, Eugene J., 213

MacKinlay, Ian, 213

MacLachlan, Cornelius & Filoni, 291

MacMahon, Charles H., 213

Macsai, John, 213

Macy, J. Douglas, 234

Madawick, Tucker P., 240

Madawick, Tucker, 240, 268

Maddox, Diane, 255

Madera, Corte, 255

Madison, Robert P., 213

Madrid, Angelina Munoz Fernandez de, 250, 254

Madsen, Peter E., 213

Maffitt, Theodore S., 213

Magaziner, Henry J., 213

Maginnis, Charles D., 36, 260

Maguire Group, 96

Maguire Thomas Partners, 42

Mahaffey, Gary, 213

Maheux, Anne Frances, 193

Mahler, Harry B., 505

Mahler, Victor C., 213

Mahlum Architects, 421

Mahlum, John E., 213

Maier-Aichen, Hansjerg, 72

Mains, Lendall W., 238

Maio, Judith Di, 190

Maitland, 209, 284

Maiwald, C. R., 213

Majekodunmi, Olufemi, 250

Makela, P. Scott, 506

Maki, Fumihiko, 19, 54, 84, 94, 97, 114, 120, 123, 195, 250

Makinen, Matti K., 250

Makinson, Randell Lee, 255

Malacara, Rutilo, 250

Malcolm Pirnie, 69

Malecha, Marvin, 214, 266

Malefane, Motlatsi Peter, 250

Mallgrave, Harry Francis, 46

Maloof, L. Vic, 214

Maltzan, Michael Thomas, 124

Malyn, Michael H., 234

Mambro, Antonio Di, 203

Man, Cameron R. J., 234, 264

Mancini Duffy, 281, 287

Mango, Joseph R., 240

Mangones, Albert, 250

Mangunwijaya, Yousef B., 33

Mangurian, Robert, 191

Manley, Donald W., 238

Manly, William M., 229

Mann, Arthur E., 214

Mann, Lian Hurst, 43

Manning, Warren H., 264

Manny, Carter H., Jr., 214

Manser, Michael, 271

Manus, Clark D., 214

Maragall, Pasqual, 84

Marco Design Group, 280

Marcus, Stanley, 255

Margarita, Rancho Santa, 215

Margerum, Roger W., 214

Mariani, Theodore F., 68

Marines, Louis L., 255

Mark Demsky Architects, 51

Markeluis, Sven Gottfrid, 105, 101

Markham, Fred L., 270

Marks, Judy, 255

Markwood, Phillip T., 214

Marmon, Harvey V., 214

Marquardt, Jud R., 214

Marr, Clinton, 214

Marsch, Dr. Oscar E., 238

Marschall, Albert R., 255

Marshall, James D., Jr., 284

Marshall, Lane L., 234, 264

Marshall, Mortimer M., 214, 238

Marshall, Richard C., 214-215, 234

Marshall, Richard K., 234

Martens, Walter F., 270

Martin, Albert C., 214

Martin, Christopher C., 214

Martin, David C., 214

Martin, Edward C., 234

Martin, Marvin, 234, 238

Martin, Robert E., 214, 234, 238

Martin, Roger B., 192, 234, 264

Martin, Sir Leslie, 101

Martin, W. Mike, 214

Martinez, Walter B., 214

Martini, Richard, 261

Moore Ruble Yudell, 39, 421

Moore, Arthur C., 215

Moore, Barry M., 215

Moore, Charles, 21, 36, 54, 65, 110

Moore, Diana K., 76

Moore, James B., 267

Moore, Kenneth J., 238

Moore, Lynn A., 234

Moore, Patrick C., 234

Moore, Richard A., 234

Moore, William B., Jr., 255

Moorhead, Gerald L., 215

Morgan, Jesse O., 215

Morgan, Julia, 303, 320, 496

Morgan, Keith N., 272

Morgan, L.A., 83

Morgan, Robert L., 215, 262

Morgan, Sherely, 265

Morgan, W. N., 215

Morgan, William, 43

Morgridge, Howard H., 215

Moriarty, Stacy T., 192

Morin, Robert J., 238

Moris, Lamberto G., 215

Moriyama, Raymond, 99

Morphosis, 47, 90, 177

Morris Architects, 421

Morris, John W., 255

Morris, Paul F., 234

Morris, Philip A., 255, 257

Morris, Robert Schofield, 101

Morris, Seth I., 215

Morrison, Darrel G., 234

Morrison, Jasper, 72

Morrison, Lionel, 215

Morrison, Mark K., 234

Morrison, Mrs. Jacob H., 314

Morse, John, 215

Morse, Joseph, 261

Mortensen, Robert H., 234, 264

Morter Architects, 284

Morter, James R., 215

Morton, Terry B., 255

Morton, Woolridge Brown, III, 255

Moses, Allen D., 215

Mosher, Robert, 215

Moskow, Keith, 124

Moskowitz, Samuel Z., 215

Moss, Eric O., 47, 215

Mostar, Stari-Grad, 32

Mostoller, G. Michael, 215

Motley, Kenneth L., 216

Motorola Inc., 80

Mott, John K., 216

Mott, Ralph O., 270

Moulthrop, Edward A., 216

Moulton, Jennifer T., 216

Mouton, Grover E., 191

Mox, Dana W., 240

Moya, Powell &, 101

Moyer, Frederic D., 216

Moynihan, Senator Daniel Patrick, 88, 314

Muchow, William C., 270

Mudano, Frank R., 216

Muhanna, Rafi, 33

Muhanna, Raif, 33

Muhanna, Ziad, 33

Mularz, Theodore, 216, 270

Mulcahy, Vincent, 191

Muldawer, Paul, 216

Mullen, John W., III, 216

Muller, Kenneth, 242

Müller, Mark, 72

Muller, Rosemary F., 216

Müller-Munk, Peter, 240

Mumford, Lewis, 101

Munari, Bruno, 84, 507

Munger, Harold C., 216

Munly, Anne, 191

Muntz, Jean G., 255

Munzer, Frank W., 216

Murase Associates, 56

Murase, Robert K., 234

Murdock, Richard C., 192

Murphree, Martha, 255

Murphy, C.F., 295

Murphy, Charles F., 216

Murphy, Frank N., 216

Murphy, Katherine Prentis, 314

Murphy/Jahn, 294, 295, 296, 421

O

Octagon, 128, 179

Odell Associates Inc., 422

Odell, A. Gould, Jr., 260

Odenwald, Neil, 234

Odermatt, Robert A., 217

Oehme, Wolfgang W., 234

Oehrlein, Mary L., 217

Oenslager, Donald, 193

Oglesby-Greene Inc., 282

Ögün, Emine, 33

Ögün, Mehmet, 33

Ohlhausen, Rolf H., 217

Ohlson Lavoie Corporation, 286

Okada, ShinIchi, 251

Olcott, Richard M., 217

Oldenburg, Claes, 40

Oldziey, Edward A., 217

Oles, Paul Stevenson, 41, 77, 217

Olin, H. B., 217

Olin, Laurie, 47, 192, 234, 255

Olin, Peter J., 234

Olinger, Edward J., 235

Olmsted, Frederick Law, 49, 264, 483

Olmsted, John C., 264

Olsen, Donald E., 217

Olsen, Harold L., 238

Olshavsky, Carole J., 217

Olson, Don H., 192, 235

Olson, James W., 217

Olson/Sundberg Architects Inc., 422

Olumyiwa, Oluwole O., 251

Omni Architects, 284

Onyx Group, 422

Oppenheimer, Herbert B., 217

Oremen, Edward L., 217

Oringdulph, Robert E., 217, 270

Orland, Brian, 235

Orland, Jerome I., 238

Orlov, Georgui M., 251

Orlov, Iosif Bronislavovitch, 105

Orr, Douglas W., 260

Orr, Gordon D., Jr., 217

Osler, David William, 217

Oslund, Thomas R., 192

Osman, Mary E., 255

Osmundson, Theodore, 55, 235, 264

Ostberg, Ragnar, 36, 101, 304

Otsuji, Dennis Y., 235, 264

Otto, Frei, 31, 35, 58, 84, 123, 254

Oudens, G. F., 217

Ove Arup & Partners, 42, 76

Overby, Osmund, 272

Overthun, Thomas, 71

Ovresat, Raymond C., 217

Owens, Hubert, 55, 264

Owings, Nathaniel A., 36

Ownby, J. Steve, 235

P

P/A Awards, 89-91

Paavilainen, Helsinki., 246

Paavilainen, Käpy, 246

Pace, Joseph De, 190

Paderewski, C. J., III, 217, 270

Padjen, Elizabeth Seward, 217

Page Southerland Page, 291, 422

Pahlman, William, 64

Painter, Michael, 235

Pairo, Edwin T., 239, 267

Palacious, Jose Luis, 124

Palermo, Gregory, 217

Paley, Albert, 43

Pallasmaa, Juhani, 37, 85, 251

Pallay, Ross D., 257

Palmer & King, 290

Palmer, Meade, 55, 235

Palu, Jay M., 262

Pan, Joshua J., 217

Pan, Solomon, 217

Panciera, Ronald J., 255

Pancoast, Lester C., 217

Pangrazio, John R., 217

Pansky, Stanley H., 191

Panton, Verner, 186, 508

Panushka, Donald H., 217

Paoletti, Dennis A., 217

Papachristou, Tician, 217

Papandrew, Thomas, 235, 264

Papp, Laszlo, 217

Rosenfeld, Myra Nan, 45

Rosenfeld, Norman, 219

Rosenman, Marvin E., 66

Rosenthal, Steve, 41

Rosenzweig, Roy, 29

Ross Barney, 38

Ross, Edgar B., 219

Ross, John R., 270

Rossant, James S., 220

Rosser International, 423

Rossetti, Louis A., 220

Rossi, Aldo, 11, 97, 251, 303

Rotchegov, Alexander, 510

Roth, Harold, 220

Roth, Richard, 220

Rothe, Edward N., 220

Rothman, Martha L., 220

Rothman, Richard, 220

Rothman, Robert S., 124

Rothschild, Bernard B., 68, 220, 239

Rothzeid, Bernard, 220

Rotival, Maurice, 220

RoTo Architects, 37

Rotondi, Michael, 47, 220

Rottet, Lauren L., 38, 220

Roudnev, L., 296

Rougerie, J., 58

Rountree, Gini, 256

Rouse, James W., 88

Rowan, Robert J., 262

Rowe, Colin, 41, 102, 110

Rowe, Judith L., 220

Rowland, Ralph T., 220

Roy Mann Associates, 56

Roy, Clarence, 235

Royal Architecture Institute of Canada, 152

Royal Australian Institute of Architects, 154

Royal Institute of British Architects, 100, 102, 155, 180, 244, 271, 497, 501

Royston, Robert N., 40, 55, 235

RTKL, 286-287, 423, 513

Rubeling, Albert W., 220

Rubenstein, Harvey M., 235

Ruble, John, 220

Rucker, J. Ronald, 220

Rucker, Robert H., 235

Rudd, J. W., 220

Rudinev, L. W., 297

Rudofsky, Bernard, 40

Rudolph, George Cooper, III, Architects, 285

Rudolph, Paul, 54

Rudy Bruner Award for Urban Excellence, 24, 104

Ruehl, Gordon E., 220

Ruffcorn, Evett J., 220

Ruffo, John A., 220

Ruga, Wayne, 242

Ruhnau Ruhnau Associates, 282

Ruhnau, Herman O., 220

Rumpel, Peter L., 220

Rupe, William W., 220

Ruprecht Schroeder Hoffman Architects, 285

Rushmore, Mount, 267

Russell, Beverly, 96, 108

Russell, Earnest J., 260

Russell, John A., 99, 231

Russell, T. T., 220

Russell, Virginia Lockett, 235

Rutes, Walter A., 220

Ruth, H. Mark, 220

Ruthazer, Jack G., 229

Ryan, James, 220, 241, 268

Ryan, Leslie A., 192

Ryan, Roger N., 220

Ryan, Terry Warriner, 235

Rybczynski, Witold, 251

Rydeen, James E., 220

Ryder, Donald P., 220

Rykwert, Joseph, 46

Ryohin Keikaku Co., 84

S

S. P. Papadatos Assoc., 82

S/L/A/M Collaborative, 423

Saarinen & Associates, 111

Saarinen, Eero, 17, 36, 71, 111-112, 169, 303, 323, 495, 515

Saarinen, Eliel, 17, 36, 101, 111

Sabo, Werner, 220

Sadler, Harold G., 220

Simonov, Nilolai Ivanovitch, 105

Simons, Lawrence L., 221

Simonsen, Paul W., 239

Simpson, Donal R., 221

Simpson, James L., 229

Simpson, Robert E., 239

Simpson, Robert T., 221

Simpson, Scott, 221

Simpson, Sir John William, 271

Simpson, Theodore A., 229

Sims, Howard F., 221

Sincoff, Jerome J., 221

Sindiong, Antonio S., 251

Singer, Donald I., 221

Singleton, E. Crichton, 221

Sink, Charles S., 221

Sinkevitch, Alice, 256

Sippel, William H., 221

Sir John Soane Museum, 183

Sir Patrick Abercrombie Prize, 105

Sir Robert Matthew Prize, 106

Siren, Heikki, 251

Siren, K., 58, 251

Siza, Alvaro, 54, 86, 94, 97, 120, 195, 252

Sizemore Floyd Architects, 280

Sizemore, Michael M., 221

Skaggs, Ronald, 221, 260

Skarl, Roy, 285

Skidmore Owings & Merrill (SOM), 31, 43, 51-52, 75, 91, 94, 111-112, 160, 280, 286, 287, 292, 293, 294, 295, 296, 297, 303, 304, 423, 494-495, 497, 505, 515

Skidmore, Louis, 36

Skilling Ward Magnusson Barkshire Inc., 70

Skilling, John B., 256

Sklarek, Norma M., 221

Skog, Gary, 221

Skoglund, William A., 239

Sky, Alison, 193

Skyscraper Museum, 184

Slaatto, Nils, 251

Slama, Murray A., 221

Slapeta, Vladimir, 251

Slater, John B., 235

Slayton, William L., 256, 511

Slutsky, Rael D., 77

Smallwood, Reynolds, Stewart, Stewart Associates, 423

Smart Design, 72, 73, 80

Smart, Clifton M., 221

Smiley Glotter Nyberg Architects, 282

Smiley, Saul C., 221

Smirke, Sir Robert, 100

Smirke, Sydney, 100

Smith & Cooper Architecture Division, 284

Smith Group Incorporated, 423

Smith Hinchman & Grylls Associates, 112

Smith, Adrian D., 221

Smith, Arthur, 222

Smith, Bill D., 222

Smith, Bruce H., 222

Smith, Charles E., 88

Smith, Christopher J., 222

Smith, Coin Stansfield, 102

Smith, Cole, 222

Smith, Colin L. M., 222

Smith, Darrell L., 222, 270

Smith, David, 73, 80, 222

Smith, Edna A., 229

Smith, Edward F., 239

Smith, Eleanor McNamara, 256

Smith, Elizabeth A.T., 92

Smith, F. Eugene, 241

Smith, Fleming W., 222

Smith, Frank Folsom, 222

Smith, Gordon H., 43

Smith, Hamilton P., 222

Smith, Harwood K., 222

Smith, Herrick H., 235

Smith, Inette L., 251

Smith, Ivan H., 222

Smith, J. M., 222, 251

Smith, James Merrick, 229

Smith, John R., 222

Smith, Joseph N., 222

Smith, Macon S., 222

Smith, Robert G., 241, 268

Smith, Roscoe D., 239

Smith, Stephen B., 222

Smith, T. Clayton, 222

Whiffen, Marcus, 44

Whisnant, Murray, 225

Whitakcr, Elliott, 265

White, Arthur B., 225

White, George F., 236, 239

White, George M., 109, 225

White, James M., 270

White, Janet Rothberg, 225

White, Norval C., 225

White, Robert F., 236

White, Samuel G., 225

Whitefield, William, 252

Whiteside, Emily M., 193

Whitney M. Young Jr. Award, 20, 121

Whitney, Stephen Q., 225

Whitney-Whyte, Ron, 243

Whyte, William H., 41, 516

Wicklund, Leonard S., 225

Wickstead, George W., 236

Widom, Chester A., 226, 260

Widseth Smith Nolting, 285

Wiedemann, Nichole, 192

Wiese, William, 226, 270

Wigginton, Brooks E., 192

Wilcox, E. D., 226

Wilcox, Glenda, 243

Wilcox, Jerry Cooper, 226

Wildermuth, Gordon L., 226

Wiley, Charles D., 192

Wiley, James E., 226

Wilkerson, Charles E., 226

Wilkes, Joseph A., 226

Wilkes, Michael B., 226

Wilkoff, William L., 230

Wilks, Barbara E., 226

Will, Philip, Jr., 260

Willen, Paul, 226

William B. Ittner, 281, 291

William D. Warner, 96, 225

William McDonough, 51, 214, 421

Williams, A. Richard, 226, 270

Williams, Allison G., 226

Williams, Daniel, 39, 54, 226

Williams, Donald, 261

Williams, E. Stewart, 226

Williams, F. Carter, 68, 226

Williams, Frank, 226

Williams, George Thomas, 226

Williams, Harold L., 226

Williams, Homer L., 226, 270

Williams, John G., 226

Williams, Lorenzo D., 226, 270

Williams, Marguerite Neel, 314, 516

Williams, Mark F., 226

Williams, Michael Ann, 29

Williams, Richard, 65, 226, 270

Williams, Roger B., 226, 443

Williams, Terence J., 252

Williams, Terrance R., 226

Williams, Tod, 54, 78, 192, 226, 424

Williams, W. Gene, 226

Williams, Wayne R., 226

Williamson Founders Architects, 50

Williamson, Frederick, 314

Williamson, Thomas, 50, 285

Willis, Beverly A., 226

Willis, Daniel, 77

Willis, Michael E., 226

Willis, Rev. Robert, 100

Willwerth, Roy W., 252

Wilmot, John C., 226

Wilson, Chris, 29

Wilson, David, 76

Wilson, Forrest, 66

Wilson, Frances, 230, 243

Wilson, Honorable Pete, 255

Wilson, John E., 226, 230

Wilson, John L., 121, 226, 230

Wilson, M. Judith, 243

Wilson, Richard A., 236

Wilson, Richard Guy, 256

Wilson, Robert, 42, 236

Wilson, Sir Hugh, 271

Wilson, William D., 226, 230

Wimberly Allison Tong & Goo, 425

Winchester, Alice, 314

Winkel, Steven R., 226

Winkelstein, Jon Peter, 226

Winkler, John H., 226

Winslow, Paul D., 226

Winstead, D. Geary, 243

Winter, Steven, 226

Wintermute, Marjorie M., 226

Wirkler, Norman E., 226

Wirt Design Group, 281

Wirth, Conrad L., 55

Wirth, Theodore J., 236, 264

Wirtz, Michael, 108, 243

Wiseman, Carter, 42

Wisner, John B., 230

Wisnewski, Joseph J., 226

Witherspoon, Gayland B., 226

Witsell, Charles, 226

Witte, D. C., 230

Wittenberg, Gordon G., 226

Wittkower, Rudolf, 41, 45

Wittwer, Gall, 192

Wnderlich, C A., 252

Woehle, Fritz, 226

Woerner, Robert L., 236, 264

Wojcik, J. Daniel, 236

Wold Architects, 425

Wold, Robert L., 226

Wolf Prize for Architecture, 123

Wolf, Arnold, 241

Wolf, Harry C., 226

Wolf, Martin F., 226

Wolf, Richard, 226

Wolfberg Alvarez and Partners, 425

Wolford, Arol, 256

Wong, Gin D., 226

Wong, John L., 192

Wong, Kellogg H., 226

Woo, Carolina Y., 226

Woo, George C., 226

Woo, Kyu S., 226

Wood, Bernard, 252

Wood, Edmund D., 230

Wood, H. A., 226

Wood, Marilyn, 256

Wood, Susan, 243

Woodbridge, John M., 226

Woodbridge, Sally B., 42

Woodcock, David, 66, 226

Woodhouse, David, 226

Woodhurst, Robert S., III, 226

Woodhurst, Stanford, Jr., 226

Wooding, Peter, 241, 268

Woodring, Cooper C., 241, 268

Woods, Hubbard, 220

Woods, Huntington, 211, 224

Woods, Lebbeus, 42

Woodward, Thomas E., 226

Woodward, William McKenzie, 313

Woollen, Evans, 226

Wooten, J. R., 226

World Heritage List, 333-341

World Monuments Fund, 42, 342, 345

Wormley, Edward J., 64

Wornum, George Grey, 101

Worsley, John C., 226

Worth, Jack, III, 261

Worthington, Sir Percy Scott, 101

Wragg, Francis R., 267

Wrenn, Tony P., 256

Wright, David G., 236

Wright, David H., 226

Wright, Frank Lloyd, 13, 18, 36, 45, 49, 101,
    111-112, 303-304, 319-320, 435, 440, 511

Wright, George S., 226

Wright, Henry L., 226, 260, 314

Wright, John L., 226

Wright, Marcellus, 226

Wright, Rodney H., 226

Wright, St. Clair, 314

Wright, Thomas W. D., 226

Wriston, Barbara, 272

WRS, 285

WTW Architects, 425

Wu, Liangyong, 85

Wurster, William Wilson, 36

Wyatt, Julie M., 230

Wyatt, Scott W., 226

Wyatt, Sir M. Digby, 100

Wyatt, Thomas Henry, 100, 271

Wynne, Brian J., 258

Wyss, Patrick H., 236

2001 ORDER FORM

We welcome you to order the upcoming 2001 edition of the *Almanac of Architecture and Design*. Please return this form to us at the address listed below. You may pay by credit card or check. Volume discounts are available, call 1.800.726.8603 for information.

Almanac of Architecture and Design $34.95

Price	Quantity	Total
$34.95		
	Shipping	$4.95
	Order Total	

☐ **Check**   ☐ **Credit card**

Card #   Expiration Date

Signature

Contact Information

Name

Address

City   State   Zip

Telephone

Fax

Email

Please return this form to:
Greenway Group
ATTN: Almanac
30 Technology Parkway South, Suite 200
Norcross, GA 30092
Tel 770.209.3770

Or email us at almanac@greenwaygroup.net

COMMENT FORM

Invitation For Comments and Suggestions
Please include any ideas, comments, or suggestions for the
Almanac of Architecture and Design.

Suggestions and Comments

_____

_____

_____

_____

_____

_____

_____

_____

_____

Contact Information

Name
_____
Address
_____
City   State   Zip
_____
Telephone
_____
Fax
_____
Email
_____

Please return this form to:
Greenway Group
ATTN: Almanac
30 Technology Parkway South, Suite 200
Norcross, GA 30092
Tel 770.209.3770

Or email us at almanac@greenwaygroup.net

CMD Group

CMD Group is a leading international provider of construction market data and a leading worldwide provider of proprietary construction information. Their information sources include *Architects' First Source*, product selection and specification information; *Clark Reports*, early planning industrial project information; *Construction Market Data* (CMD), construction project information; Associated Construction Publications, 14 regional magazines covering U.S. highway and heavy construction; Manufacturers' Survey Associates (MSA), estimating and quantity survey data.; and R.S. Means, construction cost data. CMD Group worldwide includes CMD Canada, project and product information; BIMSA/Mexico, projects and cost information for Mexico; Byggfakta Scandinavia, construction market data for Denmark, Estonia, Finland, Norway and Sweden; and Cordell Building Information Services, construction activity and cost information in Australia.

Greenway Group

The Greenway Group is a research and management-consulting firm that specializes in organizational design and strategic advisory services. Greenway Group has clients worldwide in nine foreign countries and 39 states who are served by offices in Washington D.C., Atlanta, and Chicago with staff in other cities. The firm publishes *DesignIntelligence*, a strategic change bulletin and letter published 24 times a year, *DesignTechnology*, a monthly e-publication, as well as dozens of custom and limited circulation research reports for the design professions, product manufacturers, and construction industry clients. Greenway is a firm committed to helping organizations grow faster and healthier through knowledge sharing and strategic decision support.

James Cramer

James Cramer is the founder and chairman of the Greenway Group and Adjunct Professor of Architecture at the University of Hawaii. He researches, consults, and gives seminars for over 200 leading professional firms around the world. He is the author of 120 articles and several books, including the critically acclaimed *Design + Enterprise, Seeking a New Reality in Architecture*. He is co-author of *How Firms Succeed, A Field Guide to Management Solutions*, newly released in 2000. Cramer is the former Chief Executive of The American Institute of Architects in Washington D.C. and is the former President of the American Architectural Foundation. He is currently the Co-chair of the Washington D.C. based think tank, the Design Futures Council. An educator, futurist, and business advisor, he is currently leading sessions on technology advancements and pending value migration changes in the design professions.

Paul Goldberger

Paul Goldberger is the architecture critic and a staff writer for *The New Yorker*. He joined *The New Yorker* in July 1997, following a 25-year career at *The New York Times*, where he won a Pulitzer Prize in 1984 for his architecture criticism. He lectures widely on the subject of architecture, design, historic preservation, and cities and has taught a course in architecture criticism at the Yale School of Architecture. His writing has received numerous awards in addition to the Pulitzer, including the President's Medal of the Municipal Art Society of New York, the medal of The American Institute of Architects, and the Medal of Honor of the New York Landmarks Preservation Foundation. He is also the author of several books, including *The City Observed: New York*, *The Skyscraper*, and *On the Rise: Architecture and Design in a Post-Modern Age*.

Jennifer Evans

Jennifer Evans is an Architectural Historian and Project Director at the Greenway Group and serves as the Managing Editor of the Almanac of Architecture and Design. She collaborates with other Greenway professional staff to bring forward innovative information solutions that serve the changing needs of designers and the construction industry. She has a Masters of Science in Architecture History from the Georgia Institute of Technology. She also studied at Drake University where she received her BS in Business Administration and earned a Masters Degree in Heritage Preservation at Georgia State University. As a researcher, architectural historian, and project director, she leads Greenway's initiatives that bring historical perspective and fresh insight to futures invention assignments.